PROFESSIONAL

SQL Server® 2008 Internals and Troubleshooting

PROFESSIONAL

SQL Server® 2008 Internals and Troubleshooting

Christian Bolton

Justin Langford

Brent Ozar

James Rowland-Jones

Jonathan Kehayias

Cindy Gross

Steven Wort

Wiley Publishing, Inc.

Professional SQL Server® 2008 Internals and Troubleshooting

Published by
Wiley Publishing, Inc.
10475 Crosspoint Boulevard
Indianapolis, IN 46256
www.wiley.com

Library of Congress Control Number: 2009941346

For Gemma, with all my love and thanks

—CHRISTIAN BOLTON

This is dedicated to Erika, who has been dedicated to me despite my long working hours. I love you dearly, and I love working on next chapters.

—BRENT OZAR

ABOUT THE AUTHORS

 CHRISTIAN BOLTON is the Technical Director for Coeo Ltd., a leading provider of SQL Server consulting and managed support services in the UK and Europe. Prior to this Christian worked for 5 years at Microsoft, leading the SQL Server Premier Field Engineering team in the UK. He is a Microsoft Certified Architect, Master and MVP for SQL Server, and co-author of Professional SQL Server 2005 Performance Tuning. He works out of London and lives in the south of England with his wife and children. He can be contacted at christian@coeo.com. Christian authored chapters 1, 2, 7, 13 and the online chapter 16 in addition to lending his authoring expertise where needed on other chapters and functioned as the lead author for the entire project.

 JUSTIN LANGFORD leads the Managed Support team for Coeo Ltd, delivering outsourced 24x7 operations for mission-critical SQL Server platforms. Before joining Coeo, Justin worked for Microsoft in the Premier Field Engineering team and has worked with some of Microsoft's largest finance and government customers in Europe. Justin co-authored Wrox Professional SQL Server 2005 Performance Tuning and lives in London with his girlfriend, Claire. Outside work he enjoys sailing and has a keen interest in classic British sports cars. Justin can be contacted at justinl@coeo.com. Justin authored chapters 9, 11, 12, and 15.

 BRENT OZAR is a SQL Server Expert for Quest Software. He has over a decade of broad IT experience, performing SQL Server database administration, systems administration, SAN administration, virtualization administration, and project management. In his current role, Brent trains DBAs on performance tuning, disaster recovery, and virtualization. He has spoken around the globe at events for PASS, SQLBits, SSWUG, and other organizations. Brent founded the Virtualization Virtual Chapter for the Professional Association for SQL Server (PASS), and serves as the Editor-in-Chief at SQLServerPedia.com.

Brent blogs at www.BrentOzar.com and discusses diverse topics at http://twitter.com/BrentO. When he's not talking SQL Server, he enjoys traveling, working with social media, snorkeling, and sampling new restaurants. He is the author of chapters 4 and 14.

 JAMES ROWLAND-JONES works for EMC Consulting EMEA as an Advisory Consultant. His principle focus is the delivery of large, scalable, data warehousing, and business intelligence projects. Within this field James specializes in data integration, database architecture, and performance tuning. He is very active in the technical community and is one of the organizers for SQLBits, Europe's largest SQL Server community conference. James has received the Microsoft MVP award for 2009 and 2010. You can find him online at http://consultingblogs.emc.com/jamesrowlandjones, twitter (@jrowlandjones), linkedin http://www.linkedin.com/in/jrowlandjones, or even using an old fashioned email, james.rowland-jones@emc.com. James authored chapters 6 and 10.

JONATHAN KEHAYIAS is a SQL Server MVP, MCITP Database Administrator and Developer, who got started in SQL Server in 2004 as a database developer and report writer in the natural gas industry. After spending two and a half years working in T-SQL, in late 2006, he transitioned to the role of Database Administrator. He has experience in upgrading and consolidating SQL environments, and has experience in running SQL Server in Virtual Environments on VMWare ESX 3.5+. He is a member of the Tampa SQL Server User Group and a regular speaker about SQL Server at events. Jonathan authored chapter 3.

CINDY GROSS started her SQL Server life as a DBA with a hospital and health plan company in 1993, and moved to Microsoft in 2000 where she has worked ever since. Her roles at Microsoft have included PSS Product Support Engineer, SQL Content Lead, Yukon Readiness Lead, and most recently Dedicated Support Engineer (DSE), all for SQL Server. Cindy enjoys delivering training throughout the United States as well as in Europe and India, including presentations at SQL PASS. In 2008 she started the Boise SQL Server User Group, an affiliate of the SQLCommunity.org site (where she is a worldwide SQL Server Community Leader) to share SQL Server wisdom in the Idaho SQL Server community. Most recently she obtained the Microsoft Certified Master: SQL Server Qualification, which was a hard-fought prize. Over the years Cindy has learned from many wonderful friends and colleagues and they all deserve a word of thanks for contributing to her success. Cindy authored chapter 8.

 STEVEN WORT has been working with SQL Server since the early days of SQL Server way back in 1992-93. He is currently a developer in the Windows Division at Microsoft, where he works on performance and scalability issues on large database systems for the Windows Telemetry team. Steven has been at Microsoft since 2000. Prior to working in the Windows Division, Steven spent 2 years working in the SQL Server group, working on performance and scalability. Steven's first 3 years at Microsoft were spent working in support as an escalation engineer on the SIE team. During this time, Steven was able to travel the world working with some of Microsoft's customers on their performance and scalability issues. Before coming to Microsoft, Steven spent 20 years working in the United Kingdom as a freelance consultant, specializing in database application development. When Steven isn't busy working, he can be found spending time with his family and enjoying many fitness activities in the outdoors of the Pacific Northwest. Steven authored chapter 5.

CREDITS

EXECUTIVE EDITOR
Robert Elliott

SENIOR PROJECT EDITOR
Ami Frank Sullivan

TECHNICAL EDITORS
James Boother
Jimmy May
Paul Nielsen
Tony Rogerson
James Rowland-Jones
Simon Sabin
Steven Wort

SENIOR PRODUCTION EDITOR
Debra Banninger

COPY EDITOR
Luann Rouff

EDITORIAL DIRECTOR
Robyn B. Siesky

EDITORIAL MANAGER
Mary Beth Wakefield

MARKETING MANAGER
Ashley Zurcher

PRODUCTION MANAGER
Tim Tate

**VICE PRESIDENT AND
EXECUTIVE GROUP PUBLISHER**
Richard Swadley

**VICE PRESIDENT AND
EXECUTIVE PUBLISHER**
Barry Pruett

ASSOCIATE PUBLISHER
Jim Minatel

**PROJECT COORDINATOR,
COVER**
Lynsey Stanford

COMPOSITOR
Chris Gillespie,
Happenstance Type-O-Rama

PROOFREADER
Nancy Carrasco

INDEXER
Robert Swanson

COVER DESIGNER
Michael E. Trent

COVER IMAGE
Punchstock / Glowimages

ACKNOWLEDGMENTS

FROM CHRISTIAN BOLTON: This book has been a far greater challenge and rewarding experience than I ever imagined. As with anything worth shedding blood, sweat, and tears over, it has taken a number of people, generous with their time and talents, to bring this project to life.

First of all, I'd like to thank my wife, Gemma, for her support and eternal patience during the many evenings and weekends I spent researching, writing, and reviewing content for "just a little longer." My children, Ava and Leighton, deserve a special thank you also for frequently pulling me back to what really matters with cheeky grins, demands to ride on my shoulders, spin in my chair, and an offer to draw a picture of a princess for me to put in the book.

I'd also like to thank my fellow authors and contributors for their outstanding efforts in bringing new, interesting, and well researched material to make this book unique:

- ➤ Justin Langford has been a great friend for many years and is always the first to offer support and encouragement to any project.

- ➤ James Rowland-Jones for setting impossible goals for his chapters on Locking and SQL Trace and then going past them.

- ➤ Brent Ozar, for transferring his easy-reading blog style into professional book chapters on Storage and Management Studio Reports that are a pleasure to read.

- ➤ Jonathan Kehayias for his excellent chapter on Waits and Extended Events that would have been a pale shadow of its current form had he not been involved in the book.

- ➤ Cindy Gross for bringing her years of experience at Microsoft and defining what it takes to be a Professional when troubleshooting SQL Server.

- ➤ Steven Wort for working to extremely tight timescales on the CPU and Query Processing chapter and working tirelessly to improve and expand on the original specs.

Starting a new chapter from a blank page is one of the hardest things you can do as an author, but it is ultimately rewarding when you see the finished product. I often think that Technical Editors don't get enough praise for the work they do to make the authors look good, so I want to say a big thank you to our team of Technical Editors for their diligent research, tips, advice, and patience through multiple revisions: Simon Sabin, James Rowland-Jones, James Boother, Jimmy May, Paul Nielsen, Steven Wort, and Tony Rogerson. I'd also like to thank Ami Sullivan, our Project Editor at Wiley, for keeping the schedule moving and working very hard to compensate for our writing delays, and Robert Elliott, our Executive Editor, for buying into the original vision and helping me to refine the proposal that eventually became this book.

Writing about SQL Server Internals with a sufficient abstraction in certain areas to introduce key topics and then drilling down into the heart of the product in others presents a difficult challenge for anyone, but it is much harder writing from outside Microsoft; and I'd like to thank Bob Ward,

Ewan Fairweather, and Thomas Kejser from Microsoft for their enthusiastic support for the project and for clarifying some of the finer details of exactly what the code in SQL Server is doing.

I'd also like to thank the following SQL Server professionals, MVPs, and Microsoft staff for their inspiration and support whether knowingly or not: Mark Anderson, Sunil Agarwal, Chirag Roy, Aaron Bertrand, Denny Cherry, Grant Fritchey, and Paul Randal.

Finally, I'd like to thank you for buying this book. Everyone involved has given their best game to make it stand-out; especially the authors and contributors who have given a little bit of what makes them special in their field to create a book that they're proud to put their name to. I hope it lives up to your expectations and you find it a worthy investment.

FROM JAMES ROWLAND-JONES: Firstly I'd like to thank Christian for the opportunity to be involved with the book, Simon Sabin and Tony Rogerson (my TE's) for their efforts and constructive feedback, and also to Ami Sullivan, our editor, for her endless support and patience. The management team at EMC Consulting and especially Rob Grigg have been a constant source of support; both on the book and in the community with user groups and SQLBits, so a big thank you to them. I'd also like to thank Bob Ward and Thomas Kejser for their reviews and insight during some tough times on the locking chapter. Finally, I'd like to thank all my family, but especially my wife Jane and our children Lucy, Kate, and Oliver. Without you life is strangely pointless.

FROM BRENT OZAR: Thanks to Jimmy May for hooking me up with such a great team of authors. My involvement with this book wouldn't have happened without his encouragement and trust. Similarly, I'd like to thank the authors for giving me an opportunity to work with them. I'm humbled to have my names next to such great technical minds. Thanks also to Christian Hasker, Rony Lerner, Don Duncan, and Joe Sullivan; I have consistently hit the lottery when it comes to managers, and I couldn't have picked a better string of guys to mentor me and grow my career. If anybody doesn't succeed under any of them, it's their own fault.

To my coworkers Andy Grant, Brett Epps, Heather Eichman, and everybody else at Quest Software, thanks for making my work so much fun. Thanks to everybody on Twitter for laughing with me while I keep punching harder and faster. My day is infinitely more enjoyable thanks to folks like @SQLRockstar, @SQLChicken, @SQLAgentMan, @KBrianKelley, @Wendy_Dance, @GFritchey, @MrDenny, @StatisticsIO, @MikeHillwig, @Peschkaj, @SQLSarg, @SQLCraftsman, and many others.

Finally, I'd like to thank Dad, Mom, and Caryl for my dashing good looks and brilliant wit. I just wish you'd given me some humility so that I could be perfect.

CONTENTS

INTRODUCTION

WHILE PUTTING TOGETHER THE PROPOSAL that eventually became this book, the aim was to write a troubleshooting guide that covered the additional tools available from the SQL Server community.

It soon became clear, however, that to effectively talk about the tools, so many digressions were necessary to explain the results that the flow and impact were interrupted. The decision was made to alter the approach to include architectural information, not just on SQL Server, but on the whole platform on which SQL Server depends.

If you're troubleshooting an apparent "SQL Server" issue, you need to be able to troubleshoot the underlying operating system and storage as well as SQL Server, so we wanted to bring together and simplify the architectural details of these components too.

A fair amount of Windows and storage internals information is available already, but very little of it that condenses and filters the right material to be easily consumed by SQL Server professionals. The available material is either too light or too in depth — with nothing to help bridge the gap.

Combining this need with the need for practical internals information on SQL Server, a look at building a troubleshooting methodology, and relevant information on all the extra tools, three goals for the book were established:

➤ To provide in-depth architectural information on SQL Server (and the environment on which it depends) that is easy to consume

➤ To introduce a troubleshooting approach using the same techniques and methodologies that Microsoft uses internally

➤ To present some of the additional free SQL Server troubleshooting tools that are available with real-world examples demonstrating how they can be used together to efficiently and accurately determine the root cause of issues on systems running SQL Server

WHO THIS BOOK IS FOR

This book is intended for those people who regard themselves as, or who aspire to be, SQL Server professionals in predominantly relational environments. What I mean by a SQL Server professional, is anyone that regards SQL Server as one of their core product skills and continually strives to develop their knowledge of the product and how to use it.

It is not a beginner's book and makes assumptions that the reader knows the basics of how to install, use, and configure SQL Server and is aware of some of the challenges that troubleshooting SQL Server problems using only the native tools presents. Every effort has been made however, to provide a gentle route into each area for those readers who are less confident in some of the topics presented.

The book is presented in two parts. The first covers internal information which is intended to provide an in-depth grounding in core concepts and provides the knowledge to help understand the output and positioning of the tools covered in part two. Those readers who are confident with the subject matter presented in part one will find that they can start reading from part two and dip back into part one as required to clarify any understanding.

WHAT THIS BOOK COVERS

Before launching into a description of the structure of the book and each chapter, it's important for you to understand some key drivers and assumptions that originally led to the topics the book covers.

Understanding Internals

You don't need to understand too much about how SQL Server works to be successful in many SQL Server–based job roles. You can find numerous well-established, prescriptive guidelines and a very active and helpful community to help you. Eventually, however, you will reach a point when that's just not enough (usually when something serious has gone wrong).

During an unexpected service outage, for example, you need to make quick decisions in order to balance the demands of restoring the service as quickly as possible while gathering enough data to help you diagnose the issue so you can prevent it from happening again. In that situation you cannot depend on external help or goodwill; it won't arrive fast enough to help you. Understanding internals will enable you to make quick decisions for problem resolution independently.

When I worked for Microsoft, one of our customers encountered corruption in a large business-critical database running on SQL Server. The business decided to take the database offline until it was fixed because it held financial trade data, and mistakes would have been disastrous.

They ran DBCC CHECKDB, which can be used in SQL Server to help detect and resolve corruption, but killed it after eight hours in favor of a database restore. The backup was corrupt so they had no option but to run CHECKDB again, which fixed the problem after another 12 hours. It was a time-consuming disaster and led to a large fine having to be paid by the customer for failing to provide a service to the financial markets.

The simple lessons to learn from this example are to test your backups and to know how long CHECKDB takes to run (and that it takes longer when corruption is detected, as it takes another pass with deeper checks). These are "best practices" that can be followed with little understanding of actual internals.

However, the reason for including this example is the information that resulted from the postmortem. The original error message that detected the problem contained details of a corrupt page. Armed with a data page number, the troubleshooting team could have used DBCC PAGE to look at the header and determine to which database object it belonged.

In this case it actually belonged to a non-clustered index that could have just been rebuilt without having to take the entire database down to run CHECKDB or restore the entire database. This is why it's useful to know the "internals"; so you can work things out for yourself and take the best course of action.

This book covers internals information for Windows and SQL Server that helps you understand the environment in which your application(s) works, how to configure your server to optimize for different requirements, and how to avoid making blind decisions in the heat of the moment because you don't know why you're seeing a particular behavior.

Additional Troubleshooting Tools

The second part of this book, which was actually its original source of inspiration, deals with a range of free troubleshooting tools that can be used together to form a structured, effective, troubleshooting strategy. We wanted to write a practical guide to these useful tools that can make your life so much easier on a daily basis (but which can seem overly complicated and difficult to learn to the uninitiated).

HOW THIS BOOK IS STRUCTURED

The first part of the book starts with a high-level overview of SQL Server's architecture, leading into chapters on the three core resources that are important to SQL Server: memory, storage, and CPU. Nestled in between these chapters at strategic points are additional chapters which cover material that is critical to understand for effective troubleshooting: SQL Server Waits and Extended Events, Locking and Latches, and tempdb.

This section provides an overview of each chapter to put it into context within the book and to help you decide where to start reading.

Chapter 1: SQL Server Architecture

This chapter takes you lightly through the life cycle of a query, with enough depth to help you understand fundamental concepts and architectures without getting lost in the complexities of individual components (some of which are looked at closely in later chapters).

This chapter will appeal to readers at all levels of skill, whether you're a developer, a DBA, or a seasoned SQL Server veteran.

Chapter 2: Understanding Memory

With this chapter we wanted to expand the scope of "memory" to include the physical components and Windows memory management, rather than just cover SQL Server's internal usage so you'll be able to read about the different types of memory modules you can buy and learn how Windows manages physical memory using a Virtual Memory Manager. It also compares 32-bit and 64-bit architectures and the options you have for tuning them.

For SQL Server itself, you'll learn about architectural elements such as memory nodes, clerks, caches, and the buffer pool, as well as the often misunderstood concept of memtoleave and how to measure it. You will also read all about AWE usage and how to implement it in this chapter.

The objective of this chapter is to provide you with a thorough understanding of how SQL Server uses memory. Once you understand the core architecture of SQL Server's memory management, you will be well prepared to diagnose memory-related problems as well.

Chapter 3: SQL Server Waits and Extended Events

This chapter introduces the benefits of reviewing SQL Server Waits and the architecture that supports this feature. It looks into how they occur and what they mean; the common wait types of concern; which wait types can be safely ignored; and what new wait types there are in SQL Server 2008.

It then covers a new feature in SQL Server 2008 called Extended Events and shows how they can be used to get a deeper look into what waits are occuring for individual tasks and why. Finally, it demonstrates how to implement and manage events using a freeware tool called the Extended Events Manager which was written by the author.

The objective of this chapter is to introduce and reinforce the benefits of adding waits analysis to your troubleshooting method and how to take it to the next level with Extended Events.

Chapter 4: Working with Storage

This chapter equips you with the knowledge to confidently specify and monitor your storage requirements, from understanding the uses for different types of physical disks and knowing the real-world implications for different RAID levels, to being comfortable with the technologies that make up a storage area network (SAN) and various optimization tips that you can employ on different types of storage.

We compare SANs and direct-attached storage (DAS) so you can be clear about the environment in which each is appropriate, and you'll learn about the implementation details and implications of performance-tuning tips like increasing HBA queue depth and implementing disk sector alignment.

The objective of this chapter is to ensure that you and your storage administrator can communicate using common terminology and address key storage performance bottlenecks in a cooperative and collaborative way.

Chapter 5: CPU and Query Processing

This chapter covers two key, interrelated areas. First you'll read about CPUs, looking at how they work and where the technology is heading so you can decide what features are more important to you when choosing the processors that will be available in your server.

Then, the chapter takes an in-depth look at how SQL Server processes queries because understanding how a query is processed will help you determine how to tune it. However, understanding what drives SQL Server to determine this plan will also aid you in understanding why SQL Server made that choice. Again, understanding not only how, but also why, enables you to make tuning decisions more quickly and effectively.

The objective of this chapter is to distill enough information about CPUs to help you choose what to buy (if indeed you have any influence in the process) and to help you understand how to influence the decisions that SQL Server's Query Processor makes in order to fine-tune the performance of your queries.

Chapter 6: Locking and Latches

This chapter takes a very in-depth look at how SQL Server manages isolation and concurrency and contains full details on how SQL Server implements locking and row versioning depending on how its configured.

The chapter also clarifies another type of lock that SQL Server uses internally called a *latch*, and explores the use and detailed implementation of latches within SQL Server — including what can go wrong, how to monitor for problems, and how to resolve them or mitigate against risk.

The objective of this chapter is to provide you with the knowledge to be able to choose the most appropriate isolation level for any scenario, evaluate the potential benefits of using Snapshot Isolation and row versioning, and to be able to confidently troubleshoot latch issues.

Chapter 7: Knowing Tempdb

This chapter describes which features use tempdb and what the performance implications can be for enabling them, as well as how to monitor and tune the database for best performance and availability.

You'll read about tempdb allocation problems in some depth, including how to detect, resolve, and mitigate any allocation issues by creating multiple data files, optimizing temporary object reuse, and using trace flag 1118.

The objective of this chapter is for you to not only understand how best to configure tempdb, but also to know when it is likely to be used. Once you are armed with this information, you should be able to analyze a given workload for your SQL Server and know whether or not you will need to invest significant time tuning tempdb.

The Troubleshooting Tools Chapters

Part II starts with both a human-oriented and process-driven look at how to approach troubleshooting. Then, it jumps into the tools and technologies that work well independently but are brought together into one easy solution for analysis with SQL Nexus.

The final chapters look at the built-in and customizable reporting capabilities of Management Studio, and the brand-new Management Data Warehouse feature in SQL Server 2008. Finally, you will learn several shortcuts, tips, and tricks we use on a daily basis to achieve maximum customer satisfaction by ensuring fast problem resolution with minimal impact.

Chapter 8: Defining Your Approach to Troubleshooting

Your troubleshooting will be far more effective if you do more than just rely on a "gut feeling" or your previous experience with a set of symptoms. Think of troubleshooting as a science rather than an art and you won't go far wrong.

This chapter covers the troubleshooting approach that Microsoft uses within its SQL Server support teams. It looks at having the right attitude and how to manage your sponsors, and helps you to define the problem and understand what to do after you've fixed a problem to prevent it from happening again.

Chapter 9: Viewing Server Performance with PerfMon and the PAL Tool

Performance Monitor (PerfMon) has a been a staple data gathering and reporting tool since Windows NT4, but it has obviously increased in size and scope since those early days.

This chapter demonstrates how to optimize your data collection using Performance Monitor to reduce the impact on the monitored system, and how to load the data straight into SQL Server to run your own T-SQL queries against the results. It also introduces you to the Performance Analysis of Logs (PAL) tool, which makes analysis of large data captures much easier to consume and draw conclusions from.

Chapter 10: Tracing SQL Server with SQL Trace and Profiler

This in-depth chapter covers the Profiler tool that is provided with SQL Server and the underlying technology used called SQL Trace. It will teach you tracing terminology, what you should be tracing to get the right balance of useful data while minimizing server impact, and how to build less intensive "server-side" traces from scratch instead of using Profiler.

You'll also learn about best practices for data collection, different problem scenarios for which tracing can be used, and what's new in SQL Server 2008.

Chapter 11: Consolidating Data Collection with SQLDiag and the PerfStats Script

SQLDiag is a great tool that was introduced in SQL Server 2005 to help coordinate the collection of Performance Monitor logs and SQL Traces, as well as the gathering of other system data.

In this chapter you'll learn how to configure, customize, and run SQLDiag, as well as be introduced to Microsoft's Performance Statistics (PerfStats) script, which adds locking, blocking, and wait stats to the list of collectors that SQLDiag coordinates.

This tool is one of the secrets of the trade for efficient data collection, and this chapter is a "must read" for anyone not using it extensively already.

Chapter 12: Introducing RML Utilities for Stress Testing and Trace File Analysis

This chapter describes how to configure and run OStress and ReadTrace, which are part of the RML Utilities package, and how to interpret the results. ReadTrace in particular is a very special tool that you'll come back to time and time again after you've been introduced to it, as it helps you draw conclusions within seconds — conclusions that would have been unbelievably laborious to reach in the past.

Chapter 13: Bringing It All Together with SQL Nexus

SQL Nexus is a freeware tool written by SQL Server escalation engineers at Microsoft, and it is the crown jewel of the troubleshooting tools because it consolidates the analysis and reporting from all the other tools mentioned up to this chapter.

In this chapter you'll learn how to configure, run, and draw conclusions from the reports created by this tool, which is by far the most useful piece of software in the troubleshooting kit bag of people who have taken the time to learn it.

Chapter 14: Using Management Studio Reports and the Performance Dashboard

This chapter takes you through some of the most useful Management Studio reports available, describing how you can create your own custom reports and introducing a set of custom reports written by the SQL Server support team at Microsoft, collectively known as the Performance Dashboard.

Chapter 15: Using SQL Server Management Data Warehouse

The Management Data Warehouse feature provides a centralized repository for SQL Server 2008 performance data across an organization. It is made up of three key components: the Performance Data Collector, the Data Warehouse, and the Reports.

It is intended to provide an out-of-the-box solution for performance management to SQL Server professionals who are responsible for performance and capacity management. This chapter describes what this feature can do and how to set up and configure it for yourself.

Chapter 16: Shortcuts to Efficient Data Collection and Quick Analysis

Available for download on Wrox.com

This is a web-only chapter and contains tips, tricks, and real-world scenarios for quick and easy data collection, and on-the-fly analysis of data that can be rolled out quickly and efficiently every day if necessary to give you, your customers, and your internal and external sponsors confidence in the health of a business application running on SQL Server.

This last part of the book provides complete coverage of numerous free support tools you can choose to employ. This chapter talks about the ones the authors use every day in consulting, development, and operational environments across many customers with both simple and very complex SQL Server architectures.

CONVENTIONS

To help you get the most from the text and keep track of what's happening, we've used a number of conventions throughout the book.

 Boxes like this one hold important, not-to-be forgotten information that is directly relevant to the surrounding text.

Notes, tips, hints, tricks, and asides to the current discussion are offset and placed in italics like this.

As for styles in the text:

➤ New terms and important words are *italicized* when introduced.

➤ Keyboard strokes are shown like this: Ctrl+A.

➤ Filenames, URLs, and code within the text looks like so: `persistence.properties`.

➤ Code is presented in two different ways:

```
We use a monofont type with no highlighting for most code examples.
```

```
We use bolded monofont to emphasize code that is of particular importance in
the present context.
```

SOURCE CODE

As you work through the examples in this book, you may choose either to type in all the code manually or to use the source code files that accompany the book. All of the source code used in this book is available for download at `www.wrox.com`. Once at the site, simply locate the book's title (either by using the Search box or by using one of the title lists) and click the Download Code link on the book's detail page to obtain all the source code for the book.

Code snippets that are downloadable from wrox.com are easily identified with an icon; the filename of the code snippet follows in a code note that appears after the code, much like the one that follows this paragraph. If it is an entire code listing, the filename should appear in the listing title.

Available for download on Wrox.com

This code [filename] is available for download at wrox.com

> *Because many books have similar titles, you may find it easiest to search by ISBN; this book's ISBN is 978-0-470-48428-9.*

Once you download the code, just decompress it with your favorite compression tool. Alternately, you can go to the main Wrox code download page at `www.wrox.com/dynamic/books/download.aspx` to see the code available for this book and all other Wrox books.

ERRATA

Every effort is made to ensure that there are no errors in the text or in the code. However, no one is perfect, and mistakes do occur. If you find an error in one of our books, such as a spelling mistake or a faulty piece of code, your feedback is welcome. By sending in errata, you might save another reader hours of frustration, and at the same time you will help us provide even higher quality information.

To find the errata page for this book, go to `www.wrox.com` and locate the title using the Search box or one of the title lists. Then, on the book details page, click the Book Errata link. On this page you can view all errata that has been submitted for this book and posted by Wrox editors. A complete book list, including links to each book's errata, is also available at `www.wrox.com/misc-pages/booklist.shtml`.

If you don't spot "your" error on the Book Errata page, go to `www.wrox.com/contact/techsupport.shtml` and complete the form there to send us the error you have found. Once the information is checked, a message is posted to the book's errata page and the problem is fixed in subsequent editions of the book.

P2P.WROX.COM

For author and peer discussion, join the P2P forums at `p2p.wrox.com`. The forums are a Web-based system for you to post messages relating to Wrox books and related technologies and to interact with other readers and technology users. The forums offer a subscription feature to email you topics of interest of your choosing when new posts are made to the forums. Wrox authors, editors, other industry experts, and your fellow readers are present on these forums.

At `http://p2p.wrox.com` you will find a number of different forums that will help you not only as you read this book, but also as you develop your own applications. To join the forums, just follow these steps:

1. Go to `p2p.wrox.com` and click the Register link.
2. Read the terms of use and click Agree.

3. Complete the required information to join as well as any optional information you wish to provide and click Submit.

4. You will receive an email with information describing how to verify your account and complete the joining process.

> *You can read messages in the forums without joining P2P but in order to post your own messages, you must join.*

Once you join, you can post new messages and respond to messages other users post. You can read messages at any time on the Web. If you would like to have new messages from a particular forum emailed to you, click the Subscribe to this Forum icon by the forum name in the forum listing.

For more information about how to use the Wrox P2P, be sure to read the P2P FAQs for answers to questions about how the forum software works as well as many common questions specific to P2P and Wrox books. To read the FAQs, click the FAQ link on any P2P page.

PROFESSIONAL

SQL Server® 2008 Internals and Troubleshooting

1

SQL Server Architecture

WHAT'S IN THIS CHAPTER

➤   Understanding database transactions and the ACID properties

➤   Architectural components used to fulfill a read request

➤   Architectural components used to fulfill an update request

➤   Database recovery and the transaction log

➤   Dirty pages, checkpoints, and the lazywriter

➤   Where the SQLOS fits in and why it's needed

A basic grasp of SQL Server's architecture is fundamental to intelligently approach trouble-shooting a problem, but selecting the important bits to learn about can be challenging, as SQL Server is such a complex piece of software.

This chapter distills the core architecture of SQL Server and puts the most important components into the context of executing a simple query to help you understand the fundamentals of the core engine.

You will learn how SQL Server deals with your network connection, unravels what you're asking it to do, decides how it will execute your request, and finally how data is retrieved and modified on your behalf.

You will also discover when the transaction log is used and how it's affected by the configured recovery model; what happens when a checkpoint occurs and how you can influence the frequency; and what the lazywriter does.

The chapter starts by defining a "transaction" and what the requirements are for a database system to reliably process them. You'll then look at the life cycle of a simple query that reads data, taking a walk through the components employed to return a result set, before looking at how the process differs when data needs to be modified.

Finally, you'll read about the components and terminology that support the recovery process in SQL Server, and the SQLOS "framework" introduced in SQL Server 2005 that consolidates a lot of the low-level functions required by many SQL Server components.

> *Some areas of the life cycle described in this chapter are intentionally shallow in order to keep the flow manageable, and where that's the case you are directed to the chapter or chapters that cover the topic in more depth.*

DATABASE TRANSACTIONS

A *transaction* is a unit of work in a database that typically contains several commands that read from and write to the database. The most well-known feature of a transaction is that it must complete all of the commands in their entirety or none of them. This feature, called *atomicity*, is just one of four properties defined in the early days of database theory as requirements for a database transaction, collectively known as ACID properties.

ACID Properties

The four required properties of a database transaction are atomicity, consistency, isolation, and durability.

Atomicity

Atomicity means that *all* the effects of the transaction must complete successfully or the changes are rolled back. A classic example of an atomic transaction is a withdrawal from an ATM machine; the machine must both dispense the cash *and* debit your bank account. Either of those actions completing independently would cause a problem for either you or the bank.

Consistency

The consistency requirement ensures that the transaction cannot break the integrity rules of the database; it must leave the database in a consistent state. For example, your system might require that stock levels cannot be a negative value, a spare part cannot exist without a parent object, or the data in a sex field must be male or female. In order to be consistent, a transaction must not break any of the constraints or rules defined for the data.

Isolation

Isolation refers to keeping the changes of incomplete transactions running at the same time separate from one another. Each transaction must be entirely self-contained, and changes it makes must not be readable by any other transaction, although SQL Server does allow you to control the degree of isolation in order to find a balance between business and performance requirements.

Durability

Once a transaction is committed, it must persist even if there is a system failure — that is, it must be durable. In SQL Server, the information needed to replay changes made in a transaction is written to the transaction log before the transaction is considered to be committed.

SQL Server Transactions

There are two types of transactions in SQL Server that are differentiated only by the way they are created: *implicit* and *explicit*.

Implicit transactions are used automatically by SQL Server to guarantee the ACID properties of single commands. For example, if you wrote an update statement that modified 10 rows, SQL Server would run it as an implicit transaction so that the ACID properties would apply, and all 10 rows would be updated or none of them would.

Explicit transactions are started by using the BEGIN TRANSACTION T-SQL command and are stopped by using the COMMIT TRANSACTION or ROLLBACK TRANSACTION commands.

Committing a transaction effectively means making the changes within the transaction permanent, whereas rolling back a transaction means undoing all the changes that were made within the transaction. Explicit transactions are used to group together changes to which you want to apply the ACID properties as a whole, which also enables you to roll back the changes at any point if your business logic determines that you should cancel the change.

THE LIFE CYCLE OF A QUERY

To introduce the high-level components of SQL Server's architecture, this section uses the example of a query's life cycle to put each component into context in order to foster your understanding and create a foundation for the rest of the book.

It looks at a basic SELECT query first in order to reduce the scope to that of a READ operation, and then introduces the additional processes involved for a query that performs an UPDATE operation. Finally, you'll read about the terminology and processes that SQL Server uses to implement recovery while optimizing performance.

Figure 1-1 shows the high-level components that are used within the chapter to illustrate the life cycle of a query.

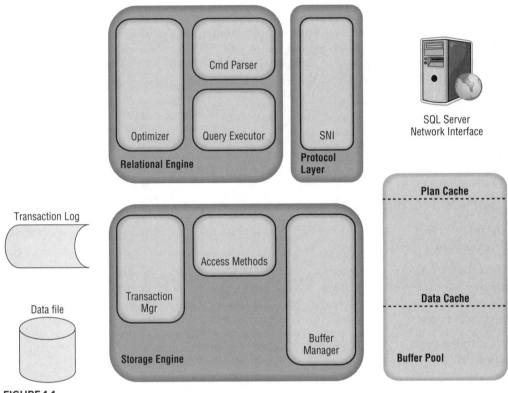

FIGURE 1-1

The Relational and Storage Engines

As shown in Figure 1-1, SQL Server is split into two main engines: the Relational Engine and the Storage Engine.

The Relational Engine is also sometimes called the query processor because its primary function is query optimization and execution. It contains a Command Parser to check query syntax and prepare query trees, a Query Optimizer that is arguably the crown jewel of any database system, and a Query Executor responsible for execution.

The Storage Engine is responsible for managing all I/O to the data, and contains the Access Methods code, which handles I/O requests for rows, indexes, pages, allocations and row versions, and a Buffer Manager, which deals with SQL Server's main memory consumer, the buffer pool. It also contains a Transaction Manager, which handles the locking of data to maintain Isolation (ACID properties) and manages the transaction log.

The Buffer Pool

The other major component you need to know about before getting into the query life cycle is the buffer pool, which is the largest consumer of memory in SQL Server. The buffer pool contains all the different caches in SQL Server, including the plan cache and the data cache, which is covered as the sections follow the query through its life cycle.

The buffer pool is covered in detail in Chapter 2.

A Basic Select Query

The details of the query used in this example aren't important — it's a simple SELECT statement with no joins, so you're just issuing a basic read request. Start at the client, where the first component you touch is the SQL Server Network Interface (SNI).

SQL Server Network Interface

The SQL Server Network Interface (SNI) is a protocol layer that establishes the network connection between the client and the server. It consists of a set of APIs that are used by both the database engine and the SQL Server Native Client (SNAC). SNI replaces the net-libraries found in SQL Server 2000 and the Microsoft Data Access Components (MDAC), which are included with Windows.

> *Late in the SQL Server 2005 development cycle, the SQL Server team decided to eliminate their dependence on MDAC to provide client connectivity. MDAC is owned by the SQL Server team but ships in the box with Windows, which means its shipped 'out-of-band' with SQL Server. With so many new features being added in SQL Server 2005, it became cumbersome to coordinate updates to MDAC with Windows releases, and SNI and SNAC were the solutions created. This meant that the SQL Server team could add support for new features and release the new code in-line with SQL Server releases.*

SNI isn't configurable directly; you just need to configure a network protocol on the client and the server. SQL Server has support for the following protocols:

➤ **Shared memory:** Simple and fast, shared memory is the default protocol used to connect from a client running on the same computer as SQL Server. It can only be used locally, has no configurable properties, and is always tried first when connecting from the local machine.

➤ **TCP/IP:** TCP/IP is the most commonly used access protocol for SQL Server. It enables you to connect to SQL Server by specifying an IP address and a port number. Typically, this happens automatically when you specify an instance to connect to. Your internal name resolution system resolves the hostname part of the instance name to an IP address, and either you connect to the default TCP port number 1433 for default instances or the SQL Browser service will find the right port for a named instance using UDP port 1434.

➤ **Named Pipes:** TCP/IP and Named Pipes are comparable protocols in the architectures in which they can be used. Named Pipes was developed for local area networks (LANs) but it can be inefficient across slower networks such as wide area networks (WANs).

To use Named Pipes you first need to enable it in SQL Server Configuration Manager (if you'll be connecting remotely) and then create a SQL Server alias, which connects to the server using Named Pipes as the protocol.

Named Pipes uses TCP port 445, so ensure that the port is open on any firewalls between the two computers, including the Windows Firewall.

➤ **VIA:** Virtual Interface Adapter is a protocol that enables high-performance communications between two systems. It requires specialized hardware at both ends and a dedicated connection.

Like Named Pipes, to use the VIA protocol you first need to enable it in SQL Server Configuration Manager and then create a SQL Server alias that connects to the server using VIA as the protocol.

Regardless of the network protocol used, once the connection is established, SNI creates a secure connection to a TDS endpoint (described next) on the server, which is then used to send requests and receive data. For the purpose here of following a query through its life cycle, you're sending the SELECT statement and waiting to receive the result set.

TDS (Tabular Data Stream) Endpoints

TDS is a Microsoft-proprietary protocol originally designed by Sybase that is used to interact with a database server. Once a connection has been made using a network protocol such as TCP/IP, a link is established to the relevant TDS endpoint that then acts as the communication point between the client and the server.

There is one TDS endpoint for each network protocol and an additional one reserved for use by the dedicated administrator connection (DAC). Once connectivity is established, TDS messages are used to communicate between the client and the server.

The SELECT statement is sent to the SQL Server as a TDS message across a TCP/IP connection (TCP/IP is the default protocol).

Protocol Layer

When the protocol layer in SQL Server receives your TDS packet, it has to reverse the work of the SNI at the client and unwrap the packet to find out what request it contains. The protocol layer is also responsible for packaging up results and status messages to send back to the client as TDS messages.

Our SELECT statement is marked in the TDS packet as a message of type "SQL Command," so it's passed on to the next component, the Query Parser, to begin the path toward execution.

Figure 1-2 shows where our query has gone so far. At the client, the statement was wrapped in a TDS packet by the SQL Server Network Interface and sent to the protocol layer on the SQL Server where it was unwrapped, identified as a SQL Command, and the code sent to the Command Parser by the SNI.

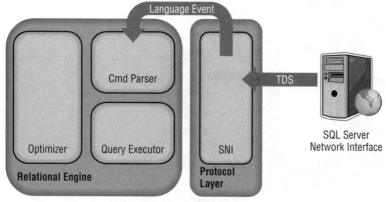

FIGURE 1-2

Command Parser

The Command Parser's role is to handle T-SQL language events. It first checks the syntax and returns any errors back to the protocol layer to send to the client. If the syntax is valid, then the next step is to generate a query plan or find an existing plan. A query plan contains the details about how SQL Server is going to execute a piece of code. It is commonly referred to as an *execution plan*.

To check for a query plan, the Command Parser generates a hash of the T-SQL and checks it against the plan cache to determine whether a suitable plan already exists. The plan cache is an area in the buffer pool used to cache query plans. If it finds a match, then the plan is read from cache and passed on to the Query Executor for execution. (The following section explains what happens if it doesn't find a match.)

Plan Cache

Creating execution plans can be time consuming and resource intensive, so it makes sense that if SQL Server has already found a good way to execute a piece of code that it should try to reuse it for subsequent requests.

The plan cache, part of SQL Server's buffer pool, is used to store execution plans in case they are needed later. You can read more about execution plans and plan cache in Chapters 2 and 5.

If no cached plan is found, then the Command Parser generates a query tree based on the T-SQL. A query tree is an internal structure whereby each node in the tree represents an operation in the query that needs to be performed. This tree is then passed to the Query Optimizer to process.

Our basic query didn't have an existing plan so a query tree was created and passed to the Query Optimizer.

Figure 1-3 shows the plan cache added to the diagram, which is checked by the Command Parser for an existing query plan. Also added is the query tree output from the Command Parser being passed to the optimizer because nothing was found in cache for our query.

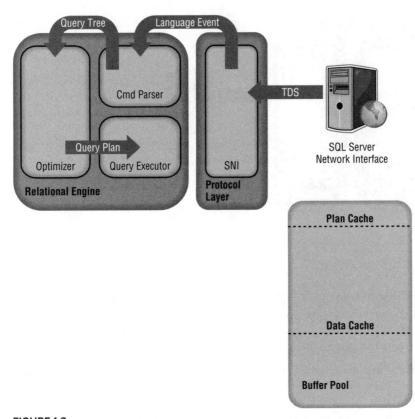

FIGURE 1-3

Optimizer

The Optimizer is the most prized possession of the SQL Server team and one of the most complex and secretive parts of the product. Fortunately, it's only the low-level algorithms and source code that are so well protected (even within Microsoft), and research and observation can reveal how the Optimizer works.

It is what's known as a "cost-based" optimizer, which means that it evaluates multiple ways to execute a query and then picks the method that it deems will have the lowest cost to execute. This "method" of executing is implemented as a query plan and is the output from the optimizer.

Based on that description, you would be forgiven for thinking that the optimizer's job is to find the *best* query plan because that would seem like an obvious assumption. Its actual job, however, is to find a *good* plan in a reasonable amount of time, rather than the *best* plan. The optimizer's goal is most commonly described as finding the most *efficient* plan.

If the optimizer tried to find the "best" plan every time, it might take longer to find the plan than it would to just execute a slower plan (some built-in heuristics actually ensure that it never takes longer to find a good plan than it does to just find a plan and execute it).

As well as being cost based, the optimizer also performs multi-stage optimization, increasing the number of decisions available to find a good plan at each stage. When a good plan is found, optimization stops at that stage.

The first stage is known as pre-optimization, and queries drop out of the process at this stage when the statement is simple enough that the most efficient plan is obvious, obviating the need for additional costing. Basic queries with no joins are regarded as "simple," and plans produced as such have zero cost (because they haven't been costed) and are referred to as *trivial plans*.

The next stage is where optimization actually begins, and it consists of three search phases:

➤ **Phase 0:** During this phase the optimizer looks at nested loop joins and won't consider parallel operators (parallel means executing across multiple processors and is covered in Chapter 5.

The optimizer will stop here if the cost of the plan it has found is < 0.2. A plan generated at this phase is known as a *transaction processing*, or *TP*, plan.

➤ **Phase 1:** Phase 1 uses a subset of the possible optimization rules and looks for common patterns for which it already has a plan.

The optimizer will stop here if the cost of the plan it has found is < 1.0. Plans generated in this phase are called *quick plans*.

➤ **Phase 2:** This final phase is where the optimizer pulls out all the stops and is able to use all of its optimization rules. It will also look at parallelism and indexed views (if you're running Enterprise Edition).

Completion of Phase 2 is a balance between the cost of the plan found versus the time spent optimizing. Plans created in this phase have an optimization level of "Full."

HOW MUCH DOES IT COST?

The term *Cost* doesn't translate into seconds or anything meaningful and is just an arbitrary number used to assign a value representing the resource cost for a plan. However, its origin was a benchmark on a desktop computer at Microsoft early in SQL Server's life (probably 7.0).

The statistics that the optimizer uses to estimate cost aren't covered here because they aren't relevant to the concepts illustrated in this chapter but you can read about them in Chapter 5.

Because our SELECT query is very simple, it drops out of the process in the pre-optimization phase because the plan is obvious to the optimizer. Now that there is a query plan, it's on to the Query Executor for execution.

Query Executor

The Query Executor's job is self-explanatory; it executes the query. To be more specific, it executes the query plan by working through each step it contains and interacting with the Storage Engine to retrieve or modify data.

> *The interface to the Storage Engine is actually OLE DB, which is a legacy from a design decision made in SQL Server's history. The development team's origi-nal idea was to interface through OLE DB to allow different Storage Engines to be plugged in. However, the strategy changed soon after that.*
>
> *The idea of a pluggable Storage Engine was dropped and the developers started writing extensions to OLE DB to improve performance. These customizations are now core to the product, and while there's now no reason to have OLE DB, the existing investment and performance precludes any justification to change it.*

The SELECT query needs to retrieve data, so the request is passed to the Storage Engine through an OLE DB interface to the Access Methods.

Figure 1-4 shows the addition of the query plan as the output from the Optimizer being passed to the Query Executor. Also introduced is the Storage Engine, which is interfaced by the Query Executor via OLE DB to the Access Methods (coming up next).

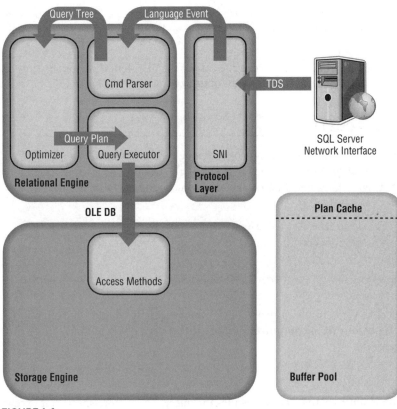

FIGURE 1-4

Access Methods

Access Methods is a collection of code that provides the storage structures for your data and indexes as well as the interface through which data is retrieved and modified. It contains all the code to retrieve data but it doesn't actually perform the operation itself; it passes the request to the Buffer Manager.

Suppose our SELECT statement needs to read just a few rows that are all on a single page. The Access Methods code will ask the Buffer Manager to retrieve the page so that it can prepare an OLE DB rowset to pass back to the Relational Engine.

Buffer Manager

The Buffer Manager, as its name suggests, manages the buffer pool, which represents the majority of SQL Server's memory usage.

If you need to read some rows from a page (you'll look at writes when we look at an UPDATE query) the Buffer Manager will check the data cache in the buffer pool to see if it already has the page cached in memory. If the page is already cached, then the results are passed back to the Access Methods.

If the page isn't already in cache, then the Buffer Manager will get the page from the database on disk, put it in the data cache, and pass the results to the Access Methods.

> The PAGEIOLATCH *wait type represents the time it takes to read a data page from disk into memory. You can read about wait types in Chapter 3.*

The key point to take away from this is that you only ever work with data in memory. Every new data read that you request is first read from disk and then written to memory (the data cache) before being returned to you as a result set.

This is why SQL Server needs to maintain a minimum level of free pages in memory; you wouldn't be able to read any new data if there were no space in cache to put it first.

The Access Methods code determined that the SELECT query needed a single page, so it asked the Buffer Manager to get it. The Buffer Manager checked to see whether it already had it in the data cache, and then loaded it from disk into the cache when it couldn't find it.

Data Cache

The data cache is usually the largest part of the buffer pool; therefore, it's the largest memory consumer within SQL Server. It is here that every data page that is read from disk is written to before being used.

The sys.dm_os_buffer_descriptors DMV contains one row for every data page currently held in cache. You can use this script to see how much space each database is using in the data cache:

```
SELECT count(*)*8/1024 AS 'Cached Size (MB)'
    ,CASE database_id
        WHEN 32767 THEN 'ResourceDb'
```

```
              ELSE db_name(database_id)
              END AS 'Database'
FROM sys.dm_os_buffer_descriptors
GROUP BY db_name(database_id) ,database_id
ORDER BY 'Cached Size (MB)' DESC
```

The output will look something like this (with your own databases obviously):

```
Cached Size (MB)   Database
3287               People
34                 tempdb
12                 ResourceDb
4                  msdb
```

In this example, the `People` database has 3,287MB of data pages in the data cache.

The amount of time that pages stay in cache is determined by a *least recently used (LRU) policy.*

The header of each page in cache stores details about the last two times it was accessed, and a periodic scan through the cache examines these values. A counter is maintained that is decremented if the page hasn't been accessed for a while; and when SQL Server needs to free up some cache, the pages with the lowest counter are flushed first.

The process of "aging out" pages from cache and maintaining an available amount of free cache pages for subsequent use can be done by any worker thread after scheduling its own I/O or by the lazywriter process, covered later in the section "Lazywriter."

You can view how long SQL Server expects to be able to keep a page in cache by looking at the MSSQL$*<instance>*:Buffer Manager\Page Life Expectancy counter in Performance Monitor. Page life expectancy (PLE) is the amount of time, in seconds, that SQL Server expects to be able to keep a page in cache.

Under memory pressure, data pages are flushed from cache far more frequently. Microsoft recommends a minimum of 300 seconds for a good PLE, but for systems with plenty of physical memory this will easily reach thousands of seconds.

The database page read to serve the result set for our `SELECT` query is now in the data cache in the buffer pool and will have an entry in the sys.dm_os_buffer_descriptors DMV. Now that the Buffer Manager has the result set, it's passed back to the Access Methods to make its way to the client.

A Basic select Statement Life Cycle Summary

Figure 1-5 shows the whole life cycle of a `SELECT` query, described here:

1.   The SQL Server Network Interface (SNI) on the client established a connection to the SNI on the SQL Server using a network protocol such as TCP/IP. It then created a connection to a TDS endpoint over the TCP/IP connection and sent the `SELECT` statement to SQL Server as a TDS message.

2.   The SNI on the SQL Server unpacked the TDS message, read the `SELECT` statement, and passed a "SQL Command" to the Command Parser.

3. The Command Parser checked the plan cache in the buffer pool for an existing, usable query plan. When it didn't find one, it created a query tree based on the SELECT statement and passed it to the Optimizer to generate a query plan.

4. The Optimizer generated a "zero cost" or "trivial" plan in the pre-optimization phase because the statement was so simple. The query plan created was then passed to the Query Executor for execution.

5. At execution time, the Query Executor determined that data needed to be read to complete the query plan so it passed the request to the Access Methods in the Storage Engine via an OLE DB interface.

6. The Access Methods needed to read a page from the database to complete the request from the Query Executor and asked the Buffer Manager to provision the data page.

7. The Buffer Manager checked the data cache to see if it already had the page in cache. It wasn't in cache so it pulled the page from disk, put it in cache, and passed it back to the Access Methods.

8. Finally, the Access Methods passed the result set back to the Relational Engine to send to the client.

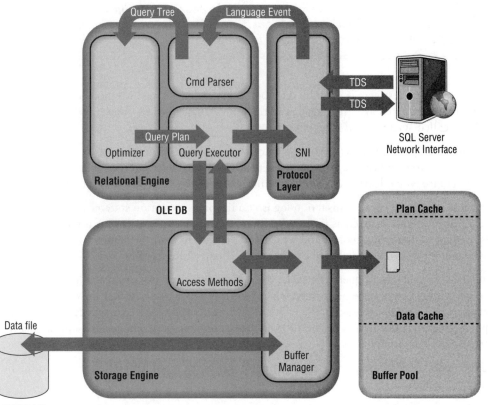

FIGURE 1-5

A Simple Update Query

Now that you understand the life cycle for a query that just reads some data, the next step is to determine what happens when you need to write data. To answer that, this section takes a look at a simple UPDATE query that modifies the data that was read in the previous example.

The good news is that the process is exactly the same as the process for the SELECT statement you just looked at until you get to the Access Methods.

The Access Methods need to make a data modification this time, so before it passes on the I/O request the details of the change need to be persisted to disk. That is the job of the Transaction Manager.

Transaction Manager

The Transaction Manager has two components that are of interest here: a Lock Manager and a Log Manager. The Lock Manager is responsible for providing concurrency to the data, and it delivers the configured level of *isolation* (as defined in the ACID properties at the beginning of the chapter) by using locks.

> *The Lock Manager is also employed during the* SELECT *query life cycle covered earlier, but it would have been a distraction, and is only mentioned here because it's part of the Transaction Manager. Locking is covered in depth in Chapter 6.*

The real item of interest here is actually the Log Manager. The Access Methods code requests that the changes it wants to make are logged, and the Log Manager writes the changes to the transaction log. This is called *Write-Ahead Logging.*

Writing to the transaction log is the only part of a data modification transaction that always needs a physical write to disk because SQL Server depends on being able to reread that change in the event of system failure (you'll learn more about this in the "Recovery" section coming up).

What's actually stored in the transaction log isn't a list of modification statements but only details of the page changes that occurred as the result of a modification statement. This is all that SQL Server needs in order to undo any change, and why it's so difficult to read the contents of a transaction log in any meaningful way, although you can buy a third-party tool to help.

Getting back to the UPDATE query life cycle, the update operation has now been logged. The actual data modification can only be performed when confirmation is received that the operation has been physically written to the transaction log. This is why transaction log performance is so crucial. Chapter 4 contains information on monitoring transaction log performance and optimizing the underlying storage for it.

Once the Access Methods receives confirmation, it passes the modification request on to the Buffer Manager to complete.

Figure 1-6 shows the Transaction Manager, which is called by the Access Methods and the transaction log, which is the destination for logging our update. The Buffer Manager is also in play now because the modification request is ready to be completed.

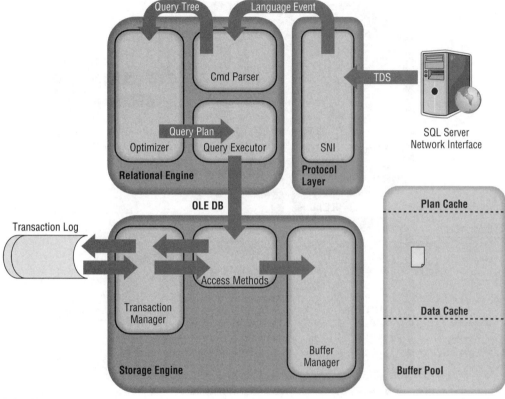

FIGURE 1-6

Buffer Manager

The page that needs to be modified is already in cache, so all the Buffer Manager needs to do is modify the page as requested by the Access Methods. The page is modified in the cache, and confirmation is sent back to Access Methods and ultimately to the client.

The key point here (and it's a big one so pay attention) is that the UPDATE statement has changed the data in the data cache, *not* in the actual database file on disk. This is done for performance reasons, and the page is now what's called a *dirty page* because it's different in memory than it is on disk.

It doesn't compromise the *durability* of the modification as defined in the ACID properties because you can recreate the change using the transaction log if, for example, you suddenly lost power to the server and therefore anything in physical RAM (i.e., the data cache). How and when the dirty page makes its way into the database file is covered in the next section.

Figure 1-7 shows the completed life cycle for the update. The Buffer Manager has made the modification to the page in cache and has passed confirmation back up the chain. The database data file was not accessed during the operation, as you can see in the diagram.

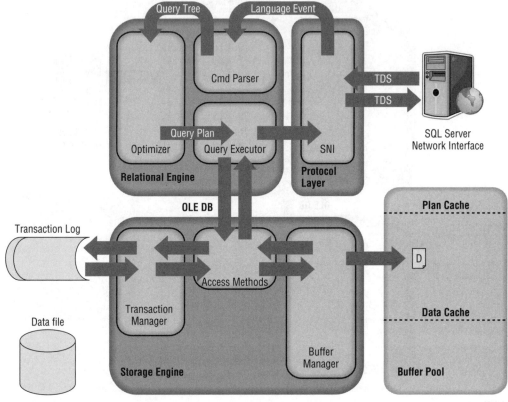

FIGURE 1-7

Recovery

In the previous section you read about the life cycle of an UPDATE query, which introduced *Write-Ahead Logging* as the method by which SQL Server maintains the *durability* of any changes.

Modifications are written to the transaction log first and are then actioned in memory only. This is done for performance reasons and because you can recover the changes from the transaction log should you need to.

This process introduces some new concepts and terminology that are explored further in this section on "recovery."

Dirty Pages

When a page is read from disk into memory it is regarded as a *clean* page because it's exactly the same as its counterpart on the disk. However, once the page has been modified in memory it is marked as a *dirty* page.

Clean pages can be flushed from cache using `dbcc dropcleanbuffers`, which can be handy when you're troubleshooting development and test environments because it forces subsequent reads to be fulfilled from disk, rather than cache, but doesn't touch any dirty pages.

A dirty page is simply a page that has changed in memory since it was loaded from disk and is now different from the on-disk page. You can use the following query, which is based on the `sys.dm_os_buffer_descriptors` DMV, to see how many dirty pages exist in each database:

```
SELECT db_name(database_id) AS 'Database',count(page_id) AS 'Dirty Pages'
FROM sys.dm_os_buffer_descriptors
WHERE is_modified =1
GROUP BY db_name(database_id)
ORDER BY count(page_id) DESC
```

Running this on my test server produced the following results showing that at the time the query was run, there were just under 20MB (2,524*8\1,024) of dirty pages in the `People` database:

```
Database Dirty Pages
People   2524
Tempdb   61
Master   1
```

These dirty pages will be written back to the database file periodically whenever the *free buffer list* is low or a *checkpoint* occurs. SQL Server always tries to maintain a number of free pages in cache in order to allocate pages quickly, and these free pages are tracked in the free buffer list.

Whenever a worker thread issues a read request, it gets a list of 64 pages in cache and checks whether the free buffer list is below a certain threshold. If it is, it will try to age-out some pages in its list, which causes any dirty pages to be written to disk.

Another thread called the *lazywriter* also works based on a low free buffer list.

Lazywriter

The *lazywriter* is a thread that periodically checks the size of the free buffer list. When it's low, it scans the whole data cache to age-out any pages that haven't been used for a while. If it finds any dirty pages that haven't been used for a while, they are flushed to disk before being marked as free in memory.

The lazywriter also monitors the free physical memory on the server and will release memory from the free buffer list back to Windows in very low memory conditions. When SQL Server is busy, it will also grow the size of the free buffer list to meet demand (and therefore the buffer pool) when there is free physical memory and the configured Max Server Memory threshold hasn't been reached. For more on Max Server Memory see Chapter 2.

Checkpoint Process

A checkpoint is a point in time created by the checkpoint process at which SQL Server can be sure that any *committed* transactions have had all their changes written to disk. This checkpoint then becomes the marker from which database recovery can start.

The checkpoint process ensures that any dirty pages associated with a committed transaction will be flushed to disk. Unlike the lazywriter, however, a checkpoint does not remove the page from cache; it makes sure the dirty page is written to disk and then marks the cached paged as clean in the page header.

By default, on a busy server, SQL Server will issue a checkpoint roughly every minute, which is marked in the transaction log. If the SQL Server instance or the database is restarted, then the recovery process reading the log knows that it doesn't need to do anything with log records prior to the checkpoint.

The time between checkpoints therefore represents the amount of work that needs to be done to *roll forward* any committed transactions that occurred after the last checkpoint, and to *roll back* any transactions that hadn't committed. By checkpointing every minute, SQL Server is trying to keep the recovery time when starting a database to less than one minute, but it won't automatically checkpoint unless at least 10MB has been written to the log within the period.

Checkpoints can also be manually called by using the CHECKPOINT T-SQL command, and can occur because of other events happening in SQL Server. For example, when you issue a backup command, a checkpoint will run first.

Trace flag 3502 is an undocumented trace flag that records in the error log when a checkpoint starts and stops. For example, after adding it as a startup trace flag and running a workload with numerous writes, my error log contained the entries shown in Figure 1-8, which indicates checkpoints running between 30 and 40 seconds apart.

2009-04-26 22:31:33.070	spid10s	About to log Checkpoint begin.
2009-04-26 22:31:33.070	spid10s	About to log Checkpoint end.
2009-04-26 22:32:05.910	spid10s	About to log Checkpoint begin.
2009-04-26 22:32:05.910	spid10s	About to log Checkpoint end.
2009-04-26 23:33:29.280	spid10s	About to log Checkpoint begin.
2009-04-26 23:33:29.370	spid10s	About to log Checkpoint end.
2009-04-26 23:34:12.000	spid10s	About to log Checkpoint begin.
2009-04-26 23:34:12.090	spid10s	About to log Checkpoint end.

FIGURE 1-8

ALL ABOUT TRACE FLAGS

Trace flags provide a way to change the behavior of SQL Server temporarily and are generally used to help with troubleshooting or for enabling and disabling certain features for testing. Hundreds of trace flags exist but very few are officially documented; for a list of those that are and more information on using trace flags have a look here: http://msdn.microsoft.com/en-us/library/ms188396.aspx

Recovery Interval

Recovery Interval is a server configuration option that can be used to influence the time between checkpoints, and therefore the time it takes to recover a database on startup — hence, "recovery interval."

By default the recovery interval is set to 0, which allows SQL Server to choose an appropriate interval, which usually equates to roughly one minute between automatic checkpoints.

Changing this value to greater than 0 represents the number of minutes you want to allow between checkpoints. Under most circumstances you won't need to change this value, but if you were more concerned about the overhead of the checkpoint process than the recovery time, you have the option.

However, the recovery interval is usually set only in test and lab environments where it's set ridiculously high in order to effectively stop automatic checkpointing for the purpose of monitoring something or to gain a performance advantage.

Unless you're chasing world speed records for SQL Server you shouldn't need to change it in a real-world production environment.

SQL Server evens throttles checkpoint I/O to stop it from impacting the disk subsystem too much, so it's quite good at self-governing. If you ever see the SLEEP_BPOOL_FLUSH wait type on your server, that means checkpoint I/O was throttled to maintain overall system performance. You can read all about waits and wait types in Chapter 3.

Recovery Models

SQL Server has three database recovery models: Full, bulk-logged, and simple. Which model you choose affects the way the transaction log is used and how big it grows, your backup strategy, and your restore options.

Full

Databases using the full recovery model have all of their operations fully logged in the transaction log and must have a backup strategy that includes full backups *and* transaction log backups.

Starting with SQL Server 2005, Full backups don't truncate the transaction log. This is so that the sequence of transaction log backups isn't broken and gives you an extra recovery option if your full backup is damaged.

SQL Server databases that require the highest level of recoverability should use the Full Recovery Model.

Bulk-Logged

This is a special recovery model because it is intended to be used only temporarily to improve the performance of certain bulk operations by *minimally-logging* them; all other operations are fully-logged just like the full recovery model. This can improve performance because only the information required to roll back the transaction is logged. *Redo* information is not logged which means that you also lose point-in-time-recovery.

These bulk operations include:

- ➤ BULK INSERT
- ➤ Using the bcp executable
- ➤ SELECT INTO
- ➤ CREATE INDEX
- ➤ ALTER INDEX REBUILD
- ➤ DROP INDEX

Simple

When the simple recovery model is set on a database, all committed transactions are truncated from the transaction log every time a checkpoint occurs. This ensures that the size of the log is kept to a minimum and that transaction log backups are not necessary (or even possible). Whether or not that is a good or a bad thing depends on what level of recovery you require for the database.

If the potential to lose all the changes since the last full or differential backup still meets your business requirements then simple recovery might be the way to go.

THE SQLOS (SQL OPERATING SYSTEM)

So far, this chapter has abstracted the concept of the SQLOS to make the flow of components through the architecture easier to understand without going off on too many tangents. However, the SQLOS is core to SQL Server's architecture so you need to understand why it exists and what it does to complete your view of how SQL Server works.

In summary, the SQLOS is a thin user-mode layer (Chapter 2) that sits between SQL Server and Windows. It is used for low-level operations such as scheduling, I/O completion, memory management, and resource management.

To explore exactly what this means and why it's needed, you first need to understand a bit about Windows.

Windows is a general purpose OS and is not optimized for server-based applications, SQL Server in particular. Instead, the goal for the Windows development team is to make sure that any application written by a wide-range of developers inside and outside Microsoft will work correctly and have good performance. Windows needs to work well for these broad scenarios so the dev teams are not going to do anything special that would be used in less than 1% of applications.

For example, the scheduling in Windows is very basic because things are done for the common cause. Optimizing the way that threads are chosen for execution is always going to be limited because of this broad performance goal but if an application does its own scheduling then there is more intelligence about who to choose next. For example, assigning some threads a higher priority or deciding that choosing one thread for execution will prevent other threads being blocked later on.

> ✎ Scheduling *is the method by which units of work are given time on a CPU to execute. See Chapter 5 for more information.*

In a lot of cases SQL Server had custom code to handle a lot of these areas already. The User Mode Scheduler (UMS) was introduced in SQL Server 7 to handle scheduling and SQL Server was managing its own memory even earlier than that.

The idea for SQLOS (which was first implemented in SQL Server 2005) was to take all of these things developed by different internal SQL Server development teams to provide performance improvements on Windows and put them in a single place with a single team that will continue to optimize these low-level functions. This then leaves the other teams to concentrate on challenges more specific to their own domain within SQL Server.

DEFINING DMVS

Dynamic Management Views (DMVs) allow much greater visibility into the workings of SQL Server than in any version prior to SQL Server 2005. They are basically just views on top of the system tables, but the concept allows Microsoft to provide a massive amount of useful information through them.

The standard syntax starts with sys.dm_ which indicates that it's a DMV (there are also Dynamic Management Functions but DMV is still the collective term in popular use) followed by the area about which the DMV provides information, for example, `sys.dm_os_` for SQLOS, `sys.dm_db_` for database, and `sys.dm_exec_` for query execution.

The last part of the name describes the actual content accessible within the view; `sys.dm_db_index_usage_stats` and `sys.dm_os_waiting_tasks` are a couple of examples and you'll come across many more throughout the book.

Another benefit to having everything in one place is that you can now get better visibility of what's happening at that level than was possible prior to SQLOS. You can access all this information through dynamic management views (DMVs). Any DMV that starts with sys.dm_os_ provides an insight into the workings of SQLOS. For example:

➤ **sys.dm_os_schedulers:** Returns one row per scheduler (there is one user scheduler per core) and shows information on scheduler load and health. See Chapters 3 and 5 for more information.

➤ **sys.dm_os_waiting_tasks:** Returns one row for every executing task that is currently waiting for a resource as well as the wait type. See Chapter 3 for more information.

➤ **sys.dm_os_memory_clerks:** Memory clerks are used by SQL Server to allocate memory. Significant components within SQL Server have their own memory clerk. This DMV shows all the memory clerks and how much memory each one is using. See Chapter 2 for more information.

Relating SQLOS back to the architecture diagrams seen earlier, many of the components will make calls to the SQLOS in order to fulfill low-level functions required to support their roles.

Just to be clear, the SQLOS doesn't replace Windows. Ultimately, everything ends up using the documented Windows system services; SQL Server just uses them in such a way as to optimize for its own specific scenarios.

> *SQLOS is not a way to port the SQL Server architecture to other platforms like Linux or MacOS so it's not an OS abstraction layer. It doesn't wrap all the OS APIs like other frameworks such as .NET, which is why it's referred to as a "thin" user-mode layer. Only the things that SQL Server really needs have been put into SQLOS.*

SUMMARY

In this chapter you learned about SQL Server's architecture by following the flow of components used when you issue a read request and an update request. You also learned some key terminology and processes used for the recovery of SQL Server databases and where the SQLOS fits into the architecture.

The key takeaways from this chapter are:

➤ The Query Optimizer's job is to find a good plan in a reasonable amount of time; not the *best* plan.

➤ Anything you want to read or update will need to be read into memory first.

➤ Any updates to data will be written to the transaction log on disk before being updated in memory so transaction log performance is critical; the update isn't written directly to the data file.

➤ A database page that is changed in memory but not on disk is known as a dirty page.

➤ Dirty pages are flushed to disk by the checkpoint process and the lazywriter.

➤ Checkpoints occur automatically, roughly every minute and provide the starting point for recovery.

➤ The lazywriter keeps space available in cache by flushing dirty pages to disk and keeping only recently used pages in cache.

➤ When a database is using the Full recovery model, full backups will not truncate the transaction log. You must configure transaction log backups.

The SQLOS is a framework used by components in SQL Server for scheduling, I/O, and memory management.

2

Understanding Memory

WHAT'S IN THIS CHAPTER

➤ Understanding physical memory and how virtual memory addressing is used

➤ Optimizing 32-bit systems with large amounts of memory

➤ Optimizing the memory configuration on 64-bit systems

➤ AWE and its uses on 32-bit *and* 64-bit environments

➤ Explaining MemToLeave

➤ SQL Server's memory clerks, caches, and pools

➤ Looking at SQL Server's plan cache

➤ Determining a setting for Max Server Memory

➤ An in-depth look at Query/Workspace memory

Memory, disk, and CPU are the holy trinity of resources in a computer system, and memory is first because it's the area that you're most likely to have an issue with. Memory issues can cause both disk and CPU saturation, so when troubleshooting a server issue (or at least a performance issue) you need to start by looking at the memory profile of the system.

This chapter explains what to expect from different system architectures, what can be configured, what the Microsoft best practices are, and, most important, how they were originally determined.

The first part of this chapter covers memory addressing, which includes physical memory, virtual memory, the Virtual Memory Manager, and the different options you have for tuning 32-bit and 64-bit systems. The second part focuses more on SQL Server's internal memory structures and consumers. It covers how to manage SQL Server's memory usage and how to view the details of each consumer.

WINDOWS AND MEMORY

This section covers topics that are generally considered to be outside the scope of a database professional, but it will give you an understanding of and appreciation for the underlying architectures on which SQL Server depends. The rationale behind this approach is to help you clarify your skill set and enable you to be more creative and inclusive as you troubleshoot.

Physical Memory

Physical memory refers to the volatile storage space most commonly referred to as RAM (random access memory). RAM is also referred to as *primary storage*, *main memory*, or *system memory* because it's directly addressable by the CPU. It is regarded as the fastest type of storage you can use, but it's volatile, meaning you lose what was stored when you reboot the computer. It's also expensive and limited in capacity when compared to nonvolatile storage such as a hard disk.

For example, Windows Server 2008 Enterprise and Datacenter Editions support up to 2TB of RAM, but buying a server with that much memory will cost you millions of U.S. dollars, whereas a single 1TB hard disk can be picked up for less than $100. Combine a few of those together and you can have tens of TBs of very cost-effective storage space. Consequently, servers use a combination of hard disks to store data, which is then loaded into RAM where it can be worked with more quickly.

By way of throughput comparison, the peak transfer rate for a mainstream RAM module would be about 5GB/sec, and the fastest hard disk I could find at the time of writing boasts "Unprecedented performance with a sustained data rate of up to 164MB/sec." That's 3.2% of the transfer rate of a reasonable RAM module.

This chapter doesn't delve deeply into different types of RAM, but it can be useful (or at least mildly interesting) to understand some of the acronyms and keywords at a high level, especially if you ever get involved in specifying new hardware for servers running Microsoft SQL Server.

SIMMs and DIMMs

Single in-line memory modules (SIMMs) and dual inline memory modules (DIMMs) refer to the physical implementation of a type of RAM. SIMMs were phased out in the mid-1990s, replaced by the more efficient DIMMs, which are the predominant type of memory today. A DIMM is what you get to plug into the motherboard when you buy a memory module.

DRAM

Dynamic RAM (DRAM) is a type of RAM that stores data in a capacitor that needs to be periodically "recharged" to prevent the data from being lost. This periodic refresh is where the term *dynamic* comes from, as opposed to *static* RAM (SRAM). SRAM does not need to be refreshed, is faster, and consumes less power, but is considerably more expensive. For this reason, DRAM is the basis for mainstream computer memory, although you will find SRAM embedded in small amounts for use in such areas as CPU cache.

SDRAM

Building upon DRAM technology, synchronous DRAM is synchronized with the computer's system bus, allowing for more complexity in its usage, including pipelining, which enables instructions to be queued, providing better efficiency.

DDR SDRAM

Double-data-rate SDRAM doubles the amount of consecutive data able to be read or written in a single instruction over standard SDRAM. *DDR2* doubles that again, and *DDR3* is double that of DDR2, providing four times the amount of consecutive data read or writes per operation compared to the original DDR1.

DDR2 is still a common choice for both the server and desktop market. However, processors based on Intel's microarchitecture (codenamed Nehalem) support only DDR3 so it will quickly become the de facto standard. You can read more about Nehalem in Chapter 5.

Dual-Channel Memory

Dual-channel architecture is technology in the memory controller that is used by a supported motherboard to increase the bandwidth to the controller by using standard memory modules in a "paired" fashion.

The CPU is the fastest component in a computer, and if the CPU bus speed is greater than the memory bus speed, then you can get a bottleneck at the memory controller. Dual-channel memory was created to relieve that pressure.

Intel's Nehalem architecture has the memory controller on the CPU, so the memory is connected directly to the processor *and* it uses three-channel memory.

Registered and Unbuffered Modules

Registered memory modules contain a "register" that reduces electrical load on the memory controller, enabling servers to remain stable with more memory modules. It also requires a supporting motherboard and is an attractive feature for servers that need a lot of memory, so you'll find that most servers require registered memory. However, because it makes the modules more expensive and adds a performance penalty, they are typically used only in servers and workstations for which scalability and stability is paramount.

When buying memory for desktop computers, you might see modules listed as "unbuffered." This simply means that the module doesn't have a register.

Error-Correcting Code (ECC) Memory

Memory is vulnerable to corruption by background radiation, among others things, which can change a stored bit value. The frequency of these errors is quite low; online research indicates an average of one bit error per gigabyte per month. Although the effect could be as severe as crashing the computer, the chances of it affecting a single bit value that you were using for a critical operation at that moment is very small.

On desktop systems that typically don't run 24/7, the chances of a corruption happening, and happening in a part of memory that you happened to be using at the time, is extremely low. Because of this and the overhead of using ECC, ECC memory and ECC-capable motherboards are not prevalent in the desktop market. For servers that are generally expected to run constantly, however, the risk is greater and the implications more severe. Most servers will support or even require that you use ECC memory modules.

FB-DIMMs

Fully Buffered DIMMs are a relatively recent technology standard based on DDR2 that uses an *advanced memory buffer (AMB)* between the memory controller and the memory module. The memory controller writes to the AMB instead of directly to the module, allowing for more memory bandwidth and error correction (with little overhead) although the addition of the AMB introduces some latency to memory requests.

FB-DIMMs need additional power to run the AMB, which means additional heat is generated. This has led to some doubt as to the future of the technology, but it's still the predominant platform for Intel-based servers a number of years after its expected decline.

Maximum Supported Physical Memory

For ease of reference, Table 2-1 shows the maximum supported physical RAM for each edition of SQL Server 2008 running on Windows Server 2008; and Table 2-2 shows the same information for Windows Server 2003 R2.

TABLE 2-1: Memory Supported by SQL Server 2008 on Various Windows Server 2008 Editions

SQL SERVER EDITION	WINDOWS DATACENTER 32-BIT	WINDOWS DATACENTER 64-BIT	WINDOWS ENTERPRISE 32-BIT	WINDOWS ENTERPRISE 64-BIT	WINDOWS STANDARD 32-BIT	WINDOWS STANDARD 64-BIT	WINDOWS WEB 32-BIT	WINDOWS WEB 64-BIT
Enterprise	64GB[1]	2TB[1]	64GB[1]	2TB[1]	4GB[1]	32GB[1]	4GB[1]	32GB[1]
Developer	64GB[1]	2TB[1]	64GB[1]	2TB[1]	4GB[1]	32GB[1]	4GB[1]	32GB[1]
Standard	64GB[1]	2TB[1]	64GB[1]	2TB[1]	4GB[1]	32GB[1]	4GB[1]	32GB[1]
Web	64GB[1]	2TB[1]	64GB[1]	2TB[1]	4GB[1]	32GB[1]	4GB[1]	32GB[1]
Workgroup	64GB[1]	4GB	64GB[1]	4GB	4GB[1]	4GB	4GB[1]	4GB
Express	1GB	n/a	1GB	n/a	1GB	n/a	1GB	n/a

[1] These limitations are the operating system (OS) maximum. Where marked, SQL Server will support the OS maximum, ensuring that SQL Server will be able to take immediate advantage of future revisions of the OS that increase these limits.

TABLE 2-2: Memory Supported by SQL Server 2008 on Various Windows Server 2003 R2 Editions with SP2

SQL SERVER EDITION	WINDOWS DATACENTER 32-BIT	WINDOWS DATACENTER 64-BIT	WINDOWS ENTERPRISE 32-BIT	WINDOWS ENTERPRISE 64-BIT	WINDOWS STANDARD 32-BIT	WINDOWS STANDARD 64-BIT
Enterprise	128GB[1]	2TB[1]	64GB[1]	2TB[1]	4GB[1]	32GB[1]
Developer	128GB[1]	2TB[1]	64GB[1]	2TB[1]	4GB[1]	32GB[1]
Standard	128GB[1]	2TB[1]	64GB[1]	2TB[1]	4GB[1]	32GB[1]
Web	128GB[1]	2TB[1]	64GB[1]	2TB[1]	4GB[1]	32GB[1]
Workgroup	128GB[1]	4GB	64GB[1]	4GB	4GB[1]	4GB
Express	1GB	n/a	1GB	n/a	1GB	n/a

[1] These limitations are the operating system (OS) maximum. Where marked, SQL Server will support the OS maximum, ensuring that SQL Server will be able to take immediate advantage of future revisions of the OS that increase these limits.

Virtual Address Space

If all the processes running on a computer could only use addresses in physical memory, there would be a bottleneck in the system very quickly. They would all have to share the same range of addresses, which would be limited by the amount of RAM installed in the computer. As physical memory is very fast to access and cannot be increased indefinitely (as just discussed in the previous section) it's a resource that needs to be used efficiently.

Windows (and many other mainstream, modern operating systems) assigns a virtual address space (VAS) to each process. This provides a layer of abstraction between an application and physical memory so that the operating system can choose the most efficient way to use physical memory across all the processes. For example, two different processes can both use the memory address 0xFFF because it's a *virtual* address and each process has its own VAS with the same address range.

Whether or not that address maps to physical memory or is determined by the operating system or, more specifically (for Windows at least), the Virtual Memory Manager, is covered in the next section.

The size of the virtual address space is determined largely by the CPU architecture. A 32-bit CPU running 32-bit software (also known as the *x86 platform*) is so named because it is based on an architecture that can manipulate values that are up to 32 bits in length. This means that a 32-bit memory pointer can store a value between 0 and 4,294,967,295 to reference a memory address. This equates to a maximum addressable space of 4GB on 32-bit platforms.

The 4GB of VAS is logically split into two ranges of 2GB: one for the process and one reserved for system use. These two ranges are commonly referred to as *user mode* and *kernel mode* address spaces and are illustrated in Figure 2-1. With a default configuration, each application process (i.e., SQL Server) can access up to 2GB of VAS, and therefore 2GB of physical memory. The options to tune this are covered in depth in the upcoming section "Tuning 32-bit Systems."

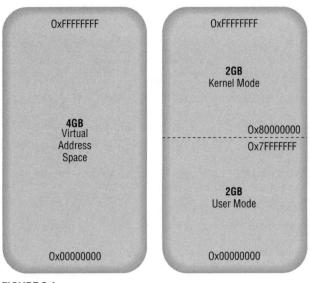

FIGURE 2-1

The limitation of 4GB exists because it's effectively the largest number that can fit in a 32-bit pointer. From here, it's an easy jump to realize that a 64-bit system with 64-bit pointers will increase this limit, but by how much?

The easiest way to work it out is to use the power function on a scientific calculator. 2^{32} gives you the 32-bit limit of 4,294,967,295, and calculating 2^{64} gives you the staggering 64-bit limit of 18,446,744,073,709,551,616.

This number is so large that in memory/storage terminology it equates to 16 *exabytes*. You don't come across that term very often, so to help understand the scale, here is the value converted to more commonly used measurements:

16 exabytes =

➤   16,777,216 petabytes (16 million PB)

➤   17,179,869,184 terabytes (17 billion TB)

➤   17,592,186,044,416 gigabytes (17 trillion GB)

As you can see, it is significantly larger than the 4GB virtual address space usable in 32-bit systems; it's so large in fact that any hardware capable of using it all is sadly restricted to the realm of science fiction. Because of this, processor manufacturers decided to only implement a *44-bit* address bus, which provides a virtual address space on 64-bit systems of 16TB. This was regarded as being more than enough address space for the foreseeable future and logically it's split into an 8TB range for user mode and 8TB for kernel mode. Each 64-bit process running on an x64 platform will be able to address up to 8TB of VAS. (For more information on processor architectures, see Chapter 5).

x64 is the predominant 64-bit architecture in use today and the main focus of this book when discussing 64-bit technologies. Figure 2-2 shows the difference between the virtual address space size per process in Windows x86 (32-bit) and Windows x64. There is an alternative architecture from Intel implemented in their Itanium chips known as IA64, and while there is a version of SQL Server 2008 available for it, there are very few production implementations so the focus in this book is on the x64 platform.

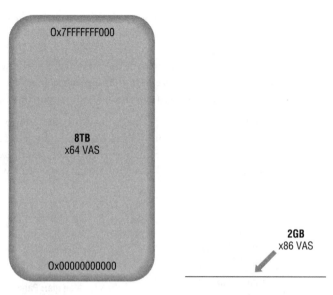

Virtual Memory Manager

Next, this chapter covers the part of Windows that joins physical memory and virtual address space together; the Virtual Memory Manager (VMM).

FIGURE 2-2

When a process wants to read from or write something into memory, it references an address in its VAS; and the VMM will map it to an address in physical memory. It isn't guaranteed, however, to still be mapped to a physical memory address the next time you access it because the VMM may determine that it needs to move your data to the page file temporarily to allow another process to use the physical memory address. As part of this process, the VMM will update the VAS address and make it invalid (it doesn't point to a physical memory address anymore). The next time you access this address, it will have to be loaded from the page file on disk so the request will be slower. This is known as a *page fault* and happens automatically without you knowing.

The portion of a process's VAS that currently maps to physical memory is known as the *working set*. If a process requests data that isn't currently in the working set, then it will need to be reloaded back into memory before use. This is called a *hard page fault* (a *soft page fault* is when the page is still on the standby list in physical memory); and to fix it, the VMM will retrieve the data from the page file, find a free page of memory, either from its list of free pages or from another process, write the data from the page file into memory, and then map the new page back into the process's virtual address space.

 The Memory\Page Faults/sec *counter in Performance Monitor includes both hard and soft page faults, so if you want to monitor just the performance sapping hard page faults you need to look at* Memory\Page Reads/sec *to get the number of times the disk was accessed to resolve hard page faults and compare it to* Memory\Pages Input/sec *to calculate the average number of pages being read in each disk access.*

On a system with enough RAM to give every process all the memory it needs, the VMM doesn't have to do much other than hand out memory and clean up after a process is done with it. On a system without enough RAM to go around, the job is a little more involved. The VMM has to do some work to provide each process with the memory it needs when it needs it. It does this by using the page file to temporarily store data that a process hasn't accessed for a while. This process is called *paging*, and the data is often referred to as having been *paged* out to disk.

The Virtual Memory Manager keeps track of each mapping for VAS addresses using a *page table*, and the mapping information itself is stored in a *page table entry (PTE)*. This is illustrated in Figure 2-3 using two 32-bit SQL Server instances as an example. Note that the dotted line indicates an invalid reference that will generate a hard page fault when accessed causing the page to be loaded from the page file.

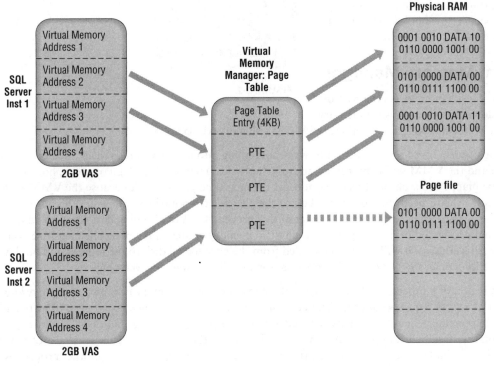

FIGURE 2-3

The system PTEs are 4KB in size and share the kernel mode address space with other system data structures and information. If you recall from the previous section, the kernel mode address space is only 2GB on a 32-bit system, which results in an inherent limitation regardless of how much physical memory the computer has. Issues with lack of system PTE space and other kernel mode space consumers are discussed in the next section.

Tuning 32-Bit Systems

The 2GB process limitation on 32-bit systems became a limiting factor long before 64-bit was ready for widespread adoption, so something needed to be done to take advantage of all the extra physical memory that hardware manufacturers were able to build systems with.

This section looks at the different ways you can configure 32-bit Windows to use more than 4GB of RAM and SQL Server to use more than the 2GB process limitation, along with the benefits and inevitable side effects that are very often overlooked. Note that this section is only applicable to 32-bit systems.

/3GB and increaseUserVA

The first technique that can be employed to increase the SQL Server process address space is to reduce the amount of kernel mode address space from 2GB to 1GB, which leaves 3GB for the user mode address space. This is implemented by using the /3GB switch, and has been referred to in the past as "4GB Tuning," or 4GT for short.

/3GB needs to be added to the OS entry in boot.ini if you're running Windows Server 2003 or earlier. To perform the equivalent operation on Windows Server 2008, you need to edit the Boot Configuration Data using BCDEdit from a command prompt using the following switch:

```
BCDEdit /set increaseUserVA 3072
```

You will find more details about increaseUserVA and /USERVA in the "/PAE and /3GB Together?" section.

Once you add /3GB and reboot, each process will have 3GB of address space instead of just 2GB, and the kernel mode address space will be reduced to 1GB. You can see this illustrated in Figure 2-4.

To be able to address the extra 1GB, your application has to have been linked with the /LARGEADDRESSAWARE flag. Thankfully, SQL Server has been linked with the appropriate flag, so you don't need to do anything else and 3GB will be available immediately.

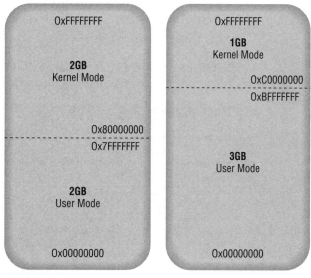

FIGURE 2-4

The downside to this configuration is the implication for consumers of the now reduced kernel mode address space — specifically, nonpaged pool, paged pool, and system PTEs (covered earlier in the section "Virtual Memory Manager").

Paged Pool and Nonpaged Pool

Paged pool and nonpaged pool are used to allocate system memory. Nonpaged pool, as its name suggests, can't be paged out to disk, and so it is used by hardware drivers to prevent the system crashes that would occur if they were paged out. You should monitor these two pools if you're using /3GB and definitely if you're using it in combination with /PAE (discussed further on).

Measuring your paged and nonpaged pool usage is straightforward; you can use Performance Monitor to view the counters for Memory/Pool Paged Bytes and Memory/Pool Nonpaged Bytes. However, these values are only useful if you know the *maximum* values for these pools on your server, which takes a bit more work to determine.

For Windows 2003, the maximum values are calculated on boot and are then fixed. To view the values, you need to use a kernel debugger; or, alternatively, you can configure the Process Explorer tool from Sysinternals to see them (you'll also need a connection to the Internet). Execute the following steps to view maximum values:

1. Download Process Explorer from here: `http://technet.microsoft.com/en-us/sysinternals/bb896653.aspx`.

2. Install the Debugging Tools for Windows to get the dbghelp.dll file: `www.microsoft.com/whdc/devtools/debugging/default.mspx`.

3. Launch Process Explorer (procexp.exe) and go to Options ➪ Configure Symbols. You'll need to configure the `Dbghelp.dll` path to use the new DLL you just installed with the Debugging Tools and the "Symbols path" to the following:

   ```
   SRV*C:\SYMBOLS*http://msdl.microsoft.com/downloads/symbols;
   ```

   If your system drive isn't C:\, then change the location appropriately. Figure 2-5 shows a screenshot of configured symbols installed where the system drive is D:\.

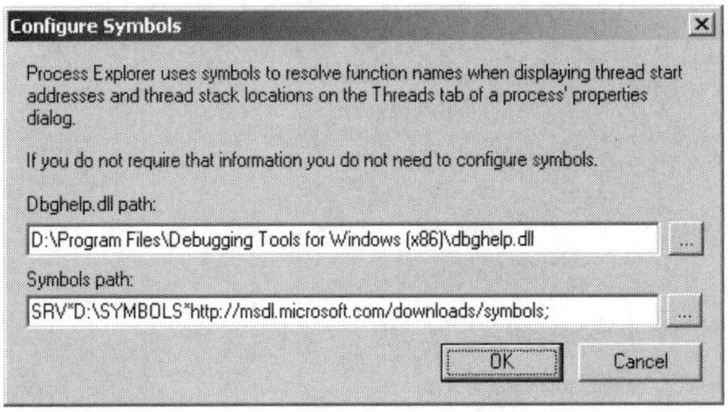

FIGURE 2-5

4. Go to View➪System Information, where the values for Paged Limit and Nonpaged Limit are now visible. Figure 2-6 shows the System Information screen after the symbols have been configured correctly.

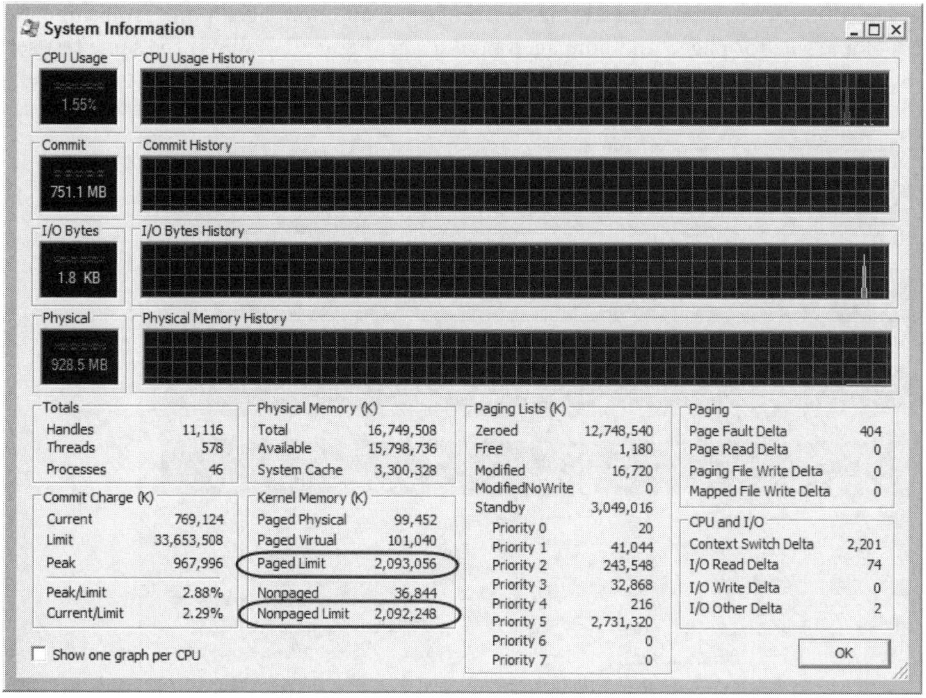

FIGURE 2-6

Enabling /3GB halves the kernel mode address space *and* the size of the paged and nonpaged pool. Table 2-3 shows typical startup values for Windows Server 2003 SP1.

TABLE 2-3: Typical Paged and Nonpaged Values for Windows Server 2003 SP1

SYSTEM RAM	PAGED MAX	NONPAGED MAX
512MB	184MB	125MB
1,024MB	168MB	202MB
1,536MB	352MB	252MB
2,048MB	352MB	252MB

A test server running Windows Server 2003 R2 SP2 with 16GB of RAM (you'll read about enabling all this memory in the PAE section coming up) has the same Paged Max and Nonpaged Max as the example in the table with only 2GB of RAM. After adding the /3GB switch, these were reduced to 156MB and 128MB, respectively, which might still be OK. Armed with the current usage and maximum values, you can make an informed decision regarding whether /3GB is restricting your paged and nonpaged pools too much.

Windows Server 2008 uses dynamic max values for the paged and nonpaged pools, so using /3GB on that OS is less of an issue for paged and nonpaged pool usage. Figure 2-7 shows the same test server as Figure 2-6 running Windows Server 2008.

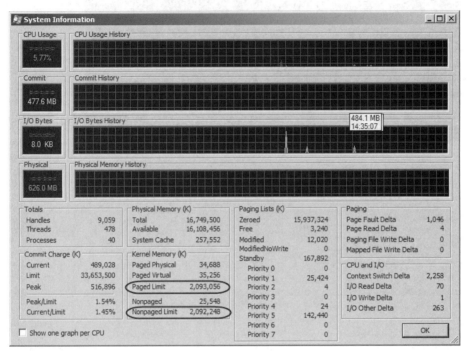

FIGURE 2-7

System PTEs

One of the symptoms of a lack of PTEs is that the server stops responding, so it's a major issue to avoid. You can monitor the number of free system PTEs using Performance Monitor and viewing the counter for Memory\Free System Page Table Entries. Microsoft recommends that this value should be at least 24,000 on boot-up and should never drop to less than 10,000 or you're considered "at risk" of running out.

The more RAM you have the more PTEs you need to manage the mapping between virtual memory and physical memory. PTEs use space in the kernel mode address space, so any reduction in the size of the kernel mode will affect how much RAM you'll be able to have in your computer.

On a Windows Server 2003 test server with 4GB of RAM, the Free System Page Table Entry count is 180,234 — well above the necessary minimum of 10,000.

After adding /3GB this drops to 26,417. It's a significant drop but still enough to meet the on-boot recommendation, and now the SQL Server instance can use 3GB of physical memory.

There is an additional switch you can use with /3GB to slightly reduce the amount of kernel mode space that's taken to allow for more system PTEs. It's called /USERVA and is covered in the upcoming section "/PAE and /3GB Together?" In Windows Server 2008, /3GB and /USERVA have been combined into a single setting called increaseUserVA, which is also covered in that section.

/PAE Switch

/3GB allows you to gain an extra 1GB for user processes but that's not a great leap in terms of capacity, so Intel introduced a technology called Physical Address Extension (PAE) that effectively increases the address bus to 36 bits and allows access to up to 128GB of RAM, depending on your OS.

The Standard Edition of Windows supports only up to 4GB of RAM, so PAE is available only in the Enterprise and Datacenter Editions. It is enabled in the same way as /3GB: by adding the /PAE switch to boot.ini or the BCD, depending on which OS you're running.

HOT-ADD MEMORY AND DATA EXECUTION PREVENTION

If you're running Windows Server 2003 Service Pack 1 or later, you may find that PAE is automatically enabled to support additional hardware-based features such as hot-add memory and data execution prevention (DEP).

Hot-add memory is self-explanatory: On a running server, it enables you to plug in additional RAM modules, which Windows will automatically detect and start using. For this to work, Windows needs to be ready in PAE mode in anticipation of this additional "hot-added" memory being greater than 4GB. If your server BIOS has support for hot-add memory enabled, Windows Server 2003 SP1 or later will automatically run in PAE mode.

DEP is a hardware-enforced security feature of Windows that prevents applications from executing code from non-executable memory, which helps to prevent exploits that might be possible via a buffer overflow. For all the possible memory ranges to be protected, Windows automatically switches on PAE if the technology is enabled in the BIOS.

On Intel motherboards, the feature is known as Execute Disable Bit (XD), and on AMD systems it's known as No-execute (NX) or Advanced Virus Protection. The point is to be aware that you're very likely to be using PAE automatically on your server without the switch being present in boot.ini or the BCD.

PAE works by modifying the system PTEs (see "Virtual Memory Manager" earlier in the chapter) to be 8KB instead of 4KB, and uses the extra space to map virtual addresses into the physical memory above 4GB. This increase in size is important to note because it effectively doubles the space required for PTEs in the kernel mode address space.

When PAE is enabled, Windows will see and manage up to 128GB of RAM on a server. You can tell if it's working by running winver.exe and checking the amount of memory that Windows has detected. If you have 16GB of RAM in the server and PAE is working, `winver` will show 16GB. Figure 2-8 shows an example of `winver` output.

You can disable PAE by adding the `/EXECUTE /NOPAE` switches to `boot.ini` or the BCD.

In order for applications such as SQL Server to use the additional memory provided by PAE, they have to be written to make use of a set of extensions known as Address Windowing Extensions (AWE), which is covered in more detail in the next section.

Address Windowing Extensions (AWE)

AWE is a Windows API that enables a 32-bit process to map memory from outside its virtual address space. That is, it enables a process to

FIGURE 2-8

reserve a portion of virtual address space (a *window*), which can then be mapped to any physical address range in a method known as *windowing*. Figure 2-9 illustrates the concept.

To reduce the additional overhead associated with mapping and remapping using AWE, the design ensures that any memory allocated using the APIs cannot be shared with any other process and is made nonpageable, or locked.

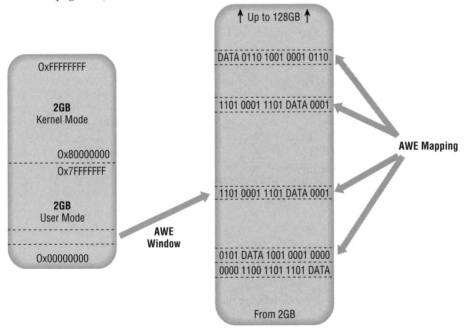

FIGURE 2-9

In order for SQL Server to use the AWE APIs, you need to enable AWE using `sp_configure` or by selecting the check box on the Memory page of a server's Properties window in Management Studio. Once enabled, the next time SQL Server is started it will attempt to lock memory pages so that it can use AWE.

To lock memory pages, the SQL Server process needs to have the "Lock Pages in Memory" Advanced User Right in Windows which is achieved by granting the permission to the SQL Server service account. This permission is not granted automatically, even if the service account is a member of the Local Administrators group.

If you enable AWE and haven't granted the right privilege to the service account, you'll see the message shown in Figure 2-10 at the beginning of the SQL Server Error Log. If the correct privilege has been granted, you'll see the message shown in Figure 2-11.

> Address Windowing Extensions (AWE) requires the 'lock pages in memory' privilege which is not currently present in the access token of the process.
> Error: 5845, Severity: 16, State: 1.

FIGURE 2-10

> Address Windowing Extensions is enabled. This is an informational message only; no user action is required.

FIGURE 2-11

To assign the "Lock pages in memory" privilege, you need to modify the Group Policy on the server using `gpedit.msc` (from the Start menu, select Run and enter **gpedit.msc**). Navigate down to User-Rights Assignment, and add the service account to the Lock pages in memory privilege, as shown in Figure 2-12.

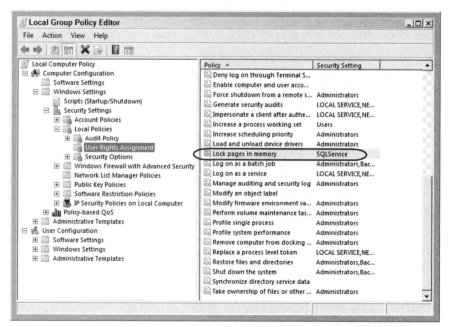

FIGURE 2-12

On Windows Server 2003 and Windows Server 2008, AWE memory is dynamically allocated by SQL Server in the same way as normal memory allocations, so you can observe SQL Server starting and taking only the minimum amount of RAM and increasing its usage as necessary.

AWE memory still isn't the perfect solution for working with large amounts of RAM. Complexity and overhead are associated with the windowing process, but the biggest drawback for SQL Server's usage is that the additional RAM can only be used for data cache. See the "SQL Server Memory" section for details on the data cache.

Only data pages can be stored in AWE mapped memory so it cannot directly help if your SQL Server is struggling to support additional users, databases, queries, locks, or other consumers of memory in SQL Server that have to run in non-AWE memory. To scale those components you need to move to a 64-bit platform.

/PAE and /3GB Together?

A common debate is whether or not you can, or, more important, *should* use /PAE and /3GB together to squeeze every last drop of physical memory for use with SQL Server.

The benefits should be obvious by now — access to more than 2GB of RAM for SQL Server's data cache *and* an additional 1GB stolen from kernel mode for use with any of SQL Server's memory requirements.

According to Microsoft's official guidelines, using /PAE and /3GB together is not recommended.

Official guidance is great and applicable to most scenarios but it's more useful to you as an IT professional to understand *why* it's not recommended so you can make a judgment call yourself.

Using both technologies can cause issues because of resulting changes that affect three key areas that depend on kernel mode address space, as mentioned earlier: paged pool, nonpaged pool, and system PTEs.

When you implement /3GB on Windows Server 2003, you significantly reduce the maximum memory available for paged pool and nonpaged pool, so you should monitor their usage as described earlier. Similarly, you also reduce the amount of space available for system PTEs as a result of losing 1GB of kernel mode address space, so you should monitor the counter for Memory\Free System Page Table Entries in Performance Monitor to ensure that it stays above 10,000.

If you then implement PAE you're effectively doubling the size of each PTE from 4KB to 8KB in an already reduced space, so a lack of free system PTEs becomes your limiting factor. More RAM requires more PTEs to manage it, so whether you can safely use /PAE and /3GB together depends on how much RAM you have. To determine the best configuration, take a look at some example memory sizes.

Table 2-4 shows the values of these components when running with different amounts of RAM on Windows Server 2003 R2 SP2 with /PAE and /3GB enabled.

As shown in Table 2-4, even with only 8GB of RAM the server had just 13,653 free system PTEs, which is almost 50% less than the recommended value of 24,000 at boot up. You could still run with this configuration if you monitored the value closely, but you can see why Microsoft doesn't recommend it.

TABLE 2-4: Paged Pool, Nonpaged Pool, and Free System PTEs on Windows Server 2003 R2 SP2 with /PAE and /3GB Enabled

SYSTEM RAM	PAGED MAX	NONPAGED MAX	FREE SYSTEM PTEs
8GB	160MB	131MB	13,653
12GB	160MB	131MB	6,500
16GB	160MB	131MB	2,000

With 16GB of RAM there are just about enough free system PTEs to start the server, so it's clear this configuration won't sustain a stable server.

To alleviate some of the pressure on systems PTEs that this setup creates, a new switch was made available in Windows Server 2003 called /USERVA. Using this switch in combination with /3GB enables you to specify a slightly lower amount of MBs for the user mode address space than 3GB, so you can leave a bit more kernel mode space for system PTEs.

Microsoft recommends trying a default value of 3030, but values between 2970 and 3030 are supported (the values are in MB). 3072 is the equivalent of /3GB without /USERVA. Table 2-5 shows the free system PTE results of testing different values for /USERVA with different amounts of RAM on Windows 2003 R2 SP2. The underlined values are optimal but any combination that results in free system PTEs greater than 24,000 at boot up is acceptable.

TABLE 2-5: Free System PTE tests with Various Values for /USERVA and amounts of RAM

	16GB RAM	12GB RAM	8GB RAM
USERVA=3030	12200	17200	<u>24500</u>
USERVA=3000	20000	<u>25000</u>	32100
USERVA=2970	<u>27400</u>	32600	39900

From the results you can see that even with 16GB of RAM you can add /3GB /USERVA=2970 to gain an extra 922MB of user mode address space and still have a supported solution.

Windows Server 2008

In Windows Server 2008, /3GB and /USERVA have been combined into a single setting called increaseUserVA, which you modify by using BCDEDIT.

Running BCDEDIT /set increaseUserVA 3072 is the equivalent to using /3GB in Windows Server 2003. Table 2-6 shows the values for the key components with different amounts of RAM on a test server running Windows Server 2008.

TABLE 2-6: Paged Pool, Nonpaged Pool, and Free System PTEs with /PAE and /IncreaseUserVA 3072 Enabled

SYSTEM RAM	PAGED MAX	NONPAGED MAX	FREE SYSTEM PTEs
8GB	1,024MB	1,024MB	110,500
12GB	1,024MB	1,024MB	105,500
16GB	1,024MB	1,024MB	95,000

You can see from the results that even with 16GB of RAM, giving 3GB to the user mode address space on Windows Server 2008 still leaves plenty of free system PTEs.

Moving to the x64 version of Windows removes all these problems with paged pool, nonpaged pool, and free system PTEs because the address space is just so large; 8TB compared to 2GB on x86 or even 1GB if you use the /3GB switch.

Figure 2-13 shows the paged maximum at 26.5GB and the nonpaged maximum at 6.5GB. This the same hardware that was used in Figure 2-6, which showed 360MB and 260MB; the only difference is the x64 version of Windows Server 2003.

Running Windows Server 2008 x64, the maximum values were 134GB and 12.5GB, but that's not so important because the maximum is dynamic in Windows Server 2008.

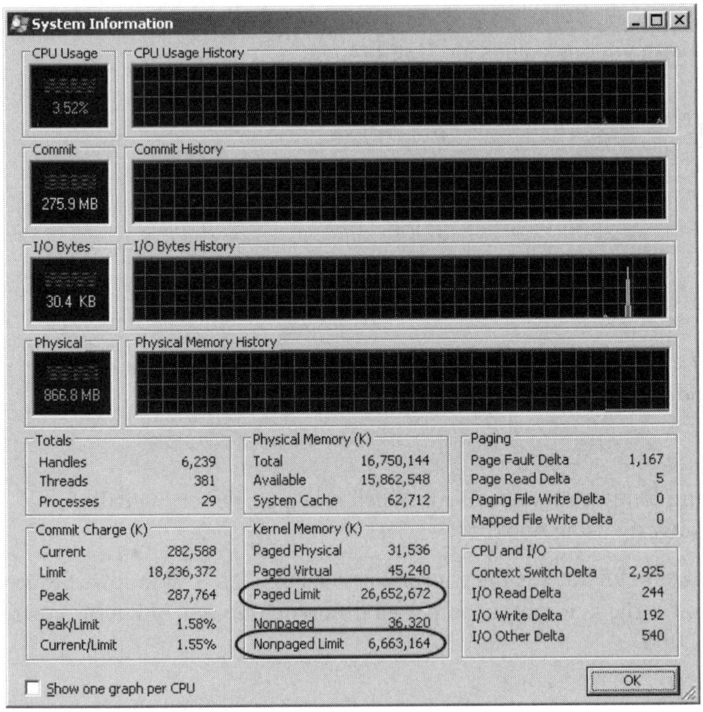

FIGURE 2-13

MemToLeave, or ReservedMemory

ReservedMemory is a part of SQL Server's address space that is reserved before SQL Server allocates its buffer pool and then freed afterwards. It's also referred to as *MemToLeave* (MTL) because that was the name of an internal variable which referenced the amount of memory to leave. Although formal documentation from Microsoft will be more likely to use the ReservedMemory term, you'll find that MemToLeave is the most commonly used term in the field, even within Microsoft's own support organization.

There is no such thing as the MemToLeave area but it is an appropriate description of the *action* that SQL Server takes when the service starts. It will leave, or reserve, a section of virtual memory before it reserves the buffer pool and will then release it afterwards so that there is some free space in the VAS for other components to reserve and commit memory using the *VirtualAlloc* Windows functions.

> VirtualAlloc, VirtualAllocEx, *and* VirtualAllocExNuma *are low-level Windows functions used by applications to reserve and then commit memory in a processes virtual address space.*

So who uses VirtualAlloc?

➤ The *heap manager* (heaps are used to allocate a lower level of granularity that VirtualAlloc normally allows) — so anything using a heap indirectly will as well.

➤ SQL Server uses VirtualAlloc for Multi-Page Allocations (MPAs),which are used when a memory request is larger than a SQL Server page (8KB).

➤ Windows will call VirtualAlloc to create a thread stack (more on this coming up).

➤ Any other components that don't know anything about the buffer pool and use their normal memory allocation routines that ultimately go to VirtualAlloc such as:

➤ OLE DB providers (including SQL Server Linked Servers)

➤ Extended Stored Procedures

➤ COM objects

> *There is no MemToLeave in 64-bit SQL Server! MemToLeave is only a part of the startup process in 32-bit SQL Server. Because the virtual address space is so large in 64-bit SQL Server reserving addresses outside the buffer pool isn't necessary. This is explored in a bit more detail later in the chapter.*

How much address space is reserved is determined by SQL Server on startup by the following formula:

memory_to_reserve = MemReserved + (NumThreads × Stack Size)

Memory_to_reserve is 256MB by default, but can be modified by using the -g startup switch.

> *Changing the memory_to_reserve option can be useful when you have more physical memory than the application virtual address space (2-3GB depending on configuration) and you're seeing messages in the error log containing "Failed Virtual Allocate Bytes". This usually indicates that SQL Server doesn't have enough VAS for the allocations it needs to make outside the buffer pool. If you get these messages and you can't reduce your linked server, extended stored procedure, and COM object usage try increasing memory_to_reserve from the default of 256 to 384 to provide more space; although be aware that the extra space you're providing will taken away from the buffer pool.*
>
> *Similarly, you can also set memory_to_reserve to a lower value to provide a bit more space in the buffer pool if you have memory intensive workloads and don't use many linked servers, extended stored procedures, or COM objects.*

NumThreads is the maximum total number of worker threads configured for your SQL Server instance. You can calculate the maximum number of worker threads you can have by using Table 2-7 (64-bit values are included out of interest only, as there is no MemToLeave in 64-bit), or by running the following query:

```
select max_workers_count
from sys.dm_os_sys_info
```

StackSize is the space required to create each thread stack. It varies according to CPU architecture. On x86 (32-bit) its 0.5MB, on x64 (64-bit) its 2MB, and on IA64 its 4MB.

TABLE 2-7: Calculating the Number of Worker Threads

NUMBER OF CPUs	32-BIT	64-BIT
≤4 processors	256	512
8 processors	288	576
16 processors	352	704
32 processors	480	960

> *SQL Server will only allocate around 35-40 worker threads on startup and then one or two more when you first connect. Additional worker threads will only be created when the worker thread pool isn't enough to satisfy all the concurrent requests, so you may have hundreds of connections but if they don't all run concurrently you may only need 5 or 10 threads to service them all.*

One of the biggest problems around the whole MemToLeave process is not running out, but rather a lack of contiguous memory addresses large enough for a requested allocation. If this happens you will see a message similar to the following in the SQL Server Error Log:

```
WARNING: Failed to reserve contiguous memory of Size=65546
```

In this example, a request for 64KB couldn't be allocated.

Determining the largest contiguous block size available for a reservation in the virtual address space was difficult in SQL Server 2000; you had to run a tool in kernel mode called vmstat, which wasn't an attractive prospect on a production SQL Server machine.

Thankfully, the introduction of dynamic management views (DMVs) in SQL Server 2005 exposed a lot more internal information without having to resort to risky low-level tools. It's still a convoluted process to determine the largest contiguous block size but at least it can be done with T-SQL. The script in Listing 2-1 will output how much space is unallocated in SQL Server's VAS, and, more important, the largest free block size (both in KB).

LISTING 2-1: Free virtual address space and largest contiguous block size

```
With VASummary(Size,Reserved,Free) AS
(SELECT
    Size = VaDump.Size,
    Reserved =  SUM(CASE(CONVERT(INT, VaDump.Base)^0)
    WHEN 0 THEN 0 ELSE 1 END),
    Free = SUM(CASE(CONVERT(INT, VaDump.Base)^0)
    WHEN 0 THEN 1 ELSE 0 END)
FROM
(
    SELECT  CONVERT(VARBINARY, SUM(region_size_in_bytes))
    AS Size, region_allocation_base_address AS Base
    FROM sys.dm_os_virtual_address_dump
    WHERE region_allocation_base_address <> 0x0
    GROUP BY region_allocation_base_address
  UNION
    SELECT CONVERT(VARBINARY, region_size_in_bytes), region_allocation_base_address
    FROM sys.dm_os_virtual_address_dump
    WHERE region_allocation_base_address  = 0x0
)
AS VaDump
GROUP BY Size)

SELECT SUM(CONVERT(BIGINT,Size)*Free)/1024 AS [Total avail mem, KB]
,CAST(MAX(Size) AS BIGINT)/1024 AS [Max free size, KB]
FROM VASummary
WHERE Free <> 0
```

This code available for download at Wrox.com [Chapter2HowMuchVAS.sql]

Using the preceding MemToLeave formula and an example 32-bit system with 2GB of RAM and two CPU cores, the formula, with all the values now known, looks like this:

```
ReservedMemory = 256MB + (256 × 0.5MB)
```

You can calculate that the ReservedMemory is 384MB, which SQL Server will reserve before reserving what's left for the buffer pool, which equates to about 1.6GB. This is why you will see SQL Server's memory usage peak at around a maximum of 1.6GB on a 32-bit server; that is what's left over after the MemToLeave process. This is illustrated in Figure 2-14.

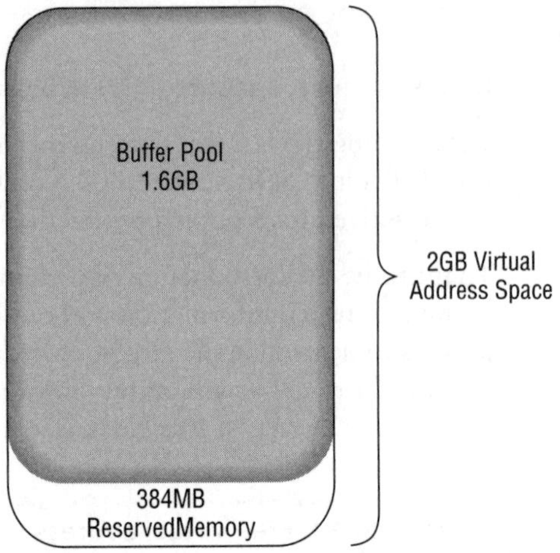

Running the script to determine free virtual address space on this system should yield results like the following:

```
Total avail mem, KB  Max free size, KB
338,856                  157,008
```

This shows that the unallocated virtual address space is 330MB and the largest contiguous block is 153MB.

To reinforce what's happening here and to show that MemToLeave is actually just VAS, you can look at what happens when there is only 1GB of RAM on the server.

The buffer pool will never be more than physical RAM, so if you take 1GB of RAM out of the example system, SQL Server will still reserve 384MB during the MemToLeave process and then reserve a buffer pool of only 1,024MB (equal to physical RAM).

You can see this illustrated in Figure 2-15. The diagram highlights the fact that the additional space not allocated to the buffer pool is exactly the same as that reserved and released for MemToLeave; it's just virtual address space not allocated to the buffer pool, which now totals 1,024MB, 640MB larger than previously.

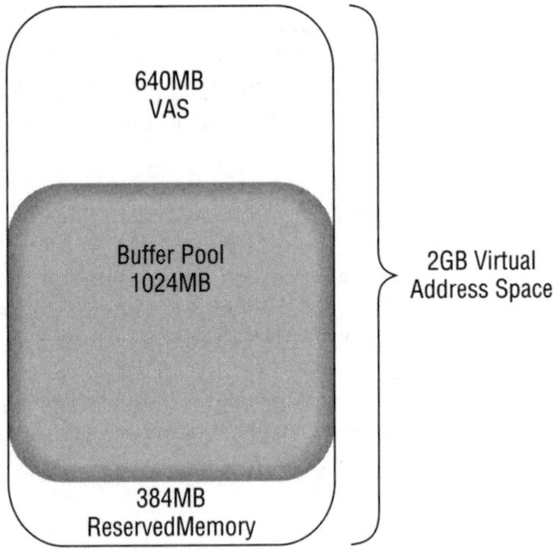

FIGURE 2-14

Buffer Pool
1.6GB

384MB
ReservedMemory

2GB Virtual
Address Space

FIGURE 2-15

640MB
VAS

Buffer Pool
1024MB

384MB
ReservedMemory

2GB Virtual
Address Space

If you run the script again on this system your results will look something like this:

```
Total avail mem, KB Max free size, KB
917,020                 364,956
```

This indicates that there is 895MB of free VAS left and that the largest block is 356MB.

Note on 64-Bit Systems

As mentioned at the start of this section, in 64-bit SQL Server there is no MemToLeave.

As you've just seen, MemToLeave is simply unallocated VAS and with the 8TB of VAS available on x64 systems, there is plenty of space and large contiguous blocks shouldn't be a problem.

To show this you can run the code in Listing 2-1 that was used to look at the VAS in previous examples. On an x64 system with four CPU cores and 16GB of RAM the results will look similar to this:

```
Total avail mem, KB  Max free size, KB
8,572,745,912        8,566,727,936
```

This shows 8,175GB of free VAS left, and the largest block is 8,169GB, which should be more than enough!

This is a big justification for moving to 64-bit, especially if you've had MemToLeave issues in the past.

Tuning 64-Bit Systems

Moving to a 64-bit system solves a lot of the memory related problems discussed so far that are related to the 32-bit platform. However, 64-bit environments bring new potential issues that you should be aware of while also learning how and when to avoid them.

AWE on 64-Bit Systems

AWE on a 64-bit system? After reading this far you might be thinking that this is either a trick question or you've misunderstood everything up to now. Thankfully, it's neither; AWE in SQL Server 64-bit systems is used as a workaround for a problem than can occur between the Windows working set manager and SQL Server, particularly on Windows Server 2003 and below.

If there isn't enough free physical memory in Windows to service a request for resources from a driver or another application, the working set manager will trim the working set (the working set reflects the physical memory usage of a process) of all applications running on the server. This is normal behavior and shouldn't have much noticeable impact.

However, if the request is for contiguous memory, the working set manager will force all applications to empty their working sets. This is known as *"aggressive working set trimming"* and will have a devastating effect on SQL Server's memory allocation and therefore performance.

In SQL Server 2005 SP2, Microsoft added a new error message so you can easily see when this happens. Here is an example:

```
2009-02-01 21:25:10.14 spid1s A significant part of sql server process memory has
been paged out. This may result in a performance degradation. Duration: 0 seconds.
Working set (KB): 1086400, committed (KB): 2160928, memory utilization: 50%.
```

The result can be as severe as SQL Server's working set dropping from tens of GB to a few hundred MB in just a few seconds, so if you see the error message there's a good chance you noticed a performance hit before looking at the error log.

Resolving this issue (or avoiding it all together) should be tackled using a combination of a few different methods:

➤ First, check for updates to all your device drivers. If the problem was caused by a device driver, it may have been fixed already in a later version.

➤ Next, set Max Server Memory in SQL Server to ensure that Windows and other processes running on the server have enough physical memory to perform their work without asking SQL Server to trim. You can read about calculating a suitable Max Server Memory value in the SQL Server Memory section.

➤ Finally, if you're still seeing the issue (or if its effects are so severe you don't want to risk seeing it again), you can configure your SQL Server to use AWE.

In the section on AWE under "Tuning 32-bit Systems" you read that it's used to access memory above the 32-bit process limitation. It also locks pages in memory to make allocations faster, and it's this facet of AWE that a 64-bit SQL Server can take advantage of. If SQL Server's memory pages are "locked," then its nonpageable and Windows can't take it when aggressively trimming.

The AWE options in `sp_configure` and SQL Server Management Studio are ignored when you're running 64-bit, but if you give the SQL Server service account the Lock Pages in Memory privilege *and* you're running the Enterprise Edition, then SQL Server will use the AWE APIs to allocate memory.

> *When SQL Server 2008 was released, being able to lock pages in memory on x64 required you to be running SQL Server Enterprise Edition.*
>
> *As a result of strong community feedback on the working set trimming issue Microsoft eventually enabled support in SQL Server Standard edition with the use of a trace flag and SQL Server 2008 SP1 with Cumulative Update 2. You can read more about this and how to enable it here:* `http://support.microsoft.com/kb/970070`

Once the pages are locked they're not considered part of available memory for working set trimming. However, AWE can only be used to lock SQL Server buffer pool allocations. Windows can still trim the working sets of other processes, affecting resources on which SQL Server depends.

AWE on 64-bit systems should be used if you continue to get working set trimming after updating your device drivers and setting a suitable max server memory *or* if the cost of SQL Server's working set being trimmed again is too risky.

It shouldn't be used as a default best practice on all your SQL Servers. It's a workaround and not intended to replace the default behavior on every 64-bit SQL Server implementation.

If AWE is working you'll see the following message in the SQL Server Error Log:

```
Using Locked Pages for Buffer Pool.
```

Windows Server 2008 has improved the way it handles requests for large or contiguous memory allocations, so in theory you shouldn't see the working set trimming problem on this platform often, if at all.

SQL SERVER MEMORY

The first part of this chapter dealt mainly with the memory environment external to SQL Server — that is, understanding and configuring memory before SQL Server starts. This second part looks at how SQL Server manages memory.

The SQL Server memory manager has a three-level structure. At the bottom are memory nodes which are the lowest level allocators for SQL Server memory, the second level consists of memory clerks which are used to access the memory nodes and cache stores which are used for caching. The top layer contains memory objects which provide a smaller level of granularity than the memory clerks allow directly.

Only clerks can access memory nodes to allocate memory, so every component that needs to allocate substantial amounts of memory needs to create its own memory clerk when the SQL Server service starts.

Memory Nodes

You can view details about the nodes on your server using the sys.dm_os_memory_nodes DMV. You will always have at least one memory node, which has a memory_node_id of 0.

You will have more than one memory node if you have configured Non-Uniform Memory Access (NUMA) *or* if your system uses AMD processors and you have more than four CPU cores. The AMD processor architecture follows the NUMA specification, and SQL Server will detect NUMA support and create multiple memory nodes if it detects four or more CPU cores.

 You can read more about NUMA in Chapter 5.

Each memory node has its own memory clerks and caches, which are distributed evenly across all nodes. SQL Server's total usage is calculated using the sum of all the nodes.

Memory Clerks, Caches, and the Buffer Pool

Memory Clerks are the mechanism by which Memory Caches are used and the Buffer Pool is far the largest consumer of memory in SQL Server. All three are discussed in this section.

Memory Clerks

Whenever a memory consumer within SQL Server wants to allocate memory it needs to go through a memory clerk, rather than going straight to a memory node. There are generic memory clerks like

MEMORYCLERK_SQLGENERAL, but any component that needs to allocate significant amounts will have been written to create and use its own memory clerk.

The buffer pool for instance has its own memory clerk (MEMORYCLERK_SQLBUFFERPOOL) as do query plans (MEMORYCLERK_SQLQUERYPLAN), which makes troubleshooting much easier because you can view the memory allocations made by each Clerk and see who has what.

You can view details about all the memory clerks using the `sys.dm_os_memory_clerks` DMV. For example, running this query against a production SQL Server 2008 Enterprise Edition x64 instance produced the results seen in Figure 2-16:

```
SELECT  [type],
        memory_node_id,
        single_pages_kb,
        multi_pages_kb,
        virtual_memory_reserved_kb,
        virtual_memory_committed_kb,
        awe_allocated_kb
FROM    sys.dm_os_memory_clerks
ORDER BY virtual_memory_reserved_kb DESC ;
```

The query orders the results by `virtual_memory_reserved_kb` so what you see in the figure are the top five memory clerks by the amount of VAS that they have reserved.

	type	memory_node_id	single_pages_kb	multi_pages_kb	virtual_memory_reserved_kb	virtual_memory_committed_kb	awe_allocated_kb
1	MEMORYCLERK_SQLBUFFERPOOL	0	0	1704	35733504	65536	29826304
2	MEMORYCLERK_SQLCLR	0	976	10096	6310592	62680	0
3	OBJECTSTORE_LOCK_MANAGER	0	0	0	131072	131072	0
4	MEMORYCLERK_XE_BUFFER	0	0	0	4224	4224	0
5	MEMORYCLERK_SQLSTORENG	0	11688	34184	3776	3776	0

FIGURE 2-16

You can also see from the results that the buffer pool has 34GB of reserved VAS with over 28GB allocated through AWE. Also note there is a column for MPAs (Multi-Page Allocations). You might recall from earlier in the chapter that the MPAs need to be allocated from VAS outside the buffer pool, which in 32-bit systems is reserved during the MemToLeave process.

Caches

SQL Server uses three types of caching mechanism: object store, cache store, and user store.

Object stores are used to cache homogeneous types of stateless data but it's the cache and user stores that you'll come across most often. They are very similar in that they're both caches; the main difference between them is that user stores need to be created with their own storage semantics using the development framework, whereas a cache store implements support for the memory objects mentioned previously to provide a smaller granularity of memory allocation.

For all intents and purposes, the user stores are mainly used by different development teams *within* Microsoft to implement their own specific caches for SQL Server features, so you can treat cache stores and user stores the same way.

You can view the different caches implemented on your SQL Server using the `sys.dm_os_memory_cache_counters` DMV. For example, running this query will show you all the caches available, ordered by the total amount of space they consume:

```
SELECT  [name],
        [type],
        single_pages_kb + multi_pages_kb AS total_kb,
        entries_count
FROM    sys.dm_os_memory_cache_counters
ORDER BY total_kb DESC ;
```

Sample output showing the top three caches by size can be seen in Figure 2-17.

	name	type	total_kb	entries_count
1	Object Plans	CACHESTORE_OBJCP	76184	198
2	SQL Plans	CACHESTORE_SQLCP	66416	730
3	Bound Trees	CACHESTORE_PHDR	22872	241

FIGURE 2-17

In the figure the caches you can see are all related to query processing (discussed further in Chapter 5). These specific caches are used for the following:

➤ **CACHESTORE_OBJCP:** Compiled plans for objects such as stored procedures, functions, and triggers.

➤ **CACHESTORE_SQLCP:** Cached plans for SQL statements or batches that aren't in stored procedures. If your application doesn't use stored procedures then the plans will be cached here. However, they are much less likely to be reused than stored procedure plans which can lead to a bloated cache taking lots of memory.

➤ **CACHESTORE_PHDR:** Algebrizer trees for views, constraints and defaults. An algebrizer tree is the parsed SQL text that resolves table and column names.

Buffer Pool

The buffer pool contains and manages SQL Server's data cache. Information on its contents can be found in the `sys.dm_os_buffer_descriptors` DMV. For example, the following query will return the amount of data cache usage in MB per database:

```
SELECT count(*)*8/1024 AS 'Cached Size (MB)'
    ,CASE database_id
        WHEN 32767 THEN 'ResourceDb'
        ELSE db_name(database_id)
        END AS 'Database'
FROM sys.dm_os_buffer_descriptors
GROUP BY db_name(database_id) ,database_id
ORDER BY 'Cached Size (MB)' DESC
```

Monitoring SQL Server's buffer pool is a great way to look out for memory pressure, and Performance Monitor provides numerous counters to help you do this. My favorites for a quick insight are as follows:

➤ **MSSQL$*<instance >*:Memory Manager\Total Server Memory (KB):** This indicates the current size of the buffer pool.

➤ **MSSQL$*<instance >*:Memory Manager\Target Server Memory (KB):** This indicates the ideal size for the buffer pool. Total and Target should be almost the same on a server with no memory pressure that has been running for a while. If Total is significantly less than Target, then it's likely that SQL Server cannot grow the buffer pool due to memory pressure, in which case you can investigate further.

➤ **MSSQL$*<instance >*:Buffer Manager\Page Life Expectancy:** This is the amount of time, in seconds, that SQL Server expects a page that has been loaded into the buffer pool to remain in cache. Under memory pressure, data pages are flushed from cache far more frequently. Microsoft recommends 300 seconds for a good PLE, but for systems with plenty of physical memory this will easily reach thousands of seconds.

Min and Max Server Memory

Min Server Memory (MB) and Max Server Memory (MB) control the allowable size of SQL Server's buffer pool. The settings do not control *all* of SQL Server's memory usage, just the buffer pool.

As its name suggests, Min Server Memory controls the minimum physical memory that SQL Server will try to keep committed. I say "try" because it can fall under that if Windows is desperate enough, but to all intents and purposes it sets a "floor" for SQL Server's buffer pool.

When the SQL Server service starts, it does not acquire all the memory configured in Min Server Memory but instead starts with only the minimal required, growing as necessary. Once memory usage has increased beyond the Min Server Memory setting, SQL Server won't release any memory below that figure.

Not surprisingly, Max Server Memory is the opposite of Min Server Memory, setting a "ceiling" for the buffer pool. Both can be set using `sp_configure` or through Management Studio on the Memory page of the SQL Server Properties window.

Configuring a maximum value for the buffer pool is the more important of the two settings and will prevent SQL Server from taking too much memory. This is particularly significant on 64-bit systems where a lack of free physical memory can cause Windows to aggressively trim SQL Server's working set. See "Tuning 64-bit Systems" for a full description of this issue.

There are a quite a few different ways to calculate an appropriate value to configure for Max Server Memory, but two of the most straightforward are as follows:

➤ Look at the buffer pool's maximum usage.

➤ Determine the maximum potential for non-buffer pool usage.

Each of these options is covered in the following sections.

Looking at the Buffer Pool's Maximum Usage

Set SQL Server to dynamically manage memory and then monitor MSSQL$*<instance>*:Memory Manager\Total Server Memory (KB) counter using Performance Monitor. This counter measures SQL Server's total buffer pool usage.

The Total Server Memory value will decrease if other processes need more physical memory than is currently free, and then increase again to use any free memory. If you monitor this counter for a period of time that is representative for your business (it includes peaks and troughs), you can then set Max Server Memory to the lowest value that was observed for Total Server Memory (KB) and you won't have to worry about SQL Server having to shrink its usage during normal operations.

Determining the Maximum Potential for Non-Buffer Pool Usage

This option is the most popular, as the aim is to calculate the worst-case scenario for memory requirements other than SQL Server's buffer pool. You should allow the following:

➤ 2GB for Windows

➤ *x*GB for SQL Server worker threads. You can figure out how many threads your instance will configure using Table 2-7, shown earlier. Each thread will use 0.5MB on x86, 2MB on x64, and 4MB on Itanium.

➤ 1GB for multi-page allocations, linked servers, and other consumers of memory outside the buffer pool. See the "Reserved Memory, or MemToLeave" section for more details and other consumers.

➤ 1–3GB for other applications that might be running on the system, such as backup programs.

For example, on a server with eight CPU cores and 16GB of RAM running SQL Server 2008 x64 and a third-party backup utility, you would allow the following:

➤ 2GB for Windows

➤ 1GB for worker threads (576 × 2MB rounded down)

➤ 1GB for MPAs, etc.

➤ 1GB for the backup program

The total is 5GB, and you would configure Max Server Memory to 11GB.

That seems like a lot to lose on a 16GB system, but remember that it's quite a rough calculation of the worst-case scenario. In this example, I'd be tempted to round up Max Server memory to 12GB and keep an eye on memory usage to get the best value.

If you added another 16GB to the system to total 32GB, the non-buffer pool maximum requirements would be the same. In that scenario, I'd probably make an allowance for the full 5GB and would set Max Server Memory to 27GB so I didn't have to worry about it again.

Both of these options can be valid in different circumstances. On a single SQL Server from which you need to squeeze every drop of performance, you might use option 1 and monitor Total Server Memory to see how often SQL Server has to give memory back to Windows. However, if you had dozens of SQL Servers to manage or a mission-critical server, you might go with option 2, as it would be easier to calculate across multiple servers and is less likely to cause a failure under exceptional circumstances.

Plan Cache

Execution plans can be time consuming and resource intensive to create so it makes sense that if SQL Server has already found a good way to execute a piece of code that it should try to reuse it for subsequent requests.

The plan cache is used to cache all the execution plans in case they can be reused.

You can view the contents of the plan cache and work out its current size by using the `sys.dm_exec_cached_plans` DMV or by running `DBCC MEMORYSTATUS` and looking for the "Procedure Cache" section, where you'll find the number of plans in cache and the cache size in 8KB pages.

> DBCC MEMORYSTATUS *provides a lot of useful information about SQL Server's memory state but you'll find that DMVs provide you far more flexibility with the output so try and get used to finding the same information from DMVs whenever you can. These DMVs are a good place to start:*
>
> ➤ sys.dm_os_memory_nodes
>
> ➤ sys.dm_os_memory_clerks
>
> ➤ sys.dm_os_memory_objects
>
> ➤ sys.dm_os_memory_cache_counters
>
> ➤ sys.dm_os_memory_pools

The following example script uses `sys.dm_exec_cached_plans` to show the number of cached plans and the total size in MB:

```
SELECT count(*) AS 'Number of Plans',
sum(cast(size_in_bytes AS BIGINT))/1024/1024 AS 'Plan Cache Size (MB)'
FROM sys.dm_exec_cached_plans
```

Running this on a client's production SQL Server system with 2GB of RAM produced the following results:

Number of Plans	Plan Cache Size (MB)
8140	848

This shows 848MB being used just for the plan cache, which is quite significant on a server with only 2GB of RAM. The Page Life Expectancy PerfMon counter was over 28,000 seconds, so the buffer pool wasn't under any pressure, but it was still worth investigating to see if the large plan cache was justified.

Running this script breaks down the plan cache size by cached object type:

```
SELECT objtype AS 'Cached Object Type',
count(*) AS 'Number of Plans',
sum(cast(size_in_bytes AS BIGINT))/1024/1024 AS 'Plan Cache Size (MB)',
avg(usecounts) AS 'Avg Use Count'
FROM sys.dm_exec_cached_plans
GROUP BY objtype
```

Results:

Cached Object Type	Number of Plans	Plan Cache Size (MB)	Avg Use Count
View	108	7	57
Check	2	0	5
UsrTab	1	0	2
Prepared	24	2	11
Adhoc	7796	808	1
Trigger	2	0	20
Proc	207	31	84

You can see from the results that most of the plan cache is taken up with ad hoc plans, with an average use of 1, indicating that they're not being reused.

Ad hoc plans are created when T-SQL commands are executed outside the context of a stored procedure, function, or trigger, and the plans created are rarely reused. This scenario often occurs because the application has been developed to use dynamically generated SQL instead of stored procedures.

If the use of stored procedures (or even parameterized queries) isn't possible due to the application design then you should monitor the space being used by ad hoc plans and either add more physical memory to the server, clear the ad hoc plans from cache, or enable the new OPTIMIZE FOR ADHOC WORKLOADS sp_configure option if you start to get memory pressure in other areas like the data cache.

> *A new sp_configure server level option was introduced in SQL Server 2008 called OPTIMIZE FOR ADHOC WORKLOADS that reduces the amount of cache used by single-use plans. Read more about it in Chapter 5.*

Running the following statement will flush the ad hoc plans (and prepared plans unfortunately but not stored procedure plans, which are more important to keep) from the cache and will free up the memory:

```
DBCC FREESYSTEMCACHE('SQL Plans')
```

This won't, of course, prevent the ad hoc plans from repopulating the cache; to do that you'd need to rewrite the code as stored procedures or as parameterized queries. After flushing the ad hoc plans, the cache looked like this:

```
Cached Object Type   Number of Plans   Plan Cache Size (MB)   Avg Use Count
View                 108               7                      57
Check                2                 0                      5
UsrTab               1                 0                      2
Adhoc                13                0                      1
Trigger              2                 0                      20
Proc                 207               31                     84
```

This left a plan cache of just 38MB. You can read more about plan reuse in Chapter 5.

The *maximum* size for the plan cache is calculated by SQL Server as follows:

➤   75% of server memory from 0 – 4GB +

➤   10% of server memory from 4GB – 64GB +

➤   5% of server memory > 64GB

Therefore, a system with 16GB of RAM would have a maximum plan cache of 3GB + 1.2GB = 4.2GB.

Query Memory/Workspace Memory

In SQL Server, *query memory* (also known as *workspace memory*) is used to temporarily store results during hash and sort operations when executing a query. It's not very widely known or documented but if you look at an execution plan (also known as an query plan) for a query and you see hash and/or sort operators, that query will need to use query memory to complete execution.

Query memory is allocated out of the buffer pool so it's definitely something to be aware of when you're building up a picture of the memory usage on a server.

You can find out how much query memory an individual query uses by looking at the properties of an *actual execution plan* in Management Studio, as opposed to an *estimated execution plan*. The estimated plan contains information about how SQL Server will run the query, and will show any hash or sort operators; but the actual plan is what SQL Server used to actually execute the query, and it contains additional run-time data, including how much query memory was used.

You can view the details of any queries that already have an allocation of query memory (memory grant) and those that are waiting for a memory grant using the sys.dm_exec_query_memory_grants DMV.

Query memory also has its own Memory Clerk which means you can view the sizing information for outstanding memory grants by querying the sys.dm_exec_query_memory_grants DMV where type = 'MEMORYCLERK_SQLQERESERVATIONS'.

> *The AdventureWorks database is a sample database originally released with SQL Server 2005 that is now maintained on the CodePlex Open Source Community website. You will find installation and download instructions here:* http://msftdbprodsamples.codeplex.com/

You can use the `AdventureWorks2008` database to look at an example memory grant:

1. Load SQL Server Management Studio and connect to your instance.

2. Press F4 to add the Properties window to your view if you don't see it already.

3. Press Ctrl+M to Include the Actual Execution Plan.

4. Run the following query:

```
USE AdventureWorks2008
GO
SELECT HireDate,LoginID
FROM HumanResources.Employee
ORDER BY HireDate
```

5. Select the Execution Plan tab near the results pane.

6. Left-click either Sort or Clustered Index Scan in the execution plan tab and then click back onto "SELECT" to update the Properties window.

You'll now see an entry called Memory Grant with a value of 1024, which is the number of pages used and equals 8MB. The query used 8MB to process the Sort operation, which was needed because the results were requested out of order based on the Clustered Index by using the ORDER BY clause.

Your screen should look similar to Figure 2-18.

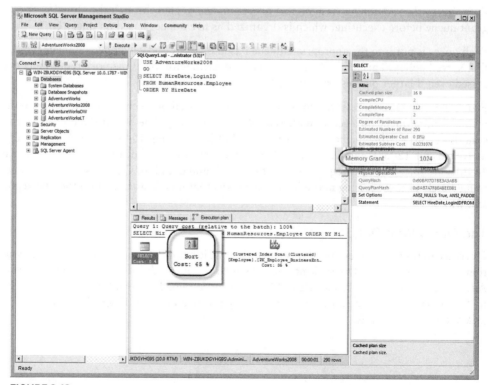

FIGURE 2-18

The memory requirements for all hash and sort operators in a plan are added together to get the total query memory requirement.

The amount of space available as "query memory" is dynamically managed between 25% and 75% of non-AWE buffer pool (remember only data pages can use AWE), but it can grow larger than that if the buffer pool is not under pressure.

> *If you're using 32-bit SQL Server with large amounts of RAM, maximum query memory will be reduced because it needs to come out of the 2GB address space, which might already be under pressure to support AWE. With 64GB of RAM, half of the 2GB address space is used just for AWE mapping information.*

Five percent of query memory is reserved for small queries that require less than 5MB of memory and have a "cost" of less than 3. SQL Server assigns a cost to queries based on how many resources will be needed to run the query. You can read more about how SQL Server assigns and uses "cost" in Chapter 5.

No individual query will get a grant for more than 20% of the total query memory, to ensure that other queries can still be executed. In addition to this safeguard, SQL Server also implements a query memory *grant queue*.

Every query that contains a hash or sort operation has to pass through the global query memory grant queue before executing, which is organized as five queues based on query cost.

Each query is put into the appropriate queue based on cost, and each queue implements a first-come first-served policy. This method enables smaller queries with lower memory requirements to be processed even if larger queries are waiting for enough free memory.

Figure 2-19 shows a representation of the five queues based on query cost that make up the global memory grant queue on a server with 1GB of query memory. The box at the bottom of the picture contains eight existing memory grants totaling 920MB, leaving 104MB free. The first request to arrive was for 120MB and went into Q3. This request can't be allocated immediately because only 104MB are free. The next request is only for 20MB and goes into Q2. This request can be fulfilled immediately because having multiple queues means that it isn't stuck behind the first request that is still waiting.

The Query Wait Option

Queries can timeout if they spend too much time waiting for a memory grant. The timeout duration is controlled by the Query Wait option, which can be modified using `sp_configure` or on the Advanced page of Server Properties in Management Studio. The default value is -1, which equates to 25 times the cost of the query in seconds. Any positive value for Query Wait will be used as the timeout value in seconds.

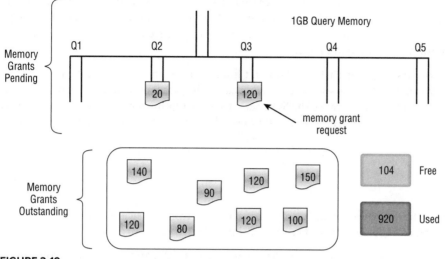

FIGURE 2-19

It is possible for a transaction that contains a query waiting for a memory grant to hold locks open and cause a blocking problem before it times out. In this situation a lower Query Wait would reduce the impact to other tasks by causing the query to timeout sooner.

However, I would first try to reduce the memory requirement for the query or increase the available memory to avoid the timeout before changing a global option like Query Wait because doing so would affect all queries running on the server.

The default setting allows for a dynamic timeout value depending on the query cost so it's generally the best option.

Query Memory Diagnostics

There are a number of different ways to get information on query memory use on your SQL Server in addition to the DMVs already discussed at the beginning of the section. Performance Monitor provides the following counters, all of which are found within the instance's Memory Manager:

➤ **Granted Workspace Memory (KB):** Total amount of query memory currently in use

➤ **Maximum Workspace Memory (KB):** Total amount of memory that SQL Server has marked for query memory

➤ **Memory Grants Pending:** Number of memory grants waiting in the queue

➤ **Memory Grants Outstanding:** Number of memory grants currently in use

The RESOURCE_SEMAPHORE wait type is a wait on a memory grant, so if you see this near the top in your results from the sys.dm_os_wait_stats DMV then your system is struggling to provide memory grants fast enough. You can read more on waits and wait types in Chapter 3.

You can also encounter performance issues other than just a query timing out waiting for a memory grant. Within an execution plan or when analyzing a SQL trace, you may notice Hash Warning or Sort Warning messages if you have selected the relevant events. These occur when the memory grant was insufficient for a query's requirements.

A hash warning occurs when the hash build doesn't fit in memory and must be spilled to disk. A sort warning occurs when a multi-pass sort is required because the granted memory was insufficient. Both warnings generally occur because the SQL Server Query Optimizer made the wrong choice, usually because of inaccurate statistics or a lack of useful statistics. You can read about statistics in Chapter 5.

SUMMARY

In this chapter you have learned about the basics of memory; from physical RAM modules to virtual memory addressing and the differences between 32-bit and 64-bit memory use.

You've read about how 32-bit systems use technologies such as /PAE and /3GB to overcome memory address limitations and how to get the most out of these environments as well as the options and best practices for configuring 64-bit systems for performance and availability.

You've also learned how and when to use AWE in both 32-bit and 64-bit environments, all about the infamous MemToLeave process, the architecture behind SQL Server 2008's memory management system and finally, the little known area within SQL Server's buffer pool known as Query Memory.

3

SQL Server Waits and Extended Events

Being able to troubleshoot problems when they happen in SQL Server is paramount to the success of any database administrator. Performance problems in particular can be a sink or swim type of test of the abilities and value a database administrator brings to the table. In an ideal world, anytime a query or batch is submitted for execution inside of SQL Server it will run immediately without delay. Most people do not, however, live in an ideal world. In fact most often, queries executed against SQL Server have to wait at some point during their execution while the resources required during their execution are gathered, latched/locked, and or other processes execute on the server. When troubleshooting performance problems and tuning SQL Server, understanding common and troublesome waits and how to eliminate them is often one of the ways to get the best bang for your buck. This chapter dives into what wait types are and how to troubleshoot them in SQL Server 2008.

In SQL Server 2000 wait statistics were aggregated and maintained at the server level, and were able to be reviewed through the use of DBCC SQLPERF. Additionally, currently waiting sessions could be viewed through the sysprocesses system view by translating the waittype column. In SQL Server 2005, the introduction of Dynamic Management Views simplified retrieving wait statistics by introducing the `sys.dm_os_wait_stats` and `sys.dm_os_waiting_tasks` views, which provided aggregate wait statistics and task-level wait information, respectively. One thing that was missing, however, was the ability to perform fine-grained analysis of wait statistics since the aggregate data was server level data, and active waiting could not easily be tracked historically. SQL Server 2008 provides the answer to this problem.

This chapter is split into two sections. The first part covers SQL Server Waits, how they occur and what they mean, the common wait types of concern, which waits can be ignored, and the new waits in SQL Server 2008. The second part will cover a new feature in SQL Server 2008 called *Extended Events* and how to use Extended Events to get a deep look into what waits are occurring in SQL Server and why. This new feature enables administrators to capture troubleshooting information in a manner that has never before been possible.

WAITS

When it comes to understanding performance problems in SQL Server there are a lot of things to look at. One of the most efficient ways to troubleshoot performance problems is to focus on how, when, and why SQL Server spends its time waiting to execute user requests. Understanding this information enables you to determine whether the problem is resource related, and if so, how to pinpoint the exact reason.

Inside SQL Server, anytime a process has to wait for something, whether it is for data to be retrieved from disk, written to disk, or even for an external process to run, the time spent waiting is tracked. A waiting process is assigned a *wait type* that identifies why the process is waiting. Wait time in SQL Server is dead time, so if you can reduce the amount of time spent waiting you'll be able to achieve better overall performance.

SQL Server Execution Model

To understand the wait types inside SQL Server, you need to first understand how SQL Server schedules and executes user requests. When SQL Server starts up, it loads its own operating system, called the SQLOS, which is essentially a resource manager for SQL Server. The SQLOS creates a scheduler for each logical CPU available on the server and then evenly divides the number of workers across the schedulers. At any given point in time, only one worker can be running on a scheduler. To accomplish this, each scheduler has five lists to which workers are assigned: worker, waiter, runnable, I/O, and timer.

The worker list is where available workers are kept until assigned to a task. Once assigned to a task, the same worker performs the task to its completion in order to reduce the need for context switching and to improve overall performance. If a worker running on the scheduler requires a resource such as a data page to be read, or a lock or latch to be acquired, it is moved into the waiter list, where it waits until the resource becomes available, enabling other workers waiting in the runnable list to execute on the scheduler. Once the resource has been acquired, the worker moves from the waiter list into the runnable list, where it waits for its turn to execute on the scheduler.

When an I/O operation is required, the executing worker creates an asynchronous I/O request and then moves into the I/O list until the I/O operation is completed, yielding the scheduler to the next worker in the runnable list. When a worker encounters a timer-based wait — for example, a WAITFOR DELAY in T-SQL code, it yields the scheduler and moves into the timer list. As each worker completes its execution on the scheduler, it checks the I/O and timer lists for completed I/O requests and expired timers, respectively, and moves workers as appropriate from the I/O and timer lists to the runnable list, where the worker(s) wait for their turn to execute on the scheduler.

The ability of the SQLOS to manage and perform cooperative scheduling in the manner just described is important to the performance of SQL Server. Because only one worker can execute on a scheduler at a time, and only one scheduler is created per processor, this voluntary yielding by workers prevents context switching on the SQL Server, improving performance. As always, there are exceptions when tasks require preemptive scheduling, such as extended stored procedure calls and linked server queries, which can cause context switching to occur.

Understanding Wait Statistics

In SQL Server 2000, the system tables and views provided limited information on waits inside of SQL Server when compared to the amount of information that is available in SQL Server 2005 and SQL Server 2008. The sysprocesses view reflected often used processes sitting in the waiter list, and it could also be used to find processes in the runnable list as well. In SQL Server 2005, dynamic management views (DMVs) were introduced, superseding the sysprocesses view, which was maintained for compatibility purposes only. While sysprocesses still works, the newer DMVs are better.

You can use the sys.dm_os_* view to look at the status of the various lists in the execution model. For example, you can find the number of schedulers (sys.dm_os_schedulers), the workers assigned to the schedulers (sys.dm_os_workers), the currently waiting tasks assigned to the wait list (sys.dm_os_waiting_tasks), the tasks in the runnable list waiting on CPU time (sys.dm_exec_requests), and the cumulative wait statistics for the entire instance (sys.dm_os_wait_stats) in the DMVs available in SQL Server.

Because this chapter's focus is on wait statistics only, it covers only three of these views, and only to the extent that they apply to understanding waiting inside SQL Server: sys.dm_os_waiting_tasks, sys.dm_exec_requests, and sys.dm_os_wait_stats.

The sys.dm_os_wait_stats DMV contains aggregated wait statistics for SQL Server. Unfortunately, the wait statistics are aggregated at the server level, with no detail level available. They are also aggregated over time, meaning that the numbers for wait times continue to accumulate as time progresses. The following example enables you to begin looking at the wait statistics that have occurred:

```
SELECT *
FROM sys.dm_os_wait_stats
WHERE wait_time_ms > 0
ORDER BY wait_time_ms DESC
```

This will return all waits with an accumulated wait time in milliseconds greater than zero in descending order. Note that not all wait types are bad for performance or avoidable. Numerous wait types are internal waits that can be ignored when reviewing the wait statistics in SQL Server. These are covered in more detail later in this chapter.

Because wait statistics are cleared by the system only when the SQL Service is restarted, when looking at waits occurring on the server it can be helpful to clear them manually using `DBCC SQLPERF("sys.dm_os_wait_stats",CLEAR)`. After clearing the values from this DMV, it can be used to analyze the current wait statistics being accumulated. If you are using third-party monitoring tools that track wait statistics, this can cause problems with what the tool reports. In this case, a temporary table and a `WAITFOR DELAY` can be used to track the changes over a period of time to determine what waits are currently occurring:

```
IF OBJECT_ID('tempdb..#wait_stats') IS NOT NULL
DROP TABLE #wait_stats

SELECT *
INTO #wait_stats
FROM sys.dm_os_wait_stats

WAITFOR DELAY '00:00:05'

SELECT ws1.wait_type,
       ws2.waiting_tasks_count - ws1.waiting_tasks_count
       AS waiting_tasks_count,
       ws2.wait_time_ms - ws1.wait_time_ms AS wait_time_ms,
       CASE WHEN ws2.max_wait_time_ms > ws1.max_wait_time_ms
THEN ws2.max_wait_time_ms
       ELSE ws1.max_wait_time_ms
END AS max_wait_time_ms,
       ws2.signal_wait_time_ms - ws1.signal_wait_time_ms
       AS signal_wait_time_ms,
       (ws2.wait_time_ms - ws1.wait_time_ms) - (ws2.signal_wait_time_ms -
  ws1.signal_wait_time_ms) AS resource_wait_time_ms
FROM sys.dm_os_wait_stats AS ws2
JOIN #wait_stats AS ws1 ON ws1.wait_type = ws2.wait_type
WHERE ws2.wait_time_ms - ws1.wait_time_ms > 0
ORDER BY ws2.wait_time_ms - ws1.wait_time_ms DESC
```

When looking at aggregated wait statistics with the `sys.dm_os_wait_stats` DMV, the `wait_time_ms` column includes the resource wait time as well as the signal wait time combined. Signal wait time reflects the time a worker spends in the runnable list before being able to continue execution after leaving the waiter list. To get the resource wait time, subtract the `signal_wait_time_ms` from the `wait_time_ms` as shown in the previous example. When looking at the difference between resource and signal waits, it can be helpful to look at the percentage of total wait time that each contributes, as shown in the following example. A high percentage of signal waits can be a sign of CPU pressure or the need for faster CPUs on the server.

```
SELECT SUM(signal_wait_time_ms) AS total_signal_wait_time_ms,
       SUM(wait_time_ms - signal_wait_time_ms) AS resource_wait_time_ms,
       SUM(signal_wait_time_ms) * 1.0 / SUM (wait_time_ms) * 100
       AS signal_wait_percent,
       SUM(wait_time_ms - signal_wait_time_ms) * 1.0 / SUM (wait_time_ms) * 100
       AS resource_wait_percent
    FROM sys.dm_os_wait_stats
```

Using the `sys.dm_os_wait_stats` DMV enables time slice analysis of wait statistics against the entire server, but it doesn't provide granular wait information for tracking which session, query, or database is actually causing the waits to occur. If the server is a shared server that hosts multiple databases, it can be difficult to determine whether high waits are being caused by a resource bottleneck. To assist with this problem, you need to look at what specific tasks are waiting.

Understanding what tasks are currently waiting is a very practical starting point to troubleshooting a performance problem, and the sys.dm_os_waiting_tasks DMV is one of the best places to start looking. When a worker moves onto the waiter list, it shows up inside this DMV until it has completed waiting and moves into the runnable list. In addition, if a blocking scenario is occurring, the blocking_session_id DMV is available to assist in troubleshooting any blocking problems that might exist.

Since SQL Server 2000, session_ids 1 through 50 are reserved for internal use; and session_ids that are greater than 50 generally represent user sessions. It is very common for internal processes to show up in the results of the sys.dm_os_waiting_tasks DMV. To look only at user sessions, which are typically the most common area of interest when looking at waiting tasks, you can use a filter on the session_id column for values greater than 50:

```
SELECT session_id,
       execution_context_id,
       wait_duration_ms,
       wait_type,
       resource_description,
       blocking_session_id
FROM sys.dm_os_waiting_tasks
WHERE session_id > 50
ORDER BY session_id
```

The preceding example query retrieves only a subset of the columns available in the view. The session_**id** column is the ID of the session associated with the task. The execution_context_id column is the execution context ID associated with the task. The value will be zero for the main thread and greater than zero for child threads. The wait_duration_ms column is the total amount of time, in milliseconds, that has been spent waiting for this wait type. This value includes any signal wait time as well. The wait_type column is the descriptive name of the wait type. The resource_description column provides description information for the resource that is being waited on. The blocking_session_id column contains the session_id of the session that is blocking the execution of this session. If the task is not blocked, then the value will be NULL.

It can also be very useful to perform aggregate queries against this DMV to find information such as the number of tasks for each wait type:

```
SELECT wait_type,
       COUNT(*) AS num_waiting_tasks,
       SUM(wait_duration_ms) AS total_wait_time_ms
FROM sys.dm_os_waiting_tasks
WHERE session_id > 50
GROUP BY wait_type
ORDER BY wait_type
```

This view can quickly indicate whether you are experiencing an abnormal kind of wait type for your server, or at least give you an idea of the most prominent waits currently occurring. An example usage of this would be a high number of waiting tasks for PAGEIOLATCH waits on a server that has never experienced I/O bottlenecks previously. It could be a sign of increased workload, the introduction of a new poorly performing query, or perhaps a process external to SQL Server that is consuming I/O heavily and affecting SQL Server performance, such as a file system defragmentation job or a heavy file copy operation.

The ability to use the `sys.dm_os_waiting_tasks` DMV to actively look at current waiters in SQL Server is very helpful, but it does not enable historical tracking of waits in a logged manner very easily. While it is possible to insert the results of querying this DMV into a table, it is highly likely that information would be missed between queries because the view is a snapshot in time. Until SQL Server 2008, no method existed to allow for detailed root cause analysis into wait statistics. However, Extended Events, which are covered later in this chapter, can solve this problem.

Wait Types

As previously mentioned, when an executing worker requires a resource that is not available, it is moved to the waiter list. As this happens, the worker is assigned a wait type that identifies why the worker is waiting, and the amount of time spent waiting begins being tracked in milliseconds.

Resource Wait Types

Resource waits are without a doubt the best place to focus your efforts when looking at improving performance on your server. This type of wait represents a point where the SQL Server had to wait to acquire a resource, which can be a sign of a bottleneck, although not necessarily. Resource waits can be grouped into potential bottleneck categories, with multiple waits in each category. In general, resource waits are a sign of CPU, memory, I/O, blocking, or network trouble on the SQL Server.

As illustrated by the scenarios discussed in the sidebar, the most visible problem isn't always the actual problem. For this reason, analysis of wait types cannot be done inside of a black box. As each category is discussed, you will notice that it may reference performance counters related to another category of waits, or even another wait category itself. This is done to ensure that the root of the problem is actually discovered, as one category of problems can impact the system to the point that waits begin to form within other categories.

Memory Waits

Memory waits occur when a process is waiting for a memory allocation from a memory object in the SQLOS. Two memory related wait types to look for are the CMEMTHREAD and RESOURCE_SEMAPHORE wait types since these occur when a process is unable to obtain the necessary memory to continue.

The CMEMTHREAD is most often a sign of plan caching problems in SQL Server. It occurs when a large number of plans are being added to or removed from the plan cache, generally indicative of an adhoc, or non-parameterized workload. In SQL Server 2005 this wait type was associated with problems in the TokenAndPermUserStore. Changes were made post Service Pack 2 in SQL Server 2005 to help address the problem, but it can still show up under certain workloads. The best fix to this problem is to change the application to utilize parameterization and reduce the number of plans being inserted and removed from the cache. However, if this is not possible, setting Forced Parameterization for the database may provide relief.

OBVIOUS ISN'T ALWAYS RIGHT

When troubleshooting wait issues, it can be very tempting to jump to the most obvious problem immediately in an attempt to quickly fix the issue. While this is a very logical approach, it can actually be counterproductive in troubleshooting waits in SQL Server. I once worked at a company with a billing system written in Transact-SQL that routinely ran with high CPU utilization during execution of the billing process. It was assumed that the load had outgrown the server and that execution times continued to increase over time. Ultimately, two missing indexes on foreign key columns solved the problem, reducing execution time from four hours to less than fifteen minutes.

In another example, I encountered a SQL Server that had very high disk utilization resulting in high ASYNC_IO_COMPLETION and PAGEIOLATCH wait types in SQL Server. The server's drive configuration was substantial enough that it should have been more than able to handle the transactional load that the system was under. The actual root cause of the problem was that the SQL Server was memory starved, running 64-bit SQL with CLR enabled and only 4GB of RAM installed. This caused the system to perform repetitive reads from disk because the buffer pool was too small. It also resulted in heavy utilization of tempdb for work tables and sorting and hashing operations. A quick upgrade to 16GB of RAM fixed the problem immediately.

The RESOURCE_SEMAPHORE wait type occurs when a memory-intensive query is unable to obtain the requested memory it needs to execute (see Workspace Memory section in Chapter 2), though it can also occur when a process has to wait during query optimization. This wait occurs when a memory request cannot be granted immediately to a process due to other concurrent processes. This wait may indicate an excessive number of concurrent processes, or excessive memory request amounts. Large sort or hash operations for example can result in this type of wait occurring. Adding an index with the correct sort order can avoid the sort operation or reduce the data in transit for the hashing operation if one is being performed.

When investigating a RESOURCE_SEMAPHORE wait problem, if the wait type is consistently occurring, the sys.dm_exec_query_resource_semaphores DMV can be queried as follows to view how many waits are occurring:

```
SELECT waiter_count,
       timeout_error_count,
       forced_grant_count
FROM sys.dm_exec_query_resource_semaphores
```

The waiter_count column shows the number of queries that are waiting on a memory grant to continue executing. The timeout_error_count column shows the number of timeout errors waiting on a memory grant that have occurred since the server last started. The forced_grant_count column shows the number of forced minimum-memory grants since the server last started. Values other than zero for any of these columns should be investigated further.

To further investigate memory waits in SQL you'll need to gather additional information from the server's performance counters for correlation. The following counters should be collected from the server:

➤ SQLServer:Memory Manager\Memory Grants Pending

➤ SQLServer:Memory Manager\Memory Grants Outstanding

➤ SQLServer:Buffer Manager\Buffer Hit Cache Ratio

➤ SQLServer:Buffer Manager\Page Life Expectancy

➤ SQLServer:Buffer Manager\Free Pages

➤ SQLServer:Buffer Manager\Free List Stalls/sec

➤ Memory: Available Mbytes

The Memory Grants Pending and Outstanding counters indicate a definite memory problem especially a non-zero value for Memory Grants Pending. If the Page Life Expectancy is consistently lower than 300 seconds the SQL Server will perform more hard reads from disk to satisfy requests. The Buffer Cache Hit Ratio is the percent of time that SQL Server was able to fetch a page from the Buffer Pool instead of having to read it from disk. It should be greater than 95% consistently for OLTP workloads. It should be noted that these values will not be accurate immediately following a service or server restart since it takes time for the buffer cache to stabilize under normal transaction load, since all data has to be read from disk initially post restart. The Free Pages counter represents the number of free pages on all lists and should generally be over 300. Values under 300 should be compared with the value for the Free List Stalls/sec, which represents the number of requests per second that had to wait for a free page. Low numbers of Free Pages associated with non-zero values for Free List Stalls can be a sign of memory pressure. The Available Mbytes counter represents the amount of memory available on the server. It should generally remain over 150MB to allow the operating system room to run.

Disk I/O Waits

Disk I/O waits occur when a process is waiting for disk I/O to complete before it can continue executing. The most common I/O waits in SQL Server are IO_COMPLETION, ASYNC_IO_COMPLETION, WRITELOG, and the PAGEIOLATCH_* waits. These wait types can be a sign that the disk subsystem is misconfigured, undersized, or overloaded for the current workload, but they can also be a sign of other non-I/O-related problems, such as a missing index, a query performing an expensive table scan being run without a WHERE predicate, or even memory pressure on the server.

When the IO_COMPLETION, ASYNC_IO_COMPLETION, or PAGEIOLATCH_* wait types are the top waits on the server, it is also common to find entries in the Error Log similar to the following:

```
SQL Server has encountered <xx> occurrence(s) of IO requests taking longer
than 15 seconds to complete on file <filename>.
```

This error message is a sign of I/O stalls on the SQL Server, and should be investigated to determine the root cause of the problem. In SQL Server, I/O stalls are tracked by the database engine and can be looked at using the sys.fn_virtualfilestats dynamic management function (DMF). This function accepts two input parameters, @DatabaseID and @FileID, both integer values that are nullable. If a default or null value is passed to the function, it will return the virtual file stats for all databases and their associated files on the server:

```
SELECT mf.name,
       mf.physical_name,
       vfs.IoStallMS,
       vfs.IoStallReadMS,
       vfs.IoStallWriteMS, *
FROM sys.fn_virtualfilestats(null,null) AS vfs
JOIN sys.master_files AS mf ON mf.database_id = vfs.DbId
       AND mf.file_id = vfs.FileId
ORDER BY vfs.IoStallMS DESC
```

Pay close attention to the physical location of files that have high I/O stall values, and determine whether the problem is isolated to a single device in the system or is more widespread. Just as with the blocking wait types, troubleshooting an I/O wait problem requires correlating information from a number of different sources.

Performance counters are important when troubleshooting I/O problems and can be used to help further guide your troubleshooting efforts. Important counters to collect for the PhysicalDisk are as follows:

➤ Average Disk sec/Read

➤ Average Disk sec/Write

➤ Average Disk Read/Write Queue Length

Disks read or write times greater than 20 ms or high queue length values should be investigated further, as these can be a sign of bottlenecking. When looking at Disk IO bottlenecks, the memory counters listed in the Memory Waits section should also be examined. In addition to the Disk and Memory counters, you should also monitor how SQL Server accesses data. Table and index scans can be expensive compared to seeks. This can be a sign of a missing index or filter criteria, requiring the database engine to read more data than would otherwise be necessary to satisfy the request. To monitor for this, collect the following performance counters:

➤ SQL Server: Access Methods\Full Scans/sec

➤ SQL Server: Access Methods \Index Searches/sec

➤ SQL Server: Access Methods \Forwarded Records/sec

High values for any of these counters should be investigated further, as these indicate that the database engine is performing excessive work to satisfy a request.

The Forwarded Records counter points to a specific problem with heaps that are frequently updated with variable-length data fields. When a row in a heap is updated and the length of the data is larger than the available space on the page, SQL Server moves the row to the end of the data file and places a forwarded record in the original allocation unit pointing to the new location of the data. If the table has non-clustered indexes, the indexes point to the original row location for lookups. To get the data, an additional page read is required for each forwarded record that exists for the row, which increases the amount of I/O required to retrieve the data. To correct this problem, consider creating a clustered index on the table, or use ALTER TABLE to rebuild the heap.

So far, the WRITELOG wait type has not been covered, and this was intentional. This wait type can occur in combination with the other I/O wait types, but it can also occur on its own. This wait type occurs when SQL Server waits to harden log entries in the database transaction log. It can occur as a result of an overall I/O subsystem problem, or it can occur as a result of improper file placement on the disk arrays on the server.

The transaction log is written to sequentially, unlike the database data files, which use random reads and writes. For this reason, it is best to separate the database transaction log onto its own disk array in order to separate its sequential workload from the random workload of the data files. Multiple log files on the same disk array can also result in WRITELOG waits as the disk heads move between files.

When a true bottleneck exists in the disk subsystem, other problems generally occur as well. Long I/O operations and I/O stalls can result in locking issues, as locks are held for the duration of the I/O operation. Locking issues lead to blocked processes on the server.

Blocking Waits

Blocking waits (LCK_* wait types) occur when one session is blocked by another session from executing. These are generally related to concurrency locking inside of the database engine. There are 21 wait types in SQL Server 2008 related to locking. Long-term locking can be a sign of a possible transaction management issue inside of user code, but it can also be a sign of memory pressure on the server.

When investigating problems involving blocking and LCK_* wait types in SQL Server, it is important to look at additional information available on the server. Performance counters such as the Page Life Expectancy and Buffer Cache Hit Ratio can help determine whether the problem is memory related. Looking at transaction duration with the sys.dm_tran_active_transactions DMV for the blocking session can help determine whether the problem is related to long-running user transactions. In addition, enable the Blocked Process Report with sp_configure and then collect it using SQL Trace to capture detailed information about blocking.

CPU

The two most common CPU-related wait types in SQL Server are the CXPACKET and SOS_SCHEDULER_YIELD waits. The SOS_SCHEDULER_YIELD wait type occurs when a task reaches the end of its quantum and yields the scheduler to the other tasks in the runnable list to allow them to execute. A worker waits with this wait type until its quantum is renewed and then returns to the runnable list to wait for its turn to execute on the scheduler again. When this wait type occurs along with a high signal wait to resource wait ratio, it can be a sign that more powerful processors are needed on the server.

The CXPACKET wait type is a parallel processing wait type that occurs when multiple tasks are used to satisfy a request in parallel. When data distribution between tasks is uneven, the task with the smaller set of data will wait with this wait type for the tasks to synchronize. This can have a negative impact on OLTP workloads, but may be acceptable for large-scale data warehouse environments. Reducing the max degree of parallelism to a value that is less than the number of physical processors, or disabling parallelism completely using sp_configure, will resolve problems with this wait type.

If the SQL Server has hyperthreading-enabled processors, disabling hyperthreading should be tested to determine if the CPU waits are related to context switching caused by running multiple threads concurrently on the same processor. This is contrary to the design and implementation of user mode schedulers by the SQLOS. Because hyperthreading doubles the physical processors as logical processors, SQL Server will have twice the user mode schedulers. This can result in SQL Server attempting to use a degree of parallelism that is greater than the physical hardware can support.

Network Waits

Network waits (ASYNC_NETWORK_IO and DBMIRROR_SEND) occur when a session has to wait to transmit information over the network interface. The ASYNC_NETWORK_IO wait type can be a sign that the current network adapter bandwidth is reaching a point of saturation. It can also be a sign that the client is not immediately consuming the results being returned by SQL Server — for example, by performing complex operations using a DataReader on the client between row fetches.

The DBMIRROR_SEND wait type can indicate that the available bandwidth is insufficient to support the volume of mirrored transactions occurring on the server. It can also indicate database mirroring oversubscription. If multiple databases are mirrored, try reducing the number of mirrored databases, or increasing the network bandwidth by upgrading to a higher-speed adapter.

When troubleshooting network waits, it can be beneficial to also investigate the configuration settings of the network adapter as well. Ensure that the server and client adapter settings match as closely as possible. Utilize full duplex and the maximum bandwidth settings available on the adapter. To monitor network adapter performance, the following network performance counters can be collected:

➤ Network\Current bandwidth

➤ Network\bytes total/sec

➤ Network\packets/sec

System Waits

As a part of its normal operation, SQL Server and the SQLOS run background tasks that perform internal system tasks. It is common for a number of these tasks to actually exist in a waiting state, which is why they appear in the sys.dm_os_waiting_tasks DMV. Internal tasks such as the deadlock monitor, lazywriter, and Extended Event Engine timer consistently wait until required. A number of these tasks generate high wait times that will show up when querying the sys.dm_os_wait_stats or sys.dm_os_waiting_tasks DMVs under normal operations. Common wait types for internal tasks include the following:

➤ LAZYWRITER_SLEEP

➤ REQUEST_FOR_DEADLOCK_SEARCH

➤ SQLTRACE_BUFFER_FLUSH

➤ XE_TIMER_EVENT

➤   `FT_IFTS_SCHEDULER_IDLE_WAIT`

➤   `LOGMGR_QUEUE`

➤   `CHECKPOINT_QUEUE`

➤   `SLEEP_TASK`

➤   `BROKER_TO_FLUSH`

When investigating wait stats in SQL Server, these wait types can often be ignored, and it is not uncommon for them to show up as the top waits for the server.

Preemptive Wait Types

As previously covered in the section "SQL Server Execution Model," SQL Server uses cooperative scheduling inside the SQLOS for most activity. However, when a process makes external code calls like OLE Automation, or uses extended stored procedures in unmanaged code, the task can't be run cooperatively. Instead, it uses the preemptive scheduling of the Windows operating system.

Preemptive tasks in SQL Server have a status of running inside of SQL Server, unlike cooperative tasks, which have a status of suspended while waiting for resources. Prior to SQL Server 2008, pre-emptive tasks either had no wait type associated with them or they had an obscure wait type like `OLEDB` associated with them, providing little information as to what the task was actually waiting for. Preemptive wait types, new to SQL Server 2008, provide the capability to track when a worker is executing code using preemptive scheduling:

```
SELECT *
FROM sys.dm_os_wait_stats
WHERE wait_type LIKE 'PREEMPTIVE%'
```

There are 190 preemptive wait types in SQL Server 2008. As you can probably guess, their names provide information about what external process is being executed. Preemptive wait type names take the following format:

```
PREEMPTIVE_<category>_<API function or class name>
```

Many of the preemptive waits are OS waits for functionality like authenticating Windows accounts that have access to SQL Server (`PREEMPTIVE_OS_AUTHENTICATIONOPS`) and external file operations (`PREEMPTIVE_OS_FILEOPS`). However, there are several COM, OLEDB, and even XE (Extended Event) waits too.

EXTENDED EVENTS

Possibly one of the best-kept secrets of SQL Server 2008 during its Community Technology Previews, and even at its release to manufacturing, Extended Events are a refreshing new method for capturing troubleshooting information in SQL Server. Replacing the much older SQL Trace in SQL Server, Extended Events was built entirely from the ground up, with performance a primary concern in its design and implementation. In addition to performance, flexibility and scalability were a chief concern in the implementation of Extended Events in SQL Server 2008.

Architecture

While a fundamental understanding of the Extended Events architecture is not required in order to use event sessions in SQL Server 2008, it is helpful when designing sessions that can scale properly and actually capture the information of interest. This section covers the Extended Event Engine, how Extended Event metadata is organized, and the life of an event.

Extended Events Engine

The foundation of Extended Events in SQL Server 2008 is the Extended Events Engine (see Figure 3-1), a service running inside the database engine that enables packages to be registered that actually contain the definition metadata of the objects available for defining event sessions. The Engine itself contains no information and has no knowledge of event information until a package is registered by a loading process in the database engine. This separation of the Engine from the package data makes Extended Events one of the most flexible troubleshooting features in SQL Server to date.

Because packages contain the definition of objects for use by the Extended Events Engine, you can add new events to the system by updating the package metadata loaded by the process into the Engine. The Customer Support Services team at Microsoft can take advantage of this flexibility by providing additional events to customers (during a support case) that may not be appropriate for standard release in the SQL Server product. It also ensures that the Extended Events Engine treats all objects equally during its execution, and ensures the same level of performance and stability for future additions to the product.

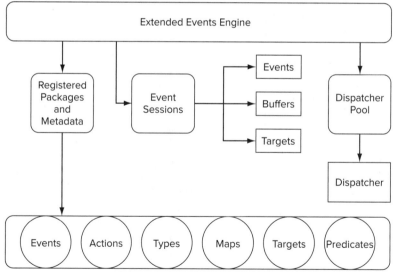

FIGURE 3-1

One of the greatest features of Extended Events is that any object from any package registered in the Engine can be used in defining event sessions. That is, a target from the *package0* package can be used with events from the *sqlos* package, which includes actions from the *sqlserver* package. This enables the correlation of data across processes in SQL Server, providing full diagnostic capabilities to resolve problems.

In addition to registering packages and providing metadata, the Extended Events Engine hosts a pool of threads (known as the *dispatcher pool*) that are used for firing events, collecting data, and buffering the information to the targets defined on event sessions. It also manages all of the active sessions defined in the SQL Server instance.

Event Firing

When a pertinent point in code execution is reached where a registered event exists, the Extended Events Engine is checked to determine whether the event is part of an active session. If so, the session is checked to determine whether the Event has any configurable columns that have been configured for it. If it does, the configured column data is retrieved, and then the base payload column data is retrieved for the event. If no configured columns exist, then only the base payload data is retrieved.

With the event data collected, any predicates defined on the event are evaluated to a Boolean pass or fail to determine whether the event needs to execute any actions before being written to the synchronous targets immediately. Once the event data has been written to the synchronous targets, it is sent to the Session Buffer memory, where it waits to be dispatched to the asynchronous targets later. This process is shown in Figure 3-2.

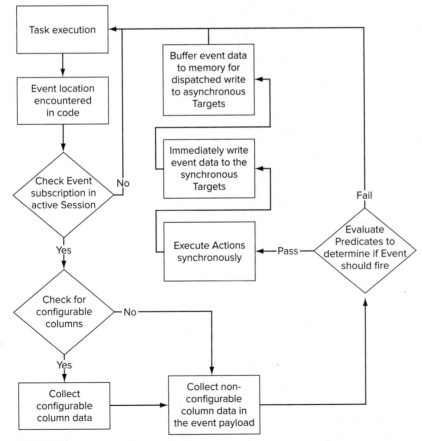

FIGURE 3-2

Once the event data has been buffered, execution continues until the next event is encountered, where the process repeats. One of the keys to the performance of Extended Events in SQL Server 2008 is that the amount of work performed on the executing thread is minimized by design unless additional requirements for synchronous execution are defined by the end user in the event session (i.e., actions and synchronous targets).

Dynamic Management Views and Functions

Because Extended Events is a new feature in SQL Server 2008, there is no UI support for them in SQL Server Management Studio. To meet this need, you can download from CodePlex a free external community tool called the Extended Events Manager, which is covered later in this chapter. For native support, the only tools available are the built-in dynamic management views and functions.

The DMVs are broken down into three subject areas: *metadata views*, *active session views*, and *session definition views*. Each subject area, including its associated views, is covered separately in its own subsection so that you can understand their relationships and appropriately query the views to obtain information from them.

Metadata Views

The metadata views contain the queryable metadata that is currently registered in the Extended Events Engine. These views contain information about the packages registered in the Engine, the objects (events, actions, predicates, types, and targets) that can be used to define an event session available in those packages, the columns available for each object, and the map values available inside the Engine.

The sys.dm_xe_packages view (see http://msdn.microsoft.com/en-us/library/bb677239 .aspx) contains a row for each package that has been registered in the Extended Events Engine. While four packages are returned from the view, only three of them can actually be used in user-defined event sessions. The capabilities_desc column in this view marks the SecAudit package as a private, internal-only package used by the Server Audit functionality in SQL Server 2008.

The sys.dm_xe_objects view (see http://msdn.microsoft.com/en-us/library/bb677276.aspx) contains a row for each object that is available in the server for use in Extended Events. Objects are categorized inside this view by their respective object_type: action, event, map, pred_compare, pred_source, target, and type. This view is joined to the sys.dm_xe_packages view by the package_guid column to the guid column as shown in the following example:

```
SELECT p.name AS package_name,
       o.name AS object_name,
       o.object_type AS object_type,
       o.description AS object_description
FROM sys.dm_xe_packages AS p
JOIN sys.dm_xe_objects AS o
    ON p.guid = o.package_guid
WHERE (p.capabilities IS NULL
  OR p.capabilities & 1 = 0)
```

The sys.dm_xe_object_columns view (see http://msdn.microsoft.com/en-us/library/ bb630367.aspx) contains the column schema definition for Extended Events objects. Two types of information are contained in this view: read-only internal information that describes the object, such as the channel and keyword for an event, and the column list available for configuring, or returned by the object. When the object type is an event, this view contains the columns carried in the default event payload, and the channel and keyword association for Event Tracing for Windows (ETW). When the object type is a target, it contains the configurable columns for the target such as filename for the asynchronous_file_target, or filtering event name for the bucketizer target. This view can be joined to the sys.dm_xe_objects view by the object_name column to the name column and object_package_guid column to the package_guid column as shown below:

```
SELECT o.name AS object_name,
       c.name AS column_name,
       c.column_id AS column_id,
       c.column_type AS column_type,
       c.column_value AS column_value,
       c.type_name as column_data_type
FROM sys.dm_xe_objects AS o
JOIN sys.dm_xe_object_columns AS c
     ON o.package_guid = c.object_package_guid
    AND o.name = c.object_name
WHERE o.name = 'wait_info'
```

The sys.dm_xe_map_values view (see http://msdn.microsoft.com/en-us/library/bb630350 .aspx) contains a row for each mapped internal key to its corresponding text value. This view can be queried and used when defining predicates for event filtering when building event sessions to identify the correct key values to use during filtering. This view can also be joined to when reading target data to translate internal keys into user-readable values.

Session Definition Views

When an event session is created on the server, the session information is stored in the master database. The session definition views provide access to session information for all sessions created on the SQL Server. The sys.server_event_sessions view (see http://msdn.microsoft.com/en-us/ library/bb677320.aspx) contains a row for each session defined in the Extended Events Engine. This view contains the session name, as well as session-level configuration information, including event retention mode, memory partition configuration, dispatch latency, and startup state.

Information about the events defined in an event session can be found in the sys.server_event_ session_events view (see http://msdn.microsoft.com/en-us/library/bb677310.aspx), which contains a row for each event defined in an event session. It includes the event id, event name, event package name, and, if defined, the predicate for the event. This view can be joined to the sys.server_event_sessions view with the event_session_id column as shown below.

```
select sese.package AS event_package,
       sese.name AS event_name,
       sese.predicate AS event_predicate
FROM sys.server_event_sessions AS ses
JOIN sys.server_event_session_events AS sese
       ON ses.event_session_id = sese.event_session_id
WHERE ses.name = 'system_health'
```

Any actions defined on an event in a session can be found in the `sys.server_event_session_actions` view (see `http://msdn.microsoft.com/en-us/library/bb677218.aspx`) view, which contains a row for each action that has been defined on an event defined in an event session. It is joined to the `sys.server_event_session_events` view by `event_session_id` and `event_id` as shown below:

```
SELECT sese.package AS event_package,
       sese.name AS event_name,
       sese.predicate AS event_predicate,
       sesa.package AS action_package,
       sesa.name AS action_name
FROM sys.server_event_sessions AS ses
JOIN sys.server_event_session_events AS sese
     ON ses.event_session_id = sese.event_session_id
JOIN sys.server_event_session_actions AS sesa
   ON ses.event_session_id = sesa.event_session_id
  AND sese.event_id = sesa.event_id
WHERE ses.name = 'system_health'
```

The targets defined on an event session can be found in the `sys.server_event_session_targets` view (see `http://msdn.microsoft.com/en-us/library/bb630370.aspx`). This view contains a row for each target defined in an event session. The configuration options for each target can be found in the `sys.server_event_session_fields` view (see `http://msdn.microsoft.com/en-us/library/bb677308.aspx`), which can be joined to the `sys.server_event_session_targets` view on `event_session_id` and the `target_id` to the `object_id` as shown below:

```
SELECT ses.name AS session_name,
       sest.name AS target_name,
       sesf.name AS option_name,
       sesf.value AS option_value
FROM sys.server_event_sessions AS ses
JOIN sys.server_event_session_targets AS sest
       ON ses.event_session_id = sest.event_session_id
JOIN sys.server_event_session_fields AS sesf
   ON sest.event_session_id = sesf.event_session_id
  AND sest.target_id = sesf.object_id
WHERE ses.name = 'system_health'
```

Active Session Views

The active session views contain information that is very similar in nature to the information contained in the session definition views. However, these views only contain information for event sessions that are active on the SQL Server. If no information is returned by the DMVs, no sessions are currently in a started state. These views can be used to get execution information and target data from an active session.

Each running session on the server will have an entry in the `sys.dm_xe_sessions` view (see `http://msdn.microsoft.com/en-us/library/bb630378.aspx`). There may also be a row for the server audits if they are enabled, which are run on top of, but are not a part of, Extended Events. This view can be used to look at and troubleshoot the impact that an Extended Events session has on the server. It contains information about the various buffer sizes, and, depending on how the session was configured, event drop rates or blocking impact.

Events that are subscribed to by an event session can be found in the `sys.dm_xe_session_events` view (see `http://msdn.microsoft.com/en-us/library/bb677260.aspx`). This view can be joined to the `sys.dm_xe_sessions` view by the `event_session_address` to the address column. Any actions defined on an event can be found in the `sys.dm_xe_session_event_actions` view (see `http://msdn.microsoft.com/en-us/library/bb677187.aspx`), which can be joined to using the `event_session_address`, `event_name`, and `event_package_guid` columns as shown below:

```
SELECT s.name AS session_name,
       e.event_name AS event_name,
       e.event_predicate AS event_predicate,
       ea.action_name AS action_name
FROM sys.dm_xe_sessions AS s
JOIN sys.dm_xe_session_events AS e
    ON s.address = e.event_session_address
JOIN sys.dm_xe_session_event_actions AS ea
    ON e.event_session_address = ea.event_session_address
    AND e.event_name = ea.event_name
WHERE s.name = 'system_health'
```

Information on the targets for an event session can be found using the `sys.dm_xe_session_targets` view (see `http://msdn.microsoft.com/en-us/library/bb677313.aspx`), which contains aggregate data for each of the targets defined on an event session. This view includes information about the target's execution count, which is the number of times the target has been executed for the session; total duration spent executing; and XML data for the target if applicable as shown in the following example:

```
SELECT s.name AS session_name,
       t.target_name AS target_name,
       t.execution_count AS execution_count,
       t.execution_duration_ms AS execution_duration,
       t.target_data AS target_data
FROM sys.dm_xe_sessions AS s
JOIN sys.dm_xe_session_targets AS t
    ON s.address = t.event_session_address
WHERE s.name = 'system_health'
```

You can find configurable options for targets and events that have customizable columns in the `sys.dm_xe_session_object_columns` view (see `http://msdn.microsoft.com/en-us/library/bb630380.aspx`), which can be joined to using the `event_session_address`, `object_name`, and `object_package_guid` columns as shown below:

```
SELECT DISTINCT s.name AS session_name,
       oc.object_name,
       oc.object_type,
       oc.column_name,
       oc.column_value
FROM sys.dm_xe_sessions AS s
JOIN sys.dm_xe_session_targets AS t
    ON s.address = t.event_session_address
```

```
JOIN sys.dm_xe_session_events AS e
    ON s.address = e.event_session_address
JOIN sys.dm_xe_session_object_columns AS oc
    ON s.address = oc.event_session_address
   AND ((oc.object_type = 'target' AND t.target_name = oc.object_name)
      OR (oc.object_type = 'event' AND e.event_name = oc.object_name))
WHERE s.name = 'system_health'
```

Extended Event Metadata

The Extended Events Metadata contains all of the necessary information required to understand and implement Extended Events. This information is loaded into the Extended Events Engine when the respective modules are loaded, and is available through the use of the dynamic management views covered in the previous section of this chapter.

Packages

Packages are basically containers of objects that are available to the Extended Events Engine for use in defining event sessions. Packages are loaded with their associated module and are registered for use by the Extended Events Engine. They may contain any combination of events, targets, actions, predicates, types, and maps.

```
SELECT *
FROM sys.dm_xe_packages
WHERE (capabilities IS NULL OR capabilities & 1 = 0)
```

At the time this chapter was written, three packages were available for user event sessions in SQL Server 2008: *package0*, a default package containing all of the standard types, maps, compare operators, actions, and targets; *sqlos*, which contains event information related to the SQL operating system; and *sqlserver*, which contains event information related to Microsoft SQL Server.

Events

Events represent a known point of execution in code inside the SQL Server Database Engine that may be of interest. Whereas SQL Trace has 180 events available for data collection and analysis, Extended Events currently has 525 events available that can be queried using the following example.

```
SELECT p.name AS package_name,
       o.name AS event_name,
       o.description
FROM sys.dm_xe_packages AS p
JOIN sys.dm_xe_objects AS o
     ON p.guid = o.package_guid
WHERE (p.capabilities IS NULL OR p.capabilities & 1 = 0)
  AND o.object_type = 'event'
```

The events in Extended Events overlap SQL Trace events, but they extend beyond the capabilities of SQL Trace, providing much more detailed information into the internal workings of SQL Server. For example, the SQL Trace SQL:StmtStarting event matches the sqlserver.sql_statement_ completed event in SQL Server, but the sqlos.wait_info and sqlos.wait_info_external events in Extended Events don't have a matching event in SQL Trace.

Each event in Extended Events has a list of columns associated with the event:

```
SELECT oc.name AS column_name,
       oc.column_type AS column_type,
       oc.column_value AS column_value,
       oc.description AS column_description
FROM sys.dm_xe_packages AS p
JOIN sys.dm_xe_objects AS o
     ON p.guid = o.package_guid
JOIN sys.dm_xe_object_columns AS oc
     ON o.name = oc.object_name
    AND o.package_guid = oc.object_package_guid
WHERE (p.capabilities IS NULL OR p.capabilities & 1 = 0)
  AND o.object_type = 'event'
  AND o.name = 'wait_info'
```

As shown in the output of this query, there are different types of columns for events, as distinguished by the `column_type` column. The data columns are the columns included in the default data payload that is collected when the event fires inside the database engine. The readonly columns are event descriptors for the event. Two readonly columns of importance are CHANNEL and KEYWORD. These are used to group events inside the Event Tracing for Windows framework of categorization. Both of these are implemented as maps inside the metadata and have corresponding lookup values in the `sys.dm_xe_map_values` DMV.

Channels are used to define to whom the event may be of interest. Currently, Extended Events includes four channels: Admin, Analytic, Debug, and Operation. Admin events are generally of interest to database administrators, and include common events like deadlocking in SQL. Analytic events are primarily of interest when analyzing performance problems in SQL Server, and include the previously mentioned `sqlserver.sql_statement_completed` event. Debug events will primarily be of interest to product support or developers when troubleshooting problems inside of SQL Server. Operational events will be of interest to administrators, and include events such as attaching or detaching a database.

Keywords are used to subdivide events within a channel, and they provide information about the subsystem that actually raised the event, such as scheduling, memory, or I/O. Keywords are optional, meaning not all events have a keyword associated with them. For example, the `user_settable` event does not have a keyword because it can be raised by a user session using the `sp_usercounter` stored procedures inside the executing T-SQL code. Its usage doesn't apply to any specific subsystem in SQL Server because it can be raised at will by a user.

In addition to the readonly and data column types, some events have a third column type of `customizable`. These optional columns can be enabled to have the event collect additional information for inclusion in its data payload. This data collection adds performance overhead, so you should limit the use of customizable columns only to scenarios in which the data is necessary to troubleshoot a specific problem.

Actions

Actions are bound to specific events and provide programmatic response to an event firing. As previously covered in this chapter, actions execute synchronously on the calling thread and can therefore have an impact on performance. There are currently 37 different actions inside Extended Events that can be queried using the following example.

```
SELECT p.name AS package_name,
       o.name AS action_name,
       o.description
FROM sys.dm_xe_packages AS p
JOIN sys.dm_xe_objects AS o
     ON p.guid = o.package_guid
WHERE (p.capabilities IS NULL OR p.capabilities & 1 = 0)
  AND o.object_type = 'action'
```

In most event sessions, the most common use of actions will be to collect further information to add to the base data for a firing event. However, actions have many different purposes, and in addition to being able to collect additional data, actions can be used to gather information about the execution context of the firing event, to capture a stack dump, and to aggregate event data.

There is also an action that can be used to create a debugging stop in the execution of SQL Server. This action should only be used in conjunction with a support incident and the Customer Support Services team, as it performs a debug break, allowing a debugger to be attached to the SQL Server process for additional investigation of a specific problem.

Targets

Targets are the event consumers inside of Extended Events. After an event fires and any actions defined for the event execute, the event and its data payload are buffered for consumption by the targets defined on the event session. Currently, six different target types are included in Extended Events that can be queried using the following example.

```
SELECT p.name AS package_name,
       o.name AS target_name,
       o.description
FROM sys.dm_xe_packages AS p
JOIN sys.dm_xe_objects AS o ON p.guid = o.package_guid
WHERE (p.capabilities IS NULL OR p.capabilities & 1 = 0)
  AND o.object_type = 'target'
```

There are two persistent targets: Event Tracing for Windows (etw_classic_sync_target) and Event File (asynchronous_file_target); and four short-term memory-resident targets: Event Bucketing (synchronous_bucketizer and asynchronous_bucketizer), Event Pairing (pair_matching), Synchronous Event Counter (synchronous_event_counter), and Ring Buffer (ring_buffer). When choosing the appropriate target to use, one of your first considerations should be the target's impact on system performance.

The Event Tracing for Windows and Synchronous Event Counter targets are synchronous targets and consume event data on the session executing when an event fires. Therefore, they can have an impact on performance. The Event Bucketing target can be either synchronous or asynchronous, and its impact depends on which one is selected. The remaining targets consume data asynchronously and will not affect performance when consuming event data.

Like events, targets have columns associated with them, but unlike event columns, which return data, target columns are used to configure the target. These can be found with the following query:

```
SELECT  oc.name AS column_name,
        oc.column_id,
        oc.type_name,
        oc.capabilities_desc,
        oc.description
FROM sys.dm_xe_packages AS p
JOIN sys.dm_xe_objects AS o
    ON p.guid = o.package_guid
JOIN sys.dm_xe_object_columns AS oc
    ON o.name = oc.object_name
    AND o.package_guid = oc.object_package_guid
WHERE (p.capabilities IS NULL OR p.capabilities & 1 = 0)
  AND o.object_type = 'target'
  AND o.name = 'asynchronous_file_target'
```

The file target has five columns that can be used to configure it: four optional columns and one mandatory one, the filename. The optional columns should look familiar to anyone with experience using server-side SQL Trace; they provide the capability to configure the maximum file size for each file and the maximum number of rollovers to keep on the server. The last column, metadatafile is the name of the metadata descriptor file that defines the information stored inside of the target file. While this name is optional, creation of a metadata file is required; the Extended Events Engine will create a metadata file for you if you don't provide it.

The memory-resident targets store event data in the sys.dm_xe_session_targets DMV in the target_data column as XML. The ETW and Event File targets store event data in the file system. Currently, there are no SQL Server–based tools for consuming ETW data, as it is intended to be combined with ETW tracing information from the Windows operating system for detailed troubleshooting.

Predicates

Predicates allow filtering to occur in the Extended Events Engine for an event to determine whether or not the event actually fires for an event session. *Predicates* are Boolean expressions that operate on local event data or state data available in the Events Engine. The local event data is defined by the columns returned as a part of the events base data payload. The available state data that can be used in the predicate definition can be found in the package metadata with the following query:

```
SELECT  p.name AS package_name,
        o.name AS source_name,
        o.description
FROM sys.dm_xe_objects AS o
JOIN sys.dm_xe_packages AS p
    ON o.package_guid = p.guid
WHERE (p.capabilities IS NULL OR p.capabilities & 1 = 0)
  AND o.object_type = 'pred_source'
```

There are 29 state data objects available in Extended Events currently. Two of these are counter objects that allow for filtering every *n*th time the event fires. The remaining objects map to common data objects in the database engine, such as `database_id` and `client_app_name`, and can be used to target events to a specific database or application.

Predicate evaluation enables short-circuiting to occur, which minimizes the amount of evaluation performed to determine whether or not the event should fire. When creating a complex predicate on an event, you can take advantage of this by ordering the criteria in ascending order of likelihood. The first false evaluation in the predicate will halt its evaluation and prevent the event from firing.

There are 111 different comparison operators, called *comparators,* available in Extended Events that can be used in defining predicates on events. These can be found in the metadata with an `object_type` of `pred_compare`:

```
SELECT p.name AS package_name,
       o.name AS source_name,
       o.description
FROM sys.dm_xe_objects AS o
JOIN sys.dm_xe_packages AS p
    ON o.package_guid = p.guid
WHERE (p.capabilities IS NULL OR p.capabilities & 1 = 0)
  AND o.object_type = 'pred_compare'
```

These operators are used similarly to how a user-defined function is used in Transact-SQL. However, the Extended Events Engine also accepts standard mathematical operators for performing comparisons. Under the covers, the Engine transforms these to their associated comparator for internal use.

Maps

Maps are tables of key/value pairs that map internal keys to user-readable values that have meaning. Currently, 59 different maps are available in SQL Server 2008 with Service Pack 1 applied. Four of these are generic maps, 15 are related to SQLOS, and 40 are related to SQL Server. A list of map keys and values for all wait types in SQL Server 2008 can be found with the following query:

```
SELECT name, map_key, map_value
FROM sys.dm_xe_map_values
WHERE name = 'wait_types'
```

Maps have no direct functionality with regard to defining an Extended Events session. They are only needed when defining session predicates for advanced filtering of events so that the correct keys are used in the predicate definition, or as lookup values when querying a target.

Event Sessions

The *event session* in Extended Events is essentially the same thing as a trace in SQL Trace. However, unlike SQL Trace, where a trace must be recreated at server restart, event sessions are persisted in the master database until the session is dropped. In simplest terms, an event session is a collection of events, and a target or targets that will consume the output from the events being fired.

The event session is a logical separation point for object definitions. The same event may be used in multiple event sessions that are started at the same time, but with different actions attached to it, and using different predicate definitions. This can be useful for advanced troubleshooting scenarios for which it may be desirable to collect additional information for a particular problem — for example, collecting the `sqlserver.sql_text` action with the `sqlos.wait_info` event for sessions that encounter a wait type longer than 10 seconds, while collecting the base event data for `sqlos.wait_info` events for waits with shorter duration.

In addition, a single event session can utilize multiple targets for event collection, which allows for different levels of event correlation. The `asynchronous_bucketizer` target can be used to group event occurrences, while the `asynchronous_file_target` collects complete event details.

As previously stated, Extended Events was designed from the ground up to minimize the impact that event collection has on server performance. However, on a busy server where events are fired faster than they can be consumed by the session targets, it is possible for a started session to affect performance. To minimize the chance of this occurring, each session has six configurable options that affect the behavior of the event session while it is running on the server.

Each event session has its own memory allocation for buffering events before they are dispatched out to the targets. By default, this is configured to 4MB, which is divided evenly across three buffers. This value can be changed using the `MAX_MEMORY` option for the session to increase or decrease the amount of memory used for buffering events. If large numbers of events occur in short bursts, then it may be beneficial to configure a larger memory size to allow the buffers to handle the bursts of events.

How the memory allocated to the buffers is partitioned can be configured using the `MEMORY_PARTITION_MODE` option. By default, one set of buffers is created for the event session. If your server uses NUMA, this option can be set to `PER_NODE`, which will create a set of buffers for each NUMA node on the server. For servers with multiple CPUs, the `PER_CPU` setting can be used to create a set of buffers for each CPU on the server, which partitions the buffers for better performance.

For the previously described scenario where events are generated faster than they can be dispatched to the targets, the `EVENT_RETENTION_MODE` option can be adjusted to meet the needs of event collection and performance requirements. The default setting, `ALLOW_SINGLE_EVENT_LOSS`, allows for single events to be dropped when the buffers are full, minimizing both the impact on performance and the amount of event information that is collected and then lost before being served to the session targets. However, this may still have an impact on performance that is unacceptable. In that case, the session option can be changed to `ALLOW_MULTIPLE_EVENT_LOSS`, which allows an entire buffer to be dropped, freeing the memory for new events being fired. The number of events lost depends on the size of the events and the `MAX_MEMORY` setting for the event session. If it is necessary when troubleshooting a specific problem for all events to be collected, without regard to the impact on server performance, then the `NO_EVENT_LOSS` option can be configured, though this is not recommended for normal usage.

In addition to these options, other options exist that control how the event session functions. The `START_STATE` option can be used to configure the event session to start automatically when SQL Server starts. The `MAX_DISPATCH_LATENCY` option can be used to configure how long after an event fires it is dispatched to the targets for consumption. By default, an event will be dispatched to the targets when the buffer fills up, or 30 seconds after it fires, whichever occurs first. To assist with event correlation, the `TRACK_CAUSALITY` option can be enabled, which causes two additional actions to be executed for each event, collecting the `package0.attach_activity_id` and `package0.attach_activity_id_xfer` with the event payload. These can be used to track the relationship between events that have fired.

system_health Session

SQL Server 2008 ships with an event session that is running by default. Named `system_health`, it was created by the Customer Service and Support Team for SQL Server to capture events that are important for troubleshooting common problems that result in calls to their team. The `system_health` event session is always on unless you prevent it from starting with SQL Server, or you drop the event session from the Extended Events Engine.

Without negatively affecting system performance, the `system_health` session collects events deemed important by the CSS Team. The event session collects the following information:

➤ The `sqlsever.error_reported` event for errors with severity ≥ 20 or the following error numbers 17803, 791, 802, 8645, 8651, 8657, or 8902

➤ The `sqlos.scheduler_monitor_non_yielding_ring_buffer_recorded` event

➤ The `sqlserver.xml_deadlock_report` event

➤ The `sqlos.wait_info` event for any sessions that have waited on a latch or other resource for >15 seconds or any sessions that have waited on a lock for >30 seconds. This event includes the `package0.callstack`, `sqlserver.sql_text`, and `sqlserver.session_id` actions as additional data in the event payload.

➤ The `sqlos.wait_info_external` event for any sessions that have waited for >5 seconds for "external" waits or "preemptive waits." This event includes the `package0.callstack`, `sqlserver.sql_text`, and `sqlserver.session_id` actions as additional data in the event payload.

The `system_health` session uses a `ring_buffer` target with 4MB of memory for event retention. As the target fills, the oldest events are discarded in a first-in, first out (FIFO) manner. The event data is available once buffered to the target and can be read by querying the `event_data` column of the `sys.dm_xe_session_targets` DMV.

While this session was intended to capture events of interest, at the time this chapter was written the XML serialization process limits the amount of information that can be output in the `event_data` column for the `ring_buffer` target. To ensure that all event data buffered can be subsequently read from the target, you can adjust the configuration of the `ring_buffer` target to set the `MAX_MEMORY` option to 2MB, which is small enough to ensure that the serialization doesn't overflow the output limits of the DMV:

```
ALTER EVENT SESSION system_health
ON SERVER
DROP TARGET package0.ring_buffer

ALTER EVENT SESSION system_health
ON SERVER
ADD TARGET package0.ring_buffer(SET max_memory=2048KB)
```

Should you decide to alter this event session in any way or accidently drop the session from the server, you can easily recreate the session from the installation script. The script for this event session can be found in the Install folder in the instance root directory by default, `C:\Program Files\Microsoft SQL Server\MSSQL10.SQL2008\MSSQL\Install\` in the `u_tables.sql` script file. It is the last script at the bottom of the file.

Managing Extended Events Sessions

Like most of the components inside SQL Server, you can manage Extended Events through DDL commands that CREATE, ALTER, and DROP the event session from the server. An event session is created using the CREATE EVENT SESSION command. This command has four sections that are used to define the objects and configuration of the event session:

```
1.  CREATE EVENT SESSION [long_duration_statements]
    ON SERVER
2.  ADD EVENT sqlserver.sql_statement_completed
    (       ACTION
            (     sqlserver.tsql_stack,
                  sqlserver.sql_text       )
         WHERE
            (     sqlserver.session_id > 50
                  AND duration > 5000000 ))
3.  ADD TARGET package0.ring_buffer
    (    SET MAX_MEMORY = 1024KB      )
4.  WITH (MAX_DISPATCH_LATENCY = 15 SECONDS)
```

Using the preceding example session, the first section provides the CREATE EVENT SESSION command and the event session name. The second section defines the event(s) that are being added to the event session for collection, any action(s) associated with the event(s), and any predicate(s) that determines whether or not the event fires. In the previous example, the `sql_statement_completed` event, has the `tsql_stack` and `sql_text` actions, which will execute when the event fires to collect these additional pieces of data. The `sql_statement_completed` event will only fire if the `session_id` >50, to capture user sessions only, and when the duration of the statement >5,000,000 microseconds, which is five seconds. The third section defines the target(s) for the session, in this case the `ring_buffer` with a MAX_MEMORY size of 1MB. The fourth section defines any session options for the event session's configuration, in this case to dispatch events to the target within fifteen seconds of them firing.

When an event session is created on the server, the session information is stored in the master database, but the event session does not immediately start collecting events. In order to start the event session it must be altered using the ALTER EVENT SESSION command:

```
ALTER EVENT SESSION [long_duration_statements]
ON SERVER
STATE=START
```

Once the event session is started, events will begin to be buffered to the targets as the predicate criteria is met and the events fire. It may happen that while an event session is running, you realize that you selected the wrong type of target for the event session. For the long statements example, the `ring_buffer` target was used, which is a memory-resident target. If the server is restarted for any reason, the information stored in the `ring_buffer` will be lost. To maintain a persistent copy of the fired events, it is possible to add a second target to the event session by altering it:

```
ALTER EVENT SESSION [long_duration_statements]
```

```
ON SERVER
ADD TARGET package0.asynchronous_file_target
(    SET filename = 'C:\WROX\CH3\long_duration_statements.xel',
         metadatafile = 'C:\WROX\CH3\long_duration_statements.mta')
```

This will add to the session an `asynchronous_file_target`, which exists until removed from the file system. An event session that is in a START state can be altered, to add or remove events and targets, without first stopping the event session. However, to change one of the session-level options — for example, changing the dispatch latency to a lower value — the session must first be stopped before being changed:

```
ALTER EVENT SESSION [long_duration_statements]
ON SERVER
STATE=STOP

ALTER EVENT SESSION [long_duration_statements]
ON SERVER
WITH (MAX_DISPATCH_LATENCY = 5 SECONDS)

ALTER EVENT SESSION [long_duration_statements]
ON SERVER
STATE=START
```

Once the option has been changed, the event session can be immediately started again. Changing the state of an event session to the STOP state stops event collection from occurring, but leaves the event session definition stored in the master database for reuse at another time.

Once an event session has been started and is collecting data, reading the collected event data is accomplished by querying the `sys.dm_xe_session_targets` DMV. The `target_data` column contains the event data collected by the target in `nvarchar(max)` format. For all of the targets the `target_data` is actually an untyped XML document that does not conform to any published schemas. To read the data from the `ring_buffer` target, an XQuery can be used to parse the XML into a tabular format:

```
SELECT event_data.value('(@timestamp)[1]', 'DATETIME') AS event_timestamp,
       event_data.value('(data[1]/value)[1]', 'VARCHAR(100)') AS database_id,
       event_data.value('(data[2]/value)[1]', 'VARCHAR(100)') AS object_id,
       event_data.value('(data[3]/value)[1]', 'VARCHAR(100)') AS object_type,
       event_data.value('(data[4]/value)[1]', 'VARCHAR(100)') AS cpu,
       event_data.value('(data[5]/value)[1]', 'VARCHAR(100)') AS duration,
       event_data.value('(data[6]/value)[1]', 'VARCHAR(100)') AS reads,
       event_data.value('(action[1]/value)[1]', 'VARCHAR(100)') AS tsql_stack,
       event_data.value('(action[2]/value)[1]', 'VARCHAR(100)') AS sql_text
FROM
(
       SELECT CAST(target_data as xml) AS target_data
       FROM sys.dm_xe_sessions AS s
       JOIN sys.dm_xe_session_targets AS t
       ON s.address = t.event_session_address
       WHERE s.name = 'long_duration_statements'
          AND t.target_name = 'ring_buffer'
) AS tab
CROSS APPLY target_data.nodes('//RingBufferTarget/event') AS tgtNodes(event_data)
```

The asynchronous file target also has an entry in the `sys.dm_xe_session_targets` DMV, but unlike the `ring_buffer` target, the event data is not stored in the DMV. Instead, the file target is read using the `sys.fn_xe_file_target_read_file` DMF. This function accepts four input parameters: `path`, `mdpath`, `initial_file_name`, and `initial_offset`. The required `path` and `mdpath` parameters represent the path to the file and its associated metadata file, and are specified when the target is created. These both accept wildcard characters in the name to allow the system to read all files matching the naming convention used. The `initial_file_name` and `initial_offset` parameters are a paired parameter set, meaning that if one is provided, the other is required. They allow partial file reading beginning at the offset value provided. If left null, then all of the files found matching the naming convention will be read by the DMF.

For performance reasons, it is best to read the file target data into a temporary table and then perform any XML parsing from the temporary table:

```
DECLARE @filename varchar(128) = 'C:\WROX\CH3\long_duration_statements*.xel'
DECLARE @metafilename varchar(128) = 'C:\WROX\CH3\long_duration_statements*.mta'

IF OBJECT_ID('tempdb..#File_Data') IS NOT NULL
DROP TABLE #File_Data

SELECT CONVERT(xml, event_data) AS event_data
INTO #File_Data
FROM sys.fn_xe_file_target_read_file(@filename, @metafilename, NULL, NULL)

SELECT event_data.value('(/event/@timestamp)[1]', 'DATETIME') AS event_timestamp,
    event_data.value('(/event/data[1]/value)[1]', 'VARCHAR(100)') AS database_id,
    event_data.value('(/event/data[2]/value)[1]', 'VARCHAR(100)') AS object_id,
    event_data.value('(/event/data[3]/value)[1]', 'VARCHAR(100)') AS object_type,
    event_data.value('(/event/data[4]/value)[1]', 'VARCHAR(100)') AS cpu,
    event_data.value('(/event/data[5]/value)[1]', 'VARCHAR(100)') AS duration,
    event_data.value('(/event/data[6]/value)[1]', 'VARCHAR(100)') AS reads,
    event_data.value('(/event/action[1]/value)[1]', 'VARCHAR(100)') AS tsql_stack,
    event_data.value('(/event/action[2]/value)[1]', 'VARCHAR(100)') AS sql_text
FROM #File_Data
```

Notice that the XQuery is slightly different for the file target than it is for the `ring_buffer`. While the actual event XML is identical between the two for a single event, the `ring_buffer` stores multiple event nodes in a single document, and the file target returns a single-event XML document for each event fired.

When the event session is no longer needed, or won't be needed again in the future, it can be removed from the system using DROP EVENT SESSION:

```
DROP EVENT SESSION [long_duration_statements]
ON SERVER
```

It is not necessary to STOP an event session before dropping it from the server. For this reason, care must be taken when using the DROP command with an event session where the target data is volatile, in-memory data. When the session is dropped, any unread events in the buffers will be lost.

Using the Extended Events Manager

Managing and using Extended Events without UI support can be a somewhat daunting task. Creating an event session requires an understanding of not only the DDL commands, but also how to query the metadata to find the events to include in the session and determine if the base data payload will contain the information needed. The complexity caused by a lack of UI support for Extended Events led to the creation of a community tool called the Extended Events Manager, which provides an easy-to-use interface for creating and managing event sessions and viewing the target data from active event sessions.

The Extended Events Manager is available for download from CodePlex as a compiled application that is ready to run. Full source code for the application can also be downloaded from the CodePlex Team Foundation Server as a part of the project. The address to the tool is `http://extendedeventmanager.codeplex.com`.

The default view (see Figure 3-3), once connected to a server, uses a multiple document interface with docking panels, much like SQL Server Management Studio, including a Server Explorer and document panel to make using the tool as simple as possible.

Just like SQL Server Management Studio, most functionality in the Server Explorer is available through a context menu, which varies according to the TreeView node that is selected when the menu is invoked by right-clicking (see Figure 3-4). At the server level are options to create a new event session, refresh the view, or view XEvent metadata in the metadata viewer, which enables easy clickable access to the metadata available on the server for defining event sessions.

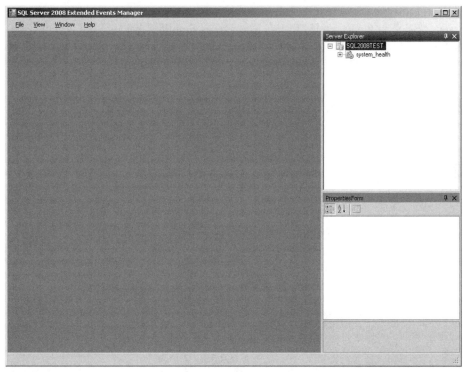

FIGURE 3-3

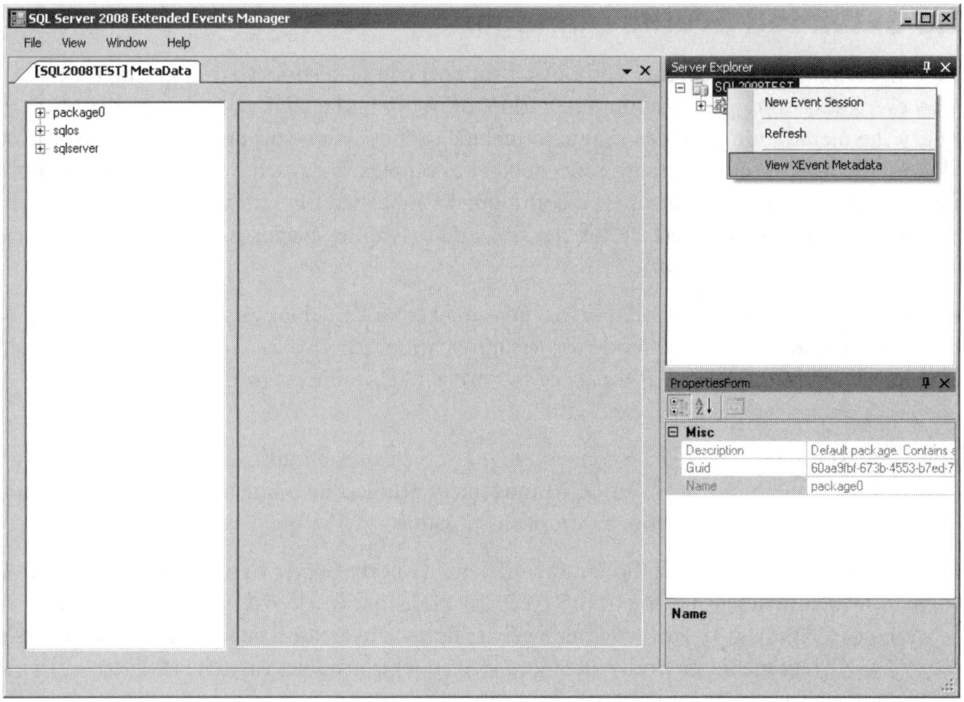

FIGURE 3-4

Defining an event session in the Extended Events Manager is simplified because the tool provides the information for adding events in the Event Editor (see Figure 3-5), sorted by package and then event name, while showing the available columns in the event data payload.

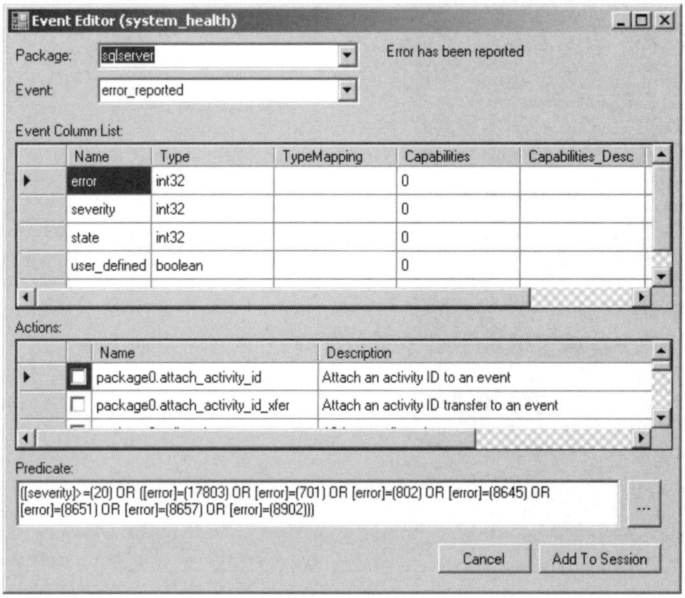

FIGURE 3-5

The available actions that can be bound to an event are also available and can be added to the event definition by checking the box for the action in the grid. Finally, the predicate definition is simplified with the Predicate Editor (see Figure 3-6), which displays the event data payload columns along with the global state columns available for the predicate definition.

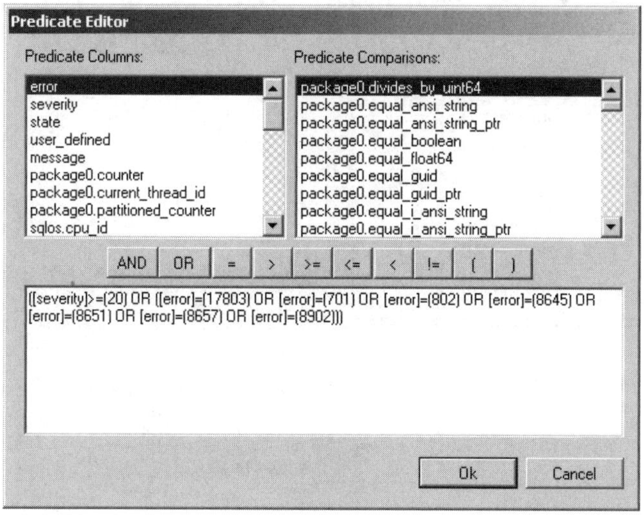

FIGURE 3-6

You can configure the target(s) for an event session using the Target Editor (see Figure 3-7), which displays all of the configurable options for the selected target and confirms that any required fields are specified before the target is added to the session.

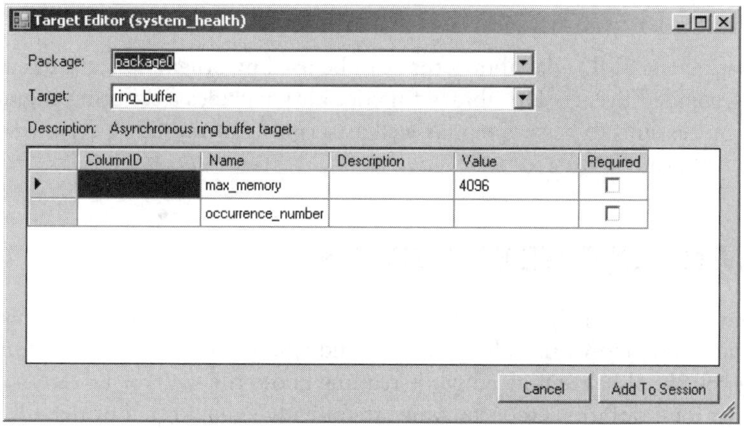

FIGURE 3-7

The Extended Events Manager also provides the capability to read and parse target data into a Profiler-like GridView (see Figure 3-8) for all target types in Extended Events except for the Event Tracing for Windows target. This removes the requirement to understand XQuery in T-SQL to consume event data, but it also parses the XML documents faster through the use of LINQ to XML in .NET.

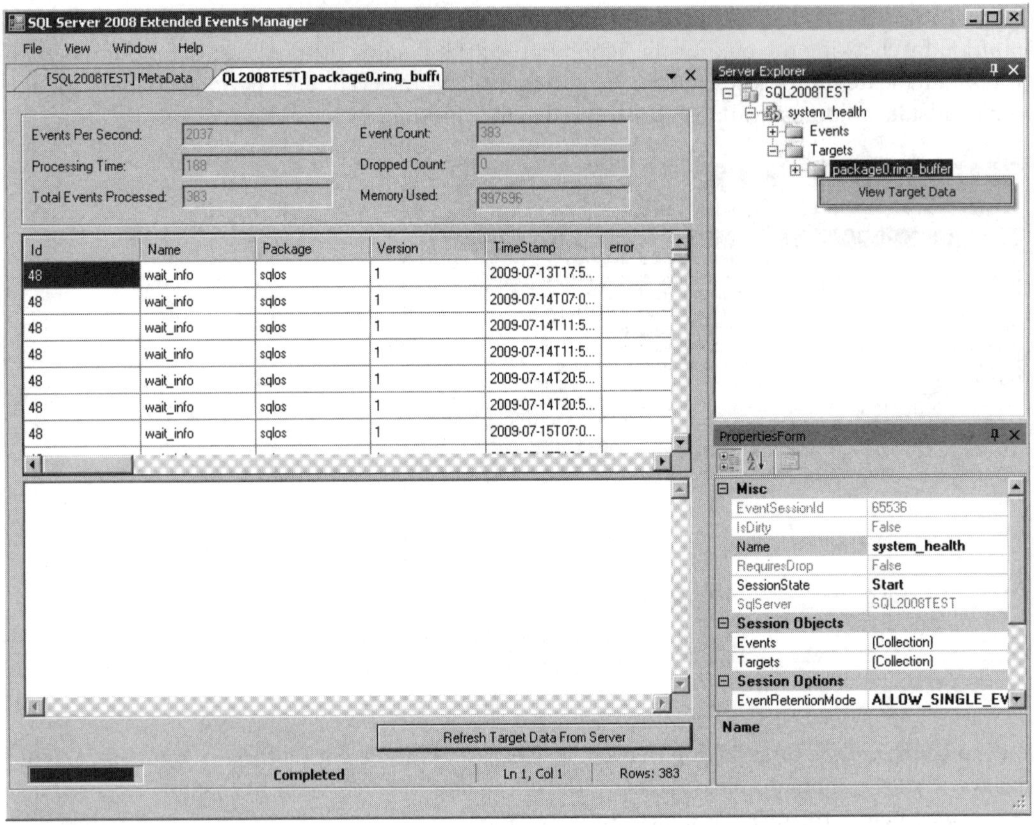

FIGURE 3-8

The foundation of the application is a SMO-like library that can be used by other applications such as PowerShell for managing Extended Events. The library functionality includes a scripting engine that allows changes in the event sessions to be scripted, as well as scripting of the entire event session for use in SQL Management Studio.

EXAMINING WAITS WITH EXTENDED EVENTS

With the essential foundations of wait statistics and Extended Events covered, the rest of this chapter focuses on putting Extended Events to work to help identify and troubleshoot waiting tasks in SQL Server 2008. One thing you should have noticed while reading about the `system_health` session in SQL Server 2008 is that long-duration resource waits are already being logged by default. The problem with this is that the duration required for the event to fire is 15 seconds for a resource or latch wait and 30 seconds for a lock wait.

If you know anything about current application development, you probably know that the default connection timeout in .NET for a `SqlConnection` object is 30 seconds, at which time the request is aborted, raising a SQL timeout back to the application. Should this happen, it is certainly beneficial to have the `system_health` session capture the event data for analysis; but for a highly transactional system, the duration for a wait of interest should actually be much lower.

One of the things that the `system_health` session provides is a shortcut for defining a custom event session for monitoring waits of interest. For performance and usability reasons, you should minimize the actual number of wait types that should be included. The `system_health` session captures 56 resource and locking wait types. You can easily use these as a basis for a custom event session to capture wait statistics.

As previously mentioned, the script to the `system_health` session, available in the Install folder under the instance root path, can be edited to create a new session with different duration values. However, the event information is also available in the session definition DMVs as well. The pertinent piece of information that should interest you is the predicate definition on the `sqlos.wait_info` and `sqlos.wait_info_external` events:

```
SELECT e.package, e.name, e.predicate
FROM sys.server_event_session_events e
JOIN sys.server_event_sessions s ON e.event_session_id = s.event_session_id
WHERE s.name = 'system_health'
  AND e.name LIKE 'wait_info%'
```

You can easily perform a replace operation on the predicate to switch `wait_type` with `map_key` to use the values in the predicate to query the `sys.dm_xe_map_values` view to look up the actual names of the wait types included:

```
SELECT map_key, map_value
FROM sys.dm_xe_map_values
WHERE name = 'wait_types'
  AND ( (map_key < 22)
      OR (map_key > 31 AND map_key < 38)
      OR (map_key > 47 AND map_key < 54)
      OR (map_key > 63 AND map_key < 70)
      OR (map_key > 96 AND map_key < 100)
      OR (map_key > 174 AND map_key < 177)
      OR (map_key > 185 AND map_key < 188)
      OR map_key = 107 OR map_key = 113
      OR map_key = 120 OR map_key = 178
      OR map_key = 186 OR map_key = 202
      OR map_key = 207 OR map_key = 269
      OR map_key = 283 OR map_key = 284)
```

Armed with this information, it is very easy to build an event session to track wait information in detail on the server, a task that was all but impossible in previous versions of SQL Server.

However, if you already know what your top wait types are, it is much easier to target the event session in its scope so that it is only firing the `sqlos.wait_info` event for problematic wait types on your server as found in the `sys.dm_os_wait_stats` aggregated values:

```
SELECT TOP 10 *
FROM sys.dm_os_wait_stats
ORDER BY wait_time_ms DESC
```

The output of this query will provide the necessary information to begin planning an event session to perform session and statement-level analysis of the top wait types on the server. For the purpose of providing an example for this chapter, assume that Table 3-1 contains the output of the preceding query, with system wait types removed.

TABLE 3-1: Sample Top Wait Statistics

WAIT TYPE	WAITING TASKS COUNT	WAIT TIME (MS)	MAX WAIT TIME (MS)	SIGNAL WAIT TIME MS
WRITELOG	234246370	2952746234	54250	54928781
PAGEIOLATCH_SH	247841947	2794660218	39468	11813843
PAGEIOLATCH_EX	25666708	342928281	20500	2464421
CXPACKET	2368839	112430296	199593	638296
SOS_SCHEDULER_YIELD	73317567	103111531	4296	103100031
ASYNC_IO_COMPLETION	213	72021906	3201421	62

The results of this query enable you to determine which wait types should be included in the event session. The aggregated wait statistics information also can be used for estimating the volume of events that may be collected based on the predicate definition. The `wait_time_ms` column can be divided by the `waiting_tasks_count` column to determine the average wait time for each wait type, enabling you to determine what an appropriate value should be for filtering on duration.

To create a predicate for these wait types, it is first necessary to get the `map_key` from the `sys.dm_xe_map_values` view for them:

```
SELECT map_key, map_value
FROM sys.dm_xe_map_values
WHERE name = 'wait_types'
AND map_value IN
('WRITELOG', 'PAGEIOLATCH_SH',
'PAGEIOLATCH_EX', 'CXPACKET',
'SOS_SCHEDULER_YIELD',
'ASYNC_IO_COMPLETION')
```

Along with these keys, the previously calculated average duration of wait can be used to define the event for the event session. Based on the value of the `waiting_tasks_count` column, it can be assumed that the event will fire a large number of times. Therefore, it's important to select the appropriate target and configure it properly.

Based on the volume of waiting tasks, the target should be configured to ALLOW_MULTIPLE_EVENT_LOSS to reduce the possibility of performance problems associated with the event session running, and it should be the `asynchronous_file_target` to allow ongoing analysis without losing events that have been dispatched to the target:

```
CREATE EVENT SESSION [track_wait_stats2]
ON SERVER
ADD EVENT sqlos.wait_info
(
    ACTION
    (
        sqlserver.database_id,
        sqlserver.client_app_name,
        sqlserver.sql_text
    )
    WHERE
    (
        duration > 1000 AND
            (wait_type = 66 OR wait_type = 68
                OR wait_type = 98 OR wait_type = 120
                OR wait_type = 178 OR wait_type = 187)
    )
)
ADD TARGET package0.asynchronous_file_target
(  SET filename = 'C:\WROX\CH3\track_wait_stats.xel',
        metadatafile = 'C:\WROX\CH3\track_wait_stats.mta',
        max_file_size = 10,
        max_rollover_files = 10)
```

To assist with the analysis, three actions have been added to the `sqlos.wait_info` event: `database_id`, `client_app_name`, and `sql_text`. These can be used after data collection analysis to determine whether a majority of the problems occur from a common database, a common client application, or a common query.

The `asynchronous_file_target` is configured to create files that are no more than 10MB in size before rolling over, and to keep the last 10 files on the server. This might seem small, but a 10MB file should hold approximately 50,000+ events depending on the size of the `sql_text` that is collected for each event. The size of the file is intentionally small to allow the files to be loaded into a temporary table efficiently.

The basic `wait_info` data can be viewed in much the same way as the `sql_statement_completed` information was previously in this chapter by loading the data into a temporary table and then using XQuery to extract the data and action nodes from the XML document for each fired event:

```
DECLARE @filename varchar(128) = 'C:\WROX\CH3\track_wait_stats*.xel'
DECLARE @metafilename varchar(128) = 'C:\WROX\CH3\track_wait_stats*.mta'

IF OBJECT_ID('tempdb..#File_Data') IS NOT NULL
DROP TABLE #File_Data

SELECT CONVERT(xml, event_data) as event_data
INTO #File_Data
FROM sys.fn_xe_file_target_read_file(@filename, @metafilename, NULL, NULL)
```

The data collected can be used in a number of different ways to troubleshoot the root cause of problems. For example, to look at how each database contributes to each `wait_type` and the wait time associated with each database, the data can be aggregated as follows:

```
SELECT wait_type,
       database_id,
       SUM(duration) AS total_duration,
       SUM(signal_duration) as signal_duration
FROM
(
  SELECT
    event_data.value('(event/data[1]/text)[1]', 'VARCHAR(100)') AS wait_type,
    event_data.value('(event/action[1]/value)[1]', 'VARCHAR(100)')
       AS database_id,
    event_data.value('(event/data[3]/value)[1]', 'int') AS duration,
    event_data.value('(event/data[6]/value)[1]', 'int') AS signal_duration
  FROM #File_Data
) as tab
GROUP BY wait_type, database_id
ORDER BY database_id, total_duration desc
```

SUMMARY

When investigating performance problems in SQL Server, an understanding of any waits occurring can reduce the time required to get to the root cause of the performance problem. Previous to SQL Server 2008, detailed and thorough analysis of wait types was not possible. Extended Events offer a new, refreshing way to dig into wait types in SQL Server at a level of detail never before possible. As explained in this chapter, when looking at wait information in SQL Server it is important to view information as an entire system to ensure that correct conclusions are drawn from the information being collected. When aggregate wait statistic information isn't enough to isolate the problem, Extended Events can be used to gather detailed information about specific wait types in a manner not previously possible.

4

Working with Storage

WHAT'S IN THIS CHAPTER

> ➤ The differences between RAID levels

> ➤ Configuring Windows and SQL Server to get the best storage performance

> ➤ Testing storage subsystems to determine if they deliver on their promises

Storage seems to be an impenetrable black box where data comes in and goes back out again, but rarely at the speeds that the database administrator expects. When storage area networking (SAN) is involved (described later in this chapter), the disks might literally be inside a black box.

This chapter will demystify what's inside the black box: the types of storage, how it attaches to the server, and how it works when it's shared between multiple servers in a SAN. After discussing basics and theories, you'll dive into testing storage performance in practice to determine whether the I/O subsystems are delivering on expectations, look at where common bottlenecks could be sapping speed, and examine free or low-cost ways to remove those bottlenecks.

Finally, these storage concepts are related to how they impact SQL Server, and how they change the decisions database administrators make about database design, configuration, and troubleshooting.

TYPES OF STORAGE

Storage is an expensive, long-term investment: It requires careful planning long before the data starts coming in. Other parts of SQL Server can be easy to change on the fly, but even minor changes in storage can require major outages. With that in mind, this section explains the basic types of drives, shows how they can be combined in groups to achieve faster performance and higher reliability, and explores how the storage can be connected to the server.

Understanding Individual Drives

Hard drives are referred to by the method of connectivity to the computer: parallel ATA, serial ATA, serially attached SCSI, or Fibre Channel. Independent of the connection method, the drive itself may be either a conventional magnetic hard drive platter or solid-state storage.

Parallel ATA (PATA, IDE, EIDE) Magnetic Drives

PATA drives were historically used in personal computers, not servers, but they're worth mentioning here because of their weaknesses. The connectivity standard wasn't particularly fast, the cables were fairly large and bulky, the cable attachment point was susceptible to bent pins, and the cables weren't designed to support hot swap capabilities.

In database storage, where many drives are packed into a tight space and a failed drive must be replaced without taking the server down, this type of drive does not suffice. The next generation of drives was designed to avoid these limitations.

Serial ATA (SATA) Magnetic Drives

The successor to PATA, IDE, and EIDE drives, SATA-connected drives support higher connectivity speeds (1.5, 3, or 6 gigabits per second). The SATA connection design means that drives can be hot swapped: A failed drive can be unplugged from a live server without damage or downtime, and a new drive can be plugged-in in its place. *Hot swapping* is plug and play capabilities for hard drives much like USB is plug and play for external peripherals.

External SATA (eSATA) drives are also available. These offer higher throughput than USB-attached hard drives, making them better candidates for backups.

Magnetic SATA drives have dominated the home computer market and low-end server market, and they're available at a very low cost with very high capacities. However, this capacity should not be mistaken for performance: Even though an entire data warehouse can fit on a single SATA drive, that doesn't mean one drive can handle the load of a data warehouse's users.

The first generations of consumer-level SATA magnetic hard drives were not built for the kind of performance that high-performance databases require. The first clue is in the drive's rotational speed. Consumer-level SATA drives spin at 5,400 or 7,200 RPM. Enterprise-quality hard drives usually spin at 10,000 RPM or 15,000 RPM. This additional speed means that more data can be pushed through the drive heads, gaining more throughput. However, higher RPMs means more susceptibility to vibration, more heat is produced, and more reliable components are required. These high-performance drives are not usually seen in SATA hard drives, and instead are seen in Serially Attached SCSI (SAS) attached drives, explored later in this chapter.

Because of the poor performance of consumer-quality SATA hard drives, SATA drives in general have a bad reputation in the database administrator community. They're not the first choice for high-performance database implementations, although they do perform well enough for low-cost storage or backup in some environments. However, there's another type of SATA drive with much higher performance capabilities.

Serial ATA (SATA) Solid-State Drives

Conventional hard drives are built with spinning magnetic platters and drive heads that dance around to grab the right sectors off the drive. When a request comes in, the drive heads have to position themselves in much the same way that a needle on a record player has to be moved to the correct track. As a result, there's a delay when the hard drive needs to access data from a different part of the drive platter. This is especially important in random access systems like OLTP databases, where data can be requested from any record in any table at any time.

Solid-state drives (SSDs), conversely, use flash memory instead of magnetic platters. Because there's no head to move around different parts of the hard drive, there's no penalty for random drive access. In effect, every access of a solid-state drive can be random.

Another benefit of not having moving parts is that solid-state drives are not susceptible to vibration. In datacenters with hundreds or thousands of hard drives vibrating in the same rack, vibration can degrade performance. One study found that yelling directly at a rack of hard drives actually caused latency in their operations. Not only are SSDs unaffected by noise and vibration, they don't produce any either.

SSDs have their own weaknesses, chief among them cost: Solid-state drives are typically several times more expensive than conventional magnetic hard drives. This cost increase may be offset by their performance gains in database server storage.

Compounding the cost problem is the fact that solid-state drives have a limited life span of writes. A given area of flash memory can only be written to so many times before it fails. Even though this number can be in the tens of thousands, that type of load occurs frequently in databases. SQL Server's temdb or log files are written to constantly, and may not make a good fit for solid-state drives.

Another weakness of solid state drives is write performance. Under heavy write load, such as database backups, SSDs can't yet match the performance of the fastest magnetic hard drives. Different types of memory chips can worsen the issue: When purchasing solid-state drives for database server use, be careful to avoid those built with MLC memory chips. Their performance is nowhere near that of drives that use enterprise-quality SLC memory chips.

Given the pros and cons of solid-state drives, they do have a place: They make for great read performance in OLTP systems. OLTP systems are smaller than large data warehouses, so less SSD drives (and less cost) are needed in order to see a performance improvement. Some storage area network vendors also use SSDs as a second tier of cache between in-memory cache and magnetic hard drives. They're considered slow memory instead of fast disks.

Serial Attached SCSI (SAS) Magnetic Drives

Serial Attached SCSI (SAS) is the successor to the original (parallel) SCSI format. The SCSI format gained wide acceptance in enterprise-quality server drives at the same time ATA became the adopted standard for desktop-quality drives. At the same time SATA replaced ATA, Serial SCSI also replaced the original SCSI.

The SAS connectivity methods don't necessarily make the drives themselves more robust, but SAS drives are targeted at enterprise use, not home use. As such, SAS drives are equipped with more performance features than SATA drives, such as platters spinning at 10,000 or 15,000 RPM, as opposed to SATA drives spinning at 5,400 or 7,200 RPM. SAS drives are typically rated for much longer runtimes between failure, referred to as MTBF. These drives are designed to run 24/7 at very high rates of speed with very high reliability rates.

SAS magnetic drives are used in enterprise-class servers for locally attached storage. They perform quite well, but for the ultimate in performance in large storage implementations, there's an even more robust (and expensive) type of hard drive.

Fibre Channel (FC) Magnetic Drives

Fibre Channel drives are similar to SAS drives: They're designed to be extremely robust, run at very high speeds, and perform very well. One difference is that Fibre Channel drives are connected with fiber-optic cables, which have historically had higher bandwidth than their SCSI or SAS equivalents—commonly 1Gbps, 2Gbps, or 4Gbps.

Fibre Channel drives are used in SANs where large numbers of drives (hundreds or thousands) need to be connected to the same system. The SAS and SATA connectivity standards only allow for a limited number of drives, but Fibre Channel controller architectures tend to scale higher.

However, depending on the architecture, all of the drives may share the same bandwidth, presenting a possible hardware bottleneck. This is discussed in the section "Storage Performance Testing" later in this chapter.

Regardless of whether a server uses solid-state drives or magnetic hard drives, one hard drive only is rarely fast enough for database storage. In order to handle the high transaction load of databases and to avoid having a single point of failure, database servers need to use multiple hard drives simultaneously.

Protecting Data with RAID

Storage faces two challenges: How can the data be moved faster and how can it be kept protected from loss? To address these challenges, storage administrators rely on *redundant arrays of inexpensive disks*, or *RAID*. The way that disks are grouped together is called a RAID level, and different RAID levels have different performance and recoverability characteristics.

RAID can be implemented in hardware or in software. Hardware RAID takes the form of storage controllers, commonly SAS or SATA controllers that hook up multiple hard drives to a single server. To that server, the storage looks as if it's a single drive: The hardware RAID controller manages the maintenance work of keeping all of the drives in sync. The RAID controller has a processor and memory to handle this data juggling, and ideally the controller can react faster than the hard drives connected to it. This dedicated hardware means that the added overhead of keeping the hard drives in sync does not slow down the server, the operating system, or the application.

Windows is capable of implementing some forms of RAID as well by doing the RAID processing at the operating system level. The DBA can attach two or more hard drives to the server, and Windows can keep the contents of those drives in sync. However, this poses two problems: One, it adds a performance penalty, and two, it has a bare minimum of features. Hardware RAID controllers offer ways to group hard drives that Windows can't, and they do it without a performance overhead. They can also achieve higher levels of performance with onboard memory (cache) that can commit writes even before the disks respond. As a result, for SQL Servers, RAID is rarely implemented in software, and is almost always implemented in hardware.

To learn about these more complex and higher-performing RAID options, the following sections discuss the common RAID levels, ways of grouping hard drives together.

RAID 1: Mirroring

RAID 1 keeps the same data on two (or more) hard drives at all times. When the operating system writes data, the RAID controller (or Windows, in the case of software RAID) knows to write that data on two identical hard drives at the same time, as shown in Figure 4-1.

One drawback of RAID 1 is the cost. It immediately doubles the cost of storing the same amount of data, because the system requires twice as many hard drives.

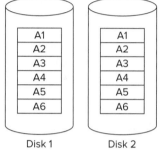

Disk 1   Disk 2

FIGURE 4-1

RAID 1 has a performance advantage for read operations because the same data exists on two drives. In theory, the two drives can be servicing two read operations for two different users at the same time, or they can retrieve the same large amount of data for one user in half the time, as each drive will retrieve half of the required data.

Depending on the RAID controller and the amount of cache, there may be a write penalty: The data has to be written to two separate drives. In most cases, however, the write penalty is minimal.

This is a good RAID level to use as an example about why hardware-based RAID controllers can have an edge over software-based RAID: Think about the performance impact of having to perform every write twice. Granted, Windows can issue two simultaneous write commands to two separate drives and in theory both drives can begin and finish their writes at the same time, but that still incurs a performance impact on the operating system to manage those writes.

The performance impact of software RAID grows in the case of failure on a RAID 1 array. When a drive starts to fail, it may take longer and longer to respond to write commands, or it may return invalid data from reads. In software RAID, Windows is tasked with the process of waiting for the drives to return data, and the operating system can slow dramatically. Even with this simple RAID level, the benefits of a hardware RAID controller start to become apparent.

When a drive fails in a RAID 1 array, no data is lost, because the other drive has a perfectly functioning copy of the data. The failed hard drive can be replaced with a new blank one, and the RAID controller will build a new copy of the data onto the new drive. During that rebuild process, performance will be degraded, because the solitary drive is reading out data to write to the new drive. It will be under a higher load than normal, which may penalize read or write speeds for the server depending on the quality and configuration of the RAID controller.

RAID controllers can be configured so that drive rebuilds take a higher or lower priority than queries from the operating system:

➤ **Low-priority rebuild:** The drive array will take longer to become completely functional, but server activity (queries, backups, data loads) will occur as fast as possible. These operations still won't be full speed, because the array is missing a drive.

➤ **Medium-priority rebuild:** The two activities will be roughly balanced.

➤ **High-priority rebuild:** The drive array will focus mainly on getting the array rebuilt as fast as possible. This penalizes server activity, but it makes sense in environments with a limited number of drives. The faster the array is fully healed, the smaller the time window of risk: Remember that the array is vulnerable to the failure of another drive. In the case of a two-drive RAID 1 array, if the second drive fails, the data is completely lost.

Regardless of performance penalties incurred during a drive rebuild, database administrators can be thankful that they don't have to restore the drive's contents from backups. End user activity can continue without an outage notice, as opposed to what happens with the RAID 0: Striping, discussed next.

RAID 0: Striping

Whereas RAID 1 keeps duplicate copies of the same data on two hard drives, RAID 0 takes a quite different approach: It splits the data in half, keeping half on each of the two drives. More than two drives can be used, and each drive will have an equal portion of the data. In a five-drive RAID 0 array, each drive will have 20% of the data, as shown in Figure 4-2.

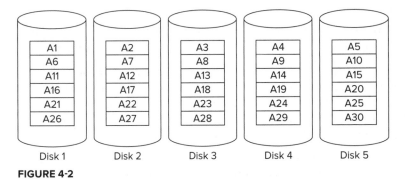

A1	A2	A3	A4	A5
A6	A7	A8	A9	A10
A11	A12	A13	A14	A15
A16	A17	A18	A19	A20
A21	A22	A23	A24	A25
A26	A27	A28	A29	A30

Disk 1 Disk 2 Disk 3 Disk 4 Disk 5

FIGURE 4-2

RAID 0 avoids the cost penalty of RAID 1: Instead of doubling costs, it adds no extra cost. Every added drive can be fully utilized in terms of capacity. If the server needs 1 terabyte of storage, the DBA can buy 1 terabyte of drives arranged in a RAID 0 configuration and use all of the volume.

There is no data redundancy with RAID 0, however, which means that when any drive fails, the entire array is unavailable and must be restored from backup. The more drives added to a RAID 0 array, the faster it will perform, but at a higher risk of data loss. If each drive fails once every 10,000 hours, then a ten-drive array will experience a drive failure every 1,000 hours.

Because of RAID 0's dangerous approach to recoverability, it's rarely seen in SQL Server implementations, but it serves as a good introduction to RAID levels 5 and 6.

RAID 5 and 6: Striping with Parity

RAID 5 is similar to RAID 0 in that each drive shares an equal part of the data, but it adds a measure of data protection to ensure that a single drive failure won't take down the entire array. Parity data is stored across the array as shown in Figure 4-3. If any one drive fails, its contents can be rebuilt from the remaining drives.

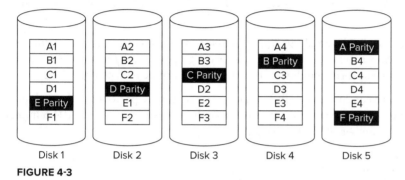

FIGURE 4-3

Calculating this parity data is processor-intensive, however: For each write, several blocks of data must be examined to come up with the parity data. These calculations can slow down writes dramatically, but modern RAID controllers have specialized processors designed to calculate this data as fast as possible. This again makes an argument for hardware RAID for database servers, as they do a large number of writes in rapid succession when doing backups, DBCC operations, or index rebuilds.

The minimum number of drives needed for a RAID 5 configuration is three: data being stored in two places, and the parity information in a third place. In practice, this does not mean data on two drives and parity on a third drive. RAID controllers balance out the stored data and parity data across all of the drives. In a RAID 5 array, each added drive's capacity contributes to the array. For example, if the server has four 500GB drives in a RAID 5 array, then the capacity would be 1.5 terabytes: three 500GB units of data, and 500GB of parity data. If another 500GB drive is added to the array, the total capacity available is now 2 terabytes: four 500GB units of data, and 500GB of parity data.

Some hardware RAID controllers can add additional drives on the fly, while the array is running, without taking down the server. The administrator can add the additional drive (assuming there's space in the server's drive bays), access the RAID controller's software application, and add the drive to the array. The RAID controller restripes the drives so that the data is evenly spread across all of them, which slows down the array while the restripe takes place, but afterwards the performance is improved by the additional spindle.

When troubleshooting performance problems on a RAID 5 array, this means that the administrator can add spindles incrementally to see the performance impact. If one additional drive does not help in a noticeable way, the DBA can pursue other performance troubleshooting methods instead of pouring a large amount of money into drives without seeing an immediate improvement.

One drawback of RAID 5 is that although it can recover from one drive failure, it can't recover from the failure of more than one drive. If two or more drives fail, the array will lose enough parity data to fail completely, and must be restored from backup. While the thought of a double hard drive failure may seem remote, keep in mind that the two drives don't have to fail at the same time. If a second drive fails anytime before the RAID array is finished rebuilding itself onto a new hot spare drive, then the array will fail. This is more of an issue with high-capacity, low-performance arrays such as SATA drives with 1 terabyte or more of capacity. The higher the drive capacity, the longer the rebuilds take.

This reinforces the low/medium/high rebuild priority discussed earlier, and now it becomes more evident why a DBA might choose to have rebuilds take a very high priority. With large SATA drives that might take hours to fully copy, the window of time for failure can be unacceptably long.

RAID 6 avoids the double-drive failure that kills RAID 5 by storing more parity data throughout the array, as shown in Figure 4-4. Capacity is reduced by two drives instead of one. RAID 6 makes good sense when using large numbers of SATA drives.

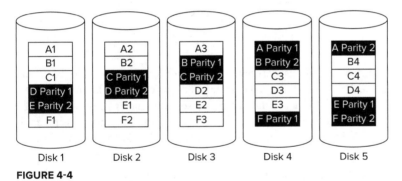

FIGURE 4-4

When relying on either RAID 5 or RAID 6, the database administrator should ensure that the RAID controller's software drivers and utilities are installed and configured correctly. RAID manufacturers have software utilities that will alert the administrator when a drive fails so that it can be quickly replaced. Remember that drive failures in a RAID array managed by a hardware RAID controller are completely invisible to the operating system: The controller might sound a beeping alarm in the datacenter, and the hard drive might be flashing a red light, but those alerts are useless if the DBA isn't standing in the datacenter. As long as a RAID 5 array has a dead hard drive, it's turned into a RAID 0 array—data spread across drives with no redundancy. It's a ticking time bomb, and the DBA has to get a new drive in as fast as possible.

In summary, RAID 5 and 6 are much more cost effective than RAID 1 (which cuts capacity in half), and just slightly more expensive than RAID 0, with a measure of data protection thrown in. Because of this high performance relative to its low cost, levels 5 and 6 are common choices for storage administrators. Where cost isn't a concern, an even higher level of performance is available.

RAID 0+1 and RAID 10: Mirroring and Striping

For the highest performance possible, RAID levels 0+1 and 10 store two identical copies of the data on two separate sets of drives. The difference between the two methods boils down to whether the data is striped and then mirrored (RAID 0+1) or mirrored and then striped (RAID 10). The differences between these two are shown in Figure 4-5.

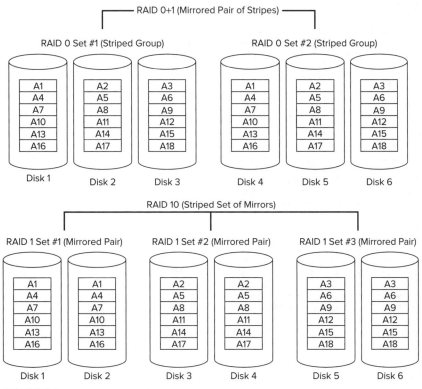

FIGURE 4-5

RAID 10 handles the failure of multiple drives in the same array, depending on where the failures occur, without data loss. RAID 0+1 handles only the failure of a single drive in each side; further failures result in data loss.

> *Like RAID 1, these methods incur a high cost penalty: They lose half of their capacity, as two copies of the data are stored at all times. However, they lend themselves well to high-performance database needs, as they allow for more recoverability than RAID 5 or 6.*

When comparing performance of these RAID levels with RAID 5, it's important to frame the discussion in terms of the number of hard drives involved. There are two ways to compare performance: by raw capacity or by usable capacity. RAID 10 cuts the amount of raw capacity in half, as two copies of the data are stored in mirrored sets. RAID 5 uses more capacity in each drive, thereby requiring fewer drives. Figure 4-6 illustrates this capacity difference.

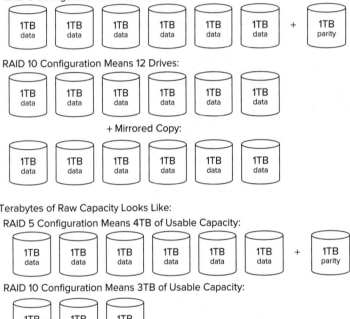

6 Terabytes of Usable Capacity Looks Like:

RAID 5 Configuration Means 7 1TB Drives:

RAID 10 Configuration Means 12 Drives:

+ Mirrored Copy:

6 Terabytes of Raw Capacity Looks Like:

RAID 5 Configuration Means 4TB of Usable Capacity:

RAID 10 Configuration Means 3TB of Usable Capacity:

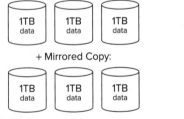

+ Mirrored Copy:

FIGURE 4-6

If you compare by available capacity, a 10-terabyte RAID 10 configuration will outperform a 10-terabyte RAID 5 configuration, but it will cost roughly twice as much. Choosing the right RAID level for a database server's needs becomes just as much an accounting decision as a technology decision.

Choosing between Performance and Price

RAID 5 is the dominant choice for non-database applications because of its cost effectiveness and density. Storage administrators love it because it minimizes the space required in the datacenter (fewer drives need fewer bays). Managers love it because of the cost efficiency. The use of very high capacity SATA hard drives gained popularity for these same reasons: high capacity, high density, and low cost.

Database administrators, however, need to weigh performance considerations before settling for RAID 5 or SATA hard drives. Either of these may be completely acceptable for an application, and perhaps even both of them together (SATA RAID 5), but each of these factors has a performance impact. In write-intensive applications such as database logs or OLTP environments, RAID 10 can be a better choice.

Microsoft has published a list of Storage Top 10 Best Practices for SQL Server: `http://technet.microsoft.com/en-us/library/cc966534.aspx`.

These guidelines recommend that all SQL Server log files be placed on RAID 10 (or RAID 1) arrays, rather than RAID 5. SQL Server log files tend to undergo large sequential write operations for long periods of time, and RAID 10 excels at that type of load. The faster the logs can be written, the faster transactions can take place.

In addition, when choosing the right RAID level for a particular database server, the decision must take into account how many drive bays are available for a given server. Servers with locally attached storage may only have a handful of drive bays and offer a limited amount of RAID configurations, whereas servers attached to a storage area network have a huge number of possibilities with more spindles, more cache, and more RAID flexibility.

Direct Attached Storage

When purchasing a server, the server will have a number of internal bays for hard drives. To add storage, simply purchase a drive and slide it into a bay. It's easy, fast to provision, and easy to support. In some cases, an external chassis with more drive bays can be added to a server as well. The chassis is attached with eSATA or SAS cables connected to the server's RAID card.

This type of storage is called *locally attached storage* because it's directly attached to the server and dedicated to that one server alone.

Direct attached storage limits a server's expansion opportunities and lacks flexibility. Servers have only a limited number of drive bays. Adding a dedicated array chassis outside of the server adds capacity, but lacks flexibility: The array chassis is dedicated to that one server alone. If the chassis supports 12 hard drives but the server only needs an additional two drives, the extra bays waste space and money.

Blade servers are especially limited when it comes to locally attached storage, as they have two to four hard drive bays available. Adding more drives can be achieved with the use of storage blades, but those consume valuable blade slots—not often available in tightly packed datacenter environments.

When servers outgrow the options available with locally attached storage, the next option is to team storage together into a large network of capacity called a storage area network (SAN).

Storage Area Networks

Storage area networks, or SANs, are pools of drive arrays linked together with a network. Each server connects into this network and can share drives, cache, and throughput with many more servers. While initially very expensive, usually in the six to seven figures, SANs can pay off with additional flexibility and cost sharing.

The resources in the SAN can be shared, even down to the individual disk level. SAN administrators can set up pools of hard drives and then designate individual spaces on each group for a specific server's use. For example, the SAN administrator may create a pool of 20 hard drives in a RAID 10 configuration, each with 1 terabyte (TB) of capacity, for a total capacity of 10 terabytes. The administrator can then allocate five 2TB spaces (called LUNs) for five separate servers. Those servers will share the same physical hard drives, but they won't see each other's data; the SAN hardware manages that access.

The drawback of this type of shared configuration is that performance may not be as predictable as when each server has its own dedicated drives. If one server suddenly creates a huge amount of data, such as when a SQL Server does a reindex job, the other servers may experience slower hard drive access.

As this section discusses the components of a SAN, consider how each component might be burdened when shared by multiple servers. Each component can be a bottleneck in the storage environment.

Storage area networks are divided into two categories according to the method of networking they use: Fibre Channel or iSCSI.

Fibre Channel Storage Area Networks

The first storage area network topology to gain widespread acceptance relied on fiber-optic networking. In the 1980s, fiber-optic networking could be used over longer distances and higher speeds than SCSI cables or Ethernet networks, so it became the standard for enterprise-quality storage connectivity.

A Fibre Channel storage area network consists of the following components:

➤ **Drives:** These can be magnetic hard drives, solid-state drives, or a combination of both.

➤ **Drawer or enclosure:** A rack-mounted chassis that contains a number of drives

➤ **Controller:** Somewhat akin to a server, the controller handles communication with the drives and groups them into arrays. A controller may have hundreds or thousands of drives, and may group them together into dozens or hundreds of arrays, each with different RAID levels. Controllers are often paired together in an active/active or active/passive configuration so that if one controller fails, the other controller can continue to manage the storage.

➤ **Switches:** SAN switches are like conventional network switches in that they pass data between devices (or in SAN terms, servers and controllers). However, SAN switches have additional capabilities: They manage security as well. SAN switches can control which servers see which ports on a given controller, thereby ensuring that one server doesn't accidentally overwrite another server's data.

➤ **Host bus adapters (HBAs):** HBAs are the equivalent of network cards for storage area networks: They plug into servers as expansion cards and connect to the network via fiber-optic patch cables. Each HBA has a unique address called a World Wide Name (WWN), and that identifier is used to designate which arrays and ports it can access on the SAN.

Figure 4-7 illustrates how these components are connected together to form what's called a *fabric*. Advanced SAN users will notice that this diagram contains only a single fabric: Two fabrics and multipathing are discussed later in the chapter.

Each of the components in the fabric has its own speed limits, commonly 1, 2, or 4 Gbits/sec. Faster standards have been developed, and are slowly trickling down through enterprises, but it's more common to see legacy 1/2/4Gbps equipment in production. Speed can be increased beyond those numbers by using multiple connections to each device, just as servers are sometimes connected to TCP/IP networks with multiple network cards in order to get more bandwidth.

When fiber-optic gear initially came out, it was much faster and more reliable than Ethernet networks, but over time, wired networks caught up in speed and far undercut it in price.

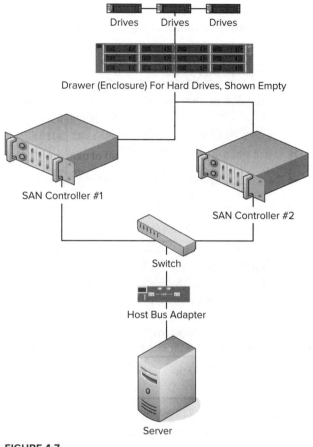

FIGURE 4-7

iSCSI Storage Area Networks

With the widespread adoption and cost effectiveness of 1Gbps and 10Gbps Ethernet, storage vendors began to offer storage connected with TCP/IP networks using conventional network cabling instead of fiber optics. iSCSI SANs have several advantages, including lower cost, the ability to use a single connection standard (CAT5/6 Ethernet) throughout the datacenter, and easier deployment via network cards and iSCSI drivers.

iSCSI SANs are no different than conventional TCP/IP networks: Connectivity is handled with the same network switches, patch cables, and network cards. In fact, iSCSI traffic can even be handled on the exact same network already being used for conventional traffic. In practice, this is rarely done because iSCSI traffic needs to be extremely fast and extremely reliable: If it shares the same network as end users surfing the Internet and streaming videos, then server storage traffic may be penalized. iSCSI SAN traffic is usually handled on a physically separate network from conventional TCP/IP traffic, with its own dedicated switches.

The storage controllers have TCP/IP addresses, and each server has a TCP/IP address just for iSCSI SAN traffic. To verify that a server can access a particular storage controller, the database administrator can simply ping the storage controller's address just like any other server. This is evidence that iSCSI SANs are easier to set up and troubleshoot than Fibre Channel SANs: Server administrators are already accustomed to implementing and troubleshooting TCP/IP networks.

ALL ABOUT ISCSI

In some implementations, specialized network cards (referred to as iSCSI HBAs to mimic the Fibre Channel HBA naming) offload some TCP processing to help the server process data faster. These iSCSI HBAs equipped with TCP Offload Engines (TOEs) can improve storage performance under very heavy loads, like virtualization servers or data warehouses. They also enable servers to boot directly off the iSCSI SAN, something not possible when using conventional network cards to access the SAN. However, if every bit of performance is critical for a server, consider implementing 10GB Ethernet or 4GB Fibre Channel before investing in iSCSI HBAs that are only connected to 1GB Ethernet.

iSCSI vendors sometimes tout that their solutions scale linearly—with every added iSCSI SAN controller, bandwidth increases. SANs with ten controllers are touted to have ten times the performance. Unfortunately, this is only true if the connecting servers have enough bandwidth to take advantage of that power. If the server only has one 1GB Ethernet iSCSI network port, then it can't send and receive more than 1GB throughput, no matter how many servers are on the other end of the network. This is especially problematic in blade server configurations, where a dozen or more servers may be sharing the same network connections out to the rest of the network.

Whether you are using Fibre Channel or iSCSI to access storage arrays, reliability is a prime concern. Servers must always be able to access their drives, or drive corruption and downtime is sure to follow. Ensuring that each server always has a path to its data is called *multipathing*.

Multipathing: Multiple Routes to the Storage

When servers lose access to their storage, bad things happen: Applications stop responding and data may not be able to be written in time to prevent a server crash. As a result, enterprise storage area networks are usually designed with extreme redundancy in mind:

➤ Two or more host bus adapters so that if one network card or patch cable fails, the server can still access its storage

➤ Two or more SAN switches so that if one fails or needs a firmware upgrade, all of the attached servers can still access their storage

➤ Two or more SAN controllers attached to the same set of drive arrays so that if one fails, a power cable becomes dislodged, or a firmware upgrade is necessary, the servers and storage still work

In a typical enterprise-quality SAN, two completely separate switch networks are used. These two networks are not cabled together in any way; every server will have two HBAs, each accessing a separate network (meaning a separate fabric). Each SAN controller will have two sets of ports, each accessing a separate network. This setup provides the ultimate in redundancy: Even a network-wide issue like an extensive switch problem will not take down the storage. This dual-fabric approach is illustrated in Figure 4-8.

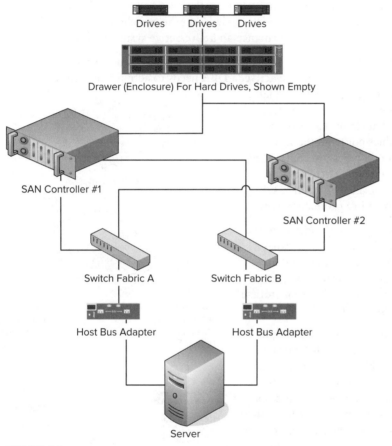

Drives   Drives   Drives

Drawer (Enclosure) For Hard Drives, Shown Empty

SAN Controller #1

SAN Controller #2

Switch Fabric A   Switch Fabric B

Host Bus Adapter   Host Bus Adapter

Server

FIGURE 4-8

To manage all of this redundancy, the server needs to know which route to take in order to access its hard drives. In conventional networks, this type of issue is handled by solutions such as network card teaming software, load balancers, and routers. In storage area networking, this concept is handled by multipathing software.

Because multipathing touches so many components from so many vendors, each multipathing system usually has a strict hardware and software qualification list. Each SAN vendor has its own proprietary multipathing software, and they all have different capabilities.

Basic multipathing is *active/passive*: Only one route to the storage is used at any given time. If the server has two host bus adapters, then only one of them is used to send and receive traffic to the storage area network. If the HBA in question is a 4GB Fibre Channel adapter, and the server needs more than 4GB of throughput, then an active/passive multipathing system won't start pushing traffic through a second HBA, even if it's sitting idle. The second HBA exists only to provide a failover mechanism if something goes wrong.

For added performance, *active/active* multipathing sends traffic over multiple paths at the same time. The more HBAs the server has, the more ports available in the switches, and the more network ports the SAN controllers have, the more performance an active/active system will see.

Unfortunately, few true active/active multipathing solutions are available, and they're not cheap. Even when a vendor touts its solution as active/active, a DBA needs to actually test this claim with the storage performance testing tools discussed later in this chapter. When doing performance testing on a multipathing system that claims to be active/active, try pulling SAN cables out from the server to test how performance and failover is affected. Users might find that the solution is active/active at the HBA level only, but not at the SAN controller. Of course, don't try this test on a live production server.

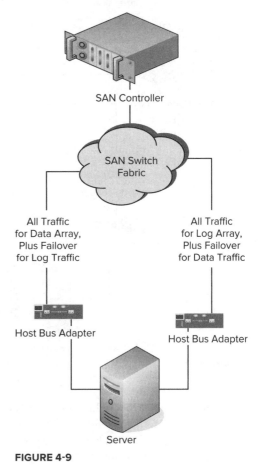

Alternatively, the solution may be active/active in the sense that it can utilize multiple HBAs simultaneously but only one per drive array: If the database needs to do a scan of a large data warehouse fact table located on a single drive array, then that storage request will still be confined to a single HBA.

When working with an active/passive multipathing solution, the DBA needs to think out-of-the-box in order to wring the best possible performance from the system. For example, the SAN may be able to place the data array on one path (one HBA and one controller) and the log array on another path (a different HBA and controller). The opposite path can be configured from failover. The system is still active/passive by array, but both paths will be utilized simultaneously for different purposes, giving you a higher throughput than you would have been able to obtain without the tweaking. Figure 4-9 shows how this type of pathing can provide additional speed, even though it's not truly active/active.

FIGURE 4-9

Choosing Shared or Dedicated Drives

In locally attached storage, all of the drives are dedicated solely for the use of the server to which they are attached, thereby ensuring consistent performance. Storage area networks can be configured in that same way: The SAN administrator can configure several drives together into a single array, and designate that array solely for the use of a single server. This is called a *dedicated configuration*, because the drives are dedicated to one server.

SANs also have the capability to pool together large numbers of hard drives into very big arrays, and then designate portions of that capacity to different servers. For example, a SAN controller might group 20 500GB drives together into one giant 9.5TB RAID 5 array, and then carve it into several 2TB chunks for four different servers. Each server is using different sections of the same underlying hard drives. This is called a shared configuration. Figure 4-10 shows how a SAN controller's arrays might be configured for several database servers sharing the same pools of drives.

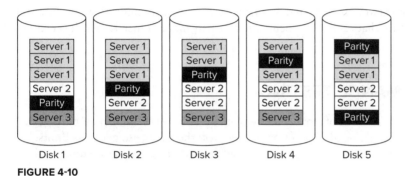

FIGURE 4-10

Shared drives are cost effective because resources can be shared between more servers. A server that only needs 50GB of storage for its databases might not be able to justify an entire RAID array by itself, especially because hard drive capacities keep increasing. It wouldn't make sense to buy a pair of 500GB SATA drives in a RAID 1 configuration and then use less than 10% of that storage capacity. In a shared array configuration, the extra space could be assigned to other servers that need more capacity.

On the other hand, this same scenario illustrates the danger of a poorly configured shared storage array. If ten database servers each need 50GB of storage, and the SAN administrator allocates just two SATA drives in a RAID 1 array for the shared use of all ten of those database servers, then performance will be horrible.

When configured correctly, shared storage arrays can give each server a large performance boost without cost. For example, if the database administrator has the following servers, it would make sense to consolidate them onto the same shared drive arrays:

➤ A sales database server that customers access frequently between 9:00 a.m. and 5:00 p.m.

➤ A reporting database server that generates and emails reports nightly at 1:00 a.m.

➤ An intranet database server with a large number of archived documents in the database, which are infrequently accessed

When combined, these servers will have different load times that rarely overlap, and thus don't have conflicting performance needs. When each of the servers needs more performance, it will be able to run faster because it has more drives to share the load. When using a system like this, be careful to schedule maintenance windows for backups and index rebuilds at staggered times, rather than schedule all servers to begin at midnight.

Shared storage empowers administrators to be more flexible with their storage designs, but it also introduces serious performance risks. Unfortunately, SAN vendors tout their shared array configurations as set-it-and-forget-it solutions, and say that their SAN controllers are fast enough to handle all loads via shared storage. This can be true, but only if the SAN administrator buys enough shared storage to overcome performance problems. All too often, SAN storage is purchased by capacity, rather than performance. As illustrated earlier in the example of ten servers sharing a pair of 500GB drives, the pure capacity numbers aren't enough to gauge whether or not a company has enough storage.

As mentioned earlier, whether you use a shared or a dedicated storage configuration, it's important to test performance to ensure that each server achieves the performance it needs, which is examined in the next section.

STORAGE PERFORMANCE TESTING

After establishing exactly what kinds of storage are hooked up to a server, but before putting the server into production, the database administrator needs to test the storage to gauge its limits. Storage performance testing involves pushing as much load as possible through the storage subsystem to probe how it reacts.

Just as SQL Server database administrators judge a server's speed by the number of transactions per second it can sustain, storage administrators have their own metrics to define a system's capabilities. To help understand these numbers, consider storage a form of shipment. Assume that the database server is a small business that needs to ship its data to a remote warehouse, and that warehouse is the storage system. You want your data to arrive as fast as possible, so you ship it in envelopes and packages via an overnight courier service.

Megabytes per second (MB/s, or throughput) indicates how much data you need to send — or in the shipping scenario, it defines whether you're trying to move an envelope or a truckload.

This is closely related to *IOPs, or input/output operations per second*, which is akin to the number of packages being shipped. You might have a large number of small packages (high IOPs, low MB/s) or a small number of large packages (low IOPs, high MB/s).

Latency defines how long it takes for a package to arrive. This number varies according to how many packages you try to ship at once, so it's not useful unless it's considered in combination with everything else. If you call the courier service to deliver a single envelope of data and they send a small station wagon, then there will be a very fast latency time. Conversely, if there are several tons' worth of data to deliver, then they will not be equipped to handle your needs. The station wagon must make a trip and then return for more of your data.

The Perfmon counter Disk Queue Length reflects the number of packages that are currently waiting to be picked up by the courier. A very high disk queue length in and of itself does not necessarily indicate a problem. The first parameters — MB/s, IOPs, latency — help describe the kind of shipping system that is needed, and are commonly used by storage administrators to gauge performance. The Disk Queue Length statistic is not commonly used by storage admins, who typically aren't concerned with the number of waiting requests — that's viewed as an operating system issue. When doing performance testing, however, you need to configure the number of packages that will be put together. When configuring storage testing software, the number of threads and the queue depth represent that number.

These metrics combine to present a picture of how the storage is performing. With this flow in mind, it's time to choose a storage performance testing tool that measures our storage's ability to deliver packages of data.

Choosing a Storage Testing Tool

When testing storage performance, either before a server goes into production or when it starts to exhibit I/O bottlenecks, it helps to be able to produce benchmark numbers without using SQL Server. Using independent programs that don't require SQL Server enables storage administrators and vendors to reproduce the speed metrics without understanding how to use SQL Server — and perhaps more important, without blaming SQL Server as the source of the problem.

SQLIO and SQLIOSim are two popular storage testing programs that do not require SQL Server to be installed. They take two separate approaches to performance testing: SQLIO is completely parameter driven and knows nothing about SQL Server's I/O characteristics, while SQLIOSim tries to mimic SQL Server as closely as possible. SQLIO is for pushing the storage boundaries as hard as possible, but the SQL Server itself may not be able to take advantage of the full performance that SQLIO discovers. Your SQL Server database application may not write or read data in the same way that your storage performs best.

When deciding between the two, consider using SQLIO if the storage and database teams are separate groups of people. Consider using SQLIOSim if there is no storage team, and the database administrator just needs to find out how fast the database will perform.

After deciding which tool makes the most sense for your environment, it's time to learn how to use it.

Using SQLIO

The name SQLIO misleads users into thinking the tool is closely related to SQL Server. In fact, the name couldn't be further from the truth: SQLIO is just a simple command-line-driven program to measure storage performance. Not only does it not require SQL Server, it doesn't even approximate SQL Server I/O performance without being explicitly instructed how to do so.

SQLIO is a free download from www.microsoft.com/downloads/
details.aspx?familyid=9a8b005b-84e4-4f24-8d65-cb53442d9e19.

After installation, SQLIO is run via batch files or the command line — there's no graphical point-and-click interface here. Usability challenges continue when the database administrator reviews the list of possible configurations and parameters, which can at first appear lengthy and obtuse.

Edit the param.txt text file in the installation directory (default is c:\program files\sqlio), which by default contains the following lines:

```
c:\testfile.dat 2 0x0 100
#d:\testfile.dat 2 0x0 100
```

The second line is commented out, so focus on the first line instead. The first parameter, c:\testfile.dat, indicates the drive letter and file path for the test file that will be created. Change this letter to point to the drive that needs to be tested.

The last parameter, 100, is the file size, in megabytes, of the test file that will be created. The test file should be much larger than the size of the storage subsystem's cache. For example, when testing a SAN with 16GB of cache, set the test file size to at least 32GB. If the file size is smaller than the SAN's cache, then the results will be artificially fast, but they would only be valid for database servers that have smaller storage needs than the SAN can accommodate in cache. Tests with large test files will take longer to set up, but the higher accuracy is worth it.

After configuring param.txt, SQLIO is run at the command line. If no parameters are specified, it uses defaults, as shown in Figure 4-11.

FIGURE 4-11

Unfortunately, however, the defaults won't tax the storage subsystem or replicate SQL Server's disk patterns. Instead, you need to run it with a long string of parameters like this:

```
Sqlio -kR -t8 -s120 -dM -o16 -fsequential -b64 -BH -LS Testfile.dat
```

The parameters are as follows:

➤ -kR: R for Read, W for Write testing.

➤ -t8: Eight threads. The more threads used, the heavier the load placed on the storage subsystem.

➤ -s120: Number of seconds the test will last. Use at least two minutes to reduce possible variations from other servers running IO activity at the same time.

➤ -dM: Drive letter to be tested — in this case, M.

➤ -o16: Number of outstanding requests that will be sent to the storage at a time. The higher the number, the more stress for the storage.

➤ -fsequential: Form of the test, either sequential or random. Magnetic storage performs quite differently based on this parameter.

➤ -b64: Block size.

Rather than test each set of parameters one at a time and document how the storage subsystem reacts, it's easier to build a batch file with a set of common parameters that mimic how SQL Server stores and reads data. Figure 4-12 shows a set of SQLIO commands in a single batch file.

```
runsqlio - Notepad                                                                    _ | 8 | ×
File  Edit  Format  View  Help
sqlio -kw -t2 -s120 -dM -o1 -frandom -b64 -BH -LS Testfile.dat
sqlio -kw -t2 -s120 -dM -o2 -frandom -b64 -BH -LS Testfile.dat
sqlio -kw -t2 -s120 -dM -o4 -frandom -b64 -BH -LS Testfile.dat
sqlio -kw -t2 -s120 -dM -o8 -frandom -b64 -BH -LS Testfile.dat
sqlio -kw -t2 -s120 -dM -o16 -frandom -b64 -BH -LS Testfile.dat
sqlio -kw -t2 -s120 -dM -o32 -frandom -b64 -BH -LS Testfile.dat
sqlio -kw -t2 -s120 -dM -o64 -frandom -b64 -BH -LS Testfile.dat
sqlio -kw -t2 -s120 -dM -o128 -frandom -b64 -BH -LS Testfile.dat

sqlio -kw -t4 -s120 -dM -o1 -frandom -b64 -BH -LS Testfile.dat
sqlio -kw -t4 -s120 -dM -o2 -frandom -b64 -BH -LS Testfile.dat
sqlio -kw -t4 -s120 -dM -o4 -frandom -b64 -BH -LS Testfile.dat
sqlio -kw -t4 -s120 -dM -o8 -frandom -b64 -BH -LS Testfile.dat
sqlio -kw -t4 -s120 -dM -o16 -frandom -b64 -BH -LS Testfile.dat
sqlio -kw -t4 -s120 -dM -o32 -frandom -b64 -BH -LS Testfile.dat
sqlio -kw -t4 -s120 -dM -o64 -frandom -b64 -BH -LS Testfile.dat
sqlio -kw -t4 -s120 -dM -o128 -frandom -b64 -BH -LS Testfile.dat

sqlio -kw -t8 -s120 -dM -o1 -frandom -b64 -BH -LS Testfile.dat
sqlio -kw -t8 -s120 -dM -o2 -frandom -b64 -BH -LS Testfile.dat
sqlio -kw -t8 -s120 -dM -o4 -frandom -b64 -BH -LS Testfile.dat
sqlio -kw -t8 -s120 -dM -o8 -frandom -b64 -BH -LS Testfile.dat
sqlio -kw -t8 -s120 -dM -o16 -frandom -b64 -BH -LS Testfile.dat
sqlio -kw -t8 -s120 -dM -o32 -frandom -b64 -BH -LS Testfile.dat
sqlio -kw -t8 -s120 -dM -o64 -frandom -b64 -BH -LS Testfile.dat
sqlio -kw -t8 -s120 -dM -o128 -frandom -b64 -BH -LS Testfile.dat

sqlio -kw -t16 -s120 -dM -o1 -frandom -b64 -BH -LS Testfile.dat
sqlio -kw -t16 -s120 -dM -o2 -frandom -b64 -BH -LS Testfile.dat
sqlio -kw -t16 -s120 -dM -o4 -frandom -b64 -BH -LS Testfile.dat
sqlio -kw -t16 -s120 -dM -o8 -frandom -b64 -BH -LS Testfile.dat
sqlio -kw -t16 -s120 -dM -o16 -frandom -b64 -BH -LS Testfile.dat
sqlio -kw -t16 -s120 -dM -o32 -frandom -b64 -BH -LS Testfile.dat
sqlio -kw -t16 -s120 -dM -o64 -frandom -b64 -BH -LS Testfile.dat
sqlio -kw -t16 -s120 -dM -o128 -frandom -b64 -BH -LS Testfile.dat

sqlio -kw -t32 -s120 -dM -o1 -frandom -b64 -BH -LS Testfile.dat
sqlio -kw -t32 -s120 -dM -o2 -frandom -b64 -BH -LS Testfile.dat
sqlio -kw -t32 -s120 -dM -o4 -frandom -b64 -BH -LS Testfile.dat
sqlio -kw -t32 -s120 -dM -o8 -frandom -b64 -BH -LS Testfile.dat
sqlio -kw -t32 -s120 -dM -o16 -frandom -b64 -BH -LS Testfile.dat
sqlio -kw -t32 -s120 -dM -o32 -frandom -b64 -BH -LS Testfile.dat
sqlio -kw -t32 -s120 -dM -o64 -frandom -b64 -BH -LS Testfile.dat
sqlio -kw -t32 -s120 -dM -o128 -frandom -b64 -BH -LS Testfile.dat

sqlio -kw -t64 -s120 -dM -o1 -frandom -b64 -BH -LS Testfile.dat
sqlio -kw -t64 -s120 -dM -o2 -frandom -b64 -BH -LS Testfile.dat
sqlio -kw -t64 -s120 -dM -o4 -frandom -b64 -BH -LS Testfile.dat
sqlio -kw -t64 -s120 -dM -o8 -frandom -b64 -BH -LS Testfile.dat
sqlio -kw -t64 -s120 -dM -o16 -frandom -b64 -BH -LS Testfile.dat
sqlio -kw -t64 -s120 -dM -o32 -frandom -b64 -BH -LS Testfile.dat
Start        runsqlio - Notepad                                              11:03 AM
```

FIGURE 4-12

The DBA can run that batch file, go about his or her business, and return 30 minutes later to review the results. Don't double-click this batch file; instead, run it from the command prompt as shown here, making sure to capture the results to a file:

```
RunSQLIO.bat > Results.txt
```

This will produce a text file as shown in Figure 4-13.

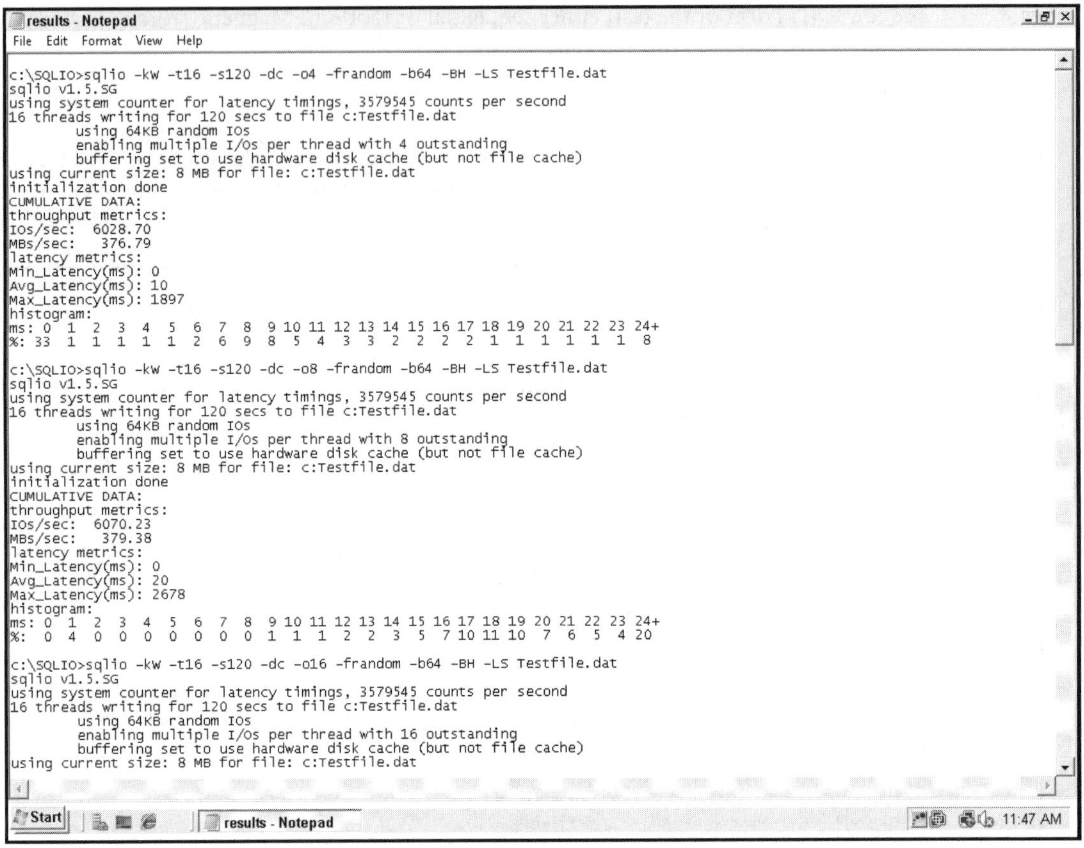

```
results - Notepad
File Edit Format View Help

c:\SQLIO>sqlio -kW -t16 -s120 -dc -o4 -frandom -b64 -BH -LS Testfile.dat
sqlio v1.5.SG
using system counter for latency timings, 3579545 counts per second
16 threads writing for 120 secs to file c:Testfile.dat
        using 64KB random IOs
        enabling multiple I/Os per thread with 4 outstanding
        buffering set to use hardware disk cache (but not file cache)
using current size: 8 MB for file: c:Testfile.dat
initialization done
CUMULATIVE DATA:
throughput metrics:
IOs/sec:  6028.70
MBs/sec:   376.79
latency metrics:
Min_Latency(ms): 0
Avg_Latency(ms): 10
Max_Latency(ms): 1897
histogram:
ms: 0  1  2  3  4  5  6  7  8  9 10 11 12 13 14 15 16 17 18 19 20 21 22 23 24+
%: 33  1  1  1  1  1  2  6  9  8  5  4  3  3  2  2  2  2  1  1  1  1  1  1  8

c:\SQLIO>sqlio -kW -t16 -s120 -dc -o8 -frandom -b64 -BH -LS Testfile.dat
sqlio v1.5.SG
using system counter for latency timings, 3579545 counts per second
16 threads writing for 120 secs to file c:Testfile.dat
        using 64KB random IOs
        enabling multiple I/Os per thread with 8 outstanding
        buffering set to use hardware disk cache (but not file cache)
using current size: 8 MB for file: c:Testfile.dat
initialization done
CUMULATIVE DATA:
throughput metrics:
IOs/sec:  6070.23
MBs/sec:   379.38
latency metrics:
Min_Latency(ms): 0
Avg_Latency(ms): 20
Max_Latency(ms): 2678
histogram:
ms: 0  1  2  3  4  5  6  7  8  9 10 11 12 13 14 15 16 17 18 19 20 21 22 23 24+
%:  0  4  0  0  0  0  0  0  0  1  1  1  2  2  3  5  7 10 11 10  7  6  5  4 20

c:\SQLIO>sqlio -kW -t16 -s120 -dc -o16 -frandom -b64 -BH -LS Testfile.dat
sqlio v1.5.SG
using system counter for latency timings, 3579545 counts per second
16 threads writing for 120 secs to file c:Testfile.dat
        using 64KB random IOs
        enabling multiple I/Os per thread with 16 outstanding
        buffering set to use hardware disk cache (but not file cache)
using current size: 8 MB for file: c:Testfile.dat
```


FIGURE 4-13

To interpret these metrics, see the section "Interpreting Storage Test Results."

> *Rather than analyze these results directly in text file format, import this data into SQL Server and slice and dice it from there. That way, historical data can be kept for all servers in a single database. For instructions on how to perform this, see* `http://sqlserverpedia.com/wiki/SAN_Performance_Tuning_with_SQLIO`.

> *If you'd like to learn even more about SQLIO and how it can be used to tune performance, pick up Professional SQL Server 2005 Performance Tuning from Wrox. Even though it covers an older version of SQL Server, the material on SQLIO is still current.*

Using SQLIOSim

SQLIOSim picks up where SQLIO leaves off: The letters SIM at the end of the tool's name hint that not only does it test I/O subsystems, it also simulates SQL Server I/O. SQLIOSim has a graphical front end, and it's favored by database administrators because its I/O load more closely simulates that of SQL Server.

One drawback of SQLIOSim is that it may not get the best performance possible from a storage subsystem because it mimics a typical SQL Server behavior. Some storage responds better to different kinds of behavior, and SQL Server's IO patterns may not get the most IOPs or highest throughput from the drive arrays. Storage administrators may discount these results by saying, "It's not my fault that SQL Server doesn't perform well." In that case, use all of the possible parameters of SQLIO as discussed earlier to determine whether the storage subsystem can sustain a load of any type at all.

Another drawback is that it produces some false alarms: It reports errors whenever the storage subsystem takes more than 15 seconds to respond to requests. While that does indeed sound like a problem, it's to be expected because SQLIOSim is designed to push load until the storage subsystem can't take any more. It should tax the storage subsystem to the limit, otherwise you wouldn't know what that limit was. As a result, don't be concerned when it shows these errors.

SQLIOSim can be downloaded at `http://support.microsoft.com/kb/231619`.

You can launch SQLIOSim either as a console application or as a graphical user interface application. It's easier to start with the GUI. Figure 4-14 shows SQLIOSim's configuration screen, which immediately seems miles beyond SQLIO's usability. An administrator can point and click through the configuration, and the configuration options feel much more like SQL Server database setup than SQLIO's cryptic parameters. The DBA can specify the data file, the log file, and growth metrics just like a user database is configured in SQL Server Management Studio.

For in-depth performance testing, however, the user still needs to edit text files in order to configure advanced settings. Look in the directory where SQLIOSim was installed, and extract the `sqliosim.cfg.zip` file. This compressed file includes several INI files with default parameter sets that will make testing easier and enable advanced configurations. Figure 4-15 shows some contents of the `sqliosim.default.cfg.ini` file: It's a text file that can be edited with Notepad to tweak parameters.

Three of the more useful parameter files included with SQLIOSim are as follows:

➤ `sqliosim.hwcache.cfg.ini`: Behaves as if the hardware cache is large enough to accommodate the database's activity. This configuration is useful with small databases hooked up to large SANs or very fast disk arrays, where the DBA needs to know that the server itself is able to keep up with the I/O.

➤ `sqliosim.nothrottle.cfg.ini`: Does not use any throttling, meaning it will pour a large volume of I/O at the storage subsystem quickly.

➤ `sqliosim.seqwrites.cfg.ini`: Simulates a large volume of sequential writes. This mimics a logging database, such as a URL filtering database for a company with a large number of employees or a sensor acquisition database.

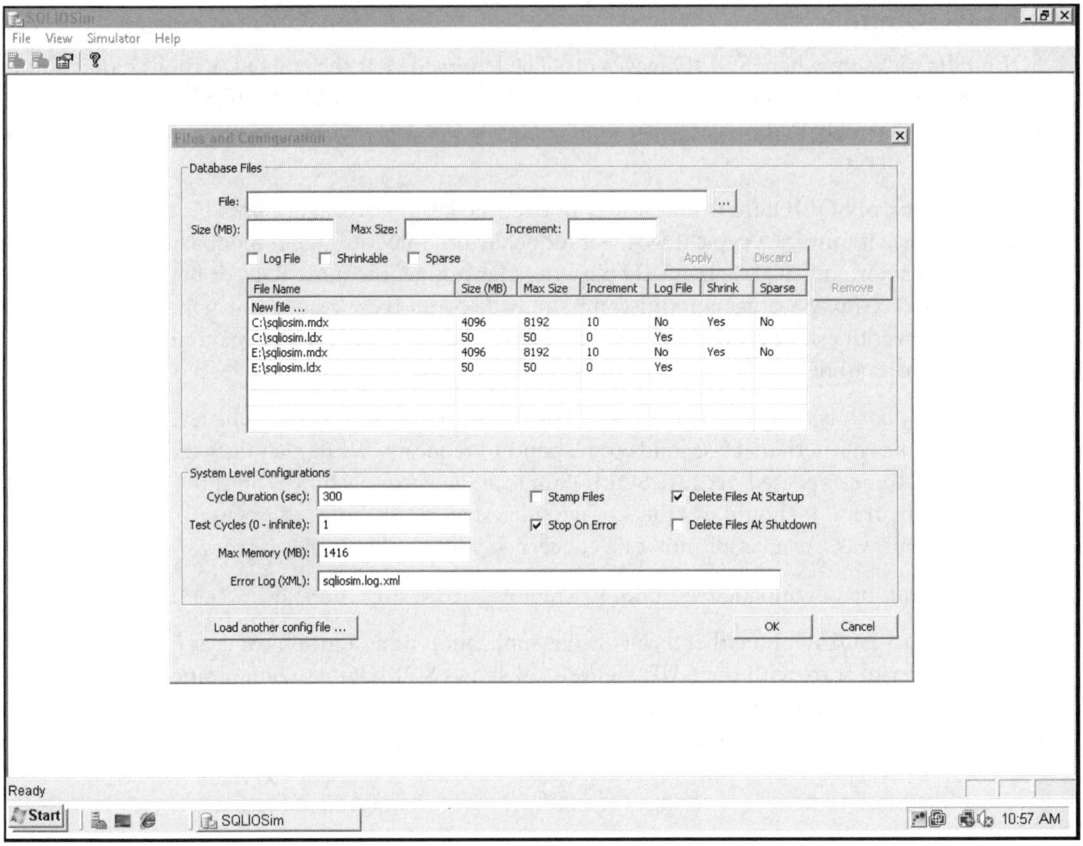

FIGURE 4-14

If none of these meet your needs, you can copy one of the INI files and tweak the parameters inside the file in order to mimic your database application. Unfortunately, it is beyond the scope of this book to discuss modeling a database's I/O requirements.

When testing with SQLIO, the database administrator can use a batch file with a wide range of configuration values to find out what parameters wring the most performance out of the storage. Conversely, with SQLIOSim, testing is geared toward long repeated iterations with the same parameters.

In environments with a storage area network (as opposed to locally attached storage), consider running several cycles with durations of an hour or more, rather than the default settings of just five minutes. The longer the tests run, the less likely that usage spikes from other servers in a shared environment will affect the benchmark results.

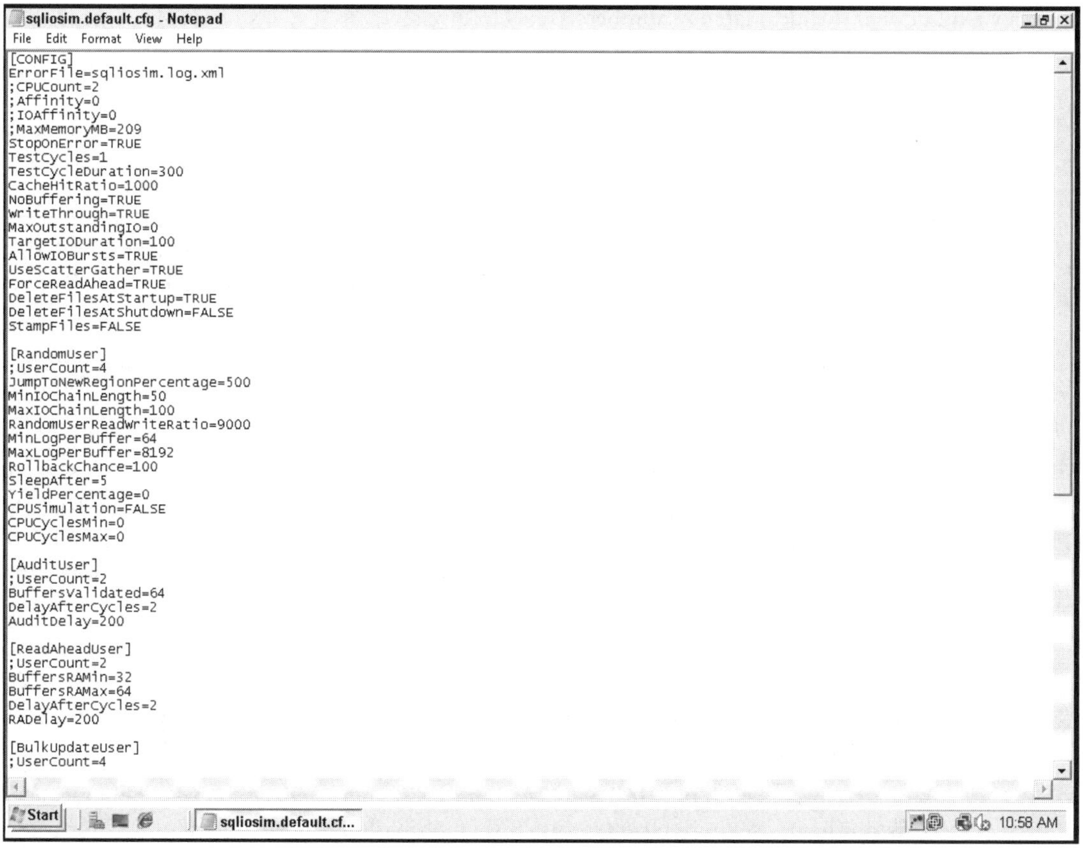

```
sqliosim.default.cfg - Notepad                                                    _ |8| x|
File  Edit  Format  View  Help
[CONFIG]                                                                                ▲
ErrorFile=sqliosim.log.xml
;CPUCount=2
;Affinity=0
;IOAffinity=0
;MaxMemoryMB=209
StopOnError=TRUE
TestCycles=1
TestCycleDuration=300
CacheHitRatio=1000
NoBuffering=TRUE
WriteThrough=TRUE
MaxOutstandingIO=0
TargetIODuration=100
AllowIOBursts=TRUE
UseScatterGather=TRUE
ForceReadAhead=TRUE
DeleteFilesAtStartup=TRUE
DeleteFilesAtShutdown=FALSE
StampFiles=FALSE

[RandomUser]
;UserCount=4
JumpToNewRegionPercentage=500
MinIOChainLength=50
MaxIOChainLength=100
RandomUserReadWriteRatio=9000
MinLogPerBuffer=64
MaxLogPerBuffer=8192
RollbackChance=100
SleepAfter=5
YieldPercentage=0
CPUSimulation=FALSE
CPUCyclesMin=0
CPUCyclesMax=0

[AuditUser]
;UserCount=2
BuffersValidated=64
DelayAfterCycles=2
AuditDelay=200

[ReadAheadUser]
;UserCount=2
BuffersRAMin=32
BuffersRAMax=64
DelayAfterCycles=2
RADelay=200

[BulkUpdateUser]
;UserCount=4                                                                            ▼
◄|                                                                                    |► |
Start |   | 🖿 ■ 🖉  ||  🗎 sqliosim.default.cf...                          🖳🌐  🔊🔉  10:58 AM
```

FIGURE 4-15

> *Also be aware that these tests should not be run on a production SQL Server, and should not be run on a shared storage environment that hosts production SQL Servers. Before running any of these tests, communicate the plan to the SAN team so they're aware of possible outages.*

Interpreting Storage Test Results

All of the storage performance testing tools described so far produce the same basic results: a report of the IOPs, MB/sec, latency, and drive queue lengths seen with a storage subsystem under different types of load. There are no hard-and-fast rules to gauge when storage is "too slow" or "fast enough," but Microsoft has produced some general guidelines for storage here: `http://technet .microsoft.com/en-us/library/cc966412.aspx`.

They explain that the ideal latency numbers are as follows:

➤ 1–5 milliseconds for log files

➤ 4–20 milliseconds for OLTP data files

➤ 30 milliseconds or less on OLAP (decision support) data files

The testing done so far in this chapter, however, hasn't been on SQL Server files, but on the arrays themselves. When reviewing performance tests, think about the files that will be placed on each particular array: If an array is delivering 4–5 milliseconds response time for writes, then it will make a good array for log files.

If your storage does not meet the minimum metrics for the type of data you'd like to store, it's time to start looking for bottlenecks and ways to improve performance.

Hitting the 100/200/400MB/sec Wall

When reviewing storage performance results for servers connected to a storage area network, it's common to find MB/sec metrics quickly hit a performance ceiling of around 100, 200, or 400MB/sec. This matches up with the 1Gbps iSCSI and Fibre Channel bottleneck, or the 2 or 4Gbps Fibre Channel bottlenecks.

Work with your storage team to whiteboard the connectivity between the database server and the SAN controller. For each component, document the number of connections upstream to the next component, and the speed of each connection. Somewhere in the chain is a single-path bottleneck that is hampering performance. Examples of this include the following:

➤ A server connected with two 1Gbps HBAs but they're in an active/passive configuration. To bypass this limit, use more HBAs, or use SAN multipathing software that allows for true active/active multipathing.

➤ A server accessing a SAN controller through several switches that are only interconnected with a single cable. To bypass this bottleneck, use more switch interconnects, or plug the server into the same switch as the SAN controller.

➤ A SAN controller plugged into the SAN only with two fiber-optic cables in an active/passive configuration. To achieve more speed, use more ports on the SAN controller.

Figure 4-16 illustrates how each individual component might seem to have a 4Gbps (400MB/sec) throughput ceiling, but the server would only be able to sustain 200MB/sec due to a switch in the middle of the fabric.

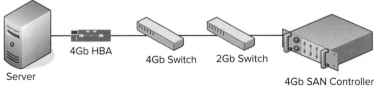

FIGURE 4-16

These solutions might all sound straightforward, but they're complicated by the fact that multipathing is not always the active/active solution it's touted to be, as discussed earlier in this chapter. The proof here is in the test results: If the results seem artificially limited to the 100/200/400MB/sec number, then contact your SAN vendor to find out exactly what's necessary to take advantage of active/active functionality.

In addition, SAN administrators may be reluctant to plug more gear into the SAN fabric due to costs. SAN administration software, monitoring software, and even switch licensing is often determined by the number of network ports in use on the SAN. The more ports plugged in, the more the SAN costs, so additional performance here can have a clear cost. To find out whether the performance gain is worth it, ask the storage team to make a temporary change in configuration in order to redo the test benchmarks, and then see whether storage performance is improved.

Cache Is Not Always King

SAN vendors and RAID controller manufacturers have been known to tout that all writes go to the storage controller's cache: For the operating system, the write is considered complete when it hits the cache. Because the cache consists of memory, the writes should be extremely fast, and in initial testing, they usually are.

Problems arise when the number and size of writes overwhelm the system's cache. With locally attached storage, this can happen during periods of intense writes, such as DBCC operations or index rebuilds. SQL Server's maintenance plan tasks to rebuild indexes will rebuild all indexes serially, whether they need rebuilding or not, which leads to a higher amount of write load — often more than the storage cache can sustain.

With shared storage area networking, the problem becomes more acute because the cache is shared across many servers. Each SAN vendor has different methods of dividing the cache, and it can be difficult to determine exactly how much cache any one server has at a given moment.

Knowing What's Happening in the Black Box

When performance testing a storage area network system that isn't dedicated to a single server, be aware of what else is going on in the SAN. The SAN controllers don't pass on information about drive failure events to the upstream servers, for example: If a drive failed and the array is in the process of rebuilding it onto a new drive, the server won't have any indication that its performance is currently impaired by this operation. This should be a relatively rare operation, but it serves as an example of events that can happen inside the SAN's "black box" that can affect performance.

Shared drive configurations are another common source of drive contention that prevent a server from reaching its full potential performance. If the load testing server is sharing drives with a file server that's currently undergoing a virus scan or a backup, performance will suffer. If it's sharing with a database server, that server might be undergoing DBCC operations or index rebuilds, both common storage performance drains. When testing storage performance on a shared array, try to test during the same time windows that the database server will need its peak performance. The closer you can duplicate real-world load conditions, the more you'll know about how the storage will perform.

Even if the drives are dedicated just to that one server, the other components in the SAN are still shared between other servers. SAN controllers have a finite amount of processing power and bandwidth shared between their drives, and that power can be taxed by operations unrelated to the database server. When a drive fails in any array in the SAN controller, performance can be affected on other arrays during the rebuild. The drives usually share the same backplane, or communication network, and that backplane has a limited amount of network bandwidth that is used up by the rebuild process.

Testing the Worst-Case Scenario

When performance testing a server that hasn't been put into production yet, the database administrator can take the testing to the next level by putting the storage subsystem under unusual strains and watching how it reacts. The right time to test the worst-case scenario is long before users begin accessing the system. This is the way to truly know whether a storage subsystem's hot swap capabilities, multipathing, and redundancy work correctly.

After finding the optimal parameters for the storage — the testing configuration that produces the absolute fastest speeds with lowest latency — run the tests again, but during testing, disconnect pieces of the storage and watch how it reacts. If the server is connected to a SAN with multiple HBAs, unplug the cables from one of them during testing. Then note the following:

➤ Does the server freeze?

➤ How long does the server pause before resuming the test?

➤ How much does performance suffer if only one cable is plugged in?

Plug the cable back in, wait a few seconds, and then pull the other cable. Does the storage subsystem recover smoothly, or does the SQL Server service stop or fail?

Another stress test example is to begin performance testing and then remove one drive from the array to simulate a failed drive. Watch how the storage subsystem reacts and verify that the administrators are properly notified about the failure. Replace that drive with a brand-new empty drive and verify that the array automatically begins rebuilding data. This is usually visible by watching the drive activity lights — even with no activity on the server, the hard-drive lights should be flashing rapidly, indicating that the rebuild is actively reading from other drives to rebuild the contents of the new drive. Run performance tests again and see what kind of performance is to be expected from the system during drive rebuilds.

These kinds of tests are well above and beyond typical storage performance tests, but they enable the database administrator to sleep peacefully at night knowing that a drive failure, cable failure, or HBA failure will be handled gracefully by the system without a production outage. The point of using RAID arrays is to get safe performance: Why not test to ensure that you're getting the desired result?

Wash, Rinse, and Repeat

Storage performance testing should be done before putting a server into production, but more important, it should be repeated periodically during maintenance windows and whenever performance problems are suspected. This process enables the database administrator to start with a known baseline of the server's performance and then compare that to current performance.

Storage performance can change over time due to the following:

➤ SAN controller firmware upgrades

➤ Networking changes (e.g., added or removed uplinks between switches)

➤   Cache configuration changes

➤   Driver upgrades

➤   Adding drives to RAID arrays

➤   New servers sharing the same SAN hardware

Storage area networks are designed to mask changes from the connected servers, so it's not always obvious when these events have taken place. The best way to gauge whether the storage has improved or deteriorated is to continue repeating these storage performance tests quarterly.

Once you understand how to repeatedly gauge your storage configuration's performance, you can begin changing Windows and SQL Server 2008 settings to improve that performance.

CONFIGURING SOFTWARE FOR STORAGE

Windows and SQL Server both have ways to tweak storage performance. Initial configurations made when the arrays are first formatted, such as sector alignment and allocation unit size, have a lasting effect on speed. Once set, these settings can only be changed using destructive methods like reformatting the drive, so be sure to pay particular attention to these right away when building a new server.

Later in a server's life cycle, other settings such as HBA queue depth, SQL Server compression, and SQL Server partitioning can help a DBA wring the last bit of performance out of the hardware. Those settings are easier to change without a complete reinstall, but still require planning and implementation time, so they're not to be taken lightly. Knowing how all of these configurations work together, and how to troubleshoot when things go wrong, empowers a database administrator to achieve improved performance without additional cost.

Configuring Windows Server

Starting with Windows 2008, Microsoft's default operating system settings do a better job of getting storage performance out-of-the-box. Users who aren't running Windows 2008 yet, however, need to pay particularly close attention to these configuration options as they default to very poor options. This section explores these settings.

Partition Alignment

Partition alignment is the single easiest and most effective way to improve storage performance without additional cost. The DBA doesn't have to change hardware configurations, recable storage area networks, or make any application schema changes. This one simple setting is easy to get right — and even easier to get wrong. Partition alignment is an obscure configuration that used to matter when individual hard drives were attached directly to servers without any form of RAID. In today's servers where RAID is the default, partition alignment ensures that the operating system's sectors line up with RAID stripe sizes. When set correctly, each operating system read will line up with as few sectors as possible in the RAID array.

Figure 4-17 illustrates the concept of partition alignment. The top partition is not aligned, and will suffer a performance penalty because read operations will span multiple sectors in cache and on disk. The bottom sector is correctly aligned, and each individual read operation will touch only one sector on the disks.

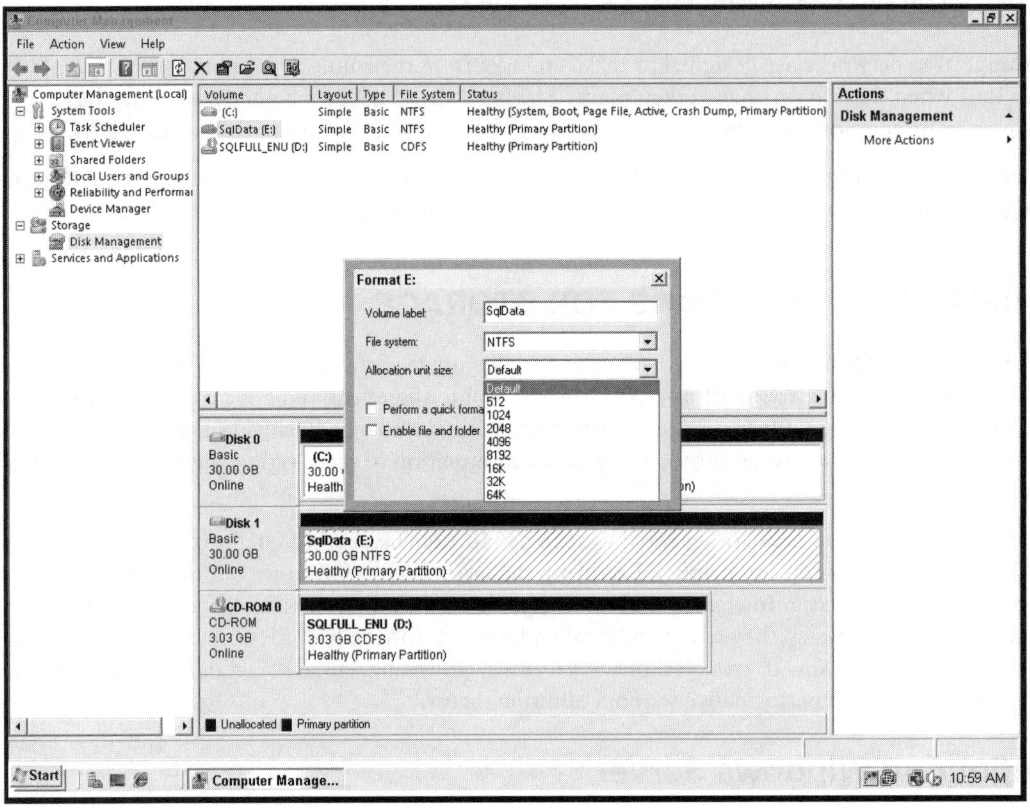

FIGURE 4-17

Beginning with Windows Server 2008, any new partitions are automatically aligned with an offset of 1024, which should work with the majority of SAN configurations. Unfortunately, this is not the case with Windows 2003 and earlier versions. In addition, if Windows Server 2008 is hooked up to arrays that have already been partitioned by an earlier version of Windows, or if Windows is upgraded in place, the partitions will not be aligned. The only way to correct partition alignment is to do the following:

1. Back up the data.

2. Erase the drives.

3. Partition the drives again with correct alignment.

4. Format the newly created partitions.

5. Restore the data from backup.

This process represents a lengthy outage for servers, so it's not usually practical to fix existing servers. Instead, this process makes the most sense when new servers or new arrays are added into the environment.

When creating a new partition on an empty disk array on Windows 2003 or earlier, simply follow the instructions in Microsoft Knowledge Base article #929491: `http://support.microsoft.com/kb/929491`.

The key instruction is the one to create a partition with `align=1024`, which aligns the partition for best performance with the vast majority of storage equipment regardless of the underlying disk hardware.

That same knowledge base article also provides instructions for checking whether a partition is already aligned correctly. For more explicit instructions, however, use the following website: `http://blogs.msdn.com/jimmymay/archive/2008/12/04/disk-partition-alignment-sector-alignment-for-sql-server-part-4-essentials-cheat-sheet.aspx`.

NTFS Allocation Unit Size

After the partition has been set up with the correct alignment, the next step in storage setup is to format the newly created partition. During the formatting process on NTFS volumes, Windows asks the user to configure NTFS allocation unit size, also known as cluster size, as shown in Figure 4-17. This unit size is the smallest amount of space that a file will take on the disk. The default size is 4KB, which makes sense when working with file servers that have a large number of small text files. If the server has thousands of 1KB–3KB text files, a lot of space will be wasted. The same concept holds true for files with a 5KB size: They would use two 4KB allocation units.

When working with a Microsoft SQL Server, however, the database administrator knows that the file sizes are going to be very large. A SQL Server database file will always be much larger than 4KB, and there won't be a great deal of files on a data or log array. Therefore, you can use higher allocation unit sizes.

The easiest way to get a performance improvement for the majority of SQL Servers is to follow Microsoft's recommendation of a 64KB allocation unit size for SQL Server. However, in some cases smaller allocation unit sizes make sense depending on the application's read/write mix and sequential versus random activity. For OLTP servers that see a high volume of small random writes, a smaller unit size of 8KB can achieve a performance benefit during that activity. If the array will be used exclusively for OLTP databases, then the 8KB unit size makes sense.

> *If you have tested this on multiple arrays but seen no performance difference, check out this article for more information:* `http://kendalvandyke.blogspot.com/2009/02/disk-performance-hands-on-series.html`

Because this setting can't be changed after the volume is formatted, consider starting with the 64KB recommendation and monitoring performance or doing benchmarking within the application itself.

Over time, as the server is moved to other storage, the allocation unit size can be tweaked with each new volume.

Be aware that using the 64KB size removes the administrator's ability to enable NTFS compression on the volume. However, this setting is not recommended by Microsoft, as it's not an efficient way to achieve compression for SQL Server data. In environments where data compression is needed, consider using SQL Server's built-in compression, discussed later in this chapter.

Configuring HBA Queue Depth

Host bus adapters in a storage area network have a queue depth setting that determines how many requests the HBA will send out over the SAN at any given time. If the operating system needs a large amount of data, the HBA will send out its requests one-by-one until it receives data back from the SAN controllers. If the HBA's queue depth setting is 32, then it will send out a maximum of 32 requests before pausing to wait to hear back from the SAN controller. Then, as each request comes back from the SAN with the appropriate data, the HBA will send out another request for more data.

In a Fibre Channel SAN environment, the HBA has to closely monitor the outgoing requests because the SAN fabric itself cannot accept more than a certain amount of traffic before encountering collisions or a full queue on the SAN controller. The maximum queue depth depends on the following:

➤ The number of SAN ports on the SAN controller

➤ The number of connected HBAs from each server (also known as *initiators*, because they initiate conversations with the SAN controller)

➤ The queue depth on each HBA

This is only the tip of the iceberg, however: Remember that each SAN typically has two fabrics to control failover. The environment would have two of these 256-queue ports, and the DBA may want to try to load balance activity between the two ports. To really maximize performance, the servers might want to pull as much load as possible through both SAN ports, but a problem arises when one of the ports fails and traffic is failed over to the other port. Suddenly, too much traffic is going through that individual port, more than its queue depth can handle.

Another complexity arises when the server administrators try to plan around load windows. If the environment has a single data warehouse that processes data only between 11:00 p.m. and 3:00 a.m., and then runs a handful of very small reports during the day, it's tempting to consider setting its HBA queue depth at 256 if you think it will be the only server using the SAN during that time window. If you max out the SAN's queue depth during that time and another server tries to do a backup or a virus scan against that same SAN, then performance problems will arise.

Setting exactly the right queue depth for your environment requires complex, detailed calculations with spreadsheets, fan-out ratios, and time windows, and is outside the scope of this book. Getting a better queue depth than the default, however, can be quite easy. Double-check your HBA queue depth on each server, because different HBA vendors and driver versions will have different HBA queue depth defaults. Use that data to whiteboard a list of connected servers and their queue depths, and get the maximum queue length supported by your SAN controller. By drawing this out as shown in Figure 4-18, the database administrator can get a rough idea of whether the SAN fabric is currently oversubscribed or undersubscribed, and adjust accordingly.

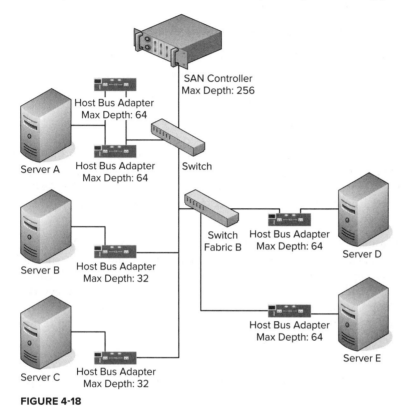

FIGURE 4-18

Starting queue depth recommendations range from 32 to 128. For a list of recommendations, see the MSDN blog post at `http://blogs.msdn.com/joesack/archive/2009/01/28/ sql-server-and-hba-queue-depth-mashup.aspx`.

Adapting to Virtual Servers

The concepts discussed so far have all focused on physical servers running Windows Server natively, without virtualization. Virtualization adds a layer of complexity between the operating system and its underlying hardware. This layer can ease the pains of administration, speed the process of moving from one brand of hardware to another, and increase uptime by avoiding unnecessary outages. Virtualization is designed to be as invisible as possible to the operating system and applications, and to abstract away the hardware.

This hardware abstraction makes management easier, but it can make performance tuning more difficult. The key is to consider the virtualization platform as another layer of settings that must be actively documented, managed, and tweaked in order to gain the best performance possible.

For example, when testing storage performance, the database administrator must be aware of the underlying hardware that's handling the database server. The make and model is not enough — the testing documentation needs to include the following:

➤ The types and quantity of host bus adapters on the host hardware

➤ How the HBA load balancing is configured

➤ The SAN fabric network topology between the host and the SAN controllers

➤ The number of other guest servers running on the same host hardware

➤ The version level of the virtualization platform

All of these things affect how much performance the server will get, and they need to be tracked as the DBA benchmarks performance over time. Updates to any of these can be completely transparent to a DBA; and if the DBA is not the person managing the virtualization platform, then he or she may not be aware of any changes made. Storage performance changes might be the only indication that something is amiss.

In addition, virtualization features such as Microsoft Hyper-V's Live Migration and VMware's VMotion enable the virtualization administrator to migrate guest servers around to different hardware in real time. If end users complain of storage performance problems on a Friday night, and the DBA doesn't check it out until Monday morning, the guest server might be already running on completely different hardware. With VMware's VMotion, the server's data might even be on a different SAN array. When servers are running in a fluid environment like this, it's important to get real-time 24/7 monitoring of storage performance and store it persistently over time.

The performance monitoring tutorials in Chapters 9 and 15 are especially helpful for servers in virtual environments. Use this information to maintain a long-term repository of performance data for troubleshooting.

Configuring SQL Server 2008

After understanding the storage subsystem, testing how it performs, and verifying that it protects data under stressful conditions, the database administrator can begin to configure SQL Server for that particular storage. SQL Server configuration can and should change depending on the storage being used. The well-educated DBA can mitigate bad storage designs with good database configuration, and can take advantage of a great storage design with an advanced database configuration.

Because storage is so expensive and can be so difficult to change after it is implemented, the database administrator needs to understand how to adapt to storage bottlenecks and work around them. Placing SQL Server data files, log files, tempdb, and other resources is all about resource allocation: Knowing which files will need the most storage performance, getting them the right resources, and monitoring to ensure that the initial decisions are still correct.

Choosing Which Files to Place on Which Disks

Best practices dictate that SQL Server data files, log files, tempdb files, and backup files are all written to separate arrays. This concept is touched on in Chapter 1 and Chapter 7 but it's worth mentioning here what types of drives can serve each purpose.

Log files, whenever possible, should be placed on RAID 10 arrays because their performance characteristics match the way RAID 10 performs best. Log files are the focus of heavy write activity, and RAID 10 specializes in high-speed writes. SAN vendors have been known to say that their RAID 5 arrays perform just as well under write conditions, but as Ronald Reagan said, "Trust, but verify." Use the performance testing tools in this chapter to back up that claim, and only accept RAID 5 for logs if this fast write performance can be conclusively demonstrated under load.

Data files, on the other hand, can be more flexibly placed on RAID 5/6 arrays in order to save money. When deciding what array to use, consider the read/write mix of the database. The Performance Dashboard Reports shown in Chapter 14 will enable database administrators to explore the current performance characteristics of their existing databases. Reviewing their read/write mix will help show which databases undergo mostly writes (and need RAID 10) versus which ones experience mostly reads (and can live on RAID 5).

Whenever possible, write backups to a different array than the array being used for data and logs. This achieves two things: faster backups and easier recovery from disaster. Backups will be written faster because they're not contending for the same drives as the data is being read from: Data can be streamed off the data drives and written to the backup drives as quickly as possible. Then, when disaster strikes and the data and/or log arrays go down for any reason, the backups will not be lost because they reside on a separate array.

A backup array can be shared between multiple SQL Servers, and this is an excellent use case for shared drive designs described earlier in the discussion about storage area networking. A RAID 10 array of SATA magnetic hard drives can often be fast enough to accommodate backups from a large number of servers simultaneously. The SATA drives will have a high capacity, which is useful in a backup environment where the DBA wants to keep as much history online as possible at one time. Configure each database server to run its backups during a slightly different time window in order to minimize the random writes: If each server is writing by itself, the writes will be mainly sequential. SATA magnetic hard drive performance suffers during random activity, so this type of array will not perform well if multiple servers try to write full backups simultaneously. Keep in mind, though, that reducing the number of drives by using large hard drives has a detrimental impact on IO throughput, which slows down backups.

Using Compression to Gain Performance

SQL Server 2008 added the capability to compress data: Tables and indexes can be stored in a compressed state, which takes up less disk capacity. In today's high-capacity SATA market, lowered storage costs may not always be an attractive benefit, but for low-capacity solid-state drives, this means that databases might be able to fit on SSDs with SQL Server's compression. Besides having the advantage of taking up less disk capacity, this also increases performance. The less data that has to be read or written off the storage, the faster the requests can be completed. If a 10GB index is compressed down to 3GB, then an index scan will be completed 70% faster simply because the data takes less time to read off the drives.

Data compression does incur a slight CPU penalty: The SQL Server engine has to compress the data before writing the page, and decompress the data after reading the page. However, in practice this penalty is far outweighed by the time saved waiting for storage (see: http://msdn.microsoft.com/en-us/library/dd894051.aspx).

Backup compression has similar payoffs: Backup times are faster because there's less data to write to disk, and restore times are faster because there's less data to read from disk. Rather than gaining more performance out of existing drives, this technique can be used to swap out fast Fibre Channel drives for slower but more cost-effective SATA drives in a backup array. With backup compression writing less data to disk, the SATA drives may be able to keep up just as well, plus deliver the added benefit of being able to keep more history on disk, as SATA drives have a much higher capacity.

Both backup compression and data compression require Enterprise Edition or Developer Edition. Backup compression is as easy as enabling a switch during backup, as shown in Figure 4-19, but data compression is not nearly as straightforward. The DBA must apply T-SQL code to each individual object that needs to be compressed. To make matters worse, compression is not something that can be scripted by default, and is not inherited from an object. If the DBA sets up a table's clustered index with compression, and developers later add more indexes, those indexes are not compressed by default. The DBA must constantly patrol for new indexes and objects, and apply compression where it makes sense from a performance perspective.

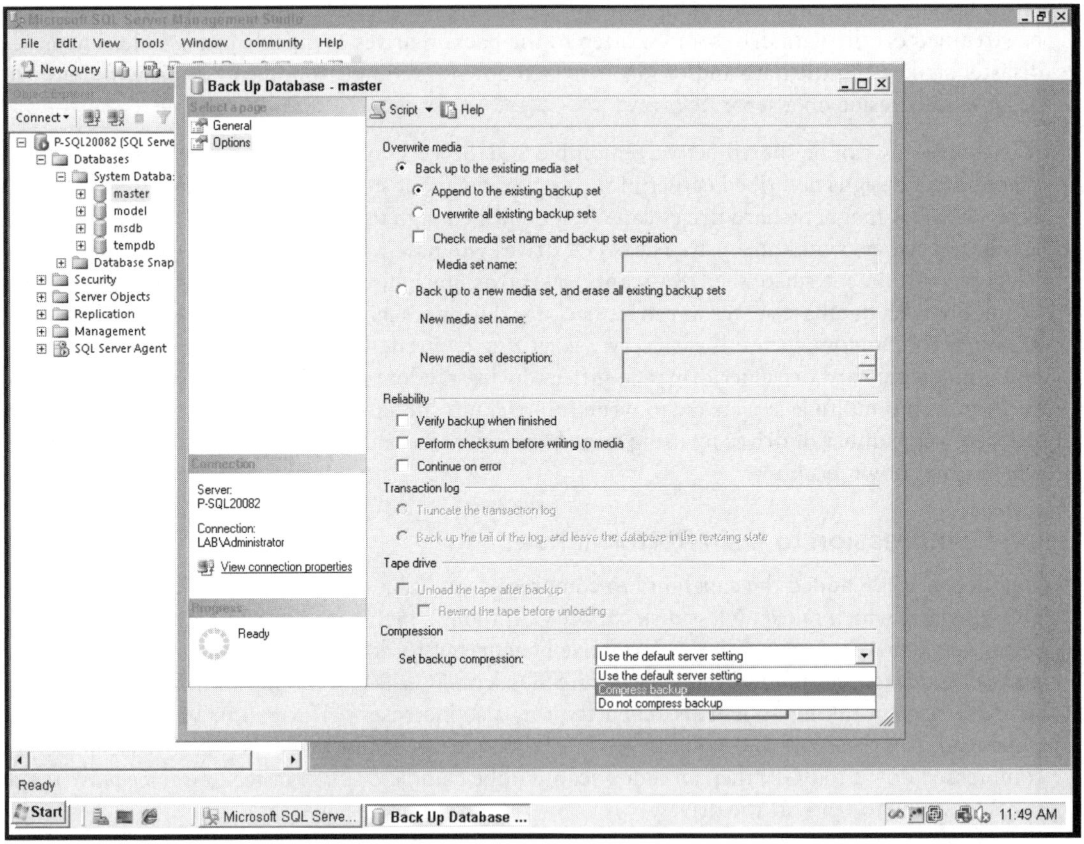

FIGURE 4-19

Storage changes over time, and applications change over time. Staying on top of SQL Server performance means being vigilant about the server's storage performance. Being an effective troubleshooter means knowing ahead of time when these changes have taken place, and how they affect the demands of the application and the users.

Corruption

When SQL Server hands off data to the operating system to write to storage, it doesn't have a way of knowing that the writes were executed correctly. Corruption often happens as data is written to storage, but SQL Server won't be aware of the problem until it tries to read that data back. The storage subsystem may have hardware, firmware or driver problems that cause it to write the wrong data to disk, or the drives themselves may not store data correctly.

Since these things happen in the background, it's important for DBAs to regularly check their databases for corruption before end users call in with query errors.

Detecting Corruption

The DBCC CHECKDB command checks a database's consistency to make sure that objects are stored correctly and don't contain invalid values. Unfortunately, the larger the database, the longer this process takes, and the more it impedes end user queries. If there's not a sufficient daily or weekly maintenance window for a full CHECKDB, consider using the PHYSICAL_ONLY option. The checks will run much faster, and they will still detect most hardware-introduced problems like pages that cannot be read. However, no logical checks of the data will be performed, such as computed columns with the wrong values or datetime fields with an invalid time. When using the PHYSICAL_ONLY option, consider running a full DBCC CHECKDB at least once per month to catch these other errors.

DBCC CHECKDB can be scheduled using SQL Server's Maintenance Plans or by using SQL Server Agent jobs to run the T-SQL directly. The method chosen usually depends on how the DBA runs regular maintenance jobs like backups. Ideally, the consistency checks are performed prior to doing a full backup; otherwise, the server is backing up a corrupt database. Whichever way the operation is scheduled, it's vital that the output is captured and sent to the database administration teams so that they can react quickly. The DBA's ability to recover from corruption depends on the ability to react quickly while valid backups are still available.

> *Unfortunately, SQL Server will often encounter corruption before DBCC CHECKDB catches it. An end user's query will try to read corrupt data, and their query will fail. SQL Server saves these error messages in the SQL Server log along with a severity level. To be alerted of these events when they happen, use SQL Server Agent to set up operators and alerts for severity levels 20 through 25. For complete instructions on accomplishing this, see the book Professional Microsoft SQL Server 2008 Administration (Wrox).*

Recovering from Corruption

Just as many hurricane deaths result from people making bad decisions after the storm passes, such as sightseeing in dangerous areas, data corruption problems can be made much worse after the initial diagnosis. Before taking any steps, review this list of actions to avoid:

➤ Don't detach the database — the corruption will still exist, and to make matters worse, SQL Server will refuse to attach the corrupt database.

➤ Don't restart SQL Server — the problem won't go away.

➤ Don't run DBCC CHECKDB REPAIR_ALLOW_DATA_LOSS — this may end up being the final solution, but it does delete data. By examining the corruption in more detail, the DBA may be able to get all of the data back more quickly.

Rather than jumping into those ill-advised options, here are the steps to take in order. Don't try jumping ahead, as the situation can get worse when steps are skipped.

Fix the Underlying Cause First

Database corruption can be caused by storage problems such as a defective SAN controller, failing hard drives, bad memory, cabling, and more. Before repairing the database, make sure that the underlying problems are fixed, or else the corruption will just keep recurring. Fixing the database corruption first is like trying to bail water out of a sinking boat: Find the hole in the boat first instead, and you'll have a fighting chance of saving the vessel.

For local storage, check the server's Windows Event Viewer in the System category. Go into Control Panel, Administrative Tools, Event Viewer, System. Depending on the server's activity levels, this screen may produce a high amount of informational alerts. These can be filtered out by clicking View, Filter, and unchecking the Information box. Any resulting errors that refer to storage should be investigated, because this is where storage controllers report their problems. Double-click on each event, and if it refers to storage, work with your system administrators and hardware vendor to fix the problems.

When using storage area networking, check the SAN controller's error logs. SAN controller errors usually don't show up in the Windows Event Viewer on the database server, and they can pinpoint exactly which storage component is failing. These errors may not repeat continuously; go back through the last several months of the SAN controller's logs looking for errors. A failing HBA may only cause problems every few weeks, for example. Work with the SAN team to make sure any problematic gear is replaced.

If other SQL Servers store data on the same SAN controller, run DBCC CHECKDB against their databases as well. They may have corruption errors that haven't surfaced yet.

Focus on the Worst Problem First

Different kinds of corruption have different repair methods, and some methods are more destructive than others. If a database has corrupt system tables, the only option may be to restore the database from backup. You don't want to waste time repairing non-clustered indexes, something easy to rebuild from scratch, if you have to end up restoring the whole database anyway.

When running DBCC CHECKDB in SQL Server Management Studio, it's unwieldy to work with dozens, hundreds, or heaven forbid, thousands of errors. Instead, check the database from a command line and capture all of the results to a text file with this command:

```
sqlcmd -E -Q"DBCC CHECKDB (master) WITH ALL_ERRORMSGS, NO_INFOMSGS"
-oC:\errorlist.txt
```

When DBCC CHECKDB returns more than one error, look for the worst error. This section covers the errors from worst to least impactful. If the database has an error that requires recovering from backup, that dictates how recovery should proceed.

Dealing with Damaged System Tables

Sadly, DBCC CHECKDB can't fix everything. Each database contains a set of metadata tables that describe where objects are stored on disk. If the clustered indexes of these system tables are damaged, SQL Server won't be able to tell where user tables are stored. Repairing something that massive is beyond the abilities of an automated tool.

In cases like this, the only options are restoring from database backups that aren't corrupted or scripting out the objects. To choose between them, find out which option involves losing the least amount of data. If the database has a recent full backup and a complete set of transaction log backups up to the point where the corruption occurred, the DBA may be able to restore those and lose the bare minimum of data. If transaction log backups weren't being performed, if the database wasn't in full recovery mode, or if the corruption is present in all of the backups, then the DBA will need to try to export data from the live database via scripting.

To script out objects in SQL Server Management Studio, right-click on the database and click Tasks, Generate Scripts. Check the box to Script All Objects in the Database, and in the Script Options step, choose as many options as you need, especially the Script Data option. During script generation, SQL Server will likely encounter errors as it runs across damaged objects, so this procedure may need to be performed one object at a time. After scripting as many objects as possible, create a new database on another server and run the scripts to recreate the data.

Dealing with Corrupt Clustered Indexes

When a table's clustered index is corrupt, the best option is to restore the database under another name, delete the table in the live database, and copy that table out of the restored copy. Depending on the table's design, this may involve dropping foreign keys, constraints, triggers, and so on. The DBA will need to make sure orphaned records are not introduced. This option may sound like a lot of work, but the other option involves a risk of data loss.

DBCC CHECKDB REPAIR_ALLOW_DATA_LOSS can fix the problem without restoring from backup, but it accomplishes the repair by outright deleting the affected rows or pages. In this case, DBCC's primary goal is to get a clean, valid copy of the table online as fast as possible without regard to saving data. It ignores constraints and triggers as it removes corrupt data. The end result is a database that is structurally sound, but may have application logic problems like orphaned parent/child records.

In rare situations where the DBA discovers corruption very quickly, there's hope for a quick fix. If the database is in full recovery mode and the corruption occurred after the last full backup, individual pages can be restored from backup. This process requires a complete unbroken log chain from the last full backup until now. Use the RESTORE DATABASE command with the PAGE option to grab the exact page(s) required, then apply all subsequent transaction logs. For more information about how to perform this process, see the following Microsoft article: `http://msdn.microsoft.com/en-us/library/ms175168.aspx.`

Dealing with Data Purity Errors

In SQL Server, times are measured with the number of minutes past midnight. This number cannot be greater than 1,440, because there's only 1,440 minutes in a day. If for some reason the storage subsystem reports back that a particular datetime field has 1,509 minutes past midnight, the database engine flags that as a data purity error because it can't possibly be correct. Other datatypes with similar possibilities for data purity errors are Unicode, real, float, decimal, and numeric.

DBCC CHECKDB can't fix data purity errors because it can't determine what the valid data should be, and it won't update user data with fake values. When repairing other corruption problems, DBCC will delete data outright, but it won't put in fake data.

The DBA has to run manual UPDATE statements against the affected rows in order to fix the data. To find out which rows are affected, use the queries in Microsoft Knowledge Base article #923247:

`http://support.microsoft.com/kb/923247`

In a perfect world, the DBA would restore the database from backup to another location (another database server or as another database name) to get the correct values to use in the UPDATE statements. If the only available database backups also have the data purity errors, the DBA will need to use default values (like midnight for a time) or use nulls.

Dealing With Corrupt Non-Clustered Indexes

In most cases, the fastest way to fix this type of corruption is to simply drop the index and recreate it. Don't try to rebuild the index – just drop it altogether before creating a new one. This method keeps the database online for end user access while the repair is performed, minimizing disruption.

Another repair option is to use DBCC CHECKDB REPAIR_REBUILD, but this method requires the database to be in single-user mode. Since that takes the database away from all end user access, it's not a preferred method.

The Final Steps After Any Repairs

After performing any corruption repairs, the DBA needs to follow up with a few more actions.

1. Run another DBCC CHECKDB. Problems may have been hidden by the first round of corruption.

2. Run DBCC CHECKCONSTRAINTS. Some methods of data repairs will get the table back online but ignore any constraints in the process.

3. Double-check the backups. If the root cause was not completely fixed, this database may become corrupt again. This would be an excellent time to proactively schedule more frequent backups.

4. Schedule regular DBCC checks. Set up a SQL Agent job to run DBCC CHECKDB on all databases at least once per week and email the results to the DBA.

SUMMARY

DBAs can avoid storage corruption and performance problems by designing, testing, and maintaining a solid storage system from the ground up. Doing so doesn't require an in-depth education in SAN technology, but rather, the DBA just needs to follow a few basic guidelines:

➤ Use the highest performing storage possible. Insist on RAID 10 where available for data, log, and tempdb arrays. Avoid SATA and IDE-based drives unless cost requirements simply can't justify faster storage.

➤ Stress test the storage before going live. Long before installing SQL Server, the DBA should use SQLIO to find out how fast the storage can really go, and what happens when the storage breaks.

➤ Set up regular DBCC checks to find corruption problems quickly. Learn how to recover from corrupted data ahead of time rather than trying to learn it under the gun.

By checking off these tasks, the DBA can stop wasting time troubleshooting storage problems and start focusing on other issues like end user queries, discussed in the next chapter.

5

CPU and Query Processing

WHAT'S IN THIS CHAPTER

➤ How CPU architecture affects SQL Server performance

➤ How SQL Server processes queries

➤ Understanding query optimization

➤ Reading query plans

➤ Using options to affect query plans

➤ Using plan hints to affect query plans

The CPU is at the core of everything that happens on a computer. This is especially true when working with SQL Server. An understanding of how the CPU works, and what it does is very valuable when trying to understand what SQL server is doing.

Query processing is one of the most critical activities that SQL Server performs when taking your T-SQL queries and returning data to you. Understanding how SQL Server process queries, how they are optimized, and executed is essential to understanding what SQL Server is doing, and why it is doing what it is doing in the way it has chosen to do it.

This chapter brings together essential information on both the CPU, and Query Processing.

In the first part of this chapter you will see how a modern CPU works, learn about the key elements of the CPU, learn about hyperthreading, and multiple core processors, and how these and other processor features can affect the performance you get from SQL Server.

In the second part of the chapter you will learn how SQL Server query processing works, looking at the details of query optimization, you will examine the various options that you can use to influence the optimization process, how SQL Server schedules activities, and executes them.

THE CPU

The modern CPU is an extremely complex combination of millions of individual transistors combined to deliver extremely high-performance computing capabilities to laptops, desktops, workstations, and servers.

The basic building blocks of the CPU, however, have not changed since the first electronic computers were built. At the core of the CPU are groups of transistors that combine to provide a set of primitive services such as moving data between memory and registers, performing basic math functions such as adding and subtracting, and comparing the contents of different registers. These basic services comprise all that's needed to build on and create the most powerful computer programs that operate today.

The basic services provided by the CPU are commonly broken down into four stages: fetch, decode, execute, and store, as shown in Figure 5-1 and described here:

➤ **Fetch:** This stage is responsible for fetching the next set of instructions of data from main memory, and making it available to the rest of the CPU.

➤ **Decode:** This stage has to decode the instructions from their external form, which is machine code, into the micro operations that the execution unit works on.

➤ **Execute:** This stage is the execution unit, where the individual micro operations are performed.

➤ **Store:** This stage is responsible for moving the results of the execution of the micro operations back into main memory.

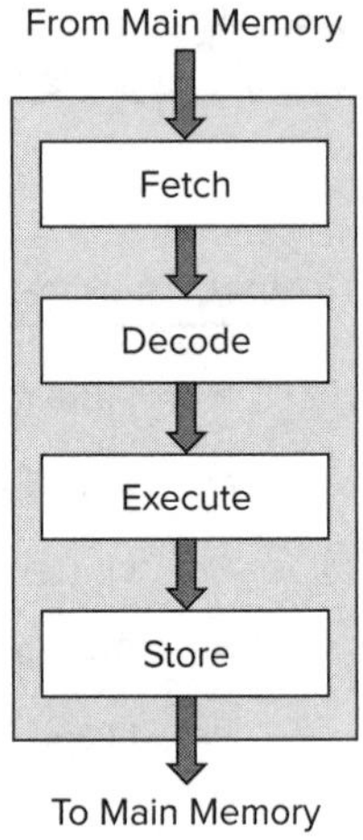

FIGURE 5-1

Modern CPUs make use of many enhancements to this basic model in order to keep data and instructions flowing to the execution unit as quickly as possible. Some of these enhancements include the use of multiple parallel "pipelines" at the fetch and decode stages. As well as having multiple parallel pipelines, these pipelines are becoming deeper so that multiple sequences of instructions can be processed in parallel at the same time. The addition of multiple pipelines led to further developments (such as hyperthreading) that will be discussed later in this chapter. Processors also include complex logic in order to predict branches in code that might invalidate the contents of a pipeline.

Figure 5-2 illustrates how the addition of pipelines affects the basic model.

This diagram shows that there are now four sets of the fetch and decode steps all working in parallel. These feed into a new out-of-order unit that arranges the various streams of micro instructions before they are passed to the execution unit. After the execution unit, another new step is responsible for reordering the results from the execution unit such that the results are consistent with the original stream of instructions.

Now that you have had a brief look inside a modern processor, in the next section you will see how SQL Server uses the CPU.

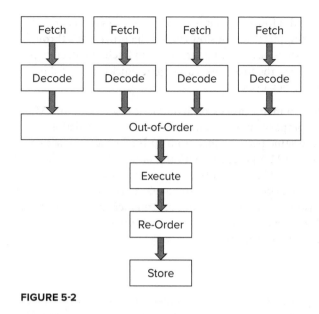

FIGURE 5-2

THE CPU AND SQL SERVER

SQL Server, like any program that runs on a modern computer, needs three resources from the computer in order to do anything: memory, storage, and CPU. You can read more about SQL Server's use of memory in Chapter 2 and storage in Chapter 4. This section describes how SQL Server interacts with the CPU.

As the heart of the modern computer, the CPU is where all the work happens, but the CPU can only remain busy doing work if memory and storage resources are fast enough to supply the CPU with everything it needs when it needs it.

Unfortunately this is not usually the case, and the CPU can end up sitting idle for periods of time while it waits for more data to arrive, or for the results it has just finished with to be put back in memory.

Different operations in SQL Server require different amounts of the three server resources, and operations that require more CPU than anything else are regarded as being processor-intensive. Some operations that fit into this category are compression, bulk load operations, compiling or recompiling queries, and executing CPU-intensive query operations. These operations reflect activities for which speed is an important factor.

Processor Speed

When you look at the specifications for a processor, one of the key numbers that is mentioned is the *clock speed*. For the current generation of processors, this ranges from 1GHz to around 3.6GHz. This value indicates how fast the processor's internal clock runs, and many people assume that this is how fast individual instructions are executed. However, that is not the case. In fact, nearly all instructions require multiple clock cycles to complete, which slows down the processor's through-put. At the same time, because modern processors have multiple-instruction fetch and decode pipe-lines, and a lot of other complicated logic to keep the processor running as quickly as possible, some instructions may approach one execution per clock cycle.

Because of internal differences between the two major processor manufacturers, Intel and AMD, it's not possible to do a direct performance comparison based on processor clock speed alone. In other words, you should not expect to get the same performance from an Intel processor with a clock speed of 2.6GHz, as you would from an AMD processor with the same 2.6GHz clock speed. However, both manufacturers are well represented in many different benchmarks, so it should be relatively easy to find benchmark results for a workload that has some relevance to what you want to do, and thus get a more realistic comparison of actual processor performance. A good place to look for benchmark results is the website for your processor manufacturer, either www.intel.com or www.amd.com. Another good place is the TPC website at www.tpc.org.

Hyper-Threading

Hyper-Threading is an optimization to the processor's design that enables one processor to appear to execute two software threads at the same time. It is an Intel-specific technology and is possible because there are a lot of steps in the actual pipeline between main memory and the execution unit, and detailed analysis performed by Intel revealed that for many workloads, a lot of the parallel steps in the pipeline were not busy at the same time.

Intel found that by adding some additional logic to maintain the concept of architectural state, they could make one processor appear to execute two threads at the same time. This is the basis for hyperthreading and is illustrated in Figure 5-3.

Unfortunately, the maximum theoretical benefit that can be gained from Hyper-Threading is just 1.3 times better than nonhyper-threaded execution, and that's in the best case. This information comes from Intel's own whitepapers, and printed material on hyperthreading. In the worst case, Hyper-Threading can cause a serious degradation in performance. There are a number of blogs and KB articles that discuss the current best practice recommenda-tions for using hyperthreading with SQL Server.

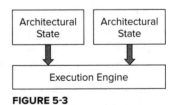

FIGURE 5-3

In a SQL Server environment, one of the optimizations that SQL Server can choose is to use paral-lelization in a query plan. This is more fully discussed in the section on parallel plans later in this chapter. Basically, *parallelization* describes the process whereby the Query Optimizer decides that a specific operation within a query would benefit from being split into multiple operations that can be run on different processors at the same time (in parallel), one piece on each of the available pro-cessors. If the available processors are hyperthreaded, then they are not really separate processors; and because each thread in a parallel plan needs to update its status to a single set of data struc-tures, on a system with Hyper-Threading enabled, a parallel plan can see a severe performance degradation.

If your system has Hyper-Threading capabilities, you need to determine whether it should be enabled. While doing so might seem an obvious choice, various SQL Server experts are split on this question. The currently accepted best practice recommendation is that you should run SQL Server with Hyper-Threading *disabled*, unless you have explicitly tested your application with it enabled and have determined that it did not cause a performance degradation.

While it's impossible to generalize about a best practice for all workloads, it is generally thought that OLTP-type workloads that don't generate parallel plans are more likely to benefit from having Hyper-Threading enabled, whereas DSS-type workloads, which are more likely to generate parallel plans, are more likely to suffer a performance degradation from having Hyper-Threading enabled.

> **OLTP VERSUS DSS WORKLOADS**
>
> An *Online Transaction Processing (OLTP) workload* is one in which a lot of small inserts are occurring, with a lot of small reads from reference data.
>
> A *Decision Support System (DSS) workload* is one in which the database consists of multiple large tables, probably with numerous indexes, running complex queries joining multiple tables, or long-running queries.

Licensing with Multicore and Hyper-Threading

Microsoft's licensing policy is the opposite of its competitors in that it licenses by the socket, not by the core or thread. This means that in some configurations it's possible for the operating system (and SQL Server) to see up to 12 processors when using a single socket(using the latest Intel Xeon hexa-core processors with Hyper-Threading enabled) and still run on a mid-range operating system such as Windows Server 2008 Standard Edition.

Cache

Modern processors need cache because they run at 2–3GHz, and main memory simply cannot keep up with the processor's appetite for this resource. To accommodate this heavy load, processor designers added several layers of cache.

The caches work by storing recently used data, pre-fetching additional data, which makes it available in very fast memory.

Pre-fetching data is the acquisition of additional data before and after the data that was explicitly requested. The amount of memory loaded on each request is determined by the cache line size and the pre-fetch parameters of the processor's caching algorithm. This behavior is based on the assumption that once the program is done with the data it just asked for, the next thing it will do is ask for data either just before or just after that data.

The cache on modern processors is typically implemented as multiple layers (L1, L2, L3, etc.). Each successive layer is physically farther from the processor core, and larger and slower relative to main memory.

Some caches are general-purpose and hold copies of any memory (L2 and L3). Other caches are very specific and hold only address lookups (TLB), data (L1 data), or instructions (instruction cache).

Typically, L1 is smaller and faster than L2, which is smaller and faster than L3. L3 cache is often physically located on a separate chip, and therefore farther from the processor core than L1 or L2, but still closer than main memory.

Processor cache is implemented as a transparent *look-through cache*. This means that controlling functions on the chip manage the process of filling the cache and managing cache entries. The process of filling and managing the cache is the job of the processor. Application developers have nothing to do with this task, and simply benefit from this feature of the processor. Thus, as far as the application is concerned, the cache is transparent.

The latest generation of Intel Xeon hexa-core processors are now available with 12–16MB of L3 cache. This design attempts to keep all six cores busy, with the memory they need located in L3 cache, enabling all six cores to keep running as fast as possible without having to wait for cache misses to be fetched from main memory.

Now for some SQL Server specifics. SQL Server 2008 is a considerably more complex product than SQL Server 2000. The cost of building in all this additional complexity is more lines of code, which appear as additional bytes in the size of the final `Sqlservr.exe` file. The exe for SQL Server 2000 was 8.9MB. The exe for SQL Server 2005 is 28MB. `Sqlservr.exe` for SQL Server 2008 now weighs in at 40MB.

In addition, simply starting the service requires more system resources. SQL Server 2000 runs in about 29MB of memory (Task Manager MEM Usage = Working Set). Connecting with OSQL or SQLCMD and issuing a simple query (`select name from master.sysdatabases`) adds another 0.5MB to that number. SQL Server 2005 uses around 50MB (49,604KB, ~35) of virtual memory just to start. Connecting with OSQL and issuing the same command makes that grow to 53MB (53,456KB). SQL Server 2008 uses around 102MB to start, and that grows to 104MB after making a single connection and executing the same query.

All this increased complexity results in a lot more code to do the same thing in SQL Server 2008 than in SQL Server 2000. This manifests itself as an increase in sensitivity to cache size: The smaller the cache, the slower the system might run; the larger the cache, the faster it might run. The net result of this is that if you have a choice between two processors running at the same speed, go for the one with the largest cache. Unfortunately, the increased cache usually comes at a price. Whether that additional cost is worth it is very difficult to quantify. If possible, running a test on both processors is the best way to determine this. Try to devise a test that delivers a specific metric that you can factor against the cost in order to get a clear indication of the cost/benefit of larger cache.

Having said all that, some of the preceding information should be qualified. SQL Server 2008's increased complexity is apparent in how it determines the best plan to execute your query. You will see this in an increase in the time it takes to compile a query — and, in most cases, a decrease in query execution time. This means that the first time a new query is run, there is a chance that it may actually take *longer* to run than in SQL Server 2000, but future executions of the plan from cache will execute considerably faster.

Please note that this difference in time is in the order of milliseconds, or in a bad case, maybe tenths of a second. If your query is only run once or twice, this isn't a problem, but in the case where your query is being compiled every time it's run, and has to be run thousands of times a second, all those extra milliseconds can add up to a big performance problem.

This is an excellent reason to make use of any feature that enables you to reuse a plan. After SQL Server has taken all that time to determine the best way to get you your data, reuse that plan as much as you can before it's thrown away. This way, you can offset the time SQL Server took to figure out a great plan for you. One way *not* to take advantage of this, and to set yourself up for worse performance, is to issue only ad-hoc statements for which the T-SQL changes significantly each time it is executed. In this case, the ad-hoc SQL is compiled into a plan that is cached each time but never reused because the T-SQL changes for the next query, Changing the T-SQL for each execution ensures that there is no plan reuse. You will spend a lot of time compiling statements that are never reused.

In summary, when considering different processors, it's important to consider the amount of cache available, and be aware that more cache is better than less cache when running SQL Server 2008.

Multicore Processors

One of the biggest challenges facing multiprocessor system designers is how to reduce the latency caused by the physical limitations of the speed of light and the distance between processors and memory. This becomes critical because the electric signals — the data being sent from memory to the processor — can't travel faster than the speed of light. As processor speeds get faster, and motherboards get larger, the speed of light starts to become a factor. One way to overcome this limitation is to put multiple processors on a single chip. This is what a multicore processor does, providing the potential for better performance than single-core systems.

This is such a good idea that it's now pretty much become the standard for server systems, and multicore processors are also appearing in high-end and middle-market desktop systems as well. Due to this prevalence, the main question now becomes not whether you should buy a system with multicore processors, but how many cores do you want? The answer depends on how much you are willing to pay, and what your longer-term plans are for the system.

Systems with fewer sockets are typically cheaper than systems with more sockets, which require more circuitry and more space on the motherboard.

Another consideration is the physical interface for the socket, and is the socket at or approaching the end of its life, or is it a newer socket that will enable you to upgrade to more cores as future generations of processors are released.

To get some idea of the relative performance of different systems, you can always check out what the hardware vendors are doing with their Transaction Processing Performance Council (TPC) benchmark numbers. These can be found on the TPC website at http://www.tpc.org. The TPC results are a great way to compare hardware, although some hardware vendors are reluctant to participate, so you may not find results for all of the systems you want to compare.

Another factor to consider is scalability. Rather than purchase a quad-socket, dual-core system, consider purchasing a dual-socket system with a quad-core processor. Make sure when doing this that the socket is compatible with the latest processors if possible, and then you'll have a better chance of being able to upgrade to the latest hexa-core processors. Intel has plans to deliver 12-core versions of some processors in the future.

Multicore Terminology

Before going further, it's worthwhile to clarify some terminology used here to avoid confusion when discussing multicore systems:

> ➤ **Socket:** New to many people is the concept of a socket. The socket is the physical component or slot into which you plug the processor die. Before multicore systems were introduced, there was a direct one-to-one relationship between sockets and execution units.

> ➤ **Core:** A core is equivalent to an execution unit, or what we would previously have considered to be a processor. A multicore processor has two or more of these per socket.

> ➤ **Thread:** A thread is only relevant in the context of hyperthreading. This is not a new execution unit, but rather a new pipeline on the front of an existing execution unit. See the section "Hyper-Threading" earlier in the chapter for more details about how this is implemented.

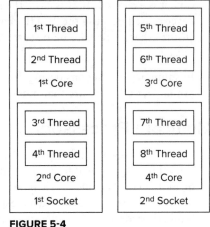

Figure 5-4 illustrates a dual-socket, quad-core computer with hyperthreading enabled, which delivers eight threads and appears to the OS as eight processors, but is licensed as two sockets.

FIGURE 5-4

SYSTEM ARCHITECTURE

System architecture refers to how the various components of the computer system are connected. The components in this context are the processor, main memory or RAM, disk drives, memory controllers, Interface controllers, and address and system buses.. Beyond the processor, other important aspects of the system have a large impact on the performance you will experience from SQL Server when running on any given computer.

This section introduces some of the more interesting aspects of system architecture that can impact SQL Server's ability to utilize the available CPU resources.

Processors are laid out and connected on the motherboard in one of two possible configurations: symmetric multiprocessing (SMP) or non-uniform memory access (NUMA). The difference between them is mostly reflected in where the memory controller lives. In systems based on AMD processors, which have a memory controller on each processor, then the architecture is NUMA. In systems based on Intel processors, where the processor design doesn't have an onboard memory controller, then architecture has been SMP.

Historically, choosing an Intel processor or an AMD processor led to different system architectures because of choices that each manufacturer made in their system design. However, Intel has recently released a new line of processors that have changed this. See the section on "AMD or Intel?" for details.

The final part of this discussion touches on the differences between processors and computer systems marketed as servers, workstations, or desktops, as the boundaries between these systems are blurring; and it's becoming increasingly difficult to determine when you should pay more money for a server that appears to have a lower specification, rather than purchase a cheaper workstation or machine with a desktop specification.

Symmetric Multiprocessing

In a symmetric multiprocessing (SMP) architecture, all processors are connected to a single pool of memory through a shared system bus. This is the typical architecture you will find on any system with less than 8 or 16 cores using Intel processors. AMD processors have a different internal architecture, one which places the memory controller inside each processor (socket) such that they are not considered to have SMP.

The SMP architecture works great on smaller systems: The physical distance between resources is small, the number of resources is small, and the demand for those resources is small. Figure 5-5 shows an eight-processor SMP system.

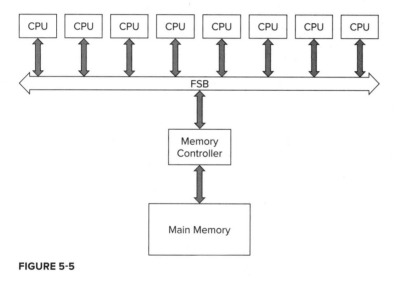

FIGURE 5-5

NonUniform Memory Access

A non-uniform memory access (NUMA) architecture refers to a system where there the total available memory is broken down into multiple *nodes*, with groups of processors connecting directly to each node of memory, which is considered the "local" memory pool. Each node also has access to all other memory on the other nodes, which are considered *remote* or *nonlocal* memory. NUMA systems are often referred to as ccNUMA, which means cache-coherent NUMA. The cache coherent (cc) part of this term reflects the fact that additional logic is built into the system to ensure that any piece of data is only ever loaded into cache at one place at any point in time.

A NUMA system architecture has the advantage that each processor in a node doesn't pay the cost of using a shared bus to access memory, provided the data it wants is in the local memory pool. If the data it wants is in remote memory, then the cost of getting access to it is a little higher than on an SMP system. Therefore, one of the objectives with a NUMA system is to try to maximize the amount of data that is used from the local memory, and avoid accessing data that is in remote memory.

NUMA systems can have a variety of configurations regarding sockets per node and cores per socket, and total processors up to the current Windows OS maximum of 256 for Windows Server 2008 R2 Data Center Edition.

One of the problems with NUMA systems is growth; as they get larger, maintaining cache coherency becomes more difficult, and introduces additional overhead that the operating system has to manage. In addition, as the number of nodes increases, it's less likely that the data needed by a newly scheduled thread will be local to the processor that is running the thread.

The operating system must also be NUMA-aware in order to schedule threads and allocate memory local to the node, which is more performant than allocating remote memory, or to schedule a thread to run on a different node. Either of these actions incurs a remote memory access — either to fetch new data from main memory or to move the thread's data from the old node to the new node.

Figure 5-6 shows an eight-processor NUMA system, comprised of two four-CPU nodes.

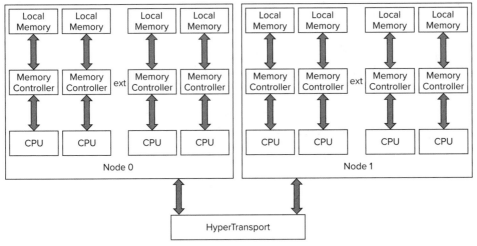

FIGURE 5-6

AMD or Intel?

One question that I hear a lot is "Should I choose Intel or AMD processors for my new server?" The answer is that it depends — both on what the best deal is at the moment, and where each company is in terms of the perpetual leapfrogging that goes on between processor capabilities of the two companies. It may also depend on which server manufacturer has been able to get the latest processor technology to market first.

Both manufacturers produce single, dual, quad, and now six-core processors; both manufacturers are discussing future versions that include options to increase to 12 cores; and both manufacturers produce processors of nearly comparable speeds, although Intel does tend to lead with higher clock speeds, but that's usually offset in performance benchmarks by AMD's ability to better utilize the available clock cycles, meaning a slower AMD processor may be able to outperform a faster Intel processor for a given benchmark.

To be consistent with both manufacturers' literature, in the following discussion, "processor" refers to what has previously been referred to as a socket, which may contain 1, 2, 4, 6, 8, or 12 cores.

Other than price, there has always been one major difference between the architecture used by these two companies. Intel has used a front-side, bus-based architecture that makes servers based on its products appear as SMP systems, unless the hardware vendor goes to a lot of trouble to build a NUMA system. AMD has a built-in memory controller per processor, and a HyperTransport technology for interprocessor communication, which means that servers based on AMD processors appear as NUMA systems without any effort from the server manufacturer.

However, this comparison is about to be made moot, as Intel is now shipping its latest generation of processors, code-named Nehalem. These processors use the new Intel QuickPath Interconnect technology, along with an on-processor memory controller. This means that servers based on this new generation of processors will appear as NUMA systems. It is also an architectural step above AMD's HyperConnect technology, which is limited to three system interconnects, limiting AMD-based servers to no more than 4–8 sockets without the need for additional system features. The Intel QuickPath Interconnect technology is a switched-system interconnect that can support 2–8 sockets, and it allows larger "super" computer systems to be built by using a hierarchy of 2–8 inter-connected nodes.

Server, Workstation, or Desktop

In today's market for computers, the lines between the specifications for a high-end desktop machine, a workstation, and a low-end server are all blurring. Combine this with the latest scalability white-papers from the likes of Google, Facebook, MySpace, etc where they talk about using "commodity" hardware, and large farms of desktop class machine to do their processing, and it is easy to see why there is a lot of renewed interest in running SQL Server on cheaper machines.

While it may seem very attractive financially to use a considerably cheaper desktop or workstation class of machine on which to run SQL Server, there are many performance, and reliability reasons why you should very carefully consider doing this.

While at an initial glance the machines' specifications may appear similar, in the server class machine you're paying more for a reason, and that reason is typically that you're getting more robust hardware that's designed to be operated 24 hours a day, 7 days a week, 365 days a year. The server may include many of the following features:

➤ **ECC memory:** to reduce the chance of data corruption from bad memory which becomes more of a problem as you add more memory to the machine

➤ **Hot swap memory:** to allow faulty memory modules to be replaced without taking the machine offline, and to allow additional memory to be added without taking the machine offline

➤ **Hot swap disks:** to allow faulty disk drives (in a RAID array) to be replaced without shutting the machine down

➤ **SCSI disk interface:** which provides higher capacity, to a more robust disk architecture than SATA drives

➤ **Dual power supplies:** to provide redundancy and keep the server up in the event of a single component failure

➤ **Greater IO capacity:** through the use of more and faster interface slots

These are just some of the features you might find on a server class machine that would be absent from a workstation, or desktop class of machine, and start to show why the server is more expensive than what may appear to be a comparable desktop or workstation computer.

QUERY PROCESSING

This section uses the AdventureWorks 2008 database, so now is a good time to download it from the SQL Server section on CodePlex if you haven't already. The AdventureWorks 2008 samples can be found at `www.codeplex.com/ SqlServerSamples`.

Query processing is done by the Relational Engine in SQL Server. It is the process of taking the T-SQL statements you write and converting them into something that can make requests to the Storage Engine and retrieve the results needed.

SQL Server takes four steps to process a query. The four steps are: Parse, Bind, Optimize, and Execute. They are shown in Figure 5-7.

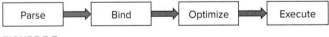

FIGURE 5-7

The first three steps are all done in the Relational Engine. The output of the third step is the optimized plan that is scheduled, and during which calls are made to the Storage Engine to retrieve the data that becomes the results of the query you are executing.

Query optimization and execution are covered later in this chapter. The following sections briefly discuss parsing and binding.

Parsing

During the parsing stage SQL Server performs basic checks on the source code (your T-SQL batch). This parsing looks for invalid SQL syntax, such as incorrect use of reserved words, column and table names, and so on.

If parsing completes without errors, it generates a parse tree, which is passed onto the next stage of query processing, binding. The parse tree is an internal representation of the query. If parsing detects any errors, the process stops and the errors are returned.

Binding

The binding stage is also referred to as the algebrizer stage after the changes made with SQL Server 2005. In SQL 2000 this stage was referred to as *normalization*. During binding, SQL Server performs several operations on the parse tree, and generates a query tree that is passed on to the Query Optimizer.

Some of the steps performed during binding are as follows:

➤ **Step 1: Name resolution** — Checks that all objects exist and are visible in the security context of the user. This is where the table and column names are checked to ensure that they exist and that the user has access to them.

➤ **Step 2: Type derivation** — Determines the final type for each node in the parse tree.

➤ **Step 3: Aggregate binding** — Determines where to do any aggregations.

➤ **Step 4: Grouping binding** — This is where any aggregations are bound to the appropriate select list.

Binding will also detect any syntax errors, at which point the optimization process halts and the error is returned to the user.

QUERY OPTIMIZATION

The job of the Query Optimizer is to take the query tree that was generated by parsing and binding your T-SQL query, and find a "good" way to retrieve the data (results) needed. Note the emphasis on "good" here, rather than best, as for any nontrivial query, there may be hundreds, or even thousands, of different ways to achieve the same results, and finding the absolutely best one could become an extremely time-consuming process. Therefore, in the interests of providing results in a timely manner, the Query Optimizer looks for a "good enough" plan, and uses that. This does mean that you may well be able to do better when you manually inspect the query plan, and different ways you can affect the decisions that SQL Server makes during optimization are covered in the upcoming section on Influencing Optimization.

The query optimization process uses the principle of cost, which is an abstract measure of work that is used to evaluate different query plan options. There is some discussion as to what the units for cost are, with some people suggesting that it's an estimate of the time in seconds the query is expected to take. However, cost should be considered to be a dimensionless value that doesn't have any units, its only value is for comparing to the cost of other plans in the search for the cheapest plan. So there are no true units for cost values.

The exact details of what SQL Server does within the optimization phase are a closely guarded secret, but it's possible to get a glimpse at some of what goes on. For the purposes of this book, you don't need to know every intimate detail, and in fact such a deep understanding isn't useful anyway.

For one thing, there is nothing you can do to alter this process; moreover, with each new service pack or hotfix, the SQL Server team tunes the internal algorithms, thereby changing the exact behavior. If you were to know too much about what was going on here, you could build in dependencies that would break with every new version of SQL Server.

Rather than know all the details, you need only understand the bigger picture. Even this bigger picture is often too much information, as it doesn't offer any real visibility into what the Query Optimizer is doing. All you can see of this secretive process is what is exposed in the DMV `sys.dm_exec_query_optimizer_info`. This can be interesting, but it's not a great deal of help in understanding why a given T-SQL statement is assigned a particular plan, or how you can "fix" what you think may be a non-optimal plan.

The current model provided by the SQL Server team works something like this:

➤ Is a valid plan cached? If yes, then use the cached plan. If no plan exists, then continue.

➤ Is this a trivial plan? If yes, then use the trivial plan. If no, then continue.

➤ Apply simplification. Simplification is a process of normalizing the query tree, and applying some basic transformations to additionally "simplify" the tree.

➤ Is the plan cheap enough? If yes, then use this. If no, then start optimization.

➤ Start cost-based optimization.

➤ **Phase 0:** Explore basic rules, and hash and nested join options.

➤ Does the plan have a cost of less than 0.2? If yes, then use this. If no, then continue.

➤ **Phase 1:** Explore more rules, and alternate join ordering. If the best (cheapest) plan costs less than 1.0, then use this plan. If not, then if MAXDOP > 0 and this is an SMP system, and the min cost > cost threshold for parallelism, then use a parallel plan. Compare the cost of the parallel plan with the best serial plan, and pass the cheaper of the two to phase 2.

➤ **Phase 2:** Explore all options, and opt for the cheapest plan after a limited number of explorations.

The output of the preceding steps is an executable plan that can be placed in the cache.

This plan is then scheduled for execution, which is explored later in this chapter.

You can view the inner workings of the optimization process via the DMV `sys.dm_exec_query_optimizer_info`. This DMV contains a set of optimization attributes, each with an occurrence and a value. Refer to SQL Books Online (BOL) for full details. Here are a few that relate to some of the steps just described:

```
select *
from sys.dm_exec_query_optimizer_info
where counter in (
'optimizations'
, 'trivial plan'
, 'search 0'
, 'search 1'
, 'search 2'
)
order by [counter]
```

The preceding will return the same number of rows as shown below, but the counters and values will be different. You will see that the value for optimizations matches the sum of the trivial plan, search 0, search 1, and search 2 counters (2328 + 8559 + 3 + 17484 = 28374):

```
Counter                occurrencevalue
Optimizations 28374        1
search 0      2328         1
search 1      8559         1
search 2      3            1
trivial plan  17484        1
```

Parallel Plans

A parallel plan is any plan where the optimizer has chosen to split an applicable operator into multiple threads that are run in parallel.

Not all Operators are suitable to be used in a parallel plan, and you will only see the optimizer choose a parallel plan if the server has multiple processors, and the maximum degree of parallelism setting allows parallel plans, and the cost threshold for `parallelization sql server configuration` option is set to a value lower than the lowest cost estimate for the current plan.

In the case where all these criteria are met, then the Optimizer will choose to parallelize the operation.

An example of this that illustrates how this works could be trying to count all the values in a table that match a particular search criteria. If the set of rows in the table is large enough, and the cost of the query high enough, and the other criteria are met, then this might be parallelized by the optimizer breaking the total set of rows in the table into equal chunks, one for each processor core. The operator is then executed in parallel, with each processor core executing one thread, and dealing with 1/ number of cores of the total set of rows. This lets the operation complete in a lot less time than if a single thread had to scan thru the whole table.

Algebrizer Trees

As mentioned above, the output of the parser is a parse tree. This isn't stored anywhere permanently, so you can't see what this looks like. The output from the algebrizer is an algebrizer tree, which isn't stored for any T-SQL queries either, but some algebrizer output *is* stored — namely, views, defaults, and constraints. This is stored because these objects are frequently reused in other queries, so caching this information can be a big performance optimization. The algebrizer trees for these objects are stored in the cache store, where `type` = CACHESTORE_PHDR.

It's only when you get to the next stage — i.e., the output from optimization — that things start to get really interesting, and here you can see quite a bit of information. This very useful data provides details about each optimized plan.

sql_handle or plan_handle

In the various execution-related DMVs, some contain a `sql_handle`, while others contain the `plan_handle`. Both are hashed values: `sql_handle` is the hash of the original T-SQL source, whereas `plan_handle` is the hash of the cached plan. Because of the auto-parameterization of SQL queries, the relationship between these means that many `sql_handles` can map to a single `plan_handle`.

You can see the original T-SQL for either using the dynamic management function (DMF) `sys.dm_exec_sql_text (sql_handle | Plan_handle)`.

You can see the XML showplan for the plan using the DMF `sys.dm_exec_query_plan (plan_handle)`.

Statistics

Statistics are a critical piece of information needed by SQL Server when performing query optimization. SQL Server statistics contain information about the data, and what the data looks like in each table within the database.

The query optimization process uses statistics to determine how many rows a query might need to access for a given query plan. It uses this information to develop its cost estimate for each step in the plan. If statistics are missing or invalid, the Query Optimizer can arrive at an incorrect cost for a step, and thus choose what ends up being a bad plan.

You can examine the statistics for any table in the database by using SQL Server Management Studio, expanding the Object Explorer to show the table you are interested in. For example, Figure 5-8 shows the `person.Address` table in the AdventureWorks2008 database. Expand the table node, under which you will see a Statistics node. Expand this, and you will see a statistic listed for each index that has been created, and in many cases you will see additional statistics listed, often with cryptic names starting with _WA. These are statistics that SQL Server has created automatically for you, based upon queries that have been run against the database.

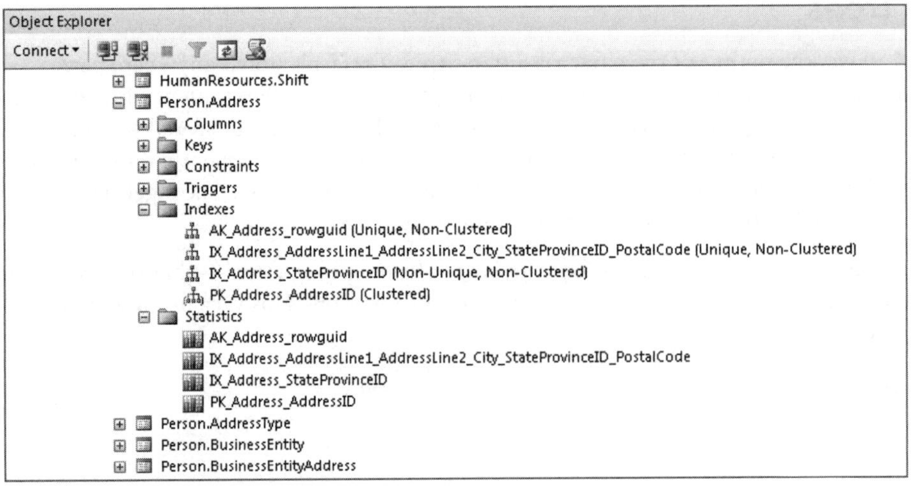

FIGURE 5-8

To see the actual statistic values, you can select an individual statistic, right-click it, and select the Properties option from the menu options. This will show you the Properties dialog for the statistic you selected. The first page, General Details, shows you the columns in the statistic, and when it was last updated. The details page contains the real guts of the statistic, and shows the data distribution. For the PK_Address-AddressID statistic on the person.address table in AdventureWorks2008, you should see something similar to Figure 5-9.

```
Table Name:        Person.Address
Statistics Name:   PK_Address_AddressID

Statistics for INDEX 'PK_Address_AddressID'.
--------------------------------------------------------------------------------
Name                           Updated                      Rows
--------------------------------------------------------------------------------
PK_Address_AddressID           Sep  7 2009  3:46PM          19614

All Density                    Average Length               Columns
--------------------------------------------------------------------------------
5.098399E-05                   4                            AddressID

Histogram Steps
RANGE_HI_KEY                   RANGE_ROWS                   EQ_ROWS
--------------------------------------------------------------------------------
1                              0                            1
1064                           1062                         1
11446                          95                           1
29846                          18399                        1
32521                          53                           1
```

FIGURE 5-9

This figure shows just part of the multi-column output, which is the same output that you get when running the following DBCC command:

```
DBCC SHOW_STATISTICS ("Person.Address", PK_Address_AddressID);
```

The following SQL Server configuration options control how statistics are created.

Auto_create_statistics

When this is on, SQL Server will automatically create statistics when it deems them necessary. That usually means when it's optimizing a query that references a table that doesn't have statistics, or when it determines that statistics are out of date. However, several other statistics-related options influence exactly when this occurs. These other options are auto_update_statistics, and auto_update_statistics_asynchronously, which are discussed in more detail in the following sections.

Auto_update_statistics

When this is on, SQL Server will automatically update statistics when it deems necessary. By default, this is done synchronously, which means that a query has to wait for the statistics to be updated before the optimization process can be completed.

Auto_update_statistics_asynchronously

When this option is on, SQL Server updates statistics asynchronously. This means that when it's trying to optimize a query and the statistics are outdated, it will continue optimizing the current query using the old stats, and queue the stats to be updated asynchronously. As a result, the current query doesn't benefit from the new stats, but it does not have to wait while stats are being updated before getting a plan and running. Any future queries can then benefit from the new stats.

Plan Caching and Recompilation

Once the Query Optimizer has come up with a plan, which may have taken a considerable amount of work, SQL Server does its best to ensure that you can leverage all that costly work again. It does this by caching the plan it just created, and taking steps to ensure that the plan is reused as widely as possible. It does this by using parameterization options.

Parameterization

Parameterization is a process whereby SQL Server will take the T-SQL you entered and look for ways to replace values that may be variables with a token, so that if a similar query is processed, SQL Server can identify it as being the same underlying query, apart from some string, or integer values, and make use of the already cached plan. For example, the following is a basic T-SQL query to return data from the Adventure Works 2008 database:

```
select *
from person.person
where lastname = 'duffy'
```

The parameterization of this query would result in the string `'duffy'` being replaced with a parameter such that if another user executes the following query, the same plan would be used, saving on compilation time:

```
select *
from person.person
where lastname = 'miller'
```

Note that this is just an example, and this particular query gets a trivial plan, so it isn't a candidate for parameterization.

The SQL Server Books Online topic on "Forced Parameterization" contains a lot of very specific details about what can and cannot be converted to a parameter.

To determine whether a query has been parameterized, you can search for it in the DMV `sys.syscacheobjects` (after first executing the query to ensure it is cached). If the SQL column of this DMV shows that the query has been parameterized, you will see that any literals from the query have been replaced by variables, and those variables are declared at the beginning of the batch.

Parameterization is controlled by the SQL Server configuration options — simple or forced:

> ➤ **Simple Parameterization:** The default operation of SQL Server is to use *simple parameterization* on all queries that are suitable candidates. Books Online provides numerous details about which queries are selected and how SQL Server performs parameterization.

Using simple parameterization, SQL Server is able to parameterize only a relatively small set of the queries it receives.

➤ **Forced Parameterization:** For more control over database performance, you can specify that SQL Server use *forced parameterization*. The Forced parameterization option forces SQL Server to parameterize all literal values in any select, insert, update, or delete statement queries. There are some exceptions to this, and these are well documented in SQL Server Books Online. Forced parameterization is not appropriate in all environments and scenarios. It is recommended that you use it only for a very high volume of concurrent queries, and when you are seeing high CPU from a lot of compilation/recompilation. If you are not experiencing a lot of compilation/recompilation, then forced parameterization is probably not appropriate. If you use forced in the absence of these symptoms, you may end up with a degradation in performance and/or throughput, as SQL Server takes more time to parameterize a lot of queries that are not then reused.

Forced parameterization can also be more finely controlled through the use of plan guides. You will learn about plan guides in more detail later in this chapter.

Looking into the Plan Cache

The plan cache is built on top of the caching infrastructure provided by the SQL OS. This provides objects called *cache stores*, which can be used to cache all kinds of objects. The plan cache contains several different cache stores used for different types of objects.

To see the contents of a few of the cache stores most relevant to this conversation, run the following T-SQL:

```
select name, entries_count, single_pages_kb, multi_pages_kb
from sys.dm_os_memory_cache_counters
where [name] in (
'object plans'
, 'sql plans'
, 'extended stored procedures'
)
```

Example output when I ran this on my laptop is as follows:

```
name                        entries_count single_pages_kb multi_pages_kb
Object Plans                54            12312           96
SQL Plans                   48            2904            232
Extended Stored Procedures 4             48              0
```

Each cache store contains a hash table that is used to provide efficient storage for the many plans that may reside in the plan cache at any time. The hash used is based on the plan handle. The hash provides buckets to store plans, and many plans can reside in any one bucket. SQL Server limits both the number of plans in any bucket and the total number of hash buckets. This is done to avoid issues with long lookup times when the cache has to store a large number of plans, which can easily happen on a busy server servicing many different queries.

To find performance issues caused by long lookup times, you can look into the contents of the DMV sys.dm_os_memory_cache_hash_tables, as shown in the following example. It is recommended that no bucket should contain more than 20 objects; and buckets exceeding 100 objects should be addressed.

```
select *
from sys.dm_os_memory_cache_hash_tables
where type in (
'cachestore_objcp'
, 'cachestore_sqlcp'
, 'cacchestore_phdr'
, 'cachestore_xproc'
)
```

Use the following DMV to look for heavily used buckets:

```
select bucketid, count(*) as entries_in_bucket
from sys.dm_exec_cached_plans
group by bucketid
order by 2 desc
```

You can look up the specific plans in that bucket using this query:

```
select *
from sys.dm_exec_cached_plans
where bucketid = 236
```

If the plans you find filling the same bucket are all variations on the same query, then the solution is to try to get better plan reuse through parameterization. If the queries are already quite different, and there is no commonality that would allow parameterization, then the solution is to rewrite the queries to be dramatically different, enabling them to be stored in emptier buckets.

Four different kinds of objects are stored in the plan cache. Although not all of them are of equal interest, each is briefly described here:

➤ **Algebrizer trees** are the output of the algebrizer, although only the algebrizer trees for views, defaults, and constraints are cached.

➤ **Compiled plans** are the objects you will be most interested in. This is where the query plan is cached.

➤ **Cursor execution contexts** are used to track the execution state when a cursor is executing, and are similar to the next item.

➤ **Execution contexts** track the context of an individual compiled plan.

The first DMV to look at in the procedure cache is sys.dm_exec_cached_plans. The following query gathers some statistics on the type of objects exposed through this DMV (note that this doesn't include execution contexts, which are covered next):

```
select cacheobjtype, objtype, COUNT (*)
from sys.dm_exec_cached_plans
group by cacheobjtype, objtype
order by cacheobjtype, objtype
```

Running the preceding on my laptop resulted in the following output; your results will vary depending on what was loaded into your procedure cache:

```
CACHEOBJTYPE    OBJTYPE    (NO COLUMN NAME)
Compiled Plan   Adhoc      43
Compiled Plan   Prepared   20
Compiled Plan   Proc       54
Extended Proc   Proc       4
Parse Tree      Check      2
Parse Tree      UsrTab     1
Parse Tree      View       64
```

To see the execution contexts, you must pass a specific plan handle to sys.dm_exec_cached_plans_dependent_objects. However, before doing that, you need to find a plan_handle to pass to this dynamic management function (DMF). To do that, run the following T-SQL:

```
-- Run this to empty the cache
-- WARNING !!! DO NOT TRY THIS ON A PRODUCTION SYSTEM !!!
dbcc freeproccache

-- Now see how many objects there are in the cache
-- There will always be a bunch of stuff here
-- from background activities SQL is always running.
select cacheobjtype, objtype, COUNT (*)
from sys.dm_exec_cached_plans
group by cacheobjtype, objtype
order by cacheobjtype, objtype
```

The output of this query can be seen here:

```
CACHEOBJTYPE    OBJTYPE    (NO COLUMN NAME)
Compiled Plan   Adhoc      5
Compiled Plan   Prepared   1
Compiled Plan   Proc       11
Extended Proc   Proc       1
Parse Tree      View       10
-- run this in the aw2008 DB, from another connection?
select lastname, COUNT (*)
from Person.Person_test
group by lastname
order by 2 desc
```

The output of the prior query is not of interest, so it's not shown here. The following query goes back and re examines the cache.

```
-- Check that we got additional objects into the cache
select cacheobjtype, objtype, COUNT (*)
from sys.dm_exec_cached_plans
group by cacheobjtype, objtype
order by cacheobjtype, objtype
```

The output from the above query is shown here:

```
CACHEOBJTYPE       OBJTYPE      (NO COLUMN NAME)
Compiled Plan      Adhoc        9
Compiled Plan      Prepared     2
Compiled Plan      Proc         14
Extended Proc      Proc         2
Parse Tree         View         13
```

At this point you can see that there are four more AdHoc compiled plans, and a number of other new cached objects. The objects you are interested in here are the AdHoc plans.

Run the following T-SQL to get the SQL text and the plan handle for the T-SQL query you ran against the AdventureWorks2008 database:

```
select p.refcounts, p.usecounts, p.plan_handle, s.text
from sys.dm_exec_cached_plans as p
    cross apply sys.dm_exec_sql_text (p.plan_handle) as s
where p.cacheobjtype = 'compiled plan'
and p.objtype = 'adhoc'
order by p.usecounts desc
```

This should give you something similar to the results shown in Figure 5-10.

```
select p.refcounts, p.usecounts, p.plan_handle, s.text
from sys.dm_exec_cached_plans as p cross apply sys.dm_exec_sql_text (p.plan_handle) as s
where p.cacheobjtype = 'compiled plan'
and p.objtype = 'adhoc'
order by p.usecounts desc
```

	refcounts	usecounts	plan_handle	text
6	2	1	0x06000F00EFA2791AB8A0E5100000000000000000000000000	select p.refcounts, p.usecounts, p.plan_handle, s.text from sys.dm...
7	2	1	0x06000F000C6F501CB8C0EE0D00000000000000000000000000	SET STATISTICS XML OFF
8	2	1	0x06000F005163130CB880EE0D00000000000000000000000000	select lastname, COUNT (*) from Person.Person_test group by last...
9	2	1	0x06000F00BA188505B800F60E00000000000000000000000000	SET STATISTICS XML ON
10	2	1	0x0600010080 4AD300B800570E00000000000000000000000000	SELECT dtb.name AS [Name], dtb.database_id AS [ID], CAST(cas...

FIGURE 5-10

To see the execution context, take the plan_handle that you got from the preceding results and plug it into the DMF sys.dm_exec_cached_plan_dependent_objects, as shown in the following example:

```
select *
from sys.dm_exec_cached_plan_dependent_objects
(0x06000F005163130CB880EE0D00000000000000000000000000)
```

The preceding code returned the following results:

```
USECOUNTS MEMORY_OBJECT_ADDRESS CACHEOBJTYPE
1         0x0DF8A038            Executable Plan
```

Another interesting thing you can examine are the attributes of the plan. These are found in the DMF sys.dm_exec_plan_attributes (plan_handle) Note that you need to pass the DMF a plan handle, and then you will get the attributes for that plan:

```
select *
from sys.dm_exec_plan_attributes
(0x06000F00C080471DB8E0691400000000000000000000000000)
```

This gave me a list of 28 attributes, a select few of which are shown here:

```
ATTRIBUTE       VALUE                                              IS_CACHE_KEY
set_options     135419                                             1
objectid        491225280                                          1
dbid            15                                                 1
language_id     0                                                  1
date_format     1                                                  1
date_first      7                                                  1
compat_level    100                                                1
sql_handle      0x02000000C080471DB475BDA81DA97B1C6F2EEA51417711E8 0
```

The sql_handle in these results can then be used in a call to the DMF sys.dm_exec_sql_text(sql_handle) to see the SQL that was being run.

Compilation/Recompilation

Compilation and recompilation are pretty much the same thing, just triggered at slightly different times. When SQL Server decides that an existing plan is no longer valid, which is usually due to a schema change, statistics changes, or some other event, it will re-optimize the plan. This only happens when someone tries to run the query. If they try and run the query when no one else is using the plan, it is a compile event. If this happens when someone else is using a copy of the plan, it is a recompile event.

You can monitor the amount of compilation/recompilation that's occurring by observing the PerfMon Object SQL Server: SQL Statistics and then looking at the following two counters: SQL compilations/sec and SQL recompilations/sec.

Influencing Optimization

There are two main ways you can influence the Query Optimizer — by using *query hints* or *plan guides*.

Query Hints

Query hints are an easy way to influence the actions of query optimization. However, you need to very carefully consider their use, as in most cases SQL Server will already be choosing the right plan. As a general rule, you should avoid using query hints, as they provide many opportunities to cause more issues than the one you are attempting to solve. In some cases, however, such as with complex queries or when dealing with complex datasets that defeat SQL's cardinality estimates on specific queries, using query hints may be necessary.

Before using any query hints, run a web search for the latest information on issues with query hints. Try searching on the keywords "SQL Server Query Hints" and look specifically for anything by Craig Freedman, who has written several great blog entries on some of the issues you can encounter when using query hints.

Problems with using hints can happen at any time — from when you start using the hint, which can cause unexpected side effects that cause the query to fail to compile, to more complex and difficult to find performance issues that occur later.

As data in the relevant tables changes, without query hints the Query Optimizer automatically updates statistics and adjusts query plans as needed; but if you have locked the Query Optimizer into a specific set of optimizations using query hints, then the plan cannot be changed, and you may end up with a considerably worse plan, requiring further action (from you) to identify and resolve the root cause of the new performance issue.

One final word of caution about using query hints: Unlike *locking hints* (also referred to in BOL as *table hints*), which SQL Server attempts to satisfy, query hints are stronger, so if SQL Server is unable to satisfy a query hint it will raise error 8622, and not create any plan.

Query hints are specified using the OPTION clause, which is always added at the end of the T-SQL statement — unlike locking or join hints, which are added within the T-SQL statement after the tables they are to affect.

 Refer to SQL Server 2008 Books Online for a complete list of query hints.

The following sections describe a few of the more interesting query hints.

FAST number_rows

Use this query hint when you want to retrieve only the first *n* rows out of a relatively large result set. A typical example of this is a website that uses paging to display large sets of rows, where the first page shows only the first web page worth of rows, and where a page might contain only 20, 30, or maybe 40 rows. If the query returns thousands of rows, then SQL Server would possibly optimize this query using hash joins, which work well with large datasets but have a higher setup time than perhaps a nested loop join, which has a very low setup cost and can return the first set of rows more quickly but takes considerably longer to return all the rows. Using the FAST <number_rows> query hint causes the Query Optimizer to use nested loop joins and other techniques, rather than hashed joins, to get the first *n* rows faster.

Typically, once the first *n* rows are returned, if the remaining rows are retrieved, then the query performs slower than if this hint were not used.

{Loop | Merge | Hash } JOIN

The JOIN query hint applies to all joins within the query. While this is similar to the join hint that can be specified for an individual join between a pair of tables within a large more complex query, the query hint applies to *all* joins within the query, whereas the join hint applies only to the pair of tables in the join it is associated with.

To see how this works, here is an example query using the AdventureWorks2008 database that joins three tables. The first example shows the basic query with no join hints.

> *These examples include plan details that are discussed in more detail later in this chapter.*

```
use adventureworks2008
go

set statistics profile on
go

select p.title, p.firstname, p.middlename, p.lastname
, a.addressline1, a.addressline2, a.city, a.postalcode
from person.person as p inner join person.businessentityaddress as b
on p.businessentityid = b.businessentityid
inner join person.address as a on b.addressid = a.addressid
go

set statistics profile off
go
```

This returns two result sets. The first is the output from the query, and returns 18,798 rows; the second result set is the additional output after turning on the statistics profile option. One interesting piece of information in the statistics profile output is the totalsubtreecost column. To see the cost for the entire query, look at the top row. On my test machine, this query is costed at 4.647023. The following shows just the `PhysicalOp` column from the statistics profile output, and this shows which operator was used for each step of the plan:

```
PHYSICALOP
NULL
Merge Join
Clustered Index Scan
Sort
Merge Join
Clustered Index Scan
Index Scan
```

This next example shows the same query but illustrates the use of a table hint. In this example the join hint applies only to the join between `person.person` and `person.businessentity`:

```
use adventureworks2008
go

set statistics profile on
go

select p.title, p.firstname, p.middlename, p.lastname
```

```
, a.addressline1, a.addressline2, a.city, a.postalcode
from person.person as p inner loop join person.businessentityaddress as b
on p.businessentityid = b.businessentityid
inner join person.address as a on b.addressid = a.addressid
go

set statistics profile off
go
```

The totalsubtree cost for this option is 8.430738. This is quite a bit higher than the plan that SQL chose, and indicates that our meddling with the optimization process has actually had a negative impact on performance.

The `PhysicalOp` column of the statistics profile output is shown next. This shows that the whole order of the query has been dramatically changed, and that the merge joins have been replaced with a loop join as requested, but this has then forced the Query Optimizer to use a `hash match` join for the other join.

```
PhysicalOp
NULL
Hash Match
Nested Loops
Clustered Index Scan
Clustered Index Seek
Index Scan
```

The final example shows the use of a join query hint. Using this forces both joins within the query to use the join type specified:

```
use adventureworks2008
go

set statistics profile on
go

select p.title, p.firstname, p.middlename, p.lastname
, a.addressline1, a.addressline2, a.city, a.postalcode
from person.person as p inner join person.businessentityaddress as b
on p.businessentityid = b.businessentityid
inner join person.address as a on b.addressid = a.addressid
option (hash join )
go

set statistics profile off
go
```

The total subtreecost for this plan is 5.249676. This is considerably better than the previous option, but still worse than the plan chosen by SQL Server.

The `PhysicalOp` column of the following statistics profile output indicates that both joins are now hash joins:

```
PhysicalOp
NULL
```

```
Hash Match
Hash Match
Index Scan
Clustered Index Scan
Index Scan
```

Using a query hint can cause both compile and run-time issues. The compile-time issues are likely to happen when SQL Server is unable to create a plan due to the query hint. Run-time issues are likely to occur when the data has changed enough such that the Query Optimizer needs to create a new plan using a different join strategy, yet is locked into using the joins defined in the query hint.

MAXDOP *n*

The MAXDOP query hint is only applicable on systems and SQL Server editions for which parallel plans are possible. On single-processor systems, multiprocessor systems where CPU affinity has been set to a single processor, or systems that don't support parallel plans, this query hint has no effect.

On systems where parallel plans are possible, and in the case of a query where a parallel plan is being generated, using MAXDOP (*n*) will allow the Query Optimizer to spawn only *n* workers.

On very large SMPs or NUMA systems, where the SQL Server configuration setting for Max Degree of Parallelism is set to some number less than the total available CPUs, this option can be useful if you want to override the system wide Max Degree of Parallelism setting for a specific query.

A good example of this might be a 16-way SMP server with an application database that needs to service a large number of concurrent users, all running potentially parallel plans. To minimize the impact of any one query, the SQL Server configuration setting Max Degree of Parallelism is set to 4, yet some activities have a higher "priority" and you want to allow them to use all CPUs. An example of this may be some operational activity such as an index rebuild, when you don't want to use an online operation, and want the index to be created as quickly as possible. In this case, the specific queries for index creation/rebuilding can use the MAXDOP 16 query hint, which allows SQL Server to create a plan that will use all 16 processors.

OPTIMIZE FOR

Because of the extensive use of plan parameterization, and the way that the Query Optimizer sniffs for parameters on each execution of a parameterized plan, SQL Server doesn't always do the best job of choosing the right plan for a specific set of parameters.

The OPTIMIZE FOR hint enables you to tell the Query Optimizer what values you expect to see most commonly at runtime. Provided the values you specify are the most common case, this can result in better performance for the majority of the queries, or at least those that match the case you optimized for.

RECOMPILE

The RECOMPILE query hint is a more granular way to force recompilation in a stored procedure than using the WITH RECOMPILE option, which forces the whole stored procedure to be recompiled.

When the Query Optimizer sees the `RECOMPILE` query hint, it forces a new query plan to be created regardless of what plans may already be cached. The new plan is created with the parameters within the current execution context.

This is a very useful option if you know that a particular part of a stored procedure has very different input parameters that can affect the resulting query plan dramatically. Using this option may incur a small cost for the compilation needed on every execution, but if that's a small percentage of the resulting query's execution time, it's a worthwhile cost to pay to ensure that every execution of the query gets the most optimal plan.

For cases in which the additional compilation cost is high relative to the cost of the worst execution, using this query hint would be detrimental to performance.

USE PLAN N 'xml plan'

The `USE PLAN` query hint tells the Query Optimizer that you want a new plan, and that the new plan should match the shape of the plan in the supplied XML plan.

This is very similar to the use of plan guides (covered in the next section), but whereas plan guides don't require a change to the query, the `USE PLAN` query hint does require a change to the T-SQL being submitted to the server.

Sometimes this query hint is used to solve deadlock issues or other data-related problems. However, in nearly all cases the correct course of action is to address the underlying issue, but that often involves architectural changes, or code changes that require extensive development and test work to get into production. In these cases the `USE PLAN` query hint can provide a quick workaround for the DBA to keep the system running while the root cause of a problem is found and fixed.

However, the preceding course of action assumes that you have a "good" XML plan from the problem query that doesn't show the problem behavior. If you just happened to capture a bunch of XML plans from all the queries running on your system when it was working well, then you are good to go. That's not likely something that anyone ever does, as you typically leave systems alone when they are working OK, and capturing XML plans for every query running today just in case you may want to use the `USE PLAN` query hint at some point in the future is not a very useful practice.

What you may be able to do, however, is configure a test system with data such that the plan your target query generates is of the desired shape, capture the XML for the plan, and use that XML plan to "fix" the plan shape on your production server.

Plan Guides

Plan guides, which were added in SQL Server 2005, are a way for the DBA to affect the optimization of a query without altering the query itself. Typically, plan guides are used by DBAs seeking to tune query execution on third-party application databases, where the T-SQL code being executed is proprietary and cannot be changed. Typical examples of applications for which plan guides are most likely to be needed would be large ERP applications such as SAP, PeopleSoft, and so on.

Although plan guides were first added in SQL Server 2005, significant enhancements, primarily regarding ease of use, have been made to them in SQL Server 2008.

There are three different types of plan guide:

➤ **Object plan guide:** Can be applied to a stored procedure, trigger, or user-defined function

➤ **SQL plan guide:** Applied to a specific SQL statement

➤ **Template plan guide:** Provides a way to override database settings for parameterization of specific SQL queries

To make use of plan guides, the first step is to create or capture a "good" plan; the second step is to apply that plan to the object or T-SQL statement for which you want to change the Query Optimizer's behavior.

QUERY PLANS

Now that you have seen how your T-SQL is optimized, the next step is to look at the query plan that the Query Optimizer generated for it.

There are several ways to view query plans, but perhaps the easiest is to view the graphical plan using SQL Server Management Studio (SSMS). SSMS makes this extra easy by providing a context-sensitive menu option that enables you to highlight any piece of T-SQL in a query window and display the estimated execution plan, as shown in Figure 5-11.

This provided the output shown in Figure 5-12.

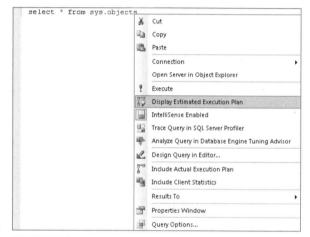

FIGURE 5-11

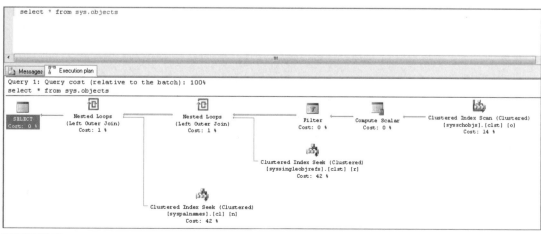

FIGURE 5-12

You can also include SET statements with your query to enable several options that provide additional output that displays the query plan for you. These options are SHOWPLAN_TEXT and SHOWPLAN_ALL. The following code example demonstrates how to use these options:

```
Use Adventureworks2008
go
set showplan_text on
go
select * from person.person
go
set showplan_text off
go
```

Following are the two result sets returned by this query. Note that this is the output after setting the query result options to *results to text*, rather than *results to grid*:

```
StmtText

select * from person.person

(1 row(s) affected)

StmtText
  |--Clustered Index Scan(OBJECT:([AdventureWorks2008].[Person].[Person]
.[PK_Person_BusinessEntityID]))

(1 row(s) affected)
Use Adventureworks2008
go
set showplan_all on
go
select * from person.person
go
set showplan_all off
go
```

Some of the output columns from this query are shown in Figure 5-13.

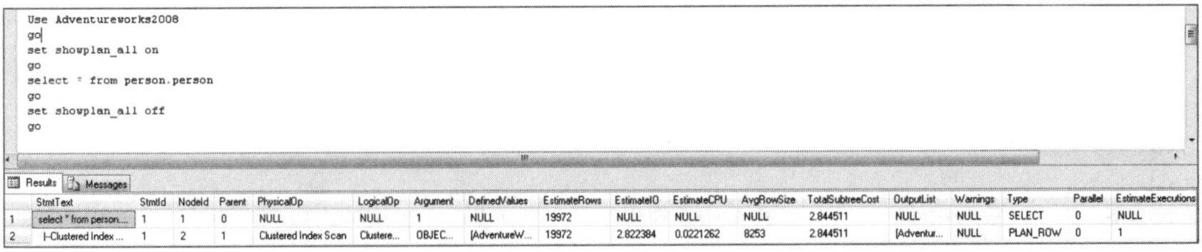

FIGURE 5-13

You can also use SHOWPLAN_XML to get the plan in an XML format:

```
Use Adventureworks2008
go
set showplan_xml on
go
select * from person.person
go
set showplan_xml off
go
```

The results from this query are shown in Figure 5-14.

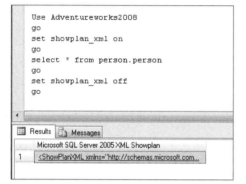

FIGURE 5-14

Clicking on the XML will display the graphical execution plan shown in Figure 5-15.

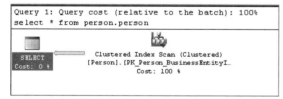

FIGURE 5-15

Another option is STATISTICS_PROFILE. Enabling this option adds statistical information to the showplan. This consists of the actual row count and number of times each operator was run when the query was actually executed:

```
Use Adventureworks2008
go
set statistics profile on
go
select * from person.person
go
set statistics profile off
go
```

Some of the columns' output from this query is shown in Figure 5-16.

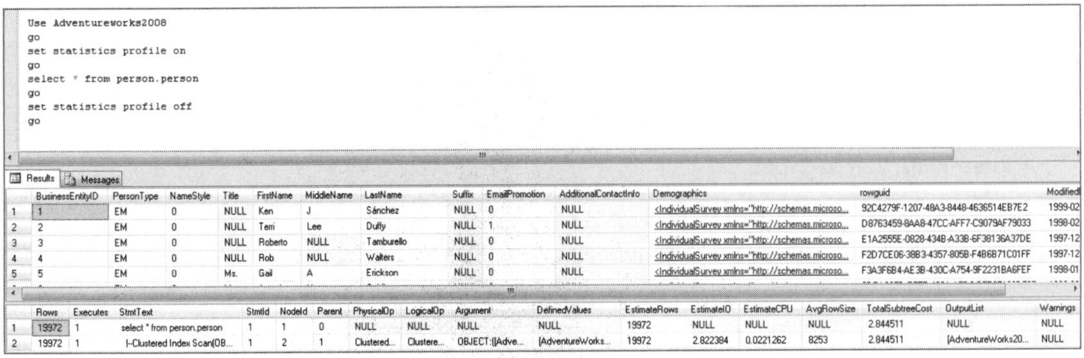

FIGURE 5-16

Another place to look for query plans is in the plan cache itself. When dealing with a lot of queries on a busy production system, it's often necessary to find the query plan for a particular query that's currently being used. To do this, use the following T-SQL to return either the XML for the plan or the text of the plan.

```
Select *
From sys.dm_exec_query_plan(plan_handle)

Select *
From sys.dm_exec_text_query_plan(plan_handle)
```

Note that you can use two DMFs here: One refers to returning the XML plan, whereas the other implies it will return the text of the plan, suggesting it would be similar to the showplan_text output, but in fact both return the XML format of the plan. The difference is that the data type of the query_plan column in one is XML, whereas the data type in the other result set is text.

Query Plan Operators

The Query Optimizer can use many different operators to create your plan. Covering them all is beyond the scope of this book, so this section instead focuses on some examples demonstrating the most common operators you will come across. For a full list of operators, refer to SQL Server Books Online (SQL BOL). Search for topics such as "graphical execution plan icons" or "logical and physical operators reference."

Join Operators

Join operators enable SQL Server to find matching rows between two tables. Prior to SQL Server 2005, there was only a single join type, the *nested loop join*, but since then additional join types have been added, and SQL Server now provides the three join types described in Table 5-1. These join types deal with rows from two tables; for a self-join, the inputs may be different sets of rows from the same table.

TABLE 5-1: SQL Server Join Types

JOIN TYPE	BENEFIT
Nested loop	Good for small tables where there is an index on the inner table on the join key
Merge join	Good for medium-size tables where there are ordered indexes, or where the output needs to be ordered
Hash join	Good for medium to large tables. Works well with parallel plans, and scales well.

Nested Loop

The nested loop join is the original SQL Server join type. The behavior of a nested loop is to scan all the rows in one table (the outer table) and for each row in that table, it then scans every row in the other table (the inner table). If the rows in the outer and inner tables match, then the row is included in the results.

The performance of this join is directly proportional to the number of rows in each table. It performs well when there are relatively few rows in one of the tables, which would be chosen as the inner table, and more rows in the other table, which would then be chosen as the outer table. If both tables have a relatively large number of rows, then this join starts to take a very long time.

Merge

The merge join needs its inputs to be sorted, so ideally the tables should be indexed on the join column. Then the operator iterates through rows from both tables at the same time, working down the rows, looking for matches. Because the inputs are ordered, this enables the join to proceed quickly, and to end as soon as any range is satisfied.

Hash

The hash join operates in two phases. During the first phase, known as the *build phase*, the smaller of the two tables is scanned and the rows are placed into a hash table that is ideally stored in memory, but for very large tables, it can be written to disk. When every row in the build input table is hashed, the second phase starts. During the second phase, known as the *probe phase*, rows from the larger of the two tables are compared to the contents of the hash table, using the same hashing algorithm that was used to create the build table hash. Any matching rows are passed to the output.

The hash join has variations on this processing that can deal with very large tables, and therefore the hash join is the join of choice for very large input tables, especially when running on multiprocessor systems where parallel plans are allowed.

HASH WARNINGS

Hash warnings are SQL Profiler events that are generated when hash recursion, or hash bailout, occurs. Hash recursion happens when the output from the has operation doesn't fit entirely in memory. Hash bailout occurs when hash recursion reaches its max level of recursion, and a new plan has to be chosen.

Anytime you see hash warnings, it a potential indicator of performance problems, and should be investigated.

Possible solutions to hash warnings are to:

➤ Increase memory on the server.

➤ Make sure statistics exist on the join columns.

➤ Make sure statistics are current.

➤ Force a different type of join.

Spool Operators

The various spool operators are used to create a temporary copy of rows from the input stream and deliver them to the output stream. Spools typically sit between two other operators: The one on the right is the child, and provides the input stream. The operator on the left is the parent, and consumes the output stream.

The following list provides a brief description of each of the physical spool operators. These are the operators that actually execute. You may also see references to *logical operators*, which represent an earlier stage in the optimization process, and are subsequently converted to physical operators before executing the plan.

➤ **Non-clustered index spool:** This operator reads rows from the child table, places them in tempdb, and creates a non-clustered index on them before continuing. This enables the parent to take advantage of seeking against the non-clustered index on the data in tempdb when the underlying table has no applicable indexes.

➤ **Row count spool:** This operator reads rows from the child table and counts the rows. The rows are also returned to the parent, but without any data. This enables the parent to determine whether rows exist in order to satisfy an EXISTS or NOT EXISTS requirement.

➤ **Table spool:** This operator reads the rows from the child table and writes them into tempdb. All rows from the child are read and placed in tempdb before the parent can start processing rows.

Scan and Seek Operators

These operators enable SQL Server to retrieve rows from tables and indexes when a larger number of rows is required. This behavior contrasts with the individual row access operators *key lookup* and *RID lookup*, which are discussed in the next section.

➤ **Scan operator:** The scan operator scans all the rows in the table looking for matching rows. When the number of matching rows is > 20 percent of the table, scan can start to outperform seek due to the additional cost of traversing the index to reach each row for the seek.

There are scan operator variants for clustered index scan, non-clustered index scan, and table scan.

➤ **Seek operator:** The seek operator uses the index to find matching rows — either a single value, a small set of values, or a range of values. When the query needs only a relatively small set of rows, seek is significantly faster than scan to find matching rows. However, when the number of rows returned exceeds 20 percent of the table, the cost of seek will approach that of scan; and where nearly the whole table is required, scan will perform better than seek.

There are seek operator variants for clustered index seek and non-clustered index seek.

Lookup Operators

Lookup operators perform the task of finding a single row of data. The following is a list of common operators:

➤ **Bookmark lookup:** Bookmark lookup is only seen in SQL Server 2000 and earlier. It's the way that SQL Server looks up a row using a clustered index. In SQL Server 2005 and later, this is done using either key lookup or RID lookup.

➤ **Key lookup:** Key lookup is how a single row is returned when the table has a clustered index. In contrast with dealing with a heap, the lookup is done using the clustering key. The key lookup operator was added in SQL Server 2005 SP2. Prior to this, and currently when viewing the plan in text or XML format, the operator is shown as a clustered index seek with the keyword lookup.

➤ **RID lookup:** RID lookup is how a single row is looked up in a heap. RID refers to the internal unique *row id*entifier (hence RID), which is used to look up the row.

Reading Query Plans

Unlike reading a typical book such as this one, whereby reading is done from top left to bottom right (unless you're reading a translation where the language is read in reverse), query plans in all forms are read bottom right to top left.

Once you have downloaded and installed the sample database, to make the examples more interesting you will need to remove some of the indexes that the authors of AdventureWorks added for you. To do this, you can use either your favorite T-SQL scripting tool or the SSMS scripting features, or run the `AV2008_person_drop_indexes.sql` sample script (available on the book's website in the

Chapter 5 Samples folder) This script drops all the indexes on the person.person table except for the primary key constraint.

After you have done this, you can follow along with the examples, and you should see the same results.

> *Because you are looking at the inner workings of the Query Optimizer, and because this is a feature of SQL Server that is constantly evolving, installing any service pack or patch can alter the behavior of the Query Optimizer, and therefore display different results.*

You will begin by looking at some trivial query plans, beginning with a view of the graphical plans but quickly switching to using the text plan features, as these are easier to compare against one another, especially when you start looking at larger plans from more complex queries.

Here is the first trivial query you will examine:

```
select firstname, COUNT (*)
from Person.Person
group by firstname
order by COUNT (*) desc
```

After running this in SSMS after enabling the "Show Execution Plan" option, three tabs are displayed. The first is the results, but the one you are interested in now is the third tab, which shows the graphical execution plan for this query.

You should see something like the image shown in Figure 5-17.

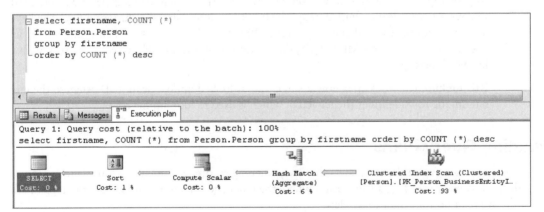

FIGURE 5-17

Starting at the bottom right, you can see that the first operator is the clustered index scan operator. While the query doesn't need, or get any benefit from, a clustered index, because the table has a clustered index and is not a heap, this is the option that SQL Server chooses to read through all the rows in the table. If you had removed the clustered index, so that this table was a heap, then this operator would be replaced by a table scan operator. The action performed by both operators in this case is identical, which is to read every row from the table and deliver them to the next operator.

The next operator is the hash match. In this case, SQL Server is using this to sort the rows into buckets by first name. After the hash match is the compute scalar, where SQL Server counts the number of rows in each hash bucket, which gives you the count (*) value in the results. This is followed by the sort operator, which is there to provide the ordered output needed from the T-SQL.

You can find additional information on each operation by hovering over the operator. Figure 5-18 shows the additional information available on the clustered index scan operator.

While this query seems pretty trivial, and you may have thought it would generate a trivial plan because of the grouping and ordering, this is not a trivial plan. You can tell this by monitoring the results of the following query before and after running it:

Clustered Index Scan (Clustered)	
Scanning a clustered index, entirely or only a range.	
Physical Operation	Clustered Index Scan
Logical Operation	Clustered Index Scan
Actual Number of Rows	19972
Estimated I/O Cost	2.82246
Estimated CPU Cost	0.0220477
Number of Executions	1
Estimated Number of Executions	1
Estimated Operator Cost	2.84451 (93%)
Estimated Subtree Cost	2.84451
Estimated Number of Rows	19972
Estimated Row Size	22 B
Actual Rebinds	0
Actual Rewinds	0
Ordered	False
Node ID	3
Object	
[AdventureWorks2008].[Person].[Person].	
[PK_Person_BusinessEntityID]	
Output List	
[AdventureWorks2008].[Person].[Person].FirstName	

FIGURE 5-18

```
select *
from sys.dm_exec_query_optimizer_info
where counter in (
'optimizations'
, 'trivial plan'
, 'search 0'
, 'search 1'
, 'search 2'
)
order by [counter]
```

Once the query has been optimized and cached, subsequent runs will not generate any updates to the Query Optimizer stats unless you flush the procedure cache using `dbcc freeproccache`.

On the machine I am using, the following results were returned from this query against the Query Optimizer information before I ran the sample query:

```
COUNTER          OCCURRENCE   VALUE
optimizations    10059        1
search 0         1017         1
search 1         3385         1
search 2         1            1
trivial plan     5656         1
```

And then again after I ran the sample query:

```
COUNTER          OCCURRENCE  VALUE
optimizations    10061       1
search 0         1017        1
search 1         3387        1
search 2         1           1
trivial plan     5656        1
```

From this you can see that the trivial plan count didn't increment, but the search 1 count did increment, indicating that this query needed to move onto phase 1 of the optimization process before an acceptable plan was found.

If you want to play around with this query to see what a truly trivial plan would be, try running the following:

```
select lastname
from person.person
```

The following T-SQL demonstrates what the same plan looks like in text mode:

```
set statistics profile on
go

select firstname, COUNT (*)
from Person.Person
group by firstname
order by 2 desc
go

set statistics profile off
go
```

When you run this batch, rather than see a third tab displayed in SSMS, you will see that there are now two result sets in the query's Results tab. The first is the output from running the query, and the second is the text output for this plan, which looks something like what is shown in Figure 5-19.

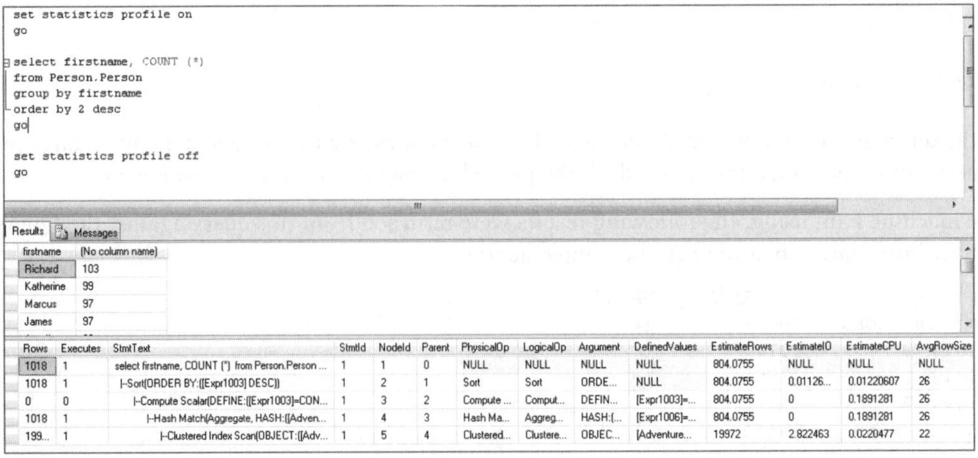

FIGURE 5-19

Figure 5-19 shows only some of the columns in the result set, as there are too many columns returned to fit onto a single screen.

The following example shows some of the content of the `StmtText` column, which illustrates what the query plan looks like, just as in the graphical plan but this time in a textual format:

```
   |--Sort(ORDER BY:())
        |--Compute Scalar(DEFINE:())
             |--Hash Match(Aggregate, HASH:( [FirstName]),
RESIDUAL:([FirstName] = [FirstName]) DEFINE:( COUNT(*)))
                  |--Clustered Index Scan(OBJECT:( [PK_Person_BusinessEntityID]))
```

The preceding output has been selectively edited to fit into the available space.

As mentioned before, this is read from the bottom up. You can see that the first operator is the clustered index scan, which is the same operator shown in Figure 5-12. From there (working up), the next operator is the hash match, followed by the compute scalar operator, and then the sort operator.

While the query you examined may seem pretty simple, you have seen how even for this query, the Query Optimizer has quite a bit of work to do. As a follow-up exercise, try adding one index at a time back into the Person table, and examine the plan you get each time a new index is added. One hint as to what you will see is to add the index `IX_Person_Lastname_firstname_middlename` first.

From there you can start to explore with simple table joins, and look into when SQL Server chooses each of the three join operators it offers: nested loop, merge, and hash joins.

EXECUTING YOUR QUERIES

So far in this chapter, you have learned how SQL Server parses, algebrizes, and optimizes the T-SQL you want to run. Now you will learn how SQL Server executes the query plan. First, however, you have to step back a little and look at the larger picture — namely, how SQL Server architecture changes with SQL Server 2005 and the introduction of SQLOS.

SQLOS

SQL Server 2005 underwent a major change in the underlying architecture with the introduction of SQLOS. This component provides basic services to the other SQL Server components, such as the Relational Engine, the Storage Engine, and so on. This architecture is illustrated in the diagram shown in Figure 5-20.

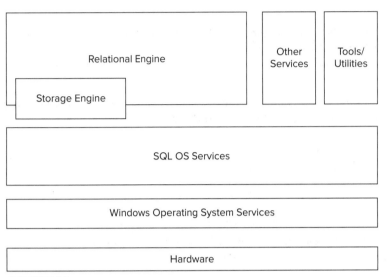

FIGURE 5-20

The main services provided by SQLOS are scheduling, which is where our main interest lies, and memory management, which we also have an interest in because the memory management services are where the procedure cache lives, and that's where our query plans live. SQLOS also provides many more services that are not relevant to the current discussion. For more details on the other services provided by SQLOS, refer to Chapter 1 or SQL Server Books Online.

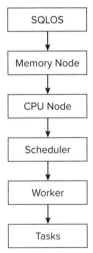

SQLOS implements a hierarchy of system objects that provide the framework for scheduling. Figure 5-21 shows the basic hierarchy of these objects — from the parent node SQLOS down to the workers, tasks, and OS threads where the work is actually performed.

The starting point for scheduling and memory allocation is the memory node.

Memory Nodes

The SQLOS memory node is a logical container for memory associated with a node, which is a collection of CPUs with shared memory. This can be either a "real" memory node, if the server has a NUMA architecture, or an artificial grouping that you created as a "soft" NUMA configuration. Refer back to the section on System Architecture for more details on NUMA vs. SMP systems.

FIGURE 5-21

Along with the memory nodes created to model the physical hardware of the server, there is always one additional memory node used by the dedicated administrator connection (DAC). This ensures that some resources are always available to service the DAC, even when all other system resources are being used.

On an eight-processor SMP system without soft NUMA, there would be one memory node for general server use, and one for the DAC. This is illustrated in Figure 5-22.

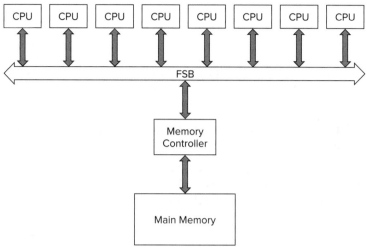

FIGURE 5-22

On an eight-processor NUMA system with two nodes of four cores, there would be two memory nodes. This is illustrated in Figure 5-23.

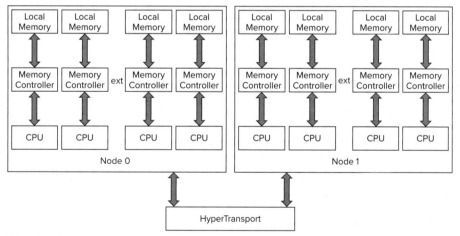

FIGURE 5-23

By querying the DMV sys.dm_os_memory_nodes, you can view the layout of memory nodes on your server. However, it makes more sense to include the node state description column from sys.dm_os_nodes using this query. Note the join between node_id in sys.dm_os_nodes and memory_node_id in sys.dm_os_memory_nodes:

```
select c.node_id, c.memory_node_id, m.memory_node_id, c.node_state_desc
, c.cpu_affinity_mask, m.virtual_address_space_reserved_kb
from sys.dm_os_nodes as c inner join sys.dm_os_memory_nodes as m
on c.node_id = m.memory_node_id
```

Here is the output from this query when run on a 16-way SMP server:

NODE_ID	MEMORY_NODE_ID	MEMORY_NODE_ID	NODE_STATE_DESC	CPU_AFFINITY_MASK	VIRTUAL_ ADDRESS_ SPACE_ RESERVED_KB
0	0	0	ONLINE	65535	67544440
64	0	64	ONLINE DAC	0	2560

In this case, Node 0 has nearly all the 64GB of memory on this server reserved, and Node 64 is reserved for the DAC, which has just 2.5MB of memory reserved.

Following is the output from this query on a 192-processor NUMA system. The server is structured as eight NUMA nodes. Each NUMA node has four sockets, and each socket has six cores (using Intel Xeon hexa-core processors), resulting in 24 cores per NUMA node:

NODE_ID	MEMORY_NODE_ID	MEMORY_NODE_ID	NODE_STATE_DESC	CPU_AFFINITY_MASK	VIRTUAL_ ADDRESS_ SPACE_ RESERVED_KB
0	0	0	ONLINE	16777215	268416
1	1	1	ONLINE	16777215	248827056
2	2	2	ONLINE	16777215	22464
3	3	3	ONLINE	16777215	8256
4	4	4	ONLINE	281474959933440	11136
5	5	5	ONLINE	281474959933440	4672
6	6	6	ONLINE	281474959933440	4672
7	7	7	ONLINE	281474959933440	5120
64	0	64	ONLINE DAC	0	2864

Soft NUMA

In some scenarios, you may be able to work with an SMP server and still get the benefit of having a NUMA-type structure with SQL Server. You can achieve this by using *soft NUMA*. This enables you to use Registry settings to tell SQL Server that it should configure itself as a NUMA system, using the CPU-to-memory-node mapping that you specify.

As with anything that requires Registry changes, you need to take exceptional care, and be sure you have backup and rollback options at every step of the process.

One common use for soft NUMA is when a SQL Server is hosting an application that has several different groups of users with very different query requirements. After configuring your theoretical 16-processor server for soft NUMA, assigning 2 × 4 CPU nodes and one 8-CPU node to a third NUMA node, you would next configure connection affinity for the three nodes to different ports, and then change the connection settings for each class of workload, so that workload A is "affinitized" to port x, which connects to the first NUMA node; workload B is affinitized to port y, which connects to the second NUMA node, and all other workloads are affinitized to port z, which is set to connect to the third NUMA node.

CPU Nodes

A CPU node is a logical collection of CPUs that share some common resource, such as a cache or memory. CPU nodes live below memory nodes in the SQLOS object hierarchy.

Whereas a memory node may have one or more CPU nodes associated with it, a CPU node can be associated with only a single memory node. However, in practice, nearly all configurations have a 1:1 relationship between memory nodes and CPU nodes.

CPU nodes can be seen in the DMV sys.dm_os_nodes. Use the following query to return select columns from this DMV:

```
select node_id, node_state_desc, memory_node_id, cpu_affinity_mask
from sys.dm_os_nodes
```

The results from this query, when run on a single-CPU system are as follows:

NODE_ID	NODE_STATE_DESC	MEMORY_NODE_ID	CPU_AFFINITY_MASK
0	ONLINE	0	1
32	ONLINE DAC	0	0

The results from the previous query, when run on a 96-processor NUMA system, comprising four nodes of four sockets, each socket with six cores, totaling 24 cores per NUMA node, and 96 cores across the whole server are as follows:

NODE_ID	NODE_STATE_DESC	MEMORY_NODE_ID	CPU_AFFINITY_MASK
0	ONLINE	1	16777215
1	ONLINE	0	281474959933440
2	ONLINE	2	16777215
3	ONLINE	3	281474959933440
64	ONLINE DAC	0	16777215

> The hex values for the cpu_affinity_mask *values in this table are as follows:*
>
> 16777215 = 0x00FFFFFF
>
> 281474959933440 = 0x0F000001000000FFFFFF0000
>
> *This indicates which processor cores each CPU node can use.*

Processor Affinity

CPU affinity is a way to force a workload to use specific CPUs. It's another way that you can affect scheduling and SQL Server SQLOS configuration.

CPU affinity can be managed at several levels. Outside SQL Server, you can use the operating system's CPU affinity settings to restrict the CPUs that SQL Server as a process can use. Within SQL Server's configuration settings, you can specify that SQL Server should use only certain CPUs. This is done using the *affinity mask* and *affinity64 mask* configuration options. Changes to these two options are applied dynamically, which means that schedulers on CPUs that are either enabled or disabled while SQL is running will be affected immediately. Schedulers associated with CPUs that are disabled will be drained and set to offline. Schedulers associated with CPUs that are enabled will be set to online, and will be available for scheduling workers and executing new tasks.

You can also set SQL Server I/O affinity using the affinity I/O mask option. This option enables you to force any I/O-related activities to run only on a specified set of CPUs. Using connection affinity as described earlier in the section "Soft NUMA," you can affinitize network connections to a specific memory node.

Schedulers

The scheduler node is where the work of scheduling activity occurs. Scheduling occurs against *tasks*, which are the requests to do some work handled by the scheduler. One task may be the optimized query plan that represents the T-SQL you want to execute; or, in the case of a batch with multiple T-SQL statements, the task would represent a single optimized query from within the larger batch.

When SQL Server starts up, it creates one scheduler for each CPU that it finds on the server, and some additional schedulers to run other system tasks. If processor affinity is set such that some CPUs are not enabled for this instance, then the schedulers associated with those CPUs will be set to a disabled state. This enables SQL Server to support dynamic affinity settings.

While there is one scheduler per CPU, schedulers are not bound to a specific CPU, except in the case where CPU affinity has been set.

Each scheduler is identified by its own unique scheduler_id. Values from 0–254 are reserved for schedulers running user requests. Scheduler_id 255 is reserved for the scheduler for the dedicated administrator connection (DAC). Schedulers with a scheduler_id > 255 are reserved for system use and are typically assigned the same task.

The following code sample shows select columns from the DMV sys.dm_os_schedulers:

```
select parent_node_id, scheduler_id, cpu_id, status, scheduler_address
from sys.dm_os_schedulers
order by scheduler_id
```

The following results from the preceding query indicate that scheduler_id 0 is the only scheduler with an id < 255, which implies that these results came from a single-core machine. You can also see a scheduler with an id of 255, which has a status of VISIBLE ONLINE (DAC), indicating that this is the scheduler for the DAC. Also shown are three additional schedulers with IDs > 255. These are the schedulers reserved for system use.

PARENT_NODE_ID	SCHEDULER_ID	CPU_ID	STATUS	SCHEDULER_ADDRESS
0	0	0	VISIBLE ONLINE	0x00480040
32	255	0	VISIBLE ONLINE (DAC)	0x03792040
0	257	0	HIDDEN ONLINE	0x006A4040
0	258	0	HIDDEN ONLINE	0x64260040
0	259	0	HIDDEN ONLINE	0x642F0040

Tasks

A task is a request to do some unit of work. The task itself doesn't do anything, as it's just a container for the unit of work to be done. To actually do something, the task has to be scheduled by one of the schedulers, and associated with a particular worker. It's the worker that actually does something, and you will learn about workers in the next section.

Tasks can be seen in the DMV `sys.dm_os_tasks`. The following example shows a query of this DMV:

```
Select *
from sys.dm_os_tasks
```

The task is the container for the work that's being done, but if you look into `sys.dm_os_tasks`, there is no sign of what work is being done. Figuring out what each task is doing takes a little more digging. First, dig out the request_id. This is the key into the DMV `sys.dm_exec_requests`. Within `sys.dm_exec_requests` you will find some familiar fields — namely, sql_handle, along with statement_start_offset, statement_end_offset, and plan_handle. You can take either sql_handle or plan_handle and feed them into `sys.dm_exec_sql_text( plan_handle | sql_handle )` and get back the original T-SQL that is being executed:

```
Select t.task_address, s.text
From sys.dm_os_tasks as t inner join sys.dm_exec_requests as r
on t.task_address = r.task_address
Cross apply sys.dm_exec_sql_text (r.plan_handle) as s
where r.plan_handle is not null
```

Workers

A worker is where the work actually gets done, and the work it does is contained within the task. Workers can be seen in the DMV `sys.dm_os_workers`:

```
Select *
From sys.dm_os_workers
```

Some of the more interesting columns in this DMV are the following:

➤ **Task_address:** Allows you to join back to the task, and from there back to the actual request, and get the text that is being executed

➤ **State:** Shows the current state of the worker

➤ **Last_wait_type:** Shows the last wait type that this worker was waiting on

➤ **Scheduler_address:** Joins back to `sys.dm_os_schedulers`

Threads

To complete the picture, SQLOS also contains objects for the operating system threads it is using. OS threads can be seen in the DMV `sys.dm_os_threads`:

```
Select *
From sys.dm_os_threads
```

Interesting columns in this DMV are the following:

➤ **Scheduler_address:** Address of the scheduler that this thread is associated with

➤ **Worker_address:** Address of the worker currently associated with this thread.

➤ **Kernel_time:** Amount of kernel time that this thread has used since it was started

➤ **Usermode_time:** Amount of user time that the thread has used since it was started

Scheduling

Now that you have seen all the objects that SQLOS uses to manage scheduling, and know how to look at what's going on within these structures, it's time to look at how SQL OS actually schedules work.

One of the main things to understand about scheduling within SQL Server is that it uses a non-preemptive scheduling model, unless the task being run is not SQL Server code. In that case, SQL Server marks the task to indicate that it needs to be scheduled preemptively. An example of code that might be marked to be scheduled preemptively would be any code that wasn't written by SQL Server that gets to run inside the SQL Server process, so this would apply to any CLR code.

PREEMPTIVE VS. NON-PREEMPTIVE SCHEDULING

With preemptive scheduling, the scheduling code manages how long the code can run before interrupting it, giving some other task a chance to run.

The advantage of preemptive scheduling is that the developer doesn't need to think about yielding; the scheduler takes care of it. The disadvantage is that the code can be interrupted and prevented from running at any arbitrary point, which may result in the task running more slowly than possible. In addition, providing an environment that offers preemptive scheduling features also requires a lot of work.

With non-preemptive scheduling, the code that's being run is written to yield control at key points. At these yield points, the scheduler can determine whether a different task should be run.

The advantage of non-preemptive scheduling is that the code running knows best when it should be interrupted. The disadvantage is that if the developer doesn't yield at the appropriate points, then the task may run for an excessive amount of time, retaining control of a CPU when it's waiting. In this case, the task blocks other tasks from running, wasting CPU resources.

SQL Server begins to schedule a task when a new request is received, after the Query Optimizer has completed its work arriving at the best plan. A task object is created for this user request, and the scheduling starts from there.

The newly created task object has to be associated with a free worker in order to actually do anything. When the worker is associated with the new task, the worker's status is set to *init*. When the initial setup has been done, the status changes to *runnable*. At this point, the worker is ready to go but there isn't a free scheduler to allow this worker to run. The worker state remains as runnable until a scheduler is available. When the scheduler is available, the worker is associated with that scheduler, and the status changes to *running*. It remains running until either it is done or it releases control while it waits for something to be done. When it releases control of the scheduler, its state moves to *suspended* (the reason it released control is logged as a wait_type. See Chapter 3 for more information). When the item it was waiting on is available again, the status of the worker is changed to runnable. Now it's back to waiting for a free scheduler again, and the cycle repeats until the task is complete.

At that point, the task is released, the worker is released, and the scheduler is available to be associated with the next worker that needs to run. The state diagram for scheduling workers is shown in Figure 5-24.

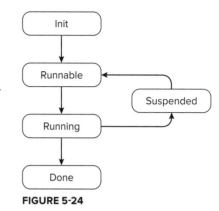

FIGURE 5-24

SUMMARY

This chapter discussed the hardware details of different processors, and looked at some of the details that differentiate different processors. You learned about the differences between SMP and NUMA architectures, how SQL Server uses CPU resources, and some of the things that SQL can do that use more CPU resources. You also learned about query execution, including the optimization process and some of the operators used by the Query Optimizer, and then you took a look at query plans, including the different ways that you can examine them, and how to read them. Finally, you learned about the objects that SQLOS uses to manage scheduling, and how scheduling works.

Some key points you should take away from this chapter include the following:

➤ The CPU is core to everything that happens on a modern computer system.

➤ Hyperthreading can provide additional CPU resources, but you have to consider its use carefully.

➤ AMD processors and the associated system architecture is typically NUMA.

➤ Intel processors before the latest Nehalem family had a SMP system architecture. Now with the Nehalem family they will have a NUMA architecture.

➤ SQL Server uses cost based optimization to find what it thinks is a good enough plan. This won't always be the best plan.

➤ Statistics are a vital part of the optimization process

➤ There are many factors that influence how SQL Server chooses a query plan.

➤ You can alter the plan chosen using a variety of plan hints, and other configuration settings.

6

Locking and Latches

WHAT'S IN THIS CHAPTER

➤ SQL Server's transactional model, with particular focus on isolation

➤ Locking internals and architecture

➤ Extensive coverage of both pessimistic and optimistic concurrency

➤ An analysis of the internals of SQL Server's version store

➤ An in-depth look at latches

Ask yourself this question: What is a lock trying to achieve? Any process that your application has to go through prior to getting to the data represents added overhead, so what is a lock's purpose?

In Chapter 1 the ACID properties of a transaction were described as the stepping-stone for understanding the life span of a query. The chapter then walked you step-by-step through an example of the sequence of events that a solitary select would need to negotiate prior to a user receiving data. This was followed by a similar pattern for the next example, that of an update. These examples were run through sequentially, as you'd expect in a book, and so the data from one query to the next was always isolated from the other as each query took its turn to execute. In this scenario there is no need for locking; a single view of the data is maintained by synchronously executing the examples.

However, suppose there were 10 different queries in the chapter, or 100 or even 1,000, but this time they are all running at once. Imagine if everyone reading the book at this very moment (here's hoping that's a lot of people) were sending their example queries to a central database. Everyone would be reading and writing data, accessing and updating the same data, all at the same time. How do you keep a single view of the data now?

Do queries form an orderly line before acting on data if they have noticed that someone else is in front? Queries aren't British! An unruly bunch, they don't like to queue, and won't if you let them. Queries are like the infamous car drivers in the city of Rome. They will go as fast as they can to achieve their goal, cutting any permitted corner possible in order to do so. What's needed, and what SQL Server provides, is a traffic officer, aka the *lock manager*.

The streets of Rome are given order by the Italian traffic police, the *vigili urbani*, who keep the traffic flowing. However, they also need to keep everyone safe. Maximum safety can be ensured by only allowing one person to use a junction at a time. Unfortunately, the safer and therefore the more isolated the cars are, the slower the process becomes. As the number of drivers increases, the situation becomes less acceptable to those left waiting, and soon becomes untenable. Everyone wants to navigate the junction at the same time — they want *concurrent* access to the junction.

Ultimately, there needs to be a trade-off between safety and practicality. The *vigili* therefore reduce the safety level for increased throughput and greater *concurrency* by allowing more than one driver to use the junction at the same time. Though drivers want to achieve different goals when using the junction, if their intent doesn't conflict with one another, all is well. Otherwise, the drivers' actions must be sequenced to avoid a collision or crash.

SQL Server is somewhat analogous to this. Rather than cars, SQL Server uses transactions to marshal activity in the database. Transactions must exhibit the four ACID properties. This chapter revisits them shortly to see how they apply to locking. One of these properties in particular is all about SQL Server "road safety" — the isolation property.

In order to isolate one's data (and keep it safe), SQL Server implements a number of isolation levels from which you can choose. These are discussed in detail later in the chapter. For now, understand that in general terms, the higher the isolation level used by the transaction, the greater the risk of impact on the level of *concurrency* that can be achieved.

SQL Server needs to provide highly concurrent access to data. Its "attitude" to concurrency is critical to understanding how locking works and what options you have when developing your applications. When transactional volume isn't high, locking might never be a problem; but on a busy system, the decisions you made when designing your system with regard to concurrency may well be the difference between a highly concurrent system and a single-user application! Concurrency, in a SQL Server context, is defined early on in the chapter, as it is a fundamental precursor to understanding SQL Server's locking architecture.

The chapter concludes with a good look at SQL Server's other locking mechanism: latches. Not much is understood or written about latches with regard to locking. However, at scale these can be the blighters that stand between you and a highly concurrent scalable system. In breaking the Extract, Transform, and Load (ETL) world record with SQL Server Integration Services (SSIS), the SQL Server Customer Advisory Team (SQLCAT) encountered a number of latch issues. The reason for including latches in this chapter is to improve your general understanding of latches, recognize their value and purpose, and aid you in troubleshooting scenarios.

However, before looking at latches or how SQL Server delivers highly concurrent data access, you should first baseline your knowledge in relation to transactions, which underpin pretty much everything in SQL Server. Without transactions there wouldn't be any need for locks or latches because there wouldn't be any feature driving a requirement to have them. Everyone would happily overwrite each other's data though, so I am glad they exist.

TRANSACTIONS

According to Wikipedia, a transaction is "a unit of work performed within a database management system (or similar system) against a database, and treated in a coherent and reliable way independent of other transactions." That's a bit of a mouthful but basically hits the spot. Simply put, transactions exist to group individual operations into a single logical unit of work. However, in order for a transaction to be deemed valid, it must exhibit the four ACID properties.

Transactions are also essentially dumb. They do what they are told and ask no questions; they provide a wrapper to a set of instructions that logically must either all succeed or fail. It is therefore your responsibility as a programmer to ensure that they are coded correctly and perform optimally. No warnings are issued that the design of a transaction could result in a long-running, resource-intensive beast that will severely impact the server. You must do all this work yourself.

So what does SQL Server provide? If you are doing all the work, what are you getting from the relational database management system (RDBMS)? Well, the role of the RDBMS is to persist whatever we encapsulate in the transaction so that we may retrieve it later — guaranteed. You also want the RDBMS to ensure that the data in the integer columns represent numbers in a valid range, and it would be very nice if it could ensure that the colleague sitting next to you doesn't destroy your work before it was finished. SQL Server does all these things because it delivers the ACID properties against any accepted type of transaction.

Let's briefly revisit the acid properties now, paying special attention to how they relate to the physical integrity of the data and, of course, locking. Feel free to skip this section if you are already well versed in the world of ACIDity. I won't hold it against you.

Atomic

The first transactional property is atomicity, which means that the set of operations contained within the transaction must be treated as a whole. The set is either atomic or it isn't. A partially complete transaction cannot be committed.

SQL Server provides this level of transaction management by guaranteeing that only complete transactions are committed. How does this affect locking? In order to allow for the transaction to be rolled back, and therefore be atomic in nature, modification locks must be held for the duration of the transaction.

Consistent

The second property that a transaction must support is consistency. The database must be in a consistent state both before the transaction begins and after the transaction has completed, irrespective of whether the transaction was a success (and therefore committed) or a failure (and therefore rolled back).

What affects consistency of data? Only valid data should make it into the database. If an insert violates a check constraint or the referential integrity of the table in question, then the transaction must be rolled back or a compensating action in the transaction must take place. The Data Definition Language (DDL) of the database determines its consistency, and SQL Server ensures that any rules imposed in the DDL are adhered to. The data must move from one consistent state to another consistent state.

Isolated

The third ACID property is isolation. SQL Server can address a great number of concurrent requests, but all users should feel like they are the only person on the system. This issue isn't one of performance, but rather one relating to the state of the data.

For example, if, as a user, you read a value in a table and that value equals 2, you expect the answer of a subsequent read in the same transaction to also be 2. If this behavior is desired (known as a repeatable read), then all other queries that want to look at this value would need to wait for your transaction to complete before gaining access to the value.

The requirement to be able to repeatedly read the same value can place a significant overhead on the concurrency of the database. In order to support this type of behavior, any lock taken would need to be held for the full duration of the transaction. This in turn affects the time that other users of the system have to wait before SQL Server can process their queries. It does, however, give you the feeling that you are the only person on the system.

Interestingly, the isolation property is also the most flexible of the four properties. In other words, you can augment its behavior.

The preceding example uses a single transaction that repeatedly reads a single value. The isolation level set when executing the transaction determines whether or not the value read back is guaranteed to be the same with each read. By altering the isolation level, you can change this behavior. For example, it could be set such that other queries could execute and change a value between your reads. This improves concurrency (as two queries are now running at the same time), but at the cost of the transaction's isolation. Instead of reading a 2, as you might expect, the value might now be 5.

Durable

The fourth and final property that a transaction must be able to support is that of durability. That is, when the transaction is committed, it stays committed. Even if the SQL Server fails one picosecond after the commit has gone through, that transaction must be imprinted on the database for all time. Similarly, if the SQL Server fails one picosecond before the commit is issued, then it must roll back the transaction on restart.

SQL Server ensures durability with the Write-Ahead Logging protocol, which represents the code used to write changes to the database's transaction log file during the commit phase. Note that this is used to update only the log file, not the data file. Just enough information is logged in the transaction log to ensure that if there were a database failure, then the transactions could be replayed in sequence to update the database and return it to the state it was in. This is known as "rolling forward." The data file or files are updated using different mechanisms — either by the tasks themselves, a checkpoint, the eager writer, or the lazywriter, so it has no bearing on the durability property of a transaction.

CONSEQUENCE OF CONCURRENT ACCESS

As mentioned earlier, you can control the isolation of a transaction by changing its isolation level. The more onerous the isolation level the greater the overall integrity of each individual transaction, but the concurrency of the application is likely to also be affected.

Concurrency can be defined in database terms as the ability of multiple processes to act on data resident in the same database at the same time. As soon as you have more than one process attempting to access data in a database at the same time, the application is operating concurrently. However, if one process is looking at orders and another is looking at products, then this is unlikely to be an issue. Concurrency is of interest when multiple processes are attempting to access the *same* table at the *same* time.

Imagine a work queue application in which all the call center staff members are picking jobs off a queue before acting on them. The call center staff may be told to process the queue of customers on a first in, first out (FIFO) basis. In this scenario, there is going to a large amount of activity and interest in a relatively small number of rows, as each staff member is focusing on the top few rows.

At this point you might be wondering which scenarios necessitate all this locking. Locking represents additional overhead in the database management system. Is it really necessary? What does it achieve?

The following sections describe the six generally accepted scenarios in which the chosen isolation level will affect the behavior of a given query. As you go through them, consider whether each scenario would be unwanted on the systems you manage. Sometimes they are; sometimes they are not.

Lost Updates

A lost update occurs when two processes read the same data and then try to update the data with a different value. Consider a scenario in which you and your partner had the romantic notion of a joint bank account. On pay day, your respective employers both deposit your salaries into the joint account. To perform the update, each process reads the data. At the time of the payments, all is well in the world and you have an outstanding balance of $10,000. Each process therefore reads $10,000 as its starting point. Your employer attempts to update the $10,000 figure with your monthly salary of $2,000, but at the same time your partner's employer updates the sum with his or her salary of $4,000. Your partner's salary is added just before yours, updating the $10,000 balance to $14,000. Your payment then runs and updates the $10,000 balance to $12,000. A look at the ATM shows $12,000. The first update has been lost, and even worse, it represented the bigger update!

Developers of transactions can introduce this behavior themselves. Consider this example:

```
/* SESSION 1*/
USE AdventureWorks2008;

DECLARE @SafetyStockLevel    int = 0
        ,@Uplift             int = 5;

BEGIN TRAN;
SELECT  @SafetyStockLevel = SafetyStockLevel
FROM    Production.Product
WHERE   ProductID = 1;

SET     @SafetyStockLevel = @SafetyStockLevel + @Uplift;

WAITFOR DELAY '00:00:05.000';

UPDATE  Production.Product
SET     SafetyStockLevel = @SafetyStockLevel
WHERE   ProductID = 1;

SELECT  SafetyStockLevel
```

```
FROM     Production.Product
WHERE    ProductID = 1;

COMMIT TRAN;
```

Does it look OK? The developer has wrapped the read and the write in an explicit transaction, but all this scenario needs is for some concurrent activity and a lost update will occur. The WAITFOR is only present to make it easier to detonate the code. In a separate session, have the following code ready:

```
/* SESSION 2*/
USE AdventureWorks2008;

DECLARE @SafetyStockLevel   int = 0
        ,@Uplift            int = 100;

BEGIN TRAN;
SELECT  @SafetyStockLevel = SafetyStockLevel
FROM     Production.Product
WHERE    ProductID = 1;

SET      @SafetyStockLevel = @SafetyStockLevel + @Uplift;

UPDATE   Production.Product
SET      SafetyStockLevel = @SafetyStockLevel
WHERE    ProductID = 1;

SELECT   SafetyStockLevel
FROM     Production.Product
WHERE    ProductID = 1;

COMMIT TRAN;
```

This code is available for download at Wrox.com [CH06 Lost Update Tran.sql]

Now run Session 1, and then as soon as you have executed it, flick over to Session 2 and execute that code. Session 2 should come back almost immediately showing that the transaction has raised the safety stock level from 1000 to 1100. See Figure 6-1 for details. If you return to Session 1, you should now be able to see that this transaction has also completed except that the Safety Stock Level has gone from 1000 to 1005 as captured in Figure 6-2. The design of the transaction is flawed, causing an update to be lost.

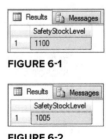

FIGURE 6-1

FIGURE 6-2

What caused this loss? The developer wrote the transaction in such a way that both sessions are able to read the data and store the stock level in a variable. Consequently, when the update is made, both transactions start with the same value. As you will see later in this chapter, the lost update can be avoided by explicitly raising the isolation level.

I know you are all too smart to code your transactions in this way, but it does show what can happen when insufficient consideration is given to the transaction design.

Dirty Reads

A dirty read takes no notice of any lock taken by another process. The read is officially "dirty" when it reads data that is uncommitted. This can become problematic if the uncommitted transaction fails or for some other reason is rolled back.

Imagine a scenario in which you are shopping on a website and place an item into your basket and proceed to payment. The site's checkout process decrements the stock by one and starts to charge your card all in the one transaction. At that time, a second unrelated process starts. The website's back office stock interface runs and makes a dirty read of all the product inventory levels, reading the reduced value. Unfortunately, there is a problem with your transaction (insufficient funds) and your purchase transaction is rolled back. The website stock level has now reverted to the original level, but the stock interface has just reported a different value.

You can run the following example against the AdventureWorks2008 database. Session 1 starts an explicit transaction to update all persons with a last name of "Jones" to have the same first name of "James." This transaction will be rolled back after five seconds, and a SELECT is run to show the original values:

```
/* SESSION 1 */
USE AdventureWorks2008;

BEGIN TRANSACTION;

UPDATE   Person.Person
SET      FirstName = 'James'
WHERE    LastName = 'Jones';

WAITFOR DELAY '00:00:05.000';

ROLLBACK TRANSACTION;

SELECT   FirstName
         ,LastName
FROM     Person.Person
WHERE    LastName = 'Jones';
```

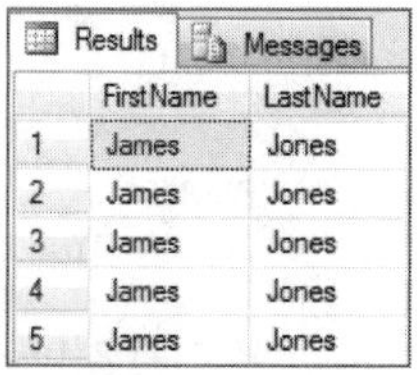

	FirstName	LastName
1	James	Jones
2	James	Jones
3	James	Jones
4	James	Jones
5	James	Jones

FIGURE 6-3

Once Session 1 is running, quickly flip over to a second session and execute the following SQL statement. The SQL in this second session will perform a dirty read. If you time it right and execute this query while the transaction in Session 1 is open (it has not yet been rolled back), then your output will match Figure 6-3 and every person with a surname of "Jones" now has a first name of "James":

Available for download on Wrox.com

```
/* SESSION 2 */
USE AdventureWorks2008;

SET TRANSACTION ISOLATION LEVEL READ UNCOMMITTED;

SELECT   FirstName
         ,LastName
FROM     Person.Person
WHERE    LastName = 'Jones';
```

This code is available for download at Wrox.com [CH06 Dirty Read.sql]

Non-Repeatable Reads

A non-repeatable read is one in which data read twice inside the same transaction cannot be guaranteed to contain the same value. This very behavior was discussed when looking at transactions earlier in the chapter. Depending on the isolation level, another transaction could have nipped in and updated the value between the two reads.

Non-repeatable reads occur because at lower isolation levels reading data only locks the data for the duration of the read, rather than for the duration of the transaction.

This behavior might well be completely desirable. Some applications may want to know the absolute, real-time value, even mid transaction, whereas other types of transactions might need to read the same value multiple times.

Consider the following example. In Session 1 the transaction reads the data for the top five people from `Person.Person` and then waits for five seconds before repeating the step. Execute the code in Session 1 before flipping to a second session and executing the code in Session 2:

```
/*SESSION 1*/
USE AdventureWorks2008;

SET TRANSACTION ISOLATION LEVEL
READ COMMITTED;
--REPEATABLE READ;

BEGIN TRANSACTION;

SELECT TOP    5
              FirstName
             ,MiddleName
             ,LastName
             ,Suffix
FROM          Person.Person
ORDER BY      LastName;

WAITFOR DELAY '00:00:05.000';

SELECT TOP    5
              FirstName
             ,MiddleName
             ,LastName
             ,Suffix
FROM          Person.Person
ORDER BY      LastName;

COMMIT TRANSACTION;

/*SESSION 2*/
USE AdventureWorks2008;

BEGIN TRANSACTION;

UPDATE  Person.Person
SET     Suffix        = 'Junior'
```

```
WHERE    LastName    = 'Abbas'
AND      FirstName   = 'Syed';

COMMIT TRANSACTION;

/*
UPDATE   Person.Person
SET      Suffix      = NULL
WHERE    LastName    = 'Abbas'
AND      FirstName   = 'Syed';
*/
```

This code is available for download at Wrox.com [CH06 Non-Repeat Read.sql]

Providing you execute the update in Session 2 in time, your results will match Figure 6-4, and the first read from Session 1, Syed Abbas, had no suffix; but in the second read he's now Syed Abbas Junior. The first read therefore hasn't been repeatable.

You can use the commented-out code in Session 2 to reset the data. Execute this code now. To get a repeatable read, change the transaction isolation level in Session 1 as indicated here:

```
SET TRANSACTION ISOLATION LEVEL
--READ COMMITTED;
REPEATABLE READ;
```

Now rerun Session 1 and Session 2 as before. You should notice that Session 2 has been blocked from performing its update until after the transaction has been completed. The first read in Session 1 is now repeatable. Your results from Session 1 should now match those in Figure 6-5.

	FirstName	MiddleName	LastName	Suffix
1	Syed	E	Abbas	NULL
2	Catherine	R.	Abel	NULL
3	Kim	NULL	Abercrombie	NULL
4	Kim	NULL	Abercrombie	NULL
5	Kim	B	Abercrombie	NULL

	FirstName	MiddleName	LastName	Suffix
1	Syed	E	Abbas	Junior
2	Catherine	R.	Abel	NULL
3	Kim	NULL	Abercrombie	NULL
4	Kim	NULL	Abercrombie	NULL
5	Kim	B	Abercrombie	NULL

FIGURE 6-4

	FirstName	MiddleName	LastName	Suffix
1	Syed	E	Abbas	NULL
2	Catherine	R.	Abel	NULL
3	Kim	NULL	Abercrombie	NULL
4	Kim	NULL	Abercrombie	NULL
5	Kim	B	Abercrombie	NULL

	FirstName	MiddleName	LastName	Suffix
1	Syed	E	Abbas	NULL
2	Catherine	R.	Abel	NULL
3	Kim	NULL	Abercrombie	NULL
4	Kim	NULL	Abercrombie	NULL
5	Kim	B	Abercrombie	NULL

FIGURE 6-5

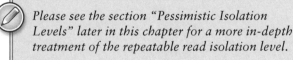

Please see the section "Pessimistic Isolation Levels" later in this chapter for a more in-depth treatment of the repeatable read isolation level.

Phantom Reads

Phantom reads occur when a row is inserted into or deleted from a range of data by one transaction that is being read by another set of data. Think back to the earlier work queue scenario. Suppose a user reads the work queue searching for new work items and gets back 10 records. Another user inserts a new work order. Shortly afterward, the first user refreshes the list of new work orders. There are now 11. This additional row is a phantom row.

Often this outcome is desirable. In cases when you need to be able to rely on the range of data previously read, however, it is not. The following example uses the `Person.Person` table to demonstrate a phantom:

```
/*SESSION 1*/
USE AdventureWorks2008;

SET TRANSACTION ISOLATION LEVEL
READ COMMITTED;
--SERIALIZABLE;

BEGIN TRANSACTION;

SELECT TOP    5
              FirstName
             ,MiddleName
             ,LastName
             ,Suffix
FROM          Person.Person
ORDER BY      LastName;

WAITFOR DELAY '00:00:05.000';

SELECT TOP    5
              FirstName
             ,MiddleName
             ,LastName
             ,Suffix
FROM          Person.Person
ORDER BY      LastName;

COMMIT TRANSACTION;
```

In Session 1 the transaction is again going to read the top five people from the `Person.Person` table twice in relatively quick succession. Session 2, however, inserts a new person who meets the criteria in the results of the query.

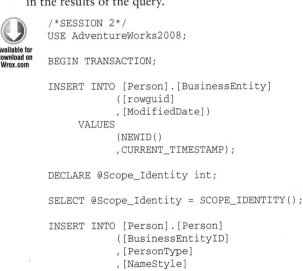

```
/*SESSION 2*/
USE AdventureWorks2008;

BEGIN TRANSACTION;

INSERT INTO [Person].[BusinessEntity]
            ([rowguid]
            ,[ModifiedDate])
      VALUES
            (NEWID()
            ,CURRENT_TIMESTAMP);

DECLARE @Scope_Identity int;

SELECT @Scope_Identity = SCOPE_IDENTITY();

INSERT INTO [Person].[Person]
            ([BusinessEntityID]
            ,[PersonType]
            ,[NameStyle]
            ,[Title]
```

```
                ,[FirstName]
                ,[MiddleName]
                ,[LastName]
                ,[Suffix]
                ,[EmailPromotion]
                ,[AdditionalContactInfo]
                ,[Demographics]
                ,[rowguid]
                ,[ModifiedDate])
        VALUES
                (@Scope_Identity
                ,'EM'
                ,'0'
                ,'Mr.'
                ,'James'
                ,'Anthony'
                ,'A'
                ,Null
                ,0
                ,Null
                ,Null
                ,NEWID()
                ,CURRENT_TIMESTAMP
                );

EXEC SP_EXECUTESQL
N'PRINT ''DELETE FROM Person.Person WHERE BusinessEntityID = '' +CAST(@Scope_
Identity as varchar(8));
  PRINT ''DELETE FROM Person.BusinessEntity WHERE BusinessEntityID = ''
+CAST(@Scope_Identity as varchar(8));'
  ,N'@Scope_Identity int',@Scope_Identity = @Scope_Identity

SELECT @Scope_Identity as BusinessEntityID

COMMIT TRANSACTION;
```

This code is available for download at Wrox.com [CH06 Phantom.sql]

Run Session 1 now before flipping over and executing Session 2. You should see in the results of the first query from Session 1 (see Figure 6-6) that Syed Abbas is the first person of five returned.

	FirstName	MiddleName	LastName	Suffix
1	Syed	E	Abbas	NULL
2	Catherine	R.	Abel	NULL
3	Kim	NULL	Abercrombie	NULL
4	Kim	NULL	Abercrombie	NULL
5	Kim	B	Abercrombie	NULL

FIGURE 6-6

However, in the result of the second query from Session 1 (see Figure 6-7) James Anthony A is now first. James Anthony A is a phantom.

To demonstrate how phantoms can be prevented, first remove James Anthony A from the table. If you revert to Session 2 and look in your message tab, you should see two delete statements. Look at Figure 6-8 for details.

	FirstName	MiddleName	LastName	Suffix
1	James	Anthony	A	NULL
2	Syed	E	Abbas	NULL
3	Catherine	R.	Abel	NULL
4	Kim	NULL	Abercrombie	NULL
5	Kim	NULL	Abercrombie	NULL

FIGURE 6-7

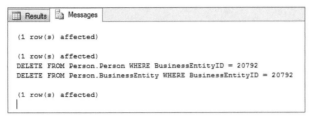

FIGURE 6-8

Copy those two rows into a new window and execute them.

In Session 1, change the transaction isolation level from Read Committed to Serializable, and repeat the example by running the code in Session 1 first, followed by that in Session 2:

```
SET TRANSACTION ISOLATION LEVEL
--READ COMMITTED;
SERIALIZABLE;
```

This time the results for selects one and two from Session 1 are the same, as shown in Figure 6-9. Note that the insert from Session 2 still happened, but only after the transaction in Session 1 had been committed.

Don't forget to remove James Anthony A from your AdventureWorks2008 database before continuing by repeating the steps mentioned above.

FIGURE 6-9

> *Please see the section "Pessimistic Isolation Levels" later in this chapter for more in-depth treatment of phantoms and the serializable isolation level.*

Double Reads

Double reads can occur when scanning data while using the default "read committed" isolation level, covered later in this chapter. During a period of concurrent activity it is possible for one query to perform a range scan on a table and, as it is scanning, a second transaction can come in and move a row thus causing it to be read twice. This can happen when the initial read during the range scan is not repeatable. The locks taken when reading data are by default released as soon as the data has been successfully read. Specific action is required to prevent this; you must increase the isolation level.

An example follows below. The code below moves Bethany Raheem and so reads her record twice. There are only five Raheems in the Adventureworks2008 database. However, in this example you will see six.

First, Session 1 creates a blocking update midway through the range scan of the Raheem data:

```
/* SESSION 1 PART 1 */
Use AdventureWorks2008;

BEGIN TRAN
UPDATE   Person.Person
SET      LastName    = 'Raheem_DOUBLE_READ_BLOCK'
WHERE    LastName    = 'Raheem'
AND      FirstName   = 'Kurt';
```

Now Session 2 starts a scan to return all persons whose surname begins with Raheem. This query will scan the index and be blocked by our uncommitted update in Session 1:

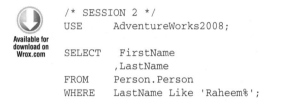
Available for
download on
Wrox.com

```
/* SESSION 2 */
USE      AdventureWorks2008;

SELECT   FirstName
         ,LastName
FROM     Person.Person
WHERE    LastName Like 'Raheem%';
```

Return to Session 1 and move Bethany Raheem ,who has already been read, to a position in the index after the row being updated in Session 1:

```
/* SESSION 1 PART 2 */
UPDATE   Person.Person
SET      LastName    = 'Raheem_DOUBLE_READ_REAL'
WHERE    LastName    = 'Raheem'
AND      FirstName   = 'Bethany';

COMMIT TRAN;
```

This code is available for download at Wrox.com [CH06 Double Read.sql]

The range scan query in Session 2 can now complete, and the results look like those in Figure 6-10.

	First Name	Last Name
1	Bethany	Raheem
2	Devon	Raheem
3	Michael	Raheem
4	Tommy	Raheem
5	Kurt	Raheem_DOUBLE_READ_BLOCK
6	Bethany	Raheem_DOUBLE_READ_REAL

FIGURE 6-10

> *For further details on the double read, please look at the following blog post from Craig Freedman:* http://blogs.msdn.com/craigfr/archive/2007/04/25/read-committed-isolation-level.aspx

Halloween Effect

The *Halloween effect* refers to a scenario in which data moves position within the result set and consequently could be changed multiple times. This effect is different from the double read because it is driven by data modification, rather than read queries.

In order to perform an update, the data must be read first. This is performed using two cursors: one for the read and the other for the write. If the data is updated by the write cursor before all the data was read in, then it is possible that a row will move position (courtesy of the update), potentially be read a second time, and consequently be updated again. In theory, this could go on forever. Reading the data using an index whose key is going to be updated by the query is an example of the Halloween effect.

This scenario is highly undesirable and thankfully the Storage Engine in SQL Server protects against it. As mentioned, SQL Server uses two cursors during an update: one to perform the read and another to perform the write. To ensure that the data available to the write has been read fully, SQL Server needs to inject a blocking operator such as a spool into the plan. It doesn't have to be the spool, but this operator is commonly selected because it invariably has the lowest cost attached to it. That said, it still isn't very efficient, as it means all the data has to be inserted into tempdb before it can be used by the write cursor. It does ensure that all the data is read before any modifications take place.

To achieve a greater level of efficiency, SQL Server actually looks out for the Halloween effect problem when creating the plan. It introduces the blocking operator only when there is a chance of the Halloween effect occurring. Even then it adds an extra one only if there is no blocking operator already present in the plan that is performing this function.

In most update scenarios the index is used to locate data, and other non-key columns are updated in the table. You wouldn't normally expect the key to be frequently updated as well, so being able to remove the blocking operator is an important optimization.

It is worth remembering the performance penalty of the Halloween effect when deciding on your indexing strategy. Perhaps that index you were thinking of adding isn't such a great idea after all. When index or performance tuning, it is always worthwhile to keep an eye on the impact that your changes have on tempdb.

> *To learn more details of how SQL Server protects you from the Halloween Effect, please see another excellent blog post from Craig Freedman*
> `http://blogs.msdn.com/craigfr/archive/2008/02/27/`
> `halloween-protection.aspx`

LOCKING

So far you have looked at transactions and why isolating them might be desirable, and what impact that might have on the overall concurrency of our systems. Now you are going to step into locking. Before moving on to look at SQL Server's "attitude" toward concurrency, you need to understand the core functionality of locking. Once you understand how locks have been implemented in SQL Server, you'll be better able to understand how they are used to facilitate both pessimistic and optimistic concurrency.

> *SQL Server can be either pessimistic or optimistic in its attitude to concurrency. Both attitudes are covered in depth later in this chapter.*

First, however, look at how you can query locks in SQL Server.

Viewing Locks — sys.dm_tran_locks

When it comes to locks, there is one dynamic management view (DMV) that rules them all, and it is the starting point for any locking analysis. Sys.dm_tran_locks is that view. Although sp_lock and sys.syslockinfo are still available, their use has been deprecated in favor of the DMVs, so you are strongly advised to take the time to learn them and break those old familiar habits. In most cases the DMVs are also more powerful and offer greater flexibility than the legacy methods. I'd like to encourage you to make the transition to DMVs, so I won't be covering the "old" ways of doing things in this chapter.

The columns available in sys.dm_tran_locks can basically be broken down into two groups. Those prefixed with request_, and those prefixed with resource_*. The resource_* columns, listed in Table 6-1, describe the resource on which the lock is requested. The request_* columns, shown in Table 6-2, are used to describe the process making the request for the lock.

It may seem counterintuitive to look at the DMV before the concepts, but it is a bit of a chicken-and-egg situation. Without the DMV it would be difficult to show you the locks, but without the explanation of the fields, the output might not be meaningful. However, most are reasonably self-explanatory, and I hope that my descriptions of the fields will help you get through any early difficulty.

TABLE 6-1: Resource Columns

COLUMN NAME	DESCRIPTION
resource_type	Describes the kind of resource that a transaction is trying to take a lock on, for example, OBJECT, PAGE, KEY, etc.
Resource_subtype	Provides a sub classification of the resource requested. Not mandatory, but good for qualifying the resource, for example, if you create a table in a transaction you will get a sub-type of DDL on the DATABASE resource_type lock.
Resource_database_id	The database in which the resource was requested

continues

TABLE 6-1 *(continued)*

COLUMN NAME	DESCRIPTION
Resource_description	Contains information describing the resource that isn't available in any other column
Resource_associated_entity_id	Describes the entity upon which the lock is being requested. It can be one of three things depending on the resource type: Object ID HoBT ID Allocation Unit ID
Resource_lock_partition	Normally 0. Lock partitioning must be available to you in order to see anything in this column, and that is only available on machines with 16 cores presented. It applies only to object locks, and even then only to those without a resource_subtype.

Of these columns, the ones that you'll pay specific attention to are the resource type, the subtype, and the associated entity. The database ID is mainly present to help you when filtering the data returned in your queries, and the lock partition has a very specialized niche usage.

TABLE 6-2: Request Columns

COLUMN NAME	DESCRIPTION
Request_mode	The mode in which the lock is requested. If the lock has a status of granted, then this is the lock mode under which the resource is currently operating, for example, IX (Intent Exclusive), X (Exclusive), etc.
Request_type	This value is always LOCK in SQL 2005 and 2008 because this view only supports locks at the moment.
Request_status	One of three values: GRANT: The requested lock is in effect. WAIT: The lock is prevented from being acquired (blocked) because the resource is already locked with an incompatible locking mode. For instance one connection has a "GRANT" X (Exclusive) lock on the object, and you are trying to also acquire an exclusive lock on the same object. CONVERT: The lock was previously granted with another status and is trying to upgrade to a more restrictive mode but is currently being blocked from doing so.
Request_reference_count	An approximate count for the number of times that a requestor has requested a lock on the given resource

COLUMN NAME	DESCRIPTION
Request_session_id	In most cases this is the session that requested the resource. Two special values: -2: An orphaned distributed transaction -3: A deferred recovery transaction
Request_exec_context_id	Execution context of the process that owns the request
Request_request_id	Batch ID of the request that owns the resource
Request_owner_type	The entity type of the owner of the request. Possible types are as follows: TRANSACTION CURSOR SESSION SHARED_TRANSACTION_WORKSPACE EXCLUSIVE_TRANSACTION_WORKSPACE
Request_owner_id	Used when the owner type is Transaction and represents the transaction ID
Request_owner_guid	Used when the owner type is Transaction and the request has been made by a distributed transaction. In that circumstance, the value equates to the MSDTC GUID for that transaction.

> *Not covered here are a couple of unsupported/internal-use only columns on* sys.dm_tran_locks *that begin with a* request_ *prefix. They are unlikely to be of interest and you aren't meant to be using them.*

The lock owner address, shown in Table 6-3, is the one column that isn't prefixed in the view with either resource_ or request_. However, it is very important. If you are embracing the new DMV world and are shying away from sp_who2, you'll need to join sys.dm_tran_locks to sys.dm_os_waiting_tasks to get a view that shows you which requests are blocking others.

TABLE 6-3: The Lock Owner Address

COLUMN NAME	DESCRIPTION
Lock Owner Address	Represents the in-memory address of the request. Use this column to join to the resource_address column in sys.dm_os_waiting_tasks to see blocking lock information.

Below is an example of how the join between `sys.dm_tran_locks` and `sys.dm_os_waiting_tasks` can be made which demonstrates how you can find out which session is causing blocking in your system using these DMVs.

Available for download on Wrox.com

```
SELECT    lok.resource_type
         ,lok.resource_subtype
         ,DB_NAME(lok.resource_database_id)
         ,lok.resource_description
         ,lok.resource_associated_entity_id
         ,lok.resource_lock_partition
         ,lok.request_mode
         ,lok.request_type
         ,lok.request_status
         ,lok.request_owner_type
         ,lok.request_owner_id
         ,lok.lock_owner_address
         ,wat.waiting_task_address
         ,wat.session_id
         ,wat.exec_context_id
         ,wat.wait_duration_ms
         ,wat.wait_type
         ,wat.resource_address
         ,wat.blocking_task_address
         ,wat.blocking_session_id
         ,wat.blocking_exec_context_id
         ,wat.resource_description
FROM      sys.dm_tran_locks lok
JOIN      sys.dm_os_waiting_tasks wat
ON        lok.lock_owner_address = wat.resource_address
```

This code is available for download at Wrox.com [CH06 Blocking Lock.sql]

Lock Granularity

SQL Server has a highly granular locking method that caters to a lot of different scenarios when needed. When a transaction interacts with data, it will typically take several locks on different resources. In general terms, the more specific, and therefore selective, the query you write, the more granular the lock that will be sought by SQL Server. This is good. High granularity means greater concurrency, but it does also mean higher resource usage.

Table 6-4 provides a list of the resources that you might see while viewing locks.

TABLE 6-4: Lock Resources

RESOURCE TYPE	EXAMPLE OF RESOURCE	DESCRIPTION
RID	1:8185:4	A Row IDentifier used to lock a single row when the table in question is a heap
		The RID Format can be understood as:
		`<FILE : PAGE : SLOT ID>`
		The lock resource RID can be retrieved with the undocumented `%%lockres%%` function.

RESOURCE TYPE	EXAMPLE OF RESOURCE	DESCRIPTION
KEY	(3a01180ac47a)	A lock on a single row on an index. This includes row locks taken on tables that have a clustered index on them. The resource is a hash value that can be retrieved against your table with `%%lockres%%`.
PAGE	1:19216	A lock on an index or data page Breaks down as `<FILE ID>:<PAGE NUMBER>` These map to the file_id and page_id fields in the sys.dm_os_buffer_descriptors DMV.
EXTENT	1:19216	A contiguous set of eight pages. Pages are allocated to tables in extents. `<FILE ID> : <FIRST PAGE NO>`
HoBT	72057594058637312	HoBT is a Heap or Balanced Tree (BTree). When a table is a heap (no clustered index), it protects the heap. Otherwise, it protects the BTree of the index.
OBJECT	2105058535	Normally a table lock but could be anything with an `OBJECT_ID`. If it's a table lock, then it will cover both data pages and all indexes on the table.
APPLICATION	0:[MyAppLock]: (6731eaf3)	An application lock. Set by `sp_getapplock`.
METADATA	xml_collection_ id = 65536	Used to lock SQL Server system metadata — e.g., when taking a schema stability lock on metadata of an XML column when querying a row.
ALLOCATION_ UNIT	72057594039828480	Allocation Unit ID seen during deferred drop operations, such as on a large table. Also visible during minimally logged operations such as `SELECT INTO`.
FILE	0	Seen when adding or removing files from a database No resource description information is published.
DATABASE	7	A lock against the entire database. This can be a shared transaction workspace lock to identify a connection in the DB or a transaction lock when altering the database. Changing from `read_write` to `read_only` would need an exclusive transaction against the database.

As mentioned in the introduction to this section, there is a cost to increased granularity. Simply put, the greater the degree of granularity the more locks that need to be taken. This consumes SQL Server resources — notably CPU and memory. Each lock equates to 96 bytes of memory, so many fine-grained locks can consume a large amount of memory in a short period of time, especially if the transaction in question is writing data and lasts a long time. Consider this trivial example:

```
USE AdventureWorks2008;

SET TRANSACTION ISOLATION LEVEL REPEATABLE READ;
BEGIN TRAN;
SELECT    LastName
          ,FirstName
          ,BusinessEntityID
FROM      Person.Person
WHERE     LastName LIKE 'SM%';

SELECT    resource_type
          ,resource_subtype
          ,request_mode
          ,COUNT(*)
FROM      sys.dm_tran_locks
WHERE     request_session_id = @@SPID
GROUP BY resource_type
          ,resource_subtype
          ,request_mode;
COMMIT TRAN;
```

This code is available for download at Wrox.com [CH06 Session Lock Count.sql]

As shown in Figure 6-11, the select returned 105 rows. That explains the 105 KEY locks — one key lock per row returned. In theory, then, if you selected all rows from the `Person.Person` table, you would see 19,974 KEY locks. Well, no. If this happened, it would translate to around 1.8MB of memory consumed just in lock resources for this one query.

SQL Server uses a heuristic locking model. Based on a number of factors, SQL Server can decide ahead of time to either use a more coarse-grained lock and lock at the page level,

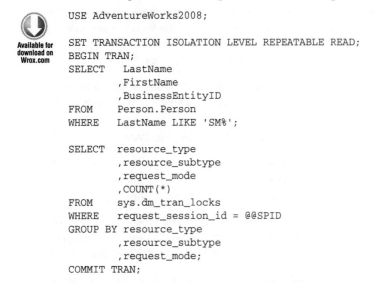

	LastName	FirstName	BusinessEntityID
1	Smith	Abigail	12032
2	Smith	Adriana	3155
3	Smith	Alexander	18069
4	Smith	Alexandra	11294
5	Smith	Alexis	11990
6	Smith	Allen	15854

	resource_type	resource_subtype	request_mode	(No column name)
1	DATABASE		S	1
2	DATABASE	ENCRYPTION_SCAN	S	1
3	KEY		S	105
4	OBJECT		IS	1
5	PAGE		IS	1

FIGURE 6-11

or as in this case, realize that it is taking too many fine-grained row locks for the query. In these situations SQL Server will attempt to escalate to a table level lock. So rather than take out nearly 20,000 row locks, SQL Server attempts, and in our case succeeds, in escalating the locking strategy to take out a single object lock (i.e. a table lock). Lock escalation is a big topic covered later, but just so you can see this for yourselves why not comment out the where clause from the select statement on `Person.Person` above and run the query again. Your query on `sys.dm_tran_locks` should now return an object (table lock) as seen in Figure 6-12.

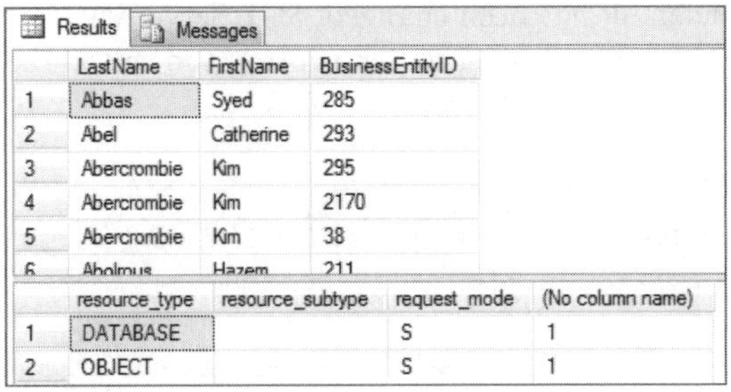

FIGURE 6-12

Think back to the original example. What were all these other locks? What were they doing there? The row locks were in place, so why did you need a lock on the page and the object? To answer these questions, you need to understand the lock mode and the lock hierarchy, covered next.

ROW LOCKS OR PAGE LOCKS?

During query runtime SQL Server will initially be taking row locks or page locks as the lowest level of lock granularity prior to any decision about lock escalation. How SQL Server decides which one is a closely guarded secret, but one factor is the number of rows that fit onto each page. Narrow tables with many rows are much more likely to see page locks when range scans are being used to query the data than wide fact or denormalized tables. Why? One factor is the sheer number of rows on the page. It has to be worthwhile for SQL Server to use page locks. If each row is wide, then the ratio of rows to pages won't be sufficient to trigger page lock usage.

The code to see SQL Server use page locks over row locks is available for download at Wrox.com [CH06 Row vs Page locks.sql]

Lock Modes

When SQL Server requests a lock, it chooses a mode in which to affect that lock. The mode determines what level of compatibility the lock will have with other locks being requested by other tasks. This applies to all locks at all levels of the hierarchy. If the lock requested is compatible with other locks, then all is well and the lock will be granted. However, if the lock mode is not compatible with an already granted lock, then that lock request will be blocked and forced to wait.

The requested lock mode will then be evident as the name of the wait type in the `sys.dm_os_wait_stats` DMV. It stays on the wait list until one of two things happens (assuming no one turns off your SQL Server in the meantime). Either the other blocking lock will be released, in which case the requesting lock will now be granted, or the lock request will time out. By default, SQL Server's lock timeout option is set to never expire, so unless the default has been changed, SQL Server will force the requesting task to literally wait indefinitely. (Users may also get fed up waiting and cancel their task, so one could say that's a third way of coming off the wait list!)

> *You can change the lock timeout setting at the connection level with SET Lock_Timeout. See Books Online for details* `http://msdn.microsoft.com/en-us/library/ms189470.aspx`

Let's now go through the requesting modes and how they relate to lock requests in the locking hierarchy.

Shared Lock Mode (S)

When a read request for a row of data is made by a task, by default SQL Server will request a lock in shared mode. Shared mode is compatible with most other locks, as it is only permitted to read the row on the data page.

Update Lock Mode (U)

Update mode is a special kind of lock. It is used when searching data during a data modification request. The process is straightforward. SQL Server uses the update lock to find the data and when located prevents others from updating it. It prevents other requests from modifying the data by virtue of the update lock's compatibility with other locks. Any other requests wishing to lock the resource with an update or exclusive lock would be forced to wait. However, in order to effect the change, the update lock must be converted to an exclusive lock. As the update lock has blocked all other data modification locks, all it needs to do is wait until it can get an exclusive lock when the last, if any, shared locks have been released. This allows for greater concurrency in the system as opposed to all writers just taking exclusive locks. If the latter were the case then blocking would be a much greater problem. Concurrent queries would be blocked for the entire duration of the update (the read part and the write) as opposed to just the write.

Exclusive Lock Mode (X)

Exclusive locks are all about data modification via insert, update, and delete. In terms of compatibility, exclusive locks are not compatible with any other kind of lock including other exclusive locks. All locks must wait for the exclusive lock to be released before they can proceed; provided your solution isn't using dirty reads and therefore bypassing the lock entirely. As mentioned earlier, exclusive locks are held until the end of the transaction, whether that is by commit or rollback.

Schema Lock Modes (Sch-S), (Sch-M)

There are actually two types of schema lock mode: *schema modification* (*Sch-M*) and *schema stability* (*Sch-S*). These locks are taken by different processes but basically boil down to the same thing. A query takes a schema-modification lock when it wants to change the schema in some way. Schema stability is designed to block schema-modification if needed. For example, when a stored procedure is compiled, a schema-stability lock is taken to ensure that no one changes the table during the compilation process. Alternatively, a schema-modification is taken when altering a table, as you have seen, but also when performing partition switching. In this case, a Sch-M is taken on both the source and the target.

Intent Lock Modes (IS), (IU), (IX)

As you saw previously in the lock granularity section, SQL Server can grant locks at various levels or degrees of granularity. These levels are used to form a hierarchy within SQL Server. A row is at the bottom of this hierarchy and belongs to a page; the page itself belongs to a table and so on. The lock hierarchy will be dealt with in detail in the next section. The purpose of the intent lock is to indicate at the higher levels of the lock hierarchy that a part of the resource actually has a lock held against it. This allows for checks to be performed at the level in which a lock is requested, which is a great performance optimization.

If an exclusive row lock is acquired on a table, the page and the table will have intent exclusive locks held against them. Consequently, if another process wishes to take out a table lock, it can check at the table level, see that there is an intent exclusive lock present, and know it's blocked without having to scan the entire table looking for conflicting locks.

Therefore, intent locks shouldn't be considered as locks in the same vein as a shared, update, or exclusive lock. They act as indicators to SQL Server and point out that an actual lock has been acquired at a lower level in that hierarchy for that resource.

Consider an ALTER TABLE statement, which needs to be executed when no other users are trying to run queries against the table. If the table changed during the query, this would be very bad news indeed. However, it would also be a massive pain to check the locks for every row of the table to see if any are being read or modified. Instead, a table-level check takes place, which would indicate immediately in a single request whether there was any other activity in the table.

Try this for yourself. In Session 1, run the following code:

```
USE AdventureWorks2008;
/* SESSION 1 */

BEGIN TRANSACTION;
UPDATE      Production.Product
SET     SafetyStockLevel = SafetyStockLevel
WHERE   ProductID =1;
--ROLLBACK TRAN;

SELECT    resource_type
        ,resource_subtype
        ,resource_description
        ,resource_associated_entity_id
        ,request_mode
        ,request_status
FROM    sys.dm_tran_locks
WHERE   request_session_id = @@spid;
```

	resource_type	resource_subtype	resource_description	resource_associated_entity_id	request_mode	request_status
1	DATABASE			0	S	GRANT
2	PAGE		1:709	72057594045595648	IX	GRANT
3	OBJECT			1717581157	IX	GRANT
4	KEY		(010086470766)	72057594045595648	X	GRANT

FIGURE 6-13

Can you see the intent locks (request_mode is "IX") on page and object in Figure 6-13? Now try to run this ALTER TABLE statement in another query window:

Available for download on Wrox.com

```
USE AdventureWorks2008;
/* SESSION 2 */

BEGIN TRANSACTION;
ALTER TABLE Production.Product
ADD TESTCOLUMN INT NULL;
--ROLLBACK TRANSACTION;
```

This code is available for download at Wrox.com [CH06 Intent Locks.sql]

The ALTER TABLE statement should be blocked. How do you know this? First, it will take forever to make that change, as the explicit transaction in Session 1 hasn't been closed. However, more important, look at row 5 in the output shown in Figure 6-14 (I have rerun the query for sys.dm_tran_locks in the Session 1 window but also included the spid used for Session 2). Note the request_mode contains a *schema modify* lock, and that the request_status is set to WAIT. This means it is on the wait list, which ties back to the fact that it is blocked. Finally, look at the resource_type. It's an object resource request. SQL Server will have checked for the existence of an object resource_type for the same resource_associated_entity_id as the one requested. Because one exists, the ALTER TABLE cannot proceed.

	resource_type	resource_subtype	resource_description	resource_associated_entity_id	request_mode	request_status
1	DATABASE			0	S	GRANT
2	DATABASE			0	S	GRANT
3	PAGE		1:709	72057594045595648	IX	GRANT
4	OBJECT			1717581157	IX	GRANT
5	OBJECT			1717581157	Sch-M	WAIT
6	KEY		(010086470766)	72057594045595648	X	GRANT

FIGURE 6-14

You might want to roll back those transactions now.

You will read about intent locks again in the lock hierarchy section later in this chapter.

Conversion Lock Modes (SIX), (SIU), (UIX)

SQL Server also provides the facility to convert shared, update, or exclusive locks to shared with intent exclusive (SIX), shared with intent update (SIU), or update with intent exclusive (UIX). This happens when a statement inside transaction already holds a lock at a course granularity (a table) but now needs to modify a component of the resource held at a much finer granularity (a row). The lock held against the course granularity needs to reflect this.

Consider this example of a SIX lock.

```
USE AdventureWorks2008;

SET TRANSACTION ISOLATION LEVEL SERIALIZABLE;

BEGIN TRANSACTION;

SELECT  BusinessEntityID
        ,FirstName
        ,MiddleName
        ,LastName
        ,Suffix
FROM    Person.Person;

SELECT  resource_type
        ,resource_subtype
        ,resource_description
        ,resource_associated_entity_id
        ,request_mode
        ,request_status
FROM    sys.dm_tran_locks
WHERE   request_session_id = @@SPID;

UPDATE  Person.Person
SET     Suffix      = 'Junior'
WHERE   FirstName   = 'Syed'
AND     LastName    = 'Abbas';

SELECT  resource_type
        ,resource_subtype
        ,resource_description
        ,resource_associated_entity_id
        ,request_mode
        ,request_status
FROM    sys.dm_tran_locks
WHERE   request_session_id = @@SPID;

ROLLBACK TRANSACTION;
```

This code is available for download at Wrox.com [CH06 SIX Lock.sql]

A transaction has selected all rows from the `Person.Person` table. This generates a table level shared lock as can be seen in Figure 06-15.

	resource_type	resource_subtype	resource_description	resource_associated_entity_id	request_mode	request_status
1	DATABASE			0	S	GRANT
2	OBJECT			1509580416	S	GRANT

FIGURE 6-15

The transaction continues though to update a single row. This triggers the need to convert the table-level shared lock to a SIX lock as the row must be exclusively locked. Figure 6-16 clearly shows that the row is locked with an exclusive KEY lock, but also that the table/object has converted its lock from shared (S) to shared with intent exclusive (SIX).

	resource_type	resource_subtype	resource_description	resource_associated_entity_id	request_mode	request_status
1	DATABASE			0	S	GRANT
2	KEY		(1d0096c50a7d)	72057594057981952	X	GRANT
3	METADATA	XML_COLLECTION	xml_collection_id = 65536	0	Sch-S	GRANT
4	METADATA	XML_COLLECTION	xml_collection_id = 65537	0	Sch-S	GRANT
5	KEY		(07038ce92446)	72057594058047488	RangeS-U	GRANT
6	PAGE		1:9992	72057594058047488	IU	GRANT
7	OBJECT			1509580416	SIX	GRANT
8	KEY		(3002fe6779f1)	72057594058047488	RangeS-U	GRANT
9	PAGE		1:36140	72057594057981952	IX	GRANT
10	OBJECT			1902629821	Sch-S	GRANT
11	OBJECT			1918629878	Sch-S	GRANT

FIGURE 6-16

Bulk Update Lock Mode (BU)

Bulk Update first appeared in SQL Server 2005. It is designed to allow multiple table level locks on a single heap while using the Bulk load API. This is important for parallel loading in data warehousing. However, in order to see it, you need to be loading into a heap and must have specified a `Tablock` on the target table. The `Tablock` is a hint to say you'll take a table lock, but this is optimized. SQL Server sees that it is the bulk API that is making the assertion, so a BU lock is issued instead. Since multiple BU locks are permitted on the same table, you are therefore empowered to perform parallel loading into the heap as each loader will take its own compatible BU lock. Note that dirty reads are also permitted against the target table.

> *If you do not specify a `Tablock` hint when bulk loading data into a heap, then you will see exclusive page locks instead. If the target table has a clustered index, then use trace flag 610 and you will also see page locks on the bulk insert. See the* Data Loading Performance Guide *from the SQLCAT team for further details.*

Look at the SQL code example below. It is using the bulk insert statement to load into a replica heap of the `dbo.factinternetsales` table. Notice that a `Tablock` hint has also been used. You can see the BU lock that is issued as a result in Figure 6-17 by querying `sys.dm_tran_locks` in a separate session as before. You'll have to be quick though! The sample data files only contain 60,398 rows.

Available for download on Wrox.com

```sql
USE AdventureWorksDW2008;

CREATE TABLE [dbo].[TestFactInternetSales](
        [ProductKey] [int] NOT NULL,
        [OrderDateKey] [int] NOT NULL,
        [DueDateKey] [int] NOT NULL,
        [ShipDateKey] [int] NOT NULL,
        [CustomerKey] [int] NOT NULL,
        [PromotionKey] [int] NOT NULL,
        [CurrencyKey] [int] NOT NULL,
        [SalesTerritoryKey] [int] NOT NULL,
        [SalesOrderNumber] [nvarchar](20) NOT NULL,
        [SalesOrderLineNumber] [tinyint] NOT NULL,
        [RevisionNumber] [tinyint] NOT NULL,
        [OrderQuantity] [smallint] NOT NULL,
        [UnitPrice] [money] NOT NULL,
        [ExtendedAmount] [money] NOT NULL,
        [UnitPriceDiscountPct] [float] NOT NULL,
        [DiscountAmount] [float] NOT NULL,
        [ProductStandardCost] [money] NOT NULL,
        [TotalProductCost] [money] NOT NULL,
        [SalesAmount] [money] NOT NULL,
        [TaxAmt] [money] NOT NULL,
        [Freight] [money] NOT NULL,
        [CarrierTrackingNumber] [nvarchar](25) NULL,
        [CustomerPONumber] [nvarchar](25) NULL) ON [PRIMARY];

BULK INSERT dbo.TestFactInternetSales
FROM    'C:\users\James.Rowland-Jones\factinternetsales.txt'
WITH    (TABLOCK
        ,FORMATFILE = 'C:\users\James.Rowland-Jones\formatFIS.txt'
        );

/* SESSION 2 */
SELECT   resource_type
        ,resource_subtype
        ,resource_description
        ,resource_associated_entity_id
        ,request_mode
        ,request_status
FROM sys.dm_tran_locks
where request_session_id = <insert your session spid here,int, 0>
```

This code is available for download at Wrox.com [CH06 BU Lock.sql, CH06 factinternetsales.txt, CH06 formatFIS.txt]

Results | Messages

	resource_type	resource_subtype	resource_description	resource_associated_entity_id	request_mode	request_status
1	DATABASE	BULKOP_BACKUP_LOG		0	NULL	GRANT
2	DATABASE	BULKOP_BACKUP_DB		0	NULL	GRANT
3	DATABASE			0	S	GRANT
4	DATABASE	ENCRYPTION_SCAN		0	S	GRANT
5	OBJECT			142623551	BU	GRANT
6	HOBT	BULK_OPERATION		72057594193969152	IX	GRANT
7	ALLOCATION_UNIT	BULK_OPERATION_PAGE		72057594202357760	S	GRANT

FIGURE 6-17

Table 6-5 provides the full list of lock modes.

TABLE 6-5: SQL Server Lock Modes

LOCK MODE	WAIT TYPE	DESCRIPTION
S	LCK_M_S	Shared — Other processes can read but not modify the locked resource when granted.
X	LCK_M_X	Exclusive — No processes can read or write to the locked resource when granted.
U	LCK_M_U	Update — Blocks other updates or exclusives. An update lock is granted when data is read as part of an update statement. The lock can then be converted to an Exclusive or X lock without risking a deadlock when the update is made.
IS	LCK_M_IS	Intent Shared — A child row or page is locked with a shared lock.
IU	LCK_M_IU	Intent Update — A child row or page is locked with an update lock.
IX	LCK_M_IX	Intent Exclusive — A child row or page is locked with an exclusive lock.
SIX	LCK_M_SIX	Shared with Intent Exclusive — A conversion lock. From shared to shared with exclusive.
SIU	LCK_M_SIU	Shared with Intent Update — A conversion lock. From shared to shared with intent update.
UIX	LCK_M_UIX	Update with Intent Exclusive — A conversion lock. From update to update with intent exclusive.
Sch-S	LCK_M_SCHS	Schema Stability — A stored procedure may be being compiled or a METADATA read may be taking place.
Sch-M	LCK_M_SCHM	Schema Modify — A partition could be being switched or a table altered.
BU	LCK_M_BU	Bulk Update — A bulk insert of data is occurring.

Lock Hierarchy

As you have just seen, SQL Server can lock at varying degrees of granularity. For data this can be at the row, page, or table (object) level. The multi-grained approach allows flexibility in determining the trade-off between many small granular locks and, for example, a single table lock. However, in truth, to fully protect the locked resource, several locks need to be taken in order to ensure that the resource is protected at all levels of the hierarchy. This is the purpose of the intent locks, which enable the lock manager to know that something at a lower level in the hierarchy is acting on the data.

Figure 6-18 shows the basic hierarchy.

At the top level of the hierarchy is the table, which contains pages belonging to one of three allocation units. Each page can have many rows. When an update occurs, an exclusive lock is ultimately sought on the row in question. As part of the process of granting the lock, SQL Server also grants intent locks on the page and the table. These facilitate other lookups by ensuring that there is a lock made at every level of the hierarchy.

Consequently, if a request is submitted to alter the structure of the table, the lock manager only needs to look for a lock at that level. An ALTER TABLE request would need to be granted a schema modification lock. However, because a process is already updating a row, this request must wait and is blocked. How do we know whether one lock is compatible with another? This leads us nicely into the next topic: lock compatibility.

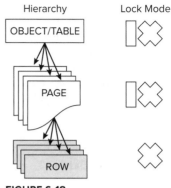

FIGURE 6-18

Lock Compatibility

Locking is a form of resource scheduling. Some resources and activities can run in parallel, whereas others must run in sequence. The mode of the lock determines its intent and its willingness to operate concurrently with other tasks. All the different modes have been mapped by Microsoft into the matrix shown in Figure 6-19, which clearly indicates which ones can co-exist with one another. I have included it here for reference, but it is available in Books Online and at `http://msdn.microsoft.com/en-us/library/ms186396.aspx`.

	NL	SCH-S	SCH-M	S	U	X	IS	IU	IX	SIU	SIX	UIX	BU	RS-S	RS-U	RI-N	RI-S	RI-U	RI-X	RX-S	RX-U	RX-X
NL	N	N	N	N	N	N	N	N	N	N	N	N	N	N	N	N	N	N	N	N	N	N
SCH-S	N	N	C	N	N	N	N	N	N	N	N	N	N	I	I	I	I	I	I	I	I	I
SCH-M	N	C	C	C	C	C	C	C	C	C	C	C	C	I	I	I	I	I	I	I	I	I
S	N	N	C	N	N	C	N	N	C	N	C	C	C	N	N	N	N	N	C	N	N	C
U	N	N	C	N	N	C	N	C	C	C	C	C	C	N	C	N	N	C	C	C	C	C
X	N	N	C	C	C	C	C	C	C	C	C	C	C	C	C	N	C	C	C	C	C	C
IS	N	N	C	N	N	C	N	N	N	N	N	N	C	I	I	I	I	I	I	I	I	I
IU	N	N	C	N	C	C	N	N	N	N	C	C	C	I	I	I	I	I	I	I	I	I
IX	N	N	C	C	C	C	N	N	C	C	C	C	C	I	I	I	I	I	I	I	I	I
SIU	N	N	C	C	C	C	N	N	C	N	C	C	C	I	I	I	I	I	I	I	I	I
SIX	N	N	C	C	C	C	N	N	C	C	C	C	C	I	I	I	I	I	I	I	I	I
UIX	N	N	C	C	C	C	N	C	C	C	C	C	C	I	I	I	I	I	I	I	I	I
BU	N	N	C	C	C	C	C	C	C	C	C	C	N	I	I	I	I	I	I	I	I	I
RS-S	N	I	I	N	N	C	I	I	I	I	I	I	I	N	N	C	C	C	C	C	C	C
RS-U	N	I	I	N	C	C	I	I	I	I	I	I	I	N	C	C	C	C	C	C	C	C
RI-N	N	I	I	N	N	N	I	I	I	I	I	I	I	C	C	N	N	N	C	C	C	C
RI-S	N	I	I	N	N	C	I	I	I	I	I	I	I	C	C	N	N	N	C	C	C	C
RI-U	N	I	I	N	C	C	I	I	I	I	I	I	I	C	C	N	N	C	C	C	C	C
RI-X	N	I	I	C	C	C	I	I	I	I	I	I	I	C	C	N	C	C	C	C	C	C
RX-S	N	I	I	N	N	C	I	I	I	I	I	I	I	C	C	C	C	C	C	C	C	C
RX-U	N	I	I	N	C	C	I	I	I	I	I	I	I	C	C	C	C	C	C	C	C	C
RX-X	N	I	I	C	C	C	I	I	I	I	I	I	I	C	C	C	C	C	C	C	C	C

Key

N	No Conflict	SIU	Share with Intent Update
I	Illegal	SIX	Shared with Intent Exclusive
C	Conflict	UIX	Update with Intent Exclusive
		BU	Bulk Update
NL	No Lock	RS-S	Shared Range-Shared
SCH-S	Schema Stability Locks	RS-U	Shared Range-Update
SCH-M	Schema Modification Locks	RI-N	Insert Range-Null
S	Shared	RI-S	Insert Range-Shared
U	Update	RI-U	Insert Range-Update
X	Exclusive	RI-X	Insert Range-Exclusive
IS	Intent Shared	RX-S	Exclusive Range-Shared
IU	Intent Update	RX-U	Exclusive Range-Update
IX	Intent Exclusive	RX-X	Exclusive Range-Exclusive

FIGURE 6-19

> *Just because you specify a hint and have therefore explicitly told SQL Server what you want to happen, do not make the mistake of thinking that this is the only lock taken by SQL Server. Even if you exclude the intent locks, you might find a few surprises in store that lead to unexpected compatibility issues. If this piques your interest, take a look at the "Read Uncommitted" section coming up under "Pessimistic Isolation Levels" for a surprising example.*

Lock Escalation

Lock escalation has been touched on briefly in this chapter, but it's worth knowing more about the details of it. That way, you can identify both when it is happening and when it is likely to happen.

Lock escalation occurs when SQL Server realizes it is locking either too many pages or too many rows. This can be identified in one of two ways. Either the number of locks required to satisfy the query has exceeded the lock threshold or the lock manager has consumed too much memory for a single query, and the memory threshold has been exceeded. When either threshold has been exceeded SQL Server will attempt an *escalation*. By this I mean SQL Server will try to grab a table lock. The only exception to this is in SQL Server 2008, where the escalation for a partitioned table would be to the HoBT, rather than to the table.

Books Online states that the threshold for a lock escalation is reached when the statement has acquired in excess of 5,000 row or page level locks on a single instance of an object (see the following note). At this point, an attempt is made to convert a higher-level lock on the object (either an IS or an IX lock) to an S lock or an X lock on the table. If this fails, perhaps because the table is being used by someone else, then SQL Server will back off and try again if it acquires another 1,250 locks on the same instance of the object. Remember that all locks attained must originate from the same object within the statement to qualify for exceeding the lock threshold, so 4,000 locks from tableA that is self-joined (i.e., another set of 4,000 locks) would not qualify.

Unlike the lock threshold, the memory threshold for lock escalation isn't managed completely internally. You can influence it both with trace flags and serverwide permissions in `sp_configure`, which is covered next as you learn how to control lock escalation.

> *The threshold for lock escalation is not a fixed limit. In basic lock threshold testing I have regularly seen a lock escalation attempt once there have been more than 6,250 individual locks attained (either row or page). The subsequent section on detecting lock escalation details how you can determine when a lock has been escalated.*

Controlling Lock Escalation

In SQL Server 2008, lock escalation can be controlled at the table level with the following syntax:

```
ALTER TABLE dbo.FactInternetSales
SET (LOCK_ESCALATION = AUTO|TABLE|DISABLE)
```

This allows lock escalation at either the HoBT level or the table level, or disables it. The latter isn't completely disabled, but it is to all intents and purposes. If a serializable transaction were issued against a heap that had to be scanned in full, then SQL Server would be forced to take a table lock to protect the transaction. This is a great step forward, as it provides much finer-grained control over this feature.

An alternative method would be to try to control it in code by using hints. By manually setting the PAGLOCK or TABLOCK hints, SQL Server is forced to take less granular locks. Be warned, however, this will be at the cost of reduced concurrency.

Trace flags 1211 and 1224 can also be used to disable lock escalation. Trace flag 1211 completely disables lock escalation. Setting this trace flag can generate a large number of lock resources and ultimately lead to a 1204 error message (unable to lock resource) due to memory starvation. Trace flag 1224 disables lock escalation based on the number of locks but allows it to operate if memory consumption becomes an issue. Exceeding either one of the following conditions will cause lock escalation to be triggered:

➤ Forty percent of the memory used by the database engine is used by lock objects when the locks property of sp_configure is set to 0.

➤ Forty percent of the value set for the locks property in sp_configure. The locks property in Sp_configure contains the total number of locks SQL Server is permitted to issue. This therefore affects the amount of memory used by SQL Server for locking. For example, if the locks option had been set to 100 and a single object in a query had exceeded 40 locks then SQL Server would attempt to escalate the lock.

Detecting Lock Escalation

Lock escalation can be seen in Profiler but only for successful attempts. Unsuccessful attempts do not appear. Unsurprisingly, this event belongs to the Locks event class.

Interestingly, The Lock:Escalation class provides additional information on the point at which the escalation occurred. Through the event subclass you can see if the escalation was triggered by the number of locks attained or was due to the amount of memory used. The IntegerData and IntegerData2 fields detail the number of locks held by the HoBT at the time of escalation and the escalated lock count (number of locks converted), respectively.

> *For full details on the* Lock:Escalation *class, please refer to the "lock escalation [SQL Server], event class" section of Books Online. Alternatively, the web version of this article can be found on msdn at* http://msdn.microsoft.com/en-us/library/ms190723.aspx.

Deadlocking

Deadlocking occurs when two processes each hold a lock or set of locks that is incompatible with a lock that the other process is trying to acquire. As neither process can complete, the two processes are said to be deadlocked. Rather than look on in morbid fascination, SQL Server chooses a victim based on which of the two processes is easiest to roll back, which is based on the amount of resources it has consumed. The victim is then rolled back.

If you have trace flags 1204 or 1222 running on the server or are using Profiler/SQL Trace to capture deadlock events, you can gather information on what processes were involved in the deadlock and which one or ones were chosen as the victim. This normally makes the identification of deadlocks a relatively straightforward process. Resolving them can be another matter entirely!

Consider this straightforward example:

1. Create the table and data:

   ```
   CREATE TABLE dbo.conn1 (col1 INT)
   INSERT dbo.conn1 (col1)
   VALUES(1)

   CREATE TABLE dbo.conn2 (col1 INT)
   INSERT dbo.Conn2 (col1)
   VALUES(1)
   ```

2. In Session 1, run the following code snippet:

   ```
   /*SESSION 1*/
   BEGIN TRAN
   UPDATE dbo.conn1 SET col1 = 1
   ```

3. Run this code in Session 2:

   ```
   /*SESSION 2 */
   BEGIN TRAN
   UPDATE dbo.conn2 SET col1 = 1
   UPDATE dbo.conn1 SET col1 = 1
   ```

4. Fire up Profiler, select the deadlock events, as shown in Figure 6-20, and click OK.

5. Return to Session 1 and run this last code snippet:

   ```
   UPDATE dbo.conn2 SET col1 = 1
   ```

You should now have an error message in the Messages tab of Session 1 that looks this:

```
Msg 1205, Level 13, State 45, Line 2
Transaction (Process ID 52) was deadlocked on lock resources with another
process and has been chosen as the deadlock victim. Rerun the transaction.
```

If your Profiler trace successfully captured the deadlock graph, then you should also have a picture that looks like the one shown in Figure 6-21.

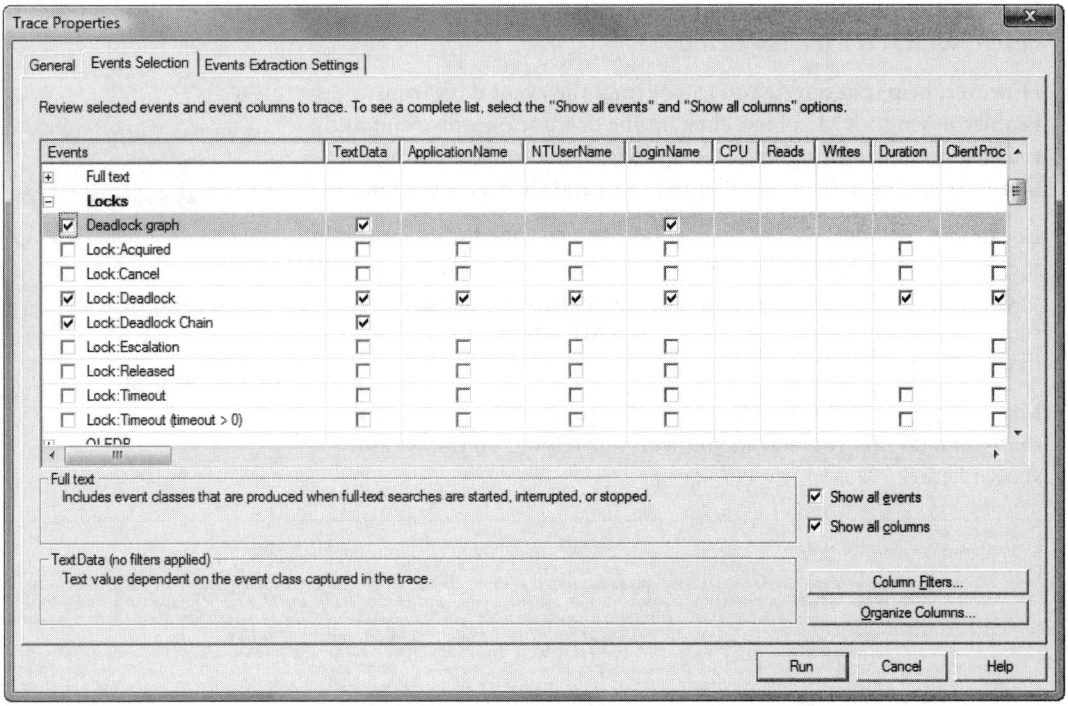

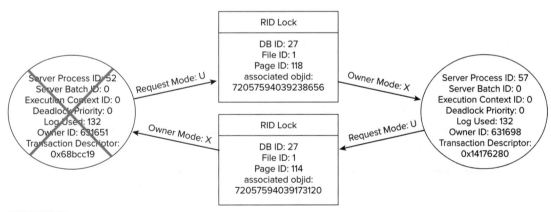

FIGURE 6-20

FIGURE 6-21

Hovering over the circles shows you the syntax of the statements made in the batch. Personally, I don't find this to be very informative. You can derive the tables involved via the associated objid's that are held in the RID Lock boxes. However, often you need to be able to see the rows involved.

If the SQL statements were actually stored procedure executions, then you might also find that the hover-over text is a lot less useful.

However, help is at hand. You can extract the event data from Profiler down to XML. First click on the deadlock graph event and then right-click to bring up some options. Look for something entitled Extract Event Data (see Figure 6-22), and then save the files.

Run Trace	
Pause Trace	
Stop Trace	
Toggle Bookmark	Ctrl+F2
Aggregated View	Ctrl+G
Grouped View	Ctrl+E
Extract Event Data...	
Properties...	

Locate the .xdl file saved at the location you specified after extracting the event data in Figure 6-22. If you just double-click the file, it will open in Management Studio and you are no further along. However, right-click this file and open it with an XML editor of your choice. I like XML Spy.

FIGURE 6-22

I have compressed the output shown in Figure 6-23, but it is hoped that you'll do this yourself so you won't be relying on the window shown here.

```
<deadlock-list>
  <deadlock victim="process5866388">
    <process-list>
      <process id="process5866388" taskpriority="0" logused="132" waitresource="RID: 27:1:118:0" waittime="211" ownerId="631651" transactionname="user_transaction" lasttranstarted="
2009-07-06T07:41:13.720" XDES="0x68bcc10" lockMode="U" schedulerid="2" kpid="3040" status="suspended" spid="52" sbid="0" ecid="0" priority="0" trancount="2" lastbatchstarted="
2009-07-06T07:41:20.600" lastbatchcompleted="2009-07-06T07:41:13.720" clientapp="Microsoft SQL Server Management Studio - Query" hostname="MYPC" hostpid="7688" loginname="JRJ"
isolationlevel="read committed (2)" xactid="631651" currentdb="27" lockTimeout="4294967295" clientoption1="671090784" clientoption2="390200">
      <process id="process5866c70" taskpriority="0" logused="132" waitresource="RID: 27:1:114:0" waittime="3649" ownerId="631698" transactionname="user_transaction" lasttranstarted="
2009-07-06T07:41:17.160" XDES="0x14176280" lockMode="U" schedulerid="2" kpid="4488" status="suspended" spid="57" sbid="0" ecid="0" priority="0" trancount="2" lastbatchstarted="
2009-07-06T07:41:17.160" lastbatchcompleted="2009-07-06T07:40:43.890" clientapp="Microsoft SQL Server Management Studio - Query" hostname="MYPC" hostpid="7688" loginname="JRJ"
isolationlevel="read committed (2)" xactid="631698" currentdb="27" lockTimeout="4294967295" clientoption1="671090784" clientoption2="390200">
    </process-list>
    <resource-list>
      <ridlock fileid="1" pageid="118" dbid="27" objectname="JUNK.dbo.conn2" id="lock1224d800" mode="X" associatedObjectId="72057594039238656">
      <ridlock fileid="1" pageid="114" dbid="27" objectname="JUNK.dbo.conn1" id="lock1224f380" mode="X" associatedObjectId="72057594039173120">
    </resource-list>
  </deadlock>
</deadlock-list>
```

FIGURE 6-23

Immediately, you can see that there is a lot more information. Key items include the following:

➤ **deadlock victim:** Always handy

➤ **logused:** One factor in determining which one to roll back is the amount of the transaction log used by either process.

➤ **waitresource:** A very important piece of info. With this, you can identify the row. For a heap this is the row id (RID). On a clustered index this is a hashed value that represents the row. A RID follows the following format `<DatabaseID>:<FileID>:<PageNumber>:<SlotID>`. An example of a hashed value used for a clustered index would be (0400b4b7d951).

➤ **lastbatchstarted:** You know when it occurred.

➤ **isolationlevel:** It's read committed, so you know that SH locks weren't being held unnecessarily.

Now it's time to go find the rows. You know the tables involved so this shouldn't take long:

```
SELECT  %%lockres%%
        , *
FROM    dbo.Conn2
WHERE   %%LockRes%% = '1:118:0'

SELECT  %%lockres%%
        , *
FROM    dbo.Conn1
WHERE   %%LockRes%% = '1:114:0'
```

The code for the deadlocking scenario is available for download at Wrox.com
[CH06 Deadlock.sql, CH06 Deadlock_XML.xdl (for reference)]

Although this little function was mentioned before, what it does was not explained. Basically, it returns the hash value or the RID for the locked resource. By taking a portion of the wait resource from the XML seen in Figure 6-23, you are able to uniquely identify the rows in question in Figure 6-24 using the SQL above.

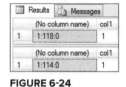

FIGURE 6-24

OK, so the rows aren't that interesting — but you have found the rows that experienced contention. A word to the wise, however: `%%lockres%%` isn't a documented function. It is also resource intensive. Therefore, use it only if necessary. You can get the file and page information through documented methods via the `sys.dm_os_buffer_descriptors` DMV but you won't get the slot or row data. However, using it in favor of `%%lockres%%` will be less resource-intensive and will reduce the cost of finding the rows in question.

For a much more advanced scenario involving `%%lockres%%`, feel free to head over to `http://blogs.conchango.com/jamesrowlandjones/archive/2009/05/28/the-curious-case-of-the-dubious-deadlock-and-the-not-so-logical-lock.aspx`.

PESSIMISTIC CONCURRENCY

SQL Server's default position is to be pessimistic. In fact, up until 2005 it was the only way it knew. Before row-level locking was introduced in SQL Server 7, this was a real issue. Entire pages were pessimistically locked, which could have quite a dramatic impact on concurrency.

What does it mean to be pessimistic about concurrency? To put it simply, it means that SQL Server is betting that concurrent access to the data is likely to cause blocking, so it sets its stall out for this kind of workload. The locking implementation by default will be such that readers will block writers and writers will block readers. Writers will always block concurrent writers, even in an optimist's world. However, it still means that multiple readers can access the same data at the same time. Optimistic concurrency will be covered in depth after we have explored the pessimistic model.

The extent to which this impacts SQL Server is largely defined by the isolation level. So without further ado, let's first look at the pessimistic isolation levels.

Pessimistic Isolation Levels

Earlier, the chapter looked at the reasons why transactions need to support isolation. To re-cap; when writing data, a transaction might exhibit certain behaviors that may be considered undesirable. Those behaviors were:

➤ Lost Updates

➤ Dirty Reads

➤ Non-Repeatable Reads

➤ Phantom Reads

To deal with these behaviors SQL Server provides five isolation levels to ensure the safety of your transactions.

Read Uncommitted

This is the lowest level of isolation offered in SQL Server. Setting this isolation level in your procedure would be the equivalent of putting a (NOLOCK) hint on every table referenced in the FROM clause of your query. This level allows data reads from uncommitted transactions (dirty reads), non-repeatable reads, and phantoms.

However, please note that read uncommitted is not the same as not having any locks — it only applies to the data locks that would otherwise be generated when reading data. Furthermore, you can still be blocked when reading data even when you use this isolation level.

Consider the following example.

In Session 1, type the following and execute it:

```
/* SESSION 1 */

USE ADVENTUREWORKS2008;
BEGIN TRANSACTION;
      ALTER TABLE Person.Person
        ADD LastName2 nvarchar(50);
--ROLLBACK TRANSACTION;
```

In Session 2, type the following and execute it:

```
/* SESSION 2 */

USE ADVENTUREWORKS2008;
SET TRANSACTION ISOLATION LEVEL READ UNCOMMITTED;

SELECT *
FROM   Person.Person
WHERE  BusinessEntityID = 1;
```

In Session 3, type the following and execute it:

```
/* SESSION 3 */

USE [AdventureWorksDW2008];

SELECT   request_session_id
        ,resource_type
        ,resource_subtype
        ,resource_description
        ,resource_associated_entity_id
        ,request_mode
        ,request_status
FROM     sys.dm_tran_locks
WHERE    request_session_id IN (54,57)
--Substitute your own SPID's here for sessions 1&2
ORDER BY request_session_id;
```

This code is available for download at Wrox.com [CH06 Read Uncommitted.sql]

Session 2 is blocked by Session 1! How can that be? Well, as you will see, locks aren't only held against the data in the database. Even for read uncommitted transactions, SQL Server needs to take locks to ensure the integrity of the read. In the preceding example Session 1 tried to alter the structure of the table; therefore, SQL Server took out a schema modification lock (Sch-M), described earlier, on the table. The output from Session 3 can be seen below in Figure 6-25 and confirms the Schema modify lock.

	request_session_id	resource_type	resource_subtype	resource_description	resource_associated_entity_id	request_mode	request_status
1	54	DATABASE	DDL		0	S	GRANT
2	54	OBJECT			5	IX	GRANT
3	54	DATABASE			0	S	GRANT
4	54	OBJECT			7	IX	GRANT
5	54	OBJECT			3	IX	GRANT
6	54	OBJECT			34	IX	GRANT
7	54	OBJECT			41	IX	GRANT
8	54	KEY		(2c02a1f36b7c)	562949956108288	X	GRANT
9	54	METADATA	DATA_SPACE	data_space_id = 1	0	Sch-S	GRANT
10	54	KEY		(8e00b9d7d978)	281474979397632	X	GRANT
11	54	KEY		(8000057524a9)	281474978938880	X	GRANT
12	54	KEY		(0e005521e822)	196608	X	GRANT
13	54	KEY		(000071f9db34)	458752	X	GRANT
14	54	KEY		(0000169f0899)	327680	X	GRANT
15	54	METADATA	SCHEMA	schema_id = 6	0	Sch-S	GRANT
16	54	OBJECT			1509580416	Sch-M	GRANT
17	57	OBJECT			1509580416	Sch-S	WAIT
18	57	METADATA	SCHEMA	schema_id = 6	0	Sch-S	GRANT
19	57	DATABASE	PLANGUIDE		0	S	GRANT
20	57	DATABASE			0	S	GRANT

FIGURE 6-25

How does the Schema modification lock impact the dirty read, you ask? The observant among you will see why from Figure 6-25. However, to understand this fully we'll look at this problem in a slightly different way. First of all you should release the schema modification lock in Session 1. If you copied the example completely, then you should see at the bottom a commented-out line of code to rollback the transaction. If you just highlight the words "Rollback Transaction" and execute that, the transaction should disappear from the system.

Now run that query again but this time with some additional trace flags on to help us see what is happening — remember these can be turned off later by using the corresponding DBCC TRACEOFF. This time, run the following code in Session 2 (you may need to run the SELECT part twice to get just the locks, as the first time will include all the plan info as well):

```
USE ADVENTUREWORKS2008

DBCC TRACEON (-1,3604)-- OUTPUT TO THE CLIENT
DBCC TRACEON(-1,1200) -- SHOWS ALL LOCK INFO

SET TRANSACTION ISOLATION LEVEL READ UNCOMMITTED

SELECT *
FROM   Person.Person
WHERE  BusinessEntityID = 1
```

You should see output similar to the following in the Messages window of Session 2:

```
Process 71 acquiring Sch-S lock on OBJECT: 10:1499152386:0  (class bit0 ref1)
result: OK
Process 71 acquiring Sch-S lock on METADATA: database_id = 10 XML_COLLECTION
(xml_collection_id = 65536) (class bit2000000 ref1) result: OK

Process 71 acquiring Sch-S lock on METADATA: database_id = 10
XML_COLLECTION(xml_collection_id = 65537) (class bit2000000 ref1) result: OK

(1 row(s) affected)
Process 71 releasing lock on OBJECT: 10:1509580416:0
```

Ignoring the METADATA locks for a moment, you can clearly see that a lock has in fact been taken on an OBJECT. The number sequence next to the OBJECT identifies it as being in Database 10, with an Object_ID of 1509580416. The final zero would normally relate to the page, but in this case that isn't relevant so it is represented by a zero. A quick check with the following query confirms our suspicions; a read uncommitted read actually does take a lock, namely a schema stability (Sch-S) lock, for the duration of the read. As we saw earlier when looking at lock compatibility, Schema Stability locks are not compatible with any other type of lock. As Session 1 was altering the table and held a schema modify lock, the read would have been incompatible with the write. Hence, the read uncommitted read was legitimately blocked.

```
USE ADVENTUREWORKS2008

SELECT     DB_ID(10)
     ,OBJECT_NAME(1509580416)
```

Refer back to Figure 6-25 down at the bottom and you will see that the object schema stability lock is present in the output. The answer was there all along! The key point here is that the request_ status is set to WAIT and not GRANT.

Read Committed

Read committed is SQL Server's default isolation level. It strikes a balance between isolation and concurrency. With read committed, it is not possible to take a dirty read without explicitly using a locking hint, covered later. However, you can, and in all likelihood will, get non-repeatable reads and phantom reads with this isolation level.

Read locks, however, are only taken for the duration of the read at this level, not for the duration of the transaction. That is why if you run a select statement in one session and try to look at the locks held in a second session you won't see them. This is the case even when you create an explicit transaction, as shown in the following example:

```
/* Run in Session 1
*/

USE ADVENTUREWORKS2008;

SET TRANSACTION ISOLATION LEVEL READ COMMITTED;

BEGIN TRANSACTION;
SELECT FirstName
       ,MiddleName
       ,LastName
       ,Suffix
FROM   Person.Person
WHERE  BusinessEntityID = 1;
--ROLLBACK TRANSACTION;

/* Run in Session 2
*/
USE ADVENTUREWORKS2008;

SELECT  request_session_id           as [Session]
        ,DB_NAME(resource_database_id) as [Database]
        ,Resource_Type               as [Type]
        ,resource_subtype            as SubType
        ,resource_description        as [Description]
        ,request_mode                as Mode
        ,request_owner_type          as OwnerType
FROM    sys.dm_tran_locks
WHERE   request_session_id > 50
AND     resource_database_id = DB_ID('AdventureWorks2008')
AND     request_session_id <> @@SPID;
```

This code is available for download at Wrox.com [CH06 Read Committed.sql]

Assuming you have no other active connections you should see three rows of data in the results of Session 2 as can be seen in Figure 6-26 below.

	Session	Database	Type	SubType	Description	Mode	OwnerType
1	54	AdventureWorks2008	DATABASE			S	SHARED_TRANSACTION_WORKSPACE
2	54	AdventureWorks2008	METADATA	DATABASE_PRINCIPAL	principal_id = 1	Sch-S	TRANSACTION
3	54	AdventureWorks2008	METADATA	SCHEMA	schema_id = 6	Sch-S	TRANSACTION

FIGURE 6-26

Look at the column named `resource_type`, which is in this `sys.dm_tran_locks` query, and is aliased as [Type]. You can see one `DATABASE` row and two more of those `METADATA` rows. What you shouldn't see are any rows that look like they are holding locks on data — because they have already been released.

As an aside, the `DATABASE` lock is present because in Session 1 you were asked to execute a `USE` statement to place the subsequent queries in the context of AdventureWorks2008. This represents our connection to this database.

Repeatable Read

With repeatable read, SQL Server needs to ensure that should the same data be read more than once in a transaction, the user can expect the same result. In the description of read committed, you saw how the locks on a read were released as soon as the data had been read. With repeatable read, those locks have to be held for the duration of the transaction. This prevents other users from modifying the data read during the lifetime of the transaction. It does not protect you from users inserting or deleting rows in between the range of rows that your query has read, however. For that level of protection see the Serializable sub-section next.

Repeatable read also enables us to see those locks in the DMV. We can modify the previous example only very slightly to get a much clearer picture of what is going on:

```
/* Run in Session 1
*/
USE ADVENTUREWORKS2008;

SET TRANSACTION ISOLATION LEVEL REPEATABLE READ;

BEGIN TRANSACTION;
SELECT FirstName
        ,MiddleName
        ,LastName
        ,Suffix
FROM    Person.Person
WHERE   BusinessEntityID = 1;
--ROLLBACK TRANSACTION;
/* Run in Session 2
*/
USE ADVENTUREWORKS2008;

SELECT  request_session_id              as [Session]
        ,DB_NAME(resource_database_id)  as [Database]
        ,Resource_Type                  as [Type]
        ,resource_subtype               as SubType
        ,resource_description           as [Description]
        ,request_mode                   as Mode
        ,request_owner_type             as OwnerType
FROM    sys.dm_tran_locks
WHERE   request_session_id > 50
AND     resource_database_id = DB_ID('AdventureWorks2008')
AND     request_session_id <> @@SPID;
```

You should now see something akin to that shown in Figure 6-27 in the Results tab for Session 2.

	Session	Database	Type	Sub Type	Description	Mode	OwnerType
1	54	AdventureWorks2008	DATABASE			S	SHARED_TRANSACTION_WORKSPACE
2	54	AdventureWorks2008	METADATA	DATABASE_PRINCIPAL	principal_id = 1	Sch-S	TRANSACTION
3	54	AdventureWorks2008	METADATA	SCHEMA	schema_id = 6	Sch-S	TRANSACTION
4	54	AdventureWorks2008	OBJECT			IS	TRANSACTION
5	54	AdventureWorks2008	PAGE		1:36120	IS	TRANSACTION
6	54	AdventureWorks2008	KEY		(010086470766)	S	TRANSACTION

FIGURE 6-27

Note the sixth row. The Type is a key lock, which equates to a row in a table (in our case a Mr. Ken J Sanchez Snr), and the Mode is a shared lock (S). The Description actually pinpoints the row being locked. We can clearly see that the lock has been taken and held until we decide to release the lock in Session 1. Try that now yourself. Roll back the lock in Session 1 and then rerun the query in Session 2. The result of rerunning the query in Session 2 should now look like that shown in Figure 6-28.

	Session	Database	Type	Sub Type	Description	Mode	OwnerType
1	54	AdventureWorks2008	DATABASE			S	SHARED_TRANSACTION_WORKSPACE

FIGURE 6-28

Now prove the repeatable read. Rerun Session 1 to generate a lock on the row and then run the following code in a third session to try to update that row:

Available for
download on
Wrox.com

```
/*SESSION 3
*/

USE AdventureWorks2008;

BEGIN TRANSACTION;

DECLARE @LastName table
        (   OldLastName nvarchar(50)
        ,   NewLastName nvarchar(50)
        );

UPDATE  Person.Person
SET     LastName = 'Rowland-Jones'
OUTPUT  DELETED.LastName
        ,INSERTED.LastName
INTO    @LastName
WHERE   BusinessEntityID = 1;

SELECT  *
FROM    @LastName;

--ROLLBACK TRANSACTION
```

This code is available for download at Wrox.com [CH06 Repeatable Read.sql]

The query in Session 3 is blocked, your query in Session 3 hasn't completed, and the update hasn't taken place. Now try running just the SELECT statement in Session 1 by highlighting that part of the code only and pressing F5. Our original row from Session 1 (Mr. Sanchez) has not had his name changed to Rowland-Jones by Session 3. You can do this any number of times, and you will always be able to repeat the read. Now flip to Session 2 and see what is going on with the locking. You should have results that look like those shown in Figure 6-29.

	Session	Database	Type	SubType	Description	Mode	OwnerType	Status
1	54	AdventureWorks2008	DATABASE			S	SHARED_TRANSACTION_WORKSPACE	GRANT
2	54	AdventureWorks2008	METADATA	DATABASE_PRINCIPAL	principal_id = 1	Sch-S	TRANSACTION	GRANT
3	54	AdventureWorks2008	METADATA	SCHEMA	schema_id = 6	Sch-S	TRANSACTION	GRANT
4	54	AdventureWorks2008	OBJECT			IS	TRANSACTION	GRANT
5	54	AdventureWorks2008	PAGE		1:36120	IS	TRANSACTION	GRANT
6	54	AdventureWorks2008	KEY		(010086470766)	S	TRANSACTION	GRANT
7	67	AdventureWorks2008	KEY		(010086470766)	X	TRANSACTION	CONVERT
8	67	AdventureWorks2008	OBJECT			Sch-S	TRANSACTION	GRANT
9	67	AdventureWorks2008	OBJECT			Sch-S	TRANSACTION	GRANT
10	67	AdventureWorks2008	KEY		(010086470766)	U	TRANSACTION	GRANT
11	67	AdventureWorks2008	DATABASE			S	SHARED_TRANSACTION_WORKSPACE	GRANT
12	67	AdventureWorks2008	PAGE		1:36120	IX	TRANSACTION	GRANT
13	67	AdventureWorks2008	OBJECT			IX	TRANSACTION	GRANT
14	67	AdventureWorks2008	METADATA	XML_COLLECTION	xml_collection_id = 65537	Sch-S	TRANSACTION	GRANT
15	67	AdventureWorks2008	METADATA	SCHEMA	schema_id = 6	Sch-S	TRANSACTION	GRANT
16	67	AdventureWorks2008	METADATA	XML_COLLECTION	xml_collection_id = 65536	Sch-S	TRANSACTION	GRANT
17	67	AdventureWorks2008	METADATA	DATABASE_PRINCIPAL	principal_id = 1	Sch-S	TRANSACTION	GRANT

FIGURE 6-29

The new session, which in this case is 67, has taken an update lock signified by the U in the Mode column on row 10 and is trying to get an exclusive lock (mode X) to perform the update on row 7. However, note the Status change on the far right. Whereas the update lock has a status of GRANT (and you'll see why that is later), the exclusive lock has a status of CONVERT. This means that SQL Server is trying to upgrade the existing update lock to a fully exclusive lock but can't because the read in Session 54 is blocking it. You can also prove this by making a join to another DMV, sys.dm_os_waiting_tasks:

```
USE AdventureWorks2008;

SELECT    lo.request_session_id                  as [Session]
          ,DB_NAME(lo.resource_database_id)      as [Database]
          ,lo.resource_type                      as [Type]
          ,lo.resource_subtype                   as SubType
          ,lo.resource_description               as [Description]
          ,lo.request_mode                       as Mode
          ,lo.request_owner_type                 as OwnerType
          ,lo.request_status                     as [Status]
          ,CASE   WHEN    lo.resource_type = 'OBJECT'
                          THEN    OBJECT_NAME(lo.resource_associated_entity_id)
                  WHEN    lo.resource_associated_entity_id IS NULL
                  OR      lo.resource_associated_entity_id = 0
                          THEN    NULL
                  ELSE            OBJECT_NAME(p.[object_id])
          END  As Associated_Entity
```

```
            ,wt.blocking_session_id
            ,wt.resource_description
FROM        sys.dm_tran_locks as lo
LEFT JOIN   sys.partitions as p
ON      lo.resource_associated_entity_id = p.partition_id
LEFT JOIN   sys.dm_os_waiting_tasks as wt
ON      lo.lock_owner_address = wt.resource_address
WHERE   lo.request_session_id > 50
AND     lo.resource_database_id = DB_ID('AdventureWorks2008')
AND     lo.request_session_id <> @@SPID
ORDER BY [SESSION]
        ,[TYPE];
```

This code is available for download at Wrox.com [CH06 Blocking Script2.sql]

Looking at the output, shown in Figure 6-30, now you can categorically see that the attempted update in Session 67 is being blocked by Session 54. You can read the same data any number of times and nothing can alter the state of that data.

	Session	Database	Type	SubType	Description	Mode	OwnerType	Status	Associated_Entity	blocking_session_id	resource_description
1	54	AdventureWorks2008	DATABASE			S	SHARED_TRANSACTION_WORKSPACE	GRANT	NULL	NULL	NULL
2	54	AdventureWorks2008	KEY		(010086470766)	S	TRANSACTION	GRANT	Person	NULL	NULL
3	54	AdventureWorks2008	METADATA	DATABASE_PRINCIPAL	principal_id = 1	Sch-S	TRANSACTION	GRANT	NULL	NULL	NULL
4	54	AdventureWorks2008	METADATA	SCHEMA	schema_id = 6	Sch-S	TRANSACTION	GRANT	NULL	NULL	NULL
5	54	AdventureWorks2008	OBJECT			IS	TRANSACTION	GRANT	Person	NULL	NULL
6	54	AdventureWorks2008	PAGE		1:36120	IS	TRANSACTION	GRANT	Person	NULL	NULL
7	55	AdventureWorks2008	DATABASE			S	SHARED_TRANSACTION_WORKSPACE	GRANT	NULL	NULL	NULL
8	67	AdventureWorks2008	DATABASE			S	SHARED_TRANSACTION_WORKSPACE	GRANT	NULL	NULL	NULL
9	67	AdventureWorks2008	KEY		(010086470766)	U	TRANSACTION	GRANT	Person	NULL	NULL
10	67	AdventureWorks2008	KEY		(010086470766)	X	TRANSACTION	CONVERT	Person	54	keylock hobtid=72057594057981952 dbid=10 id=lock...
11	67	AdventureWorks2008	METADATA	XML_COLLECTION	xml_collection_id = 65536	Sch-S	TRANSACTION	GRANT	NULL	NULL	NULL
12	67	AdventureWorks2008	METADATA	DATABASE_PRINCIPAL	principal_id = 1	Sch-S	TRANSACTION	GRANT	NULL	NULL	NULL
13	67	AdventureWorks2008	METADATA	XML_COLLECTION	xml_collection_id = 65537	Sch-S	TRANSACTION	GRANT	NULL	NULL	NULL
14	67	AdventureWorks2008	METADATA	SCHEMA	schema_id = 6	Sch-S	TRANSACTION	GRANT	Person	NULL	NULL
15	67	AdventureWorks2008	OBJECT			IX	TRANSACTION	GRANT	Person	NULL	NULL
16	67	AdventureWorks2008	OBJECT			Sch-S	TRANSACTION	GRANT	xml_index_nodes_1509580416_256000	NULL	NULL
17	67	AdventureWorks2008	OBJECT			Sch-S	TRANSACTION	GRANT	xml_index_nodes_1509580416_256001	NULL	NULL
18	67	AdventureWorks2008	PAGE		1:36120	IX	TRANSACTION	GRANT	Person	NULL	NULL

FIGURE 6-30

This can start to become problematic from a concurrency perspective. If these transactions have any significant duration, then these shared locks are going to be hanging around, affecting the ability of other users to write data.

Don't forget that you can, if needed, store data temporarily in a temp table or variable if you need to read it multiple times and reliably get the same value. Therefore, your solution only needs to use Repeatable Read isolation if you want to prevent rows read from being updated or deleted by a competing process.

Serializable

The final, and highest, level of pessimistic isolation is known as *serializable*. A transaction using serializable for its isolation level will not experience dirty reads, non-repeatable reads, or phantoms. Its name is derived from the fact that data access is serialized to prevent those side effects. It does, however, have the greatest impact by far on concurrency.

Interestingly, the default isolation level for an application transaction via, say, ADO.NET is serializable. It is always valuable to check with your application developers to ensure that when they are initiating transactions in their code, they take into account the isolation level and make the appropriate decision. It's actually quite rare for an application to need a serializable transaction; a telltale sign is when you start seeing waits appear for key range locks in the wait stats.

To see serialization in action you have to actually query for a range of data, rather than a single row. You therefore need to change the query in Session 1 slightly. Look for all persons whose `BusinessIdentityID` value is less than 10. Session 1 now reads as follows:

```
/*Session 1
*/

USE ADVENTUREWORKS2008;

SET TRANSACTION ISOLATION LEVEL SERIALIZABLE;

BEGIN TRANSACTION;
SELECT *
FROM   Person.Person
WHERE  BusinessEntityID < 10;
--ROLLBACK TRANSACTION;
```

As shown in Figure 6-31, nine rows have been returned.

	BusinessEntityID	PersonType	NameStyle	Title	FirstName	MiddleName	LastName	Suffix	EmailPromotion	AdditionalContactInfo	Demographics	rowguid	ModifiedDate
1	1	EM	0	NULL	Ken	J	Sánchez	Snr	0	NULL	\<IndividualSurvey xmlns="http://schemas.microso...	92C4279F-1207-48A3-8448-4636514EB7E2	1999-02-08 00:00:00.000
2	2	EM	0	NULL	Terri	Lee	Duffy	NULL	1	NULL	\<IndividualSurvey xmlns="http://schemas.microso...	D8763459-8AA8-47CC-AFF7-C9079AF79033	1998-02-24 00:00:00.000
3	3	EM	0	NULL	Roberto	NULL	Tamburello	NULL	0	NULL	\<IndividualSurvey xmlns="http://schemas.microso...	E1A2555E-0828-434B-A33B-6F38136A37DE	1997-12-05 00:00:00.000
4	4	EM	0	NULL	Rob	NULL	Walters	NULL	0	NULL	\<IndividualSurvey xmlns="http://schemas.microso...	F2D7CE06-38B3-4357-805B-F4B6B71C01FF	1997-12-29 00:00:00.000
5	5	EM	0	Ms.	Gail	A	Erickson	NULL	0	NULL	\<IndividualSurvey xmlns="http://schemas.microso...	F3A3F6B4-AE3B-430C-A754-9F2231BA6FEF	1998-01-30 00:00:00.000
6	6	EM	0	Mr.	Jossef	H	Goldberg	NULL	0	NULL	\<IndividualSurvey xmlns="http://schemas.microso...	0DEA28FD-EFFE-482A-AFD3-B7E8F199D56F	1998-02-17 00:00:00.000
7	7	EM	0	NULL	Dylan	A	Miller	NULL	2	NULL	\<IndividualSurvey xmlns="http://schemas.microso...	C45E8AB8-01BE-4B76-B215-820C8368181A	1999-03-05 00:00:00.000
8	8	EM	0	NULL	Diane	L	Margheim	NULL	0	NULL	\<IndividualSurvey xmlns="http://schemas.microso...	A948E590-4A56-45A9-BC9A-160A1CC9D990	1999-01-23 00:00:00.000
9	9	EM	0	NULL	Gigi	N	Matthew	NULL	0	NULL	\<IndividualSurvey xmlns="http://schemas.microso...	5FC28C0E-6D36-4252-9846-05CAA0B1F6C5	1999-02-10 00:00:00.000

FIGURE 6-31

Reuse the lock monitoring script from the repeatable read scenario above. The results contain some additional locks, as shown in Figure 6-32.

	Session	Database	Type	SubType	Description	Mode	OwnerType	Status	Associated_Entity	blocking_session_id	resource_description
1	65	AdventureWorks2008	DATABASE			S	SHARED_TRANSACTION_WORKSPACE	GRANT	NULL	NULL	NULL
2	65	AdventureWorks2008	KEY		(03000d8f0ecc)	RangeS-S	TRANSACTION	GRANT	Person	NULL	NULL
3	65	AdventureWorks2008	KEY		(0900696fb3a3)	RangeS-S	TRANSACTION	GRANT	Person	NULL	NULL
4	65	AdventureWorks2008	KEY		(07005a186c43)	RangeS-S	TRANSACTION	GRANT	Person	NULL	NULL
5	65	AdventureWorks2008	KEY		(010086470766)	RangeS-S	TRANSACTION	GRANT	Person	NULL	NULL
6	65	AdventureWorks2008	KEY		(06003f7fd0fb)	RangeS-S	TRANSACTION	GRANT	Person	NULL	NULL
7	65	AdventureWorks2008	KEY		(0a0087c006b1)	RangeS-S	TRANSACTION	GRANT	Person	NULL	NULL
8	65	AdventureWorks2008	KEY		(08000c080f1b)	RangeS-S	TRANSACTION	GRANT	Person	NULL	NULL
9	65	AdventureWorks2008	KEY		(0400b4b7d951)	RangeS-S	TRANSACTION	GRANT	Person	NULL	NULL
10	65	AdventureWorks2008	KEY		(020068e8b274)	RangeS-S	TRANSACTION	GRANT	Person	NULL	NULL
11	65	AdventureWorks2008	KEY		(0500d1d065e9)	RangeS-S	TRANSACTION	GRANT	Person	NULL	NULL
12	65	AdventureWorks2008	METADATA	SCHEMA	schema_id = 6	Sch-S	TRANSACTION	GRANT	NULL	NULL	NULL
13	65	AdventureWorks2008	METADATA	XML_COLLECTION	xml_collection_id = 65536	Sch-S	TRANSACTION	GRANT	NULL	NULL	NULL
14	65	AdventureWorks2008	METADATA	DATABASE_PRINCIPAL	principal_id = 1	Sch-S	TRANSACTION	GRANT	NULL	NULL	NULL
15	65	AdventureWorks2008	METADATA	XML_COLLECTION	xml_collection_id = 65537	Sch-S	TRANSACTION	GRANT	NULL	NULL	NULL
16	65	AdventureWorks2008	OBJECT			IS	TRANSACTION	GRANT	Person	NULL	NULL
17	65	AdventureWorks2008	PAGE		1:36120	IS	TRANSACTION	GRANT	Person	NULL	NULL

FIGURE 6-32

Note that you now have rows being returned from the sys.dm_tran_locks view with a mode of RangeS-S. But wait. On closer inspection, there are 10 RangeS-S locks but only nine rows have been returned. What is the purpose of the additional lock? Fire up a new session (Session 3) and insert a row:

```
/* Session 3 */
USE AdventureWorks2008;

BEGIN TRANSACTION;

SET IDENTITY_INSERT Person.BusinessEntity ON;

INSERT INTO [Person].[BusinessEntity]
            ([BusinessEntityID]
            ,[rowguid]
            ,[ModifiedDate]
            )
      VALUES
            (0
            ,NEWID()
            ,getdate()
            );

SET IDENTITY_INSERT Person.BusinessEntity OFF;

Select  *
FROM    Person.BusinessEntity
WHERE   BusinessEntityID = 0;

INSERT INTO [Person].[Person]
            ([BusinessEntityID]
            ,[PersonType]
            ,[NameStyle]
            ,[Title]
            ,[FirstName]
            ,[MiddleName]
            ,[LastName]
            ,[Suffix]
            ,[EmailPromotion]
            ,[AdditionalContactInfo]
            ,[Demographics]
            ,[rowguid]
            ,[ModifiedDate])
      VALUES
            (0
            ,'EM'
            ,0
            ,'Mr'
            ,'James'
            ,'Anthony'
            ,'Rowland-Jones'
            ,'III'
            ,1
            ,NULL
            ,NULL
```

```
                    ,newid()
                    ,getdate());
    --ROLLBACK TRANSACTION;
```

This code is available for download at Wrox.com [CH06 Serializable.sql]

To insert a row into `Person.Person`, first insert a row into `Person.BusinessEntity`. In order to show the blocking for a phantom based on our query running in Session 1, it is necessary to manually pick an identity value for `BusinessEntityID`. I have chosen 0. If you now try to run this query in Session 3, you are blocked.

Figure 6-33 shows the partial output of the locking query in Session 2.

	Session	Database	Type	Sub Type	Description	Mode	OwnerType	Status	Associated_Entity	blocking_session_id	resource_description
3	65	AdventureWorks2008	KEY		(010086470766)	RangeS-S	TRANSACTION	GRANT	Person	NULL	NULL
4	65	AdventureWorks2008	KEY		(03000d8f0ecc)	RangeS-S	TRANSACTION	GRANT	Person	NULL	NULL
5	65	AdventureWorks2008	KEY		(0900699fb3a3)	RangeS-S	TRANSACTION	GRANT	Person	NULL	NULL
6	65	AdventureWorks2008	KEY		(08000c080f1b)	RangeS-S	TRANSACTION	GRANT	Person	NULL	NULL
7	65	AdventureWorks2008	KEY		(0400b4b7d951)	RangeS-S	TRANSACTION	GRANT	Person	NULL	NULL
8	65	AdventureWorks2008	KEY		(020068e8b274)	RangeS-S	TRANSACTION	GRANT	Person	NULL	NULL
9	65	AdventureWorks2008	KEY		(06003f7fd0fb)	RangeS-S	TRANSACTION	GRANT	Person	NULL	NULL
10	65	AdventureWorks2008	KEY		(0a0087c009b1)	RangeS-S	TRANSACTION	GRANT	Person	NULL	NULL
11	65	AdventureWorks2008	KEY		(0500d1d065e9)	RangeS-S	TRANSACTION	GRANT	Person	NULL	NULL
12	65	AdventureWorks2008	METADATA	XML_COLLECTION	xml_collection_id = 65536	Sch-S	TRANSACTION	GRANT	NULL	NULL	NULL
13	65	AdventureWorks2008	METADATA	DATABASE_PRINCIPAL	principal_id = 1	Sch-S	TRANSACTION	GRANT	NULL	NULL	NULL
14	65	AdventureWorks2008	METADATA	XML_COLLECTION	xml_collection_id = 65537	Sch-S	TRANSACTION	GRANT	NULL	NULL	NULL
15	65	AdventureWorks2008	METADATA	SCHEMA	schema_id = 6	Sch-S	TRANSACTION	GRANT	NULL	NULL	NULL
16	65	AdventureWorks2008	OBJECT			IS	TRANSACTION	GRANT	Person	NULL	NULL
17	65	AdventureWorks2008	PAGE		1:36120	IS	TRANSACTION	GRANT	Person	NULL	NULL
18	70	AdventureWorks2008	DATABASE			S	SHARED_TRANSACTION_WORKSPACE	GRANT	NULL	NULL	NULL
19	70	AdventureWorks2008	KEY		(ea020122f943)	X	TRANSACTION	GRANT	BusinessEntity	NULL	NULL
20	70	AdventureWorks2008	KEY		(010086470766)	RangeI-N	TRANSACTION	WAIT	Person	65	keylock hobtid=72057594057981952 dbid=10 id=lock...
21	70	AdventureWorks2008	KEY		(0000e320bbde)	X	TRANSACTION	GRANT	BusinessEntity	NULL	NULL
22	70	AdventureWorks2008	METADATA	SCHEMA	schema_id = 6	Sch-S	TRANSACTION	GRANT	NULL	NULL	NULL
23	70	AdventureWorks2008	METADATA	XML_COLLECTION	xml_collection_id = 65537	Sch-S	TRANSACTION	GRANT	NULL	NULL	NULL
24	70	AdventureWorks2008	METADATA	DATABASE_PRINCIPAL	principal_id = 1	Sch-S	TRANSACTION	GRANT	NULL	NULL	NULL
25	70	AdventureWorks2008	METADATA	XML_COLLECTION	xml_collection_id = 65536	Sch-S	TRANSACTION	GRANT	NULL	NULL	NULL

FIGURE 6-33

Sure enough, our query is again blocked. Check the details of the blocking information provided, as shown in Figure 6-34.

X	TRANSACTION	GRANT	BusinessEntity	NULL	NULL
RangeI-N	TRANSACTION	WAIT	Person	65	keylock hobtid=72057594057981952 dbid=10 id=lock9cd64c0 mode=RangeS-S associatedObjectId=72057594057981952
X	TRANSACTION	GRANT	BusinessEntity	NULL	NULL

FIGURE 6-34

You are once again blocked, but this time by a lock using mode RangeS-S. This is a range key lock. Recall that there were 10 locks but only nine rows returned. This is the tenth lock. It is preventing us from inserting a phantom row that would otherwise occur by an insert of a `BusinessEntityID` with a value of 0. In fact, that last lock will stop us from inserting any value from -2,147,483,648 to 0.

Did you also notice the lock mode we were blocked from using? The Range I-N mode, which stands for Insert Range Null Resource, is specific to serialized transactions. It is used to test a range before inserting a new key into the index. However, you were trying to insert a value of zero into the key, and the original query in Session 1 had the following WHERE clause:

```
WHERE  BusinessEntityID < 10
```

Therefore, there was no chance of us getting that row in until Session 1 released the lock.

For reference, Table 6-6 shows all the Key Range lock modes.

TABLE 6-6: Key Range Lock Modes

RANGE	ROW	MODE	DESCRIPTION
RangeS	S	RangeS-S	Shared lock on the key range and a shared lock on the ending resource key value
RangeS	U	RangeS-U	Shared lock on the key range and an update lock on the ending resource key value
RangeIn	Null	RangeIn-N	Used to test ranges before adding a new key into the index
RangeX	X	RangeX-X	Exclusive lock on the key range and an exclusive lock on the ending resource key value

Concurrency vs. Isolation

To conclude our look at pessimistic concurrency, I've included an extra table (Table 6-7) to help you remember which isolation levels you should use to protect yourself from the concurrency issues we saw earlier on.

TABLE 6-7: Concurrency vs. Isolation

		CONCURRENCY ISSUE					
		HALLOWEEN	DIRTY READ	LOST UPDATE	DOUBLE READ	NON REPEATABLE READ	PHANTOMS
ISOLATION LEVEL	Read Uncommitted	✔					
	Read Committed	✔	✔				
	Repeatable Read	✔	✔	✔	✔	✔	
	Serializable	✔	✔	✔	✔	✔	✔

OPTIMISTIC CONCURRENCY

Optimism came late to SQL Server. Prior to SQL Server 2005 there only existed pessimistic methods of concurrency control. As a reminder, that meant readers of data blocked writers, and writers blocked readers.

All that changed in SQL Server 2005 with the advent of new functionality called *row versioning*. This was in part a response to competing vendors that offered optimistic concurrency solutions, but it also enabled the development of other new features that can also leverage this technology. Now, not only can writers write at the same time that readers are reading, but SQL Server is able to provide online index operations and Multiple Active Result Sets (MARS). In addition, row versioning is used to build the inserted and deleted tables seen in Triggers. This means you don't need to issue I/O read requests against the transaction log anymore. There are plenty of reasons to be cheerful!

However, before anyone gets too carried away and starts looking for the options to set their databases into an optimistic model immediately, it is worth considering a couple of points.

First, there is no free lunch! In order to provide optimistic concurrency, SQL Server has a different workload to perform. This may make your system better or faster, but it may not. It depends on how the applications interact with their data, i.e., the mixture of reads and writes, whether multiple users are accessing the same data, if blocking is currently a problem, that sort of thing.

Second, optimistic isn't always best — personally, I prefer a pessimistic DBA than an optimistic one! With regard to concurrent access by multiple writers, this will still cause blocking. From this perspective, nothing has really changed — you still need to know about lock modes, lock compatibility, and blocking, except now you might make your situation worse by enabling optimistic concurrency and introducing even greater strain or side effects to your system. In short, your concurrency may improve, but the performance of the individual queries may also be affected. You will look at the causes for performance degradation under optimistic concurrency as you make your way through this chapter.

This section looks at row versioning in depth, as it is the core functionality that underpins the optimistic transaction isolation levels. However, first you need to understand the new isolation levels and what they offer us as system builders.

Optimistic Isolation Levels

Two new isolation levels have been enabled by row versioning. The first is known as *read committed snapshot isolation* and is a natural extension of the pessimistic read committed isolation level. The second is entirely new and is called *snapshot isolation*. The minimum objective of both these isolation levels is to prevent the readers blocking writers scenario. However, snapshot isolation is also designed to provide a greater degree of isolation, as you will soon see.

Note that there are some incompatibilities in SQL Server with regard to optimistic concurrency. For example, you can't use either option if there are filestream file groups in the database. If you try, you'll get an error message like this one:

```
Msg 5099, Level 16, State 3, Line 1
ALTER DATABASE failed because the READ_COMMITTED_SNAPSHOT
and the ALLOW_SNAPSHOT_ISOLATION options cannot be set to ON when a database
has FILESTREAM filegroups.  To set READ_COMMITTED_SNAPSHOT or ALLOW_SNAPSHOT_
ISOLATION to ON,
you must remove the FILESTREAM filegroups from the database.
Msg 5069, Level 16, State 1, Line 1
ALTER DATABASE statement failed.
```

> *It is not unusual for the SQL Server Product Team to restrict the applicability of a new feature. In my opinion, it's much better to release the functionality and find a market for it than hold onto it until every possible area supports the new feature. This way, everyone gets to see many more features in each release than they would otherwise. However, it is always a good idea to be aware of restrictions like these early on in your design process.*

Read Committed Snapshot Isolation

Read committed snapshot isolation (RCSI) is essentially delivering the same isolation to a transaction that read committed provides in the pessimistic concurrency model. However, it achieves this without taking any shared locks when reading data.

When RCSI is enabled in a database, SQL Server will use it as the default transactional isolation level for *all* transactions that don't explicitly specify their isolation level.

To put your database into RCSI mode (and note that this is a database-level setting, *not* a server-level setting), simply execute the following statement (note there cannot be any connections — sleeping or active — that have their database context set to the database you are trying to change):

```
ALTER DATABASE AdventureWorks;

SET READ_COMMITTED_SNAPSHOT ON;
```

Once set, SQL Server starts versioning the data immediately, and all subsequent requests with no explicit isolation level requests will be satisfied using RCSI. However, while single-user mode isn't required to enable this setting, you need to be the only user connected to the database at the time. Your ALTER DATABASE request will be blocked until this is the case. In order to make the change SQL Server needs to take two locks. First it takes out a schema modify (Sch-M) lock on the metadata of the database held in master; then it acquires a full database Exclusive (X) lock to effect the change in the user database. Naturally, this is also the case if you wish to reverse your optimistic decision.

You can force the database into single user mode with the following script. However, be warned that this version throws everyone out forcibly.

```
USE AdventureWorks;

ALTER DATABASE AdventureWorks
SET SINGLE_USER WITH ROLLBACK IMMEDIATE;
--SET MULTI_USER WITH ROLLBACK IMMEDIATE;
```

In RCSI the data that the user can read is the data provided at the time the statement inside the transaction starts. In that sense it is every bit the same as a pessimistic read committed transaction. This does distinguish it from its more heavyweight partner in optimistic crime, covered in detail next.

Snapshot Isolation

Whereas RCSI might be considered a revision of an existing isolation level, snapshot isolation is completely new. It is designed to give users the option of optimistic concurrency but with protection from phantoms and implementing repeatable read.

With snapshot isolation, data that is read during a snapshot transaction will be transactionally consistent. The view is of the data that existed in the system at the point the transaction started. In other words, changes to data that occurred before the transaction begins are visible, but those made during it are not. Once the transaction starts, time effectively stands still for that data until it is committed. In essence it is a picture of the data. From the user's perspective, their changes are the only ones that they should see.

Snapshot transactions do not take share locks when reading data unless the database is in recovery. Snapshot transaction reads also do not block other transaction writes.

Transactions writing data are still possible in other transactions (otherwise it wouldn't be very optimistic), and data can be updated inside the snapshot transaction. Updates made inside the snapshot transaction can be seen by the transaction (as you'd expect), and they will take locks to isolate those changes; but updates made outside the transaction are not visible. In this situation, the snapshot transaction is given a versioned row.

Enabling snapshot isolation is a two-step process. First, the database must be enabled to permit snapshot transactions:

```
ALTER DATABASE AdventureWorks
SET ALLOW_SNAPSHOT_ISOLATION ON;
```

Once enabled, SQL Server waits for all open transactions to be completed before allowing you to create a snapshot transaction. For as long as open transactions exist in the database, SQL Server will have this setting in a state of in_transition_to_on as you can see in Figure 6-35. Once all previously open transactions have been closed out, the status will be set to on. You can see the current state by querying sys.databases as follows:

```
SELECT   name
        ,snapshot_isolation_state
        ,snapshot_isolation_state_desc
FROM sys.Databases;
```

	name	snapshot_isolation_state	snapshot_isolation_state_desc
1	master	1	ON
2	tempdb	0	OFF
3	model	0	OFF
4	msdb	1	ON
5	ReportServer	0	OFF
6	ReportServerTempDB	0	OFF
7	AdventureWorks	3	IN_TRANSITION_TO_ON

FIGURE 6-35

Second, because this is a new isolation level (and not modifying the default as per RCSI), anytime you want a snapshot isolated transaction you must explicitly ask for one:

```
SET TRANSACTION ISOLATION LEVEL SNAPSHOT;
BEGIN TRAN
    SELECT  FirstName
            ,LastName
            ,ContactID
    FROM    AdventureWorks.Person.Contact
    WHERE   ContactID IN (991,992);
COMMIT TRAN;
```

If you have not enabled snapshot isolation at the database level first, you will receive this error:

```
Msg 3952, Level 16, State 1, Line 4
Snapshot isolation transaction failed accessing database 'AdventureWorks2008'
because snapshot isolation is not allowed in this database.
Use ALTER DATABASE to allow snapshot isolation.
```

One very important thing to note with snapshot transactions is that the transaction itself begins with the BEGIN TRAN statement:

```
SET TRANSACTION ISOLATION LEVEL SNAPSHOT;
BEGIN TRAN   --<-- Transaction Starts here
    SELECT  FirstName
            ,LastName
            ,ContactID
    FROM    AdventureWorks.Person.Contact
    WHERE   ContactID IN (991,992);
COMMIT TRAN;
```

The Snapshot Achilles Heel — Update Conflicts

Snapshot isolation does, however, have an Achilles heel: update conflicts. It is possible that while one snapshot transaction is reading the data, another transaction makes an update to the data. If this is all that happens, then there is nothing to worry about. However, if the snapshot transaction also decides to update the same row, SQL Server will kill the snapshot transaction, as it cannot resolve this conflict.

Consider this example, which requires two sessions running in order to work. Gustavo phones customer services for AdventureWorks and requests that his telephone number be changed. The customer services rep looks him up on the system:

```
/*Session 1*/
USE AdventureWorks;

SET TRANSACTION ISOLATION LEVEL SNAPSHOT;

BEGIN TRANSACTION;
SELECT  *
FROM    Person.Contact
WHERE   FirstName = 'Gustavo'
AND     LastName = 'Achong';
```

At that moment, the marketing department decides to perform an update to the customer data based on some new data they have purchased. Gustavo's email address has changed and they decide to update it:

```
/*Session 2*/
USE AdventureWorks;

BEGIN TRANSACTION;
Update Person.Contact
SET     EmailAddress = 'GustavoIsTHEMAN@live.com'
WHERE   ContactID = 1;
COMMIT TRANSACTION;
```

In the meantime, the customer services employee has been talking to Gustavo about whether he should buy the new RADBike3000 even though he only asked for his phone number to be changed. However, now the customer services rep is ready to take Gustavo's information and make the update:

```
/*Session 1*/
UPDATE Person.Contact
SET     Phone       = '555-911-999'
WHERE   FirstName   = 'Gustavo'
AND     LastName    = 'Achong';
```

Disaster!

```
Msg 3960, Level 16, State 5, Line 2
Snapshot isolation transaction aborted due to update conflict.
You cannot use snapshot isolation to access table 'Person.Contact' directly or
indirectly in database 'AdventureWorks' to update, delete, or insert the row
that has been modified or deleted by another transaction. Retry the transaction
or change the isolation level for the update/delete statement.
```

This code is available for download at Wrox.com [CH06 SI Update Conflict.sql]

The transaction has been aborted because of an update conflict. All isn't lost, however. The IT department at AdventureWorks predicted this might happen and proactively developed a shiny retry button on their application. The customer services rep tries again:

```
SET TRANSACTION ISOLATION LEVEL SNAPSHOT;

BEGIN TRANSACTION;
UPDATE Person.Contact
SET     Phone       = '555-911-999'
WHERE   FirstName   = 'Gustavo'
AND     LastName    = 'Achong';
COMMIT TRANSACTION;
```

Success! The earlier snapshot transaction had been rolled back and the marketing transaction was completed. This time our transaction didn't conflict with any other concurrent write, so all was well.

Note several points about this example.

First, long-running transactions are never going to be good. Optimistic concurrency in its current form does bring them to light in more obvious ways — either by their impact on tempdb (which we will see later on in this section) or by forcing retry logic as is the preceding example.

Second, the marketing transaction affected different data. However, the unit that is compared is the row and not the column. Even though the updates didn't actually impact one another in terms of the data being changed, they did cause an irreconcilable issue at the row level.

Third, and most important, the IT department had to *design for snapshot isolation.* They had built retry logic into their application. This is the Achilles heel. Snapshot isolation can force applications to change. The double whammy for snapshot is that read committed snapshot isolation does not have this limitation. Therefore, you really, really have to need the repeatable read or phantom level protection to consider this option.

> *Do not use snapshot isolation unless you have fully tested your solution and are aware of the risks you are taking. Have you built retry logic into the calling application? Do you really need repeatable read or phantom-level isolation? If either answer is no, then consider your alternatives. Read committed snapshot isolation may be more than sufficient for your needs, so consider your options carefully.*

Other Limitations of Snapshot Isolation

Bear in mind some other limitations with snapshot isolation should you decide to use it. It's worth highlighting these because there are quite a few; and compared to read committed snapshot isolation, it has quite a few more pitfalls.

Consider this next example. If you wish to query across databases in a snapshot transaction, then you need to alter the isolation level in all the databases involved. Assuming that you ran the earlier AdventureWorks example, try to run this:

```
CREATE DATABASE AW2;
GO
USE AW2;

CREATE TABLE dbo.Contact
    (ContactID INT
    ,FirstName nvarchar(50)
    ,LastName nvarchar(50)
    );

INSERT INTO dbo.Contact
(    ContactID
    ,FirstName
    ,LastName
)
SELECT    ContactID
        ,FirstName
        ,LastName
```

```
FROM      AdventureWorks.Person.Contact
WHERE     ContactID IN (991,992);

SELECT *
FROM dbo.Contact;

SET TRANSACTION ISOLATION LEVEL SNAPSHOT;

BEGIN TRANSACTION;

SELECT    c1.ContactID
         ,c1.FirstName
         ,c1.LastName
         ,c2.ContactID
         ,c2.FirstName
         ,c2.LastName
FROM      AdventureWorks.Person.Contact c1
JOIN      AW2.dbo.Contact c2
ON        c1.ContactID = c2.ContactID;

COMMIT TRANSACTION;
```

SQL Server returns the following error:

```
Msg 3952, Level 16, State 1, Line 27
Snapshot isolation transaction failed accessing database 'AW2' because snapshot
isolation is not allowed in this database. Use ALTER DATABASE to allow snapshot
isolation.
```

Now rerun the transaction like this:

**Available for
download on
Wrox.com**

```
SET TRANSACTION ISOLATION LEVEL SNAPSHOT;

BEGIN TRANSACTION;

SELECT    c1.ContactID
         ,c1.FirstName
         ,c1.LastName
         ,c2.ContactID
         ,c2.FirstName
         ,c2.LastName
FROM      AdventureWorks.Person.Contact c1
JOIN      AW2.dbo.Contact c2 WITH (REPEATABLEREAD)
ON        c1.ContactID = c2.ContactID;

COMMIT TRANSACTION;
```

This code is available for download at Wrox.com [CH06 SI Cross DB.sql]

It works! That's because the isolation level is now sympathetic to the snapshot isolation cause. While you can understand why this is the case, it does mean that for those applications that query across databases, some application coding changes need to be made before this option could be enabled, just to get it to work.

Nor can you switch into snapshot isolation from another isolation level mid transaction. For example, in a new query window try to do the following:

```
BEGIN TRANSACTION;
SET TRANSACTION ISOLATION LEVEL SNAPSHOT;

    SELECT  FirstName
            ,LastName
            ,ContactID
    FROM    AdventureWorks.Person.Contact
    WHERE   ContactID IN (991,992);

COMMIT TRANSACTION;
```

Note in the preceding code that the BEGIN TRAN is now before the SET statement. The preceding will throw the following exception:

```
Msg 3951, Level 16, State 1, Line 4
Transaction failed in database 'AdventureWorks' because the statement was run under
snapshot isolation but the transaction did not start in snapshot isolation. You
cannot change the isolation level of the transaction to snapshot after the
transaction has started unless the transaction was originally started under
snapshot isolation level.
```

Finally, when using snapshot isolation, distributed transactions aren't possible:

```
SET TRANSACTION ISOLATION LEVEL SNAPSHOT;

BEGIN DISTRIBUTED TRANSACTION;

SELECT  c1.ContactID
        ,c1.FirstName
        ,c1.LastName
        ,c2.ContactID
        ,c2.FirstName
        ,c2.LastName
FROM    AdventureWorks.Person.Contact c1
JOIN    AW2.dbo.Contact c2 WITH (REPEATABLEREAD)
ON      c1.ContactID = c2.ContactID

COMMIT TRANSACTION;
```

The preceding returns the following error:

```
Msg 3996, Level 16, State 1, Line 3
Snapshot isolation level is not supported for distributed transaction.
Use another isolation level or do not use distributed transaction.
```

Bear in mind, however, that only snapshot isolation is allowed to be configured in msdb, master, and tempdb; so if your optimistic concurrency model needs to extend into these databases, then you need to look closely at snapshot isolation and determine whether the benefits (repeatable reads without phantoms) outweigh the costs.

How Row Versioning Works

Happily, row versioning is one of the few technologies whose name precisely describes what it does. This makes explaining (and remembering) the process that much easier.

When row versioning is enabled, SQL Server maintains a complete copy of the row every time it is changed. Prior to updating a row, SQL Server copies the row and stores it in tempdb in a set of pages known collectively as the *version store*. There it is held until the data is no longer needed.

SQL Server knows how long to keep the rows because each row is marked with the transaction ID of the update that caused it to appear in the version store in the first place. The Storage Engine tracks the minimum transaction ID and then uses this to purge the version store of transactions that no longer need to be supported.

The writers bear the brunt of the cost for setting up the row version, but it is the readers who pay when it comes to navigating pointer chains. Readers have to hit the version store to find the record that is appropriate for them. This affects the overall speed of the read but it might well be completely acceptable, especially when compared to the cost of being continually blocked.

The only exception to these rules concern large object (BLOB) data types and their data. Row versioning only keeps the fragment of a BLOB that was changed, rather than the whole object. This makes sense as blobs are big things.

At a superficial level that's all there is to say about row versioning. However, I think it's much more interesting, and beneficial, to really get under the skin of something, and understanding row versioning will help you make the right decision about whether optimistic concurrency is right for you and your organization.

Row Versioning Deep Dive

This section is going to get into the bowels of row versioning to fully understand this process in depth. The scenario I am going to describe uses a very simple database, a table with fixed columns, and a solitary row of data. However, to pull this together I have used some undocumented DBCC commands, so please don't try this on your production servers!

First of all, create the baseline database, in a new query window:

```
CREATE DATABASE RowVsn;
GO
ALTER DATABASE RowVsn SET READ_COMMITTED_SNAPSHOT ON;

USE RowVsn;

CREATE TABLE VersionTable
(    Col1 INT
    ,Col2 INT
);

INSERT INTO VersionTable
(    Col1
    ,Col2
)
```

```
VALUES
(    1
    ,1
);
```

To confirm we have nothing in the version store, now execute the DMV
sys.dm_tran_version_store:

```
SELECT  *
FROM    sys.dm_tran_version_store
WHERE   database_id = DB_ID('RowVsn');
```

The DMV should be empty. Keep in mind that inserts do not generate row versions. Now update
your single row and generate some versioning information:

```
UPDATE  VersionTable
SET     Col2 = 2;
SELECT *
FROM    sys.dm_tran_current_transaction;
UPDATE  VersionTable
Set     Col2 = 3;
SELECT *
FROM    sys.dm_tran_current_transaction;
UPDATE  VersionTable
SET     Col2 = 4;
SELECT *
FROM    sys.dm_tran_current_transaction;
UPDATE  VersionTable
SET     Col2 = 5;
SELECT *
FROM    sys.dm_tran_current_transaction;

BEGIN TRAN
    UPDATE  VersionTable
    SET     Col2 = 6;

    SELECT *
    FROM    sys.dm_tran_current_transaction;
--COMMIT TRAN;
```

I deliberately made the last update inside an explicit transaction and haven't closed it off so you can
see what's going on inside the DMVs at your leisure. Don't forget to commit the transaction after
you have finished, however, or you might get a nasty surprise, which I'll come to shortly. Figure 6-36
displays all the results from the sys.dm_tran_current_transaction DMV queries.

You can see that with each transaction, the transaction id has increased, as has the last transaction
sequence number. The first useful sequence number hasn't increased, as the version store has identified that as the minimum sequence number it must keep in the version store to support RCSI.

	transaction_id	transaction_sequence_num	transaction_is_snapshot	first_snapshot_sequence_num	last_transaction_sequence_num	first_useful_sequence_num
1	65801	0	0	NULL	1803	1804

	transaction_id	transaction_sequence_num	transaction_is_snapshot	first_snapshot_sequence_num	last_transaction_sequence_num	first_useful_sequence_num
1	65803	0	Click to select the whole column	NULL	1804	1804

	transaction_id	transaction_sequence_num	transaction_is_snapshot	first_snapshot_sequence_num	last_transaction_sequence_num	first_useful_sequence_num
1	65805	0	0	NULL	1805	1804

	transaction_id	transaction_sequence_num	transaction_is_snapshot	first_snapshot_sequence_num	last_transaction_sequence_num	first_useful_sequence_num
1	65807	0	0	NULL	1806	1804

	transaction_id	transaction_sequence_num	transaction_is_snapshot	first_snapshot_sequence_num	last_transaction_sequence_num	first_useful_sequence_num
1	65808	1807	0	NULL	1807	1804

FIGURE 6-36

Now run a select on the `sys.dm_tran_version_store` DMV. For now, I am reducing the number of columns so I can easily show the results (see Figure 6-37):

```
SELECT  transaction_sequence_num
        ,min_length_in_bytes
        ,record_length_first_part_in_bytes
        ,record_image_first_part
FROM    sys.dm_tran_version_store
WHERE   database_id = DB_ID('RowVsn');
```

	transaction_sequence_num	min_length_in_bytes	record_length_first_part_in_bytes	record_image_first_part
1	1803	12	29	0x50000C0001000000010000000200000000000000000000F90600000000
2	1804	12	29	0x50000C0001000000020000000200000E80A000001000B000B0700000000
3	1805	12	29	0x50000C0001000000030000000200000E80A000001000C000C0700000000
4	1806	12	29	0x50000C0001000000040000000200000E80A000001000D000D0700000000
5	1807	12	29	0x50000C0001000000050000000200000E80A000001000E000E0700000000

FIGURE 6-37

This view shows us some interesting things right away. First, you can see there is one row for every update. That's because each update occurred inside its own transaction. Before moving on to look at other aspects, run this next code snippet:

```
Update VersionTable
Set Col2 = Col2+1;
```

This code is available for download at Wrox.com [CH06 Row Versioning1.sql]

Now run the select on `sys.dm_tran_version_store` again. The number of records is the same! Because the preceding update was already inside our open transaction, there was no need to version the row, as other writers are already blocked and the previous version of the row has already been versioned. This is different from other new technologies and features released for SQL Server, such as Change Data Capture (CDC), which captures and versions all changes to the row, or Change Tracking, which keeps only the latest change. In this instance, you are keeping only versions that we need to support transactional isolation.

What else is there to see? The transaction sequence number (XSN) has been pulled out for us to work with and join to. You can clearly see that this number increments by one every time a new record is added to the version store. It can also be cross referenced using the transaction sequence numbers in the `sys.dm_tran_current_transaction` DMV seen in Figure 6-36 and other transaction-based DMVs.

Now look at the `record_image_first_part` column. In this example, it represents the entire row that has been copied into the version store prior to the update on the page in the `VersionTable` table. This isn't always the case, though.

The version store does not use special pages to hold its data, so each page can only hold 8,060 bytes of row data. Because the version store also has its own columns, sometimes the versioned row data needs to be split across two rows in the version store. However, when presenting this data through the `sys.dm_tran_version_store` DMV, SQL Server pivots out this information to present it on a single row:

Available for download on Wrox.com

```
USE RowVsn;

CREATE TABLE bigrow
(    col1 CHAR(8000)
);
INSERT INTO bigrow ( col1 )
VALUES(REPLICATE(1,8000));

UPDATE  bigrow
SET col1 =  REPLICATE(2,8000);

SELECT  transaction_sequence_num
        ,status
        ,record_length_first_part_in_bytes
        ,record_image_first_part
        ,record_length_second_part_in_bytes
        ,record_image_second_part
FROM    sys.dm_tran_version_store
WHERE   database_id = DB_ID('RowVsn');
```

This code is available for download at Wrox.com [CH06 Row Versioning2.sql]

The status flag (see Figure 6-38) tells us that the row has been split. To see and evaluate the row, one would need to stitch those two pieces of data together to get the full picture of the actual row.

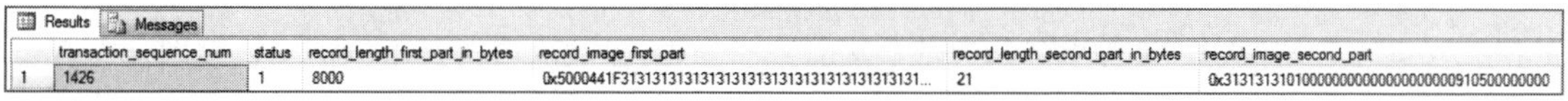

Results | Messages

	transaction_sequence_num	status	record_length_first_part_in_bytes	record_image_first_part	record_length_second_part_in_bytes	record_image_second_part
1	1426	1	8000	0x5000441F3131313131313131313131313131313131313131...	21	0x313131310100000000000000000000910500000000

FIGURE 6-38

Now revert back to the original example. I have copied the results in Figure 6-37 again for convenience.

	transaction_sequence_num	min_length_in_bytes	record_length_first_part_in_bytes	record_image_first_part
1	1803	12	29	0x50000C0001000000010000000200000000000000000000F90600000000
2	1804	12	29	0x50000C000100000002000000020000E80A000001000B000B0700000000
3	1805	12	29	0x50000C000100000003000000020000E80A000001000C000C0700000000
4	1806	12	29	0x50000C000100000004000000020000E80A000001000D000D0700000000
5	1807	12	29	0x50000C000100000005000000020000E80A000001000E000E0700000000

FIGURE 6-37

Notice just how big that varbinary value in the `record_image_first_part` column is. Our eight bytes of data with two columns translates to 29 bytes per row when you include the row's internal structure. Consider what impact this might have then on your tempdb — remember, it is copying the *whole row,* not just the values for that row.

The row value, as mentioned earlier, is held as varbinary but SQL Server returns this data in hex for us here to look at. Table 6-8 breaks down the row structure to highlight what else can be gleaned at this stage.

TABLE 6-8: Byte Breakdown for Version Store Record Images

BYTE							
0	1	2–3	4–8	9–12	13–14	15	16–29
50	00	0C00	01000000	01000000	0200	00	0000000000000000F90600000000
50	00	0C00	01000000	02000000	0200	00	E80A000001000B000B0700000000
50	00	0C00	01000000	03000000	0200	00	E80A000001000C000C0700000000
50	00	0C00	01000000	04000000	0200	00	E80A000001000D000D0700000000
50	00	0C00	01000000	05000000	0200	00	E80A000001000E000E0700000000

In case you aren't familiar with the byte breakdown for a record, I have mapped it in the following list, with a brief explanation of these values. However, I hope you can clearly see that row versioning applies to the *whole row* and not just the data values.

- **Byte 0:** The record type. A value of 50 means the record is a primary record with two additional attributes:
  - Nullable Columns bit 0x10
  - Supports Row Versioning bit 0x40
- **Byte 1:** Indicates a forwarded or unforwarded record
  - 0 indicates records that haven't been forwarded.
  - 1 indicates records that have been forwarded.

➤ **Bytes 2–3:** Forward pointer to the end of the fixed data type column data to locate the Null Bitmap

➤ **Bytes 4–8:** Our first column of data — 4 bytes long for an integer

➤ **Bytes 9–12:** Our second column of data

➤ **Bytes 13–14:** The fixed column count

➤ **Byte 15:** Null Bitmap. Actual indicator of which fields are nullable (only one byte because there are only two columns).

➤ **Bytes 16–29:** Row versioning information, including transaction sequence number and pointers to the previous row. Six bytes are for the XSN and eight bytes are allocated for the pointer to the previous row.

Reading the XSN and Pointer

The bytes that we are interested in looking at in detail are the XSN and pointer bytes, which in this case are bytes 16–29 (see Table 6-9):

TABLE 6-9: Row Versioning Data — As Seen on the Page

PAGE	FILE	SLOT	XSN
00000000	0000	0000	F90600000000
E80A0000	0100	0B00	0B0700000000
E80A0000	0100	0C00	0C0700000000
E80A0000	0100	0D00	0D0700000000
E80A0000	0100	0E00	0E0700000000

Notice that the oldest row, the one at the top, is zeroed out for page and file. That's because this is our insert row. The page, file, and slot values provide the pointer to the previous row. To illustrate further, in Table 6-10 I have also converted these hex values to decimal to make things easier.

> *Wintel platforms use the Little Endian form to represent numeric data when stored as bytes. Therefore when reading the hex values you must read them from right to left to get the correct value. To learn about "Endianness" check out the following sage information on Wikipedia* http://en.wikipedia.org/wiki/Endianness

TABLE 6-10: Row Versioning Data —
Decimal Values

PAGE	FILE	SLOT	XSN
0	0	0	1785
2792	1	11	1803
2792	1	12	1804
2792	1	13	1805
2792	1	14	1806

Can you see how the data is chained together in the version store? The most recent record shows slot 14 is the location for its predecessor, and 13 before that. The XSN that is stamped in the row data is the XSN of the transaction but the XSN that is held in the transaction_sequence_num field of sys.dm_tran_version_store is the XSN of the row that caused the transaction to be placed in the version store. That's important, as it not only provides the other linkage in the row versioning, but also facilitates joins to the current state of the transaction. Without both XSNs you wouldn't be able to join to the current transaction and also recurse down through the history. Now bring the current row in to confirm what you have seen; it should point to your most recent addition to the version store in slot 14.

By the way, notice that you can repeatedly query sys.dm_tran_version_store and see all those rows. Our open transaction is preventing SQL Server from removing them. Close this now (in order to do the next bit) but keep in mind that they were there for an awfully long time. . . .

To see the current row on the VersionTable table you'll need to use DBCC IND and DBCC PAGE (remember that these are still undocumented commands, so play safely!):

```
DBCC IND(rowvsn,'VersionTable',-1)

DBCC TRACEON(3604)   -- To return output of DBCC to Console
DBCC PAGE('RowVsn',1,79,3)

Record Type = PRIMARY_RECORD    Record Attributes =  NULL_BITMAP VERSIONING_INFO
Record Size = 29
Memory Dump @0x61E1C060

00000000:   50000c00 01000000 07000000 020000e8 †P.............è
00000010:   0a000001 000f000f 07000000 00†††††††††............

Version Information =
        Transaction Timestamp: 1807
        Version Pointer: (file 1 page 2792 currentSlotId 15)


Slot 0 Column 1 Offset 0x4 Length 4 Length (physical) 4

Col1 = 1

Slot 0 Column 2 Offset 0x8 Length 4 Length (physical) 4

Col2 = 7
```

I have highlighted all the information that relates to versioning, some of which was touched on earlier. First, you can clearly see that the Record Size is 29 bytes but we only have eight bytes of information. Second, the Record Attributes have been pulled out from the first byte. Third, the 14 extra bytes of data held on the row are visible. By using option 3 on DBCC PAGE, it has kindly done the hex to decimal for you. Clearly, then, the current row indicates that our XSN is 1807, and the pointer information is sending us back to the version store slot 15, which is exactly what you'd expect.

You can join your current row in VersionTable to the most recent row in the version store and establish two links to this data — first via the pointer information and second through the XSN held in the version store (transaction_seq_num of sys.dm_tran_version_store) to the XSN held in the version information in the current row.

MORE XSN

While you are in the middle of the deep dive, I thought I'd pose a question: Did anyone think it odd that the XSN is a six-byte integer? I am not aware of such a data type — a six-byte integer. The sys.dm_tran_current_version shows the XSN as a bigint, so I can only assume that this is an internal optimization to save two bytes. It never ceases to amaze me how far the Storage Engine team will go to optimize SQL Server. Still, six bytes does result in a rather large number of positive values.

```
SELECT (POWER(CAST(256 as bigint),6)/2)-1
```

140,737,488,355,327 to be precise. Even split over all the transactions in all the databases on the server that's a very large number of row versions. SQL Server also resets the XSN when it is restarted, so it is highly unlikely that you'll ever run out of XSNs.

Rogue Transaction

I hope you recall that you did have something of concern going on with the DMVs. When the transaction was open none of the rows from the version store were lost, which implies that a rogue transaction could have some rather unexpected side effects and cause tempdb to balloon in size — possibly even filling the disk, which, as we have established, is much more likely than running out of XSNs. Should this happen, SQL Server isn't able to write version rows any longer; and while the application will still perform writes, readers of data will start seeing errors.

You can therefore start to get a clearer picture of where this technology is best served. Write-heavy workloads, for example, might not be ideal candidates, whereas read-centric applications would benefit. Ideally, concurrent access will also be minimal, as that will keep the version store small.

You might also want to consider what impact this will have on the size of your tempdb database, and the additional overhead this places on it as well. For example data warehouse workloads will often run into tempdb issues if Snapshot Isolation is used. I strongly recommend reading Chapter 7, "Knowing Tempdb," as these two areas are closely connected. For now, however, it would seem an opportune moment to discuss how SQL Server actually does clean up after itself when row versioning.

Garbage Collection

Approximately every 60 seconds SQL Server's version store garbage collector kicks in, looking for redundant data that isn't required any further. Internally, SQL Server achieves this by tracking the lowest XSN it needs to keep in the version store, and then performs a set-based delete on anything lower than this number. You can see what that number is with the following query:

```
SELECT    transaction_id
          ,transaction_sequence_num
          ,transaction_is_snapshot
          ,first_snapshot_sequence_num
          ,last_transaction_sequence_num
          ,first_useful_sequence_num
FROM      sys.dm_tran_current_transaction;
```

In the result, shown in Figure 6-39, the `first_useful_sequence_num` tells us that any transaction sequence numbers in the version store that are less than 4024604 can be safely removed. However, this view also states that in this instance the `last_transaction_sequence_num` is actually less than the first useful figure.

	transaction_id	transaction_sequence_num	transaction_is_snapshot	first_snapshot_sequence_num	last_transaction_sequence_num	first_useful_sequence_num
1	77541	0	0	NULL	2622	2623

FIGURE 6-39

`Last_transaction_sequence_num` is the last sequence number generated by the system. Because it is less, assume that in this case the version store is either empty or about to be made empty very soon.

If you haven't already done so, go ahead and commit your transaction. You might need to wait for a minute but very shortly you will not see those records in your version store any longer.

But what of that transaction issue? Why was that such a problem? Is it going to prevent you from deploying optimistic concurrency options? Is this behavior going to affect other features like online index rebuilds? These are all valid concerns and we will address them in turn. However, it should be clear by now that although it is as simple as flicking a switch, using this functionality does need some careful consideration. In order to address the transactional issue, it is necessary to delve deeper into the world of the version store and garbage collection. There you discover a second store in place called the *append-only store*. As updates and deletes are made to the base table, and row versions are being captured, SQL Server groups them into batches for future cleansing. The rows — from all databases on the SQL Server, not just one database — are collected in a physical unit, the append-only store.

These stores are created every minute by the background garbage collector, so in normal operation any one store will have one minute's worth of row versions contained within it. In order for SQL Server to delete the rows contained in the append-only store, all the rows must be deemed to be no longer useful. I should emphasize that this append-only store for that minute is the only repository for the instance of SQL Server, and all databases using row versioning will be sharing this one space.

However, in the case of a long-running transaction — for example, one running for several minutes — all rows belonging to that transaction will end up in the one store. That isn't the problem, though. SQL Server needs to guarantee that no one is interested in this data. Therefore, three rules need to be satisfied before an append-only store can be deleted:

> ➤ All transactions that started in the time window for that append-only store have completed.

> ➤ All transactions that started in a subsequent time window but rely on rows from the current time window (and therefore the current append-only store) have also completed.

> ➤ All previous append-only stores have been deleted.

Therefore, if a transaction is left open — perhaps at the beginning of the day — then no append-only store can be deleted until that transaction is committed or rolled back. Granted, that is an extreme example and one that points to an issue elsewhere in the application, but it is well worth considering. It might be a good idea to read Chapter 9, "Viewing Server Performance with PerfMon and the PAL Tool," to make sure you have a good understanding of what, if any, long-running transactions exist in your system before making this jump.

Having long-running transactions in a system is rarely desirable, and row versioning's use of tempdb is likely to increase the likelihood of this being an issue. Consequently, you might want to also think about making this change on a SQL Server that isn't co-hosting multiple applications, as performance issues based on anticipated workloads may be difficult to predict; and with the focus on an already shared resource, namely tempdb, it might be a good idea to consider isolating any databases appropriate for this setting.

One thing you don't have to worry about is the issue of online index rebuilds. Online reindexing SQL Server uses its own internal append-only store, so it doesn't get caught up in user application issues.

Monitoring Row Versioning

This section might just as easily have been entitled "Monitoring Tempdb," and indeed you can look at Chapter 7 to learn more about that. However, this discussion would not be complete without looking at some of the other counters that you can use to keep an eye on your SQL Server. Just because you are optimistic doesn't mean you need to be foolhardy!

I recommend keeping an eye on the following:

> ➤ Overall size and growth of the version store over time

> ➤ Who is generating the rows and how frequently are they generating them?

> ➤ Version generation and cleanup: How long do versions last in the system?

> ➤ Transaction duration: These can be deadly. You should definitely understand this *before* enabling optimistic concurrency options.

> ➤ Free space in tempdb: However, also ensure you have sufficient drive space allocated for unexpected situations and growth.

The good news is that the majority of these issues can be captured by PerfMon. They even all exist under the `SQLServer:Transactions` object (see Figure 6-40).

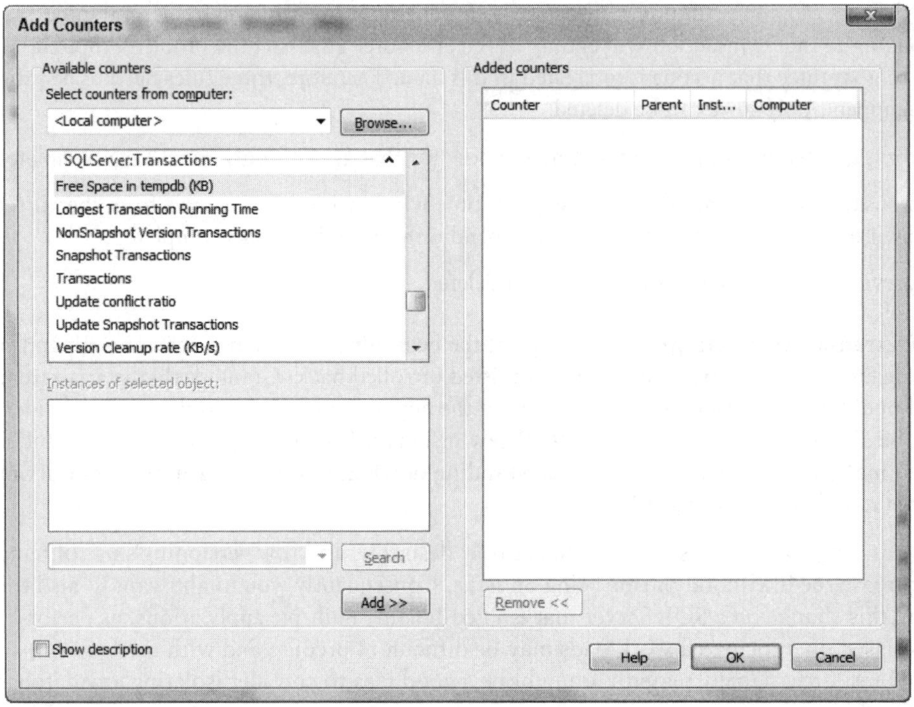

FIGURE 6-40

sys.dm_tran_top_version_generators

This DMV addresses the "Who is generating all these row versions?" question raised in the preceding section:

```
SELECT  database_id
        ,rowset_id
        ,aggregated_record_length_in_bytes
FROM    sys.dm_tran_top_version_generators;
```

This is one of the DMVs whose statistics you need to track over time. It reports on only what is currently in the version store, and is essentially an aggregation of `sys.dm_tran_version_store`. By summing up the length of the records in the version store, you get a good idea as to which databases and rowsets are placing the greatest burden on it. In order to minimize overhead on the SQL Server, this DMV returns only the top 256 database/rowset ID combinations.

This would be a rather innovative way of tuning tempdb and validating a SQL Server's health post deployment. By simply running the preceding query on my laptop, it is pretty clear that one write-heavy application is causing the load on it, as shown in Figure 6-41.

	database_id	rowset_id	aggregated_record_length_in_bytes
1	13	72057594038779904	18531
2	4	72057594039828480	656
3	4	72057594040811520	520
4	4	72057594040483840	306
5	4	72057594040942592	228
6	4	72057594039894016	70

FIGURE 6-41

LATCHES

Latches are lightweight synchronization objects that are used to protect SQL Server's internal in-memory structures. They are used by the Storage Engine internally and operate independently of any user configuration of SQL Server. They most certainly are not exposed as functionality to the user. In other words, the properties of a transaction (including isolation) have no bearing on latching, and users cannot invoke a latch in their application code. Users of SQL Server have no direct control over latching. However, by their very actions, users will cause latches to be taken by the engine.

Latches are closely aligned with locking, and they exhibit similar behavior. It is often said that SQL Server's locking implementation could have been used instead of latching. The reason for having two locking paradigms was performance. However, the reverse isn't true. Although latches exhibit some of the functionality of a lock, they are heavily optimized and therefore do not exhibit all of the same behaviors. For example, a latch can be blocked by another latch, but a latch could not be used to prevent a non-repeatable read (read on to find out why).

While similar, locks and latches are trying to achieve very different goals. A lock is present to uphold a transaction's integrity; the latch's role is to protect the database's physical integrity and to co-ordinate threading in the engine.

The following sections dive into the world of the latch, looking at what types of latch exist and how they can block each other. You will notice a focus on buffer (BUF) latches, as these are the latches that you are most likely to see when troubleshooting. Finally, the section ends by considering a real-world example of how latching is used to secure data page access and prevent lost updates.

The objective of this section of the chapter is to provide a basic understanding of latching. Subsequent chapters draw heavily on this knowledge, so acquiring a solid grounding here should stand you in good stead later.

Latch Types

Latches exist to protect in-memory data. There are hundreds of different types of latch, most of which you are unlikely to encounter in any meaningful way when you are working with SQL Server. While latch waits will occasionally show up in `sys.dm_os_wait_stats`, you do normally have to go looking for them. As a rule they don't come to you. To explain them here, I have taken the traditional approach and divided them into two distinct areas with a focus on the BUF latches.

Latches in SQL Server either serve the buffer pool, in which case they are known as BUF latches (showing up as PAGELATCH in `sys.dm_os_wait_stats`), or they don't, in which case they are grouped under the non-buffer (Non-BUF) heading. (Some sources refer to a third group, the TRANMARK latches, but I believe that these reflect a form of implementation, rather than a separate type, so I have chosen to leave them in with the NON-BUF boys.)

Non-Buffer (Non-BUF) Latches

This group of latches describes a very wide variety of latches, but the one thing they have in common is that they aren't used to synchronize access to the buffer pages. When they are forced to wait for a resource, their wait time is grouped under the LATCH_* wait types. Their role is to provide synchronization services to other in-memory data structures or semaphores for concurrency-sensitive code.

Non-BUF latches can be readily identified by their latch class in SQL Server, and can be seen by querying the `sys.dm_os_latch_stats` DMV with the following query:

```
SELECT   latch_class
FROM     sys.dm_os_latch_stats
WHERE    latch_class <> 'BUFFER'
```

In SQL Server 2008, this view returns 144 different classes of latch as seen in Figure 6-42. Each class name has a naming convention applied to it that reflects the role that those latches play in SQL Server. The following query returns all those latches that play some part in tracing:

```
SELECT   latch_class
FROM     sys.dm_os_latch_stats
WHERE    latch_class LIKE 'TRACE%'
```

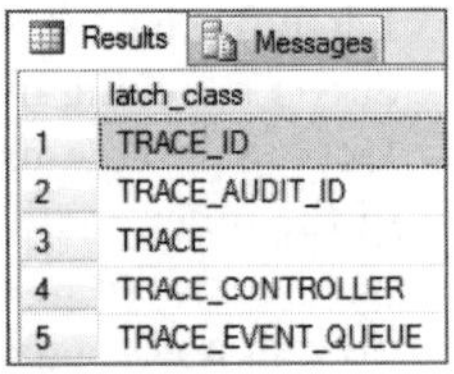

Results	Messages	
	latch_class	
1	TRACE_ID	
2	TRACE_AUDIT_ID	
3	TRACE	
4	TRACE_CONTROLLER	
5	TRACE_EVENT_QUEUE	

FIGURE 6-42

To further explore the example of a Non-BUF latch, let's look at the TRACE_CONTROLLER latch. This latch must be acquired in exclusive mode whenever a trace is stopped or started. This prevents other threads from accessing the trace controller's in-memory data structures during the act of changing the state of the trace. It therefore ensures that the change can happen by forcing single-threaded physical access.

Buffer (BUF) Latches

Buffer latches protect data pages as they are accessed from the buffer pool. They are grouped together under a single latch class known as BUFFER. However, they can also be identified and grouped by the first part of their wait type name: PAGE*.

BUF latches are the most visible of the latch classes. If you encounter an issue with latching on your SQL Server, it most likely results from a BUF latch. All BUF latches appear in the `sys.dm_os_wait_stats` DMV in full. This is in contrast to the NON-BUF latches, which are grouped under the LATCH_* wait type. BUF latch waits convey two pieces of information: not only which BUF latch is waiting, but also which *mode* it is requesting. There is more on latch modes coming up shortly.

BUF latches are used to marshal access to data. A BUF latch might be taken, for example, while the Storage Engine takes data from the buffer pool and passes it to the Relational Engine.

However, unlike locks, BUF latches aren't held for the duration of a transaction. Latches are always only held for the duration of the operation, after which they are immediately released. This is even the case with writes.

Another differentiating factor between locks and latches is that BUF latches only affect the page, not the row. Locking can be much more granular, as it is not trying to synchronize and serialize physical access to the data page.

Recall that earlier in the chapter, when looking at lock granularity, you queried the `Person.Person` table, returning all people whose `LastName` began with "SM%." 105 row locks were taken. However, how many pages were brought into cache to satisfy this query? The following example code tells you:

```
USE AdventureWorks2008;

DBCC FREEPROCCACHE;
DBCC DROPCLEANBUFFERS;

SET TRANSACTION ISOLATION LEVEL REPEATABLE READ;
BEGIN TRAN;
SELECT    LastName
         ,FirstName
         ,BusinessEntityID
FROM      Person.Person
WHERE     LastName LIKE 'SM%';   --Index Seek on Person.IX_Person_LastName_FirstName

SELECT    COUNT(*)           AS buffer_cache_page_count
         ,SUM(buf.row_count) AS rows_on_page_count
         ,DB_Object_name
         ,IX_Object_name
FROM      sys.dm_os_buffer_descriptors AS buf
JOIN      (   SELECT   OBJECT_NAME([object_id])               AS DB_Object_name
                     ,(  SELECT   ind.name
                         FROM     sys.indexes ind
                         WHERE    ind.index_id = p.index_id
                         AND      ind.[object_id] = p.[object_id]
                      )                                        AS IX_Object_name
                     ,allocation_unit_id
              FROM     sys.allocation_units     AS au
              JOIN     sys.partitions           AS p    ON     au.container_id =
      p.hobt_id
                                                        AND    (  au.[type]   = 1
                                                        OR au.[type]   = 3
                                                        )
              WHERE    [object_id] = object_id('Person.Person')

              UNION ALL

              SELECT   OBJECT_NAME([object_id])               AS DB_Object_name
                     ,(  SELECT   ind.name
                         FROM     sys.indexes ind
                         WHERE    ind.index_id = p.index_id
                         AND      ind.[object_id] = p.[object_id]
                      )                                        AS IX_Object_name
                     ,allocation_unit_id
```

```
            FROM    sys.allocation_units   AS au
            JOIN    sys.partitions         AS p     ON      au.container_id =
        p.partition_id
                                                    AND     au.[type]      = 2
                WHERE   [object_id] = OBJECT_ID('Person.Person')
            )                                                AS obj
    ON      buf.allocation_unit_id = obj.allocation_unit_id
    WHERE   database_id = DB_ID()
    GROUP BY DB_Object_name
            ,IX_Object_name
    ORDER BY buffer_cache_page_count DESC;

    COMMIT TRAN
```

This code is available for download at Wrox.com [CH06 Buffer Pages In Memory to satisfy Query.sql]

As shown in Figure 6-43, nine data pages belonging to IX_Person_LastName_FirstName_MiddleName were brought into memory. A quick double-check of the execution plan confirms that this index was scanned to perform the select.

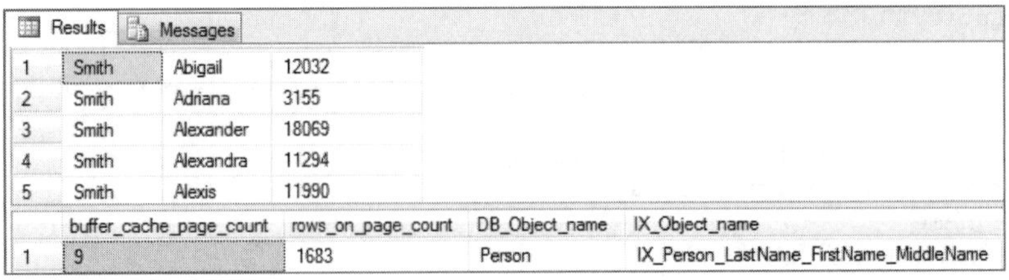

1	Smith	Abigail	12032
2	Smith	Adriana	3155
3	Smith	Alexander	18069
4	Smith	Alexandra	11294
5	Smith	Alexis	11990

	buffer_cache_page_count	rows_on_page_count	DB_Object_name	IX_Object_name
1	9	1683	Person	IX_Person_LastName_FirstName_MiddleName

FIGURE 6-43

Latches have therefore more in common with semaphores than they do with locks. However, as you will see, the process of physically updating a database page must be performed sequentially; otherwise you will incur lost updates. BUF latches therefore support the locking process.

One BUF latch is associated with each allocation unit. However, it's the BUF latches that are associated with certain page types, notably the PFS, IAM, GAM and SGAM pages that cause issues; especially with tempdb. However, contention with tempdb, and the allocation contention issues associated with latching, are outside the scope of this chapter. Fortunately, it is covered in Chapter 7 "Knowing Tempdb," so if you are interested in reading about BUF latch contention you may wish to skip ahead. However, this chapter covers sub-latching and super-latching and how they can ease latching contention.

IO (BUF) Latches

I/O latches are a particular subset of BUF latches. They are used whenever there is an outstanding I/O operation against either the data page or the index page when synchronizing it with the buffer pool.

This subset of latches can be seen as a `PAGEIOLATCH_*` prefixed wait stat and will show up in the `sys.dm_os_waiting_tasks` view.

The I/O latches are used for disk-to-memory transfers. Significant `PAGEIOLATCH` waits are a positive indication that the I/O subsystem is not keeping up with demand. Unless you are working with very high-end systems, it should be expected to see some element of `PAGEIOLATCH`. However, it is worthwhile to keep an eye on just how long your system is waiting for the latches to occur.

BUF Latch Architecture

At this point, you now know a few things about BUF latches, including the fact that there is a 1:1 mapping between buffer pool pages and a latch. But how does that relate to data pages? This section looks at the basic architecture of BUF latches, as a complete description is only really known by the developers at Microsoft. It is explained here from the top down and specifically in relation to data pages. Figure 6-44 shows the overall picture.

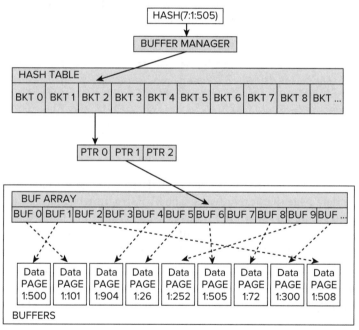

FIGURE 6-44

Buffer Manager

The buffer pool is accessed via the Buffer Manager, which receives requests from the Storage Engine for data pages. The Storage Engine will pass in a hashed value that includes the database id, the file id, and the page number. This gives the Buffer Manager enough information to service the request.

Hash Table

In order to find out whether the page is already in the buffer pool or whether it needs to schedule a read from disk, SQL Server needs to scan the *hash table* to determine whether it is there or not..

The hash table contains a series of *hash buckets*. The hashed value passed into the Buffer Manager maps to a hash bucket in the hash table. These buckets contain the pointers, in a linked list, to the BUF array. This data is spread across buckets in the hash table.

Theoretically, SQL Server could just scan the data pages in memory but this would be very inefficient and involve numerous memory lookups. Even though all your data is in memory, this would still be orders of magnitude slower than it needs to be. Instead, it does something like this: When requesting a page, SQL Server has enough information to help direct the Buffer Manager. It therefore passes in the database id, the file id, and the page number. As previously mentioned, to make it useful to the Buffer Manager, these values are hashed. The Buffer Manager uses this hash value to scan the hash table to determine which bucket the page is in. Assume for this example there is a match. Using a linked list of pointers, the memory address is found for the BUF structure in the BUF array. The BUF structure can then be latched. Once latched, the BUF structure can divulge the in-memory location of the data page.

> In a NUMA-enabled environment the buffer hash buckets are now also partitioned by NUMA node.

Buffer

A buffer is essentially made up of two components: the header, or BUF structure, and a physically separate in-memory object for the data page that it represents. The BUF structure belongs in the BUF array and contains one BUF structure for every data page reserved in the buffer pool. When SQL Server is started, it determines how many data pages it will reserve and then ensures it creates the same number of BUF structures. In order for data to be read, it must first exist in a buffer.

Buffers are rarely removed or sent to the free list. It is much more efficient to keep the buffer than be forced to read it in again from disk. Buffers are only sent to the free list when under memory pressure. This might occur more frequently because of insufficient physical memory or a manual change to the max server memory setting.

For details on memory allocation at system startup, please see Chapter 2.

BUF Arrays and BUF Structures

The BUF structure contains the in-memory mapping to the data page, in addition to the reference count for the page, and the page's latch and status information, such as whether an I/O is pending or dirty. In that sense the BUF structure acts as the gateway to the data page.

The key point to remember here is that when a latch is taken it is taken against the BUF structure, not against the data page. This is in part why a latch is so lightweight. The BUF structure is only

64 bytes in size. The part of the buffer that is moved to and from the free list is the buffer structure, not the data page. This makes perfect sense, as it means that only 64 bytes are being moved around, not 8KB. The latch is however an altogether more lightweight operation than a lock. Locks have a lot more checking to do than a latch, and this is the biggest factor in the performance difference between the two mechanisms.

To place this into a SQL Server context, imagine the following scenario. A write operation such as the lazywriter has kicked in. It scans the BUF array looking for dirty pages to write to disk. Note it doesn't scan the data pages. In the case of the lazywriter, it looks in the headers for the dirty page flag where the ref count is zero — i.e., the data page hasn't been accessed recently and has been updated in the buffer. When this happens the lazywriter will latch the page, write it to disk, un-hash the data page from the hash table, and move the BUF structure back to the free list, releasing the latch.

You can see the BUF structure associated with a data page by using DBCC PAGE:

```
BUFFER:

BUF @0x04281E48

bpage = 0x0D0FC000          bhash = 0x00000000          bpageno = (1:79)
bdbid = 23                  breferences = 0             bUse1 = 9462
bstat = 0x1c00009           blog = 0x21212159           bnext = 0x00000000
```

Data Pages

These are the pages that hold the actual row information for your tables. By looking at the page header information using DBCC PAGE, you can see how a data page maps back to the BUF structure:

```
PAGE HEADER:


Page @0x0D0FC000

m_pageId = (1:79)               m_headerVersion = 1     m_type = 1
m_typeFlagBits = 0x4            m_level = 0             m_flagBits = 0xa000
m_objId (AllocUnitId.idObj) = 29     m_indexId (AllocUnitId.idInd) = 256
Metadata: AllocUnitId = 72057594039828480
Metadata: PartitionId = 72057594038779904              Metadata: IndexId = 0
Metadata: ObjectId = 2105058535     m_prevPage = (0:0)     m_nextPage = (0:0)
pminlen = 12                    m_slotCnt = 1          m_freeCnt = 8065
m_freeData = 125                m_reservedCnt = 0      m_lsn = (46:185:4)
m_xactReserved = 0              m_xdesId = (0:0)       m_ghostRecCnt = 0
m_tornBits = 2025830588


Allocation Status

GAM (1:2) = ALLOCATED            SGAM (1:3) = NOT ALLOCATED
PFS (1:1) = 0x61 MIXED_EXT ALLOCATED  50_PCT_FULL          DIFF (1:6) = CHANGED
ML (1:7) = NOT MIN_LOGGED
```

I have highlighted the hashed page value at the top of the page header. If you refer back to the BUF structure shown earlier, you'll see that its `bpage` value is the same value as that on the page header. However, the `bpage` value on the BUF structure is the volatile one.

When a data page is written to disk, the buffer is returned to the free list. This process is optimized. The data page itself is not affected during this process. The BUF structure is updated to remove the association with the data page; thereby marking the page as being free. The data page will be over-written when the next page is read in.

Latch Modes

Because latches are taken for various purposes, they have several modes of operation. For example, a read request may have been received, in which case a mode suitable to that need must be available. Likewise, should an update, insert, or delete have been executed against the data, then an appropriate latch must be taken. Latch modes also dictate compatibility. Table 6-11 contains a complete list of latch modes. Table 6-12 shows the compatibility between the respective modes.

TABLE 6-11: Latch Modes

LOCK MODE	DESCRIPTION
NL	Null Latch - Internal - Not used
KP	Keep Latch - Can be held by multiple tasks simultaneously - Only blocked by a latch in a DT mode
SH	Shared Latch - Used when reading a data page - Can be held by multiple tasks simultaneously - Blocks EX and DT latches from being taken (see Table 6-12)
UP	Update Latch - Used when writing to a system allocation page and versioning pages in tempdb - A latch can only be held in this mode by a single task.
EX	Exclusive Latch - Used when writing to a data page - A latch can only be held in this mode by a single task.
DT	Destroy Latch - Rarely used - A latch can only be held in this mode by a single task.

TABLE 6-12: Latch Mode Compatibility

		WAIT LIST CHILD LATCH REQUEST				
		KP	SH	UP	EX	DT
WAIT LIST HEAD LATCH REQUEST	**SH**	Y	Y	Y	N	N
	UP	Y	Y	N	N	N
	EX	Y	N	N	N	N
	DT	N	N	N	N	N

Keep (KP) Latch

Keep latches are used in the code for two purposes. Their first and primary purpose is to maintain the reference counts in the BUF structure. However, they also have a secondary use. In some places in the code they are used to *keep* the data page in the buffer. This could be while the Engine decides whether or not to take an SH or EX latch, for example. There can be multiple keep latches against a BUF structure at the same time from concurrent requests.

Keep latches are quite special. They are only ever blocked by destroy latches, and they are not part of the relaxed first in, first out (FIFO) system used to determine the grant order.

Shared (SH) Latch

A shared latch is taken when a request to read the data page has been made. It is subject to the FIFO grant order but can be held by multiple takes simultaneously. The FIFO grant order is how SQL Server stops a queue of SH latches from preventing exclusive (EX) or destroy (DT) latches from getting to the page.

Update (UP) Latch

An update latch is different from a lock. Its use is much more specific. This latch mode is most frequently seen when updating system allocation pages and row versioning in tempdb, rather than processing update statements from a client application. However, these are the exception to the rule, rather than the norm. Head over to Chapter 7, "Knowing Tempdb," to see an example of tempdb under pressure, resulting in latch waits for allocation. In general terms, when SQL Server needs to modify a data page in the buffer, it will take an exclusive (EX) latch, not an UP latch.

You'll see UP latches when pages are being written to disk and the "page verify" option is set to checksum or none. An UP latch is taken for the duration of the write to ensure that no one else messes with the buffer data page during the write. In this mode, the latch is being used to block other write-based latches from being taken. However, it still allows latches in shared mode to read the data, which is nice because this helps the concurrency of the system.

Another example would be when the bitmaps need updating on the page free space (PFS) pages. It's an indicator of there being too few files in a database that's subject to high insert rates. For an in-depth treatment of this specific issue please see Thomas Kejser's blog post on the SQLCAT site `http://sqlcat.com/technicalnotes/archive/2008/03/07/` `How-many-files-should-a-database-have-part-1-olap-workloads.aspx`.

Exclusive (EX) Latch

An exclusive latch is taken when modifying the buffer data page. An example might be adding a row. However, another example is when data is being read in from disk. Although the request is to read data, you actually need to write it into the data page of the buffer first (if it doesn't already exist), before it can be read. Therefore, SQL Server needs to prevent others from trying to read the BUF structure or the data page, and therefore uses an EX latch to do this.

It's almost needless to say that data access is serialized by the EX latch and that this latch can only be held by one task at a time.

If the table that owns the page in question has a "page verify" option of Torn Pages, then an EX latch is taken when writing the page back to disk. This is because the implementation of torn pages modifies the page during the write process, a process sometimes known as *bit-flipping*. An EX latch is therefore needed.

EX latch waits will also start showing up when there are lots of insert operations trying to add rows to the same data page. Remember it is the page that is latched even when it's only a single row being inserted.

Destroy (DT) Latch

Destroy (DT) latches are used to remove a BUF structure from the buffer pool and return the data page to the free list. This is one of the reasons why KP latches exist — to prevent a DT latch from being granted, thereby *destroying* a BUF structure while it is being looked at.

When a DT latch has been granted, no other latch can be granted against that BUF structure.

Grant Order

As stated earlier, latches can be blocked by other latches. Broadly speaking, this is resolved in a FIFO system; but once a latch has been granted, all other requests, including new requests, must wait until that latch is released before latches are reconsidered for the next round of latching. There is no latch compatibility at this point. A shared latch request would need to wait even though the current latch mode was also SH. However, there are two notable exceptions to this.

First, keep latches are not blocked unless the latch is currently in destroy mode. In this case, it is blocked. The second exception is related to what occurs when the latch is released. Although the granting system is largely FIFO, the entire wait list is evaluated at this point, so if compatible latch requests are present, then SQL Server will process these requests at the same time. For example, imagine a page had just finished being written to, i.e., an EX latch and the first in the queue was a SH request. SQL Server would scan the wait list for all compatible requests with that SH request. Consequently, other SH requests — for example, in positions 3, 5, and 6 on the wait list — would also be processed immediately, even though there were EX requests at positions 2 and 4. Once the SH request was complete, the EX latch that would be first in the queue would then be processed in isolation. For a more detailed example, see the section "Latching in Action" later in the chapter.

Latch Waits and Blocking

As you have seen with latch compatibility, some latches can come into contention with one another. This is intended and desirable as part of the need to serialize access. However, as with locking, this does raise the prospect of blocking, and consequently latch waiting.

A *latch wait* can be defined as a latch request that cannot be granted immediately. This could result from one of two reasons. The first reason is that the latch is already being accessed. As stated earlier, new latches are evaluated at the closure of the existing request. The second reason follows from the first. When the wait list is accessed following the closure of the previous latch, the next wait in that list may be a conflicting lock with other waits. If you refer back to the grant order example, when an EX request is processed no other latch may be granted at the same time.

Unfortunately, there are side effects to keeping latches lightweight. They do not provide full blocking task information when forced to wait. Blocking task information is only known when the latch is held in one of the write latch modes — namely, UP, EX, and DT. Given that only one task can hold a latch in one of these modes at any one time, identifying it as the blocker is relatively straight forward. If the blocker is a read latch (either KP or SH) then this could be held by many tasks simultaneously, so identifying the task that is the blocker is not always possible. When the blocker is known, all waiting tasks will report that the one task is the cause of the block. Logically, then, the wait type is that of the requester, not the blocker.

It is possible for this blocking information to change during a single task's wait. Consider this example: An UP latch has been granted. Another task has requested an EX latch and therefore has been forced to wait. At this point the blocker is reported, as the latch held is an UP latch. By definition this can only be a single task. Before the UP latch has been released, a KP latch sneaks in and is granted (remember that KPs don't respect the FIFO rules). The UP latch is then released, leaving the KP in place to do its thing. It can no longer be guaranteed that this KP is the only latch in play. The EX latch is still forced to wait because the KP is already there. However, now there is no serialized write latch mode in effect and the blocking information is lost. What can be said though at this point is that the blocker is either a KP latch or a SH latch.

It is also possible for a task to be shown to block itself in certain scenarios. This is due to the asynchronous nature of data access. Again, this is probably best illustrated with an example. Consider this scenario: A read request is made to the Buffer Manager, but when the hash table is checked it is found that the page doesn't exist in memory. An I/O request is scheduled and an EX latch is taken (assume granted) on a BUF structure to allow the page to be read into the data page for the buffer. The task that initiated the request will then submit an SH latch to read the data. However, this can appear as being blocked by the EX latch if there is a lag retrieving the page from disk.

You'll hear more about latch blocking in the section "Latching in Action."

SUB-LATCHES AND SUPER-LATCHES

Simply put, super-latches and sub-latches are part of the same process of partitioning a single BUF structure. In normal situations a single BUF structure services all requests from all schedulers. As you have seen from DBCC PAGE, this includes all the state information relating to the buffer. However, in certain heavy read scenarios, this can put a lot of pressure on the BUF structure, thereby reducing performance.

The solution is to partition the latch. A sub-latch is created and aligned to each SQL Server scheduler. Any read request now only needs to latch the local, partition-aligned sub-latch. Because the BUF structure is so small (64 bytes), it is more likely that it will stay in local CPU cache where the scheduler resides, thus further optimizing the process.

The super-latch is the parent of all sub-latches. It still receives the requests but passes them out without having to burden itself with the state requests.

While this is all very good news for reads, the story isn't so great for writes. As the state is now split across all the sub-latches, a single EX latch request must now be granted against all sub-latches. On a 16-core server, that means 16 EX latches granted before the request can be satisfied. In this situation, the super-latch will be demoted, as the cost outweighs the benefits.

Place this into a real-world context. Imagine a reporting SQL Server that has just been rebooted. It is unlikely you will see super-latching on a cold SQL Server, even though all the requests may be exclusively read. That's because the buffers will all be empty and therefore need to be filled with EX write requests! Once this has happened though and the server is warm, this reporting SQL Server may be a very strong beneficiary of super-latches.

There is a DMV, sys.dm_os_sublatches, for monitoring the sub-latches, but it is undocumented and not officially supported. It doesn't offer much in terms of information (there are only three columns), but you will be able to see whether your system is promoting latches to sub-latches and on which tables this is occurring, as the partition_id is present.

Super-latches can also be monitored using performance monitor (PerfMon). In PerfMon you can see how many super-latches there are in addition to measuring super-latch volatility as latches are promoted to super-latches and subsequently demoted. See Figure 6-45 for details.

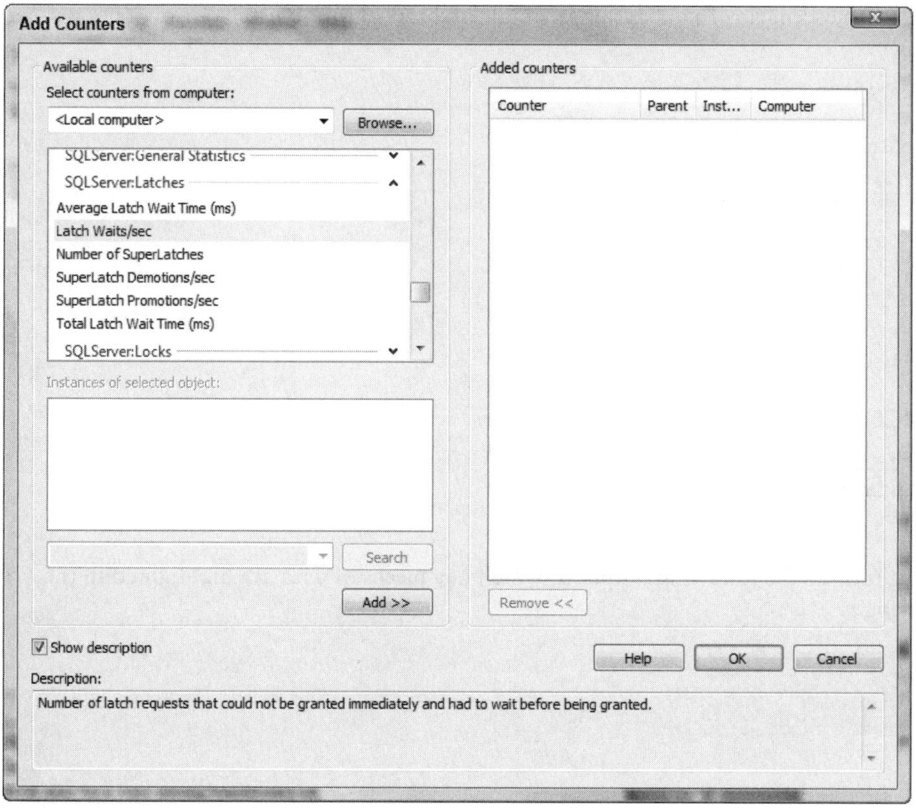

FIGURE 6-45

LATCHING IN ACTION

When the Relational Engine is processing a query, each time a row is needed from a base table or index, the Relational Engine uses the OLE DB API to request that the Storage Engine return the row. While the Storage Engine is actively transferring the row to the Relational Engine, the Storage Engine must ensure that no other task modifies either the contents of the row or certain page structures, such as the page offset table entry locating the row being read. The Storage Engine does this by acquiring a latch, transferring the row in memory to the Relational Engine, and then releasing the latch.

This section pulls all that you have learned about latches into a pseudo-real scenario. This illustration is a fictitious and massaged example of what would happen both with and without latches. SQL Server (thankfully) works so this isn't actually possible to repeat but it serves to illustrate the value of latches. This scenario concerns two concurrent writers who are both trying to add new rows to the same table. Session 1 contains transaction 1, which is trying to insert "2,200." Session 2 contains transaction 2, which wants to insert the values "3,300" into the table.

To begin, create the scenario. To make things simple and repeatable, create your own database and insert one row:

```
CREATE DATABASE LatchInAction;
GO
USE LatchInAction;

CREATE TABLE LatchTable
(       COL1 INT
        ,COL2 INT
);

INSERT INTO LatchTable ( COL1, COL2 )
VALUES (1,100);
```

Now run DBCC PAGE to get the output of the table:

```
DBCC TRACEON(3604)
DBCC IND(LatchInAction,'LatchTable',-1)
DBCC PAGE('LatchInAction',1,79,1)
```

The preceding returns the following output in which key pieces of data are highlighted in the explanation following :

```
PAGE: (1:79)


BUFFER:


BUF @0x04174970

bpage = 0x05F98000          bhash = 0x00000000         bpageno = (1:79)
bdbid = 26                  breferences = 0            bUse1 = 41669
bstat = 0x1c0010b           blog = 0x212121bb          bnext = 0x00000000

PAGE HEADER:


Page @0x05F98000

m_pageId = (1:79)           m_headerVersion = 1        m_type = 1
m_typeFlagBits = 0x4        m_level = 0                m_flagBits = 0x8000
m_objId (AllocUnitId.idObj) = 29    m_indexId (AllocUnitId.idInd) = 256
Metadata: AllocUnitId = 72057594039828480
Metadata: PartitionId = 72057594038779904                 Metadata: IndexId = 0
Metadata: ObjectId = 2105058535     m_prevPage = (0:0)    m_nextPage = (0:0)
pminlen = 12                m_slotCnt = 1              m_freeCnt = 8079
m_freeData = 111            m_reservedCnt = 0          m_lsn = (46:68:21)
m_xactReserved = 0          m_xdesId = (0:0)           m_ghostRecCnt = 0
```

```
m_tornBits = 0

Allocation Status

GAM (1:2) = ALLOCATED                    SGAM (1:3) = ALLOCATED
PFS (1:1) = 0x61 MIXED_EXT ALLOCATED  50_PCT_FULL          DIFF (1:6) = CHANGED
ML (1:7) = NOT MIN_LOGGED

DATA:


Slot 0, Offset 0x60, Length 15, DumpStyle BYTE

Record Type = PRIMARY_RECORD   Record Attributes =  .NULL_BITMAP Record  Size = 15

Memory Dump @0x6443C060

00000000:   10000c00 01000000 64000000 020000†††††........d......

OFFSET TABLE:

Row - Offset
0 (0x0) - 96 (0x60)
```

From this you can see that the single row is in Offset 96 (the page header consumes the earlier byte count) and our record length is 15 (note there is no read committed snapshot isolation here for those of you who have read that section). In the page header is a value called M_freedata. This is the pointer to the next available location for a row. In this case it is 111. That makes sense, as 96+15 = 111.

At this point, concurrent inserts begin:

```
/*TRANSACTION 1 SESSION 1*/
    INSERT INTO LatchTable
    VALUES (2,200);

/*TRANSACTION 2 SESSION 2*/
    INSERT INTO LatchTable
    VALUES (3,300);
```

Both these inserts are concurrent and are received by the lock manager at the same time. Neither row exists, so there is no Exclusive (X) lock available on the row just yet. Both sessions receive an Intent Exclusive (IX) lock on the page which are compatible with one another.

The transactions now proceed to the Buffer Manager to write their respective rows. A lookup in the hash table shows that our page is in memory, and both proceed to the BUF structure to read it. The following sections describe what happens next. Look at the fictitious scenario where latches do not exist. Then, once you have seen the danger in the "Without Latching" section, you will see how latches prevent this from happening in the "With Latching" section.

Without Latching

The next steps represent a world without latches. Say for the sake of argument that the row inserting the values "2,200" in Transaction 1 arrived at the page a fraction of a second before Transaction 2 and the values "3,300" are written. Transaction 1 writes to the page:

```
Page @0x0EF84000

m_pageId = (1:79)              m_headerVersion = 1      m_type = 1
m_typeFlagBits = 0x4           m_level = 0              m_flagBits = 0x8000
m_objId (AllocUnitId.idObj) = 29   m_indexId (AllocUnitId.idInd) = 256
Metadata: AllocUnitId = 72057594039828480
Metadata: PartitionId = 72057594038779904             Metadata: IndexId = 0
Metadata: ObjectId = 2105058535    m_prevPage = (0:0)    m_nextPage = (0:0)
pminlen = 12                       m_slotCnt = 1         m_freeCnt = 8062
m_freeData = 111                   m_reservedCnt = 0     m_lsn = (46:72:5)
m_xactReserved = 0                 m_xdesId = (0:0)      m_ghostRecCnt = 0
m_tornBits = 0

DATA:


Slot 0, Offset 0x60, Length 15, DumpStyle BYTE

Record Type = PRIMARY_RECORD    Record Attributes =  NULL_BITMAP    Record Size = 15

Memory Dump @0x633DC060

00000000:   10000c00 01000000 64000000 020000††††........d......

Slot 1, Offset 0x6f, Length 15, DumpStyle BYTE

Record Type = PRIMARY_RECORD    Record Attributes =  NULL_BITMAP    Record Size = 15

Memory Dump @0x633DC06F

00000000:   10000c00 02000000 c8000000 020000††††........È......

OFFSET TABLE:

Row - Offset
0 (0x0) - 96 (0x60)
```

As can be seen in bold above, the update has gone through as you have a second row in the page in slot 1 with the hex values 02 and c8 or 2 and 200, respectively. However, the page header and the slot offset haven't yet had a chance to be updated. Look at the value from m_freedata — it's still 111 and the m_slotcnt is still 1. It's too late. Transaction 2 has arrived and wants to write a row with its "3,300" values. There is no mechanism to stop it. Look what happens to the page now:

```
Page @0x0FA12000

m_pageId = (1:79)              m_headerVersion = 1      m_type = 1
m_typeFlagBits = 0x4           m_level = 0              m_flagBits = 0x8000
```

```
m_objId (AllocUnitId.idObj) = 29      m_indexId (AllocUnitId.idInd) = 256
Metadata: AllocUnitId = 72057594039828480
Metadata: PartitionId = 72057594038779904              Metadata: IndexId = 0
Metadata: ObjectId = 2105058535       m_prevPage = (0:0)       m_nextPage = (0:0)
pminlen = 12                          m_slotCnt = 2            m_freeCnt = 8062
m_freeData = 126                      m_reservedCnt = 0        m_lsn = (46:72:2)
m_xactReserved = 0                    m_xdesId = (0:0)         m_ghostRecCnt = 0
m_tornBits = 0

DATA:


Slot 0, Offset 0x60, Length 15, DumpStyle BYTE

Record Type = PRIMARY_RECORD    Record Attributes =  NULL_BITMAP   Record Size = 15

Memory Dump @0x6821C060

00000000:   10000c00 01000000 64000000 020000†††††........d......

Slot 1, Offset 0x6f, Length 15, DumpStyle BYTE

Record Type = PRIMARY_RECORD    Record Attributes =  NULL_BITMAP   Record Size = 15

Memory Dump @0x6821C06F

00000000:   10000c00 03000000 2c010000 020000†††††........,......

OFFSET TABLE:

Row - Offset
1 (0x1) - 111 (0x6f)
0 (0x0) - 96 (0x60)
```

Before the "2,200" transaction could update the metadata, the "3,300" transaction was in. "3,300" looked at the m_freedata, saw where to write the row, and updated the offset accordingly. But what do we have here? Only two rows . . . a lost update has occurred! Harking back to the earlier section on transactions, you know that this mustn't happen; otherwise, those inserts can't be defined as transactions. This is one of the prime uses for latches: serializing writes to prevent lost updates.

Happily, you won't be able to repeat this demonstration. SQL Server wouldn't let you. It didn't let me — remember I massaged the output to present this scenario. Now let's see what actually happens in a normal scenario.

With Latching

I won't repeat all the steps again because I am sure you know what would happen. However, I thought it might be worthwhile to describe why it happens like this.

When Transaction 1 with values "2,200" gets to the BUF structure it takes out an EX latch. The "3,300" transaction would have been forced on to the wait list, as it also would have wanted an EX latch. Two tasks can't have an EX latch granted at the same time.

The "2,200" transaction would have held the EX latch for as long as it needed to write the row and update the page header and offset. Only then would it have released the exclusive latch and allowed another transaction in. Note that the "2,200" transaction does not wait for the end of its transaction before releasing the latch. The latch isn't tied to the transaction in that sense.

Once the latch has been released the "3,300" transaction can get in with its own EX latch and insert its row of data, updating the header and offset accordingly.

This is a prime example of why latches exist within SQL Server. When writing to the data pages in the buffer, SQL Server must do so serially to ensure that modifications to the data aren't lost.

SUMMARY

This chapter delved deep into the bowels of SQL Server's internal locking and latching mechanisms. You should now understand the core concepts of transactions and how the isolation property in particular can be modified to alter locking behavior. By extending these core principles, you can understand how locking affects concurrency and how SQL Server's "attitude" toward concurrency can have a significant impact on the performance of the system.

More specifically, you've looked into the pessimistic isolation levels and compared them to the newer optimistic levels before diving headfirst into tempdb's version store. While looking at the version store, you decomposed a row and saw for yourself the overhead of optimistic concurrency that comes in the form of the XSN.

The chapter concluded with an architectural overview of latches and how they are used by SQL Server to marshal access to data pages. You saw several points of possible contention where latch waits may manifest themselves. The chapter also looked at some of the ways to monitor latches, both with PerfMon and with the DMVs, and how SQL Server scales its latching implementation by using super-latches.

7

Knowing Tempdb

This chapter is about the system database called tempdb, which is used for storing temporary objects and has been a key component of SQL Server since its inception. Since SQL Server 2005, however, the role of tempdb has been brought to the forefront with a plethora of new features and optimizations that depend on temporary objects.

All these features have increased the visibility and requirement for good tempdb performance, which is why there is a full chapter dedicated to a thorough grounding in what it's used for, how to troubleshoot issues, and how it should be configured.

In the first section you'll get a look at the facets that make tempdb special, which SQL Server components use it, and specifically how it's used. The next section covers common issues and how to troubleshoot them, which sets the scene nicely to help justify the configuration recommendations. Finally, you'll find an especially useful best practices section at the end of the chapter.

OVERVIEW AND USAGE

You can think of tempdb as the "scratch" database for SQL Server; it's a temporary data store used by both applications and internal operations. It is very similar to other databases in that it has a data file and a log file and can be seen in SQL Server Management Studio, but it does have some unique characteristics that affect the way you use and manage it.

The first fact to note is that everyone using an instance shares the same tempdb; you cannot have any more than one within an instance of SQL Server.

I worked with an investment banking customer many years ago that ran a database hosting service for internal customers based on SQL Server 2000. They had many databases belonging to different internal teams running on a single instance, and because tempdb is a shared resource they were having frequent issues with bad code in one database affecting all the others. A rogue connection would fill up tempdb, which affected the entire instance.

Although Microsoft received numerous requests about multiple tempdb databases as a feature in a future release, it never made it into SQL Server 2005 or 2008 because it would have meant a significant architectural change but they did introduce some DMVs to help determine who is using what in tempdb. These DMVs are discussed in the section on troubleshooting common issues later in the chapter.

The following features and attributes should be considered when learning about, using, tuning and troubleshooting tempdb:

➤ Nothing stored in tempdb persists after a restart because tempdb is to all intents and purposes recreated every time SQL Server starts. This "feature" also has implications for the *recovery* of tempdb — namely, it doesn't need to be done, so most of the extra work carried out in a normal database for recovery purposes can be avoided.

➤ Tempdb is always set to "Simple" recovery mode, which, if you remember from Chapter 1, means that transaction log records for committed transactions are marked for reuse after every checkpoint. This means that you don't need to back up the transaction log for tempdb, and in fact you can't back up tempdb at all. Transaction log usage is optimized even further because *redo* information isn't written to the log.

➤ Redo information in a transaction log is used during the recovery process in order for a database to "redo" committed transactions, but because SQL Server creates a fresh copy of tempdb each time you don't actually need it.

➤ Tempdb can also only have one filegroup (the PRIMARY filegroup), you can't add more.

➤ New for SQL Server 2008 is the ability to configure database page checksums to detect corruption caused outside of SQL Server.

➤ Tempdb is used to store three types of objects: user objects, internal objects, and the version store.

User Temporary Objects

To store data temporarily you can use local temporary tables, global temporary tables, or table variables, all of which are stored in tempdb (you can't change where they're stored). A local temporary table is defined by giving it a prefix of # and is scoped to the session in which you created it. This means that no one can see it and when you disconnect, or your session is reset with connection pooling, the table is dropped. Here is an example that creates a local temporary table, populates it with one row, and then selects from it:

Available for
download on
Wrox.com

```
CREATE TABLE #TempTable ( ID INT, NAME CHAR(3) ) ;
INSERT  INTO #TempTable ( ID, NAME )
VALUES  ( 1, 'abc' ) ;
GO
SELECT  *
FROM    #TempTable ;
GO
DROP TABLE #TempTable ;
```

This code available for download at Wrox.com [Chapter7CreateTempObjects.sql]

Global temporary tables can be seen by all sessions connected to the server and are defined by a prefix of ##. They are used in exactly the same way as local temporary tables, the only difference being that everyone can see them. They are not used very often because if you had a requirement for multiple users to use the same table, you're more likely just to implement a normal table in a user database, rather than a global temporary table. Here is exactly the same code as above but implemented as a global temporary table:

Available for
download on
Wrox.com

```
CREATE TABLE ##TempTable ( ID INT, NAME CHAR(3) ) ;
INSERT  INTO ##TempTable ( ID, NAME )
VALUES  ( 1, 'abc' ) ;
GO
SELECT  *
FROM    ##TempTable ;
GO
DROP TABLE ##TempTable ;
```

This code available for download at Wrox.com [Chapter7CreateTempObjects.sql]

As you can see, the only difference is the prefix; both local temporary tables and global temporary tables are dropped when the session that created them is closed. This means it is not possible to create a global temporary table in one session, close the session, and then use it in another.

> *It's easy to be caught out by the scope of a temporary table with SSIS (SQL Server Integration Services). By default, each task in SSIS uses a different connection, which rules out the use of local temporary tables. You can configure SSIS to use a single connection for all tasks, which allows local temporary tables to be used, but be aware that you'll probably be sacrificing some performance.*

A table variable is used similarly to a local temporary table. The differences are explored in the next section.

Here is the same sample again, this time implemented as a table variable:

Available for
download on
Wrox.com

```
DECLARE @TempTable TABLE ( ID INT, NAME CHAR(3) ) ;
INSERT   INTO @TempTable ( ID, NAME )
VALUES   ( 1, 'abc' ) ;
SELECT   *
FROM     @TempTable ;
```

This code available for download at Wrox.com [Chapter7CreateTempObjects.sql]

The syntax for declaring a table variable is slightly different to a temporary table but a more important difference is that table variables are scoped to the batch, rather than the session. If you kept the GO batch delimiter as in the previous examples, then an "object does not exist" error would be raised for the last SELECT statement because the table variable does not exist in the scope of the statement.

Temp Tables vs. Table Variables

Having touched on the concept and scope of temporary tables and table variables in the previous section, the mechanism used to store temporary results usually boils down to the differences in features between temporary tables (#table) or a table variable.

Statistics

The major difference between temp tables and table variables is that statistics are not created on table variables. This has two major consequences, the first of which is that the Query Optimizer uses a fixed estimation for the number of rows in a table variable irrespective of what data is in it. Moreover, adding or removing data doesn't change the estimation.

To illustrate this, executing the code found in Listing 7-1 and looking at the properties of the table scan in the actual execution plan will give you the properties shown in Figure 7-1. To understand the example you need to first understand the Query Optimizer, statistics, and execution plans, which you can read up on in Chapter 1 and Chapter 5.

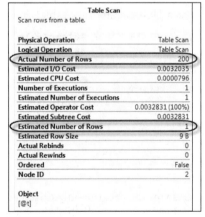

FIGURE 7-1

Available for
download on
Wrox.com

LISTING 7-1: Creating, populating, and reading a table variable with 200 rows
(Chapter7TempTableVsTableVariable.sql)

```
DECLARE @TempTable TABLE ( c1 INT ) ;
DECLARE @i INT ;
SET @i = 0 ;
WHILE ( @i < 200 )
```

```
BEGIN
    INSERT  INTO @TempTable ( c1 )
    VALUES  ( @i ) ;
    SET @i = @i + 1 ;
END ;
SELECT  COUNT(*)
FROM    @TempTable ;
```

What you can see highlighted is that the optimizer based the plan on an estimation of one row being returned, whereas 200 rows were actually returned when it was executed. Regardless of the number of rows in the table variable, the optimizer will always estimate one row because it has no statistics with which to generate a better estimation, and this could cause a bad execution plan to be used.

You can do the same test but using a temporary table instead by executing the code in Listing 7-2.

LISTING 7-2: Creating, populating, and reading a temporary table with 200 rows

```
CREATE TABLE #TempTable ( c1 INT ) ;
DECLARE @i INT ;
SET @i = 0 ;
WHILE ( @i < 200 )
    BEGIN
        INSERT  INTO #TempTable ( c1 )
        VALUES  ( @i ) ;
        SET @i = @i + 1 ;
    END ;
SELECT  COUNT(*)
FROM    #TempTable ;
```

The properties for the table scan in this scenario can be seen in Figure 7-2 which shows an accurate row estimate of 200 because statistics were automatically created when the SELECT statement was run.

Indexes

You can't create indexes on table variables although you can create constraints. This means that by creating primary keys or unique constraints, you are able to have indexes (as these are created to support constraints) on table variables.

Even if you have constraints and therefore indexes that will have statistics, the indexes will not be used when the query is compiled because they won't exist at compile time, nor will they cause recompilations.

Table Scan	
Scan rows from a table.	
Physical Operation	Table Scan
Logical Operation	Table Scan
Actual Number of Rows	200
Estimated I/O Cost	0.0032035
Estimated CPU Cost	0.0002985
Number of Executions	1
Estimated Number of Executions	1
Estimated Operator Cost	0.003502 (97%)
Estimated Subtree Cost	0.003502
Estimated Number of Rows	200
Estimated Row Size	9 B
Actual Rebinds	0
Actual Rewinds	0
Ordered	False
Node ID	2
Object	
[tempdb].[dbo].[#tmpTable]	

FIGURE 7-2

Schema Modifications

Schema modifications are possible on temporary tables but not on table variables. While schema modifications are possible on temporary tables, avoid using them because they will cause recompilations of statements that use the tables.

Table 7-1 provides a brief summary of the differences between temporary tables and table variables.

TABLE 7-1: Temporary Tables versus Table Variables

	TEMPORARY TABLES	TABLE VARIABLES
Statistics	Yes	No
Indexes	Yes	Only with constraints
Schema modifications	Yes	No
Available in child routines including `sp_executesql`	Yes	No
Use with `INSERT INTO ... EXEC`	Yes	No
In memory structures	No	No

BUT I THOUGHT TABLE VARIABLES WERE CREATED IN MEMORY?

There is a common misconception that table variables are in-memory structures and so will perform quicker than temporary tables. Thanks to a DMV called `sys.dm_db_session_space_usage` introduced in SQL Server 2005, which shows tempdb usage by session, you can prove that's not the case. After restarting SQL Server to clear the DMV, run this script to confirm that your `session_id` returns 0 for `user_objects_alloc_page_count`:

```
SELECT   session_id,
         database_id,
         user_objects_alloc_page_count
FROM     sys.dm_db_session_space_usage
WHERE    session_id > 50 ;
```

Now you can check to see how much space a temporary table takes up by running this script to create a temporary table with one column and populate it with one row:

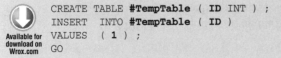
Available for download on Wrox.com

```
CREATE TABLE #TempTable ( ID INT ) ;
INSERT  INTO #TempTable ( ID )
VALUES   ( 1 ) ;
GO
```

```
SELECT    session_id,
          database_id,
          user_objects_alloc_page_count
FROM      sys.dm_db_session_space_usage
WHERE     session_id > 50 ;
```

This code available for download at Wrox.com [Chapter7TempTableVsTableVariableSpace.sql]

The results on my server (shown in Figure 7-3) indicate that the table was allocated one page in tempdb.

session_id	database_id	user_objects_alloc_page_count
51	2	1

FIGURE 7-3

Now run the same script but use a table variable this time:

```
DECLARE @TempTable TABLE ( ID INT ) ;
INSERT  INTO @TempTable ( ID )
VALUES  ( 1 ) ;
GO
SELECT    session_id,
          database_id,
          user_objects_alloc_page_count
FROM      sys.dm_db_session_space_usage
WHERE     session_id > 50 ;
```

Available for download on Wrox.com

This code available for download at Wrox.com [Chapter7TempTableVsTableVariableSpace.sql]

You can see in Figure 7-4 that using the table variable caused another page to be allocated in tempdb, so table variables are not created in memory.

session_id	database_id	user_objects_alloc_page_count
51	2	2

FIGURE 7-4

Table variables and temporary tables are both likely to be cached, however, so in reality, unless your server is memory constrained and you're using particularly large tables, you'll be working with them in memory anyway.

Internal Temporary Objects

Internal temporary objects are objects used by SQL Server to store data temporarily during query processing. Operations such as sorts, spools, hash joins, and cursors all require space in tempdb to run. You can read more about query processing in Chapter 5.

You can see how many pages have been allocated to internal objects for each session by looking at the internal_object_alloc_page_count column in the sys.dm_db_session_space_usage DMV. You'll find more details on looking at tempdb usage in the "Troubleshooting Common Issues" section later in the chapter.

The Version Store

Many features in SQL Server 2008 require multiple versions of rows to be maintained, and the *version store* is used to store these different versions of index and data rows. The following features make use of the version store:

➤ **Triggers:** These have used row versions since SQL Server 2005, rather than scan the transaction log as they did in SQL Server 2000.

➤ **Snapshot Isolation and Read-Committed Snapshot Isolation:** Two new isolation levels based on versioning of rows, rather than locking. You can read more about them in Chapter 6.

➤ **Online Index Operations:** Row versioning to support index updates during an index rebuild.

➤ **MARS (Multiple Active Result Sets):** Row versioning to support interleaving multiple batch requests across a single connection. You can search SQL Server Books Online for more information on this.

Version Store Overhead

The overhead of row versioning is 14 bytes per row, which consists of a transaction sequence number referred to as an *XSN* and a row identifier referred to as a *RID*. You can see this illustrated in Figure 7-5.

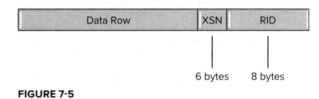

FIGURE 7-5

The XSN is used to chain together multiple versions of the same row; the RID is used to locate the row version in tempdb.

The 14-byte overhead doesn't reduce the maximum possible row size of 8,060 bytes and is added the first time a row is modified or inserted when:

➤ you're using snapshot isolation;

➤ or the underlying table has a trigger;

➤ or you're using MARS;

➤ or an online index rebuild is running on the table;

and will be removed when:

➤ snapshot isolation is switched off;

➤ or the trigger is removed;

➤ or you stop using MARS;

➤ or an online index rebuild is completed.

You should also be aware that creating the additional 14 bytes could cause page splits if the data pages are full and will affect your disk space requirement.

Append-Only Stores

The row versions are written to an append-only store of which there are two; index rebuilds have their own version store and everything else uses the common version store. To increase scalability, each CPU scheduler has its own page in the version store to store rows, as illustrated in Figure 7-6 with a computer with four CPU cores. You can read about CPU cores and schedulers in Chapter 5.

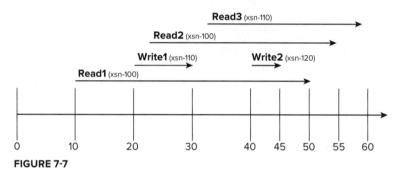

FIGURE 7-6

You can view the entire contents of the version store using the `sys.dm_tran_version_store` DMV but use it with care as it can be resource intensive to run.

For an example demonstrating how row versioning is used, Figure 7-7 illustrates an example of multiple read and write transactions operating under snapshot isolation.

FIGURE 7-7

Along the bottom of the diagram a timeline is represented from 0 to 60; the horizontal arrows represent the duration of a specific transaction. The sequence of events occurs like this:

➤ At timeline 10 a transaction called Read1 starts and reads the row associated with XSN-100.

➤ At 20 another transaction starts called Write1 that wants to modify the row. Snapshot isolation guarantees a repeatable read for Read1 and ensures that any new readers can read committed data at the point a write starts. Therefore, it copies the rows associated with XSN-100 to the version store and allows Write1 to modify the row under XSN-110.

➤ Read2 starts before Write1 has committed, so the version chain is traversed from XSN-110 to XSN-100 in the version store to get the last committed value.

➤ Read3 starts *after* Write1 has committed and reads the value from XSN-110.

➤ Write2 now starts and wants to modify the row. Read1 and Read2 still need the version under XSN-100 and Read3 needs the version under XSN-110, so a new version is created for XSN-120, and XSN-110 is moved to the version store in tempdb.

➤ Write2 commits XSN-120.

➤ Read1 completes, but XSN-100 is still being used by Read2.

➤ Read2 completes and XSN-100 is now stale.

➤ Read3 completes and XSN-110 is now stale.

A background thread removes stale versions of rows from tempdb every minute, so at that point only the result of the write operation carried out by transaction Write2 will be stored and no previous versions will be available or stored in tempdb.

Figure 7-8 represents the state of the row on the data page and the versions stored in tempdb at timeline 0. You can see that the only available result is the currently committed value as of XSN-100.

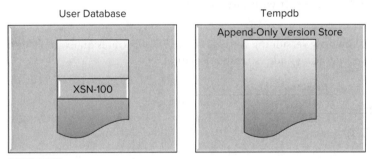

FIGURE 7-8

Figure 7-9 shows the state at timeline 45. Two versions are being maintained in tempdb to provide a repeatable read for the Read1, Read2, and Read3 transactions.

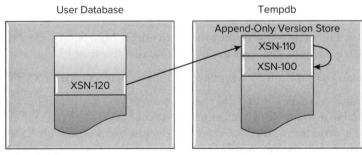

FIGURE 7-9

Figure 7-10 shows timeline 60. All transactions that required previous versions to maintain the snapshot isolation level have now completed, so the stale versions stored in tempdb have been cleaned up by a background thread.

You'll find more in-depth information on snapshot isolation, including its uses and its drawbacks, in Chapter 6.

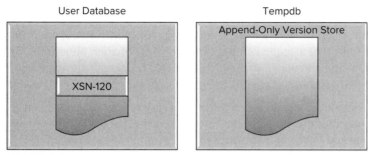

User Database   Tempdb

Append-Only Version Store

XSN-120

FIGURE 7-10

TROUBLESHOOTING COMMON ISSUES

The unique nature of tempdb as a shared resource for temporary objects makes it more prone to specific performance problems than other databases. In this section you'll read about the most common issues that tempdb is vulnerable to and how to troubleshoot and avoid them.

Latch Contention

Compared to a normal database, tempdb's use as a temporary storage area makes the workload pattern likely to contain a disproportionate amount of the creation and destruction of many small objects.

This type of workload can lead to latch contention on the pages required to allocate objects in a database.

If you've read the previous chapter on locking and latches, you should have a good grasp of what a latch is, so it's covered only briefly here for the sake of context.

What Is a Latch?

A latch is a short-term synchronization lock used by SQL Server to protect *physical* pages.

You can't influence latching behavior by changing the isolation level or by using "hints," as you can with normal locks; latches are used automatically behind the scenes to protect pages in memory from being modified by another task while the content or structure is being changed or read from disk.

Allocation Pages

When you create an object such as a temporary table in tempdb, it needs to be allocated space in exactly the same way as creating a table in a normal database. There are three pages in the allocation process that you need to be aware of: Page Free Space, Global Allocation Map, and Shared Global Allocation Map, all of which are covered in the following sections.

PFS (Page Free Space)

The PFS page stores 1 byte of information for each page, containing how much free space is on it and what it's used for, which means that a single PFS page can store information about roughly 64MB of pages. Therefore, you'll find a new PFS page at close to 64MB intervals throughout a database data file.

The first page on any database data file is always a PFS page so it's easy to spot the page in an error message. If you see "2:1:1" anywhere it's referring to the first page on the first data file in database_id 2, which is tempdb. "5:3:1" would be the first PFS page in file_id 3 in database_id 5.

GAM (Global Allocation Map)

The GAM page tracks 1 bit per *extent* (an extent is 8 pages) showing which extents are in use and which are empty. SQL Server reads the page to find free space to allocate a full extent to an object.

Storing only 1 bit for each extent (instead of 1 byte per page like the PFS page) means that a single GAM page can track a lot more space and you'll find a new GAM page at roughly 4GB intervals in a data file. However, the first GAM page in a data file is always page number 2, so "2:1:2" would refer to the first GAM page in tempdb.

SGAM (Shared Global Allocation Map)

The SGAM page (pronounced *ess*-gam) also stores 1 bit per extent but the values represent whether the extent is a mixed extent with free space or a full extent. SQL Server reads this page to find a mixed extent with free space to allocate space to a small object.

A single SGAM can track 4GB of pages, so you'll find them at 4GB intervals just like GAM pages. The first SGAM page in a data file is page 3, so "2:1:3" is tempdb's first SGAM page.

Allocation Page Contention

Imagine that you take an action within an application that needs to create a temporary table. To determine where in tempdb to create your table, SQL Server will read the SGAM page (2:1:3) to find a mixed extent with free space to allocate to the table.

SQL Server will take out an exclusive latch on the SGAM page while it's updating the page and will then move on to read the PFS page to find a free page within the extent to allocate to the object.

An exclusive latch will also be taken out on the PFS page to ensure that no one else tries to allocate the same data page, which is then released when the update is complete.

This is quite a simple process (but maybe not to explain) and works very well until tempdb becomes overloaded with allocation requests. The threshold can be hard to predict, but in SQL Server 2005 a few changes were made to the allocation process for tempdb that makes this issue far less likely.

Even with the improvements brought forward from SQL Server 2005, however, there is still the potential for the issue to arise. The next section describes several things you can do to proactively avoid it.

The issue itself manifests as a PAGELATCH wait with 2:1:1 or 2:1:3 as the resource description. See Chapter 3 for more details on waits.

Figure 7-11 shows contention on the allocation pages because multiple users are trying to allocate many objects at the same time.

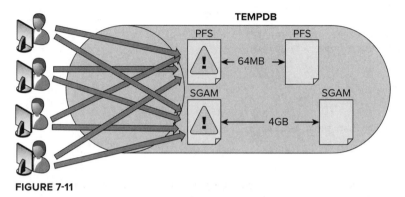

FIGURE 7-11

Allocation Page Contention Example

In order to demonstrate page contention I've created a couple of stored procedures and a table in an empty database called demo. If you want to step through the example yourself, I have provided all the necessary steps and scripts, starting with the creation script in Listing 7-3.

LISTING 7-3: Allocation contention demo stored procedure that uses tempdb (Chapter7AllocationContentionSetup.sql)

```
-- Create stored procedure that creates a temp table, a clustered index and
populates with 10 rows
-- The script expects a database called Demo to exist
USE [demo] ;
GO
CREATE PROCEDURE [dbo].[usp_temp_table]
AS
    CREATE TABLE #tmpTable
        (
          c1 INT,
          c2 INT,
          c3 CHAR(5000)
        ) ;
    CREATE UNIQUE CLUSTERED INDEX cix_c1 ON #tmptable ( c1 ) ;
    DECLARE @i INT = 0 ;
    WHILE ( @i < 10 )
        BEGIN
```

continues

LISTING 7-3 *(continued)*

```
                INSERT  INTO #tmpTable ( c1, c2, c3 )
                VALUES  ( @i, @i + 100, 'coeo' ) ;
                SET  @i += 1 ;
            END ;
GO
-- Create stored procedure that runs usp_temp_table 50 times
CREATE PROCEDURE [dbo].[usp_loop_temp_table]
AS
    SET nocount ON ;
    DECLARE @i INT = 0 ;
    WHILE ( @i < 100 )
        BEGIN
            EXEC demo.dbo.usp_temp_table ;
            SET @i += 1 ;
        END ;
```

The `usp_temp_table` stored procedure creates a table in tempdb with three columns and a unique clustered index on column 1. The table is then populated with 10 rows. The `usp_loop_temp_table` stored procedure runs the `usp_temp_table` procedure 100 times.

To simulate multiple users trying to run the same procedure at the same time, I'm going to use a tool called *OStress,* which is part of a download called RML Utilities, covered in detail in Chapter 12, for stress testing and trace file analysis.

For the purpose of the demo I'm just going to use OStress very simply to run the `usp_loop_temp_table` procedure using 300 connections. The aim is to simulate 300 people running a stored procedure that recursively calls another stored procedure 100 times.

OStress needs to be run from the command prompt:

```
C:\"Program Files\Microsoft Corporation"\RMLUtils\ostress -Scosimo\reading -E
-Q"EXEC demo.dbo.usp_loop_temp_table;" -ooutput.txt -n300
```

Of course, *cosimo\reading* is my SQL Server instance name, so change it to your own if you're following along.

While OStress is running, take a look at the `sys.dm_os_waiting_tasks` DMV (see Chapter 3 for more details) using the following script:

```
SELECT  *
FROM    sys.dm_os_waiting_tasks
WHERE   resource_description = '2:1:1'
OR resource_description = '2:1:2'
OR resource_description = '2:1:3' ;
```

You should see results similar to those shown in Figure 7-12.

waiting_task_address	session_id	wait_duration_ms	wait_type	blocking_session_id	resource_description
0x0800D558	984	51	PAGELATCH_UP	NULL	2:1:1
0x068F1000	971	74	PAGELATCH_UP	NULL	2:1:1
0x0800D720	985	51	PAGELATCH_UP	NULL	2:1:1
0x0800B000	981	53	PAGELATCH_UP	NULL	2:1:1
0x07B93558	986	91	PAGELATCH_UP	NULL	2:1:1
0x07D74AA8	979	17	PAGELATCH_UP	NULL	2:1:1
0x0800D390	975	69	PAGELATCH_UP	NULL	2:1:1
0x091171C8	734	77	PAGELATCH_UP	NULL	2:1:1
0x07441558	713	59	PAGELATCH_UP	NULL	2:1:1
0x088EC8E0	680	68	PAGELATCH_UP	NULL	2:1:1
0x094D0E38	715	69	PAGELATCH_UP	NULL	2:1:1
0x07445E40	732	74	PAGELATCH_UP	NULL	2:1:1
0x07487558	751	77	PAGELATCH_UP	NULL	2:1:1
0x07445720	733	60	PAGELATCH_UP	NULL	2:1:1
0x074411C8	696	60	PAGELATCH_UP	NULL	2:1:1

FIGURE 7-12

At the time I took this snapshot of `sys.dm_os_waiting_tasks`, more than 200 tasks were waiting for a PAGELATCH on page 2:1:1 (which is the PFS page), so there is evidence of allocation page contention.

Before moving on to reducing the contention, I'm going to use the `sys.dm_os_wait_stats` DMV to provide another benchmark, as well as the timings from OStress in order to measure any improvements. If you haven't already done so, you can read all about wait stats and the `sys.dm_os_wait_stats` DMV in Chapter 3.

To quickly recap, the `sys.dm_os_wait_stats` DMV is an aggregation of all the waits that have occurred within the SQL Server instance since the last service restart. It contains one row for every wait type and has columns showing the following:

➤ Total number of tasks that have waited for that wait type

➤ Total time they've spent waiting

➤ Maximum time that a single task has spent waiting

➤ Total signal wait time for that wait (indicates CPU pressure)

Although `sys.dm_os_wait_stats` aggregates information since the last service restart, you can clear the information using the following command:

```
DBCC sqlperf('sys.dm_os_wait_stats',clear) ;
```

This can be very useful in a dev or test environment (if you're the only user) before running a batch that you want to test because you'll then have the aggregated wait stats for just your batch of code. This is exactly what we want to do for the OStress load.

Clear the wait stats and run SELECT * FROM sys.dm_os_wait_stats just to ensure that all the values are zero. Now, if you start the OStress tool you'll be gathering all the wait information for this DMV.

As soon as OStress completes, run this script:

```
SELECT  *
FROM    sys.dm_os_wait_stats
ORDER BY wait_time_ms DESC ;
```

On my server, OStress completed in 4 minutes and 5 seconds. The top three wait types are shown in Figure 7-13.

	wait_type	waiting_tasks_count	wait_time_ms	max_wait_time_ms	signal_wait_time_ms
1	PAGELATCH_UP	550155	54618443	468	188976
2	PAGELATCH_EX	324988	10549340	721	236638
3	PAGELATCH_SH	2678448	5385302	684	1617161

FIGURE 7-13

These page latch waits are consistent with my expectations based on the sys.dm_waiting_tasks results in Figure 7-12, although they may not all relate to waits against the allocation pages. Based on these statistics you can conclude the following baseline for this workload:

➤ **Duration:** 4 minutes 5 seconds

➤ **Total tasks waiting on PAGELATCH:** 3,553,591

➤ **Total time waiting on PAGELATCH:** 70,553 seconds

➤ **Maximum single wait for a PAGELATCH:** 721 milliseconds

Now that a baseline has been established, you can look into what can be done to alleviate the problem.

Resolving and/or Avoiding Allocation Page Contention Problems

Once you've determined that you're suffering from allocation page contention in tempdb (or even if you're not sure), there are a few different ways to reduce the likelihood of it happening.

Multiple Tempdb Data Files

If you're a DBA rather than a developer, you might be tempted to opt for this solution first. Recall that there is a set of allocation pages at the start of each data file, so if you have more than one file and can balance the load between them you'll be less likely to get a hot spot on the allocation pages compared to a single file.

It's a good best practice to have multiple tempdb files for your instance anyway because doing so is a simple, risk-free way of reducing the likelihood of contention occurring.

Tempdb works with multiple data files by using a *proportional fill* algorithm to try to balance the amount of free space across all the files. The effect of this is to favor the file with the most free space until it equals all the other files. This is a bad scenario if you're trying to balance the allocation requests evenly across the files, so you need to ensure that all the tempdb data files are the same size. This is illustrated in Figure 7-14.

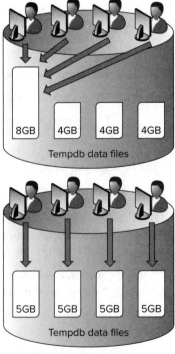

FIGURE 7-14

You can learn more about how to configure multiple tempdb data files in the last major section of this chapter, "Configuration Best Practices."

To determine whether simply adding more files can make a measurable difference to the contention example from the previous section, we can configure the server to have four equally sized tempdb data files. It's not important for them to be on separate drives because you're not doing it to improve I/O performance but simply to have more allocation pages.

Listing 7-4 contains the script used to configure the data files, which are all on the same disk.

LISTING 7-4: Modifying tempdb to have four data files of equal size (Chapter7AddingNewTempdbFiles.sql)

```
ALTER DATABASE tempdb
MODIFY FILE (name=tempdev,size=512MB) ;
GO
ALTER DATABASE tempdb
ADD FILE (name=tempdev2,size=512MB,filename='D:\data\tempdev2.ndf') ;
GO
ALTER DATABASE tempdb
ADD FILE (name=tempdev3,size=512MB,filename='D:\data\tempdev3.ndf') ;
GO
ALTER DATABASE tempdb
ADD FILE (name=tempdev4,size=512MB,filename='D:\data\tempdev4.ndf') ;
```

Clearing `sys.dm_os_wait_stats`, running OStress, and viewing the wait stats again returns the results shown in Figure 7-15.

wait_type	waiting_tasks_count	wait_time_ms	max_wait_time_ms	signal_wait_time_ms
PAGELATCH_EX	315507	28757230	1799	406988
PAGELATCH_SH	381829	21106028	1771	1711046
PAGELATCH_UP	30643	3154089	622	34799

FIGURE 7-15

Totaled up along with the OStress timings, this provides a performance measurement as follows:

➤ **Duration:** 3 minutes 10 seconds

➤ **Total tasks waiting on PAGELATCH:** 727,979

➤ **Total time waiting on PAGELATCH:** 53,017 seconds

➤ **Maximum single wait for a PAGELATCH:** 1799 milliseconds

This represents a significant improvement in all results except the maximum single wait, but the net impact has been enough to reduce the overall run time by 55 seconds, which isn't bad for a configuration change.

Temporary Object Reuse

This optimization is a little-known feature called *temporary object reuse*. If you're a developer and you manage the code rather than the server, the first thing you'll likely look at is optimizing the code, rather than reviewing server best practices. In most scenarios changing the code will yield the best performance improvements anyway, so it's not a bad starting approach.

Beginning with SQL Server 2005, it's possible for SQL Server to cache temporary object definitions so that they can be reused if the same object needs to be created again. To be more specific, one IAM page (Index Allocation Map) and one extent are cached.

Objects that are reused don't have to be allocated new space and therefore won't contribute to any allocation problems. Optimizing your code to ensure that your temporary tables are being cached will help to reduce any potential problems.

SQL Server tries to cache temporary tables by default, so the first thing you need to check is whether or not SQL Server is caching yours. To check this you can run your code in a loop and monitor the difference between the "temp table creation rate" performance monitor counter at the start and end of the loop. Fortunately, Sunil Agarwal from Microsoft has written a nice wrapper script that does it for us, which you'll find in Listing 7-5.

LISTING 7-5: Script to show how many temporary tables are created by your code (Chapter7HowManyTempTablesCreated.sql)

```
SET NOCOUNT ON ;
GO
DECLARE @table_counter_before_test BIGINT ;
SELECT  @table_counter_before_test = cntr_value
FROM    sys.dm_os_performance_counters
WHERE   counter_name = 'Temp Tables Creation Rate' ;
DECLARE @i INT = 0 ;
WHILE ( @i < 10 )
    BEGIN
        EXEC demo.dbo.usp_loop_temp_table ;
        SELECT  @i += 1 ;
    END ;
DECLARE @table_counter_after_test BIGINT ;
SELECT  @table_counter_after_test = cntr_value
FROM    sys.dm_os_performance_counters
WHERE   counter_name = 'Temp Tables Creation Rate' ;
PRINT 'Temp tables created during the test: '
    + CONVERT(VARCHAR(100), @table_counter_after_test
    - @table_counter_before_test) ;
```

To use the script yourself simply change the stored procedure name you want to test from `usp_loop_test_table` to whatever code you want.

If the code you want to test is complicated, you might want to set the loop iterations to 1 the first time you run this script just to be sure how many *different* temporary tables are created. Once you know that, you can set it back to 10 loop iterations as in the example.

In my example code I know that I only have one temporary table creation statement that's called many times, so if the value returned from Listing 7-5 is more than 1, then I can be confident that I'm not getting temporary object reuse.

Running the script as shown in Listing 7-5 gives me the following result:

```
Temp tables created during the test: 1000
```

During 10 executions, 1,000 temporary tables were created, so I can conclude that the table isn't being cached (remember that the looping procedure executes the procedure creating the temp table 100 times, 10 * 100 = 1,000).

There's obviously a problem in the example code somewhere, so what I need to understand now is under what circumstances SQL Server *will* cache temporary tables so I can determine whether any changes can be made to the code.

Temporary objects will be cached as long as:

➤ Named constraints are not created.

➤ DDL (Data Definition Language) statements that affect the table, such as CREATE INDEX or CREATE STATISTICS, are not run after the table has been created.

➤ The object is not created using dynamic SQL; using sp_executesql, for example.

➤ The object is created inside another object such as the following:

➤ Stored procedure

➤ Trigger

➤ User-defined function

➤ The return table of a user-defined table-valued function

If you look back at Listing 7-3 you'll notice that a unique clustered index is created after the table definition, which breaks the rules for cached temporary objects:

```
CREATE UNIQUE CLUSTERED INDEX cix_c1 ON #tmptable ( c1 ) ;
```

All is not lost, however, because you can utilize a constraint within the temp table definition to achieve the same results without breaking the rules for temporary object caching. Listing 7-6 shows the new definition with the old CREATE INDEX statement commented out.

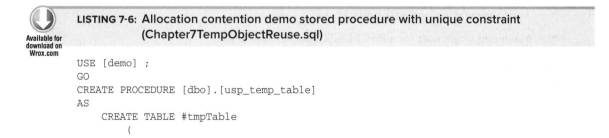

LISTING 7-6: Allocation contention demo stored procedure with unique constraint (Chapter7TempObjectReuse.sql)

Available for download on Wrox.com

```
USE [demo] ;
GO
CREATE PROCEDURE [dbo].[usp_temp_table]
AS
    CREATE TABLE #tmpTable
        (
```

continues

LISTING 7-6 *(continued)*

```
                c1 INT UNIQUE CLUSTERED,
                c2 INT,
                c3 CHAR(5000)
            ) ;
    --CREATE UNIQUE CLUSTERED INDEX cix_c1 ON #tmptable ( c1 ) ;
    DECLARE @i INT = 0 ;
    WHILE ( @i < 10 )
        BEGIN
            INSERT  INTO #tmpTable ( c1, c2, c3 )
            VALUES  ( @i, @i + 100, 'coeo' ) ;
            SET @i += 1 ;
        END ;
GO
```

You can see that I've added a unique clustered constraint to the c1 column, which SQL Server will enforce internally by using a clustered index, so I've been able to keep exactly the same functionality.

Testing the new stored procedure using the temp table creation test now returns the following result:

```
Temp tables created during the test: 1
```

The stored procedure has been successfully optimized for temporary object reuse, but what effect will it have on the allocation page contention example earlier in this chapter?

Clearing dm_os_wait_stats, running OStress, and viewing the wait stats again returns the results shown in Figure 7-16.

wait_type	waiting_tasks_count	wait_time_ms	max_wait_time_ms	signal_wait_time_ms
PAGELATCH_UP	179049	14476227	539	85970
PAGELATCH_EX	68998	3230830	676	55548
PAGELATCH_SH	304180	648729	454	237505

FIGURE 7-16

Those results, totaled up along with the OStress timings, provide the following performance measurement:

➤   **Duration:** 1 minutes 13 seconds

➤   **Total tasks waiting on PAGELATCH:** 552,227

➤   **Total time waiting on PAGELATCH:** 18,355 seconds

➤   **Maximum single wait for a PAGELATCH:** 676 milliseconds

These figures are a result of the combined optimizations for temporary object caching and multiple tempdb data files, and are a vast improvement over the original baseline. Combined, they shaved off 2 minutes and 52 seconds from the original workload duration — a performance improvement of over 70%.

Trace Flag 1118

This trace flag was introduced in SQL Server 2000 to help alleviate contention on the SGAM page (2:1:3) by disabling nearly all mixed extent allocations in tempdb.

You might remember from earlier in the chapter that SGAM pages track mixed extents that have free space available. Every time you create a new table that's not big enough to fill an extent (which happens a lot in tempdb), the SGAM page is read to find a mixed extent with enough free space to allocate to your table.

The effect of enabling this trace flag is that every object you create in tempdb will be allocated its very own extent (a *uniform* extent). The only downside to this is the extra disk space that's needed because every table needs at least 64KB; although that's unlikely to be an issue on most systems.

SQL Server 2008 contains an improved algorithm for allocating space in mixed extents so you'll be unlikely to encounter this issue often if at all with SQL Server 2008. This is why the allocation page contention example used previously only shows contention on 2:1:1, the PFS page.

Comparing the results from the same contention example run against SQL Server 2005, you can see in Figure 7-17 that all the PAGELATCH waits were on 2:1:3, the SGAM page. The PFS page is the next page to be accessed when allocating objects so you can conclude that SQL Server 2008 doesn't suffer from the same problem.

Even though you're unlikely to find SGAM contention in SQL Server 2008, trace flag 1118 still works exactly the same as it does in SQL Server 2000 and 2005; it disables mixed extent allocations in tempdb.

waiting_task_address	session_id	wait_duration_ms	resource_description
0x06F2DB58	204	62	2:1:3
0x06F2D2E8	229	62	2:1:3
0x0C7306B8	216	47	2:1:3
0x0C731798	232	47	2:1:3
0x06FD4E38	310	62	2:1:3
0x06FD4D48	313	16	2:1:3
0x06BCDE28	153	47	2:1:3
0x0C7304D8	176	78	2:1:3
0x0C730A78	175	47	2:1:3
0x071511F8	178	62	2:1:3
0x0C7311F8	190	47	2:1:3
0x06FD5F18	196	62	2:1:3
0x0C730C58	201	78	2:1:3
0x06FD5E28	200	62	2:1:3
0x07AF1F18	202	47	2:1:3
0x06F2CA78	203	0	2:1:3

FIGURE 7-17

Monitoring Tempdb Performance

Troubleshooting SQL Server implies a very *reactive* activity; an issue has occurred that now needs to be fixed. That may be true but one of the differences that separates an average SQL Server professional from a good one is knowing about a problem *before* it has an impact on a live system.

You should be aware by now of tempdb's importance to the overall health of an entire instance, so it shouldn't be a hard sell to realize the benefits of being proactive and monitoring tempdb to get early warning of potential problems before they affect a production system. This section covers the specifics of monitoring tempdb: What you should be looking at and what thresholds should prompt you to do something.

I/O Performance

The speed at which requests to store and retrieve data are processed against tempdb is important to the overall performance of any SQL Server instance and can even be critical where tempdb is either heavily used or part of an important business process.

Whether you have tempdb on local storage or a SAN (storage area network), on a RAID10 volume or RAID1, the simplest method of checking I/O system performance is to look at the latency of I/O requests. You'll find a lot more detailed information about storage, including SANs, RAID levels, and benchmarking performance, in Chapter 4.

There are two methods for measuring disk latency: using Performance Monitor (see Chapter 9) and using SQL Server DMVs. Which one you should choose depends on how you want to monitor performance and how accurate you need it to be.

Performance Monitor

The PerfMon counters that you should be interested in are as follows:

➤ Avg. Disk sec/Transfer

➤ Avg. Disk sec/Read

➤ Avg. Disk sec/Write

You'll find them grouped under "Logical Disk," which shows the logical drives and drive letters presented in Windows as you would see them in Explorer; and "Physical Disk," which shows the drives as Windows sees them internally. Which group you get the counters from won't matter in the majority of cases so I tend to use the Logical Disk counters because it's easier to work with drive letters.

The counters themselves all provide the average latency in milliseconds for I/O requests. "Avg. Disk sec/Transfer" is the combined average for both reads and writes to a drive. This counter provides the simplest measurement for regular long-term monitoring.

"Avg. Disk sec/Read" and "Avg. Disk sec/Write" separate the requests into read and write measurements that can be useful for determining how to configure disk controller cache (see Chapter 4). For example, if you're seeing poor read performance and excellent write performance, you might want to optimize the cache more for reads.

SQL Server DMVs

Monitoring the performance of a disk volume using Performance Monitor is a useful indicator of a potential storage performance issue, but you can get a further level of granularity from SQL Server itself. The script in Listing 7-7 uses the `sys.dm_io_virtual_file_stats` DMV to calculate the read and write latency for all database files that have been used since the SQL Server service was last started.

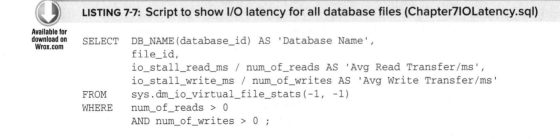

LISTING 7-7: Script to show I/O latency for all database files (Chapter7IOLatency.sql)

```
SELECT   DB_NAME(database_id) AS 'Database Name',
         file_id,
         io_stall_read_ms / num_of_reads AS 'Avg Read Transfer/ms',
         io_stall_write_ms / num_of_writes AS 'Avg Write Transfer/ms'
FROM     sys.dm_io_virtual_file_stats(-1, -1)
WHERE    num_of_reads > 0
         AND num_of_writes > 0 ;
```

You can see part of the output from running the script on a busy production SQL Server in Figure 7-18. Tempdb has four data files with file_id's 1, 3, 4, and 5, and a transaction log with file_id 2. All the data files have the same read and write latency, which is a positive indicator that the I/O is balanced across all the files, and all the results indicate good performance from tempdb.

Database Name	file_id	Avg Read Transfer/ms	Avg Write Transfer/ms
master	1	11	3
master	2	6	2
tempdb	1	7	5
tempdb	2	4	3
tempdb	3	7	5
tempdb	4	7	5
tempdb	5	7	5

FIGURE 7-18

Thresholds

Microsoft suggests the following performance thresholds for disk latency on drives containing SQL Server database files:

Database data files

➤   **Target:** <10ms

➤   **Acceptable:** 10–20ms

➤   **Unacceptable:** >20ms

Database log files

➤   **Target:** <5ms

➤   **Acceptable:** 5–15ms

➤   **Unacceptable:** >15ms

You should use these thresholds for guidance only because some systems will never be able to achieve the target latency. If you don't have any performance issues with your application and you're seeing latency of 20ms, then it's not so important; but you can still look at Chapter 4 to see if there's anything you can do to optimize your existing storage investment.

I tend to use 20ms as a rule of thumb target on most systems unless SQL Server is spending a lot of time waiting for I/O requests. Chapter 3 explains how to measure SQL Server I/O waits.

Troubleshooting Space Issues

The beginning of this chapter mentioned that there is only one tempdb that all the databases on an instance have to share. During the development of SQL Server 2005, pressure was put on Microsoft by some of its largest SQL Server customers to provide a means for multiple tempdbs to be used to help isolate workloads. This proved to be too big of an architectural change to make it into the product, however, so Microsoft focused instead on improving the visibility of what was being used in tempdb and by whom. The result was three new DMVs, which are the focus of this section.

sys.dm_db_file_space_usage

This DMV provides a view of the number and types of pages that are allocated in tempdb by file. Looking at a simple SELECT * FROM sys.dm_db_file_space_usage on my server gave me the results shown in Figure 7-19

database_id	file_id	unallocated_extent_page_count	version_store_reserved_page_count	user_object_reserved_page_count	internal_object_reserved_page_count	mixed_extent_page_count
2	1	65320	0	40	0	176
2	3	65512	0	8	8	8
2	4	65520	0	0	0	16
2	5	65520	0	0	0	16

FIGURE 7-19

You can tell based on the number of rows that there are four data files configured. The columns are as follows:

➤ **database_id:** the integer used by SQL Server to reference each database. The only database_id here is 2 so the DMV works only for tempdb.

➤ **file_id:** the integer used to reference each file that makes up a database. You can see that the numbers are incremental and that number 2 is missing. That's because it's the transaction log file and the DMV is reporting only on data files.

➤ **unallocated_extent_page_count:** shows the number of free 8KB pages in each file. This could be used in a tempdb free space calculation.

➤ **version_store_reserved_page_count:** the number of pages in use for row versioning.

➤ **user_object_reserved_page_count:** shows the number of pages in use by user objects such as temporary tables or table variables.

➤ **internal_object_reserved_page_count:** the number of objects in use for internal use to support operators such as sorts, spools, hash joins, and cursors.

➤ **mixed_extent_page_count:** shows the number of allocated and unallocated pages in allocated mixed extents.

This DMV is most useful when totaling the values across all the files to get a single view of the breakdown of tempdb usage, which can help you to narrow down the scope of the problem in the event of unexpected usage. An example script for this can be found in Listing 7-8.

LISTING 7-8: Script to total tempdb usage by type across all files (Chapter7TempdbSpaceUsage.sql)

```
SELECT  SUM(user_object_reserved_page_count) AS user_object_pages,
        SUM(internal_object_reserved_page_count) AS internal_object_pages,
        SUM(version_store_reserved_page_count) AS version_store_pages,
        total_in_use_pages = SUM(user_object_reserved_page_count)
        + SUM(internal_object_reserved_page_count)
        + SUM(version_store_reserved_page_count),
        SUM(unallocated_extent_page_count) AS total_free_pages
FROM    sys.dm_db_file_space_usage ;
```

On my server the script produced the results shown in Figure 7-20.

user_object_pages	internal_object_pages	version_store_pages	total_in_use_pages	total_free_pages
48	8	0	56	261856

FIGURE 7-20

sys.dm_db_task_space_usage

This DMV provides details of tempdb usage for currently running tasks. The values are set to 0 at the start of the task and deleted when the task completes, so it's useful for troubleshooting live issues with currently executing tasks. For example, running the query in Listing 7-9 will give you the topfive sessions currently using space in tempdb, ordered by the total amount of space in use.

LISTING 7-9: Script to find the top five sessions running tasks that use tempdb (Chapter7TempdbSpaceUsage.sql)

```
SELECT TOP 5
       *

FROM    sys.dm_db_task_space_usage
WHERE   session_id > 50
ORDER BY user_objects_alloc_page_count + internal_objects_alloc_page_count DESC ;
```

Running this on my server returned the results shown in Figure 7-21.

session_id	request_id	exec_context_id	database_id	user_objects_alloc_page_count	user_objects_dealloc_page_count	internal_objects_alloc_page_count	internal_objects_dealloc_page_count
57	0	0	2	717008	717008	0	0
58	0	0	2	673184	673184	0	0
56	0	0	2	661488	661488	0	0
53	0	0	2	593024	593024	0	0
60	0	0	2	542416	542416	0	0

FIGURE 7-21

From these results you can see that my top consumer of space in tempdb is a task running under session_id 57, which has so far allocated 717,008 pages in tempdb. You can also see that it has subsequently deallocated the same amount of pages so at the time of the snapshot the task wasn't consuming any space.

To help investigate this further I can use a feature that was added in SQL Server 2005 that enables users to view the execution plan (see Chapters 1 and 5) for a currently running task.

For many previous versions of SQL Server, it has been possible to get at least some of the query text for an executing task, but until SQL Server 2005 it just wasn't possible to get the execution plan for a query that was already running.

This meant that troubleshooting a "live" issue was very difficult because you couldn't see what decisions the optimizer (see Chapter 1) had made for the execution of that query; instead, you had to rely on a "post-mortem" approach (see Chapter 8) or set up some data collection and wait for the problem to reoccur.

To help in this situation, a column called plan_handle was added to the sys.dm_exec_requests DMV and a system table-valued function (TVF) called sys.dm_exec_query_plan was provided to get the actual execution plan in use based on the plan_handle.

The script in Listing 7-10 returns the session_id, the text of the query that is running, and the execution plan in XML format for all sessions that are running application code. It uses the

CROSS APPLY operator to evaluate the two TVFs for every row returned from sys.dm_exec_
requests and returns only rows that produce a result.

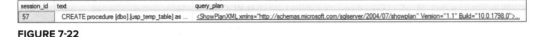

LISTING 7-10: Script to return currently running T-SQL with Execution Plans
(Chapter7TempdbSpaceUsage.sql)

Available for
download on
Wrox.com

```
SELECT   session_id,
         text,
         query_plan
FROM     sys.dm_exec_requests
         CROSS APPLY sys.dm_exec_sql_text(sql_handle)
         CROSS APPLY sys.dm_exec_query_plan(plan_handle) ;
```

I'm only interested in session_id 57 so I added a WHERE clause to return only the details for that
session, and got the result shown in Figure 7-22.

session_id	text	query_plan
57	CREATE procedure [dbo].[usp_temp_table] as ...	\<ShowPlanXML xmlns="http://schemas.microsoft.com/sqlserver/2004/07/showplan" Version="1.1" Build="10.0.1798.0">...

FIGURE 7-22

When you return the sql_text for a running stored procedure it contains the stored
procedure definition, so you can determine
from my results that session 57 was running
dbo.usp_temp_table, rather than creating it
as you might first assume.

SQL Server Management Studio has also
recognized that the query_plan is an XML
document and has provided a link to display
it. When you click the link, Management
Studio detects that it contains an execution
plan and renders it properly, as you can see in
Figure 7-23.

This is a new feature for the tools in SQL
Server 2008, and it will also work against
a SQL Server 2005 instance. If you're still
using the SQL Server 2005 toolset, the XML
version of the plan is displayed, but if you
save it with a ".sqlplan" extension and load it
into Management Studio again it renders the
graphical plan for you.

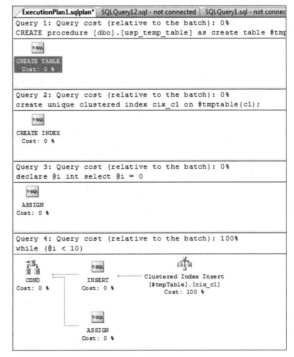

FIGURE 7-23

> *You can read about how to interpret SQL Server execution plans in Chapter 5.*

As a quick summary, you've just seen how to view the most active tempdb sessions using `sys.dm_db_task_space_usage`, how to get the code that a session is running, and the execution plan that's being used.

sys.dm_db_session_space_usage

When a task completes, the values from `sys.dm_db_task_usage` are aggregated by session, and these aggregated values are viewable using `sys.dm_db_session_space_usage`.

The example code in Listing 7-11 demonstrates how to use this DMV, showing you all the sessions in order of total tempdb usage.

LISTING 7-11: Script to find historic tempdb usage by session(Chapter7TempdbSpaceUsage.sql)

Available for
download on
Wrox.com

```
SELECT   *
FROM     sys.dm_db_session_space_usage
WHERE    session_id > 50
ORDER BY user_objects_alloc_page_count + internal_objects_alloc_page_count DESC ;
```

You can see the results from running this script on my server in Figure 7-24.

session_id	database_id	user_objects_alloc_page_count	user_objects_dealloc_page_count	internal_objects_alloc_page_count	internal_objects_dealloc_page_count
54	2	1116800	1116816	0	0
53	2	939056	939040	0	0
56	2	919792	919776	0	0
55	2	898912	898912	0	0
59	2	165	130	8	0

FIGURE 7-24

The results show that `session_id` 54 has been the top consumer of tempdb during its connection period. This won't include any currently executing tasks so it's not very useful for a live issue, but you can look up the `session_id` in sys.dm_exec_requests to gather information on who's using that `session_id`, such as their login details, the server they're connecting from, and the application that they're using.

Transaction Log Growing Too Big?

I've experienced this issue twice with two different customers and since then have read a few forum posts from other people having the same issue.

Chapter 1 covered how and why the transaction log is used, and the beginning of this chapter established that tempdb is always in *Simple* recovery mode. Every time a checkpoint occurs, log records from all committed transactions are marked for reuse, so you shouldn't have to worry about the transaction log for tempdb unless you have a very long running transaction that prevents part of the log from being reused.

One scenario to keep an eye out for is when there are no active transactions in tempdb but the transaction log keeps filling up and autogrowing until it runs out of disk space. It's a puzzling scenario to work with until you realize that issuing a manual checkpoint using the T-SQL CHECKPOINT command with tempdb as the database context clears the transaction log completely (and safely).

It's easy to conclude from an observation like this that automatic checkpointing for tempdb is broken, but in both the scenarios that I came across the problem was actually due to poor I/O performance.

Checkpoints happen automatically roughly every minute, starting with the user databases followed by the system databases. Automatic checkpoints are all handled by a single process; there is nothing specific just for tempdb. In both cases that I worked on, I/O performance wasn't good enough for the checkpoints on the user databases to complete fast enough to move on and checkpoint the system databases, including tempdb.

Issuing a manual checkpoint forced a checkpoint to occur outside of the automatic checkpointing process and clears the transaction log, inevitably preventing downtime.

The correct solution, of course, is to fix the cause of the issue, which is poor I/O performance, but that can be difficult and sometimes expensive to achieve. Another sensible solution is to create an alert that triggers a manual checkpoint in tempdb if the transaction log becomes 70% full. It may not fix every tempdb transaction log problem but you've got nothing to lose by running it, and automating it might just save you some downtime.

Available for download on Wrox.com

Sample code [Chapter7CheckpointAlert.sql] to set this up is available for download at Wrox.com.

CONFIGURATION BEST PRACTICES

Because several of the issues addressed in this chapter have required configuration changes, this section consolidates all the best practices for configuring tempdb. You won't just find prescriptive rules here, but also the background to the recommendations and guidance on how to choose the best configuration for any particular environment. In this section you read about:

➤ Where to place tempdb

➤ Initial sizing and autogrowth

➤ Configuring multiple files

Tempdb File Placement

It's quite a well-known best practice to "separate data, transaction logs, and tempdb" for performance reasons. What this means is that as a rule of thumb, performance will be better if you store these components on separate physical disk arrays (separate spindles) because they can have different patterns of I/O.

However, one thing they do have in common is the recommendation to store them on a RAID 10 disk array, which provides the best overall combination of disk protection and performance levels.

In determining the best disk configuration for data, log, and tempdb, I'm going to assume RAID10 as a fixed requirement. You can read more details about storage terminology and RAID levels in Chapter 4.

Many questions come up time and time again with regard to this best practice, but the two most common are these:

➤ "I don't have many disks; what should I prioritize?"

➤ "I can't guarantee separate spindles so should I bother separating the components?"

The following two scenarios address these questions.

Scenario 1: Single Instance Failover Cluster with 12 Disks in a Shared Disk Array

This is the most common scenario that I come across among clients with mid-size systems for which they're unlikely to have a large corporate-wide SAN for storage, but instead have an entry-level disk array with space for 12 disks.

Best practice for a single SQL Server instance in this scenario requires you to separate data, log, and tempdb but also provision a quorum disk for the cluster (in the most common cluster configuration scenario). This translates to a minimum requirement of the following:

➤ **Database files:** 4 disks in RAID 10

➤ **Transaction log files:** 4 disks in RAID 10

➤ **Tempdb:** 4 disks in RAID 10

➤ **Quorum disk:** 2 disks in RAID 1 (mirrored)

The total number of disks required is 14, so already you're going to have to make some compromises — and this is where the heated debates start about what to prioritize. You're going to have to make some decisions that some people would applaud and others would passionately disagree with; there's no perfect answer, so the most important thing for you to do is to be aware of all the arguments before making your choice.

The Quorum Disk

The first decision point is about the quorum disk, which, among other things, is used to arbitrate who should have control of the disks in the event that the cluster nodes lose communication.

It's a very important resource in the cluster but the disk space requirement for the quorum will be <100MB and its I/O usage will be negligible, which prompts the question about consolidating it onto another array. Should you waste 100's of GB's of disk space and, more important, two of your 12 disks on it?

If you wanted to keep as much isolation as possible between the internal cluster resources and your SQL Server resources, then you might argue that using two disks for the quorum is simply the price you have to pay for having a failover cluster.

The alternative is to create a small volume of 100MB (using the array configuration software, not Windows) on the same array as your data files, for example. The justification is that if your array containing the data files was lost, then you wouldn't be worried about the stability of a cluster with no databases.

It's also worth noting that by "losing" the array I mean that more physical disks break down than your configured RAID level can handle.

Assume you've decided to create the quorum as a volume on the same disk array as the data volume. Now your disk requirements are down to twelve and you have twelve disks, so you could just go ahead and set things up according to best practice.

However, don't forget that best practices exist only as a general *rule of thumb* for guidance in the most common scenarios, so you should also consider the alternatives.

More Disks in an Array vs. Workload Separation

With 12 disks and a leaning towards separating data, log, and tempdb, you have several options for configuration, some of which you can explore in Table 7-2. Don't forget you're assuming RAID 10 as a fixed requirement, which needs a minimum of four disks.

TABLE 7-2: Disk Array Configuration Options

OPTION	DESCRIPTION
One array with all 12 disks	No separation of workload but provides a single volume in the best-performing configuration possible.
	Great performance but differing workload patterns could reduce the performance of all components.
Three arrays of 4 disks each	Meets the best practice recommendation but only providing 4 disks to each component may not provide enough raw performance to any single component.
Two arrays: one of 8 disks and one of 4	Separate one component, leaving the other two on a faster array because it's spread over 8 disks instead of 4.
	The choice in most scenarios is whether or not to separate the transaction logs or the tempdb files onto the 4-disk array because you'll want the data files to be on the 8-disk array.

In a lot of circumstances the benefit of separating the data files and transaction log files is increased performance of the data files, so you shouldn't just look at the I/O latency on your transaction log files when determining whether or not to put them on their own disk array.

I have seen many SQL Server implementations in which the data file performance has increased dramatically when the transaction log was moved to a separate disk even though the log itself already had excellent performance on the same drive as the data files.

In scenario 1 the options tend to boil down to whether or not to separate data, log, and tempdb or which ones to prioritize.

In general, I would start with two arrays (of 8 and 4 disks), separating the transaction logs onto 4 disks configured as RAID10 from the data files, and tempdb, which will be on 8 disks configured as RAID10. This should provide the ideal balance of performance unless you're expecting particularly heavy tempdb usage.

As always, though, there is no hard-and-fast rule that works best for every system, so try to make an educated choice before testing it thoroughly.

Scenario 2: Single Instance Connected to an Enterprise SAN

What defines the difficult element in this scenario is the inability to guarantee separate spindles for data, log, and tempdb as defined by the best practice recommendation.

In a long-running debate, DBAs have insisted on the use of separate spindles, with SAN administrators replying that it's not possible and isn't necessary.

Essentially, what happens is that your SQL Server is presented with multiple LUNs (logical unit numbers), which are just like disk volumes. Which physical disks those LUNs actually reside on can be dynamically managed by the SAN hardware to avoid hot spots and maintain good performance for all users of the SAN.

The effect is that you can't guarantee separate spindles but should get good performance anyway. Therefore, on an Enterprise SAN you should focus on the I/O performance you get from your LUNs, rather than worry about the underlying disk implementation.

Once you've come to terms with that, the question then arises of whether you should even bother separating data, log, and tempdb if the SAN adapts the underlying disk configuration to meet the performance requirements anyway.

 The short answer is yes but it's mainly for administrative purposes, rather than performance. If you put a data, log, or tempdb file onto its own LUN and it grows quickly to fill the disk, then you minimize the impact on other components because the file is isolated. This is particularly relevant for tempdb because it's a shared resource.

Ideally you would have separate LUNs for the data files, transaction log files, and tempdb files in order to isolate them, which is much easier to achieve on a SAN because the size and number of LUNs isn't tied to the number of physical disks.

Listing 7-12 shows sample code to move your tempdb files to a new location. When you run this, the system metadata is updated; and the next time you start SQL Server it creates the tempdb files in the new location.

LISTING 7-12: Script to move tempdb data and log files to a new
location(Chapter7MoveTempdb.sql)

```
USE master ;
GO
ALTER DATABASE tempdb
MODIFY FILE (NAME = tempdev, FILENAME = 'T:\data\tempdb.mdf') ;
GO
ALTER DATABASE tempdb
MODIFY FILE (NAME = templog, FILENAME = 'T:\data\templog.ldf') ;
GO
```

Once tempdb has its own drive letter, whether it's a volume on a small disk array or a LUN on an enterprise SAN, you can then size the database, which is the topic of the next section.

Tempdb Initial Sizing and Autogrowth

A default installation of any SQL Server edition will create a tempdb database with an 8MB data file and a 1MB transaction log file. For a lot of SQL Server installations these file sizes won't be enough, but they are configured to autogrow by 10% as needed. You can see the properties window for tempdb on a default installation of SQL Server 2008 Developer Edition in Figure 7-25.

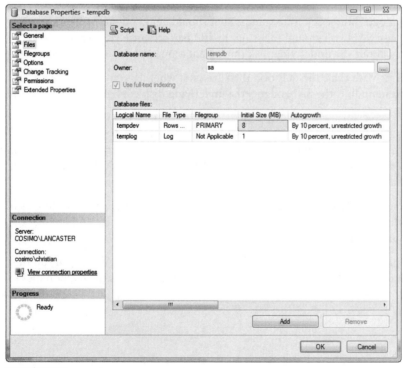

FIGURE 7-25

Although the autogrow feature enables a more hands-off approach to maintaining many SQL Server installations, it's not necessarily desirable because the files cannot be used while they are autogrowing and it can lead to fragmentation of the files on the hard disk, leading to poor performance.

This is a recommendation that would apply to any SQL Server database, but for tempdb it's even more relevant. When you restart your SQL Server instance, tempdb is re-initialized to the size specified in the database properties, which as you've just seen is only 8MB for the data file and 1MB for the log file by default.

I've reviewed many SQL Server installations with tempdb files of tens of GBs that have autogrown to that size and have the default properties set. The next time SQL Server is restarted, tempdb will be just 8MB and will have to start autogrowing all over again.

Figure 7-26 illustrates an example scenario of tempdb sizing.

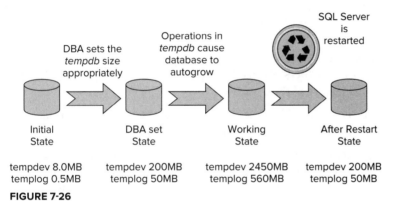

FIGURE 7-26

As shown in the diagram, you can see the size of the initial files, which the DBA has set to 200MB and 50MB.

The workload running against SQL Server has then caused the tempdb files to autogrow to 2450MB and 560MB.

SQL Server is then restarted and tempdb has gone back to 200MB and 50MB, as set by the DBA, and would have to autogrow again to fulfill the workload.

How Big Should I Set My Tempdb Database?

This is, of course, a difficult question to answer without more details about the workload but there is still some guidance that you can use.

First of all, unless you're running SQL Server Express, set tempdb to be bigger than the default; that's an easy one.

Next, if you can give tempdb its own disk, then configure it to almost fill the drive. If nothing else will ever be on the drive, then you're better off setting it to be larger than you'll ever need. There's no performance penalty and you'll never have to worry about autogrow again. Many internal SQL Servers are run by Microsoft IT with 200GB LUNs for tempdb, and tempdb configured to be

180GB (to avoid <10% free disk space warnings from the monitoring tools). It's more than they'll probably ever need but they don't need to worry about managing tempdb size.

If you can't put tempdb on its own disk, then you'll need to manage size and autogrow a bit more closely. You could just let it autogrow for a while and then manually set it to be bit larger than what it grows to or you could just make it a reasonable size in relation to your other databases and set large autogrow amounts.

What Should I Set Autogrow To?

If you've moved tempdb to its own drive and configured it to almost fill the disk, then arguably you don't need to enable autogrow. That would be a reasonable choice in this scenario but it may be worth leaving it on if you still have a small amount of disk space left over.

The best way to think of autogrow for any database, not just tempdb, is as a last resort. Your databases should be sized appropriately so they don't need to autogrow, but you still configure it just in case you need it.

Using fixed growth amounts is generally a better approach for autogrow because it makes autogrow events more predictable. Autogrowing a 10GB transaction log by 10%, for example, is going to take a long time and will affect the availability of the database.

The Instant File Initialization (IFI) feature in Windows Server 2003 and later can make things a bit easier for autogrowing the data files but it doesn't work for log files because of the way they are used.

IFI is used automatically by SQL Server if the service account is a local administrator (which it shouldn't be as a security best practice) or if the account has the "Manage Volume Maintenance Tasks" advanced user rights. To give the service account the necessary rights, you can use the group policy tool, as shown in Figure 7-27, by running gpedit.msc.

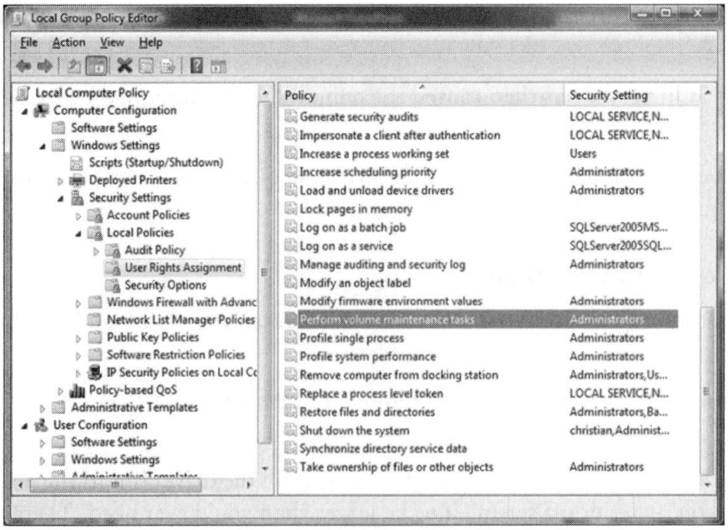

FIGURE 7-27

Once IFI is working you can set autogrow to be large fixed amounts for data files. 50MB or 500MB are good values depending on the size of the database, but any size will be created virtually instantly so you avoid any downtime.

For transaction log files, however, you need to be a lot more conservative and use a figure that balances the time it takes to autogrow and the usefulness of the extra space. Autogrowing by 1MB, for example, will be quick but you might need to do it so often that it becomes a bottleneck. Autogrowing by at least 10MB for the transaction log is a good place to start, but you may need it to be higher to provide enough space to avoid autogrowing again quickly. The best way to manage it is to avoid autogrowing in the first place by correctly sizing the files.

Configuring Multiple Tempdb Data Files

The use of multiple data files for tempdb was covered earlier in the chapter as an aid to reducing allocation contention problems.

Reducing the occurrence and risk of allocation contention on tempdb is the only reason for configuring multiple tempdb data files. You can't add filegroups to tempdb, so there is no way for you to create a temporary object on a specific data file and no reason for any of your data files to be on separate disks.

When you create multiple data files they will all be in the primary filegroup and SQL Server will use a proportional fill algorithm to determine which file to use for each request to create an object. If all the files are exactly the same size, then SQL Server uses the files in a "round robin" fashion, spreading the load equally across the files. This is, of course, exactly what you want.

For SQL Server 2005 and 2008, Microsoft recommends creating ¼ to ½ the number of files per CPU core, up to a maximum of 8 files, so on an 8-core server you would configure 2 or 4 files.

This is just for guidance, though; the important point is not to exceed 8 files, as Microsoft's tests indicate no performance benefit beyond that.

Whether or not you configure multiple data files as a best practice on all your SQL Servers or just on those for which you've detected allocation issues is a choice only you can make. As a best practice, I prefer to configure them on all the servers I work with as a proactive measure, as it's hard to see a downside.

SUMMARY

This chapter introduced the concept of and many uses for the tempdb database in SQL Server 2008 as well some of the most common problems you might encounter and how to avoid them.

The key takeaways from this chapter are:

➤ There are three types of objects that can be found in tempdb: user-created, internally created, and the version store.

➤ Latch contention is a common problem even in SQL Server 2008 but is easy to resolve and avoid.

➤ You should learn to be familiar with these DMVs to help you troubleshoot urgent tempdb space issues:

   ➤ sys.dm_db_file_space_usage

   ➤ sys.dm_db_task_space_usage

   ➤ sys.dm_db_session_space_usage

➤ Appropriate sizing and configuration of tempdb should be paramount for any SQL Server installation to avoid performance issues later on.

8

Defining Your Approach To Troubleshooting

WHAT'S IN THIS CHAPTER

➤ How to approach troubleshooting

➤ Defining the problem you're working on

➤ Knowing your SLAs and baselines

➤ Defining the exit criteria

➤ Choosing how to gather data

➤ Your options for analyzing a data collection

➤ Troubleshooting components like failover Clustering, Replication, and Analysis Services

No matter what sort of problem you are approaching, there are certain factors you should always consider. Whether you are helping your kids with their homework, dealing with a mechanical issue, or troubleshooting a SQL Server problem there are common steps such as making sure you understand the problem and the people involved. If you can step back and think through these steps you can become a better problem solver.

In addition to the common steps, some steps are specific to SQL Server. Some of these steps are obvious; others only become important after you feel the results of skipping them.

This chapter provides the framework for how to approach problems with SQL Server. It serves as a foundation for all the remaining chapters. After walking through both the human and technical aspect of an effective troubleshooting methodology, later chapters will expand to fill in the details of troubleshooting specific problems.

APPROACHING THE PROBLEM CORRECTLY

How you approach a problem can make a huge difference in when, how, and even whether it is resolved. Your mind-set, or attitude, for example, can positively or negatively impact your project long term.

Likewise, how you decide to approach your management team can either short-circuit your efforts or enable your problem to be satisfactorily resolved depending on how you involve them in the problem-solving process.

Finally, you need to be aware of your own limitations; if you've never experienced a certain problem and it's going to cost a lot of downtime, you might consider bringing in outside help. The following sections outline how to positively approach a problem so that everyone benefits from the experience.

Having the Right Attitude

Having the proper attitude not only leads to a better, possibly faster resolution, but also makes you and your coworkers less stressed during the troubleshooting process.

Consistently solving problems by breaking them down scientifically is a proven and effective method. The right attitude can even lead to more opportunities when management and your coworkers see that you are able to approach a problem methodically and with a purpose.

Remain Calm

Remain calm and objective about any problem that arises, no matter how urgent it is. This can be difficult if your end users or management are in a panic. However, remaining calm enables you to slow down and assess the problem, which will result in a better, and often faster, resolution.

When we get caught up in the stress of a situation, we often hurry, skip steps, or ignore warning signs. Any of those things can easily lead to mistakes and actually delay the resolution of a problem.

When you are troubleshooting, you must remain composed and approach the problem rationally and logically. When you remain calm you project your calmness to the situation as a whole and give confidence to those working with you and relying on you.

Avoid Prejudice

Never assume that you know how to solve a problem until you have fully fleshed out the problem description and done some basic testing. It is not necessary to prove that you know everything about the product, environment, or anything else by providing an instant answer.

The fact that the same, or even a superficially similar, scenario came up in the past does not necessarily mean that the underlying problem and resolution are the same. Many errors are fairly generic and only have meaning in a specific context.

Scenarios such as blocking locks or cluster failover can have many different causes and potential resolutions.

Avoid Rushing or Plodding

Never assume you have to solve something immediately before you fully define the problem. Even the most urgent problem can benefit from taking the time to think through the problem and test possible resolutions.

If you rush, you may implement something that makes the problem worse or causes unexpected side effects. However, you cannot let yourself become so bogged down in analyzing the problem that you never get around to solving it. This can be a difficult balancing act, and you will get better at it over time.

Think Ahead

Try to proactively consider potential roadblocks. For example, if there's a good chance you might need to restore the database, and you know it will take hours or even days to get a backup file from a tape restored to the system, start that process now.

Dealing with Management

Management understandably wants problems resolved right away and with the fewest possible resources used. They are under pressure to answer to users, their own managers, and sometimes even outside interests such as auditors or the press. In some cases this can lead to managers hovering, asking for constant updates, and basically just getting in your way. Sometimes this can make the resolution take much longer than necessary or even lead to mistakes being made along the way as you deal with the distractions and pressure.

To mitigate problems with management, I recommend enlisting their help:

➤ Ask them to be a buffer between you and everyone else who isn't directly involved in solving the problem.

➤ Negotiate a schedule for providing updates and stick to that schedule to reduce distractions from random, possibly too frequent requests for information.

➤ Identify one person to whom you will give your updates, let that person deal with anyone else who needs that, or other information. If more than one person is directly involved in the technical aspects of the troubleshooting, choose just one technical person to talk to your management contact.

Management can also help by determining exactly what the real impact is to the business. As a guideline, try to establish the following:

➤ If this is a production problem, how severely is the system impacted?

➤ Are there users who cannot work?

➤ Is revenue directly impacted?

➤ Does the problem have high visibility?

➤ Are the affected users internal only or are external customers affected?

➤ How long can the problem persist before there are serious consequences?

Management can also help you find mitigating factors. For example, if there's only an hour until closing time for the affected users and no one else will use the system until the next day, can the users be sent home early to avoid paying their hourly costs while they can't work anyway? Can they work on some other system or project for a while? All of these factors can be used to help shape the solution.

For example, if you're rapidly losing a large amount of money, then you may need to look for an interim solution that gets you back online, even if it has a high cost in some other way or doesn't solve the problem completely. Then you can work on a better, more permanent resolution offline.

Conversely, if you have enough time to thoroughly investigate the problem and test the potential solutions, then you may not want to settle for a workaround.

When to Call for Outside Help

It is not always necessary to solve a problem yourself. Often the barrier to hiring a consultant or calling Microsoft Support is the money involved; but in reality, many scenarios can be much more expensive if you do not ask for outside help.

The time, resources, and opportunity costs of taking a long time to solve a problem, solving it in an inappropriate or inefficient way, or not solving it at all can be high. Make sure you take these other factors into account when deciding if and when to ask for outside help. It can actually be cheaper to call for help right away in some cases.

For example, if the hourly cost of a consultant is half the cost of what you are losing per hour while the system is unavailable, it may make sense to bring in a consultant immediately. Some examples of when this makes sense is if the problem is with a feature you don't use often, a feature you don't have deep expertise in, or the product is producing an error message that you can find no information on.

Another barrier to asking for help is that you want to be seen as the expert in a technology or an area of the business. No one can realistically expect to know everything about SQL Server, even if your knowledge is limited to just the components and features used by one particular line of business. If you bring in an outside expert you can use the opportunity to learn more about the product and increase your value to the business. You can also see and learn different approaches to troubleshooting, which can sometimes be even more important than the technical skills themselves.

Some types of problems are tailor-made for asking for outside help. For example, you might be more inclined to call for help if you experience corruption in your database. This is a very serious problem and many of the urban legends and "common wisdom" about how to address corruption can actually make the problem worse while avoiding solving the underlying cause of the problem.

If you do bring in Microsoft Support, a consultant, or other outside assistance, you will need to provide them with some basic information. As a starting point, consider the following:

➤ As you do your troubleshooting, document both the steps you have already taken and the results of each step.

➤ Keep basic logs and other data gathered into a single location.

➤ In most cases you will need to provide at least a basic snapshot from SQLDiag or something else that shows versions, configuration settings, and other basic information.

➤ Many problems will also require a SQLTrace, though which events you need to capture will vary greatly. PerfMon output is often a valuable tool as well.

DEFINING THE PROBLEM

If you take the time to understand the problem and environment, you can achieve a higher-quality resolution.

It is very common to skip this step, but doing so can often lead to unexpected problems further down the line; if you do not define the problem, then you cannot understand what is really happening, and you will just be guessing at the resolution.

You have to know enough about the problem to ensure that you are working on its most critical aspect. You may get lucky and cover up a problem for a while, but if you do not take the time to understand what's going on, you will be back to troubleshoot it again later after an imperfect resolution.

The next few sections offer tips for identifying the problem, breaking up the problem into workable steps, and solving bottlenecks you might encounter along the way.

Tips for Identifying a Problem

Use the following guidelines to fully comprehend the exact problem you are facing:

➤ Take screenshots or cut and paste pop-up screens indicating errors. Sometimes a missed word, a typo, or ignored state information in an error will completely change the trouble-shooting steps you take.

➤ Obtain copies of all relevant logs such as the Event Viewer logs, the SQL Server Error Log, dump files, and application-specific logs. Sometimes different logs will have different levels of detail or even different information captured.

➤ Understand the steps necessary to reproduce the problem. Often, if you dig a little deeper when you ask the user about how and when the problem occurs, you will find that the problem happens only some of the time, under certain circumstances, for certain login accounts, or only with certain data. You may also discover other information that the user didn't mention initially. These pieces of information can be vital to troubleshooting.

➤ When you gather your information, make sure you understand the context. Know whether the logs are from a client workstation, a middle tier server, or a server running SQL Server. Pay attention to the exact time, including the time zone, on each machine from which you gather data. In some scenarios it is vital to synchronize the data from multiple sources, and you must take differing times into account to get accurate information.

Part of understanding the problem is understanding why the issue is occurring now. If this is a new system, perhaps you haven't seen this level of load on the system before.

If it is an existing system, look back at your change control documents to see what has changed recently on the system. Any change, even if seemingly unrelated, should be reviewed.

This can mean any alteration no matter how small, such as a Windows or SQL Server patch, a new policy or removed permission, a configuration option, or an application or database schema change, needs to be reviewed.

Bite-Size Chunks

Once you understand the overall problem you can break it down into manageable pieces and isolate the various pieces, which enables you to concentrate on the most troublesome part first. The following is a list of troubleshooting by category.

Connectivity Issues

Check if the problem only occurs with one protocol such as Named Pipes or TCP/IP. Are there some applications, users, client workstations, or particular subnets that can connect while others cannot?

Does the problem only happen with double hops, whereas direct connections work? Will local connections work but remote ones fail? Can you connect using the dedicated administrator connection (DAC)?

Performance Issues

For a performance problem you need to determine if the issue is on the client, the middle tier, the server on which SQL Server runs, or the network. If you've isolated the problem to the server, is the main problem with SQL Server or some other application?

In some cases you may find that another application on the server is using all the available CPU resources and leaving nothing for SQL Server to use. This can make SQL Server seem unresponsive or slow.

In this case, no amount of tuning within SQL Server will solve the problem and sometimes hours or days are spent trying to figure out what is wrong with SQL Server when the problem lies elsewhere.

If the problem is within SQL Server, is the main bottleneck the network stack, memory, I/O, or CPU?

If the problem is with a particular screen in the application, can you narrow it down to one function or button? What stored procedure calls are issued by that application function?

Once you have a stored procedure identified, break it down into component queries and concentrate on the worst one. Once you know your bottleneck, you can quickly determine the best troubleshooting steps.

Memory or Compilation Issues

If you are able to identify one user query that is slow, the most common causes are insufficient resources (network, memory, I/O, CPU), blocking, out-of-date statistics, or inefficient indexes. Sometimes the problem is not with the query execution but with the compilation. Often, analyzing the plan cache can lead to resolving the problem.

Service-Level Agreements

Know how long you have to resolve a problem, when it is essential to fall back on a workaround, and when to rollback a change rather than continue to troubleshoot it.

You also need to know the agreed performance expectations; hopefully there are documented service-level agreements (SLAs) that have already defined this for you.

For example, if you need to find out why a clustered instance failed over and the troubleshooting involves taking the system down for some of the testing, when you'll be able to do that will depend on the SLA.

If your SLA specifies that each application function must complete in less than two seconds, does it make sense to tune the only query that answers that functionality to execute in less than one second when it already takes less than the SLA of two seconds?

You also need to understand what an acceptable solution looks like. Does it have to be perfect or can it be approximate? How fast is "fast enough" for performance tuning? What baseline information are you comparing to if "it used to be faster" and what has changed since then? Do you have time to get an upgrade working no matter what or do you have to make a decision to roll back after a certain amount of time has passed? If you cannot get an upgrade to complete, is it better to troubleshoot the upgrade process or uninstall and reinstall with the newer version?

Defining Exit Criteria

Once you have fully defined the problem, it is usually fairly simple to understand when the problem is resolved. But you should still make sure you understand how to recognize when you've reached this step.

Explicitly state how you will know you are done. Doing so enables you to focus your efforts and helps structure your troubleshooting steps. For example, you may not want to spend days tuning a query to get it from two seconds to 100 milliseconds if the SLA requires only a one-second response time and that was reached with an hour of tuning.

Unfortunately, it's common to spend a lot of time troubleshooting numerous issues that have nothing to do with the main source of the problem. If you fully define both the problem and the exit criteria, you are more likely to spend your time on the main problem and resolve it faster. It also helps you define your test cases so you can prove you have achieved your objective.

Understanding Your Baselines

For performance issues it is essential to know what you are comparing performance to. Are there previous baselines such as PerfMon and Profiler traces or other testing output? What were the circumstances when they were gathered? Were they taken at the same time of day and day of the week or whatever circumstances make a pattern in your environment? How fast has this particular screen, stored procedure, or query been in the past? What has changed since then? When were the statistics last updated? How fast is "fast enough" to the user? How fast is realistic given the existing environment and other business requirements?

Once you understand the circumstances surrounding how and when the data was gathered, you know what caveats to make with any comparisons to other baselines.

For example, if you compare the average number of transactions per hour in a retail environment for Super Bowl Sunday to an average Sunday you will probably see a drastically different number but it will probably not be due to system problems. Users love to say "it's slow" but it can be difficult to pin them down on exactly how much slower and how they determined that.

Make sure it's not just a perception problem. If you regularly take baselines, you can find a baseline from a similar time period and compare the queries associated with the part of the application they are using with the current performance metrics. This will give you an objective set of data to compare to.

For example, you may see that if you compare the query durations from the same day in the prior month, the query durations are the same but the time between queries is much longer. This might lead you to discover that network bandwidth is more limited on that day of the month due to something like a monthly backup process.

It is important to gather the same data for each baseline. The exact Performance Monitor (PerfMon) counters to use will vary depending on where you have historically seen bottlenecks in your environment and on exactly how you are using the system. However, most baselines will include the basic Memory, I/O, CPU, and other counters described throughout this book.

As an example, a basic data collection will capture the following counters (the SQL Server counter names will vary depending on the instance name).

- **LogicalDisk and PhysicalDisk:**
    - Avg. Disk Bytes/{Read, Write, or Transfer}
    - Disk Bytes/sec
    - Disk Transfers/sec
    - Avg. Disk sec/Read
    - Avg. Disk sec/Write
- **Memory:**
    - Available Mbytes
    - Free System Page Table Entries
- **SQL Server Buffer Node:**
    - Page Life Expectancy
    - Target Pages
    - Total Pages

- ➤ **SQL Server Databases:**
  - ➤ Active Transactions
  - ➤ Log File(s) Size (KB)
  - ➤ Log File(s) Used Size (KB)
  - ➤ Percent Log Used
  - ➤ Transactions/sec
- ➤ **SQL Server General Statistics:**
  - ➤ Processes Blocked
  - ➤ User Connections
- ➤ **SQL Server Latches:**
  - ➤ Average Latch Wait Time (ms)
  - ➤ Latch Waits/sec
- ➤ **SQL Server Locks:**
  - ➤ Average Wait Time (ms)
  - ➤ Lock Requests/sec
  - ➤ Lock Timeouts/sec
  - ➤ Lock Waits/sec
  - ➤ Number of Deadlocks/sec
- ➤ **SQL Server Memory Manager:**
  - ➤ Optimizer Memory (KB)
  - ➤ SQL Cache Memory (KB)
  - ➤ Target Server Memory (KB)
  - ➤ Total Server Memory (KB)
- ➤ **SQL Server SQL Statistics:**
  - ➤ All counters
- ➤ **SQL Server Transactions:**
  - ➤ Free Space in tempdb (KB)
  - ➤ Longest Transaction Running Time
  - ➤ The other counters if you are using any type of snapshots, including triggers
- ➤ **SQL Server Wait Statistics:**
  - ➤ All counters

➤ **Process (Choose at least your SQL Server instance(s) as well as any other applications/processes that might compete with SQL Server.):**

  ➤ % Processor Time

  ➤ Private Bytes

  ➤ Virtual Bytes

  ➤ Working Set

➤ **Processor ("<All instances>" and Total):**

  ➤ % Processor Time

Chapter 9 covers PerfMon data collections in-depth.

For I/O you will also want to capture whatever data your storage hardware will provide. The specifics will vary by storage vendor and product line. Keep in mind that direct storage monitoring usually captures just the pure disk time, whereas PerfMon I/O counters capture the entire duration from the time the request is made by SQL Server, down through the OS layers, through the hardware layers including but not limited to the disks and controllers, and back to SQL Server. Therefore storage vendor I/O counters and PerfMon I/O counters rarely match and you have to understand the purpose and scope of each.

Generally you will want to collect some information about the rate and intensity of blocking and some of the basic SQL Server PerfMon counters as well. If you have historically seen problems with some particular area, such as SQL Server replication or your network, you will want to capture the relevant counters for those areas as well.

A SQLTrace may have different levels of detail. The more events you choose, the bigger the trace file and the greater the overhead of capturing the data. A big trace file gives you more data to analyze but may become too large to realistically manage even with rollover files. Some events, such as locks and even some of the performance events, are much more intensive than others.

An event like autogrow that (hopefully) is occurring infrequently or even better, never, should always be captured. Something that occurs frequently or has large output like the query plan will generally only be captured in very short running traces. Some of the events you will commonly see in a baseline are:

➤ Some or all of the "completed" events from the RPC and T-SQL categories

➤ Most or all of the events from the "Errors and Warnings" category

➤ All of the "Database" category events (grow, shrink, etc.)

➤ The "Locks" category Deadlock Graph event and possibly the escalation and timeout events but generally NOT any of the other lock related events. There are other ways to troubleshoot blocking that are much less intensive.

➤ The "Progress Report" category events

➤ Some, all, or none of the Performance events. These events can take a lot of space so consider the trade-offs carefully.

Chapters 10-13 cover SQLTrace extensively.

Events and Alerts

Windows has built in event logs, SQL Server has an Error Log, and your application may have a log as well. When you experience a problem, check to see if there are recent log events or alerts, or even in the last few days, weeks or months, that might indicate some underlying or related problem.

For example:

➤ I/O errors from SQL Server are often accompanied by hardware errors in the Windows event logs.

➤ The cause of a cluster failover might be apparent from looking in the cluster log or the Windows event logs.

➤ A series of monitoring tool alerts warning that a disk is approaching capacity might indicate whether an out of space error is due to a sudden problem or steady growth over time.

➤ Repeated Policy-Based Management validation failures might help you narrow down the source of a problem to a previous change in the system.

Keep in mind that monitoring a system *will* have an effect on the system itself however slight, so in some circumstances it may help to turn off alerts to reduce the load on the system, to prevent logs from filling up, or to reduce "noise" from known issues in the logs or alerting system.

Of course, if you turn off any monitoring, make sure you turn it back on once the problem is resolved.

GATHERING DATA

Now that you have defined the problem and your exit criteria, you need to gather some data, but the sort of data depends on the type of problem. For performance issues you usually need basic configuration information, a SQLTrace and a PerfMon collection. For connectivity and security issues you will need a SQLTrace with basic session, login, and error information, and maybe a Network Monitor trace. Other problems may require a different combination of data collections.

Understanding the Data Gathering Process

Data gathering is a delicate balance between getting enough information to get the full picture and not gathering so much that you either impact the system or have too much data to efficiently analyze.

If you can reproduce the problem easily or it always happens in a predictable pattern, you can usually confine your data gathering to a short period of time and gather a full portfolio of information.

Conversely, if the problem happens randomly, you will need a different strategy because a normal data collection will likely gather too much data over a long period, and you usually cannot wait for the problem to start before you gather data because the events that happen just before the problem starts are often important.

The approach in this scenario is to proactively start a a data collection like a light-weight trace and let it run until the problem occurs again. You may be able to configure the data to be overwritten by newer data until the problem actually occurs to avoid filling your drives.

Chapters 9-11 and 15 cover data collection in depth.

Tools and Utilities

The following is a list of some information-gathering tools and utilities that are available. The specifics of how to use some of these tools will be discussed in the following chapters.

SQLDiag

SQLDiag ships with SQL Server. It can be used to gather basic environmental information such as the SQL Error Logs, event logs, and SQL Server configuration settings with the /x option. It can also be used to capture time-synchronized SQLTrace and PerfMon information. Which events are captured is controlled by an XML file. For more details see Chapter 11.

PSSDiag

This is a wrapper around SQLDiag with some extensions that Microsoft Support configure and send to customers to help troubleshoot a specific issue. It comes with a GUI tool that's used to generate the XML configuration files used by SQLDiag and generates a single executable for customers to run. Unfortunately, the GUI tool isn't currently distributed by Microsoft. You can find some more details on the background to PSSDiag in Chapter 11.

Windows Event logs (Application, System, and Security)

These logs are often useful to show you what errors, warnings, and informational messages have occurred in the recent past. Sometimes you can match performance problems to I/O errors, for example.

Custom Application Logs

If your application is instrumented to write errors or diagnostic information, then these logs can be useful in narrowing down the problem.

User Dumps

If you see an exception in the SQL Error Logs you should also see a mini-dump file with the extension .mdmp in the same directory. This can be used by Microsoft Support to help determine why the exception occurred. Under some circumstances they may direct you to capture full memory dumps which are much larger.

PerfMon

Performance Monitor ships with Windows and can be used to gather information on the resources used on the server. It can track system information such as CPU and memory usage, I/O statistics, and network activity. When SQL Server is installed it adds some SQL Server–specific counters that can be useful in various troubleshooting and monitoring scenarios. Chapter 9 covers Performance Monitor.

NetMon

Network Monitor is a free network packet analyzer tool that is used to look at data as it is sent over the network. It is often used to diagnose connectivity or authentication problems. Wireshark is another great packet analyzer and is also free.

Management Data Warehouse

This is used for performance trending and can be used to see how performance has changed over time. It can be configured to collect and consolidate various data over time. See Chapter 15 for more details.

Policy-Based Management

PBM can be used to validate whether pre-determined standards have been followed. Some policies allow you to prevent certain actions from ever occurring.

ANALYZING DATA

To analyze data, you need to determine where your bottleneck is. For example, for a performance problem where you don't already know the query(s) involved, you can find the longest-duration queries in Profiler. You can also review PerfMon output to see whether I/O, CPU, memory, or the network is the bottleneck.

Often, once you remediate one bottleneck another will appear. This is where it is important to understand your SLAs so you know when to stop troubleshooting.

The following is a list of tools and utilities you can use to analyze your data.

SQL Nexus

SQL Nexus, available from `www.codeplex.com`, imports data from SQLTrace, PerfMon, and PerfStats into a SQL Server database and generates reports showing the most common performance issues based on that data.

For example, it can show you all statements captured in your trace that were blocked for more than 30 seconds. SQLNexus is commonly used to show you the stored procedures or queries that had the highest duration, were executed most frequently, or used the most CPU and to help navigate blocking lock chains. Nexus is a great tool for taking a large amount of data and quickly finding the pain points that will require a more thorough follow up. You can read all about it in Chapter 13.

Profiler

Profiler can be used to replay statements if the right events are captured. There is a "Replay" template built into Profiler that you can use to make sure you have all those events. This is useful if you want to test the same queries over and over against a database where you have made changes, such as altering the file layout or modifying indexes. You can then measure the impact of the changes to the overall workload using this consistent set of replay data.

Most of us are more familiar with using Profiler to view statements that were sent to SQL Server, and some of the internal information about those statements such as the query plan and transactional boundaries. Often you will sort by duration, I/O, or CPU so you can easily find the most painful queries. Profiler is also used for troubleshooting security and connectivity problems as you can capture login and session information that is useful for diagnosis.

See Chapter 10 for in-depth coverage of Profiler and SQLTrace.

Database Tuning Advisor

The DTA can take an individual query or an entire SQLTrace as its input. It will make recommendations for possible index or partitioning changes that you can test. You should never blindly implement suggestions from DTA; always review the recommendations and seek to justify them yourself.

Visual Studio Database Edition

A full discussion of this product is well beyond the scope of this book but at a high level, some of the functionality available includes schema compare, data compare, test data generation, reverse engineering, and deploying schemas.

TESTING SOLUTIONS

Once you think you have a possible solution you should test it. Ideally, reproduce the problem on a test or development system and try the fix there first. You may want to test the change within a transaction but not commit the transaction until you are sure it has worked.

It is usually best to test each change in isolation. If you change several things at once, it may not be clear which change resolved the problem. Moreover, it is harder to roll back multiple changes than single, individual changes. Make sure you understand the consequences of any change, including whether or not that change can be undone.

You should always document each change; note the behavior before and after the change, as well as exactly what change was made.

TROUBLESHOOTING OTHER COMPONENTS

Within this section you'll find additional information that covers specifics of troubleshooting discrete SQL Server components not covered directly in the rest of the book.

Failover Clustering

Your troubleshooting steps will be basically the same on a clustered or a standalone instance for most problems. Even if the problem is that you need to understand why a cluster failover happened, you are usually just troubleshooting either a performance problem that makes the system seem unresponsive to the cluster service or some other perceived "hang" of SQL Server. Some of the major differences in troubleshooting on a cluster are as follows:

➤ When you collect a full user dump from SQL Server it will appear that SQL Server is unresponsive. If you need to gather a user dump from a clustered instance, you need to increase the time that the cluster service waits before it decides to do an automatic failover.

➤ Any files you expect to be available, regardless of which node owns the clustered instance, should be put on one of the shared drives on which this particular instance of SQL Server depends.

➤ To start the instance in single-user mode, you need to start it outside the cluster so that the cluster service does not take the only available connection. Take the SQL Server, SQL Agent, and Full-Text resources offline. Do *not* take the SQL Server name, IP, or disks offline. After this you can start SQL Server from the command line using –m parameter and whatever other parameters are necessary for your troubleshooting steps. Once you finish with those steps you should stop the command-line version of SQL Server and then bring SQL Server, SQL Agent, and Full Text online.

➤ The SQL Server service depends on an IP address, a name (DNS entry), and at least one disk. If any of these dependent resources are offline, SQL Server cannot be brought online (started).

➤ If SQL Server's behavior varies depending on which node owns the SQL Server group, look for differences in the nodes. Differences might include installed software, services, or utilities, hardware, configuration, or errors. Are there differences in the Windows version, Windows hotfixes, policies, firmware, BIOS, SQL Server binary versions, or certificates?

➤ Do the other applications (such as other instances of SQL Server) already have resources in use that this instance cannot use?

➤ Are the permissions to directories, files, and Registry keys the same on all nodes?

Some queries you may want to use when troubleshooting a clustered instance:

➤ Check to see if the instance is clustered: `SELECT SERVERPROPERTY('IsClustered')`

➤ Use the below DMV to list the drives that can be used by this clustered instance of SQL Server for database files, transaction logs, and SQL Server backups. If a drive is not in this list, then data and logs cannot be created on that drive. Also, in order for any file to be available, no matter which node owns the SQL Server instance, it must be on a drive in this list: `SELECT * FROM sys.dm_io_cluster_shared_drives`

➤ Get a list of the possible owners of this SQL Server instance. `SELECT * FROM sys.dm_os_cluster_nodes`

Replication

There are several variations of replication and various problems that can occur with it, but they all share many basic concepts. In many respects you can treat replication as a third party product that happens to use SQL Server as a backend.

Replication activity occurs via "agents" that are SQL Agent jobs that call replication executables. Each agent makes calls to stored procedures that result in data movement between replicated databases so you can trace and troubleshoot those stored procedure calls just like you would any other application. It helps if you understand the application, in this case replication, but there are certain common troubleshooting steps regardless of the application.

You can use SQLTrace or Profiler to find out what procedure calls replication is making at any given time. In most cases you have at least some network traffic to deal with as most production systems involve at least 2-3 different servers. If you have a performance problem, you can look at SLAs, baselines, and network traces just like with any other application.

Security is basically the same as for any other SQL Agent job, with a few minor additions. The exact security requirements for each replication activity are specified in SQL Server Books Online.

If any of the replication databases are on a clustered instance, replication works the same way as it does on a standalone instance; however, just as with any other clustered application, the files that replication references must be on a clustered shared drive. For replication those files are specified in *snapshot* properties for each type of replication.

For transactional replication latency problems you can use *tracer tokens*. Latency means that there is a longer than expected delay in getting data between the publisher and the subscriber, this is a special type of performance problem. A tracer token is basically just a sample bit of data sent through the system. It is used to measure the elapsed time from the publisher to the distributor and from the distributor to the subscriber(s). The tracer token can help narrow down where the problem is and whether the problem is specific to just one article (SQL Server object).

You should break down the problem into where it occurs and which agent is running when the problem occurs. The agents can be configured to run in various places and local resources are used for the execution of the agent. However, most of the work of the agent occurs within SQL Server.

The executable called by the replication agent (a replication job in SQL Server Agent) initiates the connection to SQL Server and passes it data and parameters. The parameters can be specified directly in the agent job or in an agent profile. The parameters passed into each replication agent can greatly impact performance. For example, with transactional replication you sometimes have to influence the batch/command ratios.

Most replication performance problems can be handled with normal SQL Server performance troubleshooting. Replication is in many ways just another application that runs on top of SQL Server.

It is important to understand how and when each agent runs; once you do so, it becomes easier to narrow down the problem and concentrate on the correct instance of SQL Server. To help you understand the role of each agent, here are some descriptions:

Snapshot Agent

The Snapshot Agent reads data on the publisher and writes the output to a file. It is used in all types of replication. Sometimes it can cause blocking or performance problems on the publisher. The job that initiates the snapshot has to be able to read the data in the database and write to the designated snapshot folder. If the snapshot folder is not local to the subscriber, you have to consider whether network bandwidth impacts any performance issues you may see.

Log Reader Agent

The Log Reader Agent is used only for transactional replication but this includes peer-to-peer replication. It reads the transaction log on the publishing database and sends the data to the distribution database. This adds some load to the publisher and in particular adds load to the directory where the log file of the publishing database resides.

When the log reader is running it changes the log from a purely sequential operation to a semi-random operation. On a system that is already stressed, the additional movement of the disk read heads (they no longer get to stay in one place purely doing sequential writes) may cause some increased response times for that drive. The log reader is writing to the distribution database which may be on a different server (a *remote distributor*) from the publisher so once again you may need to consider network bandwidth in performance problems.

Distribution Agent

The Distribution Agent is used in transactional (including peer-to-peer) and snapshot replication. It moves data from the distribution database to the subscriber(s).

Initially this data movement is through the application of a snapshot. If the article (SQL Server object involved in replication) is configured so that the object is recreated when a snapshot is applied, applying the snapshot through the Distribution Agent will read the snapshot folder, find the CREATE statements stored there in various files when the Snapshot Agent ran, and apply those statements to the subscriber.

If the article is configured to replace the data on the subscribers (this is almost always true) then the Distribution Agent will Bulk Copy the data from the snapshot folder into the subscriber tables.

It reads from the distribution database tables and inserts data on the subscribers. The majority of the time the Distribution Agent is not applying a snapshot, it is applying changes captured by the log reader. This involves reading the T-SQL statements that modified data from the distribution database and applying the data statements (as defined in the article, usually a simple mapping where a modification on the publisher is applied exactly the same way on the subscribers) on the subscribers. Network bandwidth can be an issue with this agent as well.

Merge Agent

The Merge Agent is used only in merge replication, it moves data between the publisher and subscribers. Merge replication is not as straight forward as the other types of replication. The distribution database plays a much smaller role as data is moved directly between the publisher and the various subscribers.

Each database involved in merge replication contains several tables that maintain the data that has been modified, and complex logic helps determine if and how to apply each change to each database involved.

Triggers on the tables involved in merge replication populate these metadata tables on the local database. Sometimes, performance problems with merge are due to the extra resources needed by the triggers, though much more often merge performance problems are due to the resources involved in the metadata management, such as *conflict resolution*. Network bandwidth can sometimes contribute to performance issues.

Cleanup Agents

Cleanup Agents remove metadata that is no longer needed by replication. The Cleanup Agents may modify large amounts of data at once which can cause a surge in log usage and possibly blocking. These agents are running on the local instance so network bandwidth is not an issue.

Replication Monitor

SSMS has a Replication Monitor that is used to monitor the health of the replication topology and indicate the status of each replication job. This is a very useful tool that can provide immediate feedback about the health of your replication topology. You can use SQLTrace/Profiler to see what commands are issued by Replication Monitor and model those commands to create your own custom monitoring or reports if necessary.

Analysis Services

Many of the same basic concepts apply to both SQL Server and Analysis Services troubleshooting. For performance troubleshooting, you need baselines to compare to, for test systems you need data that is as close to production as possible, and Profiler and PerfMon are two of your main troubleshooting tools.

You should always ask what the expected performance is and whether that is realistic. However, the specifics of what to look for are different for Analysis Services and some of the terminology will seem strange to those used to the relational world.

For Analysis Services the first question to ask is whether you are troubleshooting processing, MDX queries, or XMLA queries. Processing will generally occur on some schedule while MDX and XMLA queries are somewhat random depending on user activity.

MDX queries will usually make up the majority of the query activity; MDX is used to read existing data. Those queries are almost always read-only as few people use the writeback functionality.

XMLA on the other hand is for administrative activity such as backing up or restoring a database, processing data, and creating cubes and dimensions.

XMLA Queries

XMLA is the language used to submit administrative queries to Analysis Services. Processing, for example is a collection of XMLA commands. The exact troubleshooting steps will depend on which activity is having problems. The key Profiler events to capture for an XMLA query problem are:

➤ **Command Events:** All

➤ **Errors and Warnings:** All

➤ **Progress Reports:** All

Processing Performance

Processing is the method by which Analysis Services reads data from a source relational database (often SQL Server) and posts it to an Analysis Services database. This is all done with XMLA queries, though most people use the processing interface in the client tools.

If you are troubleshooting processing, you first have to determine whether the problem is with reading the data from the data source or from building the data in Analysis Services. The queries that are issued to the relational database are formed based on the design of the Analysis Services database and in most cases cannot be directly modified. If a relational query needs to change, you usually have to change the Analysis Services design.

If the problem is with reading the data from a SQL Server data source, then it should be approached as a SQL Server performance tuning issue. The key Profiler events to capture for a processing problem are:

- ➤ **Command Events:** All
- ➤ **Errors and Warnings:** All
- ➤ **Progress Reports:** All

For example, if the Analysis Services profiler events show that an unexpectedly long time is spent in executing the SQL queries on the underlying relational database (event 25- ExecuteSQL), then you will want to tune that relational database or the network bandwidth/utilization.

You might also want to change indexes, update statistics, or defragment the database. Always check to see if blocking is part of the problem. In the case of a properly formed query that is slow on the relational side, Analysis Services can be treated pretty much as a third party application that is issuing queries against SQL Server (or another supported source database).

In some cases where the source relational database is used for other activity, Analysis Services processing may slow down the other activity. If you can afford to throttle your Analysis Services processing you may want to use Resource Governor to limit the resources available within SQL Server to satisfy the SQL queries generated by Analysis Services during the processing phase so that other activity can continue at the cost of a longer processing time.

Where you have placed Analysis Services and the data source is very important for processing. If they are on the same box, they will compete for resources.

With this scenario you have to be very aware of the peak performance needs of each application (Analysis Services and SQL Server) and provide for them properly. If you put Analysis Services and SQL Server on separate boxes they are not competing for resources, but you do have the added network usage as the T-SQL query results are sent over the network to the Analysis Services box. A fast network connection between them will be essential to fast processing. Along with a fast network you need a fast I/O subsystem for Analysis Services and as much memory as Analysis Services can use.

If a significant amount of time is spent in populating the cubes or dimensions, building the aggregations and indexes, or anywhere else that is not directly related to querying the source database then you have two ways to approach it.

One method is to tune the processing activity. For example, you may want to change your processing schedule or do incremental instead of full processing.

Another processing option that often helps is to change whether you use one transaction for the entire processing job or if you use a separate transaction for each step. See the Books Online topic "Processing Settings and Options" for more details.

The other way is to change the Analysis Services design. For example, if the problem is with the time it takes to create aggregations you may want to change the aggregation levels or the attribute relationships. For most cubes 10-20% performance gain is a good aggregation level, for larger cubes you will often choose something like 5%.

The higher the aggregation level the more MDX queries will be satisfied by aggregated data and will therefore run faster. The tradeoff however, is longer processing time.

If most queries can be satisfied with a lower aggregation level then you may choose the improved processing time at the cost of an occasional slower MDX query. Some designs such as "distinct count" are always intensive and should be isolated and used only when necessary. The key size and the dimension attribute properties "optimized," "ordered," and "visible" often make a big difference in processing performance.

There are various Analysis Services configuration settings that can affect performance and a very good whitepaper from the SQL Server Customer Advisory Team at Microsoft discusses these at length. The whitepaper can be found here: `http://msdn.microsoft.com/en-us/library/dd542635.aspx` although with Analysis Services 2008 the default values will serve you well in most cases.

MDX Queries

When an end user complains about slow performance they are usually referring to an MDX query. Front end tools like Reporting Services, ProClarity, and Excel all generate MDX queries behind the scenes after the user finishes dragging and dropping. Different tools may generate the underlying MDX query and even the connection string properties differently. Connection string properties are more likely to have a performance impact for Analysis Services than for SQL Server.

If the problem has not been narrowed down to one query, ask yourself these questions:

➤ Are all queries slower than expected?

➤ Is there one query that is slower than usual?

➤ Is there a particular type of query that is slow?

➤ Is there anything common about the slow queries?

➤ Was it faster on a different version of the product or of the database design?

➤ Does the problem differ depending on which tool or user executes the query?

If you cannot narrow it down to one query you should first make sure that there is not some sort of overall system problem, such as another service taking all the resources away from Analysis Services or failing hardware. If you still cannot narrow it down, then pick one query to concentrate on and stick with that one query through all your troubleshooting. This allows consistent test results throughout the troubleshooting process.

Unexpected MDX Query Results

For unexpected MDX query results you need to understand the design, how the data is processed, and what data is in the system.

The first step must be to clearly define your expected results. Make sure your expected results make sense given your data and design, then see if you can reproduce the problem with slight variations or against other databases such as a test system.

If the problem happens with multiple queries with similar characteristics check your attribute relationships to make sure they are all defined properly. If it only happens on test or production but not both, what is different?

Security

In many ways security in Analysis Services is much simpler than for SQL Server. There are fewer built-in roles and basic security assignments are very simple. However, Analysis Services has the option of dynamic security which allows a custom function to limit security at the time a query runs based on data in the Analysis Services database. Dimension security is also an option and database roles can be added. There are also some settings and properties that affect which members are visible to a given user.

When troubleshooting security issues, you can use SQLTrace/Profiler to capture the Security Audit and Session Events information. The session events will allow you, for example, to see what roles a user is a member of. You need to understand what types of security are defined and exactly how the user came into the system.

If you want to test the effective security of a user or a role, Business Intelligence Development Studio offers the "Change User" option so you can see what data is returned for a particular user. You can also pass "Roles=" or "EffectiveUserName=" in the connection string.

Connectivity

A failure to connect to Analysis Services involves the same basic troubleshooting as with SQL Server. You need to start with defining the exact error and the scenario where the problem occurs. The error will usually make it apparent whether the failure is with the user connection to Analysis Services or with a subsequent attempt of Analysis Services to connect to a relational back end, such as SQL Server. For instance, during processing or MDX queries against ROLAP data two connections are made: one to Analysis Services and another to the relational back end. If either fails the user will receive a connection failure message.

Some questions to ask about the failure:

➤ Could it be a name resolution problem?

➤ Do connections work from only some machines or accounts?

➤ Are you connecting to a named or a default instance?

➤ Will the connection work from some tools or providers?

➤ Is AS configured to allow remote connections?

➤ Check the Profiler Security Audit:
Audit Login events to see if the expected user is listed.

➤ Check the event log for any login or security errors.

➤ If Analysis Services is a named instance, is the SQL Browser started on the box?

➤ What port(s) is Analysis Services listening on and is the firewall configured to allow connections to that port?

HTTP

Analysis Services allows users to connect to an IIS box with HTTP or HTTPS and then the IIS box controls the connection to Analysis Services. If you can connect directly to the Analysis Services box but cannot connect through HTTP, ask yourself these questions:

➤ Verify non-HTTP connectivity works from the IIS box to AS.

➤ Check to see if msmdpump.dll configured correctly: `http://technet.microsoft.com/en-gb/library/cc917711.aspx`

➤ Verify the msmdpump.ini is pointing to the correct Analysis Services instance.

➤ The msmdpump.dll must be the same platform as IIS, regardless of the platform of Analysis Services. For example, with an x64 Analysis Services server and a 32-bit IIS server you will use the 32-bit msmdpump.dll.

➤ Is IIS configured to allow connectivity per your business needs?

➤ From the Internet Explorer instance you use for testing, always turn off "Show friendly HTTP error messages" so you can see the more detailed messages.

Kerberos

Kerberos is a security protocol that commonly comes into play with something called double hops. When you connect from your workstation directly to SQL Server or Analysis Services, that is a single hop. If you add another machine in the middle, such as client to IIS to Analysis Services or client to SQL Server to Analysis Services or client to Analysis Services to SQL Server this is known as a "double hop."

If the second connection is using the Windows credentials entered on the client then you must use Kerberos to "delegate" the "impersonated" credentials. In Windows this means that a Service Principle Name (SPN) is created for the SQL Service and this SPN must belong to one and only one Active Directly "container." The "container" in this case is the account used to start the service.

The existence of the SPN plus some configuration options in the domain indicates the domain administrators have allowed delegation to occur for that service. Some things to consider if you suspect a Kerberos problem:

➤ Determine if the problem only happens with double hops but not with single hops.

➤ Verify the domain level settings as outlined in SQL Server Books Online.

➤ Refer to this KB article to check the steps you used to enable Kerberos for Analysis Services: `http://support.microsoft.com/kb/917409/en-us`

➤ Does a valid SPN belong to the Analysis Services startup account ONLY?

➤ Use Profiler to view the Security Audit: Audit Login events. See if any connection attempt or error is visible in the trace.

Analysis Services troubleshooting is in many ways similar to SQL Server, but it does require specific knowledge as well. The above section ties together the general steps with the Analysis Services specific information.

SUMMARY

Solving the problem is not enough; you must understand *why* it happened. If you changed code to fix the problem, perhaps you need to update your coding standards or code review practices. If it was a security breach, you should review current access to the system, whether minimal permissions have been granted, and how new accounts are added and permissions chosen for them. Performance problems focused on one table may indicate similar problems lurking for other tables.

If you understand what happened this time you can reduce the chance that a similar problem will happen again on this system or on another system. Sometimes once you find the true source of a recent problem you will realize your resolution is not the most appropriate for a long term solution.

Sometimes you are able to put a solution in place that resolves the immediate problem, but you should always come back to the problem later and review it. Was there any underlying cause you have not yet addressed? Is there something that would be more efficient, more in line with your standards, or otherwise more appropriate as a resolution in addition to or instead of what you implemented during the initial troubleshooting process?

Keep in mind that a problem on one system often points to similar problems elsewhere. Most of us set up the same environment repeatedly even if no specific standards or checklists are in place. A problem is an opportunity to create or update your skills, your standards, and your systems.

How you approach a problem is critical to your success. Your attitude, willingness to ask for and accept help, and ability to "handle" management are essential troubleshooting skills and are, in their own way just as important as your technical skills to a successful career.

It doesn't matter if you are looking at a performance problem, healing a security breach, or fixing a connectivity issue. Take it a step at a time, break the problem into manageable chunks and you'll soon have the issue resolved!

9

Viewing Server Performance with PerfMon and the PAL Tool

WHAT'S IN THIS CHAPTER

➤ When and how to use Perfmonance Monitor

➤ How to baseline server performance

➤ Using sample thresholds to identify performance problems

➤ Automating data analysis with Performance Analysis for Logs (PAL)

Performance Monitor, widely known as PerfMon, is a Windows tool for measuring real-time server performance and recording system performance to a file over time. Understanding when and how to use Performance Monitor enables you to quickly and effectively narrow the scope of problems from entire IT systems to specific servers, components, or resources. When used effectively, Performance Monitor can assist with resolving complex problems, some of which may seem random or intermittent, by narrowing the focus to the root cause.

Knowing which PerfMon counters to include for a given scenario will enable you to interpret the data and draw useful conclusions, following these with constructive recommendations for remediation. Capturing too much, too little, or the wrong type of data can lead you to draw no conclusion or an inaccurate conclusion, which may be then followed by incorrect recommendations. Bad or missing performance data might mean you miss correlations or patterns in the data that could support a hypothesis regarding the problem's cause.

Engineers or DBAs unfamiliar with PerfMon often look at the data generated in the performance log and ask themselves questions like the following:

➤ Is value X acceptable?

➤ Why is my system running so slow?

➤ What does "normal" look like?

➤ How can I tell if there's a problem?

This chapter addresses these questions in three main ways:

➤ It provides key counters and thresholds for issues.

➤ It helps you gather a baseline from a healthy server.

➤ It demonstrates tools to assist with analyzing performance logs.

This chapter consists of four main sections that together provide a complete view on PerfMon data capture and log analysis, including an overview of Performance Monitor, how to use it, and working with Performance Analysis for Logs (PAL) and other PerfMon log analysis tools.

After reading this chapter you should have a good understanding of using PerfMon, and you'll know which counters to monitor and what values are acceptable. Additionally, you'll be aware of a selection of tools and utilities to help with log analysis.

PERFORMANCE MONITOR OVERVIEW

PerfMon provides server-wide, real-time and logged performance monitoring. First introduced with Windows NT 4.0, the core features and user interface have barely changed from the first Microsoft Management Console (MMC) snap-in. Windows Server 2003 saw the tool renamed to System Monitor, although the data logging functionality of System Monitor retained the name Performance Monitor. In Windows Server 2008, PerfMon has been incorporated into the Reliability and Performance Monitor.

Use Performance Monitor for the following common tasks:

➤ View real-time performance data on your server.

➤ See performance data represented visually.

➤ Record performance data over an extended time frame.

➤ Quantify the performance impact of hardware or software changes.

➤ Save and export performance data.

➤ Fire alerts based on performance thresholds.

➤ Compare performance data from different servers.

Reliability and Performance Monitor in Windows Server 2008

The latest refresh for PerfMon in Windows Server 2008 brings a new look and a new name to the parent snap-in: Reliability and Performance Monitor, although real-time performance monitoring retains the PerfMon name.

Reliability and Performance Monitor comprises three main components: Monitoring Tools, Data Collector Sets, and Reports. The focus for this chapter is Performance Monitor and Data Collector Sets. Monitoring Tools comprises Performance Monitor (PerfMon), which is the tool of choice when investigating server-wide problems or resource problems, and Reliability Monitor, which reports on system stability.

Resource Overview

Once Performance and Reliability Monitor is launched, the Resource Overview is the initial screen displayed, showing real-time performance data. The Resource Overview provides a visual representation of each of the four key hardware elements: CPU, Disk, Network, and Memory. Each element can be expanded to reveal a list of processes, listed in descending order by the resource type — for example, when CPU is expanded, all processes are listed ordered by Average CPU descending, as shown in Figure 9-1.

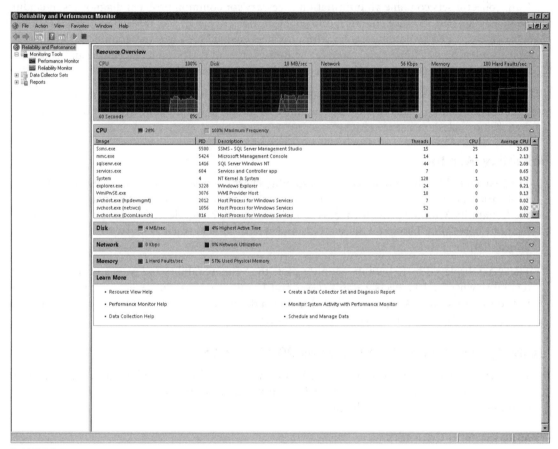

FIGURE 9-1

In addition to the four individual performance graphs displayed across the top of the Resource Overview, each major component shows resource utilization details in a horiztonal bar — CPU, Disk, Network and Memory. Each bar can expand/ collapse to show more detailed resource information. In the collapsed position, each bar displays two mini-charts showing resource, utilization metrics. Figure 9-1 shows CPU in the expanded view and other resources in the default collapsed view with only the mini-charts visible.

It's worth noting that for CPU, the left mini-chart indicates current CPU utilization, while the right mini-chart indicates maximum CPU frequency. Some computers (mostly laptops) may have maximum CPU frequency less than 100% when operating in energy-saving modes. The memory resource element displays hard (page) faults per second in the left mini-chart (more on hard page faults later in this chapter), and the percentage of physical memory in use is shown on the right mini-chart.

Data Collector Sets

Data collector sets combine all information necessary for common problem diagnostics, including event tracing, performance counters, and configuration (Registry and WMI classes). Data collector sets can be created by administrators with providers enabled for trace and counter data. Once a collector set has been defined, it is stored in the Reliability and Performance Monitor, and you can start and stop the collector at any point in the future without recreating it, or control it on a schedule.

Three predefined system data collector sets are included: LAN Diagnostics, System Diagnostics, and System Performance. Each collects performance counters, trace data, and system configuration for common troubleshooting scenarios.

Reliability Monitor

The Reliability Monitor provides a system stability chart. Here, events such as hardware failures, application failures, or Windows failures are tracked against a timeline. The data presented by the Reliability Monitor provides access to failure activity data, plotted against a time chart to facilitate correlation between failure events and system activity, such as software installation or uninstallation.

The chart displayed by Reliability Monitor plots the System Stability Index — a rating system for reliability whereby 10 reflects a stable server and 1 reflects an unstable server. The intention of the Index is to assist in making correlations between a decrease in system stability and a specific change, such as an updated device driver or hotfix installation.

Usability Enhancements in Windows 2008 PerfMon

There are some nifty enhancements to the PerfMon user interface in Windows Server 2008, although if you're familiar with the changes to PerfMon in Windows Vista these won't be new. This section contains a brief précis of the highlights.

Auto-Scaling Counters

Counter values often appear way off the top of the PerfMon graph or are dwarfed by other counters — neither situation allows changes in counter values to be seen clearly. Prior to Windows Server 2008, scaling counters could be a painful process of trial and error, selecting each counter in turn and attempting to choose a reasonable value to scale the counter by. The process is made much simpler in Windows Server 2008 because it's possible to select a group of counters, right-click, and choose "Scale selected counters." PerfMon will then adjust the scale of each counter to a reasonable value so that all lines are plotted in or around the middle of the graph.

> *Don't let counter scaling in PerfMon catch you out — always check scaling of counters before comparing two counters, particularly when comparing between servers. Auto-scaling in Windows 2008 PerfMon can adjust instances of the same counter to use different scales.*

Show/Hide Counters

Anothersmall but useful enhancement to PerfMon in Windows Server 2008 is that counters can be shown or hidden from the graph. This is useful when monitoring in real time because you can capture many counters while displaying fewer of them. Showing/hiding counters enables you to record the data (including min, max, and average values) and display as needed, which is also faster than adding counters and provides historic data for reference.

New Counters for SQL Server 2008 in PerfMon

SQL Server 2008 has some new PerfMon counters to provide performance logging for new features such as Resource Governor, and there are new counter instances for improved features, such as for monitoring compression in database mirroring. Later sections look in more detail at some new SQL Server counters, focusing particularly on the database mirroring improvements, as this feature is widely used.

Also included with SQL Server 2008 is a PerfMon counter called Deprecated Features, which is a great counter to help reduce the risk of upgrading SQL Server 2008 in the future. Deprecated features are features that still operate but will be removed in a future version. The new counters can be captured in a lightweight PerfMon trace to record calls to deprecated features such as COMPUTE BY, database compatibility mode 90, some SET options, and a number of DBCC commands such as DBREINDEX and INDEXDEFRAG. Previously, customers undertaking an upgrade project had to rely on detailed application knowledge and rigorous testing to ensure code compatibility.

Table 9-1 summarizes the new counters for widely used, common functionality within SQL Server. There are two new counters for Resource Governor called Resource Pool Stats and Workload Group Stats, each containing more than ten instances relating to the new Resource Governor functionality. If you're using Service Broker, a number of new counters and instances relating to Service Broker functionality are included.

SQL Server 2008 includes backup compression, and this functionality can be utilized by database mirroring, such that logs can be compressed prior to transmission and uncompressed at the destination. Using these new counters it is possible to calculate database mirroring recovery time, in the event of a failure. Table 9-2 describes the new counters for database mirroring.

TABLE 9-1: New PerfMon Counters for SQL Server 2008

COUNTER		DESCRIPTION
SQL Server Access Methods	Page compression attempts/sec	Number of attempts to compress a database page per second
	Pages compressed/sec	Number of times a database page was compressed
SQL Server Databases	Commit table entries	Size of the in-memory part of the commit table for the database
	Tracked transactions/sec	Number of committed transactions recorded in the commit table for the database
	Write transactions/sec	Number of transactions that wrote to the database in the last second
SQL Server Buffer Node	Local node page lookups/sec	Number of lookup requests from this node that were satisfied from this node
	Remote node page lookups/sec	Number of lookup requests from this node that were satisfied from other nodes
SQL Server General Statistics	Connection reset/sec	Total number of connection resets per second
	Tempdb recovery unit ID	Number of duplicate tempdb recovery unit ID generated
	Tempdb rowset id	Number of duplicate tempdb rowset ID generated
SQL Server SQL Statistics	Guided plan executions/sec	Number of plan executions per second in which the query plan has been generated by using a plan guide
	Misguided plan executions/sec	Number of plan executions per second in which a plan guide could not be honored during plan generation. The plan guide was disregarded and normal compilation was used to generate the executed plan.
Deprecated Features	*<feature>*	Lists usage of deprecated features such as COMPUTE BY, GROUP BY ALL, various DBCC commands and SET options.

TABLE 9-2: New Counters for Database Mirroring

COUNTER	DESCRIPTION
Log Bytes Redone from Cache/sec	Number of log bytes that were redone from the Database Mirroring log cache per second
Log Bytes Sent from Cache/sec	Number of log bytes that were sent from the Database Mirroring log cache in the last second
Log Compressed Bytes Rcvd/sec	Number of compressed bytes of the log received in the last second
Log Compressed Bytes Sent/sec	Number of compressed bytes of the log sent in the last second
Log Harden Time (ms)	Milliseconds that log blocks waited to be hardened to disk in the last second
Log Remaining for Undo KB	Total number of log kilobytes that remain to be scanned by the new mirror server after failover
Log Scanned for Undo KB	Total number of log kilobytes that have been scanned by the new mirror server after failover
Log Send Flow Control Time (ms)	Milliseconds that log stream messages waited for send flow control in the last second
Mirrored Write Transactions/sec	Number of transactions written to the mirrored database in the last second, that waited for logged transactions to be sent to the mirror
Send/Receive Ack Time	Milliseconds that messages waited for acknowledgment from the partner per second

Troubleshooting SQL Server Problems

It's unusual for complete fault information to be provided when an incident is escalated. Application performance is often closely related to database performance and as such server-wide problems often impact database response times immediately and operations DBAs are notified rapidly. High-impact database problems reach support teams by phone or walk-up much faster than automated alerts or formal support-ticket escalation. Typically, escalated support cases contain insufficient data to make any kind of decision, and further analysis is required before any kind of remediation can begin.

When accepting a problem to investigate, it's useful to know the following information:

➤ The problem statement, in order to understand the user experience and expected application behavior

➤ What troubleshooting steps have been carried out already (by the users and first- or second-line support engineers)

➤ What data has already been gathered about the problem

In order to resolve a problem, it's first necessary to understand the problem fully. Often, one of the most effective methods to gain a better understanding of the problem is to reproduce it. Depending on the nature of the problem, the complexity of the infrastructure, and the availability of test or pre-production environments, this may be possible.

REPRODUCING PROBLEMS

If possible, take the time to reproduce the problem. When you reproduce a problem, you're half the way to fixing it, as recreating the exact scenario in which a problem condition occurred requires a thorough understanding of the problem itself. When the problem and conditions are well understood, the options for remediation become clearer. Once a problem can be reliably reproduced, the potential causes will be fewer, as the environment variables are being managed. After the potential causes are understood, the problems can be worked to elimination or incrimination. When a specific component or resource has been indentified, an action plan can be developed for resolution.

PerfMon is a great tool to start troubleshooting most kinds of problems. It can be used to do either of the following:

➤ Prove a problem condition

➤ Narrow the problem scope

If practical, establish and prove the problem condition. The next step is to narrow the scope of the problem. Ideally, a specific component or server has been identified as the problem. PerfMon can then be used to eliminate areas of doubt or identify specific areas where further investigation is required.

PerfMon is especially valuable in problem situations where resource contention such as hardware is suspected as a potential root cause. Additionally, PerfMon is vital in situations where SQL Server is co-resident with another application or a Windows feature such as Internet Information Server (IIS). In situations where SQL Server is co-hosted with other applications (perhaps Small Business Server), PerfMon is key to early identification of the problem source.

Data-Driven Troubleshooting

Data-driven troubleshooting refers to an iterative approach to troubleshooting problems whereby each decision or recommendation is based on data gathered about the problem. This approach avoids the hearsay and speculation that often surrounds high profile, high-impact problems.

Data-driven troubleshooting relies on three components:

➤ Tools to collect data

➤ Engineers to read data and understand the problem (us)

➤ Any one of a number of people to assist with problem resolution (server hardware engineers, storage engineers, or developers)

The iterative troubleshooting approach doesn't necessarily deliver the final solution immediately, but focuses on the worst component first — providing actionable items to work toward a resolution. Applying this approach to SQL Server problems, many built-in and third-party tools are available to help collect data — the most obvious two are PerfMon and SQL Profiler. Chapter 10 contains details of how to get the most from SQL Profiler.

PerfMon should reside right at the top of ever SQL Server engineer's decision flowchart for troubleshooting most problems. The cause of a problem is often unclear from the problem symptoms and PerfMon can provide data necessary to reduce the scope, identify the source, and reduce the problem.

Choosing the Right Tool for the Job

There are many tools available for problem analysis and fault diagnosis. By familiarizing yourself with the strengths and weaknesses of each and common usage scenarios, you'll be able to employ the right tool the first time when a problem does occur, rather than waste valuable time experimenting with or attempting to learn how to use these tools under pressure.

> *Use PerfMon early in the troubleshooting process to help narrow the scope and focus your effort. If you're tackling a performance problem, PerfMon will help you identify the problem area. For example, if you note that CPU is higher than usual, or disk reads are slow, you can focus on high CPU queries or queries with expensive disk access as necessary.*

Selecting the right tool for the job is hard when the problem isn't well understood. Troubleshooting is an iterative approach, but having a good grasp of the nature and features of the problem combined with knowledge of the tools means you're more likely to reach a resolution with fewer steps. Here's a (non-exhaustive) list of tools available for troubleshooting SQL Server problems:

➤ SQL Server error logs

➤ Windows event logs

➤ SQL Profiler

- ➤ Performance Monitor (PerfMon)
- ➤ Stored procedures
- ➤ Dynamic management views
- ➤ DBCC
- ➤ Replication Monitor
- ➤ Wait stats
- ➤ Performance Data Warehouse
- ➤ SQL Nexus
- ➤ PSSBlocker script
- ➤ PerfStats script
- ➤ SQL Server Management Studio Reports
- ➤ Database Tuning Advisor
- ➤ Trace flags
- ➤ Execution plans
- ➤ Stack dumps

These tools each provide different information about the server and environment. PerfMon provides a server-level view of hardware utilization. It also includes a comprehensive set of counters for SQL Server, although in some situations a statement-level view is required, which only SQL Profiler can provide.

You've already read that PerfMon is a Windows monitoring tool; as such it can be used to monitor any application — from Microsoft Exchange to SAP. When an application is installed, a number of PerfMon counters are installed to provide visibility of internal activity for diagnostic purposes.

GETTING STARTED WITH PERFMON

PerfMon is a component of the Reliability and Performance Monitor, which can be launched from Start ➪ All Programs ➪ Administrative Tools. Alternatively, just type **perfmon** into the Run box and press enter.

When an application is installed, performance counters are registered; and you can monitor the counters in real time or trace to a log file. PerfMon isn't designed specifically for SQL Server, so you'll need to add the relevant Windows and SQL Server counters to a log file in order to monitor resource utilization and SQL Server activity.

Monitoring Real-Time Server Activity

One of the most common uses for PerfMon is viewing real-time server activity. PerfMon provides data instantly on system workload, performance, and resource consumption. Reading the data presented by PerfMon can rapidly narrow the scope of a problem.

Within the Reliability and Performance Monitor, the following steps provide an overview of server activity:

1. Select Performance Monitor from the Monitor Tools folder. Immediately you'll see a line chart plotting "% Processor Time" from your own computer. You'll add a few counters to get a feel for CPU, disk, and memory activity on your own PC.

2. Right-click anywhere in the chart area and choose Add Counters.From here you'll be able to choose from hundreds of counters to monitor!

3. Scroll through the list of counters until you see Memory, and click to expand.

4. Select Available Mbytes and click Add.

5. Scroll to locate the LogicalDisk counter and select Avg. Disk sec/Transfer. If you have multiple disks, then select each disk individually from the instance list and click OK, as shown in Figure 9-2.

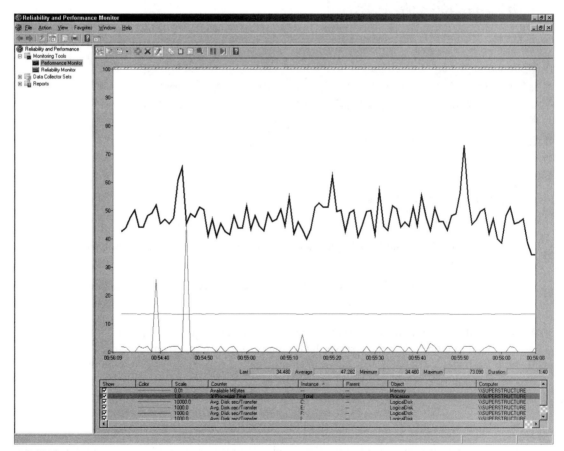

FIGURE 9-2

You'll see the counters added to the performance graph immediately; as the time line moves across the screen, each counter will be populated with data as shown in Figure 9-3.

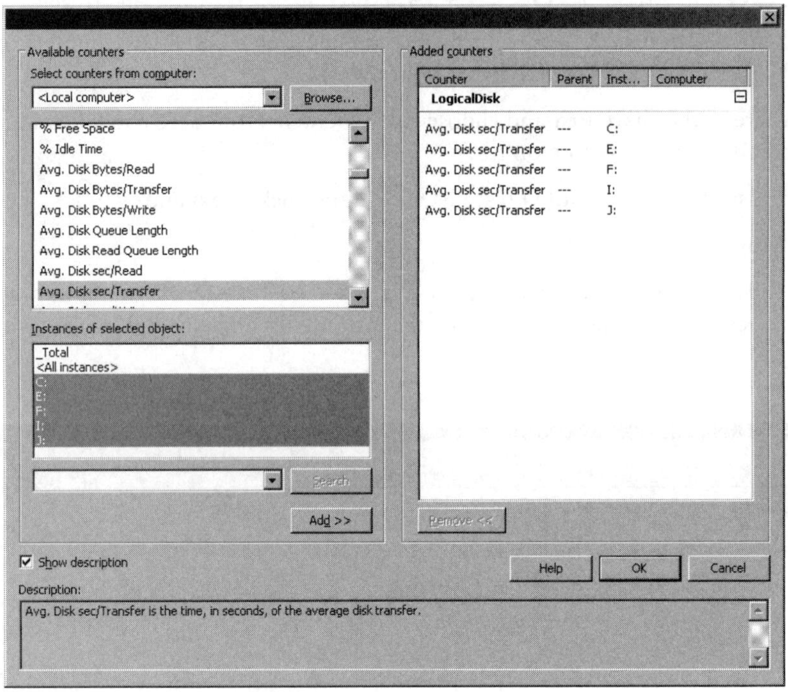

FIGURE 9-3

A couple of pointers to help out:

➤ Organize the columns so you can read each row more easily.

➤ Press Ctrl+H to enable highlighting for the selected counter — this means the line graph is highlighted.

➤ Select all counters, right-click, and choose Scale Selected Counters to ensure that they are all displayed within the screen.

Mostly you'll want to monitor a server (rather than your own workstation), and it's possible to use PerfMon to monitor a remote server by typing the server name from the Add Counters dialog. If you're adding a lot of counters, the graph can become a little unwieldy as individual counters become difficult to read. Three options can help:

➤ Remove surplus counters.

➤ Hide nonrequired counters (uncheck the Show button).

➤ Use a report view instead of the line graph (select Report from the mini drop-down on the top menu bar).

Starting Out with Data Collector Sets

Data Collector Sets are groups of data gathering tools, and can include kernel tracing, performance logs, and configuration data. Three data collector sets are provided out-of-the-box with Windows Server 2008, including a System Performance collector that consists of a kernel trace and PerfMon log. To utilize a predefined data collector, expand Data Collector Sets ⇨ System, right-click System Performance, and choose Start.

The System Performance collector will run for 60 seconds. Once collection has finished, navigate to Reports ⇨ System ⇨ System Performance, and choose the most recent report. As shown in Figure 9-4, the report presents data in a very readable layout.

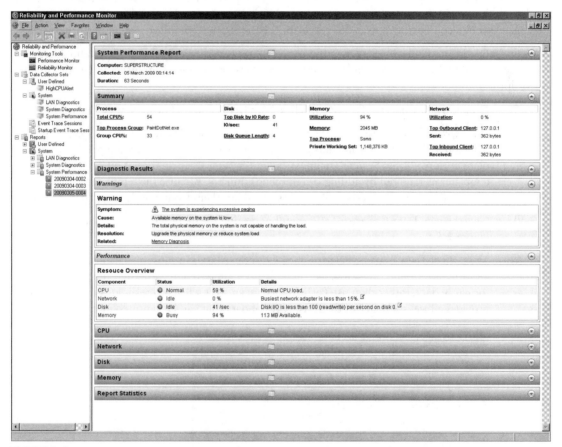

FIGURE 9-4

The System Performance report begins with a summary of the four key resources: CPU, Disk, Memory, and Network. Figure 9-4 shows memory utilization at 94%, and the diagnostic results report excessive paging and low memory, recommending adding more memory or reducing system load. The performance report component shows memory with a busy status, highlighting a potential memory issue.

The small effort required to start the System Performance collector, wait 60 seconds, and launch the report results in a conclusive initial investigation. In this case, the top process shown in the memory summary is Ssms (SQL Server Management Studio), so the next step would be to identify the problem session and resolve.

Working with User-Defined Data Collector Sets

In addition to the provided Data Collector Sets, it's also possible to create user-defined Data Collector Sets consisting of your own counters and settings. Real-time monitoring is great when a quick snapshot is required, but it can be difficult to identify patterns and trends when observing a server "live." It's usually more convenient to capture performance data to a file and then analyze that log file — either manually or using one of the tools looked at later in this chapter. This section walks through configuring a user-defined Data Collector Set to monitor system performance.

User-Defined Data Collector Sets in Windows 2008 replace the Performance Logs and Alerts from Windows 2000/ 2003 but the principle is the same. Start from the Reliability and Performance Monitor and follow the steps below:

1. Expand Data Collector Sets. Right-click User Defined and choose New ➪ Data Collector Set.

2. Short wizard launches to create the new Data Collector Set. The first choice is whether to create from a template or create manually. Creating a collector from a template provides three template options: Basic, System Diagnostics, and System Performance. You can modify these templates as required by adding or removing counters. Because the templates are Windows-generic, there's nothing especially interesting about them from a SQL Server perspective.

3. Give the new Data Collector Set a useful name and create it manually, as shown in Figure 9-5.

4. Next select Data Logs or Performance Counter Alerts. In most situations, you'll use the Performance Counter data log, as you'll likely be interested in gathering some system-wide performance data, rather than use PerfMon to fire an alert when a threshold is exceeded. Table 9-3 provides a brief summary of the three types of data that can be captured in the data log.

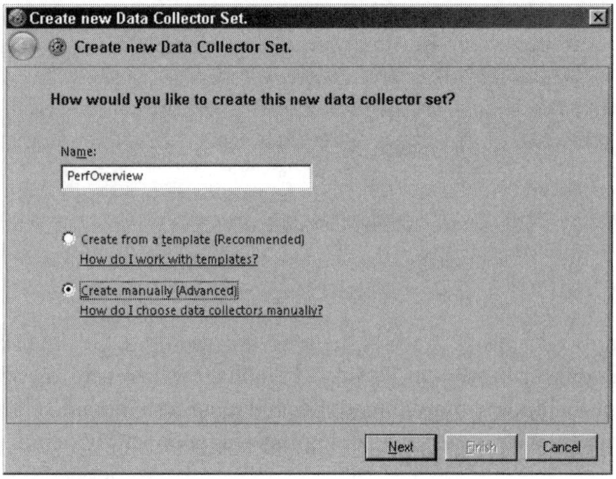

FIGURE 9-5

TABLE 9-3: Data Collector Set Logging Options

LOG TYPE	DESCRIPTION
Performance Counter	PerfMon counters provide performance data for most aspects of Windows and SQL Server.
Event trace data	Using Event Tracing for Windows provides low-level operating system tracing.
System configuration information	This captures Registry keys.

5. Select the Performance Counter log type and click Next to continue. Now you'll add a small selection of interesting counters to get an overview of system performance.

6. Click Add, and select all counters as shown in Figure 9-6.

7. Leave sample interval at 15 seconds — the impact of the sampling interval is covered in the next section.

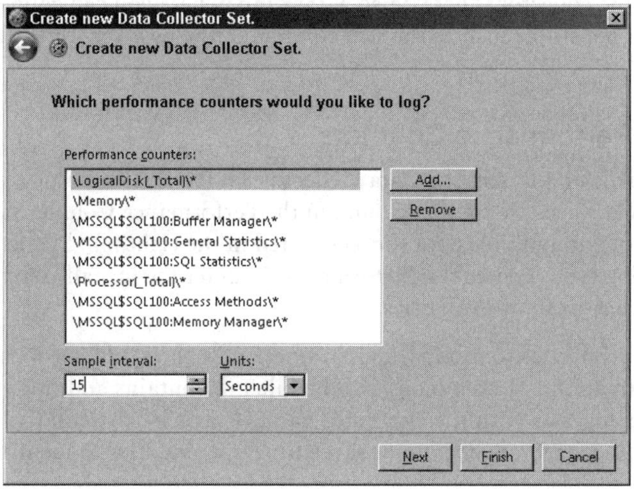

FIGURE 9-6

8. Once you've added the counters, select a folder to store the trace data. Ensure there's sufficient space on the disk to hold the trace file (size will vary according to how long the trace is running, but normally 2GB free space should be fine for a few hours of tracing).

9. Click Next after you've entered a location for the logs at the final confirmation dialog.

10. Click Finish to create the collector.

11.   At this point, the data collector set has been defined, but no data has actually been captured because the collector has never been started. To start a collector, right-click the collector name and choose Start. Collectors with no stop condition configured will run until they're stopped manually.

12.   To stop the collector, right-click on the collector name and choose Stop. Collectors can be started and stopped as a whole, but performance logs or traces within a collector cannot be started independently of the collector; you must define a new collector if this is required.

Configuring Collector Properties

Collectors can be scheduled using the Schedule tab on the collector's Properties dialog. When combined with a stop condition, the start and stop of a collector can be fully scheduled.

Note two points of interest in the Properties dialog: the Directory tab, where you can change the folder used to store the log files, and the Stop Condition tab. The Stop Condition enables administrators to configure the duration of the collector — in seconds, minutes, hours, days, or weeks. Once the time configured in the stop condition has elapsed, the collector is automatically stopped.

Also included in the Data Collector Set Properties dialog is the Schedule tab, which enables administrators to schedule the start of the collector. There's also a Task tab, where you can configure a task to run when the Data Collector Set stops, such as the msg command (the new version of NET SEND) on completion.

Configuring Properties for Performance Counters

You may have noticed that there is no place in the Data Collector Set Properties dialog to add or remove PerfMon counters — that's because they are found in the Performance Counter properties. Because collectors could contain multiple data sources (listed in the right-hand pane), these properties are specific to each log type. Locate the Performance Counter log (usually named DataCollector01) and double-click to show Properties.

Use the Performance Counter properties to modify log parameters, such as adding or removing counters, and changing log format and sample interval. The File tab contains additional settings, including a check box to prefix log files with the computer name — this is particularly useful when comparing logs from multiple servers because it saves time opening files to identify the source server.

PerfMon Log Formats

There are four options for PerfMon log format: Comma Separated, Tab Separated, SQL, and Binary. The default, Binary log (BLG) type, is suitable for most situations. Choosing SQL will require a data source name (DSN) to connect to SQL Server. There are some performance considerations when using this option, as you want to try to limit the impact of monitoring to genuine user or server activity, and outputting trace data to the same instance being monitored is unlikely to help. Performance data can be imported into a data post-capture for easier/better analysis; as such, avoid logging directly to SQL Server unless there's a good reason to do so and you're confident of the impact to the monitored instance.

PERFMON AS A CAPACITY PLANNING TOOL

Using activity data captured with PerfMon can be a powerful tool for performance and capacity planning. Analyzing the data will allow accurate forecasts to be made assessing the lifetime of servers and identifying spare capacity.

It's possible to capture a lightweight PerfMon trace and cycle the log files daily. The log data could be imported to a Data Warehouse using ReLog.exe (see below) or SQL Server Integration Services where analysis and reporting could identify trends and forecast growth.

Using the Relog.exe tool it's possible to manipulate log files, converting files between types; and if you're working with large log files, it's possible to narrow the time frame or extract some interesting counters.

Running PerfMon Remotely

Like many server management tools, an instance of PerfMon can be connected to a remote server for remote monitoring. This avoids the need to connect via Remote Desktop. To run PerfMon against a remote server, when adding counters, specify the target server name, replacing <Local computer> in the "Select counters from computer" drop-down (see Figure 9-7). In order to use PerfMon remotely, you'll need to be a local administrator on the target server, and the remote Registry service should be running.

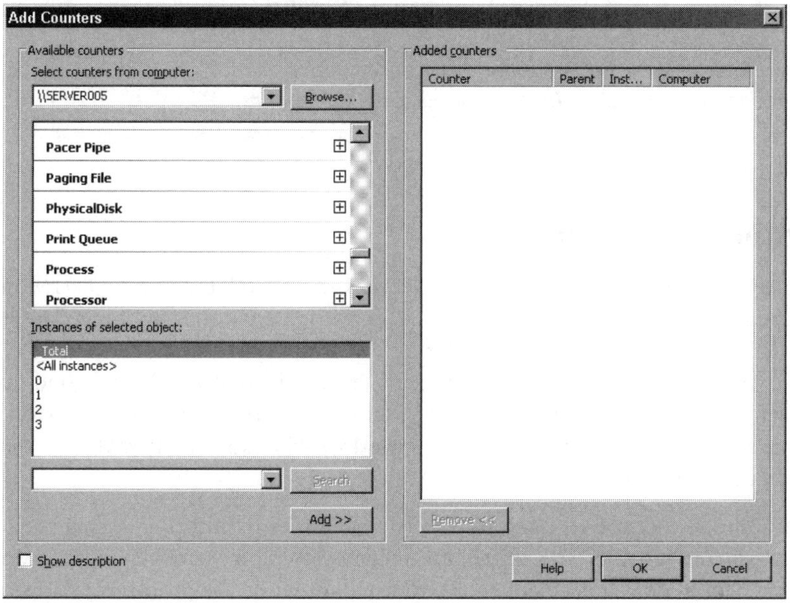

FIGURE 9-7

What to Be Aware of When Running PerfMon

There's no free lunch when monitoring servers. Any monitoring method you use adds overhead — the challenge is to minimize this overhead. When monitoring, consider performance implications with a view to reducing overhead and minimizing risk of the following:

➤ Making problems worse

➤ Affecting monitoring results

PerfMon counters are themselves updated by the application, regardless of whether they're being consumed by PerfMon. Therefore, the performance overhead with PerfMon is only usually encountered when polling (or sampling) these counters and when writing them to disk if a collector has been set up.

Not to panic you with running PerfMon — the overhead of monitoring normal servers with a typical workload is generally minimal. Performance often becomes a discussion point when monitoring servers operating in time-sensitive environments (e.g., trading platforms) or with servers suffering acute performance problems — where the monitoring overhead could tip the server over the edge.

Given that the act of reading PerfMon counters is the only real overhead of concern, you should consider network time and disk activity during monitoring.

> *One of the challenges with many performance problems is that we must obtain a PerfMon log to identify the cause of the problem. Without a log, engineers and managers can observe poor application performance and hypothesize about potential causes and remedies; but in order to diagnose the problem and take remedial action, we must obtain performance data. Sometimes you just have to accept the risk and overhead of running PerfMon because there simply is no better way to obtain performance data that will help solve a problem.*

The Impact of Running PerfMon

PerfMon is a lightweight tool and its impact on any given server is partly related to how PerfMon is configured and partly dependent on the workload of that server while PerfMon is running. To illustrate this scenario, consider two servers: Server A is suffering under heavy workload with 99% CPU utilization and poor disk performance, while server B currently runs with 20% CPU and good disk response times. In this scenario, it's likely that the impact to server A is greater because PerfMon could consume 1 or 2% of available CPU capacity, whereas the 1 or 2% added by PerfMon to server B will have negligible detectable impact.

Many organizations attempt to reduce the risk and impact to systems by monitoring during periods of low activity, such as during lunch or late afternoon, when user volumes are generally lower. However, this is usually the worst idea! It is essential to capture data while the problem is happening, not on either side of the problem (typically when concurrency is at its peak). Additionally, the worse the problem, the easier it is to spot. Often, problems are accentuated with user activity; if they're more likely to occur and be worse, then you have the best chance possible to capture a log containing the problem.

The following sections describe three key factors to consider when determining the impact of PerfMon: sample interval, number of counters, and disk performance.

Sample Interval

The sample interval controls the frequency with which PerfMon polls counters to read their values. The more often PerfMon samples, the greater the impact to the server and the more log data generated. The default is 15 seconds, which is usually fine when tracing for a few hours only; however, when tracing over longer periods, reducing the sample interval (frequency) for example from 30 seconds to 60 seconds will reduce the overhead of PerfMon and the size of the file generated.

Consider a situation where you have a busy system with a high workload but very short transactions — sampling every 60 seconds could miss many of these very short transactions. The sample interval can affect the shape of the data, so always be aware of it and the overall timeframe (i.e., a 5 minute sample during s peak period compared with 3 hours during a low activity period) for monitoring when reviewing performance logs, especially when looking at min, max, and average values. Occassionally problems can be caused by short, sharp spikes in resource utilization (such as CPU usage), and if the sample interval is set too high (its samples are taken infrequently) it is possible this problem may be overlooked. Take into account system activity and usage patterns to ensure that the log is representative of a typical workload.

Number of Counters

A consideration with a similar impact to sample interval is the number of counters. More counters result in a higher sampling cost and additional storage of those counter values. Most instance counters have a _TOTAL counter, which is a total of the individual counter instances combined. In some cases, such as for disk counters, this total has limited use, since often the details of each disk (instance) counter are required to identify disk performance problems. The total can hide actual problems because an average might give the appearance of a healthy system, masking disks with high activity.

Disk Performance

When capturing performance data using Data Collectors Sets, consider where the log files will be stored. The objective is to minimize the impact to SQL Server; log performance data to a file on disk (not a database); and, where available, use a disk that will not contend with any databases — i.e., avoid any disks where data or log files are stored.

PerfMon logs grow in a linear and predictable pattern (unlike SQL Profiler trace logs, which are workload dependent). For example, sampling 100 counters every 15 seconds for five minutes might create a 2MB PerfMon log file, so it would be reasonable to estimate that logging 100 counters for six hours would generate a 144MB log file. Generally, try to avoid capturing data to a system drive, as the implications should that drive fill up are much greater than if logging to a non-system drive.

Servers with Very Poor Performance

When capturing PerfMon logs on servers with acute performance problems, run PerfMon with consideration to reducing the overhead while still harvesting performance data. Here are some guidelines:

➤ Run PerfMon remotely.

➤ Reduce the sampling interval.

➤ Include as few counters as possible.

➤ Log to disk.

Common PerfMon Problems

In some cases you may have problems with PerfMon itself, specifically counters could be missing or aren't displayed correctly, or there could be problems connecting to servers remotely. This section contains a summary of some common issues and how to resolve them.

Using PerfMon on 64-bit Systems Using WOW

When running x64 Windows with x86 SQL Server, you're using Windows-on-Windows, or WOW, which means x64 Windows is emulating an x86 environment to host x86 SQL Server. If you're using IA64 processor architecture or x64 Windows and x64 SQL Server, this section isn't relevant to you since you're not using WOW.

When PerfMon runs on an x64 host, none of the counters pertaining to x86 applications are available because the x64 PerfMon cannot load x86 counters. You can overcome this limitation by launching the x86 version of the Microsoft Management Console (MMC), with the PerfMon snap-in. Run the following to launch the PerfMon x86 from an x64 Windows computer:

```
mmc /32 perfmon.msc
```

> *If you're running SQL Server in a Windows-on-Windows (WOW) mode, i.e., x86 SQL Server on x64 Windows, you'll be unable to run PerfMon remotely from other x64 machines because the remote Registry service is an x64 process; therefore, counters will only be visible to x86 processes.*

Remote Monitoring Failures

If you're trying to monitor remote servers and this is failing, the most likely cause is permissions problems. Here are some common causes:

➤ Ensure that the account is the local administrator on the target server.

➤ Confirm NetBIOS access to the target server.

➤ Ensure that the remote Registry service is running on the target server.

➤ Ensure that no local security policy or Active Directory group policy is restricting access.

Missing SQL Server Counters

It may happen that when you open PerfMon, there are no SQL Server counters available in the counter list. This problem occurs more often on clustered instances. If counters are missing, check the SQL Server error log and Windows Event Application log to determine whether any errors are logged regarding the failed counters. If there are no errors in either log, then you can unload the counters as follows:

```
unlodctr mssqlserver
```

Once the counters have been unloaded, verify the path to `sqlctr.ini` and use this next command to reload the counters:

```
lodctr C:\Program Files\Microsoft SQL Server\MSSQL10.1\MSSQL\Binn\sqlctr.ini
```

As with any change, test the process on a nonproduction server (even if there is no problem on the test server, you can still test the commands) to gain confidence in the process. If, after reloading the counters, they still aren't listed, you will need to rebuild them.

Missing Counters or Numbers Instead of Names

If when you attempt to add performance counters the list contains numbers instead of counter names, the counters could have been corrupted by a process incorrectly modifying the Registry. This problem can be overcome by rebuilding the counters. For details, see the Microsoft KB article 300956 at `http://support.microsoft.com/kb/300956`.

GETTING MORE FROM PERFORMANCE MONITOR

This section is intended to build on the introduction to PerfMon and provide specific counters and prescriptive guidance on acceptable counter thresholds. With so many counters available, it can be difficult to know which to use when; and no single counter is sufficient to make any decision or recommendation. More often, PerfMon is the better option with which to construct a picture of workload and resource consumption.

> *Your aim when troubleshooting is to narrow the focus as quickly as possible to home in on the problem. To do this effectively, use an iterative approach whereby each iteration has a specific objective or component, such as CPU, disk, or memory, to eliminate or identify as the cause. At the end of each data-gathering cycle and log analysis (an iteration), you should be able to determine with some certainty that a particular component of the solution has been ruled in or out of the problem scope.*

This section looks at hardware, operating system, and SQL Server bottlenecks, considering each major component in order of problem likelihood: memory, disk, and CPU. It also explores SQL Server performance counters to provide a plan for using PerfMon to identify specific SQL Server problem conditions.

Identifying SQL Server Bottlenecks

A bottleneck is any resource that significantly restricts database performance. There will always be bottlenecks of one kind or another — the important thing to avoid is any single component that significantly delays the entire transaction processing system. Identifying bottlenecks enables us to prioritize our troubleshooting; in the event of numerous problems, a clear and specific bottleneck provides an area of focus.

This section considers some different types of bottlenecks and offers some prescriptive guidance that can help identify resource contention. It's normal for an active database server to read from and write to disk lots where locking and blocking is part of normal usage patterns. However, a resource or component that consumes a significant portion of query completion time can cause a problem.

The responsiveness of SQL Server is closely related to overall server performance because query processing duration is heavily dependent on sufficient available memory, disk, and CPU performance. Since SQL Server is dependent on each of these resources, they're listed in likelihood of causing a problem, but each should be configured correctly and performing well to service SQL Server and provide optimal transaction throughput for the hardware.

Types of Bottleneck

Most bottlenecks can be categorized as one of two types: configuration-based bottlenecks or schema-based bottlenecks. Each bottleneck category can cause bottlenecks within each resource type (CPU, memory, and disk). Of course, not every performance problem (or bottleneck) will fit neatly into any model ever developed, but most seem to be either configuration-based or schema-based. Most server-wide or instance-wide bottlenecks tend to be configuration-based, whereas schema-based bottlenecks are database specific (since each database has its own schema).

Configuration-Based Bottlenecks

SQL Server doesn't require any specialized knowledge to install, and the default values in many scenarios are sufficient for most deployments. When performance and scalability are critical, you can make many optimizations, both to the operating system and to SQL Server. Knowing which to change and when is key to getting the most from the hardware and SQL Server itself. Quantifying the change through precise performance measurement is absolutely necessary to validate whether changes have made system performance better, worse, or had no effect at all. This before and after picture can be built using some core PerfMon counters to quantify system performance.

Always consider system performance in the context of workload and don't be tempted to compare performance data from two consecutive days without including data about system workload (such as Batches/Second for SQL Server).

Configuration-based bottlenecks include any operating system configuration, such as memory settings, including /3GB and /PAE in boot.ini; I/O performance tuning such as disk sector alignment; and HBA queue depth optimization. Additionally, there are many SQL Server configuration-based optimizations such as disk and log file placement, database auto-growth settings, and any sp_configure options.

Schema-Based Bottlenecks

Schema-based bottlenecks are application-specific, as they relate to the schema of a specific database (whereas configuration bottlenecks are server-wide or instance-wide). In most cases, the best time to optimize the schema is during application design because schema changes have the least impact on the application when the application is still under development. Schema-based bottlenecks illustrate why performance testing must be included as an integral part of software build projects, as it can be incredibly difficult to retro-fit performance to an application that's already live.

Schema-based bottlenecks include problems such as normalization issues, where the schema is either overnormalized, requiring denormalization, or not fully normalized, such as when tables contain duplicate data. Additional schema-based bottlenecks include missing or surplus indexes, missing statistics, and poor choice of a clustering key, such as using a GUID instead of an incrementing ID column.

Prescriptive Guidance

The guidance provided in this section includes details of interesting PerfMon counters to include when troubleshooting each resource type, and prescriptive advice for ensuring "healthy" counter values. Because the prescriptive guidance offered here cannot be exhaustive, you should use both the indicators presented and other evidence you gather before making a decision or recommendation to form an action plan. No single item of evidence is usually enough to form a reasonable decision: Plan to gather several aspects before you make any decision or change — always get a complete picture.

These values are experience based, and are unlikely to apply to every server indefinitely. However, they provide a reference point to begin troubleshooting, and will highlight any significant resource problems early in the troubleshooting cycle.

Each resource group section includes a table with details of the main PerfMon counters, a description of what to look for, and a value for a problem condition. A counter value that falls within the problem condition threshold warrants further investigation.

Investigating CPU Problems

The availability of CPU cycles to service SQL Server in a timely manner is critical to database server performance. Configuration-based CPU bottlenecks include the following:

➤ Hyperthreading

➤ Max degree of parallelism

➤ Cost threshold of parallelism

It's important to recognize the difference between *kernel mode* and *application mode* CPU consumption because this will provide an important and useful indicator when troubleshooting. This concept applies to both CPU and memory consumption.

Kernel mode refers to internal Windows operations in which the kernel has unrestricted access to system hardware, such as the full memory address range, external devices, and so on.

Application mode (also known as *user mode*) is responsible for everything else, including running applications such as SQL Server. All user mode applications access hardware resources through the executive, which runs in kernel mode. An application requiring disk I/O submits the request through the kernel mode executive, which carries out the request and returns results to the requesting user mode process.

CPU Performance Counters

SQL Servers suffering from performance problems caused by high CPU usage is one of the most frequently occurring performance problems. It can be easy to identify `sqlservr.exe` using Task Manager, but Table 9-4 describes counters that will provide further evidence to assist troubleshooting.

TABLE 9-4: Key CPU PerfMon Counters

COUNTER		WHAT TO LOOK FOR	PROBLEM CONDITION
Processor	% Processor Time	Percent of total time the CPUs are busy servicing productive requests	> 80%
Processor	% Privilege Time	Percent of total CPU time spent servicing kernel mode requests	> 30%
Process	% Processor Time (sqlservr)	Percent of total time SQL Server spent running on CPU (user mode + privilege mode)	> 80%
Process	% Privilege Time (sqlservr)	Percent of time SQL Server was executing in Privilege mode	> 30% of % Processor Time (sqlservr)

Common Causes of CPU Problems

The three common causes of high CPU conditions are:

➤ **Missing or Outdated Statistics:** The Query Optimizer is dependent on relevant statistics to determine a good execution plan — missing or outdated statistics could cause it to select a sub-optimal plan, causing excessive CPU consumption.

➤ **Missing Indexes:** A lack of useful indexes can result in a high-CPU condition. SQL Server is dependent on meaningful indexes to retrieve data efficiently, and missing indexes can often cause excessive CPU utilization. A lack of useful indexes can result in expensive operations such as hash joins and sorts that could otherwise be avoided with improved indexes.

➤ **Excessive Recompilations:** Poor plan reuse can cause a high-CPU condition whereby SQL Server consumes excessive CPU cycles while generating query plans. Recompilations can be caused by ad hoc or dynamic queries or by a lack of memory (procedure cache), causing plans to be dropped from cache.

Investigating Memory-Related Problems

SQL Server performance is closely related to the availability and performance of sufficient memory. SQL Server configuration-related memory settings include the following:

➤ SP_CONFIGURE:

➤ Min/max server memory

➤ AWE Enabled

➤ Min memory per query

➤ Windows:

➤ /3GB, /USERVA, /PAE

➤ Lock Pages in Memory privilege

Typically, using Windows Task Manager doesn't provide a representative measure of the memory consumed by SQL Server because Task Manager only reflects the buffer pool, and SQL Server makes memory allocations outside this space for objects such as extended stored procedures, linked servers, and the CLR. Additionally, when SQL Server is using AWE on 32-bit servers, Task Manager will not reflect the correct memory allocation.

Types of Memory Pressure

SQL Server can suffer from internal or external memory pressure, and understanding how to identify and troubleshoot each will enable more targeted troubleshooting.

External memory pressure occurs most often when SQL Server is running on a shared computer and several processes are competing for memory. In this situation, the Resource Monitor within the SQL Server Operating System (SQLOS) will receive a signal from Windows requesting SQL Server to reduce its committed memory. This will cause SQL Server to recalculate its target commit level, reducing it if required.

Internal memory pressure occurs when internal SQL Server resources compete with each other for memory. This is typically caused by SQL Server shrinking the buffer pool. Use the DBCC MEMORYSTATUS command to gain visibility of SQL Server memory consumption.

Virtual Address Space

Every Windows process has its own virtual address space (VAS), the size of which varies according to processor architecture (32-bit or 64-bit) and the operating system edition. The VAS is a fixed-size resource that can be exhausted, even on 64-bit computers, and even when there might be physical memory available.

Memory Performance Counters

Table 9-5 describes the PerfMon counters that are key to gaining visibility of memory availability and consumption.

TABLE 9-5: Key Memory PerfMon Counters

COUNTER		WHAT TO LOOK FOR	PROBLEM CONDITION
Memory	Available MB	Amount of free physical memory in MB; values below 100MB could indicate external memory pressure.	< 100MB
Memory	Pages/sec	A high value doesn't necessarily mean a problem. Review this counter if you suspect external memory pressure, and always consider it within the context of other memory counters.	> 500
Memory	Free System Page Table Entries	Page table entries are most likely to become depleted (i.e., a bottleneck) on x86 servers, particularly where /3GB or /USERVA switches are used in boot.ini.	< 5,000
Paging File	% Usage, % Usage Peak	Generally, workload increases demand for virtual address space (VAS), which increases demand for page filing. Heavy reliance on page file use is usually an indication of memory problems.	> 70%
MSSQL Buffer Manager	Page Life Expectancy	Duration, in seconds, that a data page resides in the buffer pool. A server with sufficient memory has high page life expectancy.	< 300 seconds
MSSQL Buffer Manager	Buffer Cache Hit Ratio	Percent of page requests satisfied by data pages from the buffer pool	< 98%
MSSQL Buffer Manager	Lazy Writes/sec	Number of times per second SQL Server relocates dirty pages from buffer pool (memory) to disk	> 20

Disk or Storage Problems

SQL Server read/write performance is closely related to the ability of Windows to retrieve and write data pages to disk efficiently. Chapter 4 is dedicated to correct storage configuration and tuning best practices. Efficient and timely data access is dependent on both configuration- and schema-based factors, such as data and log file sizing and placement, useful indexes, and index fragmentation.

Optimizing disk and storage performance can be a hugely complex and protracted exercise, often confused by terminology and logical abstractions that can make it hard to identify the root cause. However, regardless of storage hardware, disk layout, or path configuration, the only aspect of real interest is the time required to read from or write to disk because this is a great indicator of whether disk access performance is likely to cause SQL Server problems.

Typically, once disk access has been identified as a bottleneck, tools more specialized than PerfMon must be employed to detect bottlenecks (most SAN vendors provide performance monitoring tools).

Disk performance problems have wide and varied potential resolutions, including extensive disk reconfiguration, such as changing RAID level, disk group membership, and stripe size. You can also make many enhancements within SQL Server, including right-sizing data and log files; pre-allocating space; and, for very large databases, table partitioning. Table 9-6 describes the main disk-related PerfMon counters.

TABLE 9-6: Key Disk PerfMon Counters

COUNTER		WHAT TO LOOK FOR	PROBLEM CONDITION
Physical Disk	Avg. disk sec/Read	Average time in seconds to complete a read from disk	> 0.010 Sub-optimal > 0.020 Poor
Physical Disk	Avg. disk sec/Write	Average time in seconds to complete a write to disk	> 0.010 Sub-optimal > 0.020 Poor

SQL Server Performance Problems

Sometimes server hardware resources do not cause bottlenecks but application performance is still bad. In this situation, internal SQL Server resources can become exhausted or depleted. Table 9-7 represents the principal counters for monitoring internal SQL Server resources.

TABLE 9-7: Key SQL Server PerfMon Counters

COUNTER		WHAT TO LOOK FOR	PROBLEM CONDITION
MSSQL SQL Statistics	Batch Requests/sec	Number of T-SQL batches processed by SQL server. Higher is better. Useful for baseline and should be considered when making any comparisons.	> 1,000 Indicates a server with high activity

continues

TABLE 9-7 *(continued)*

COUNTER		WHAT TO LOOK FOR	PROBLEM CONDITION
MSSQL SQL Statistics	SQL Compilations/ sec	Number of batches requiring plan compilations per second. High compilations indicates either poor plan reuse or many ad hoc queries.	> 20% Batch Requests/sec
MSSQL SQL Statistics	SQL Recompilations/sec	Number of statement recompiles per second	> 20% Batch Requests/sec
MSSQL General Statistics	Processes Blocked	The number of currently blocked processes	Investigate when > 0
MSSQL Locks	Lock Waits/sec	Number of user requests waiting for locks, per second. Can be indicative of blocking.	> 0
MSSQL Locks	Lock Timeouts/sec	Number of lock timeouts per second. Anything greater than 1 should be investigated.	> 0
MSQQL Transactions	Free Space in Tempdb (KB)	Reports free space in Tempdb in KB	< 100MB

Wait Stats Analysis

SQL Server Wait Stats record the resource and time SQL Server spends waiting for each resource. A number of these wait types are exposed as PerfMon counters:

- ➤ Lock waits
- ➤ Log write waits
- ➤ Network I/O waits
- ➤ Non-page latch waits
- ➤ Page I/O latch waits
- ➤ Page latch waits

It may be easier to access these wait stats from the DMVs within SQL Server; however, collecting them as part of a system-wide data gathering exercise with PerfMon minimizes the logistics effort involved in collecting the data.

Getting a Performance Baseline

A performance baseline is simply a PerfMon log from a time frame representing "normal" performance, retained for future review. The PerfMon log should contain counters that provide a complete picture of hardware and SQL Server resources during a representative workload period.

The performance baseline can provide answers to questions that no person will be able to answer otherwise. When performance problems occur, the baseline will be available for comparison; and by mapping the SQL Server batch requests per second against other values, it will be possible to compare problem server activity/workload with the workload of a known good data capture.

The baseline should be kept current; otherwise, configuration changes or tuning optimizations could alter the output and invalidate any comparison. It's useful to get into the habit of taking a fresh baseline periodically. The frequency to create a baseline depends on the system purpose (i.e. is the business/ application cyclic) and the rate of change; generally speaking, the rule is the more changes (hardware, application, business logic stored in the database) the more frequently a baseline should be created. As a rule of thumb, it's useful to run a basic baseline for each server quarterly, unless there is a specific reason to do so more or less frequently (such as many changes or no changes within the environment).

GETTING STARTED WITH PERFORMANCE ANALYSIS FOR LOGS (PAL)

When faced with reviewing many gigabytes of PerfMon logs, it can be very time consuming and difficult to discern problems from noise generated by daily activity. Often the log analysis task involves knitting logs together to attempt to form a picture for forensic analysis. In the absence of a system baseline it can be difficult to highlight problem areas to focus on, as it can be easy to perceive either no problems or dozens of problems, any of which could be the root cause.

Performance Analysis for Logs is a tool created by engineers from the product support organization within Microsoft to automate log file analysis to provide rapid identification of problems within log files. PAL works using templates to analyze performance data and will flag values outside the acceptable range as determined in the templates.

PAL was designed to reduce the labor-intensive log analysis tasks and help engineers provide faster turnaround in log analysis. Since its original release PAL has been enhanced to include templates to analyze performance logs for many popular Microsoft server products, such as IIS, BizTalk, Exchange, Active Directory, and SQL Server. Templates are based on thresholds used by product support teams at Microsoft when troubleshooting customer problems. Using PAL simplifies the task of log analysis, providing a report that highlights key problem areas.

PAL uses templates and widely-tested thresholds that correlate performance data from multiple counters, which means reports provide a robust and reliable solution for log file analysis. However, there is always potential for unusual or outlying problems that have not been included or are out of scope of the templates. As such you should view PAL as a tool to assist troublehooting, not a complete solution to identify performance problems. PAL is not a replacement for good methodology and usual troubleshooting steps!

Templates and PAL

The PAL tool uses templates that consist of performance rules, each called an Analysis within the tool. System-wide Analyses include Processor, Memory, and Disk. These are present in the System Overview template as well as each of the product-specific templates.

An example Analysis from the Processor group is "Excessive Processor Use by Processes." This Analysis consists of a single PerfMon counter `\Process(*)\% Processor Time`. Two thresholds are specified to determine alert criteria and warning condition (which can be either Information, Warning, or Critical states) where the color and priority is also specified, as follows:

➤ **Significant Processor Use Suspected:** More than 60% CPU Utilization (warning — yellow, priority 50)

➤ **Excessive Processor Use Suspected:** More than 80% CPU Utilisation (critical — red, priority 100)

Within the SQL Server 2005 template there are also Analysis configured using more than one PerfMon counter to handle more complex conditions/ warnings. One such example can be found in the SQL Server: SQL Statistics group, where an Analysis is configured for SQL Compilations/ sec. This Analysis operates using the following two source counters:

➤ `SQLServer:SQL Statistics\Batch Requests/sec`

➤ `SQLServer:SQL Statistics\SQL Compilations/sec`

Using these two counters allows a ratio comparison of the number of compilations per second to the number of batches each second. The template threshold provides an alert if the ratio exceeds 1 compilation for every 100 batch requests per second.

The PAL release at time of writing includes the following templates for log analysis from SQL Server machines:

➤ SQL Server 2000

➤ SQL Server 2005

➤ SQL Server Replication

These templates provide a starting point for log analysis and thresholds, and Analysis can be edited and tuned to values meaningful within your environment.

Capturing PerfMon Logs

Using the PAL tool to successfully analyze performance logs is dependent on the source logs containing the right counters. Each analysis in the threshold file can consist of one or more performance counters. If any of the counters are missing PAL will skip analysis for the threshold and the report becomes less useful. To resolve this, ensure all counters required by the Analysis within PAL are gathered during data capture and the PAL tool can help with this.

The PAL tool can be used to export a PerfMon template file. The PerfMon template can then be used to capture the data required by PAL for log analysis. To use this feature, choose the Export to Perfmon Template File button. When saving the file, an information box is displayed notifying that the PerfMon counter does not support named instances. The PAL tool supports log analysis from named instances, but the template creation process does not because of the path setup for named instance counters.

This means if you are using named instances or failover clusters you will need to configure the PerfMon log to capture data the counters required (the HTM file containing the counters can be viewed in Internet Explorer for a complete list). This PerfMon file export creates a file with an HTM extenstion that can be drag/ dropped to PerfMon to start data capture immediately.

Using PAL for Log Analysis

PAL is available from Microsoft's Open Source community project, CodePlex. PAL works on computers running Windows XP SP2, Windows Vista, and Windows Server 2003 or newer. PAL requires LogParser 2.2 as a pre-requisite, and if setup detects LogParser isn't installed the installer opens a web browser window to the download page on `www.microsoft.com`. LogParser requires Microsoft Office Web Components (OWC) 11. This is because LogParser uses the OWC to generate charts and graphs for reporting. Since the OWC were only released in 32-bit versions, the PAL tool is currently only supported on 32-bit machines.

> *There is no need to install the PAL on a production server. Performance analysis is resource intensive; therefore, to avoid impacting performance of a production server, capture the logs on the server suffering the problem and copy these to a desktop or test server for analysis with PAL.*

The PAL User Interface (UI) requires .NET Framework v2.0; however, all functionality of the PAL tool is available from the command line. Therefore, the UI is optional and there is no need to install .NET 2.0 if the UI isn't required. The PAL tool itself is a Visual Basic Script (VBS) and the UI provides a convenient way to construct the command line with parameters to start the tool with the desired settings.

1. Download and install the latest release of PAL and LogParser (linked from the PAL homepage on codeplex) `www.codeplex.com/PAL`.

2. Once installed, launch PAL from the Start menu, and the Welcome page will appear as seen in Figure 9-8.

3. Select the Counter Log tab and browse to select the PerfMon log illustrated in Figure 9-9.

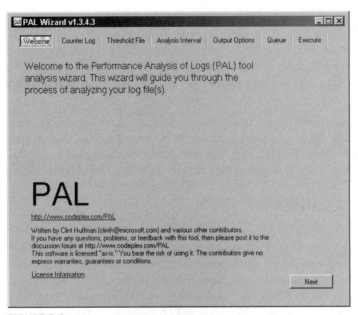

FIGURE 9-8

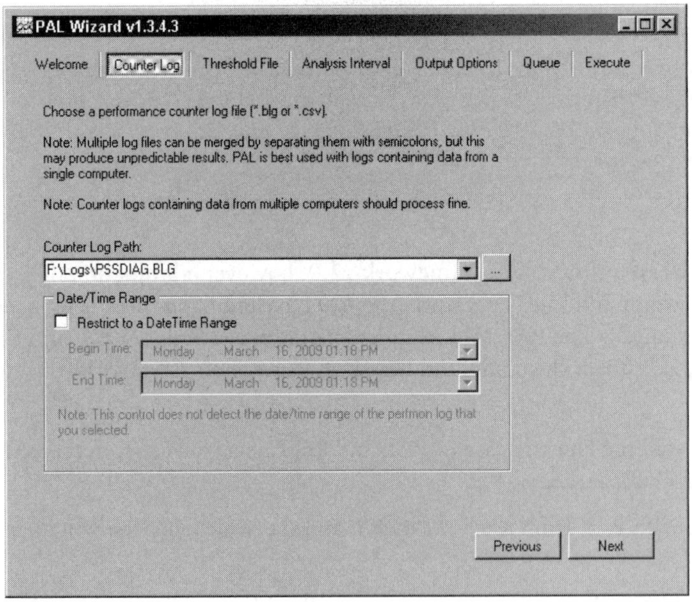

FIGURE 9-9

4. Click Next or select the Threshold File option from the top menu bar. Select the required Threshold File from the drop-down selection box. At time of writing the current release of PAL doesn't have a SQL Server 2008 template, so the SQL Server 2005 template provides the closest match (these templates can be configured and adapted as required). This is shown in Figure 9-10.

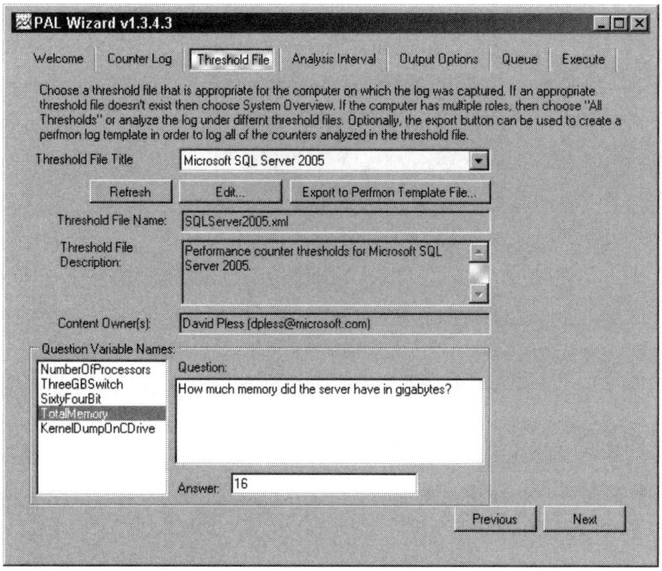

FIGURE 9-10

5. There are five further questions to answer from the Variables dialog at the bottom left of the Thresholds screen. Respond to these questions to provide output with thresholds tailored to the server on which the PerfMon log was captured. Ensure that you populate logical cores, not physical sockets, when choosing the number of CPUs.

6. Click Next, or choose the Analysis Interval menu item. Use this tab to control the time interval used by PAL to sample log files for analysis.

> *The default (Auto) uses 30 time slices. For a log file captured in 30 minutes, the log file will be sampled every 1 minute and a 60 minute log file will be sampled every 2 minutes. Be careful when choosing All from the drop-down box, because doing so causes PAL to analyze every single data point in the log file (this could be very many) and analysis will be lengthy. Generally, leave this set to Auto unless you have a specific reason to change it.*

7. Click Next or choose the Output Options item from the menu bar. Here it's possible to control the output types and location. The default settings are usually fine unless something specific is required.

8. Move to the Execute tab, where usually the default settings are adequate. Click Finish to begin log analysis, which launches the script shown in Figure 9-11.

Once the PAL tool has finished, an MHT file will be displayed in Internet Explorer containing the results. A recent 254MB log file analyzed by PAL on a quad-core computer took around 45 minutes to analyze. Figure 9-12 shows the report.

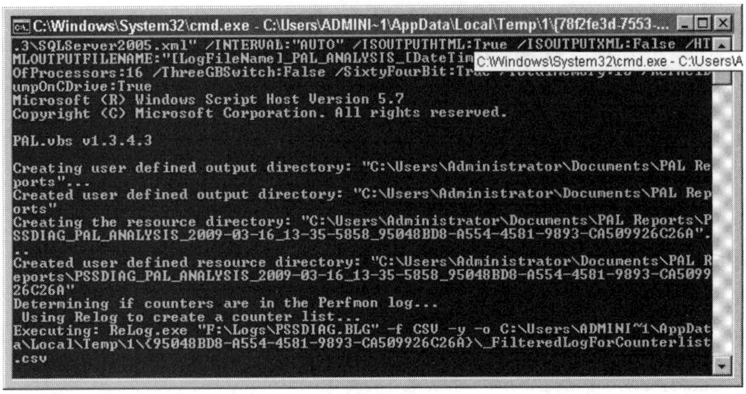

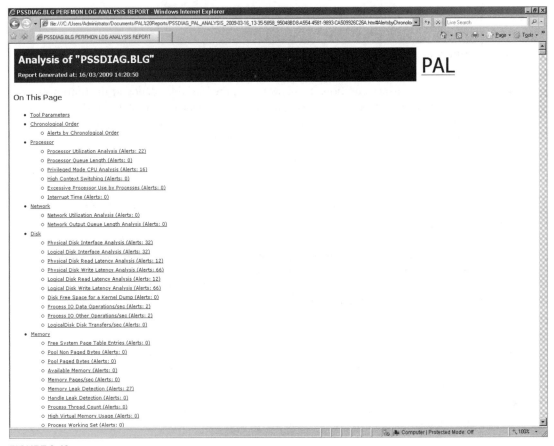

FIGURE 9-11

FIGURE 9-12

The report produced by PAL analyzes performance metrics for the key hardware resources: Processor, Network, Disk, Memory, and SQL Server. The report is color-coded to help identify problem areas more quickly. Figure 9-13 shows the output for a particular server suffering a performance problem, although the figure is printed in black and white. Three alert levels are displayed: Disk C is green (OK); Disk E is yellow (warning — spike of more than 25ms for disk access); Disk G is red (critical — disk responsiveness is very slow, more than 24ms).

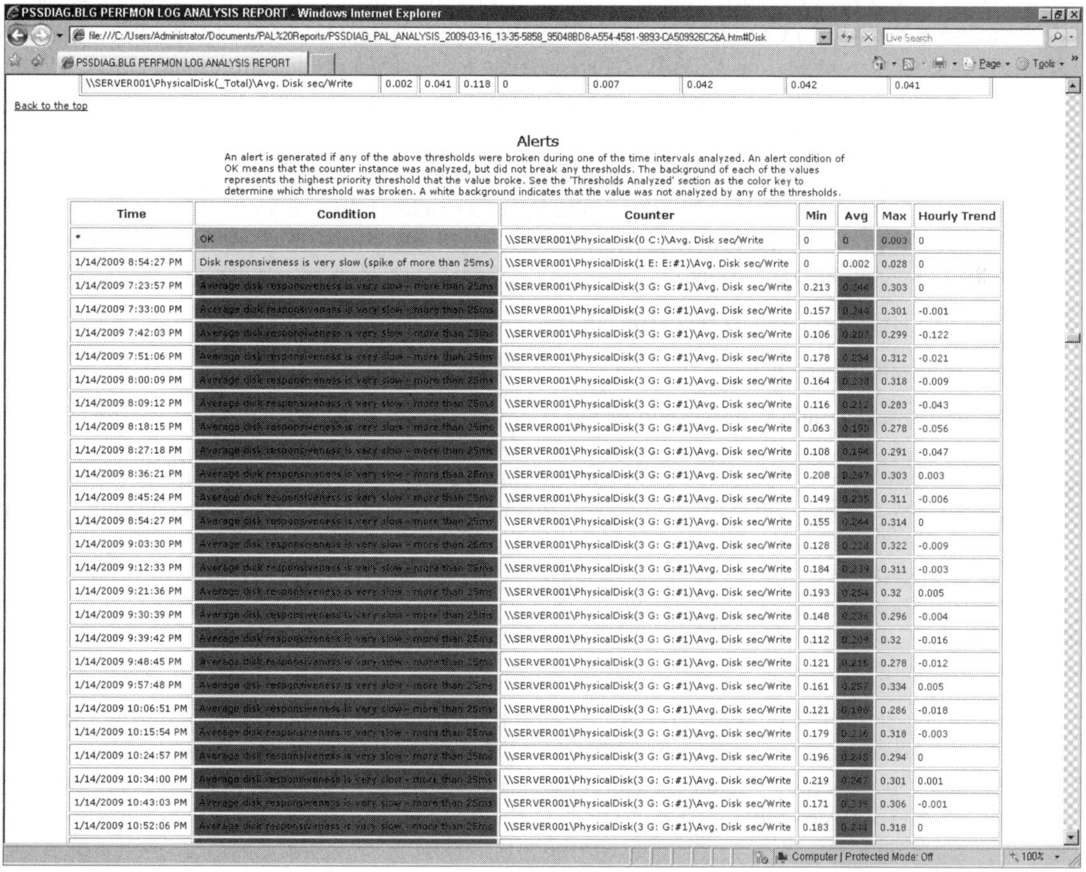

FIGURE 9-13

OTHER PERFMON LOG ANALYSIS TOOLS

This section of the chapter evaluates common tools for managing, manipulating, and interpreting PerfMon logs. Since PerfMon logs can be saved or converted to comma-separated value (CSV) files, you have many options for data analysis, including loading the file into SQL Server, analysis with Microsoft Excel, and almost any other data manipulation tool.

Using SQL Server to Analyze PerfMon Logs

Analyzing large quantities of performance logs with SQL Server can be a useful solution when data analysis through other methods could be cumbersome and labor intensive. The data load process from CSV files could simply make use of the ad hoc Import/Export Wizard launched from SQL Server Management Studio; alternately, this process could be automated and scheduled.

SQL Server can't read the native Binary Log File (BLG) file type, so PerfMon logs should either be written to a log file as a CSV file type, or use the Relog utility to convert the file post-capture (more detail to follow) from BLG to CSV. It is also possible for PerfMon to log directly to a SQL Server database through a DSN, although additional overhead is associated with this process, which can be avoided by logging to a file.

Analyzing PerfMon logs from within a database has the benefit of data access through the familiar language of T-SQL, meaning problems should be easier to identify and you can write queries looking for specific problem conditions. In the following example, three counters could be combined to identify a low-memory condition:

➤ Available memory less than 100MB

➤ Page life expectancy less than 60 seconds

➤ Buffer cache hit ratio less than 98%

If the PerfMon logs have already been imported into SQL Server, the following query could be used to identify any instance during the data capture window when the low memory condition existed:

```
SELECT *
FROM subset
WHERE Mem_Avail_Bytes < 1000000
AND Buff_Mgr_PLE < 60
AND Buff_Cache_Hit_Ratio < 98
```

This example should be modified to reflect the table and column names specified during the data import, of course, and you can see how the concept could be adapted for any number of scenarios. Additionally, this method could be used to manage performance data across a number of servers, and Reporting Services could be used to present the data.

Combining PerfMon Logs and SQL Profiler Traces

A feature first available in SQL Server 2005 was the capability to combine PerfMon logs with SQL Profiler traces. Using Profiler to combine logs in this way enables you to view T-SQL code that's running on the server, combined with the hardware impact of running the code, such as high CPU or low memory.

The combined view presents a time axis, which can then be navigated by selecting a moment when a CPU spike occurred; the Profiler trace automatically relocates to the T-SQL that was executing at the time of the spike.

Using Relog

Relog is a command line tool that can be used to create new log files with a different sampling rate or a different file format from existing PerfMon logs. Relog was first included in Windows XP and can be useful when handling large logs or in situations where many surplus counters are included. Additionally, in some cases a log may contain data for many hours but the time frame of interest is much shorter. Relog can assist in extracting the interesting time window for easier analysis. Table 9-8 summarizes the parameters you can use with Relog.

TABLE 9-8: Relog Parameters

OPTION	DESCRIPTION
-?	Display context-sensitive help
-a	Append output to the existing binary file
-c <path [path ...]>	Counters to filter from the input log
-cf <filename>	File listing performance counters to filter from the input log. The default is all counters in the original log file.
-f <CSV|TSV|BIN|SQL>	Output file format
-t <value>	Only write every nth record into the output file. The default is to write every record.
-o	Output file path or SQL database
-b <dd/MM/yyyy HH:mm:ss[AM|PM]>	Begin time for the first record to write into the output file
-e <dd/MM/yyyy HH:mm:ss[AM|PM]>	End time for the last record to write into the output file
-config <filename>	Settings file containing command options
-q	List performance counters in the input file
-y	Answer yes to all questions without prompting

The following section provides three examples of the scenarios and syntax for Relog.

Extracting Performance Data for a Specific Timeframe

This technique can be useful when using PerfMon to log over many hours or days. Were a problem to occur at 10:30 a.m. on March 15, it would be useful to extract the time frame from 10:00 a.m. to 11:00 a.m. to provide a manageable log size, without losing any data points, as shown in the following example:

```
Relog Server001_LOG.blg -b 15/03/2009 10:00:00 -e 15/03/2009 11:00:00 -o
Server001_LogExtract.blg
```

Extracting Specific Performance Counters

When monitoring tools (or sometimes other engineers) gather logs containing extraneous counters; you can extract specific counters for analysis using Relog. The Relog parameter -c enables a subset of counters to be specified. In the following example, just the memory counters would be extracted to a new log file:

```
Relog Server001_Log.blg -c "\Memory\*" -o Server001Memory_Log.blg
```

Further, it is possible to perform more complex filtering by passing Relog a text file containing a subset of counters from the original performance log. The following command creates a new log file containing only counters included in the filter file (CounterList.txt in the example) from the original log:

```
Relog Server001_Log.blg -cf CounterList.txt -o Server001Overview_Log.blg
```

The preceding example requires `CounterList.txt` to contain a single counter per line with those counters to be extracted.

Converting Log Files to New Formats

PerfMon creates log files in a binary log format (BLG) by default. In some situations it can be desirable to convert a performance log to a new format to enable applications other than PerfMon to read the log. For example, this can be useful when importing the data to SQL Server or analyzing performance in Excel. The following example shows how to convert the BLG file to a CSV file:

```
Relog Server001_Log.blg -f CSV -o Server001_Log.csv
```

Using LogMan

LogMan is a command line tool used to create and manage PerfMon logs. The LogMan tool can be used to schedule the starting and stopping of logs. This can be a useful alternative to using the Windows AT scheduler or the scheduler functions available within PerfMon. The great benefit of using LogMan is that you can centrally start and stop performance monitoring.

Using LogMan it's possible to define a data collector and copy that collector to multiple servers from a single, central location. To use LogMan, here's the syntax:

```
logman [create|query|start|stop|delete|update|import|export] [options]
```

Table 9.9 describes the parameters used to control LogMan.

The following example creates a collector named DBOverviewLog, which contains all Processor, Memory, and LogicalDisk counters with a sample interval of 30 seconds, and a max log file size of 254MB:

```
Logman create counter "DBOverviewLog" -si 30 -v nnnn -max 254 -o
"D:\logs\DBOverview" -c "\Processor(*)\*" "\Memory(*)\*" "\LogicalDisk(*)\*"
```

TABLE 9-9: LogMan Usage

VERB	DESCRIPTION
Create	Create a new data collector.
Query	Query data collector properties. If no name is given, all data collectors are listed.
Start	Start an existing data collector and set the start time to manual.
Stop	Stop an existing data collector and set the stop time to manual.
Delete	Delete an existing data collector.
Update	Update properties of an existing data collector.
Import	Import a data collector from an XML file.
Export	Export a data collector to an XML file.

Table 9-10 shows the four options available with LogMan, including the useful -s parameter, which enables the collector to be created, started, and stopped on remote computers.

TABLE 9-10: LogMan Options

OPTION	DESCRIPTION
`-?`	Display context-sensitive help.
`-s <computer>`	Perform the command on the specified remote system.
`-config <value>`	Settings file containing command options
`-ets`	Send commands to event trace sessions directly without saving or scheduling.

Using LogMan it's possible to script a collection for a baseline dataset from an entire application environment. This could be incredibly useful when performing performance testing, baselining application performance, or troubleshooting live problems.

Using LogParser

LogParser is a simple to use yet powerful tool for log file analysis, popularized for analyzing logs from IIS web servers. LogParser can be used to examine a range of log types, and can provide output in various forms. Once installed, LogParser also allows pseudo-SQL querying of log files! This can be great when searching Windows event logs, IIS logs, or PerfMon logs.

LogParser is part of the Windows Resource Kit and is available as a standalone download from www.microsoft.com. PerfMon logs must be converted to CSV (using ReLog) prior to analysis with LogParser.

SUMMARY

PerfMon is often the first choice tool when troubleshooting performance problems since it can be used to capture system-wide performance data and gain visibility of server behavior with little overhead. PerfMon can be useful in narrowing the problem scope and determining whether hardware performance is a major bottleneck.

This chapter includes details on when and how to capture a system baseline and sample values that can be used to identify specific resources as problem areas.

Performance Analysis for Logs (PAL) is a tool to reduce time and effort required to analyze PerfMon log files. The tool uses customizable templates with predefined values to build a report containing color-coded alerts to help quick assessment of problems. Problem areas are highlighted based on green (ok), yellow (warning), and red (critical) status.

10

Tracing SQL Server with SQL Trace and Profiler

WHAT'S IN THIS CHAPTER

- ➤ An overview of why tracing is important
- ➤ Deep look into the Architecture of SQL Trace
- ➤ Comprehensive coverage of the Tracing views, functions, and stored procedures
- ➤ An extended analysis of Security and SQL Trace
- ➤ Profiler, Profiler, and more Profiler

Profiler is a GUI; SQL Trace is the juice. That's the message for this chapter. SQL Trace is the architecture upon which server-side tracing and Profiler are built. Those who know and understand how SQL Trace works use server-side tracing to minimize the impact on their production servers. Profiler is a very useful tool and is a great option for ad-hoc performance analysis. However, it does tend to get used in situations where it should not be used.

In this chapter you will learn all about SQL Trace. Once you understand its architecture you'll come to appreciate the subtleties between server-side tracing and Profiler. Both methods have their advantages and disadvantages as you will soon see.

This chapter is going to take a deep dive into the guts of SQL Trace. You will learn all about its strengths and weaknesses. You will also learn much about security issues that arise from Profiler traces. The objective is for you to really understand the best ways to use both Profiler and server-side tracing so that ultimately you also understand your SQL Server.

TRACING 101

Before diving headfirst into the guts of SQL Trace it's probably worth stepping back and asking some fundamental questions about why SQL Server provides us with the ability to trace in the first place. Anything you add to a system is an overhead and will consume resources — resources that could be spent servicing requests for data. This section then covers the basic why, when, where, what, and how questions of tracing and remind ourselves of its importance in our role as DBAs.

Why Trace

As a DBA, SQL Trace is one of the most important tools in your arsenal. Without it you wouldn't have a clue about what was happening to your SQL Server. Your insight would be restricted to the performance counters found in Performance Monitor (PerfMon) and any information you might be able to glean from the dynamic management views (DMV). Therefore, you would be able to see how much memory or CPU was being consumed but not which queries were being run, their durations, or frequencies. At least you wouldn't be able to see that very easily. SQL Trace gives you a real-time, run-time insight into SQL Server without having to use Trace Flags or any black magic. I find not having to resort to a SQL Server Shaman to tell me what is going on with my SQL Server to be a great bonus! The fact that this information is very easy to gain access to is also a great plus. Therefore, a trace should be one of the first diagnostic options you should turn to when faced with a problem.

When to Trace

Now you understand the why; then the next question to ask yourself is when. When should you be tracing my SQL Server? In production I would say: All the time!

Imagine your business sells children's shoes. Your business is very popular, and you have measured that, on average, your website sales volume is $100,000 an hour. However, one day the SQL Server encounters a problem and the site is effectively down. Without having a trace running you have minimal information to go on to diagnose your issue. How long does the site have to be down before that trace would have paid for itself? On modern hardware it could be as little as 5 minutes. A slightly more powerful server (if it is required at all) costs a fraction of the business of a website outage. To compound the situation without the trace you might not be able to diagnose the problem. Consequently you then have to set up your trace and wait for it to happen again. In other words you actually need your problem to re-occur to find out what the first fault was. Rather than one outage of an hour ($100,000 cost to the business) you now have two outages ($200,000). Now that the trace is up you can monitor your SQL Server and pro-actively look out for anomalies. Clearly then, tracing the activity of your SQL Server *and analyzing the results* is a key part of the DBA role.

Where to Trace

The beauty of tracing is that it can help you in different ways depending on where you are in the product life-cycle. In development for example a .NET developer can use Profiler to make sure his calls to the stored procedures are getting through to the database. Whereas a development DBA might also be running a trace to see what calls the same developer is making. By running a trace the DBA can answer the following questions:

➤ How many calls are being made to the database?

➤ How long are the calls taking?

➤ Are the calls synchronous or asynchronous in nature?

➤ Has the developer used stored procedures or are the calls all ad-hoc SQL statements?

The information collected might indicate facets of the design choices made during development, if there are no stored procedure calls, for example, that might indicate that the data access layer is using a persistence framework such as Entity Framework or nHibernate. It might therefore be a good idea, given the dynamic generation of T-SQL from such frameworks, to keep an even closer eye on performance as the DBA has no real control on what queries will be issued to the database.

In my experience you will reap huge dividends from keeping a close eye on what is happening in the development cycle and discover early on any performance issues.

Likewise if you have integration or system test and UAT environments you should also be running traces there as well. However, in these environments, rather than looking at a single page or user you might be looking at an applications performance. Why might you do this? Well what if the SQL Server in production was host to many applications. You might need to benchmark the resources consumed and for that you'd more than likely use PerfMon, but what if you needed to see why the CPU suddenly spiked during a test? Having a trace running will help you understand what caused that spike.

What to Trace

The SQL Trace architecture is present to answer three types of questions. The first, as you have seen, relates principally to performance. SQL Server can tell you via SQL Trace what was being executed when and by whom. The "by whom" part of the last sentence leads me nicely into the second type of question: The "what has changed" question.

SQL Trace captures lots of information relating to change. It can answer the "who accessed the system and changed a table" question but also the "who changed the permissions for a given user" question as well. Using SQL Trace you can build your own auditing solution.

The third type of question is the "what went wrong" question. SQL Trace enables you to track errors and warnings and can guide you to answer some problems in your solutions. You can get some of this information from the SQL log or the windows event log. However, the nice bit about capturing this data in SQL Trace is that it makes it easy to see those errors *in context*. Knowing that a certain stored procedure had just started prior to an exception being raised may be critical to diagnosing a fault or issue.

How to Trace

There are only two ways to trace information out of SQL Server and both of these methods use the SQL Trace architecture. The first method is to use Profiler and the second method is to build and execute a server-side trace.

Profiler is a graphical user interface (GUI) which you can use to interactively build and execute a tracing session. You can select any combination of events and SQL Trace will return them to the GUI so you can see what is happening in real time. Whilst the basics of setting up a trace in Profiler won't be covered in this book, it does also offer lots of extended functionality, and these more advanced aspects of Profiler are indeed covered in this book.

The server-side trace however is the main event, in my opinion, when it comes to tracing SQL Server, especially in production environments. You create server-side trace by executing a number of system stored procedures against SQL Server. The server-side trace then writes the events that you have asked it to capture to a file on the file system. For auditing style traces you should always use a server-side trace. You will discover why when you look at the architecture of SQL Trace.

THE ARCHITECTURE OF SQL TRACE

The best way to understand SQL Trace is to think of SQL Server in terms of any mature application. All well written applications instrument the application source code by writing out tracing messages. This helps developers understand what code is executing at a given point. This information is invaluable for understanding what was going on when something unexpected happened.

As important as knowing what these events are, developers also need to know and understand the sequence of those events. This makes the process of debugging much easier. It certainly helps if you know the path the code took by examining the sequence of the events.

Ideally, a developer will normally also want to reduce the events being raised to only those they are interested in. Otherwise the number of events being raised on the server might result in them having to find a needle in a haystack. This can be done by supplying additional information to the trace or by putting conditional logic into the tracing code. This helps reduce the volume of trace information — possibly down to the actions of a single user, for example.

In SQL Server, this tracing information is implemented as a series of *events*. The various components of the database engine are collectively known as *event producers*.

Producing events can be expensive. You only want events to be raised if someone has said that they are interested in receiving them. If no one is interested, then what is the point of raising them? In a regular custom application, this might be a setting in a configuration file. This setting might even have a verbosity flag so you can tune the level at which the tracing information is created.

SQL Server provides the *trace controller*, shown in Figure 10-1. The trace controller component tells the rest of the database engine, via a bitmap, which events are being requested by a tracer. Don't worry about who that tracer might be right now — suffice it to say it could be you, using Profiler; it could be me, using a server-side trace; or it could be SQL Server itself. If someone, anyone, has an open trace running and wants a given event, then the database engine will generate that event when it occurs. An open trace equates to a *trace session*.

Once the event has been generated by the event producer, the trace controller decides what to do with it. The event is held in a queue and synchronized while the trace controller determines what it needs to do with it. Because the trace controller knows what events each trace has requested, it passes the complete event down the line to each trace session that has asked for it.

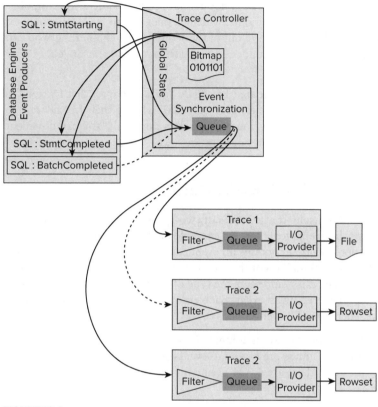

FIGURE 10-1

The trace session can now act on the trace data it has received from the controller. Each event received contains a complete set of columns which can be used to further filter the data that is captured in the trace. For example, you might be interested in only those events generated by the actions of a single user, consequently you may have created a filter to only keep events from a specific SPID. In addition to filtering the rows, this step also removes any columns that have not been requested to be kept.

You might be asking yourself why SQL Server filters the columns in the trace session rather than earlier in the process. Simply put, by deferring this process to session filtering, SQL Server ensures that it only needs to track which events the sessions are interested in and raise the event once and nothing more. The tracing session knows which columns have been requested and can safely remove the others. Remember the session has its own copy of the event. A tracing session cannot adversely affect other tracing sessions.

After the events have been filtered, the event can be sent to the *I/O provider* for the trace. The I/O provider is the determining factor for the endpoint of the trace event. The event is either written to a file or sent to a rowset provider, where it is consumed by an application such as Profiler.

It's worth pointing out that the consumer of trace data doesn't have to be Profiler. You can, of course, build your own, using the built-in object model, which enables you to build your own tracing applications. Details about this object model are out of the scope of this chapter, but you can find all the information you need to get started at `http://msdn.microsoft.com/en-us/library/ms162565.aspx`.

An example of a custom tracing application is the free Trace File Source Adapter that Darren Green and Allan Mitchell created for SQL Server Integration Services (SSIS). Using their free adapter for reading trace files, you can process them any way you like in a data flow task. You can download a copy of this source adapter at `http://sqlis.com/post/Trace-File-Source-Adapter.aspx`.

EVENT CLASSIFICATION AND HIERARCHIES

Event data is classified by a mini-hierarchy that consists of two levels. The top level is the *event category*, which logically groups the events together. An example might be locks or stored procedures. Note that there is no root level that contains all event categories. There are 21 different categories in SQL Server 2008. The second level of the hierarchy reflects the events themselves and is known as the *event class*. The event class represents the type of event that can be traced and contains all the columns that can be reported by an event. Each event class belongs to a single category in a parent-child relationship. There are 180 event classes in the database engine.

As I have just mentioned events are *bound* to event columns to form the event class. There is a distinct list of 66 event columns. Event columns are *bound* to events according to whether they are applicable to the event or not. In total, there are 4,304 permissible *bindings* between events and event columns.

An event class can also be sub-classified. An *event subclass* consists of a *subclass name* and a *subclass value*. An event subclass is grouped together by the event column and the event class to create a unique list of permissible names and values for an event column. The event subclass is then bound to the event class as part of the column binding process. Some event subclasses have the same names and sometimes even have the same values, so it looks as though they have been repeated. You must look at the context for the sub-classification. Each event and column combination that wishes to use a sub-classification must create its own list of subclass names and values. In other words it is a different sub-classification even though the names are the same. To determine the correct list of sub-classifications you must know both the event class to be raised *and* the column that is subject to the sub-classification. Take a look at Figure 10-2 for a graphical example of how event categories, event classes, the binding, and the subclass all fit together.

> *Although there may be many event subclasses with the same name they may not have the same value associated with them. Look at the Authenticate subclass name as an example. For the "Audit Server Operation Event" event class it uses the value 4 for the subclass in the* `EventSubClass` *column. However, for the "Audit Database Operation Event" it uses the subclass value 3 in the* `EventSubClass` *column.*

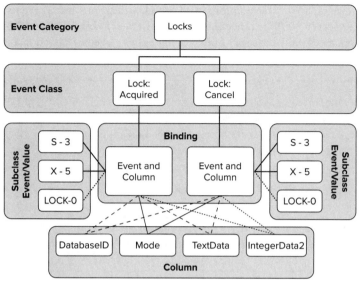

FIGURE 10-2

Happily, you can use catalog views to access this information. There is one view for each of the six grey boxes seen in Figure 10-2 above. Notice how the binding box wires everything together. The `sys.trace_event_bindings` view holds the many-to-many relationships between events and event columns to form the event class. Let's look at how the views can be brought together:

```
SELECT    cat.name            AS category_name
         ,ev.name             AS event_name
         ,col.name            AS column_name
         ,col.is_filterable   AS column_is_filterable
         ,col.max_size        AS column_max_size
         ,col.[type_name]     AS column_type_name
         ,sub.subclass_name   AS subclass_name
         ,sub.subclass_value  AS subclass_value
FROM      sys.trace_categories cat
JOIN      sys.trace_events ev
ON        cat.category_id    = ev.category_id
JOIN      sys.trace_event_bindings bi
ON        bi.trace_event_id  = ev.trace_event_id
JOIN      sys.trace_columns col
ON        bi.trace_column_id = col.trace_column_id
LEFT JOIN sys.trace_subclass_values sub
ON        sub.trace_column_id = bi.trace_column_id
AND       sub.trace_event_id  = bi.trace_event_id
ORDER BY cat.name
         ,ev.name
         ,col.name
         ,sub.subclass_value
```

This code is available for download at Wrox.com: CH10 Trace View.sql

This is the full list of categories, events, applicable columns, and sub-classifications for all events. If you run this query on your SQL Server 2008 instance it should return 9,477 rows! Figure 10-3 shows a sample of this output from the T-SQL category and `StmtRecompile` event, in particular to illustrate the information available.

6	SQL:StmtRecompile	EventSequence	0	8	bigint	NULL	NULL
7	SQL:StmtRecompile	EventSubClass	1	4	int	Schema changed	1
8	SQL:StmtRecompile	EventSubClass	1	4	int	Statistics changed	2
9	SQL:StmtRecompile	EventSubClass	1	4	int	Deferred compile	3
10	SQL:StmtRecompile	EventSubClass	1	4	int	Set option change	4
11	SQL:StmtRecompile	EventSubClass	1	4	int	Temp table changed	5
12	SQL:StmtRecompile	EventSubClass	1	4	int	Remote rowset changed	6
13	SQL:StmtRecompile	EventSubClass	1	4	int	For browse permissions changed	7
14	SQL:StmtRecompile	EventSubClass	1	4	int	Query notification environment changed	8
15	SQL:StmtRecompile	EventSubClass	1	4	int	PartitionView changed	9
16	SQL:StmtRecompile	EventSubClass	1	4	int	Cursor options changed	10
17	SQL:StmtRecompile	EventSubClass	1	4	int	Option (recompile) requested	11
18	SQL:StmtRecompile	EventSubClass	1	4	int	Parameterized plan flushed	12
19	SQL:StmtRecompile	EventSubClass	1	4	int	Test plan linearization	13
20	SQL:StmtRecompile	EventSubClass	1	4	int	Plan affecting database version changed	14
21	SQL:StmtRecompile	GroupID	1	4	int	NULL	NULL

FIGURE 10-3

Clearly, the event subclass for a statement recompile can have one of 14 permissible values, which can be used for diagnosing the cause of the recompile.

SQL TRACE CATALOG VIEWS

In the previous section you saw and queried the majority of the tracing catalog views. However, in some respects, that section missed the most important view: `sys.traces`. This is the view that actually shows you the list of trace definitions on the server. All the other tracing views are present to provide the metadata, but `sys.traces` shows the actual object definitions of user-defined and system-defined traces.

This section takes a more in-depth look at the information provided by `sys.traces` before reviewing the purpose and applicability of the other views.

sys.traces

This is the catalog view to see all traces that have been configured against the SQL Server. A trace will appear in this view when a SQL trace definition has been created using `sp_trace_create`. A server-side trace is first created with a status of "stopped."

The reason for creating the status in a "stopped" state is simple. `sp_trace_create` only creates the trace definition, which in itself is much like a container — at this point the trace hasn't been configured to request events to be sent to it, so there is no point in starting this trace yet. SQL Trace stored procedures are covered later in the chapter.

The stopped state is mentioned here because the status of the trace determines its visibility in `sys.traces`. A trace is visible when in two states: stopped or started. However, using `sp_trace_setstatus` you can also close the trace. As soon as the trace is "closed" the definition is removed from the system.

Therefore, it is no longer visible — and to all intents and purposes that trace definition never existed. Table 10-1 shows the columns of the sys.traces view.

> *If you want to audit the creation and deletion of traces on a SQL Server, you can always create a trace to do this yourself. You can't use triggers on system catalogs, and so creating a trace is your best option here. You can see the mechanics of creating a trace definition with Profiler in the "Exporting a Trace Definition" section toward the end of this chapter.*

TABLE 10-1: Columns of sys.traces

COLUMN NAME	DATA TYPE	DESCRIPTION
ID	Int	This is the trace ID. You need to know this value when modifying the trace — for example, adding events to a trace definition using sp_trace_addevent.
Status	Int	The current state of the trace. 0 = Stopped (value on creation) 1 = Running Change this value with sp_trace_setstatus.
Path	Nvarchar (260)	Nullable value that shows the path to the trace file when tracing to a file. Null when trace is using a rowset provider. 260 values are possible, as this is the maximum character length for a file path in Windows.
Max_Size	Bigint	Nullable value that highlights the maximum size of a trace file. If the trace has been configured to *roll over,* it will grow to this size first and then create another file.
Stop_Time	Datetime	Date and time to stop running a trace
Max_Files	Int	Maximum number of files that a trace can generate. This is only used in conjunction with *rollover.*
Is_rowset	Bit	Identifies a trace definition as one using the rowset provider. Profiler creates trace definitions using the rowset provider when tracing interactively. 0 = File Provider Trace 1 = Rowset Provider Trace
Is_rollover	Bit	States whether the trace is allowed to *roll over* events into a new file once the current file has reached Max_Size. The trace will continue to do this until it hits Max_Files. 1 = RollOver Enabled

continues

TABLE 10-1 *(continued)*

COLUMN NAME	DATA TYPE	DESCRIPTION
Is_shutdown	Bit	States whether SQL Server should shut down if it is unable to write events. 1 = Shutdown Enabled
Is_default	Bit	States whether the trace in question is the "default trace." Should only be Trace ID 1. This is a special trace that SQL Server always runs by default.
Buffer_count	Int	A count of the number of in-memory buffers the trace is consuming
Buffer_size	Int	The size of each buffer in KB
File_position	Bigint	Populated for file provider only. Denotes the last trace file position.
Reader_spid	Int	Populated when the rowset provider is used as the output provider for a trace. Contains the SQL Server SPID of the reading session (i.e., Profiler's SPID).
Start_time	Datetime	Date-time of trace start
Last_event_time	Datetime	Time that the last event was raised
Event_count	Bigint	Total number of events that have occurred
Dropped_event_count	Int	Total number of dropped events. This should be zero when the output provider is a file, but a positive value may be present when used with a rowset provider. If the output is a file and events are dropped, keep an eye on the is_shutdown bit flag, as SQL Server should shut down.

Of the columns presented in the preceding table, some are naturally of more interest than others. Those worth another look in particular are the bit flags and their associated columns.

Is_rowset

Of the bit flags, this one is the least interesting. It is used to identify traces that are being consumed by a consumer such as Profiler or the SMO trace provider. Using the READER_SPID column, it is easy to see which SPID is responsible for the trace and then track down that user courtesy of his or her login information:

Available for download on Wrox.com

```
SELECT   trc.id                 AS Trace_ID
        ,trc.[status]           AS Trace_Status
        ,trc.start_time         AS Trace_StartTime
        ,trc.last_event_time    AS Trace_LastEventTime
        ,trc.event_count        AS Trace_EventCount
```

```
            ,trc.dropped_event_count         AS Trace_DroppedEventCount
            ,ses.login_time                  AS Session_LoginTime
            ,ses.[host_name]                 AS Session_HostName
            ,ses.[program_name]              AS Session_ProgramName
            ,ses.login_name                  AS Session_LoginName
            ,ses.nt_domain                   AS Session_NTDomain
            ,ses.nt_user_name                AS Session_NTUserName
            ,ses.cpu_time                    AS Session_CPUTime
            ,ses.memory_usage                AS Session_MemoryUsage
            ,ses.reads                       AS Session_Reads
            ,ses.writes                      AS Session_Writes
            ,ses.logical_reads               AS Session_LogicalReads
            ,ses.last_request_start_time     AS Session_LastRequestStartTime
            ,ses.last_request_end_time       AS Session_LastRequestEndTime
FROM        sys.traces trc
JOIN        sys.dm_exec_sessions ses         ON trc.reader_spid = ses.session_id
WHERE       is_rowset = 1
```

This code is available for download at Wrox.com: CH10 Trace Rowset.sql

The results of this query (transposed to fit on the page) are shown in Table 10-2.

TABLE 10-2: Rowset Query Results

COLUMN NAME	VALUES
Trace_ID	2
Trace_Status	1
Trace_StartTime	19/07/2009 02:18:21.3
Trace_LastEventTime	19/07/2009 02:29:17.8
Trace_EventCount	2264
Trace_DroppedEventCount	0
Session_LoginTime	19/07/2009 02:18:16.1
Session_HostName	HostName
Session_ProgramName	SQL Server Profiler - 3092c2ca-08f2-4fea-9e2a-198029dd057b
Session_LoginName	DOMAIN\UserName
Session_NTDomain	DOMAIN
Session_NTUserName	UserName
Session_CPUTime	63

continues

TABLE 10-2 *(continued)*

COLUMN NAME	VALUES
Session_MemoryUsage	2
Session_Reads	0
Session_Writes	0
Session_LogicalReads	0
Session_LastRequestStartTime	19/07/2009 02:18:21.3
Session_LastRequestEndTime	19/07/2009 02:18:21.3

Is_rollover

Tracing can generate a large amount of data. When writing to a file, this can quickly translate to something large and unwieldy. When files get beyond a certain size, then they become more difficult to move and administer making house-keeping more difficult — especially if you need to move these files over unreliable network links.

> By keeping files under 2GB you can also use the windows compression functions to conserve space.

SQL Trace provides a feature in the file provider known as *rollover*. When enabled, SQL Trace will generate a new linked file when the current file reaches the size set in the MAX_SIZE parameter. Both the IS_ROLLOVER and the MAX_SIZE values need to be set for this to work. Without MAX_SIZE, SQL Trace wouldn't know when to roll over the file so it uses its default value of 5MB instead.

If rollover isn't enabled and the file has reached the MAX_SIZE, then SQL Server will simply stop tracing — the trace will be stopped and closed, resulting in the definition being deleted from the system. However, if rollover is enabled, then SQL Trace will create a new file and write events to it instead. The new file will have the same name as the original file, but with an incremented suffix. For example, when rolled over, C:\Tmp\MyTrace.trc would become C:\Tmp\MyTrace_2.trc.

This continues until the maximum number of files has been reached (if this value has been specified) or until the trace is stopped. Once the MAX_FILES value has been reached, SQL Server eliminates the oldest file before creating a new file. SQL Server attempts to maintain the number of files at the MAX_FILES number, but if for some reason it is prevented from deleting the file, then it will just ignore it. This file would need to be cleaned up manually. To continue our example, if MAX_FILES had been set to 2 and C:\Tmp\MyTrace_2.trc was filled, then SQL Server would delete C:\Tmp\MyTrace.trc before creating C:\Tmp\MyTrace_3.trc.

> It is worth remembering how rollover works when performing security or audit tracing, as invariably you don't want to ever lose the trace data that you are collecting. Ensure that you haven't set the MAX_FILES option when performing security or audit tracing to avoid having your audit data overwritten by the roll-over functionality.

Is_shutdown

If this flag is set in the trace definition, then SQL Server will shut itself down if for any reason it isn't able to write out the trace information successfully. This setting is normally used during security or audit tracing, where the trace is the definitive log of access to the SQL Server.

This option should only be set by a trace using the file provider, as the rowset provider isn't designed to guarantee that all events are persisted. Using this option with the rowset provider therefore makes it much more likely that a SQL Server might be shut down.

Interestingly, the sys.traces catalog view also provides the number of dropped events by a trace. From this value you can infer just how dangerous it would be to use this feature with a given trace configuration.

Is_default

The default trace is a SQL Trace that is always running and is designed to be a lightweight trace that ticks along in the background. It was added at the request of the Microsoft Customer Support Team to help troubleshoot issues, and is a step up from the optional black box trace that a DBA could enable in SQL Server 2000.

Unfortunately, the black box trace needed to be started manually, so in order to have this running in an automated fashion, DBAs needed to create system startup stored procedures to make all this work. Not so with the default trace. The default trace is started at system startup and is managed as a server-wide session. Its objective is similar to the black box trace in as much as it stores only the most recent activity on the system.

You might by now be asking yourself a few questions about the default trace.

➤ Where is it located?

➤ Can I change the location?

➤ Can I read it?

➤ What events does it capture?

➤ What impact does it have on my server?

Some of these questions are easier to answer than others. However, starting from the top, the files are located in the MSSQL\Log location of your SQL Server. You cannot change this location. You can, however, read the data — by using either Profiler or a user-defined function that hasn't been discussed yet called `fn_trace_gettable`. Using the latter, it is very straightforward to query the files and load the data into a table where the data can be manipulated further:

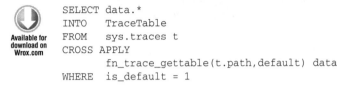

```
SELECT  data.*
INTO    TraceTable
FROM    sys.traces t
CROSS APPLY
        fn_trace_gettable(t.path,default) data
WHERE   is_default = 1
```

This code is available for download at Wrox.com: CH10 Trace Insert Simple.sql

The next questions are slightly trickier to answer. In order to get at the trace definition and convert it into something human readable, you actually need to do quite a bit of work. This is because there are no catalog views for the events, columns, or filters defined in SQL Server 2008. Instead, you must use some of the user-defined functions and translate the integers they provide to the textual descriptions:

```
DECLARE @vTraceID INT;
SET     @vTraceID = 1;

WITH filter AS
(   SELECT   columnid
            ,CASE   logical_operator
                    WHEN 0 THEN 'AND'
                    WHEN 1 THEN 'OR'
                    ELSE 'err'
            END AS logical_operator
            ,CASE   comparison_operator
                    WHEN 0 THEN ' = '
                    WHEN 1 THEN ' <> '
                    WHEN 2 THEN ' > '
                    WHEN 3 THEN ' < '
                    WHEN 4 THEN ' >= '
                    WHEN 5 THEN ' <= '
                    WHEN 6 THEN ' LIKE '
                    WHEN 7 THEN ' NOT LIKE '
            END AS comparison_operator
            ,value
    FROM    ::fn_trace_getfilterinfo(@vTraceID)
)
SELECT   cat.name AS CategoryName
        ,evt.name AS EventName
        ,col.name AS ColumnName
        ,STUFF  (   (   SELECT ' | ' + child_fil.logical_operator
                                     + child_fil.comparison_operator
                                     + CAST(child_fil.value AS VARCHAR(MAX)
                    )
                        FROM    filter child_fil
                        WHERE   parent_fil.columnid = child_fil.columnid
                        FOR XML PATH ('')
```

```
                ),1,1,''
            ) AS ColFilters
FROM     fn_trace_geteventinfo(@vTraceID) evi
JOIN     sys.trace_events evt
ON       evi.eventid          = evt.trace_event_id
JOIN     sys.trace_categories cat
ON       evt.category_id      = cat.category_id
JOIN     sys.trace_columns col
ON       evi.columnid         = col.trace_column_id
LEFT JOIN filter parent_fil
ON       col.trace_column_id = parent_fil.columnid
GROUP BY cat.name
        ,evt.name
        ,col.name
        ,parent_fil.columnid
ORDER BY cat.name
        ,evt.name
        ,col.name
```

This code is available for download at Wrox.com: CH10 Trace Definition.sql

What this query returns is a list of all categories, event classes, and columns collected by the default trace. This includes seven different categories with 35 different events, as shown in Table 10-3.

TABLE 10-3: Default Trace Categories and Events

CATEGORY NAME	EVENT NAME
Database	Data File Autogrow
Database	Data File AutoShrink
Database	Database Mirroring State Change
Database	Log File Autogrow
Database	Log File AutoShrink
Errors and Warnings	ErrorLog
Errors and Warnings	Hash Warning
Errors and Warnings	Missing Column Statistics
Errors and Warnings	Missing Join Predicate
Errors and Warnings	Sort Warnings
Full text	FT:Crawl Aborted
Full text	FT:Crawl Started

continues

TABLE 10-3 *(continued)*

CATEGORY NAME	EVENT NAME
Full text	FT:Crawl Stopped
Objects	Object:Altered
Objects	Object:Created
Objects	Object:Deleted
Performance	Plan Guide Unsuccessful
Security Audit	Audit Add DB User Event
Security Audit	Audit Add Login to Server Role Event
Security Audit	Audit Add Member to DB Role Event
Security Audit	Audit Add Role Event
Security Audit	Audit Addlogin Event
Security Audit	Audit Backup/Restore Event
Security Audit	Audit Change Audit Event
Security Audit	Audit Change Database Owner
Security Audit	Audit Database Scope GDR Event
Security Audit	Audit DBCC Event
Security Audit	Audit Login Change Property Event
Security Audit	Audit Login Failed
Security Audit	Audit Login GDR Event
Security Audit	Audit Schema Object GDR Event
Security Audit	Audit Schema Object Take Ownership Event
Security Audit	Audit Server Alter Trace Event
Security Audit	Audit Server Starts And Stops
Server	Server Memory Change

Looking at these events, you can see that there are no SQL data modification language (DML) statement-based events in this list. Quite the contrary; this list of events is primarily looking at database change, audit, and errors. It is therefore not anticipated that the default trace would cause any meaningful degradation of your SQL Server. Disabling the default trace therefore isn't going to achieve anything apart from leaving you in the dark when there is a problem caused by a change to the server. If you had left this enabled you would have a record in the default trace.

> *You might see the default trace get disabled during extreme performance tests such as those carried out during TPC benchmarking. Have a look at the disclosure documents and see if you can tell if they have done this.*

Black Box vs. Default Trace

Now that you know about the default trace it might be of interest to compare and contrast its definition with that of the old black box trace we mentioned earlier.

Table 10-4 shows what is included in the black box trace.

TABLE 10-4: Black Box Trace Categories and Events

TRACE CATEGORY	TRACE EVENT
Errors and Warnings	Attention
Errors and Warnings	Exception
Stored Procedures	RPC:Starting
T-SQL	SQL:BatchStarting

Interestingly, this trace definition captures an entirely different set of events than the default trace. The default trace configuration would seem to represent a refinement of the black box trace. The Attention and Exception events are generic, whereas the default trace captures much more specific events. Furthermore, by capturing the `RPC:Starting` and `SQL:BatchStarting` events, the black box trace captures potentially heavily called events.

In addition, the black box trace can't be tweaked in any shape or form. This includes the fact that the black box is always written to the same location, which, depending on where your database files are located, might be undesirable for writing out trace data. While the same is also true for the default trace, the volume of data captured is much less and so the location issue is not so significant.

> *The black box can only use two files. Each file can be a maximum size of 5MB. Therefore the maximum amount of information is constrained to 10MB. Given that the black box is capturing* `RPC:Starting` *and* `SQL:BatchStarting` *events don't expect the data in these files to hang around for long!*

Given the onerous restrictions of the black box, my advice is to configure your own version of it if you want to capture these events rather than use this feature. With your own implementation you can retain full flexibility of the trace definition and have total control over file placement.

sys.trace_categories

This catalog view is used to provide the textual descriptions for the categories of event classes used by SQL Trace. There is an additional grouping of Category Type; however, as this hasn't been heavily used (only two categories fall outside of the Normal category), there isn't much value to it.

The following code demonstrates how to query this catalog view and also provides the textual descriptions of the category types.

Available for
download on
Wrox.com

```
SELECT   category_id AS Category_ID
        ,name        AS Category_Name
        ,[type]      AS Category_TypeID
        ,CASE [type]
                WHEN 0 THEN 'Normal'
                WHEN 1 THEN 'Connection'
                WHEN 2 THEN 'Error'
                ELSE 'Unknown'
         END     AS [Category_TypeName]
FROM     sys.trace_categories
```

This code is available for download at Wrox.com: CH10 sys.trace_categories.sql

The preceding example returns the 21 available categories in SQL Server 2008, as shown in Figure 10-4.

	Category_ID	Category_Name	Category_TypeID	Category_TypeName
1	1	Cursors	0	Normal
2	2	Database	0	Normal
3	3	Errors and Warnings	2	Error
4	4	Locks	0	Normal
5	5	Objects	0	Normal
6	6	Performance	0	Normal
7	7	Scans	0	Normal
8	8	Security Audit	0	Normal
9	9	Server	0	Normal
10	10	Sessions	1	Connection
11	11	Stored Procedures	0	Normal
12	12	Transactions	0	Normal
13	13	TSQL	0	Normal
14	14	User configurable	0	Normal
15	15	OLEDB	0	Normal
16	16	Broker	0	Normal
17	17	Full text	0	Normal
18	18	Deprecation	0	Normal
19	19	Progress Report	0	Normal
20	20	CLR	0	Normal
21	21	Query Notifications	0	Normal

FIGURE 10-4

sys.trace_events

The `sys.trace_events` catalog view is also primarily used for converting the event id back to a text-based description. However, it also carries the ID for the category to which the event belongs:

```
SELECT   trace_event_id      AS Event_ID
         ,evt.name           AS Event_Name
         ,evt.category_id    AS Event_CategoryID
         ,cat.name           AS Category_Name
FROM     sys.trace_events evt
JOIN     sys.trace_categories cat
ON       evt.category_id = cat.category_id
ORDER BY cat.name
         ,evt.name
```

This code is available for download at Wrox.com: CH10 sys.trace_events.sql

Running the query returns the full list of events available in SQL Server. Figure 10-5 shows a subset of this data containing all events for the Errors and Warnings category.

	Event_ID	Event_Name	Event_CategoryID	Category_Name
1	16	Attention	3	Errors and Warnings
2	193	Background Job Error	3	Errors and Warnings
3	212	Bitmap Warning	3	Errors and Warnings
4	137	Blocked process report	3	Errors and Warnings
5	214	CPU threshold exceeded	3	Errors and Warnings
6	213	Database Suspect Data Page	3	Errors and Warnings
7	22	ErrorLog	3	Errors and Warnings
8	21	EventLog	3	Errors and Warnings
9	33	Exception	3	Errors and Warnings
10	127	Exchange Spill Event	3	Errors and Warnings
11	67	Execution Warnings	3	Errors and Warnings
12	55	Hash Warning	3	Errors and Warnings
13	79	Missing Column Statistics	3	Errors and Warnings
14	80	Missing Join Predicate	3	Errors and Warnings
15	69	Sort Warnings	3	Errors and Warnings
16	162	User Error Message	3	Errors and Warnings

FIGURE 10-5

sys.trace_columns

This view contains the list of all possible columns. Again, its use is predominantly for translating the column ID values back to textual descriptions for each of the columns. As mentioned earlier, a total of 66 columns are available in SQL Trace. Each row in the result set equates to a possible event column. Not all columns map to all events, but you'll learn more about that when you look at the `sys.trace_event_bindings` view later.

However, a couple of columns on the catalog view does reveal some interesting information. I'd like to focus your attention on two columns in particular: the `is_repeatable` and `is_repeated_base` bit flags:

```
SELECT  trace_column_id
        ,name
        ,type_name
        ,max_size
        ,is_filterable
        ,is_repeatable
        ,is_repeated_base
FROM    sys.trace_columns
WHERE   is_repeatable = 1
OR      is_repeated_base = 1
```

This code is available for download at Wrox.com: CH10 sys.trace_columns.sql

The preceding code returns the result set shown in Figure 10-6.

So what is interesting about the `is_repeatable` and `is_repeated_base` flags? Note that only one column has the `is_repeated_base` flag set to true. This is the key for all repeated data. All the other columns marked as `is_repeatable` contain session-based information that relate to that SPID.

A repeatable column means that SQL Server doesn't have to send this data to the trace more than once and ensures that subsequent events inherit this information. In short, it is an optimization.

Actually, the best description for repeatable data can be found in the U.S. Patent for SQL Trace, where the following statements can be found:

	trace_column_id	name	type_name	max_size	is_filterable	is_repeatable	is_repeated_base
1	6	NTUserName	nvarchar	512	1	1	0
2	7	NTDomainName	nvarchar	512	1	1	0
3	8	HostName	nvarchar	512	1	1	0
4	9	ClientProcessID	int	4	1	1	0
5	10	ApplicationName	nvarchar	512	1	1	0
6	11	LoginName	nvarchar	512	1	1	0
7	12	SPID	int	4	1	0	1
8	26	ServerName	nvarchar	512	0	1	0
9	41	LoginSid	image	1073741824	1	1	0
10	60	IsSystem	int	4	1	1	0

FIGURE 10-6

The "trace repeated data" column indicates a desired repetition of data from a preceding event. The "trace repeated data" column is preferably followed by a range of column identifiers in which to insert the repeated data. Such repetition is available only for columns specifically defined as repeatable columns

. . .

Repeatable element 630 provides an indication of whether column 610 is repeatable. Server 220 desirably need not resend data corresponding to a repeatable column in a subsequent trace. If a repeatable column is selected to be repeated, then it is indicated in the 'trace repeated data' trace special column set forth above.

> *The patent documentation itself is very interesting and you can read it for yourself at* www.patents.com/System-monitoring-performance-a-server/US7155641/en-US/.

sys.trace_subclass_values

When an event is raised, data is passed down from SQL Server's Trace Controller to the trace session. This data contains the values for the columns bound to that event. Some of these columns are dynamic in nature with no two events likely to produce the same value. An example of a dynamic column would be TextData. TextData contains the readable call to the database. Each query therefore will have a different value. Other columns however, contain a fixed sub-classification as you saw earlier. These columns, such as Mode, can only contain a fixed range of values.

The sys.trace_subclass_values catalog view provides the permissible list of values for a given event and column combination. The following SQL example shows the subclass values for the Lock:Acquired event and Mode column. Before reading ahead, see if you notice something slightly curious about the results based on the way I revised the query from one used earlier:

```
SELECT    cat.name                        AS category_name
          ,ev.name                        AS event_name
          ,col.name                       AS column_name
          ,sub.subclass_name              AS subclass_name
          ,sub.subclass_value             AS subclass_value
          ,datalength(sub.subclass_name)  AS subclass_name_length
FROM      sys.trace_categories cat
JOIN      sys.trace_events ev
ON        cat.category_id    = ev.category_id
JOIN      sys.trace_event_bindings bi
ON        bi.trace_event_id  = ev.trace_event_id
JOIN      sys.trace_columns col
ON        bi.trace_column_id = col.trace_column_id
LEFT JOIN sys.trace_subclass_values sub
ON        sub.trace_column_id = bi.trace_column_id
AND       sub.trace_event_id  = bi.trace_event_id
WHERE     sub.subclass_name IS NOT NULL
AND       cat.name             = 'Locks'
AND       ev.name              = 'Lock:Acquired'
AND       col.name             = 'Mode'
ORDER BY cat.name
         ,ev.name
         ,col.name
         ,sub.subclass_value;
```

This code is available for download at Wrox.com: CH10 sys.trace_subclass_values.sql

The preceding code returns the values shown in Figure 10-7.

	category_name	event_name	column_name	subclass_name	subclass_value	subclass_name_length
1	Locks	Lock:Acquired	Mode	NULL	0	8
2	Locks	Lock:Acquired	Mode	Sch-S	1	10
3	Locks	Lock:Acquired	Mode	Sch-M	2	10
4	Locks	Lock:Acquired	Mode	S	3	2
5	Locks	Lock:Acquired	Mode	U	4	2
6	Locks	Lock:Acquired	Mode	X	5	2
7	Locks	Lock:Acquired	Mode	IS	6	4
8	Locks	Lock:Acquired	Mode	IU	7	4
9	Locks	Lock:Acquired	Mode	IX	8	4
10	Locks	Lock:Acquired	Mode	SIU	9	6
11	Locks	Lock:Acquired	Mode	SIX	10	6
12	Locks	Lock:Acquired	Mode	UIX	11	6
13	Locks	Lock:Acquired	Mode	BU	12	4
14	Locks	Lock:Acquired	Mode	RangeS-S	13	16
15	Locks	Lock:Acquired	Mode	RangeS-U	14	16
16	Locks	Lock:Acquired	Mode	RangeI-N	15	16
17	Locks	Lock:Acquired	Mode	RangeI-S	16	16
18	Locks	Lock:Acquired	Mode	RangeI-U	17	16
19	Locks	Lock:Acquired	Mode	RangeI-X	18	16
20	Locks	Lock:Acquired	Mode	RangeX-S	19	16
21	Locks	Lock:Acquired	Mode	RangeX-U	20	16
22	Locks	Lock:Acquired	Mode	RangeX-X	21	16

FIGURE 10-7

The very observant among you might have noticed that in the WHERE clause I added a filter excluding NULL against the event subclass name. However, subclass_value 0 returns a name of "NULL." With that information you probably realize what the issue is. The value shown is actually the word NULL, not a NULL value per se. The hint is the white background, and the additional field of subclass_name_length confirms this. The value of this field is 8, representing the byte count for the subclass name. Clearly, then, subclass_name is a Unicode data type — hence the double-byte count for every character.

In addition to listing permitted values to aid filtering, sys.trace_subclass_values could also be used to drive drop-downs of permitted values in custom application development. However, currently only the Lock category and Mode column contain a character-based NULL. In normal circumstances there simply is no mapping where there is no set of values for that event and column combination.

The following code snippet returns all events that have a subclass_name of 'NULL' and Figure 10-8 shows all nine examples of this in SQL Server 2008.

```
SELECT   evt.name
         ,col.name
         ,sub.subclass_name
         ,sub.subclass_value
FROM     sys.trace_subclass_values sub
JOIN     sys.trace_columns col
ON       sub.trace_column_id = col.trace_column_id
JOIN     sys.trace_events evt
ON       sub.trace_event_id  = evt.trace_event_id
WHERE    subclass_name = 'NULL'
```

This code is available for download at Wrox.com: CH10 NULL subclass names.sql

	name	name	subclass_name	subclass_value
1	Lock:Deadlock Chain	Mode	NULL	0
2	Lock:Released	Mode	NULL	0
3	Lock:Acquired	Mode	NULL	0
4	Lock:Deadlock	Mode	NULL	0
5	Lock:Cancel	Mode	NULL	0
6	Lock:Timeout	Mode	NULL	0
7	Lock:Escalation	Mode	NULL	0
8	Lock:Timeout (timeout > 0)	Mode	NULL	0
9	Blocked process report	Mode	NULL	0

FIGURE 10-8

It is also worth noting that only eight of the 66 columns use this feature as can be seen in the following code snippet. However, these eight columns are used across 111 of the available events, as shown in Figure 10-9.

	distinct_trace_columns	distinct_trace_events
1	8	111

FIGURE 10-9

```
SELECT   COUNT(DISTINCT sub.trace_column_id) AS distinct_trace_columns
        ,COUNT(DISTINCT sub.trace_event_id)  AS distinct_trace_events
FROM    sys.trace_subclass_values sub;
```

For reference, the columns that map to specific subclass values are as follows (the results of which can be seen in Figure 10-10):

Available for download on Wrox.com

```
SELECT   col.trace_column_id                AS trace_column_id
        ,col.name                           AS column_name
        ,COUNT(DISTINCT sub.subclass_value) AS subclass_value_count
FROM    sys.trace_subclass_values sub
JOIN    sys.trace_columns col
ON      sub.trace_column_id = col.trace_column_id
GROUP BY col.trace_column_id
        ,col.name
ORDER BY col.name
```

This code is available for download at Wrox.com: CH10 subclass count.sql

With a few notable exceptions that use this feature heavily (`ObjectType`, `EventSubclass`, `Mode`, and `Type`) it's fair to say that not many of the other columns make use of this feature, which I believe is a shame for those building custom applications as mentioned earlier.

	trace_column_id	column_name	subclass_value_count
1	31	Error	4
2	21	EventSubClass	23
3	55	IntegerData2	1
4	32	Mode	22
5	28	ObjectType	80
6	58	OwnerID	7
7	30	State	1
8	57	Type	12

FIGURE 10-10

sys.trace_event_bindings

The `sys.trace_event_bindings` catalog view simply provides the association between all events and all columns to create the permissible list. The best way to visualize this is probably through the Trace Properties dialog box in Profiler, shown in Figure 10-11.

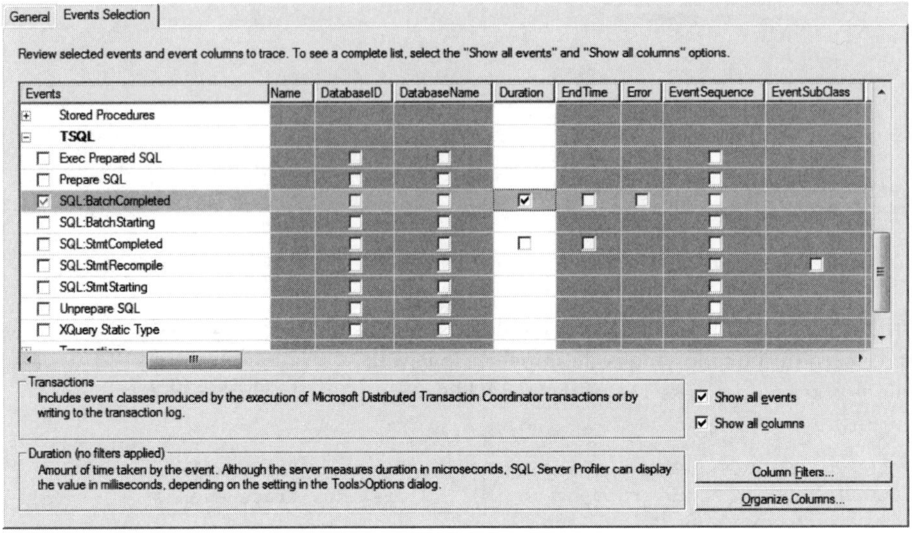

FIGURE 10-11

Anything with a check box in the cross-referenced co-ordinate equates to a row in the event binding catalog view. After looking at them for a while, it becomes quite intuitive as to when they may or may not be available.

Let's look at the example provided in Figure 10-11. The Duration column is available for `SQL:BatchCompleted` but not available for `SQL:BatchStarting`. Since SQL Server hasn't yet achieved the feat of time travel, it makes sense that it can only tell you the duration of a batch after it has finished.

SQL TRACE PROCEDURES AND FUNCTIONS

The last section looked at each catalog view in order to highlight all the metadata exposed for creating a trace. However, at present you are no closer to creating your own trace. For this you need some stored procedures.

Actually, the interface for building a trace is pretty clunky, as you will soon see. However, this is where Profiler comes into its own. There is no better interface for building a trace definition from scratch.

This section describes the stored procedures available and demonstrates how to use them to build a trace definition by hand. Once you understand how to do this manually (as in, the hard way), you can look at ways to make your use of SQL Trace much more pleasant.

sp_trace_create

To start the process off, a trace definition needs to be created. This is performed by using `sp_trace_create`. This stored procedure is responsible for setting the ground rules for the trace.

Note that SQL Trace is able to output only to a file (i.e., the flat file I/O provider) when invoked via this stored procedure. Moreover, this flat file should be located on a local drive so as not to incur network I/O, and it shouldn't be a UNC path. By avoiding UNC paths, the need to invoke the network stack is removed completely.

> *Don't forget that the SQL Server service account will need sufficient permission in Windows to write the trace file in the target directory.*

We actually covered all the options you have at your disposal when we talked about sys.traces. Therefore, to avoid repetition, we are more interested here in how the options map back to those descriptions given for the fields in sys.traces (see Table 10-5).

TABLE 10-5: sp_trace_create Parameters

PARAMETER	DATA TYPE	DEFAULT	MAPPING TO SYS.TRACES COLUMN
TraceID	Int	NULL	ID This is an output parameter. You will need to capture this ID to work with the trace in future stored procedure calls to add events and columns for example.
Options	Int	N/A	2 - Rollover - Is_rollover 4 - Shutdown - Is_shutdown 8 - Black Box - NO MAPPING
TraceFile	Nvarchar (245)	N/A	Path
MaxFileSize	Bigint	5	Max_size
StopTime	Datetime	NULL	Stop_time
FileCount	Int	NULL	Max_files

Of all the options, only the setting of the black box trace isn't mapped back to a column on sys.traces. A trace configured as the black box does, however, show up in the sys.traces catalog view:

```
DECLARE  @trace_id  INT
        ,@rc         INT = 0;

EXEC     @rc = SP_TRACE_CREATE   @traceid = @trace_id OUTPUT
                                ,@options =  8;

SELECT   @trace_id as TraceID
```

```
            ,@rc as ReturnCode;

select    id
          ,[path]
          ,max_size
          ,max_files
FROM      sys.traces
```

This code is available for download at Wrox.com: CH10 blackbox trace.sql

However, as shown in the file path in Figure 10-12, the only way to determine that the trace in question is a black box trace is by parsing the filename. The reason for this is unclear, but it may be that the default trace represents the future direction of system-based tracing and that the black box trace is present only for backward compatibility.

	TraceID	ReturnCode			
1	2	0			

	id	path	max_size	max_files
1	1	C:\Program Files\Microsoft SQL Server\MSSQL10.MSSQLSERVER\MSSQL\Log\log_392.trc	20	5
2	2	\\?\C:\Program Files\Microsoft SQL Server\MSSQL10.MSSQLSERVER\MSSQL\DATA\blackbox.trc	5	2

FIGURE 10-12

All the tracing stored procedures make heavy use of return code values to inform you of problems at run time. They aren't covered explicitly in this chapter but they are documented in Books Online at the following address `http://msdn.microsoft.com/en-us/library/ms187346.aspx`

> *sp_trace_create will not overwrite a file that already exists. If you try and do this you will get the following error message:*
>
> ```
> Windows error occurred while running SP_TRACE_CREATE. Error =
>     0x80070050(failed to retrieve text for this error. Reason: 15100).
> Msg 19062, Level 16, State 1, Procedure sp_trace_create, Line 1
> Could not create a trace file.
> ```

sp_trace_setevent

In order to capture a trace event, you need to mark it so that SQL Server knows to capture it and pass it through to your session. This stored procedure performs that function. However, somewhat painfully, it is necessary to call sp_trace_setevent for every column that you wish to capture for the event — for example, if you want to capture 1 event and 10 or its columns, then you must call this procedure 10 times. A more accurate name for this procedure would have been sp_trace_SetEventColumn. When you have seen how the On parameter works in the next example, you'll understand why — pay particular attention to it! Table 10-6 describes the parameters available for sp_trace_setevent.

TABLE 10-6: sp_trace_setevent Parameters

PARAMETER	DATA TYPE	DEFAULT	DESCRIPTION
TraceID	Int	NULL	ID field of sys.traces
EventID	Int	N/A	ID field of sys.trace_events
ColumnID	Int	N/A	ID field of sys.trace_columns
On	Int	N/A	Conditional logic: When ColumnID is populated, states whether the column is captured or not. When ColumnID is not populated, adds or removes the event to or from the trace definition but always removes all previous columns specified.

Consider the following example:

```
-- Create a Queue
declare @rc int
declare @TraceID int
declare @maxfilesize bigint
set @maxfilesize = 5

exec @rc = sp_trace_create @TraceID output
                ,0
                ,N'C:\tmp\TraceEventExample1'
                ,@maxfilesize
                ,NULL

-- Set the events
declare @on bit
set @on = 1
exec sp_trace_setevent @TraceID
                ,20
                ,NULL
                ,@on
```

The preceding code generates the definition shown in Figure 10-13 using the SQL we built earlier to see which events were included in the default trace (note that On is set to 1).

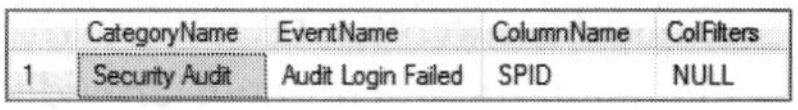

	CategoryName	EventName	ColumnName	ColFilters
1	Security Audit	Audit Login Failed	SPID	NULL

FIGURE 10-13

> *The SPID column is always included for each event added to a trace definition. You cannot exclude it.*

Now consider this more advanced scenario (remember that On is again set to 1 in all cases):

```
-- Set the events
declare @on bit
            ,@TraceID int

set @on = 1
set @TraceID = 3

exec sp_trace_setevent @TraceID, 20, 6, @on

exec sp_trace_setevent @TraceID, 20, NULL, @on

exec sp_trace_setevent @TraceID, 20, 1, @on
```

This code is available for download at Wrox.com: CH10 sp_trace_setevent.sql

This preceding code first calls sp_trace_setevent and adds one column to event 20 (Audit Login Failed). The second procedure call uses the same stored procedure against the same event. However, the second execution adds the event without specifying any columns. Finally, we have added another column to event 20. However, how many will be included in the trace definition? The answer is, of course, two (see Figure 10-14). The addition of event 20 without a ColumnID parameter effectively reset the event.

	CategoryName	EventName	ColumnName	ColFilters
1	Security Audit	Audit Login Failed	SPID	NULL
2	Security Audit	Audit Login Failed	TextData	NULL

FIGURE 10-14

Conversely, setting the On parameter to 0, or off, works pretty much as expected. If the ColumID parameter is specified, then this column is removed for the event. If the ColumnID parameter is not specified and the On parameter is set to 0, then the whole event is removed from the trace definition.

In short, there is no way to state that you wish to include all columns for a given event in a single stored procedure execution and then possibly remove specific columns. All columns have to be set first.

Performance Considerations

Some events can be very costly to include in your server-side trace, so forethought should be given to how frequently the event is raised prior to selecting it. As you saw in the section "The Architecture of SQL Trace," every new event you select in the trace definition adds a burden to SQL Server. Consider carefully, therefore, what it is you are trying to achieve in your tracing session. Some of the template trace definitions provided in Profiler offer a good starting point for your own definition, but do you really need, for example, the Audit Login and Audit Logout events in your trace? Picking high-volume trace events generates high-volume trace files — the more you collect the more you'll need to process. An example of this is the Lock:Acquired event. A single range scan query can generate thousands of rows of data all by itself. Couple this with the Lock:Released event and you'll have a truly massive trace in no time at all!

The most common causes of trace performance issues arise when DBAs opt to trace at the detail level — i.e., most commonly at the statement level. On systems where there is a large amount of ad-hoc or dynamic SQL then it can be desirable to capture at the statement level. Applications that use persistence frameworks such as NHibernate also draw you to trace at this level. However, on a busy OLTP system this can lead to very big trace files in a relatively short period. More specifically, if your workload includes scalar functions, then, depending on the event captured, this can seriously affect the performance of the SQL Server. This is because the scalar function can raise an event per row processed. This acts as a massive multiplier to the volume of trace data captured. Take a look at this in action:

```
USE AdventureWorks;

CREATE FUNCTION FormatName    (@FirstName NVARCHAR(50)
                              ,@MiddleName NVARCHAR(50)
                              ,@LastName NVARCHAR(50)
                              )
RETURNS NVARCHAR(200)
AS
BEGIN
    RETURN (RTRIM(LTRIM(@FirstName))
           +COALESCE(' '+RTRIM(LTRIM(SUBSTRING(@MiddleName,1,1)))
           +' ',' ')+RTRIM(LTRIM(@LastName)))
END;

SELECT TOP 10
            dbo.FormatName (FirstName
                           ,MiddleName
                           ,LastName
                           ) AS FullName
FROM        Person.Contact
ORDER BY LastName
        ,FirstName
        ,MiddleName;
```

This code is available for download at Wrox.com: CH10 evil scalar function.sql

If you simply trace SP:StmtCompleted while executing the preceding SELECT statement, then you do not get one row as you might expect. Instead, you would see what is shown in Figure 10-15.

EventClass	TextData
Trace Start	
SQL:StmtCompleted	USE AdventureWorks;
SP:StmtCompleted	RETURN (RTRIM(LTRIM(@FirstName)) +COALESCE(' '+RTRIM(LTRIM(...
SP:StmtCompleted	RETURN (RTRIM(LTRIM(@FirstName)) +COALESCE(' '+RTRIM(LTRIM(...
SP:StmtCompleted	RETURN (RTRIM(LTRIM(@FirstName)) +COALESCE(' '+RTRIM(LTRIM(...
SP:StmtCompleted	RETURN (RTRIM(LTRIM(@FirstName)) +COALESCE(' '+RTRIM(LTRIM(...
SP:StmtCompleted	RETURN (RTRIM RETURN (RTRIM(LTRIM(@FirstName)) +COALESCE('+RTRIM(LTRIM(
SP:StmtCompleted	RETURN (RTRIM(LTRIM(@FirstName)) +COALESCE(' '+RTRIM(LTRIM(...
SP:StmtCompleted	RETURN (RTRIM(LTRIM(@FirstName)) +COALESCE(' '+RTRIM(LTRIM(...
SP:StmtCompleted	RETURN (RTRIM(LTRIM(@FirstName)) +COALESCE(' '+RTRIM(LTRIM(...
SP:StmtCompleted	RETURN (RTRIM(LTRIM(@FirstName)) +COALESCE(' '+RTRIM(LTRIM(...
SP:StmtCompleted	RETURN (RTRIM(LTRIM(@FirstName)) +COALESCE(' '+RTRIM(LTRIM(...
SQL:StmtCompleted	SELECT TOP 10 dbo.FormatName (FirstName ...
Trace Stop	

FIGURE 10-15

That's 10 rows! One row is returned for each row evaluated as part of the TOP statement. That represents a ten-fold increase in anticipated trace data volume. As pointed out in

Simon Sabin's excellent blog (`http://sqlblogcasts.com/blogs/simons/archive/2008/11/03/`
`TSQL-Scalar-functions-are-evil-.aspx`), the impact of scalar functions on a production system
can be quite horrific. That however was only ten rows. Now try repeating the test but now add the
scalar function in the `where` clause with the following code:

```
SELECT TOP 10
            dbo.FormatName   (FirstName
                             ,MiddleName
                             ,LastName
                             ) AS FullName
FROM        Person.Contact
WHERE       dbo.FormatName (FirstName,MiddleName,LastName) like '%Abercrombie%'
ORDER BY LastName
          ,FirstName
          ,MiddleName;
```

Almost 20,000 rows in Profiler! Ouch. Did you also notice how much longer that query took to
run? More on this later.

This can be mitigated in part by applying a filter to exclude the rows generated as a result of the
function. You can achieve this by adding a filter (20038) on `ObjectType` to remove scalar functions,
which can be seen in Figure 10-16 below.

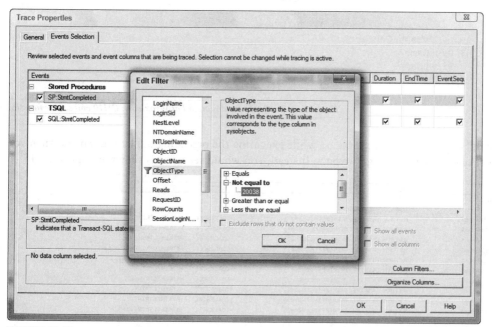

FIGURE 10-16

Unfortunately there is a side-effect to adding this filter. In the preceding example, the entire set of
`SP:StmtCompleted` rows have now been filtered out from the trace. If your workload uses scalar
functions liberally you might find you have little or no trace data left.

Unfortunately, SQL Server still has to raise all these events. The saving, as you saw earlier, is about the reduction in the volume of the trace data written to file, rather than avoiding the impact on SQL Server.

There are, however, options. How successful they will be will depend on your scenario but may be good workarounds for you. By selecting the `SQL:StmtCompleted` event, rather than the `SP:StmtCompleted` event, only one call is recorded (see Figure 10-17).

However, if the SQL is encapsulated in a stored procedure, then you would only see the execution call of that stored procedure in the trace output and the statement level is lost. The procedure is taken to be the statement being executed — i.e., the stored procedure name. This may be enough to point you in the right direction, however, because the duration of the procedure may have been sufficient to indicate the performance issue in the first place. Unfortunately, it doesn't end there. If the stored procedure call was made from a client machine using a remote procedure call, the `SQL:StmtCompleted` event won't be fired at all. In this situation only the events from the stored procedures event category are raised.

EventClass	TextData
Trace Start	
SQL:StmtCompleted	SELECT TOP 10
Trace Stop	

```
SELECT TOP 10
            dbo.FormatName  (FirstName
                            ,MiddleName
                            ,LastName
                            ) AS FullName
FROM           Person.Contact
ORDER BY LastName
            ,FirstName
            ,MiddleName;
```

FIGURE 10-17

The best method for reducing the impact of tracing activity without re-writing the application source code, however, is to not trace at the statement level in the first place. If the system uses stored procedures, then ask yourself whether you can get what you need from tracing at a procedure level, rather than at a statement level. Where there is a 1:1 mapping between the procedures and the statements contained inside them, you should be tracing at the procedure level already. However, in many systems the stored procedures represent a layer of complexity that encapsulates and wraps up a number of statements in each procedure. In these situations, try tackling the problem as a two-stage process.

First, measure execution duration at the stored-procedure level and devise a list of candidate poor performers. Then, if you can't break it down yourself based on the parameters captured, define a much tighter trace definition for these troublesome procedures only. Bear in mind, though, that if you have scalar functions embedded in the stored procedures, you will get one row in your output per row scanned. Therefore, the situation can go from bad to horrific if that scalar function is involved in some form of aggregation.

Another way of slightly modifying the earlier example to the following SQL also demonstrates just how bad things can get:

```
SELECT MAX(
            dbo.FormatName  (FirstName
                            ,MiddleName
                            ,LastName
                            )) AS FullName
FROM           Person.Contact
```

Notice that the scalar function `dbo.FormatName` is now wrapped in the loving embrace of a `MAX` aggregate function. As you'd expect, SQL Server returns a single row for this select statement (see Figure 10-18).

Results	Messages
FullName	
1	Zoe W Watson

FIGURE 10-18

However, now take a look at the Profiler output for this query, shown in Figure 10-19.

EventClass	ApplicationName	CPU	ClientProcessID	DatabaseID	Datab
SP:StmtCompleted	Microsoft SQ...	0	4896	7	Adve
SP:StmtCompleted	Microsoft SQ...	0	4896	7	Adve
SP:StmtCompleted	Microsoft SQ...	0	4896	7	Adve
SP:StmtCompleted	Microsoft SQ...	0	4896	7	Adve
SP:StmtCompleted	Microsoft SQ...	0	4896	7	Adve
SP:StmtCompleted	Microsoft SQ...	0	4896	7	Adve

```
SELECT MAX(
         dbo.FormatName   (FirstName
                          ,MiddleName
                          ,LastName
                          )) AS FullName
FROM       Person.Contact
```

Trace is stopped.   Ln 19974, Col 1   Rows: 19975

FIGURE 10-19

19,975 rows! This equates to one row per contact in the Contacts table, plus the start and stop trace events. In both cases (the MAX and the where clause) the scalar function has triggered an event for every row during the table scan.

Linchi Shea, in his blog (`http://sqlblog.com/blogs/linchi_shea/archive/2009/06/15/performance-impact-sql-trace-and-user-defined-scalar-functions.aspx`), provides even more details on the performance impact and consequences of tracing scalar functions, and I encourage you all to take a look.

sp_trace_setfilter

As the name suggests, `sp_trace_setfilter` is used when building a server-side trace to filter the results that are captured to a file. A filter is placed on a column in the trace and is not aligned to a specific event per se. Furthermore, not all columns can have a filter applied to them. The `sys.trace_columns` catalog view has a column called `is_filterable` (see Figure 10-20) that you can use to check whether you can place a filter against the column:

	is_filterable	filter_count
1	0	3
2	1	63

FIGURE 10-20

```
SELECT   is_filterable
        ,COUNT(*) AS filter_count
FROM     sys.trace_columns
GROUP BY is_filterable;
```

This code is available for download at Wrox.com: CH10 column is filterable.sql

The vast majority of columns are filterable.

The three columns that aren't filterable are as follows:

➤ EventClass

➤ EventSequence

➤ ServerName

The most common filter you are likely to see applied is self-imposed by Profiler. It is the filter that excludes Profiler itself from the trace:

```
declare @TraceID int
set     @TraceID = 2

exec sp_trace_setfilter
 @traceid              = @TraceID
,@columnid             = 10          -- ApplicationName
,@logical_operator     = 0           -- AND
,@comparison_operator  = 7           -- NOT LIKE
,@value                = N'SQL Server Profiler -
   180a71e3-2916-4eb5-b5cf-cb625d702f39'
```

This code is available for download at Wrox.com: CH10 sp_trace_setfilter.sql

If you generate your trace definition from Profiler, you will always see this filter in your trace, as Profiler inserts this filter by default when you specify the trace. Note you wouldn't necessarily want this filter on your server-side trace, as you might be very interested to see those Profiler calls!

Table 10-7 shows the parameters available for `sp_trace_setfilter`.

TABLE 10-7: sp_trace_setfilter Parameters

PARAMETER	DATA TYPE	DEFAULT	COMMENT
TraceID	Int	N/A	The id of the trace. Relates to the ID column found on `sys.traces`.
Columnid	Int	N/A	The id of the column. Relates to the ID column found on `sys.trace_columns`.
Logical_operator	Int	N/A	Can be one of two values: 0 = AND 1 = OR
Comparison_operator	Int	N/A	Determines how the filter value is applied to the column. Can be one of eight values: 0 - Equal (=) 1 - Not Equal (<>) 2 - Greater Than (>) 3 - Less Than (<) 4 - Greater Than or Equal To (>=) 5 - Less Than or Equal To (<=) 6 – Like 7 - Not Like

continues

TABLE 10-7 *(continued)*

PARAMETER	DATA TYPE	DEFAULT	COMMENT
Value	variant	N/A	Provides the value on which the filter is applied to the column. The data type of the value being passed to the procedure must match the data type of the field being filtered (contrary to normal procedure calls when values can get explicitly cast). If NULL is specified to remove null values, then only 0 (=) or 1 (<>) comparisons are valid.

Note that traces which are actively capturing data cannot be dynamically filtered. Therefore, the trace must have a status of 0 — that is, stopped — in order for this stored procedure to work.

Filtering a Range

In order to create a range filter with sp_trace_setfilter it is necessary to execute it twice. The first time sets the lower boundary; the second time creates the upper boundary. For example, you might wish to create a range on the Duration column, in which case it would look something like this:

```
declare @TraceID int
set     @TraceID = 2

exec sp_trace_setfilter  @traceid               = @TraceID
                        ,@columnid              = 13        -- Duration
                        ,@logical_operator      = 0         -- AND
                        ,@comparison_operator   = 2         -- Greater Than
                        ,@value                 = 100
exec sp_trace_setfilter  @traceid               = @TraceID
                        ,@columnid              = 13        -- Duration
                        ,@logical_operator      = 0         -- AND
                        ,@comparison_operator   = 3         -- Less Than
                        ,@value                 = 1000
```

This code is available for download at Wrox.com: CH10 range filter.sql

Bear in mind that while filters are excellent at reducing the file output, they also incur extra overhead — especially complex text-based filters. If you want to set up complex filtering, then you need to balance the cost associated with this. One additional factor is the location of the file you are tracing to and the performance of the disk subsystem. It may well be preferable to create your trace with a simplified filter and then upon completion, load the events into a table — filtering either during the load process or as part of the query. We haven't looked at loading a trace file yet. If you are interested in this specifically, skip ahead to the "fn_trace_gettable" section.

sp_trace_setstatus

`sp_trace_setstatus` is the stored procedure used to start, stop, and destroy trace definitions. As you have seen, traces need to be put into the right state before events are captured and prior to being read.

The parameters for `sp_trace_setstatus`, shown in Table 10-8, are very straightforward.

TABLE 10-8: sp_trace_setstatus Parameters

PARAMETER	DATA TYPE	DEFAULT	COMMENT
TraceID	Int	N/A	The ID of the trace to be modified. Relates to the ID column found on `sys.traces`.
Status	Int	N/A	States the action to take against the trace. Three values are possible: 0- Stop Trace 1- Start Trace 2- Close Trace (also deletes the trace definition from SQL Server) 3 - Pause trace (shows up as 0 in `sys.traces`) is used by Profiler. Pausing a trace is specific Profiler functionality. If you try and use this parameter it will delete your trace. When Profiler unpauses a trace it actually recreates it. The difference is that Profiler doesn't flush the GUI of events captured prior to the pause being requested.

Although the parameters are quite straightforward, note the following subtleties to the sequence of these statuses.

A trace must be stopped before it can be closed. Trying to execute the following statement on a running trace will result in an error:

```
EXEC sp_trace_setstatus    @TraceID = 2
                          ,@Status = 2
Msg 19052, Level 16, State 2, Procedure sp_trace_setstatus, Line 1
The active trace must be stopped before modification.
```

In order to read a file reliably without issue in Profiler, you must have first stopped and closed the trace. The key word in that last sentence is *reliably*. Books Online maintains that an actively running trace cannot be viewed unless stopped and closed. However this is perfectly possible with admin

FIGURE 10-21

access. You may need to open Profiler with the Run as administrator option shown in Figure 10-21. Remember the file isn't always completely up to date because SQL Server is caching the data, so even though you opened the trace it might not be 100% up to date.

You may, however, find you are unable to read the tail of the file if it is being written to at the same time you try to read it. If this happens, you might see the error message shown in Figure 10-22.

A refresh of the file usually resolves this.

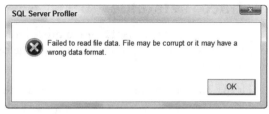

FIGURE 10-22

> *If you are planning to open trace files with SQL Profiler, try to ensure that the file sizes are manageable by rolling the file fairly frequently. Profiler also tries to be helpful by offering to load in subsequent rolled over files for you, which is nice.*

sp_trace_generateevent

`sp_trace_generateevent` enables you to instrument your SQL code with user-defined events. It is quite limited, as you are only given 10 distinct user-defined events to play with. Nor is it frequently used by application developers who normally instrument code outside of the stored procedure layer.

Table 10-9 shows the parameters for this stored procedure.

TABLE 10-9: sp_trace_generateevent Parameters

PARAMETER	DATA TYPE	DEFAULT	COMMENT
EventID	Int	N/A	The custom event ID. It can be any number between 82 and 91.
UserInfo	Nvarchar (256)	NULL	Optional information providing insight for the triggering of the event
UserData	Varbinary (8000)	NULL	Optional data providing insight for the triggering of the event

For example, the following code uses event ID 82 to generate an event every time a row is added to the `AdventureWorks` build version table:

```
DECLARE @sysinfoID tinyint = 1

WHILE @sysinfoID <=10
BEGIN
    Set @sysinfoID = @sysinfoID + 1

INSERT INTO dbo.AWBuildVersion
(   [Database Version]
    ,VersionDate
    ,ModifiedDate
```

```
        )
    VALUES
    (   '10.00.80404.00'
        ,CURRENT_TIMESTAMP
        ,CURRENT_TIMESTAMP
    )

    EXEC sp_trace_generateevent
        @eventID = 82
        ,@userinfo = N'EID:82 - New Row in Adventureworks Build Table'

    END
```

This code is available for download at Wrox.com: CH10 sp_trace_generateevent.sql

To capture this data you need a running trace definition looking for Event ID 82. Unfortunately, this is where the process starts to fall down. The mapping from event IDs 82–91 is most certainly not obvious. Figure 10-23 shows how they appear in Profiler.

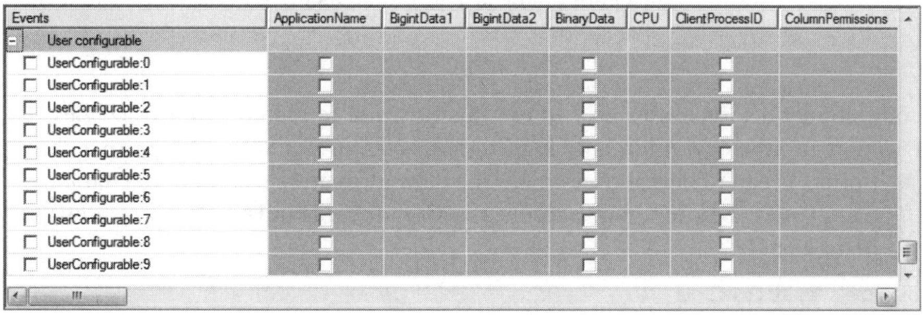

FIGURE 10-23

Event IDs 82–91 map to events `UserConfigurable:0`–`UserConfigurable:9`, as shown in Figure 10-24. There is no way to change these event names. Therefore, the user is forced to remember this mapping or sacrifice some of the text available in the user info column to help.

So when might this be useful? Consider user-defined transactions as a case in point. Logging and instrumenting transactions in SQL code can be a bit problematic, as data logged inside the transaction is rolled back along with the transaction. In short, you have to log outside the transaction scope. However, events raised via `sp_trace_generateevent` inside a transaction aren't capable of being rolled back, which makes instrumenting the code a much simpler task. Furthermore, using a user-defined event for important transactions increases the tracing potential of SQL transactions without having to capture them all and then filter the result.

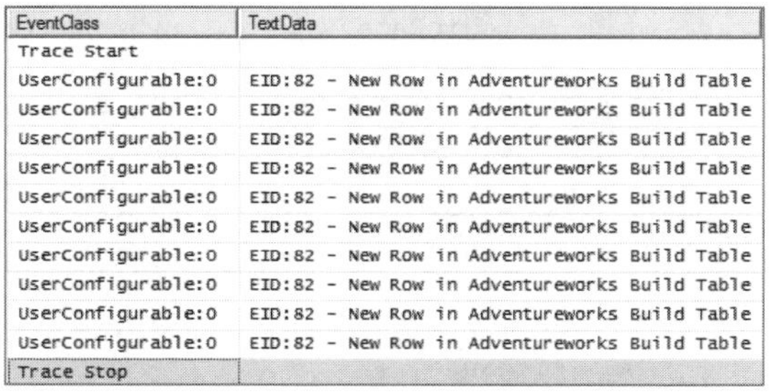

FIGURE 10-24

fn_trace_gettable

Of all the trace functions available, `fn_trace_gettable` is the most interesting and useful in every-day use. This function enables you to read a trace file even while it is open and being written to. It can therefore be used to process trace data collected in trace files and load it into tables in SQL Server for a more detailed analysis. Once loaded into a table, the data is much more easily digested and analyzed.

`fn_trace_gettable` takes only two parameters, as shown in Table 10-10. The first identifies the trace file. The second is used to limit the number of files to process if the trace has rolled over.

TABLE 10-10: fn_trace_gettable Parameters

COLUMN	DATA TYPE	COMMENT
filename	Nvarchar(256)	The path and filename of the first file to be read
Number of Files	Int	States the number of rollover files to be read. If Number of Files is specified as the default, then all rollover files are processed.

The following code snippet demonstrates how to use this function to load up your trace files. Personally, I like to now use the new minimally logged inserts feature of SQL 2008, rather than `SELECT...INTO`, as it offers greater control over where the data ultimately resides in the database data files. The `fn_trace_gettable` function outputs a very wide table indeed, so using a minimally logged process is a good idea.

```
CREATE TABLE dbo.DefaultTrace
(        DefaultTraceID      int identity(1,1)    NOT NULL
        ,TextData            ntext                    NULL
        ,BinaryData          image                    NULL
        ,DatabaseID          int                      NULL
        ,TransactionID       bigint                   NULL
        ,LineNumber          int                      NULL
        ,NTUserName          nvarchar(256)            NULL
        ,NTDomainName        nvarchar(256)            NULL
        ,HostName            nvarchar(256)            NULL
        ,ClientProcessID     int                      NULL
        ,ApplicationName     nvarchar(256)            NULL
        ,LoginName           nvarchar(256)            NULL
        ,SPID                int                      NULL
        ,Duration            bigint                   NULL
        ,StartTime           datetime                 NULL
        ,EndTime             datetime                 NULL
        ,Reads               bigint                   NULL
        ,Writes              bigint                   NULL
        ,CPU                 int                      NULL
        ,[Permissions]       bigint                   NULL
        ,Severity            int                      NULL
        ,EventSubClass       int                      NULL
        ,ObjectID            int                      NULL
        ,Success             int                      NULL
```

```
            , IndexID               int                     NULL
            , IntegerData           int                     NULL
            , ServerName            nvarchar(256)           NULL
            , EventClass            int                     NULL
            , ObjectType            int                     NULL
            , NestLevel             int                     NULL
            , [State]               int                     NULL
            , Error                 int                     NULL
            , Mode                  int                     NULL
            , Handle                int                     NULL
            , ObjectName            nvarchar(256)           NULL
            , DatabaseName          nvarchar(256)           NULL
            , [FileName]            nvarchar(256)           NULL
            , OwnerName             nvarchar(256)           NULL
            , RoleName              nvarchar(256)           NULL
            , TargetUserName        nvarchar(256)           NULL
            , DBUserName            nvarchar(256)           NULL
            , LoginSid              image                   NULL
            , TargetLoginName       nvarchar(256)           NULL
            , TargetLoginSid        image                   NULL
            , ColumnPermissions     int                     NULL
            , LinkedServerName      nvarchar(256)           NULL
            , ProviderName          nvarchar(256)           NULL
            , MethodName            nvarchar(256)           NULL
            , RowCounts             bigint                  NULL
            , RequestID             int                     NULL
            , XactSequence          bigint                  NULL
            , EventSequence         bigint                  NULL
            , BigintData1           bigint                  NULL
            , BigintData2           bigint                  NULL
            , [GUID]                uniqueidentifier        NULL
            , IntegerData2          int                     NULL
            , ObjectID2             bigint                  NULL
            , [Type]                int                     NULL
            , OwnerID               int                     NULL
            , ParentName            nvarchar(256)           NULL
            , IsSystem              int                     NULL
            , Offset                int                     NULL
            , SourceDatabaseID      int                     NULL
            , SqlHandle             image                   NULL
            , SessionLoginName      nvarchar(256)           NULL
            , PlanHandle            image                   NULL
            , GroupID               int                     NULL
) ON [PRIMARY];
GO

INSERT INTO DefaultTrace WITH (TABLOCKX)
SELECT data.*
FROM   sys.traces t
CROSS APPLY
       fn_trace_gettable(t.path,default) data
WHERE  is_default = 1
ORDER BY EventSequence
```

This code is available for download at Wrox.com: CH10 fn_trace_gettable Minimal_log.sql

Once the data has been loaded into a table you can now analyze it. Remember you are looking for patterns as well as spikes. Ask yourself this question: Is it more important to find the one procedure that took 10 seconds to run and tune it to run in a 100 milliseconds or identify a second procedure that was executed 100,000 times (each execution taking 300 milliseconds) and expend effort there? I'd argue that the pattern is in many ways more important than the single instance as the cumulative effect has a far greater total impact on the system.

To aid you in your analysis you may want to consider performing some additional cleansing on the trace data you have loaded. You might want to consider splitting the table, for example, to move some of the wide or infrequently used columns into a separate structure. You can always take the EventSequence field into this second table so you can join the data back together if needed. Alternatively, you might want to invest more time and normalize the data. Finally you might want to simply remove a bunch of events that aren't helping you perform the analysis. Integration Services is a great tool for this kind of work. I have already mentioned the free data source adaptor available at http://www.sqlis.com you can download to help you do this.

> *You can also use a free tool called ClearTrace to load trace files into SQL Server. It provides some handy additional features such as normalization and param- eterization of SQL, as well as providing some performance statistics on the data imported. Try it for yourself at* www.cleardata.biz/cleartrace/default.aspx.

fn_trace_geteventinfo

This function returns all the events and columns specified for a currently defined trace. It's essen- tially an enabling function that is used by tool providers and DBAs who want to know what events are being captured in trace sessions.

For example, you can see the list of events specified by the default trace with the following query:

Available for download on Wrox.com

```
SELECT    evt.name AS EventName
          ,col.name AS ColumnName
FROM fn_trace_geteventinfo(1) inf
JOIN sys.trace_events evt   ON inf.eventid  = evt.trace_event_id
JOIN sys.trace_columns col  ON inf.columnid = col.trace_column_id
ORDER BY eventid
         ,columnid
```

> *This code is available for download at Wrox.com: CH10 fn_trace_geteventinfo.sql*

I am sure you noticed that the preceding example specifies an extra couple of joins to trace the cata- log views sys.trace_events and sys.trace_columns. This is because fn_trace_geteventinfo only returns the IDs for the event and column, respectively.

fn_trace_getfilterinfo

`fn_trace_getfilterinfo` acts similarly to `fn_trace_geteventinfo`. Its job is to retrieve all filters specified for a given trace, and its output is identical to the values used to create it. Therefore, Table 10-11 should be reminiscent of what was shown earlier in the section on `sp_trace_setfilter`.

TABLE 10-11: fn_trace_getfilterinfo Parameters

COLUMN NAME	DATA TYPE	COMMENT
Columnid	Int	The ID of the column on which the filter is applied. Relates to the ID column found on `sys.trace_columns`.
Logical_operator	Int	Can be one of two values: 0 = AND 1 = OR
Comparison_operator	Int	Determines how the filter value is applied to the column. Can be one of eight values: 0 - Equal (=) 1 - Not Equal (<>) 2 - Greater Than (>) 3 - Less Than (<) 4 - Greater Than or Equal To (>=) 5 - Less Than or Equal To (<=) 6 - Like 7 - Not Like
Value	variant	The value by which the filter is applied to the column

Remembering these values can be a pain, so you can incorporate the following SELECT statement into your own view or function to help make sense of the output:

```
SELECT   CASE   fil.logical_operator
         WHEN 0 THEN 'AND'
         WHEN 1 THEN 'OR'
         ELSE        '#ERROR#'
         END AS logical_operator_desc
        ,col.name
        ,CASE   fil.comparison_operator
         WHEN 0 THEN '='
         WHEN 1 THEN '<>'
         WHEN 2 THEN '>'
         WHEN 3 THEN '<'
         WHEN 4 THEN '>='
         WHEN 5 THEN '<='
         WHEN 6 THEN 'LIKE'
         WHEN 7 THEN 'NOT LIKE'
         ELSE        '#ERROR#'
```

```
            END AS comparison_operator_desc
            ,fil.value
    FROM    fn_trace_getfilterinfo(2) fil
    JOIN    sys.trace_columns col            ON fil.columnid = col.trace_column_id
    ORDER BY col.name
```

Figure 10-25 shows the output.

	logical_operator_desc	name	comparison_operator_desc	value
1	AND	ApplicationName	NOT LIKE	SQL Server Profiler - 467ad2d0-0fe9-4154-86cf-34...
2	AND	ApplicationName	NOT LIKE	Report Server%

FIGURE 10-25

> *There are no parentheses options when configuring a trace, so use* OR *very carefully. Nor is there an event filter ID. You therefore must sequence your* ANDs *and* ORs *very carefully against a single column when mixed together.*

SECURING SQL TRACE

Back in the days of SQL Server 2000, anyone wishing to run a trace needed to be a systems administrator — i.e., a member of the sysadmin role. This proved to be a problematic level of granularity. On the one hand, access to tracing was locked down to ensure that only persons with the highest level of permissions could run a trace and see potentially compromising data. On the other hand, it was particularly restrictive in terms of who could use this incredibly useful functionality. It made it impossible to grant permission to trace without granting a whole host of other privileges.

To resolve this predicament, SQL Server 2005 changed the security dynamic for tracing. A new permission was created called ALTER TRACE. This permission was granted in the normal way via a GRANT permission, like so:

```
GRANT ALTER TRACE TO Trace;
```

This meant that a login could be allowed to trace against the SQL Server but without being allowed to perform any other action. This was certainly a step in the right direction. However, ALTER TRACE is still a server principal security setting. This hasn't changed in SQL 2008. Consequently, *any* event raised by the SQL Server can be captured by a person running a trace. This therefore leaves us with some security challenges:

➤   A login can alter any trace, even one it did not create.

➤   A login can view definitions of objects to which they might not have access.

➤   A login can see the parameters passed into stored procedures. Consider the stored procedure parameters for inserting a contact record or, more seriously, a credit card against a user's profile.

➤   A tracing application might be able to see a password that is being changed.

➤   A tracing application might be able to see the passwords for other logins as they are created.

The following sections look at each of these areas to see if and how they have been addressed by the SQL Server Product Team.

Tracing Login Creation/Deletion

There is mixed news here. If the WITH PASSWORD syntax is picked up by the trace controller, then the text relating to this event will be modified to prevent a user from seeing it. This occurs no matter what privileges the owner of the trace has. For example, the following code generates the results shown in Figure 10-26:

```
CREATE LOGIN Trace WITH PASSWORD = 'ArsenalAreTheBest',CHECK_POLICY = OFF;
```

EventClass	TextData
Trace Start	
SQL:BatchStarting	--*CREATE LOGIN--
SQL:StmtStarting	-- 'CREATE LOGIN' was found in the text of this event. -- The text has been replaced with this comment for security reasons.
SQL:StmtCompleted	-- 'CREATE LOGIN' was found in the text of this event. -- The text has been replaced with this comment for security reasons.
SQL:BatchCompleted	--*CREATE LOGIN--
Trace Stop	

FIGURE 10-26

Great news! SQL Server has obscured the result, so you cannot see any part of the login in question.

However, the WITH PASSWORD syntax is required only when creating SQL logins (something I hope everyone is doing less and less with each passing day). How does SQL Server behave when a Windows login is created?

```
CREATE LOGIN [BUILTIN\Users] FROM WINDOWS;
```

Figure 10-27 shows what the preceding generates in Profiler:

Not so clever. Although the password isn't compromised, a malicious user now at least knows what accounts to target.

Dropping of either the Windows or the SQL login also reveals the login name. This is unsurprising but consistent, as in both cases the WITH PASSWORD is not required.

EventClass	TextData
Trace Start	
SQL:BatchStarting	CREATE LOGIN [BUILTIN\Users] FROM WINDOWS;
SQL:StmtStarting	CREATE LOGIN [BUILTIN\Users] FROM WINDOWS;
SQL:StmtCompleted	CREATE LOGIN [BUILTIN\Users] FROM WINDOWS;
SQL:BatchCompleted	CREATE LOGIN [BUILTIN\Users] FROM WINDOWS;
Trace Stop	

FIGURE 10-27

```
DROP LOGIN [BUILTIN\Users];
DROP LOGIN Trace;
```

Figure 10-28 shows what is generated by the preceding code.

EventClass	TextData
Trace Start	
SQL:BatchStarting	DROP LOGIN [BUILTIN\Users]; DROP LOGIN Trace;
SQL:StmtStarting	DROP LOGIN [BUILTIN\Users];
SQL:StmtCompleted	DROP LOGIN [BUILTIN\Users];
SQL:StmtStarting	DROP LOGIN Trace;
SQL:StmtCompleted	DROP LOGIN Trace;
SQL:BatchCompleted	DROP LOGIN [BUILTIN\Users]; DROP LOGIN Trace;
Trace Stop	

FIGURE 10-28

Logins Changing Passwords

There are two ways a SQL login password can be changed:

➤   sp_password

➤   ALTER LOGIN

Let's check to see what happens in both these situations. First, the legacy method: sp_password. Note that this method is ripe for removal from SQL Server, as the ALTER syntax method is available:

```
USE MASTER;
CREATE LOGIN Trace WITH PASSWORD = 'ArsenalAreTheBest',CHECK_POLICY = OFF;
GRANT ALTER TRACE TO Trace;
EXECUTE AS Login = 'Trace';
EXEC sp_password 'ArsenalAreTheBest','Arsene Wenger is a football genius',Trace
REVERT
DROP LOGIN Trace;
```

Figure 10-29 shows what is generated by the preceding example.

EventClass	TextData
Trace Start	
SQL:BatchStarting	USE MASTER; --*CREATE LOGIN------------------------------
SQL:StmtStarting	USE MASTER;
SQL:StmtCompleted	USE MASTER;
SQL:StmtStarting	-- 'CREATE LOGIN' was found in the text of this event. --
SQL:StmtCompleted	-- 'CREATE LOGIN' was found in the text of this event. --
SQL:StmtStarting	GRANT ALTER TRACE TO Trace;
SQL:StmtCompleted	GRANT ALTER TRACE TO Trace;
SQL:StmtStarting	EXECUTE AS Login = 'Trace';
SQL:StmtCompleted	EXECUTE AS Login = 'Trace';
SQL:StmtStarting	-- 'sp_password' was found in the text of this event. -- T
SQL:StmtCompleted	-- 'sp_password' was found in the text of this event. -- T
SQL:StmtStarting	REVERT
SQL:StmtCompleted	REVERT
SQL:StmtStarting	DROP LOGIN Trace;
SQL:StmtCompleted	DROP LOGIN Trace;
SQL:BatchCompleted	USE MASTER; --*CREATE LOGIN------------------------------
Trace Stop	

FIGURE 10-29

As you can see, the event text data for the execution of sp_password has been masked. Now consider the SQL Server 2005 and later method for changing your password:

```
USE MASTER;

CREATE LOGIN Trace WITH PASSWORD = 'ArsenalAreTheBest',CHECK_POLICY = OFF;

GRANT ALTER TRACE TO Trace;

EXECUTE AS Login = 'Trace';

ALTER LOGIN Trace
WITH PASSWORD = 'No. Really. Arsenal are the best'
OLD_PASSWORD  = 'ArsenalAreTheBest';

REVERT

DROP LOGIN Trace
```

The preceding example generates the output shown in Figure 10-30 in Profiler.

EventClass	TextData
Trace Start	
SQL:BatchStarting	SELECT dtb.name AS [Name], dtb.database_id AS [ID], CAST(
SQL:StmtStarting	SELECT dtb.name AS [Name], dtb.database_id AS [ID], CAST(
SQL:StmtCompleted	SELECT dtb.name AS [Name], dtb.database_id AS [ID], CAST(
SQL:BatchCompleted	SELECT dtb.name AS [Name], dtb.database_id AS [ID], CAST(
SQL:BatchStarting	USE MASTER; --*CREATE LOGIN-----------------------
SQL:StmtStarting	USE MASTER;
SQL:StmtCompleted	USE MASTER;
SQL:StmtStarting	-- 'CREATE LOGIN' was found in the text of this event. --
SQL:StmtCompleted	-- 'CREATE LOGIN' was found in the text of this event. --
SQL:StmtStarting	GRANT ALTER TRACE TO Trace;
SQL:StmtCompleted	GRANT ALTER TRACE TO Trace;
SQL:StmtStarting	EXECUTE AS Login = 'Trace'; [GRANT ALTER TRACE TO Trace;]
SQL:StmtCompleted	EXECUTE AS Login = 'Trace';
SQL:StmtStarting	-- 'ALTER LOGIN' was found in the text of this event. --
SQL:StmtCompleted	-- 'ALTER LOGIN' was found in the text of this event. --
SQL:StmtStarting	REVERT
SQL:StmtCompleted	REVERT
SQL:StmtStarting	DROP LOGIN Trace
SQL:StmtCompleted	DROP LOGIN Trace
SQL:BatchCompleted	USE MASTER; --*CREATE LOGIN-----------------------
Trace Stop	

FIGURE 10-30

Clearly then the output is again masked to protect the passwords submitted in the batch. However, one key assumption has been made by the development team: The user submitting the query gets the syntax 100% correct. Consider this slight tweak to the preceding SQL batch:

```
GO
ALTER LOGIN Trace
SET PASSWORD = 'No. Really. Arsenal are the best'
OLD_PASSWORD = 'ArsenalAreTheBest';
GO
ALTER LOGIN Trace
WITH PASSWORD = 'No. Really. Arsenal are the best'
OLD_PASSWORD = 'ArsenalAreTheBest';
```

The preceding code includes an invalid ALTER LOGIN statement inside its own batch. However, now look at the output in Profiler, shown in Figure 10-31.

EventClass	TextData
Trace Start	
SQL:BatchStarting	USE MASTER; --*CREATE LOGIN-- GRANT ALTER TRA
SQL:StmtStarting	USE MASTER;
SQL:StmtCompleted	USE MASTER;
SQL:StmtStarting	-- 'CREATE LOGIN' was found in the text of this event. -- The text has been replaced with this comment for s
SQL:StmtCompleted	-- 'CREATE LOGIN' was found in the text of this event. -- The text has been replaced with this comment for s
SQL:StmtStarting	GRANT ALTER TRACE TO Trace;
SQL:StmtCompleted	GRANT ALTER TRACE TO Trace;
SQL:StmtStarting	EXECUTE AS Login = 'Trace';
SQL:StmtCompleted	EXECUTE AS Login = 'Trace';
SQL:BatchCompleted	USE MASTER; --*CREATE LOGIN-- GRANT ALTER TRA
SQL:BatchStarting	ALTER LOGIN Trace SET PASSWORD = 'No. Really. Arsenal are the best' OLD_PASSWORD = 'ArsenalAreTheBest';
SQL:BatchCompleted	ALTER LOGIN Trace SET PASSWORD = 'No. Really. Arsenal are the best' OLD_PASSWORD = 'ArsenalAreTheBest';
SQL:BatchStarting	--*ALTER LOGIN---- -- ---------------------------------
SQL:StmtStarting	-- 'ALTER LOGIN' was found in the text of this event. -- The text has been replaced with this comment for se
SQL:StmtCompleted	-- 'ALTER LOGIN' was found in the text of this event. -- The text has been replaced with this comment for se
SQL:StmtStarting	REVERT
SQL:StmtCompleted	REVERT
SQL:StmtStarting	DROP LOGIN Trace
SQL:StmtCompleted	DROP LOGIN Trace
SQL:BatchCompleted	--*ALTER LOGIN---- -- ---------------------------------
Trace Stop	

FIGURE 10-31

The new batch has been captured in the trace with my login name, my old password, and my new password all in clear text! If I saved this trace to a file, I could potentially be facing a serious breach of the security policy.

In fact, the comment in the Text Data output is misleading:

```
-- 'ALTER LOGIN' was found in the text of this event.
-- The text has been replaced with this comment for security reasons.
```

It is actually the words WITH PASSWORD in the event text data that forces the replacement, not the words ALTER LOGIN. Given that some days I wouldn't trust my users to tie their own shoelaces together much less assume that their SQL batch is 100% perfect *before* submitting it, I think I'd much prefer it if the comment were actually correct. Perhaps using sp_password isn't so bad after all. . .

When Tracing Login Can View Object Definitions and Parameter Values

As a direct result of the tracing permission being set at the server principal level, rather than at a database principal, a tracing login can see object definitions for which it has no permissions in SQL Server. This might be an issue for you when considering server consolidation, especially with third-party applications.

To illustrate the point, let's create a login with no explicit access granted to any user database and then set up a Profiler session using this login. Once this is created, you'll execute a stored procedure in a separate session from Management Studio. Here is the login:

```
CREATE LOGIN Trace WITH PASSWORD = 'Arsenal',CHECK_POLICY = OFF;
GRANT ALTER TRACE TO Trace;
```

Now execute the following stored procedure:

```
USE [AdventureWorks]
GO

DECLARE        @return_value int
BEGIN TRAN
EXEC    @return_value = [HumanResources].[uspUpdateEmployeePersonalInfo]
                @EmployeeID = 1,
                @NationalIDNumber = N'999-911-555',
                @BirthDate = N'19660520',
                @MaritalStatus = N'M',
                @Gender = N'M'
ROLLBACK TRAN
SELECT 'Return Value' = @return_value
```

The results aren't important, but the trace output, shown in Figure 10-32, clearly shows the UPDATE statement for an object for which you do not have VIEW DEFINITION permissions.

EventClass	TextData
SP:Starting	EXEC @return_value = [HumanResources].
SP:StmtStarting	SET NOCOUNT ON;
SP:StmtCompleted	SET NOCOUNT ON;
SP:StmtStarting	BEGIN TRY
SP:StmtCompleted	BEGIN TRY
SP:StmtStarting	UPDATE [HumanResources].[Employee]
SP:StmtCompleted	UPDATE [HumanResources].[Employee]

```
UPDATE [HumanResources].[Employee]
    SET [NationalIDNumber] = @NationalIDNumber
       ,[BirthDate] = @BirthDate
       ,[MaritalStatus] = @MaritalStatus
       ,[Gender] = @Gender
    WHERE [EmployeeID] = @EmployeeID;
```

FIGURE 10-32

It stands to reason, having just seen the object definitions returned, that the `BatchStarting` and `BatchCompleted` statements will contain the stored procedure call, including the parameters to that call. Rerunning the previous query confirms this, as shown in Figure 10-33.

EventClass	TextData
Trace Start	
SQL:BatchStarting	USE [AdventureWorks]
SQL:StmtStarting	USE [AdventureWorks]
SQL:StmtCompleted	USE [AdventureWorks]
SQL:BatchCompleted	USE [AdventureWorks]
SQL:BatchStarting	DECLARE @return_value int BEGIN TRAN EXEC
SQL:StmtStarting	BEGIN TRAN

```
DECLARE @return_value int
BEGIN TRAN
EXEC    @return_value = [HumanResources].[uspUpdateEmployeePersonalInfo]
            @EmployeeID = 1,
            @NationalIDNumber = N'999-911-555',
            @BirthDate = N'19660520',
            @MaritalStatus = N'M',
            @Gender = N'M'
ROLLBACK TRAN
SELECT  'Return Value' = @return_value
```

FIGURE 10-33

Clearly, the `BatchStarting` event has revealed the employee's national ID number, birth date, and employee ID. What does SQL Server offer in mitigation? Not a great deal. You can encrypt the stored procedure, and this will impact what is shown for query plans and statements.

Encrypting a stored procedure is a simple case of creating or altering the stored procedure using the `WITH ENCRYPTION` option. Following is the modified stored procedure, which is part of the `AdventureWorks` database:

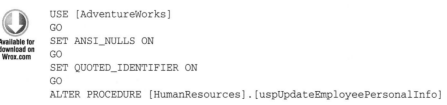

Available for
download on
Wrox.com

```
USE [AdventureWorks]
GO
SET ANSI_NULLS ON
GO
SET QUOTED_IDENTIFIER ON
GO
ALTER PROCEDURE [HumanResources].[uspUpdateEmployeePersonalInfo]
```

```
        @EmployeeID [int],
        @NationalIDNumber [nvarchar](15),
        @BirthDate [datetime],
        @MaritalStatus [nchar](1),
        @Gender [nchar](1)
WITH EXECUTE AS CALLER,ENCRYPTION
AS
BEGIN
    SET NOCOUNT ON;

    BEGIN TRY
        UPDATE [HumanResources].[Employee]
        SET [NationalIDNumber] = @NationalIDNumber
            ,[BirthDate] = @BirthDate
            ,[MaritalStatus] = @MaritalStatus
            ,[Gender] = @Gender
        WHERE [EmployeeID] = @EmployeeID;
    END TRY
    BEGIN CATCH
        EXECUTE [dbo].[uspLogError];
    END CATCH;
END;
GO
```

This code is available for download at Wrox.com: CH10 AdventureWorks Encrypted HumanResources.uspUpdateEmployeePersonalInfo.sql

The results are shown in Figure 10-34.

The following events, therefore, reveal the parameter values passed into a stored procedure:

➤ SQL:BatchStarting

➤ SQL:BatchCompleted

➤ SQL:StmtStarting

➤ SQL:StmtCompleted

The only statements affected by the encryption option are those contained inside the stored procedure, but not the stored procedure itself. Consequently, although the definition of the object is protected from prying eyes, the parameter values are not.

EventClass	TextData
SQL:StmtCompleted	BEGIN TRAN
SQL:StmtStarting	EXEC @return_value = [HumanResource...
SP:Starting	EXEC @return_value = [HumanResource...
SP:StmtStarting	-- Encrypted text
SP:StmtCompleted	-- Encrypted text
SP:StmtStarting	-- Encrypted text
SP:StmtCompleted	-- Encrypted text
SP:StmtStarting	-- Encrypted text
SP:StmtCompleted	-- Encrypted text
SP:StmtStarting	-- Encrypted text
SP:StmtCompleted	-- Encrypted text
SP:Completed	EXEC @return_value = [HumanResource...
SQL:StmtCompleted	EXEC @return_value = [HumanResource...

```
EXEC    @return_value = [HumanResources].[uspUpdateEmployeePersonalInfo]
        @EmployeeID = 1,
        @NationalIDNumber = N'999-911-555',
        @BirthDate = N'19660520',
        @MaritalStatus = N'M',
        @Gender = N'M'
```

FIGURE 10-34

Logins Changing Trace Definitions

Another aspect of the tracing security model is that once a login has been granted ALTER TRACE, it can affect all user-defined traces defined on the system. This includes stopping and starting, as well as amending and even deleting those traces. There is no real concept of a trace owner, and therefore no ownership chain.

There is one exception to this: the default trace. This is a system-generated trace, which we looked at in detail earlier in the chapter. Suffice it to say, if you used your "Trace" login and tried to affect the default trace, then you will see an error:

```
EXEC sp_trace_setstatus 1,0
```

The default trace is always TraceID number 1. The preceding statement attempts to stop the default trace. However, look at the message you receive:

```
Msg 19070, Level 16, State 1, Procedure sp_trace_setstatus, Line 1
The default trace cannot be stopped or modified. Use SP_CONFIGURE to turn it off.
```

Using the same login, let's try to stop the default trace:

```
EXEC sp_configure 'default trace enabled',0
```

The preceding returns the following message:

```
Msg 15247, Level 16, State 1, Procedure sp_configure, Line 94
User does not have permission to perform this action.
```

That's because the user doesn't have the ALTER SETTINGS permission. This permission is implicitly granted to the sysadmin and serveradmin roles only. It is recommended that you not assign this permission to any one user of the SQL Server to facilitate tracing, as you would again be facing the dilemma of assigning more privileges than necessary. These permissions would allow someone to make some significant server-wide changes to SQL Server behavior that would impact its overall performance. You can see the full list of settings that could be affected by querying the sys.configurations catalog view. For example, it would be possible to set min and max memory values for SQL Server.

> The ALTER SETTINGS *permission also grants the login the rights to successfully execute the* RECONFIGURE *statement.*

From a tracing perspective, the only other time you might need ALTER SETTINGS permission is to enable C2-level auditing. C2-level auditing was introduced in SQL Server 2000 to help push the product into highly secure organizations (think Army, Navy, Ministry of Defense, CIA, and so on). However, if your environment needs this level of audit in place, then you will probably find it quite hard to get the DBAs to grant you ALTER TRACE in the first place, let alone ALTER SETTINGS. Therefore, you might need to find a higher authority to enable this for you.

C2 has now been superceded by the Common Criteria. This is not based on tracing, but rather affects SQL Server in other ways: enabling statistical output in DMVs, protecting data when resident in memory, and affecting the permissions hierarchy. An in-depth analysis of the Common Criteria is outside the scope of this book.

> *To learn more about the Common Criteria standard, check out their portal at* www.commoncriteriaportal.org/ *or Microsoft's common criteria website* (www.microsoft.com/sql/commoncriteria/certifications.mspx).

Securing the Output of SQL Trace

As you have learned, there are two I/O providers for SQL Trace events:

- ➤ Flat-file provider
- ➤ Rowset provider

The rowset provider is used by Profiler, and the flat-file provider is used by server-side tracing. Having spent a significant amount of time ensuring that only authorized persons are allowed to create traces, you now must ensure that the data is similarly well protected when this information is persisted.

SQL Trace File Protection

Simply put, the flat files generated when running a server-side trace contain all the data captured by the events subscribed to in the trace definition. However, you can protect these files to some extent by using Windows permissions on a folder structure, which will also help to organize the files.

In order for SQL Trace to be able to write to a location, the service account of SQL Server must have write access to that path and file location. The same goes for read. By ensuring that only the SQL Server service account and the user(s) in question has access to the folder being written to, the files should be safe from prying eyes.

In addition, don't forget about file system backups! You might want to put exclusion rules in place to prohibit these files from being backed up. This has two benefits:

- ➤ It reduces backup times and size of the backup.
- ➤ It eliminates the possibility that the files could be restored to another server from the backup device.

What you want to be left with is a nicely organized folder structure, which, coupled with a good file-naming convention, will help keep your systems neat and tidy.

My suggestion is that you give each tracer a folder under a root and then three subfolders within that. The three subfolders are entitled Read, Write, and Archive. To help secure the trace files, and to prevent another tracer loading up a file they didn't create, only allow the SQL Server Service to have read permission on the read folder and write permission on the write folder. In order to load up the data, a tracer would need to move the file from the write folder to the read folder. Switching the files between locations should only be a quick pointer change on the disk, and the move could easily be achieved with a simple PowerShell script. Your folder structure would look something like Figure10-35.

FIGURE 10-35

This may seem over the top and for some places that may well be the case but consider this situation. You, as the DBA, might be tracing the tracer's activity. You may need to audit what is going on and must prevent anyone seeing what could be highly sensitive data. Would you consider such a structure over the top then?

Rowset Provider Protection

Ultimately it is the user's responsibility to securely manage the data received from the SQL Trace rowset provider. In the case of Profiler, users have two options should they decide to persist the trace data, but neither option is inherently secure — you have to make it secure. Should you wish to save the trace data, you can do one of the following:

➤ Save to a table

➤ Save to a file (which may or may not be XML)

You have already seen what you can do to protect a flat file. However, what about when you save this data to a table? What can you do here?

As a DBA, you can do a couple of things. First things first: You can decide to not grant the permissions necessary to make this a viable option. However, it can be very handy to be able to query this data, rather than merely look at it in a file. Perhaps, then, you ought to let tracers save data to a table. Let's assume for a moment that you are a nice, friendly DBA, rather than the "don't bother asking" variety, and see how you can make this happen.

When I am faced with this situation I like to create an empty database, normally called `TraceDB`, which is appropriately sized to hold tracing information. I can then decide whether or not this database is backed up, and what recovery model is used. Restricting access to this database is now a simple case of locating those logins with the `ALTER TRACE` permission and making the necessary grants. If there are multiple tracers, then rather than grant `db_owner` privilege, I tend to give each tracer a schema within that database to load up and query their tracing data. This isolates tracers from one another and prevents them from reading each other's trace information — a Chinese wall if you will.

If you were to implement something like this yourself, you might end up with a script similar to the following:

```
CREATE DATABASE TraceDB
GO
ALTER DATABASE TraceDB SET RECOVERY SIMPLE
GO
CREATE LOGIN JRJ
WITH PASSWORD = 'D@r3D3vilR0ck5'
,DEFAULT_DATABASE=[TraceDB]
,CHECK_POLICY = OFF;

USE TraceDB;
GO
CREATE USER JRJ FOR LOGIN JRJ WITH DEFAULT_SCHEMA=JRJ
GO
CREATE SCHEMA JRJ AUTHORIZATION JRJ;
GO
```

```
GRANT CREATE TABLE TO JRJ AS dbo
GO
GRANT CONNECT TO JRJ AS dbo
GO
```

This script contains sufficient permissions to create a table in the JRJ schema only; query it and delete it. The JRJ login can also query the tracing catalog views, which will also prove to be useful when determining which events are contained in the table. This is because the event names or column names aren't inserted into the saved trace table, only the IDs. In order to retrieve the IDs, a join is required to the sys.trace_columns and sys.trace_events catalog view.

PROFILER

As mentioned at the beginning of this chapter, Profiler is a graphical user interface (GUI) tool that is often used to run traces against production systems. However, using Profiler in this way can cause heartache.

Not only does it consume CPU and make heavy use of the TEMP folder on your production system, it is also an implementation of a rowset provider. Therefore, it is not designed to guarantee the capture of all events specified in a trace. Under heavy load you may well see that a tracing session using Profiler drops events.

You might think then that Profiler should come with some sort of government health warning to prevent people from using it at all. However, such a strong caveat is a complete disservice to the tool. Profiler certainly has pride of place in the DBA toolbox. It has several advanced features and it's a great productivity aid for the configuration of server-side traces and for reading trace files. With the advent of SQL Server 2008, you can also use Profiler to create a T-SQL Data Collection Set definition for the Management Data Warehouse.

Profiler can also be used to "replay" a trace. However, replaying traces with Profiler has now been superseded by the RML Utilities, and the ReadTrace, OStress, and ORCA utilities in particular. You can read all about the RML Utilities in Chapter 12, "Introducing RML Utilities for Stress Testing and Trace File Analysis."

This section about Profiler focuses on some of the advanced features of Profiler with special attention paid to the functionality provided to configure a trace definition and export it for later use. The chapter then closes with some hints and tips on how best to use this tool.

Advanced Features of Profiler

A key message for this chapter has been to encourage you to use server-side tracing as much possible. While server-side tracing can be a bit of a pain to set up it should be your preferred way to trace, especially in production. That said, Profiler does have some really nice features and is much more intuitive to use. Because some of those features aren't immediately obvious, the next few sections highlight a few.

Grouping Events

Sometimes it can be difficult to see what is going on with Profiler. Auto Scroll might be on (in which case just switch that off on the menu bar), but you also might have a lot of other events getting in the way. Thankfully, Profiler allows you to Group by one or many events.

By opening up your trace's properties and clicking the Events Selection tab you expose the Organize Columns button. Click this button to see the organize columns dialog box, shown in Figure 10-36.

You can use the up and down buttons to change the sequence of the event columns and you can also move one or more columns up into the Groups area. This changes how the events appear in Profiler's GUI. By default the events are shown in tree control style. This is ok but can be frustrating to navigate when the tree suddenly closes on you unexpectedly. The Tree (or Aggregated) view can be seen in Figure 10-37.

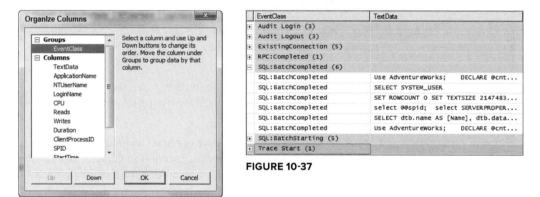

FIGURE 10-36

FIGURE 10-37

However, you can also right click on the events and select a different view. This view is called the Grouped view and is shown in Figure 10-38. With this view all events are immediately visible but they are grouped together, which makes it easier to see what is going on.

EventClass	TextData
Audit Logout	
Audit Logout	
ExistingConnection	-- network protocol: LPC set quote...
ExistingConnection	-- network protocol: LPC set quote...
ExistingConnection	-- network protocol: LPC set quote...
ExistingConnection	-- network protocol: LPC set quote...
ExistingConnection	-- network protocol: LPC set quote...
RPC:Completed	exec sp_executesql N'SELECT dtb.col...
SQL:BatchCompleted	Use AdventureWorks; DECLARE @cnt...
SQL:BatchCompleted	SELECT SYSTEM_USER
SQL:BatchCompleted	SET ROWCOUNT O SET TEXTSIZE 2147483...
SQL:BatchCompleted	select @@spid; select SERVERPROPER...
SQL:BatchCompleted	SELECT dtb.name AS [Name], dtb.data...
SQL:BatchCompleted	Use AdventureWorks; DECLARE @cnt...
SQL:BatchStarting	SELECT SYSTEM_USER
SQL:BatchStarting	SET ROWCOUNT O SET TEXTSIZE 2147483...
SQL:BatchStarting	select @@spid; select SERVERPROPER...
SQL:BatchStarting	SELECT dtb.name AS [Name], dtb.data...
SQL:BatchStarting	Use AdventureWorks; DECLARE @cnt...
Trace Start	

FIGURE 10-38

I have grouped these examples by the `EventClass`. However, an alternative method would be to group by a `ClientProcessID`, `SPID`, `HostName`, `NTUserName`, `LoginName`, or `SessionLoginName` to help isolate a single user in the context of all other event data.

Extracting Event Data

There are three primary ways to extract event data from a Profiler trace. Firstly you can highlight one or many rows and watch as Profiler concatenates the event statements together in the lower grey window. Secondly, you can highlight an event or events and then right click on your mouse and select the "Extract Event Data" option. Finally, you can also use the menu bar as follows: File ⇨ Export ⇨ Extract SQL Server Events ⇨ Extract Transact-SQL Events.

> *Make sure you highlight at least one row before using the menu bar to extract an event. If you don't, Profiler generates a server-side trace definition based on your Profiler output. This is not undesirable per se but it can be quite confusing.*

For SQL statements these options only work for `SQL:BatchStarting`, `SQL: BatchCompleted`, `RPC:Starting`, and `RPC:Completed` events. You can however always copy the text from the lower grey box for a single event as the text data is shown there.

You can also extract plan and deadlock information if you have opted to include this in your trace definition. For a deadlock example please refer to the Deadlocking section in Chapter 6 because the example there uses this feature. However, here you will see how to do this for the Showplan XML events.

First, create a trace in Profiler that includes the following events and start running:

> SQL:BatchStarted
>
> Showplan XML for Query Compile
>
> Showplan XML Statistics Profile

Once Complete execute the following code:

```
DBCC     FREEPROCCACHE;

Use      AdventureWorks;

EXEC     dbo.uspGetBillOfMaterials 777, '20040101';
```

Your Profiler window should now be populated with each of the preceding events. You may now highlight one or all of the rows, right-click and select extract event data or use the menu bar as follows: File ⇨ Export ⇨ Extract SQL Server Events ⇨ Extract Showplan Events. Note you must highlight the rows you wish to extract first before using *either* method.

> *To make it easier to extract events you may want to consider grouping the events by the* EventClass *as shown in the previous sub-section "Grouping Events."*

Importing PerfMon Data into Profiler

This is Profiler's ace in the pack. Profiler can consume a Performance Monitor trace and synchronize it with the event data it has also captured. The beauty of this is that you can, for example, use Profiler to drill into both sets of data and pinpoint the query/queries that caused the CPU spike. Neither dataset needs to have been collected by Profiler for this to work.

Let's illustrate how easy this is to achieve. First create a new Data Collector Set using the System Performance template. Pick all the defaults and start it running. Next create a basic server-side trace. Select SP:Starting, SP:Completed, SP:StmtStarting, and SP:StmtCompleted as a minimum and then start this running. Finally, generate some load with the following script.

```
Use AdventureWorks;

DECLARE @cnt int =1;

WHILE @cnt < 1000
BEGIN
    EXEC dbo.Top10Names;

    SET  @cnt = @cnt +1;
END
```

Once this loop has finished executing you should have enough data to collect some results. Stop the trace — the Data Collector Set should have stopped after a minute.

Now you must join the results together. First, use Profiler to open the server-side trace file. Then click File ⇨ Import Performance Data and navigate to the Performance Counter.blg file created by the Data Collector Set. Normally, this file is located in a subfolder of %systemdrive%\PerfLogs\Admin\. A new dialog box (see Figure 10-39) should now be in front of you. Select the % Processor Time Box and any

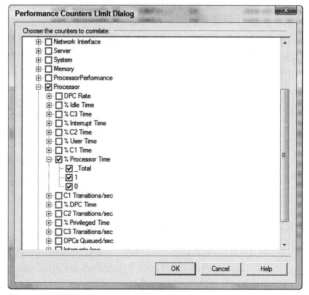

FIGURE 10-39

other counters you think may be of interest and then click OK.

You should now be blessed with an interface containing all the Profiler events *and* the PerfMon data you collected and subsequently imported as shown in Figure 10-40.

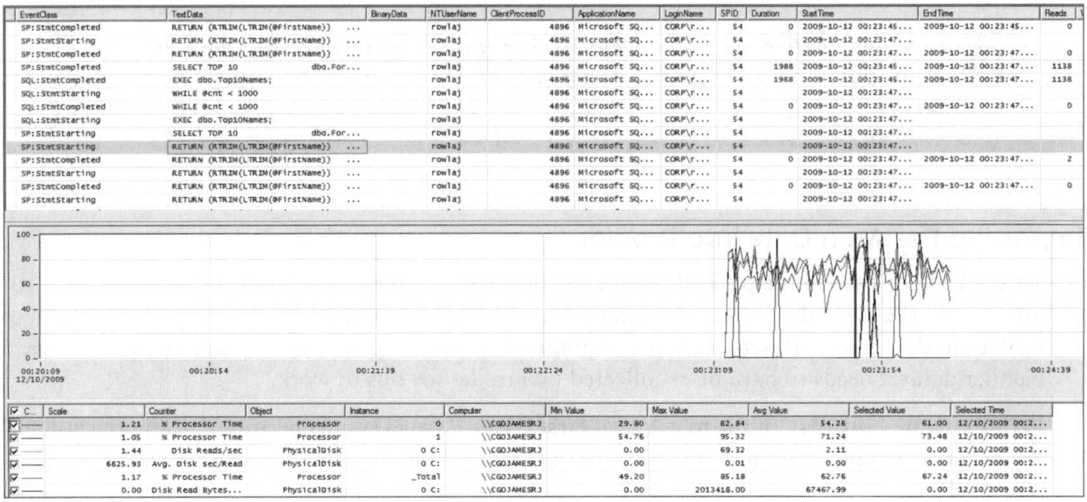

FIGURE 10-40

Please also make sure you pay special attention to the red vertical bar on the PerfMon graph. You will notice that my PerfMon counters didn't start for a while. Rather than trawl through a log, all I need to do is click on the performance graph and immediately the red bar moves to the relevant point. However, something else happened. Did you see that the Profiler data moved when you clicked the performance graph? Both datasets are synchronized by their respective timestamps. Wherever you click on the graph (or if you choose to select a specific event in the Profiler trace) the other set of data moves to its nearest position so that all the information available is provided in context. Bear in mind that the precision of Performance Monitor isn't the same as the events captured in Profiler. PerfMon's sampling interval is at best one second. Therefore it's not likely that the two datasets will synchronize exactly. Still, Profiler is certainly putting you in the right ball park.

Finally if you let your mouse hover over the red vertical bar then you will notice that the mouse icon changes. If you click and hold the vertical bar you move it to cover a span of time, which causes you to zoom into the graph for deeper analysis.

Exporting a Trace Definition

Defining a server-side trace is a relatively straightforward process in Profiler. To get started, select the General tab of the Trace Properties dialog, where you can choose from a list of predefined trace templates, which you can then modify as desired (see Figure 10-41).

On this screen you can then decide whether the output of your trace is saved to a file or a table. Note that if you select a table, you are in fact using the rowset provider. There is no part of the SQL Trace architecture that allows for data to be saved to a table. Therefore, by selecting the "save to table" option you are actually using Profiler's rowset provider, which is in turn inserting the data into the table. Not only will your trace take the hit of having to write each event back to the database, it might not contain all the events you expected to capture. Interestingly, saving to a file also uses the rowset provider unless, as shown in Figure 10-42 the server processes trace data configuration option is set. (This option is not set by default, but doing so reduces the impact of your tracing activity and guarantees that your events will be captured.)

One final point to mention is that you can also set the trace stop date and time, as shown in Figure 10-42. This screen therefore reflects the sp_trace_create stored procedure discussed in some detail earlier.

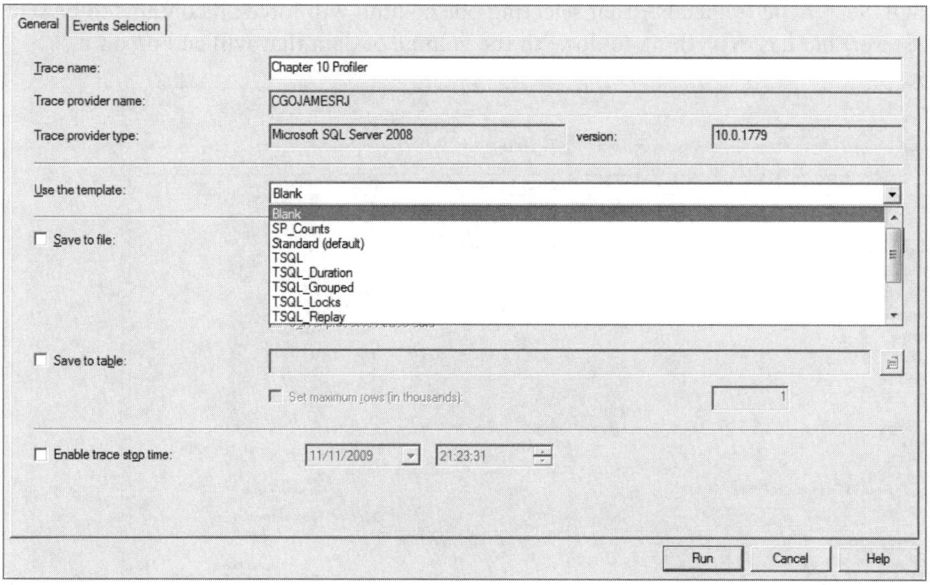

FIGURE 10-41

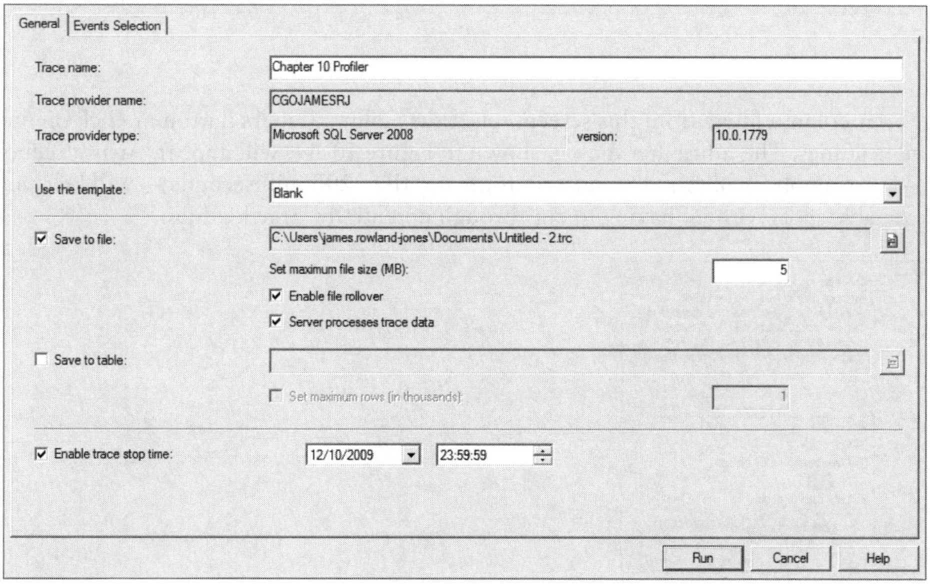

FIGURE 10-42

Flipping to the Events Selection tab, shown in Figure 10-43, enables you to configure the events and columns you wish to trace. If you have specified a template other than blank, some of these settings will be preset for you. However, when selecting the blank template, you will need to choose events and columns from scratch. Be careful not to get too cavalier here. Selecting the check box to the left of the event name will select all columns currently displayed, but the best practice is to select only the columns you need. If you want all possible columns you must first check the show all columns checkbox before selecting the check box to the left of the event name. This isn't for performance reasons at the SQL Server end (remember that selecting one column will force all columns to be sent out by SQL Server) but has everything to do with the volume of data that will end up on disk.

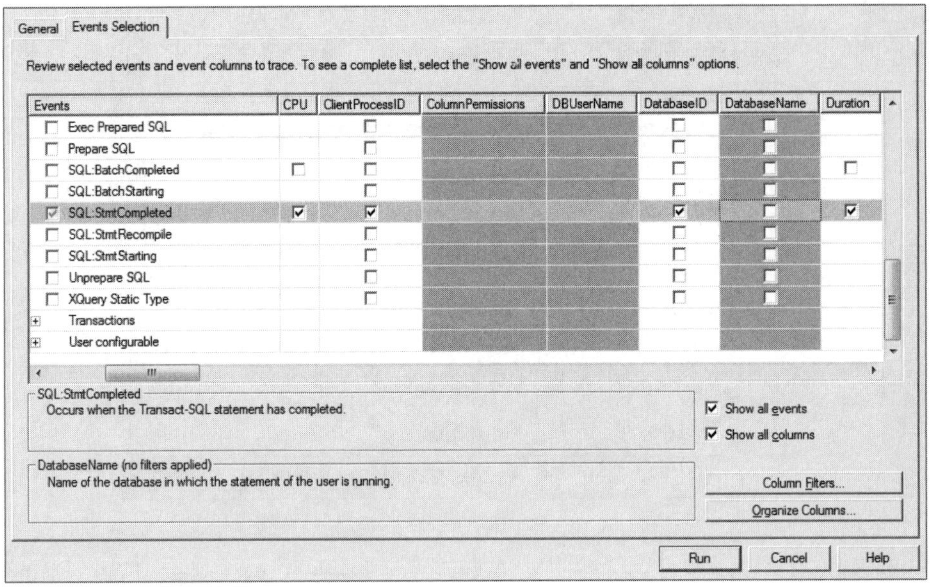

FIGURE 10-43

To configure your column filters from this screen, select the Column Filters button or click on one of the column headings. The Edit Filter dialog, shown in Figure 10-44, will appear. Again, reducing the output — for example, by filtering on durations greater than 200 milliseconds — will help you focus on the trouble spots without having to cut through potentially large log files.

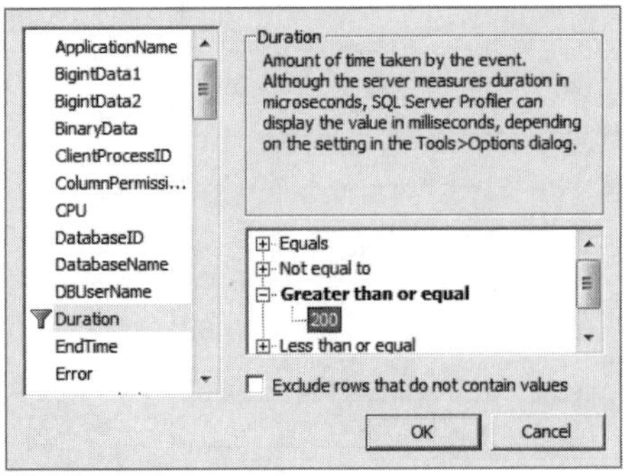

FIGURE 10-44

> By default, duration is displayed in milliseconds in Profiler. However, by select-
> ing Tools ⇨ Options you can make Profiler display the microsecond value. This
> works only for SQL Server 2005 and later, and it allows for greater precision.
> When this option is set, any value specified in a duration filter will be converted
> to a microsecond value in the GUI.

The Events Selection screen is the equivalent of using the `sp_trace_setevent` and `sp_trace_setfilter` stored procedures. Once all the values have been selected, clicking Run will start the trace. The trace can be stopped immediately but it is unfortunately a necessary precursor. All you need to do now is export this definition. Simply navigate to File ⇨ Export ⇨ Script Trace Definition and pick your target, as shown in Figure 10-45.

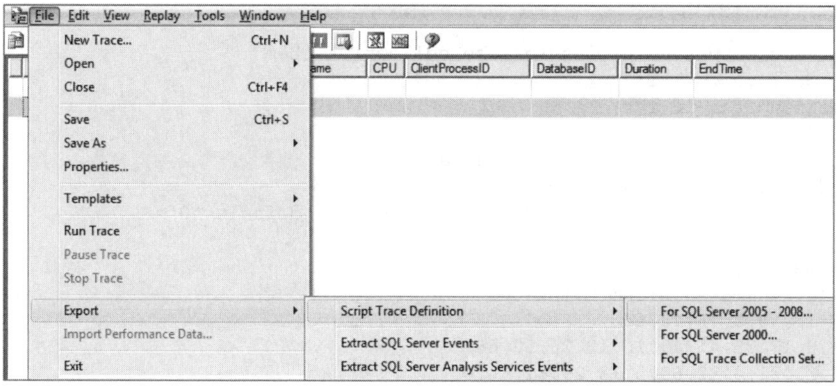

FIGURE 10-45

Of particular interest is the SQL Trace Collection Set, as this is a new feature in SQL Server 2008. I particularly like how the trace definition is created as an XML definition. If the interface for regu-lar SQL trace definitions were the same, then I'd be a very happy man, rather than the cumbersome method of repeatedly calling the same stored procedure. However, for completeness, both defini-tions follow in Listings 10-1 and 10-2.

LISTING 10-1: Exported SQL Trace Collection Set (CH10 Sample Trace Collection Set.sql)

```
/****************************************************************/
-- SQL Trace collection set generated from SQL Server Profiler
-- Date: 30/08/2009  20:39:01
/****************************************************************/

USE msdb
GO

BEGIN TRANSACTION
BEGIN TRY

-- Define collection set
```

continues

LISTING 10-1 *(continued)*

```
-- ***
-- *** Replace 'SqlTrace Collection Set Name Here' in the following script
-- *** with the name you want to use for the collection set.
-- ***
DECLARE @collection_set_id int;
EXEC [dbo].[sp_syscollector_create_collection_set]
    @name = N'SqlTrace Collection Set Name Here',
    @schedule_name = N'CollectorSchedule_Every_15min',
    @collection_mode = 0, -- cached mode needed for Trace collections
    @logging_level = 0, -- minimum logging
    @days_until_expiration = 5,
    @description = N'Collection set generated by SQL Server Profiler',
    @collection_set_id = @collection_set_id output;
SELECT @collection_set_id;

-- Define input and output varaibles for the collection item
DECLARE @trace_definition xml;
DECLARE @collection_item_id int;

-- Define the trace parameters as an XML variable
SELECT @trace_definition = convert(xml,
N'<ns:SqlTraceCollector xmlns:ns="DataCollectorType" use_default="0">
<Events>
  <EventType name="TSQL">
    <Event id="41" name="SQL:StmtCompleted"
columnslist="7,15,55,8,16,48,64
            ,1,9,17,25,41,49,10,18,26,50,66
            ,3,11,51,4,12,60,5,13,29,61,6,14" />
  </EventType>
</Events>
<Filters>
  <Filter columnid="13" columnname="Duration"
          logical_operator="AND"
          comparison_operator="GE" value="200L" />
</Filters>
</ns:SqlTraceCollector>
');

-- Retrieve the collector type GUID for the trace collector type
DECLARE @collector_type_GUID uniqueidentifier;
SELECT @collector_type_GUID = collector_type_uid
FROM [dbo].[syscollector_collector_types]
WHERE name = N'Generic SQL Trace Collector Type';

-- Create the trace collection item
-- ***
-- *** Replace 'SqlTrace Collection Item Name Here' in the following script
-- *** with the name you want to use for the collection item.
-- ***
EXEC [dbo].[sp_syscollector_create_collection_item]
    @collection_set_id = @collection_set_id,
    @collector_type_uid = @collector_type_GUID,
```

```
    @name = N'SqlTrace Collection Item Name Here',
    @frequency = 900, -- specified the frequency for checking to see if
trace is still running
    @parameters = @trace_definition,
    @collection_item_id = @collection_item_id output;
SELECT @collection_item_id;

COMMIT TRANSACTION;
END TRY

BEGIN CATCH
ROLLBACK TRANSACTION;
DECLARE @ErrorMessage nvarchar(4000);
DECLARE @ErrorSeverity int;
DECLARE @ErrorState int;
DECLARE @ErrorNumber int;
DECLARE @ErrorLine int;
DECLARE @ErrorProcedure nvarchar(200);
SELECT @ErrorLine = ERROR_LINE(),
       @ErrorSeverity = ERROR_SEVERITY(),
       @ErrorState = ERROR_STATE(),
       @ErrorNumber = ERROR_NUMBER(),
       @ErrorMessage = ERROR_MESSAGE(),
       @ErrorProcedure = ISNULL(ERROR_PROCEDURE(), '-');
RAISERROR (14684, @ErrorSeverity, 1 , @ErrorNumber, @ErrorSeverity,
@ErrorState, @ErrorProcedure, @ErrorLine, @ErrorMessage);
END CATCH;
GO
```

LISTING 10-2: Exported SQL Trace Definition (CH10 Sample Server-Side Trace)

```
/****************************************************/
/* Created by: SQL Server 2008 Profiler           */
/* Date: 30/08/2009  20:42:34        */
/****************************************************/


-- Create a Queue
declare @rc int
declare @TraceID int
declare @maxfilesize bigint
set @maxfilesize = 5

-- Please replace the text InsertFileNameHere, with an appropriate
-- filename prefixed by a path, e.g., c:\MyFolder\MyTrace. The .trc extension
-- will be appended to the filename automatically. If you are writing from
-- remote server to local drive, please use UNC path and make sure server has
-- write access to your network share

exec @rc = sp_trace_create @TraceID output
                           ,0
                           ,N'InsertFileNameHere'
                           ,@maxfilesize
                           ,NULL
```

continues

LISTING 10-2 *(continued)*

```
if (@rc != 0) goto error

-- Client side File and Table cannot be scripted

-- Set the events
declare @on bit
set @on = 1
exec sp_trace_setevent @TraceID, 41, 7, @on
exec sp_trace_setevent @TraceID, 41, 15, @on
exec sp_trace_setevent @TraceID, 41, 55, @on
exec sp_trace_setevent @TraceID, 41, 8, @on
exec sp_trace_setevent @TraceID, 41, 16, @on
exec sp_trace_setevent @TraceID, 41, 48, @on
exec sp_trace_setevent @TraceID, 41, 64, @on
exec sp_trace_setevent @TraceID, 41, 1, @on
exec sp_trace_setevent @TraceID, 41, 9, @on
exec sp_trace_setevent @TraceID, 41, 17, @on
exec sp_trace_setevent @TraceID, 41, 25, @on
exec sp_trace_setevent @TraceID, 41, 41, @on
exec sp_trace_setevent @TraceID, 41, 49, @on
exec sp_trace_setevent @TraceID, 41, 10, @on
exec sp_trace_setevent @TraceID, 41, 18, @on
exec sp_trace_setevent @TraceID, 41, 26, @on
exec sp_trace_setevent @TraceID, 41, 50, @on
exec sp_trace_setevent @TraceID, 41, 66, @on
exec sp_trace_setevent @TraceID, 41, 3, @on
exec sp_trace_setevent @TraceID, 41, 11, @on
exec sp_trace_setevent @TraceID, 41, 51, @on
exec sp_trace_setevent @TraceID, 41, 4, @on
exec sp_trace_setevent @TraceID, 41, 12, @on
exec sp_trace_setevent @TraceID, 41, 60, @on
exec sp_trace_setevent @TraceID, 41, 5, @on
exec sp_trace_setevent @TraceID, 41, 13, @on
exec sp_trace_setevent @TraceID, 41, 29, @on
exec sp_trace_setevent @TraceID, 41, 61, @on
exec sp_trace_setevent @TraceID, 41, 6, @on
exec sp_trace_setevent @TraceID, 41, 14, @on


-- Set the Filters
declare @intfilter int
declare @bigintfilter bigint

set @bigintfilter = 200
exec sp_trace_setfilter @TraceID, 13, 0, 4, @bigintfilter

-- Set the trace status to start
exec sp_trace_setstatus @TraceID, 1

-- display trace id for future references
select TraceID=@TraceID
goto finish

error:
```

```
select ErrorCode=@rc

finish:
go
```

Exporting an Existing Server-Side Trace

Unfortunately, once a server-side trace has been executed against the SQL Server there is no way to script it out again. You must either generate one yourself by writing SQL against the various tracing catalog views; create a replica by hand; or save the original.

You can use the following script (Listing 10-3) to help you generate or hydrate a server-side trace definition once it has been created inside SQL Server. When you have trace definitions that consist of many events and columns, this sort of script can be a mini lifesaver if the original script has been lost:

LISTING 10-3: Hydrate SQL Trace (CH10 Trace Hydrate.sql)

```
DECLARE @TraceID int
SET     @TraceID = 1

SELECT
'
DECLARE  @rc            int
        ,@TraceID       int
        ,@MaxFileSize   bigint
        ,@BigIntfilter  bigint
        ,@on            bit = 1
'
UNION ALL
SELECT 'SELECT @MaxFileSize = '+ CAST(max_size as varchar(20))
FROM    sys.traces
WHERE   ID = @TraceID
UNION ALL
select 'EXEC @rc = sp_trace_create @traceid output ,'
        +
        CASE    WHEN [path] like
'\\?\C:\Program Files\Microsoft SQL Server\MSSQL__.MSSQLSERVER\MSSQL\DATA\blackbox%'
                THEN '@options = 8'
        ELSE
                CASE    WHEN is_shutdown = 1
                        AND  is_rollover = 1    THEN '6'
                        WHEN is_shutdown = 1    THEN '4'
                        WHEN is_rollover = 1    THEN '2'
                        ELSE '0'
                END + ',N'''
                + REVERSE(SUBSTRING(SUBSTRING(REVERSE([path]),5,LEN([path]))
                 ,CHARINDEX('_',SUBSTRING(REVERSE([path]),5,LEN([path])),1)+1
                 ,LEN([path])))
                +''', @MaxFileSize'
                +','+ coalesce(''''+convert(varchar(20),stop_time,126)
                +'''','NULL')
                + CASE WHEN is_rollover = 1
```

continues

LISTING 10-3 *(continued)*

```
                                  THEN ','+cast(max_files as varchar(20))
                                   ELSE ''
                          END
              END
from      sys.traces
WHERE     ID = @TraceID
UNION ALL
SELECT 'if (@rc != 0) goto error'
UNION ALL
SELECT  CASE WHEN [path] like
'\\?\C:\Program Files\Microsoft SQL Server\MSSQL%.MSSQLSERVER\MSSQL\DATA\blackbox%'
          THEN ''
          ELSE
          'EXEC @rc = sp_trace_setevent @traceid'
          +','+CAST(EventID as varchar(20))
          +','+CAST(columnid as varchar(20))
          +', @on'
          END
FROM      ::fn_trace_geteventinfo(@TraceID) evi
CROSS APPLY   sys.traces trc
WHERE     trc.id = @TraceID
UNION ALL
SELECT  CASE   WHEN col.type_name = 'int'
               OR   col.type_name = 'bigint'
               THEN  'SELECT @BigIntFilter = '
                    +CAST(CAST(value as bigint)AS varchar(20))
               ELSE  ''
          END
FROM      ::fn_trace_getfilterinfo(@TraceID) fil
JOIN      sys.trace_columns col
ON        fil.columnid = col.trace_column_id
UNION ALL
SELECT  'EXEC @rc = sp_trace_setfilter @traceid'
          +','+CAST(columnid as varchar(20))
          +','+CAST(logical_operator as varchar(20))
          +','+CAST(comparison_operator as varchar(20))
          +','+CASE   WHEN col.type_name = 'int'
                      OR   col.type_name = 'bigint'
                      THEN  '@BigIntFilter'
                      ELSE  ''''+CAST(value as varchar(8000))+''''
                      END
FROM      ::fn_trace_getfilterinfo(@TraceID) fil
JOIN      sys.trace_columns col
ON        fil.columnid = col.trace_column_id
UNION ALL
SELECT
'--Starting Trace
exec sp_trace_setstatus @traceid, 1

-- Stop Trace ' +CAST(@TraceID as varchar(20))+'
-- EXEC sp_trace_setstatus '+CAST(@TraceID as varchar(20))+', 0
```

```
-- Close and Delete Trace  '+CAST(@TraceID as varchar(20))+'
-- EXEC sp_trace_setstatus '+CAST(@TraceID as varchar(20))+', 2
-- display trace id for future references
select TraceID=@TraceID
goto finish
'
UNION ALL
SELECT
'error:
select ErrorCode=@rc

finish:'
```

Tips & Tricks

To conclude the chapter I thought it might be worth spending a few moments highlighting a few extra Profiler tips and tricks to help you use the tool as effectively as possible. Some tips have come throughout the chapter. The following sections cover others that did not.

Turn Auto Scroll Off

It's a shame but there is no hotkey for this and no way to disable it by default. However, if you want to keep your sanity, then turn Auto Scroll off. The button on the menu bar has a blue downwards arrow on it as shown in Figure 10-46. You can also use the Menu Bar as follows: Windows ⇨ Auto Scroll.

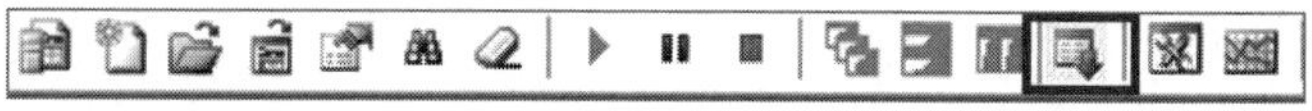

FIGURE 10-46

Edit the Base Template

I don't know about you but it drives me mad when I set up a trace and its "contaminated" by SQL Server Agent and Report Server Messages. The trick here is to change your templates so they automatically exclude these applications, much the same way as Profiler can also exclude itself.

To do this, simply use the menu bar as follows: File ⇨ Template ⇨ Edit Template. This will fire up the Trace Template Properties dialog box as seen in Figure 10-47.

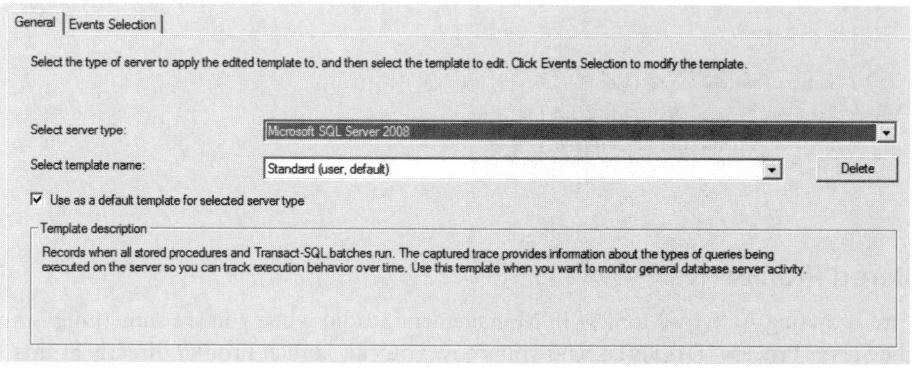

General | Events Selection |

Select the type of server to apply the edited template to, and then select the template to edit. Click Events Selection to modify the template.

Select server type: Microsoft SQL Server 2008

Select template name: Standard (user, default)   Delete

☑ Use as a default template for selected server type

Template description

Records when all stored procedures and Transact-SQL batches run. The captured trace provides information about the types of queries being executed on the server so you can track execution behavior over time. Use this template when you want to monitor general database server activity.

FIGURE 10-47

From here you can select the template you wish to edit and alter which template is seen as the default. Clicking the Events Selection Tab (Figure 10-48) allows you to then add / remove events, columns, and filters for your chosen template in the normal way.

Events	TextData	ApplicationName	NTUserName	LoginName	CPU	Reads	Writes	Duration	ClientProc
☐ SP:StmtCompleted	☐	☐	☐	☐	☐	☐	☐	☐	☐
☐ SP:StmtStarting	☐	☐	☐	☐					☐
⊟ **TSQL**									
☐ Exec Prepared SQL		☐	☐	☐					☐
☐ Prepare SQL		☐	☐	☐					☐
☑ SQL:BatchCompleted	☑	☑	☑	☑	☑	☑	☑	☑	☑
☑ SQL:BatchStarting	☑	☑	☑	☑					☑
☐ SQL:StmtCompleted	☐	☐	☐	☐	☐	☐	☐	☐	☐
☐ SQL:StmtRecompile	☐	☐	☐	☐					☐
☐ SQL:StmtStarting	☐	☐	☐	☐					☐
☐ Unprepare SQL		☐	☐	☐					☐

Review selected events and event columns to trace when using this template. To see a complete list, select the "Show all events" and "Show all columns" options.

Unprepare SQL
Indicates that the SqlClient, ODBC, OLE DB, or DB-Library has unprepared (deleted) a prepared Transact-SQL statement or statements.

☑ Show all events
☑ Show all columns

ClientProcessID (no filters applied)
The process ID of the application calling SQL Server.

Column Filters...
Organize Columns...

FIGURE 10-48

Click the Column Filters button, and you can now remove those applications by adding filters to the ApplicationName event as shown in Figure 10-49.

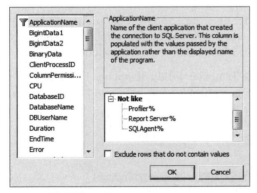

FIGURE 10-49

Firing Pre-Filtered Profiler

Imagine you are browsing Activity Monitor in Management Studio when you see something is awry with one of the Server Process IDs (SPID). Did you know you can launch Profiler directly at this point? Are you aware that when you do this, the trace it creates is pre-filtered so you will only see data from that SPID? I like this feature very much. It also helps you by filtering out Profiler at the same time.

All you need to do, as shown in Figure 10-50, is right click on a SPID in Activity Monitor and select Trace Process in SQL Server Profiler. Presto!

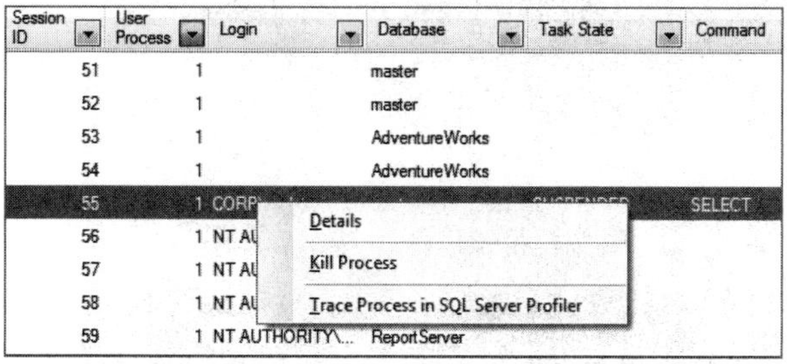

Session ID	User Process	Login	Database	Task State	Command
51	1		master		
52	1		master		
53	1		AdventureWorks		
54	1		AdventureWorks		
55	1	CORP		SUSPENDED	SELECT
56	1	NT AU			
57	1	NT AU			
58	1	NT AU			
59	1	NT AUTHORITY\...	ReportServer		

Details
Kill Process
Trace Process in SQL Server Profiler

FIGURE 10-50

SUMMARY

This chapter covered a wide spectrum of issues concerning the use of SQL Trace using either a server-side trace or more interactively with Profiler. My strong recommendation to you is to get into the habit of using a server-side trace. It can be painful and is less intuitive to use but when it comes to production it is the only way to go. By ensuring that you are familiar with server-side tracing then you won't be daunted by it when you need to use it. Remember you can always use Profiler to view the results of your tracing activities. I certainly hope that the scripts I have included as part of this chapter will help you to use it regularly.

When you are about to start a trace think back over what you have read and ask yourself some important questions:

How busy is the system?

Which events do I need to capture?

What columns do I need to capture?

Are there any filters I need to apply?

Do I really need to capture statement level events?

Will the trace I create contain sensitive information?

What should happen if I can't capture an event?

Will I need to have Performance Monitor running as well?

Do I need to guarantee that I capture all the results?

Where should my trace files be stored?

How will the data be analyzed?

Will Profiler suffice or should I load the data into a table?

How should I load this data?

My final point to you is this: When you are tracing you are tracing SQL Server. You are not tracing a database. Be very careful who you grant `ALTER TRACE` to on a production system, especially on a consolidated system. Tracing is the window to SQL Server's soul.

11

Consolidating Data Collection with SQLDiag and the PerfStats Script

WHAT'S IN THIS CHAPTER

➤ An approach to collecting performance data for complex or challenging SQL Server problems

➤ When to use SQLDiag and the PerfStats script

➤ How to configure SQLDiag and the PerfStats script

➤ Extending the capability of SQLDiag and the PerfStats script

When handling complex SQL Server problems, gathering the right information to be able to solve the problem can be labor intensive, time consuming and error prone, especially when working remotely or in a multi-level support organization. This chapter contains information about tools that simplify and automate data collection to provide the best possible chance of collecting the data necessary to fix a problem, the first time.

SQLDiag and the PerfStats script provide data collection that can be used as input to SQLNexus, a GUI tool for processing data to assist identifying problem queries and performance bottlenecks. Chapter 13 focuses on getting the best results from SQLNexus. Combining the data collection functionality of SQLDiag and PerfStats with the analysis capabilities of SQLNexus and Performance Analysis for Logs (PAL) provides engineers with many of the same tools available to Microsoft support engineers. Using these tools at the right time and in the correct way enables engineers to tackle some of the most complex and hard to resolve SQL Server issues.

Someone once said that a DBA is only as good as his or her last outage, and these tools are a great asset to reduce the resolution time for complex or serious SQL Server problems. If there's been a problem and insufficient data was captured to determine the root cause (the problem may have been temporarily resolved), configure these tools in preparation for a reccurence of the problem. Familiarity with SQLDiag and the PerfStats script means you'll be confident that if the problem does recur, the complete data required to resolve the problem will be captured.

This chapter provides a detailed look at SQLDiag and the PerfStats script. SQLDiag is an out-of-the-box data capture utility used to automate collection of PerfMon logs, SQL Trace files, application and SQL Server error logs, and other troubleshooting data. The PerfStats script utilizes SQLDiag alongside other troubleshooting scripts, extracting DMV data and capturing blocking information. The PerfStats script uses SQLDiag and extends this functionality to provide a comprehensive activity capture from the problem server. The PerfStats script provides all the data necessary for detailed problem analysis with SQLNexus. The PerfStats script is little known and can be tough to track down — see the later section "Where to Get the PerfStats script" for details of its location.

> *You need to download the PerfStats script from CodePlex, although locating the scripts isn't easy, the section later in this chapter describing the location should help.*

APPROACHING DATA COLLECTION

When production SQL Server problems occur, systems engineers and DBAs work as quickly as possible to restore service. Often, fault resolution of live systems involves a number of tools for problem analysis and restoration, and sometimes several actions will be taken before the problem is resolved.

Once the priority of restoring service is achieved, DBAs often face questions:

➤   What caused the problem?

➤   How can the problem be prevented from happening again?

➤   What steps should be taken if the problem does happen again?

Complex problems on systems comprising many moving parts can be difficult to troubleshoot, and once a problem has been resolved it isn't always possible to determine the root cause because the problem condition no longer exists.

One frustrating aspect of tackling serious production issues is the stress and pressure engineers face — often there isn't sufficient time to consider and capture the right data required to perform a thorough root-cause analysis, as the first priority is restoring service. This situation is fairly common — a problem is cleared but the team who resolved the incident didn't collect sufficient data to identify/resolve the root cause.

Following a service-impacting incident, probably one of the hardest messages to deliver to a service manager or anyone in the business is that insufficient data was captured to determine the root cause. This frustrating aspect of many IT systems results in two options:

➤   Reproduce the problem in a test environment

➤   Wait for the problem to recur

While the problem symptoms and sequence of steps to clear the problem condition may be known, often the underlying cause and long-term fix is not well understood.

In such cases, the engineers tackling the problem should be ready to capture as much information about the problem as possible prior to following the steps used previously to clear the problem condition. Occasionally data capture may slightly extend the duration of the outage, and service managers and users should be briefed to expect this. Good preparation and familiarity with the tools will reduce the time needed to capture the necessary data and ensure that no important data is missed.

An important tool used in troubleshooting SQL Server problems is SQL Trace which is a set of system stored procedures used to create traces in SQL Server, but you may be more familiar with the SQL Server Profiler tool which uses SQL Trace.

SQL Trace has such an important role in troubleshooting that Chapter 10 is dedicated to SQL Server Profiler and tracing. In this chapter tracing in SQL Server is referred to as SQL Trace because the SQLDiag and PerfStats script use server-side tracing to reduce the performance impact of monitoring. The same data can be captured with SQL Server Profiler; however, there's a greater overhead when using the Profiler interface — therefore server-side tracing is preferred, and as such, tracing is referred to as SQL Trace throughout this chapter.

> **TO SQLDIAG OR NOT TO SQLDIAG**
>
> It's likely that experienced SQL Server engineers will be already familiar with SQL Server Profiler and scripts such as `sp_blocker_pss08`. When run together, these two tools can help investigate performance issues caused by locking and blocking problems — with little fuss and without bloating data capture with event logs and SQL Server error logs.
>
> One drawback of this manual approach is that the `sp_blocker_pss08` stored procedure must be created on the target servers in advance; additionally, capturing a SQL Trace can be time consuming to prepare and initiate. In some cases, SQL Profiler and `sp_blocker_pss08` provide exactly the data required to handle a problem; and if that is the case, SQLDiag probably can't add much in terms of what data is captured. However, with a little investment of time, SQLDiag could be tailored to meet your needs by excluding any redundant data collectors and capturing any additional data that might be useful. In the event of a problem, SQLDiag can be configured and begin data capture very quickly.

WHAT IS SQLDiag?

SQLDiag is a general-purpose data collection utility for SQL Server. It can be configured for automated data collection to reduce the burden and manual nature of collecting server configuration information, activity, and performance data. SQLDiag can be adapted for different problem types and helps engineers become more effective by reducing the time required to gather data for fault diagnosis.

As the SQL Server product family matures, support tools that were once only internally available to Microsoft engineers have become integrated into the product. Microsoft recognizes that an important aspect of enhancing customer support options and increasing customer satisfaction is to provide tools enabling customers to identify and resolve problems themselves.

SQLDiag is one such tool and is shipped with the product and used extensively by the customer support teams at Microsoft while assisting customers to resolve problems. Ideally, customers shouldn't need specialist tools, deep product expertise, or frequent support from the vendor, but SQL Server is used is so many different ways even within a single organization that it's difficult to deliver a product that works consistently well in every situation. Although Microsoft has done a great job with SQL Server, problems can still occur.

An Overview of SQLDiag

SQLDiag is the latest evolution of a combined data capture utility known in previous releases as SQLDiag and PSSDiag. PSSDiag is used by Microsoft Customer Service and Support (CSS used to be known as Product Support Services or PSS) when capturing diagnostic data on customers' servers relating to SQL Server problems under investigation.

PSSDiag originally spawned from a customer support requirement at Microsoft to extend the functionality of SQLDiag to reliably gather data on customer servers. Prior to PSSDiag, many support cases handled by CSS contained incomplete or mismatched data. Customers would often omit critical Performance Monitor (PerfMon) counters, miss events from SQL Traces, or not capture blocking information. Sometimes a correctly defined PerfMon log and complete SQL Trace were provided by customers, but each covered different time frames.

In the days of SQL Server 2000, the customer support team responded to this problem with PSSDiag. This tool provides a number of templates, enabling a CSS engineer to customize a data collection, defining the PerfMon counters and SQL Server Profiler events, and package these to send to the customer. The customer receives a single self-extracting executable, which once extracted requires another executable to run (PSSD.exe). A version of PSSDiag with reduced functionality was made available to the public and an associated Microsoft Knowledge Base article was published characterizing the utility.

In addition to capturing PerfMon logs and SQL Traces, PSSDiag also captures environment information, collecting data such as msinfo32 results, replication configuration, SQL Server error logs, and Windows event logs.

It is almost impossible to design a one-size-fits-all diagnostic tool for a product as diverse and widely deployed as SQL Server. As such, it's important to understand the limitations of SQLDiag and the types of data that will *not* be gathered, since there is no silver bullet for every problem type. For example, SQLDiag does not collect data about missing indexes, missing statistics, or index fragmentation — all of which are common performance problems. This data collection could be added using a script executed by a custom collector, but it isn't collected by default (see the PerfStats section later in the chapter).

SQLDiag in SQL Server 2005 and SQL Server 2008

Microsoft support wanted to simplify the data-collection process to reduce the burden on customers and improve the reliability of data collection. Instead of distributing the PSSDiag tool to each customer for every problem, the SQL Server product team at Microsoft renamed the tool to SQLDiag and included it with the product when it shipped.

This way, the members of the CSS team at Microsoft can send customers solely an XML configuration file, along with execution instructions. PSSDiag was a specialist support tool used only by support engineers from Microsoft — recently customer perceptions have changed, as SQLDiag is now considered part of the SQL Server product. Typically there is much less resistance when customers seek authorization from change managers to run SQLDiag on production servers.

Components of SQLDiag

SQLDiag is designed to make data collection easier. It doesn't do any unique data collection itself; each of the data collection methods could be performed manually if desired. SQLDiag provides a convenient and repeatable method to gather data from servers using a number of *collectors*. These collectors gather system configuration, log, and performance data from servers. Collectors can be configured to exclude specific data or to collect data from additional scripts or collectors. SQLDiag can be used to collect the following data:

SQL Server configuration data, including the following:

- ➤ `sp_configure`
- ➤ `sp_helpdb`
- ➤ `sp_helpextendedproc`
- ➤ `sysdatabases`
- ➤ `DBCC TRACESTATUS`

Contents of many system stored procedures and DMVs, including these:

- ➤ `sp_who`
- ➤ `sp_lock`
- ➤ `sys.dm_exec_sessions`
- ➤ `sys.dm_os_schedulers`
- ➤ `sys.dm_io_virtual_file_stats`
- ➤ Blocking information
- ➤ Server-side tracing
- ➤ Performance Monitor (PerfMon) logs
- ➤ Collectors:
- ➤ Event logs
- ➤ SQL error logs
- ➤ Mini-dumps
- ➤ msinfo32

SQLDiag captures a comprehensive point-in-time snapshot of a server with these collectors. All SQL Server and Windows Event logs are collected; and MSInfo32 is used to capture system configuration information, including details of the hardware components and driver versions.

> *SQLDiag is provided with three XML configuration files. These files are unpacked on first execution of SQLDiag — no parameters are necessary; just run SQLDiag from the command prompt.*
>
> *If the server has User Access Control (UAC) enabled, an elevated command prompt should be run to prevent the files from failing to extract because of denied access when writing to the folder.*

Registering SQLDiag as a Service

In some situations it may be useful to register SQLDiag as a service, enabling collection to start using the following command:

```
NET START SQLDiag
```

This could be useful when starting data collection from a SQL Agent job or monitoring product. The arguments specified when registering SQLDiag as a service are persisted, meaning the template and output location will remain intact. Use the /R switch to register SQLDiag as a service, and the /U switch to unregister.

Where to Find SQLDiag

SQLDiag is located in the SQL Server folder within Program Files: `C:\Program Files\Microsoft SQL Server\100\Tools\Binn`.

There's a useful operating system function called WHERE that displays all files matching a given string. It is simple to use and returns only matching rows. This is demonstrated in Figure 11-1, which shows two matching results because this server has SQL Server 2005 (version 90) and SQL Server 2008 (version 100) installed.

FIGURE 11-1

Working with SQLDiag Configuration Files

SQLDiag uses templates based on XML or INI files to control which collectors are enabled — and in the case of PerfMon and Profiler, specifically which counters and events will be captured. SQLDiag provides three templates, which can be used as-is or customized as necessary.

Additionally, SQLDiag uses an XSD (XML Schema Definition) file named `SQLDiag_Schema.XSD`, which is extracted to the same folder as the configuration files. Table 11-1 briefly summarizes the three templates and the scope of each.

TABLE 11.1: SQL Diag Template Overview

FILENAME	DEFAULT	EVENT LOGS	PERFMON	SQLDIAG*	BLOCKING	PROFILER
SQLDiag.XML	Yes	No	No	Yes	No	No
SD_General.XML	No	No	Yes	Yes	No	Light
SD_Detailed.XML	No	No	Yes	Yes	No	Medium

*The collector named SQLDiag gathers SQL Server configuration-specific data such as output from sp_configure, SQL Server Error Logs, and data from many DMVs.

The collectors used by SQLDiag can be controlled using the XML templates. Each can be switched on or off using `<enabled=true>` or `<enabled=false>` within the configuration file. Avoid deleting entire collectors from the XML files, as SQLDiag will subsequently fail to load the XSD if the XML file doesn't match. Of course, it is possible to amend the XSD too, but it's usually quicker and more convenient to toggle the enabled value to true or false for each collector.

Using SQLDiag without any modification will collect information from all SQL Server instances on the local machine. During the first execution, three XML configuration files are created. The following example shows an extract from the `SQLDiag.XML` file:

```
<Collection setupver="3.0.1.7" casenumber="SRX000000000000">
        <Machines>
            <Machine name=".">
                <MachineCollectors>
          <EventlogCollector enabled="false" startup="false" shutdown="true" >
            <Eventlogs>
              <EventlogType name="Application" enabled="true"/>
              <EventlogType name="Security" enabled="true"/>
              <EventlogType name="System" enabled="true"/>
            </Eventlogs>
          </EventlogCollector>
<PerfmonCollector enabled="false" pollinginterval="5" maxfilesize="256">
                </MachineCollectors>
                <Instances>
                <Instance name="*" windowsauth="true" ssver="10" user="">
                        <Collectors>
      <SqldiagCollector enabled="true" startup="false" shutdown="true" />
        <BlockingCollector enabled="false" pollinginterval="5" maxfilesize="350"
filecount="1"/>
<ProfilerCollector enabled="false" template="_GeneralPerformance90.xml"
pollinginterval="5" maxfilesize="350" filecount="1">
```

In the preceding configuration file extract, the local computer is the target, which is expressed as a period: `<Machine name=".">`. If SQL Server is running on a failover cluster, SQLDiag will detect this and collect data from all virtual servers. If data is required for a single specific virtual server, just specify the virtual server name as the machine name, such as `<Machine name="LONSQL01">` in `SQLDiag.XML`. Remember that the virtual machine name is different from the instance name, and the virtual server name is configured in the failover cluster resource group.

> *In addition to developing and editing Transact-SQL and DMX scripts, SQL Server Management Studio (SSMS) also supports editing XML files. Using SSMS is a quick and convenient way to customize XML-based SQLDiag configuration files.*

The next important customization controls which SQL Server instances are targets for the data capture. The default setting means SQLDiag will capture data for all instances running on a target computer. This is expressed using an asterisk: `<Instance name="*"...>`. If the target is a stand-alone machine with a single SQL Server instance, this does not need to be changed. If the target has multiple instances, such as a default instance and several named instances, and the problem instance is known, then restrict the data collection to just the problem instance. This will reduce the overhead of monitoring and make data analysis simpler because the dataset to analyze will be smaller.

When working with XML configuration files, it is useful to be aware of the nested structure of elements within the file, as this can save some configuration effort. The XML document consists of many named elements, which may contain any number of child or sub-elements. If the parent element is disabled (i.e., `enabled="false"`), then the child elements will be ignored.

For example, consider the `<Eventlogs>` element, which contains three child elements (Application, Security, and System) controlling collection of the Windows event logs. Each child log is enabled, but the event logs will not be collected because the parent element — `<Eventlogcollector>` — is disabled. In this situation, if the event logs are required for collection, then this can be specified at the `<Eventlogcollector>` element. Otherwise, the event logs will not be collected and it is not necessary to set each of the child elements to `<enabled="false">`.

Using SQLDIAG

Out-of-the-box, SQLDiag provides a configurable tool to administer data collection for the purposes of troubleshooting. SQLDiag can be run from the command line or as a service. Because it can run as a service, this also means data collection can be scheduled, avoiding the need to manually start and stop collection during non-business hours, such as at night or during weekends.

SQLDiag is administered through configuration files, which can be either XML or INI type files. Three templates are provided with SQLDiag and these can be run as is or, in some situations, customized prior to running SQLDiag.

SQLDiag must be run directly on the server; there's no method to execute remotely. Here's a straightforward execution of SQLDiag from the command prompt, using an XML configuration file called `sqldiag_blocking.xml` and writing all output to the folder `D:\TEMP`:

```
sqldiag /I sqldiag_blocking.xml /O D:\TEMP
```

SQLDiag can also be configured to save space by using NTFS compression for the output folder. To enable compression, use the /C parameter. You can find complete syntax details and parameters by checking Books Online or by querying as follows:

```
sqldiag /?
```

When SQLDiag begins, it goes through some initialization steps to gather the data configured for collection in the XML file. How long initialization takes depends in part on the options enabled for collection and the size of event logs or error logs to be collected. Frequently, servers suffering problems may have large error logs containing spurious errors and warnings — writing out large event logs or error logs can be time consuming. As such, initialization may take several minutes. It isn't complete until the following message, shown in Figure 11-2 is displayed:

```
SQLDIAG Collection started. Press Ctrl+C to stop it.
```

The initialization process on an otherwise idle machine, with the default collector options enabled, took around 14 seconds.

```
SQLDIAG                                                                          _ □ ×
C:\Program Files\Microsoft SQL Server\100\Tools\Binn>sqldiag /I sqldiag_blocker.xml /O E:\TEMP
2009/05/20 03:13:16.92 SQLDIAG Collector version
2009/05/20 03:13:16.92 SQLDIAG

IMPORTANT:  Please wait until you see "Collection started" before attempting to reproduce your issue

2009/05/20 03:13:16.92 SQLDIAG Output path: E:\TEMP\
2009/05/20 03:13:17.05 SQLDIAG Collecting from 1 logical machine(s)
2009/05/20 03:13:17.06 SUPERSTRUCTURE\* SQL Server version: 10
2009/05/20 03:13:17.06 SUPERSTRUCTURE\* Machine name: SUPERSTRUCTURE (this machine)
2009/05/20 03:13:17.06 SUPERSTRUCTURE\* Target machine is not a cluster
2009/05/20 03:13:17.07 SUPERSTRUCTURE\* Instance: SQL100 (32-bit)
2009/05/20 03:13:18.06 SQLDIAG Initialization starting...
2009/05/20 03:13:20.02 SUPERSTRUCTURE\* Starting Profiler trace
2009/05/20 03:13:21.03 SUPERSTRUCTURE\* MsInfo: Get MSINFO32
2009/05/20 03:13:21.33 SUPERSTRUCTURE\* MsInfo: Get default traces
2009/05/20 03:13:21.62 SUPERSTRUCTURE\* MsInfo: Get SQLDumper log
2009/05/20 03:13:21.90 SUPERSTRUCTURE\* Adding Perfmon counters...
2009/05/20 03:13:29.06 SQLDIAG Initialization complete
2009/05/20 03:13:29.06 SUPERSTRUCTURE\* Starting Perfmon
2009/05/20 03:13:29.06 SUPERSTRUCTURE\* Perfmon started
2009/05/20 03:13:29.06 SUPERSTRUCTURE\* Collecting diagnostic data

2009/05/20 03:13:30.06 SQLDIAG Collection started.  Press Ctrl+C to stop.
```

FIGURE 11-2

If you're attempting to recreate a problem for the purpose of troubleshooting, wait until the preceding message (which appears in green onscreen) has displayed before starting the steps to recreate the problem.

Using SQLDiag on Failover Clusters

When running SQLDiag in the default configuration on a multi-instance failover cluster, the command window will show numerous red errors. In this situation, because SQLDiag.XML has not been changed to reflect a specific virtual server of instance names, SQLDiag automatically detects the cluster and gathers logs and configuration information for every virtual server and instance. Errors are displayed in the command window because SQLDiag attempts to connect to each instance at every virtual server, resulting in several failures, e.g., a two-instance cluster will generate two failures because SQLDiag will attempt to connect to each instance at both virtual servers.

In this case, either configure the SQLDiag.XML file with the required target's virtual server name or ignore these errors. If any errors are displayed, they can be safely ignored. Likewise, the log file (##SQLDIAG.LOG) is usually easier to read and interpret to identify errors that can be safely ignored.

Configuring the PerfMon Collector

There are three SQLDiag templates: SQLDiag.XML, SD_General.XML, and SD_Detailed.XML. The SD_General.XML and SD_Detailed.XML templates are both configured to collect PerfMon data. These two templates set up PerfMon collections to files using a five-second polling interval and .BLG log files, which roll over to a new file at 256MB. The SD_General.XML and SD_Detail.XML templates both capture exactly the same PerfMon counters.

Within the XML configuration files, the SQL Server counters are conveniently located at the top of the file. All SQL Server counters and instances are enabled by default, capturing everything, including Analysis Services, SQL Agent, SSIS, and Full-Text Search.

Additionally, all key hardware performance counters are included, such as Processor, Memory, LogicalDisk, PhysicalDisk, and NetworkInterface. The only routine addition to the template could be the PagingFile counter, unless troubleshooting a specific problem elsewhere within Windows, when other counters such as Process, PagingFile, and System may be necessary.

Configuring the Profiler Collector

The same two templates that capture PerfMon logs also run a SQL Trace but collect slightly different SQL trace events. The SD_Detailed.XML template includes more events than SD_General.XML. Review the XML content of either template for details of events that are the same across templates; Table 11-2 shows only the extra events captured by SD_Detailed.XML.

TABLE 11-2: Profiler Collector Templates

EVENTS		SD_GENERAL.XML	SD_DETAILED.XML
Broker	Broker:Message Classify	No	Yes
Broker	Broker:Conversation	No	Yes
Cursors	CursorOpen	No	Yes
Performance	Showplan XML Statistics Profile	No	Yes
Stored Procedures	SP:StmtCompleted	No	Yes
T-SQL	SQL:StmtCompleted	No	Yes

Exercise caution when working on systems with high transaction throughput or limited free system resources, as capturing the events with the SD_Detailed.XML template could be prohibitively expensive. The templates are set up to create 350MB trace files, and once this is reached the trace rolls over to a new file. Increase the file size for busy servers to avoid an unmanageable number of 350MB trace files.

Adding Custom Collectors

The configuration information and performance data collection by SQLDiag is comprehensive, and one of the most powerful aspects is that it can be adapted to meet almost any requirement for data collection. You can add new custom collectors to the SQLDiag XML configuration file and they will be run as part of the normal collection.

In situations where a problem is transitive, it may be necessary to run the same query successively to gain insight into SQL Server activity or behavior over time. The following query will run a loop and output size, in kilobytes, of the TokenAndPermUserStore, an area of memory that can become quite large with certain workloads on some builds of SQL Server:

```
WHILE 1=1
BEGIN
        SELECT SUM(single_pages_kb + multi_pages_kb) AS
    'CurrentSizeOfTokenCache(KB)'
    FROM sys.dm_os_memory_clerks
    WHERE name = 'TokenAndPermUserStore'
    WAITFOR DELAY '00:05:00'
END
GO
```

The preceding query runs in a loop, executing every five minutes, and should be saved as a .sql file located on the server. In order to add this script as a custom collector in SQLDiag, insert the following code above </CustomDiagnostics>, which is toward the bottom of the template XML configuration file:

```
<CustomGroup name="CustomScripts" enabled="true" />
<CustomTask enabled="true" groupname="CustomScripts" taskname="Get
TokenAndPermUserStore" type="TSQL_Script" point="Startup" wait="No"
cmd="TokenAndPermUserStore.sql"/>
```

The contents of the script can be adapted to run any required query, and the frequency — controlled by the WAITFOR DELAY statement — should be adapted as necessary.

Running SQLDiag in Production

In almost all cases, if there's a problem, gathering data is a necessary evil in order to resolve it. There are a couple of things to consider when running SQLDiag in a production environment, primarily performance overhead and disk space.

Always log to nonsystem drives, as the impact of a disk filling to capacity is less and recovery is simpler. The performance impact of increased disk I/O activity to SQL Server while writing SQL Trace files can be minimized by writing to a dedicated disk, if a suitable volume is available for this purpose. Avoid writing trace files to a disk group hosting the data files or transaction logs.

PerfMon logs have linear growth based on the number of counters and the polling frequency. Sampling 100 counters every 15 seconds may produce a 100MB log file each hour, so it's reasonable to predict 800MB PerfMon logs after eight hours. Required disk space can be harder to predict if SQL tracing is enabled because the size of the trace (.trc) files is directly related to workload: The busier the server, the larger the trace files will be, so it can be difficult to predict the size of trace files based on current sizes.

Trace file forecasts should be made based on knowledge of usage patterns and volumes — for example, a 1GB file generated every 15 minutes during the day may be small compared to what's generated in an evening if the platform supports website users whose usage pattern is predominately in the evening. Minimizing the number of events included in the trace will reduce the size of the trace files. Some guidelines to follow include the following:

➤ There is a direct relationship between overhead and the number of trace events and Performance Monitor (PerfMon) counters captured.

➤ Capture only data that can be analyzed.

➤ Take an iterative approach whereby a high-level set of counters and events are captured initially, and then focus on the problem.

➤ Be methodical about adding more counters in a targeted and logical approach, remembering to remove any nonrequired counters.

➤ If the cause of a problem is unknown, avoid the temptation to capture data on everything "just in case" — use an iterative approach, ruling elements in or out of a list of potential causes.

When carrying out performance planning and capacity analysis, consider ensuring sufficient free capacity to run SQLDiag. Since many serious SQL Server problems will require some kind of data gathering, there should be enough capacity to enable these tools to run. There may, of course, be situations in which a resource becomes completely depleted — for example, high CPU or low memory conditions. Such a situation could be caused by a missing index, a poor query plan, or another problem that causes the CPUs to be pegged (utilization is consistently at 100%), and in this case it may still be necessary to run SQLDiag.

Test and monitor the overhead of SQLDiag. If possible, run SQLDiag with an appropriate configuration in a representative test environment, generate a workload, and note whether system response times are affected. If you are nervous about the impact of using SQL Trace, start small with data capture and add additional events slowly, as required.

Alert-Driven Data Collection with SQLDiag

Intermittent problems are often the hardest to solve, whether it's a problem with a car, a hot water supply, or the performance of a database server. The ability to reproduce a fault on demand goes a long way toward solving a problem, as it reflects a basic understanding of the conditions under which the problem occurs. Equipped with the knowledge of a sequence of events or simultaneous operations that cause a specific problem, it's much easier to recreate the problem in a controlled environment, such as a test platform, and interrogate the problem until the root cause is identified.

Unfortunately, this isn't always possible because sometimes the elapsed time between problem conditions is so long that no correlation is made, or pressure from the business to clear the fault (restarting SQL Server, freeing caches, etc.) is so high that little or no relevant data is captured about the problem.

In such situations, it is often undesirable to leave detailed monitoring running indefinitely because the ongoing performance cost can be high and disk space requirements can be large. In addition, the data to analyze could be unmanageable. However, it is possible to launch SQLDiag based on a SQL Server Agent alert configured to fire when a performance condition is encountered. Once an alert has fired, a SQL Server Agent job can be nominated to take an action in response to the alert. For this purpose, a SQL Server Agent job can be prepared, which starts SQLDiag using a custom template and runs for a designated period.

An example illustrates the concept of alert-driven data capture with SQLDiag. A good example of an intermittent performance problem that can be hard to pinpoint is excessive blocking. Because intermittent blocking problems can appear when multiple instances of a problem batch or stored procedure execute simultaneously, or when two different stored procedures execute simultaneously, there could be a long period between occurrences of the blocking problem, which makes the problem harder to resolve.

The first step is to create a job that will start SQLDiag. This requires a single `CmdExec` command to call SQLDiag, as shown here and in Figure 11-3:

```
start /min cmd.exe /C"sqldiag.exe /E +00:15:00 /Q /O E:\TEMP"
```

Depending on the nature of the problem, SQLDiag can be configured to capture any range of data. In this case, the default template is used, and the /E switch means SQLDiag will collect data for 15 minutes before stopping.

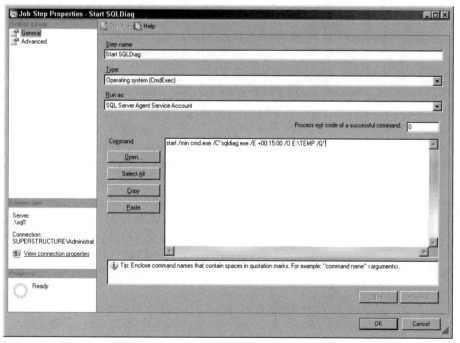

FIGURE 11-3

Next, create the alert that will watch for the performance condition, and when the blocked processes threshold is met, the SQL Agent job will be fired. Create a new SQL Server performance condition alert, specifying the General Statistics object and the Processes blocked counter. The number of blocked processes before performance is affected depends on the system; setting the threshold to alert if it exceeds 4 means an alert will be fired for five blocked processes, as shown in Figure 11-4. The alert-driven solution could also be implemented by registering SQLDiag as a service, and the SQL Server Agent job step could then consist of a single command: NET START SQLDiag.

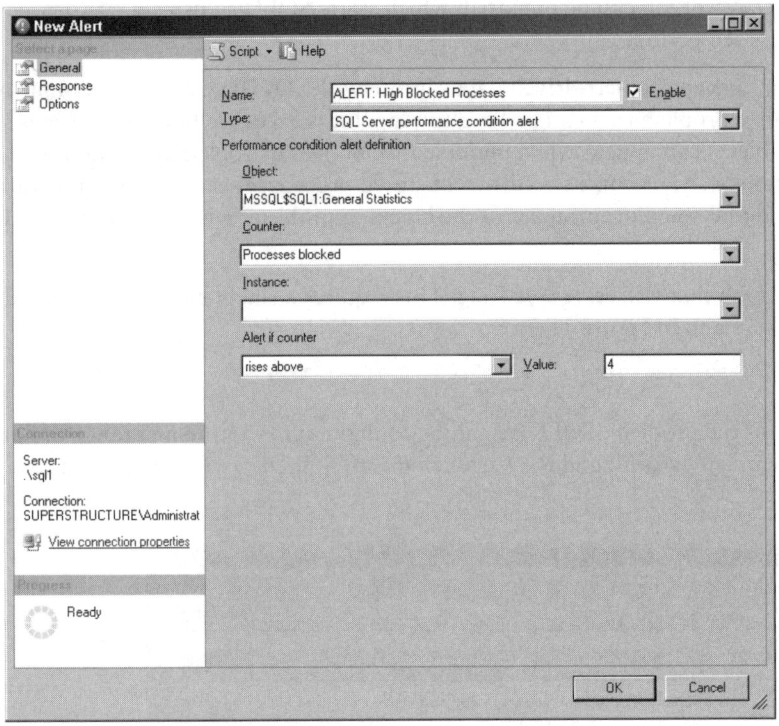

FIGURE 11-4

Finally, configure an alert response. This step associates the job to start SQLDiag with the performance alert. As shown in Figure 11-5, simply select the SQL Agent SQLDiag job from the drop-down list.

Using the Options tab, an alert can be configured to send an email or use a message sent via net send to notify an administrator when the alert has fired and the data has been captured to avoid the need to check the output folder or job history repeatedly. Finally, confirm the Agent job works as expected, this can be done by running the job manually, verifying the output folder to ensure the alert fires, and then creating a blocking chain of five sessions to ensure SQLDiag starts automatically.

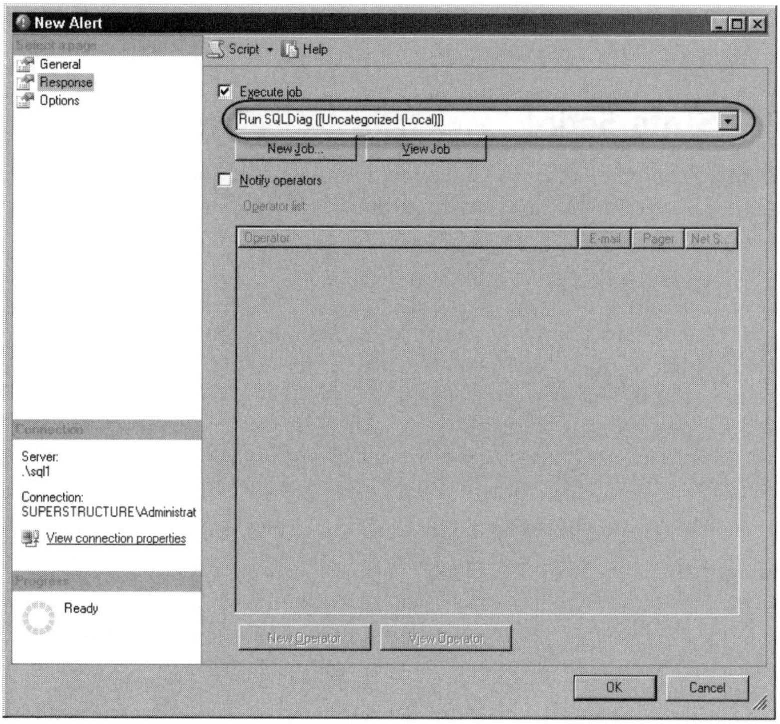

FIGURE 11-5

USING THE PERFSTATS SCRIPT

The PerfStats script was created by the SQL Server support group at Microsoft in addition to the already great SQLDiag templates. Make use of these ready-made data gathering tools to reduce the time and effort needed to gather meaningful data from problem servers. You can further reduce the time it takes to resolve performance problems and gain valuable insight by combining data gathering with PerfStats and data analysis with SQLNexus.

What Is the PerfStats Script?

The PerfStats script helps reduce the time and complexity required to gather performance data by controlling the start and stop of data collection. The PerfStats script extends the capability of SQLDiag by capturing additional blocking data and gathering more dynamic management view (DMV) data.

Out-of-the-box, three templates are provided to collect the necessary data for three common scenarios:

➤ General performance statistics

➤ Blocking details

➤ Latch contention

The PerfStats script can be used as a general-purpose troubleshooting utility in place of SQLDiag, as the data gathered is more detailed and provides information for more problem scenarios.

Where to get the PerfStats Script

The PerfStats script is available for download from CodePlex; however, it is not a standalone solution, but rather is integrated with SQL Nexus, and locating the scripts isn't intuitive! Use the following steps to navigate to the download page:

1. Browse to `www.codeplex.com/sqlnexus`.

2. Locate point 4 in the Highlights section and select "SQL 2005 Perf Stats Script or SQL 2008 Perf Stats." If the Highlights section is not available, use the following URL to navigate directly to the SQL Nexus Wiki page: `http://sqlnexus.codeplex.com/Wiki/ View.aspx?title=Sql2005PerfStatsScript`.

3. Click Page Info from the navigation bar.

4. Scroll down to locate the File Attachments section.

5. Click to download `PerfStatsScript2008.zip`.

After downloading the PerfStats zip file, extract it to a working folder. Table 11-3 lists the eight files included in the download.

TABLE 11-3: What's Included in the PerfStats Download

FILENAME	PURPOSE
SQLDiagPerfStats_Detailed_Trace2008.XML	SQLDiag XML configuration files control data to be captured.
SQLDiagPerfStats_Trace2008.XML	
SQLDiagReplay2008.xml	Three templates are provided and can be configured as necessary.
SQL_2008_Perf_Stats.sql	Captures DMV output and detailed blocking information
SQL_2008_Perf_Stats_Snapshot.sql	
StartSQLDiagDetailed_Trace2008.cmd	Batch files are used to start and stop data capture by passing the filename for the XML template.
StartSQLDiagForReplay2008.cmd	
StartSQLDiagTrace2008.cmd	
StartSQLDiagNoTrace.cmd (only included in the SQL Server 2005 download)	

Three templates are provided, each with a corresponding command script that is preconfigured with the XML template name for convenience. In situations where no customization is required, choose a template and double-click the command script to begin collection immediately.

All three templates capture the same following information:

➤ Event logs

➤ PerfMon

➤ SQLDiag

➤ Blocking information

➤ SQL Trace

The SQLDiag templates provided with PerfStats are somewhat different than the native templates provided with SQLDiag and an additional custom collector to gather more data from the server. The additional custom collector, called SQL 2008 Perf Stats, executes two T-SQL scripts and executes a test with the RDTSC utility. The collector consists of three TSQL_Script tasks; one script is executed twice (on startup and again on shutdown) and the second script is executed once.

The RDTSC utility is used to check drift between CPU clocks, which can lead to SQL Server recording inaccurate query duration.

The difference between the templates is the events captured in the Profiler configuration. The following table summarizes each SQLDiag template and the Profiler template used.

TABLE 11-4: SQLDiag PerfStats Template Summary

SQLDIAG TEMPLATE	PROFILER TEMPLATE	PURPOSE
SQLDiagPerfStats_Trace2008.XML	_GeneralPerformance10.xml	General performance data capture
SQLDiagPerfStats_Detailed_Trace2008.XML	DetailedPerformance10.xml	Detailed Profiler Trace events
SQLDiagReplay2008.xml	PSSReplay10.xml	Use to capture workload for replay in test environment

Select the most appropriate template based on the objectives of the data gathering activity. There will always be a compromise between data to be captured and performance overhead. Each additional event included in the SQL trace will add an element of overhead. However, there are times when knowing the poorly performing stored procedure is not enough and statement-level information is required to understand the long-running batch or problem statement within the stored procedure; and this level of detail can only be obtained with statement-level tracing.

The Replay template can be used to capture activity on a production server to be replayed in a test environment. The OStress utility, part of the Replay Markup Language (RML) Utilities, can be used to replay a trace generated using this template. OStress can also be used to generate a specific workload or activity, which can be useful when load and performance testing.

The General Purpose template should be used when a SQL Trace is required to capture high level, lightweight, performance and activity. This template will capture batch activity using the `SQL:BatchStarting` and `SQL:BatchCompleted` events and `RPC:Starting` and `RPC:Completed`.

The Detailed Performance template provides an extra level of detail by adding statement-level activity and stored procedure actions with the following additional events:

➤   `SQL:StmtStarting` and `SQL:StmtCompleted`

➤   `SP:Starting` and `SP:Completed`

➤   `SP:StmtStarting` and `SP:StmtCompleted`

Additional overhead is required to trace these events compared with the general-purpose data capture, but this may be necessary and justified in some performance troubleshooting scenarios.

Configuring the PerfStats Script

The XML configuration files used for PerfStats are an extended version of those used for SQLDiag; some additional custom collectors are added to gather the extra information by PerfStats. As with SQLDiag, the default configuration collects data from all SQL Server instances on the local machine. The machine name needs to be configured with the virtual server name if PerfStats is running on a failover cluster. Always specify the instance name to reduce the performance overhead and the volume of data collected.

➤   **Machine name:** `<Machine name=".">`

➤   **Instance name:** `<Instance name="*" windowsauth="true" ssver="10" user="">`

Finally, consider changing the output location, because by default a new folder named `SQLDiagOutput` will be created in the same location as the configuration files. The PerfMon and Profiler logs can grow very large and affect read/write performance on the volume, so it is usually beneficial to relocate the output folder to a temporary or scratch volume. To do this, edit the relevant command file and use /O to specify the required output folder.

> *When customizing the SQLDiag XML configuration files provided with the PerfStats download, note that these files have the Read-only property set. Open the working folder where the files are extracted, right-click, and remove the Read-only check box. Now the files can be edited and saved with the original filename.*

Running the PerfStats Script

The PerfStats script must already be running at the time a problem occurs for you to be able to capture data on it. However, if there is no problem condition exhibited during your data collection the data gathered could still be useful to form a baseline. The SQL Trace and PerfMon logs are necessary to gain visibility of the problem; and if the problem doesn't happen, these should be archived and kept as a baseline. The narrower the window of monitoring, the better the chance of resolution, although this is largely dependent on the nature of the problem, e.g., some problems occur reliably at 3:00 p.m. daily, in other situations performance degrades during the working day. Narrowing the focus of data gathering means less data to analyze, less monitoring overhead, and a shorter collection period.

Choose the right template. Ensure the objectives of data collection are understood and there is a clear goal for the activity. This will help identify one of the existing templates to meet the requirements; otherwise, a template should be customized to capture the data needed to satisfy the objectives.

Monitor the output folder. PerfMon logs (.blg) will grow with a predictable linear size, whereas the size of Profiler (.trc) files is workload dependent and therefore less easy to predict.

When running PerfStats on a failover cluster; the XML template file should be customized to include the virtual server name and SQL Server instance name. Additionally, the command script (which is used to call SQLDiag and pass required parameters) may also need to be modified if the output folder is to be moved to a volume on the shared storage for better performance.

PERFSTATS OVERHEAD

The most frequently asked question by engineers or managers when logging or tracing on a production server is, "What's the overhead?" Typically, they want to know the performance cost of the data capture, and the answer is largely dependent on the configuration of the tool.

There have been users who perceived PSSDiag as a tool that hinders performance, although they would routinely run PerfMon captures and SQL Traces without issue. This perception could be accurate, as any misconfigured monitoring tool can significantly affect performance, but this doesn't mean that SQLDiag or PSSDiag are bad tools!

The component tools (Profiler, PerfMon, etc.) could be run individually and manually, with much more human effort and administration required, and the burden on the server would be the same.

In most cases, in order to resolve a problem you need to understand the server activity, resource utilization, and SQL Server behavior; and in many situations the only method available is additional monitoring on the server.

Analyzing PerfStats Output

The PerfStats collector generates three output files (.OUT) with quite similar filenames. All files are prefixed by server name and instance name:

```
ServerName_InstanceName_SQL_2008_Perf_Stats_Snapshot_Startup.OUT
ServerName_InstanceName_SQL_2008_Perf_Stats_Startup.OUT
ServerName_InstanceName_SQL_2008_Perf_Stats_Snapshot_Shutdown.OUT
```

The first and third output files are snapshots taken as the collector starts and completes. This snapshot script contains details of missing indexes, and conveniently includes the CREATE INDEX statement for each missing index. Both snapshot output files also contain the top 50 worst-performing queries (by disk, CPU, and duration) from sys.dm_exec_query_stats. This is a non-intrusive method to retrieve the worst-performing query data without requiring a SQL Trace. Be aware that frequently querying this DMV can tax a system and have other limitations because it is based on the plan cache. Not every query plan will be inserted into the plan cache (there are more details in the header of the output file); therefore, poorly performing queries without a cached plan could be overlooked.

The second output file in the preceding list (without snapshot in the filename) has the main content and will be much larger than the other two files. This output file contains data collected on two polling cycles: Information on active queries is collected every 10 seconds and instance-wide data is collected once per minute.

Active Queries

The active queries polling cycle gathers the following data every 10 seconds, grouped in three sections:

- ➤ Requests
- ➤ Head Blocker Summary
- ➤ Notable Active Queries

The Requests section contains extensive and detailed information for every session with an active query. This information includes CPU time, memory usage, reads, writes, program name, login name, wait type, duration and blocking details, plus many more columns.

> *When reviewing the output file in Notepad or WordPad, use the Find feature (Ctrl+F) to quickly locate these sections. Search for string text — requests, head, or notable — to navigate directly to these sections.*

The Head Blocker Summary section will be displayed if blocking is detected. When blocking is detected, session information such as the head of the blocking chain, number of sessions blocked, and statement text is recorded in the output file.

The Notable Active Queries output section contains procedure name, statement text, and execution statistics.

Instance-Wide Data

The same output file also captures some basic instance-wide performance data once per minute. This performance data includes a subset of the SQL Server PerfMon counters, virtual file stats, and waitstats data.

SUMMARY

Investing a little time to become familiar with SQLDiag and the PerfStats script will save time when troubleshooting difficult or complex problems. Knowledge of the common command-line arguments and awareness of the template contents will enable you to resolve production problems effectively.

Combining SQLDiag and the PerfStats script for data gathering with SQLNexus and Performance Analysis for Logs (PAL) provides a powerful combination for analyzing the toughest problems. These are the same tools used by Microsoft to support its customers, and using these tools effectively reduces the occasions when external assistance is required to resolve a SQL Server problem.

12

Introducing RML Utilities for Stress Testing and Trace File Analysis

WHAT'S IN THIS CHAPTER

➤ How and when to use RML Utilities

➤ Using RML Utilities to replay workload

➤ Ensuring fair and representative replay testing

Like many of the utilities presented in this book, the RML Utilities are a set of tools originally developed by the SQL Server support organization within Microsoft to help engineers effectively resolve customer support incidents. The RML Utilities consist of four key components: ReadTrace, OStress, ORCA, and Reporter. When combined, these utilities enable developers and administrators to replay workload, identify problems, and compare performance.

The high-level process to generate real production workload on a test server is as follows:

1. Capture a trace on a production server.

2. Convert the trace with ReadTrace.

3. Replay the trace on the test server using OStress.

The Replay Markup Language (RML) is an XML-like language that can be used to replay workload against a SQL Server. A trace containing the statements executed against a server are captured using SQL Server Profiler, then ReadTrace is used to convert the .TRC (profiler trace output) to .RML files, which can then be replayed using OStress.

It can be difficult to simulate production workload in a test environment, and RML Utilities addresses this challenge. In addition to providing a testing platform, the tools within RML Utilities can provide powerful insight into performance data. Moreover, the tools are easy to learn, flexible, and available for free.

WHEN TO USE RML UTILITIES

The RML Utilities are useful in situations where testing will be undertaken to identify database system performance or capacity problems. The motivation for such performance testing activities can usually be grouped into the following categories:

➤ Testing new applications before going live

➤ Validating the impact of a change

➤ Identifying problems in a current environment

➤ Baselining

> *Commercial load generation tools typically simulate user activity and provide workload generation for an end-to-end application environment, including web servers, application servers, middleware, and load balancers. RML Utilities can be used to replay trace data against SQL Server only, therefore they are useful (but limited to) generating traffic and testing the database server only.*
>
> *RML Utilities is designed to support effective troubleshooting of SQL Server, so it is not a competitor of these tools. RML Utilities can be used very effectively in conjuction with such tools.*

Database administrators, engineers, and developers may each want to replay a trace or generate a test workload on a server for many different reasons. In many troubleshooting situations it is important to undertake a structured approach and attempt to prove or disprove a given hypothesis about the cause of a problem. When tackling problems with complex systems, often multiple hypotheses must be ruled out before the root problem is identified. It's often necessary to iterate through this process systematically, and use the early stages of troubleshooting to eliminate common and easy-to-resolve problems. Once any relevant but obvious or easy to resolve problems are excluded as potential problem sources — only then is it necessary to move onto more detailed problems.

As troubleshooting continues, steps to prove or disprove a hypothesis become more time consuming, invasive, risky, and less easy to reverse, while the degree of certainty as to the actual cause may be reduced. In situations with long-running problems, it can prove invaluable to reproduce the problem in a test environment.

Assuming a trace representative of the live environment and containing the problem can be captured — RML Utilities can be used to replay the workload and simulate the problem in the test environment. This can be a useful test in itself to determine whether the problem is resident within the database code (T-SQL) or is environment specific, such as data access components, drivers, hardware, resource usage. When using RML Utilities to replay traces, consider the hardware specification used for replay. When the hardware used for replay is identical to the production hardware where the trace was captured — direct performance comparison can be made between the servers. If their servers utilize different hardware, for example they could be virtualized, replay results are less easy to compare. In situations when the replay hadware is different from the source hardware, the best comparison can be made by creating a baseline and observing the difference, then applying a factor for the difference to all subsequent results.

If the problem does manifest itself while replaying in the test environment, then you can narrow the replay window in order to zoom in on the problem. An iterative approach to identifying the source of the problem will almost always yield results, after which you can determine the best remediation actions. Finally, the remediation steps can be carried out in the test environment and the trace replayed to confirm the desired outcome with no undesirable impact on the production system. Note: This is especially useful if the systems are identical. If not, RML Utilities can be used to replay on the production system to identify and quantify any environment differences.

The trace replay capability and processes with RML Utilities described above are intended to provide DBAs with the ability to reproduce production workload and provide repeatable testing. It is important that confidence is gained in test results and the testing process is rigourous and valid — this confidence can be built by executing several iterations of trace replay using a trace file.

Testing New Applications before Going Live

Most applications have some form of performance or application response time target in the form of a service-level agreement (SLA). Developers, DBAs, and architects need to be confident that once a platform is commissioned and servicing live users, the database platform will be capable of handling the volume of requests generated by the application. Although there are tools available to simulate user workload for website visitors, few of these focus on the database or provide the level of workload replay that RML Utilities provides.

Testing the database should be considered in the wider context of the application environment, and an approach to testing that includes other middle and application or presentation tiers of the application solution should also be considered.

Validating the Impact of a Change

Once an application is in service (i.e., users are actively working with the application and the business has a database that is required for daily operations, revenue generation, and payment settlements), one of the most high-risk activities is changes to the environment.

Application functionality and performance might be acceptable, but the organization may require the following:

➤ Application Release

➤ New functionality

➤ Bug fixes to existing functionality

➤ Performance improvements (database indexes, statistics)

➤ System Software Upgrade

  ➤ Operating system upgrade or service pack

  ➤ SQL Server upgrade or service pack

  ➤ BIOS, firmware, or driver updates

➤ Hardware Upgrade

➤ Memory, CPU, or disk performance improvements

➤ Upgraded storage capacity

The approach to managing the risk of changes through testing remains the same regardless of software or hardware changes. RML Utilities provide an effective tool to help rigorously test changes, limiting the risks that changes might cause in the live environment, and thereby ensuring predictable post-change performance. When capturing the trace baseline that is used for repeatable testing — ensure the trace is representative including any seasonal variations or re-capture the trace regularly to ensure complete coverage of application usage scenarios.

RML Utilities can be helpful in establishing a baseline for known good performance. Using this approach pre-change and post-change means performance can be compared, enabling you to more readily identify discrepancies. Once the trace captured from production is known to provide as near complete code coverage as possible — plus the shape of the trace data matches production (i.e. the number of requests in relation to each other are representative), this trace can be used in replay scenarios for validating impact and effective in reducing risk.

Determining the Purpose of Testing

This may seem obvious but it's important to clearly define and understand the intention of testing. In many situations, multiple tests are required to satisfy all requirements for testing. Testing labels such as performance testing, load testing, capacity testing, and functional testing are often used interchangeably and may have different meanings for project managers, developers, database administrators, and hardware engineers.

If a problem occurs subsequent to the change or going live, it can be useful to review test plans to determine whether the same test passed successfully earlier in the project or whether the testing could be improved. Closing the loop to reduce repeat occurrences of problems improves the test cycles and ensures completeness.

WHAT ARE RML UTILITIES?

As mentioned earlier, the RML Utilities are tools built around the Replay Markup Language (RML) to enable engineers to create production-like workload in test environments. The ReadTrace component of RML Utilities is used to convert SQL Server trace files to an XML-like structure that can be used by OStress to generate the same workload against another server.

RML Utilities allow you to replay traces at the same rate they were captured. That means you get a better representation of true user activity and server workload than you do with other tools that condense the statements and execute them in sequence.

The Reporter component of RML Utilities provide a useful reporting capability, similar to SQL Nexus. Reporter will identify like queries executing with different parameters and these will be aggregated and grouped in the report based on unqiue query structure. Although it's not as comprehensive, because SQL Nexus can also import the PerfStats script output, the Reporter utility still provides useful Top N reports for worst-performing queries by duration, CPU, reads, or writes.

History of RML Utilities

RML Utilities were developed by Keith Elmore and Bob Dorr from the SQL Server Escalation team in Texas. The Replay Markup Language itself has been around since 1998 and was the product of an evolving troubleshooting toolset used by the SQL Server Escalation team to enable support engineers to resolve customer problems by reproducing them on demand.

These tools have subsequently been released for wider use by the SQL Server user community, and the Customer Support Services (CSS) team continues to support and provide assistance for these tools as best as it can outside the product (i.e., it isn't possible to raise a case or bug against these tools).

RML Utilities are used by SQL Nexus, discussed in detail in Chapter 13.

What's in the Download

The RML Utilities can be downloaded from `http://support.microsoft.com/?kbid=944837`. After the download completes, run setup, which requires elevated privileges if User Account Control (UAC) is enabled. Common setup issues and known workarounds are included in the document titled "Errors and Info" located in the Help folder.

The toolkit provides support for SQL Server 2000, 2005, and 2008, and is available in x86 and x64 versions. It consists of the executables shown in Table 12-1.

TABLE 12-1: Executables from the Toolkit

FILE	PURPOSE
CABPipe.exe	Streams .TRC(s) files from a .CAB over a secure named pipe so ReadTrace can process it directly from memory
ORCA.exe	The OStress Replay Control Agent is used to coordinate sequencing between one or more OStress instances. It provides replay sequencing in addition to DTC import and export functionality.
OStress.exe	An ODBC application used to read .RML and .SQL files for replay against SQL Server
ReadTrace.exe	Converts SQL Server Profiler trace files (.TRC) into Replay Markup Language (.RML) format. Provides filtering, mirroring, and performance analysis.
Reporter.exe	Report Viewer-based application providing interactive performance analysis
ZIPPipe.exe	Streams .TRC(s) files from a .ZIP over a secure named pipe so ReadTrace can process it directly from memory

The latest version of RML Utilities contains a very detailed PDF user guide called "RML Help." The user guide explains the command-line syntax, the architecture, and detailed design information about each of the RML Utilities.

RML Utilities also includes a compressed file (SAMPLES.CAB) containing sample files. These assist with getting started because they contain examples to set up and generate trace workload.

Once the samples compressed file is extracted, you can access several SQL scripts, batch files, and ReadMe files to create an environment and a working example demonstrating use of the tools. Select a non-production SQL Server for trace file analysis (a test machine or desktop will suffice providing the trace files are of a manageable size (<10GB).

➤ Start by running the `Setup.SQL` script to create the `PrecisionPerformance` database.

➤ Next, start a trace (choose one of the three traces based on the testing objective), replacing the filename and using the `sp_trace_setstatus` to control the server-side trace start/stop.

➤ Next, run `Workload.SQL` to generate load.

At the end of this process, stop the trace and use ReadTrace to analyze the output. Detailed steps are included in the Quick Start section of the user guide PDF (RML Help.PDF).

Components of RML Utilities

This section provides an overview of the four main RML Utilities — ReadTrace, Reporter, ORCA, and OStress — including usage details and guidance where relevant.

ReadTrace

ReadTrace is a tool for processing SQL Trace (TRC) data, either raw or compressed in .ZIP or .CAB format. ReadTrace extracts session-specific information from the trace files to build an RML file for each session (SPID), containing the commands of that session.

Query Templates

It is necessary for ReadTrace to identify statements that are the same query but with different values, in the similiar way SQL Server uses auto parameterization for execution plan reuse. An example of such parameterization and substitution is shown here:

```
SELECT name, DOB, address FROM customers WHERE country='UK'
```

The preceding SQL statement will be parameterized to

```
SELECT name, DOB, address FROM customers WHERE country=@p1
```

This allows reuse of a query plan for the query above where only the country differs (e.g., US).

When consuming trace data, ReadTrace builds a normalized query template in much the same way — by substituting parameters and identifying queries that are effectively the same albeit with different values. ReadTrace creates a hash ID of the normalized query and uses it to identify multiple calls of the same stored procedure where the query `hashID` matches.

This step is vital in identifying stored procedures or queries that have short execution times but execute frequently. For example, a query that consumes 5ms of CPU time and executes 100 times per minute is more expensive for the CPU than another query that executes once and consumes 400ms of CPU. Without this analysis, it would be impossible to spot the lower cost query as the target for optimization.

GROUPING AND AGGREGATING TRACE DATA

One solution adopted by some DBAs is to use `fn_trace_gettable` to load trace data from the TRC files into a SQL Server database. Once trace data is held in a SQL Server database, it is fairly trivial to query this data — looking, for example, for queries with long duration, high CPU, and so on, with a view to optimizing these queries.

The primary drawback of this method is that no grouping or aggregation of trace data is performed. In this situation two queries with the same query text — but different parameters — will be handled as two unique queries. This technique is limited since the recurrences of identical queries is usually low in an OLTP environment. Often performance problems are the result of inefficient queries that complete quickly, and execute extremely frequently. Because each execution completes in, for example, less than 100ms, the individual query is unlikely to appear in any Top N worst performing query reports. However when looking at this query which executes thousands of times per second, reducing the individual query completion time from 100ms to 50ms could constitute a significant overall performance gain.

For this reason the results from non-grouped data analysis might be useful for identifying the single longest-running query or procedure, but this approach is unlikely to yield truly useful results (mostly, results are misleading), as identifying the most resource-intensive queries or procedures requires additional steps to group and aggregate the data.

Using ReadTrace to handle grouping and aggregation of trace data and Reporter to present this data is more likely to deliver useful results with considerably less effort than loading and querying trace data manually.

Getting Started with ReadTrace

ReadTrace must be executed with at least one parameter, which is the path to the first TRC or compressed trace file. Where trace or zip files roll over, ReadTrace automatically detects this and consumes all files (the parameter `-r` can be used to set a maximum number of files to consume).

ReadTrace requires access to a SQL Server database where query templates and plans are stored for comparison. By default, ReadTrace connects to a local default instance, but if this instance is named or remote, use the `-S` parameter to express the servername\instancename, and `-U` and `-P` to specify username and password, respectively. The ReadTrace database, called `PerfAnalysis`, is created automatically on first execution, and the contents are automatically cleared with each execution of ReadTrace.

An example of a simple command execute from the RML Utilities Command Prompt, to get ReadTrace running is:

```
readtrace -Ssuperstructure\sql100 -Ie:\tracedata\sql1_trace.trc -oD:\traceout
```

Once running, ReadTrace will process the trace data, loading it into the `PerfAnalysis` database. It is possible to provide a different target database using the `-dServer01PerfDB` parameter with the target database name. Figure 12-1 shows the progress status.

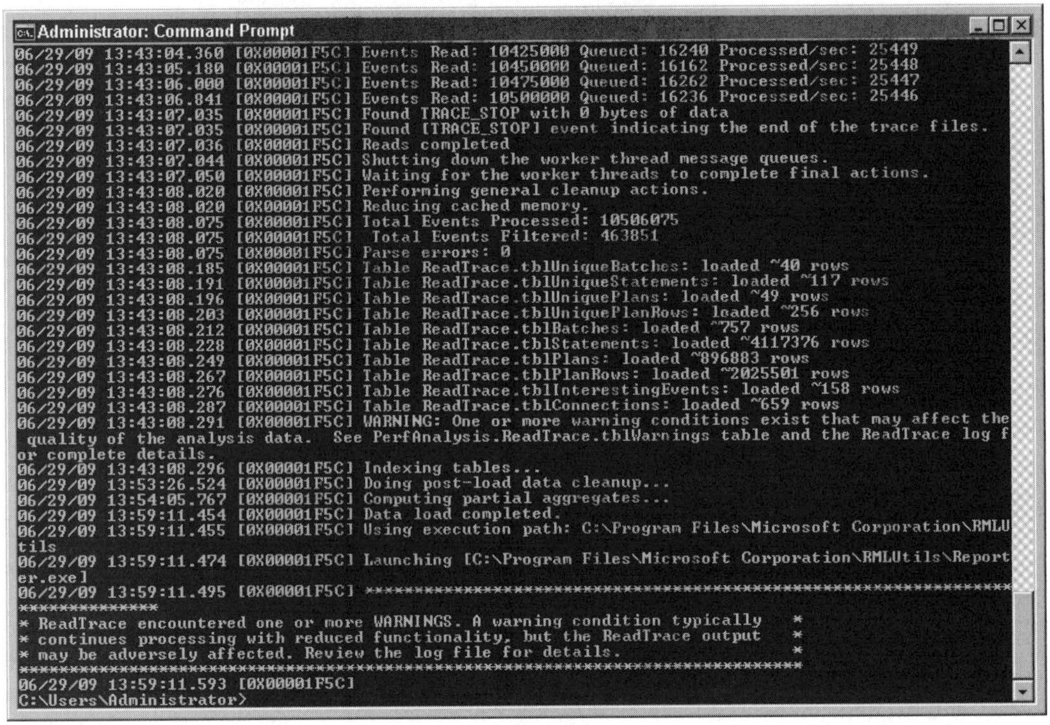

FIGURE 12-1

The load time will vary according to the size and number of trace files. Status messages will report progress and the number of events processed each second. Expect this process to take between a few minutes and several hours, depending on the size of the trace data and the performance of the computer running ReadTrace. Following completion of the data load, ReadTrace creates indexes and calculates aggregates prior to launching Reporter. The trace load will perform best when source trace files are located locally and the PerfAnalysis database and tempdb are adequately sized to avoid file autogrowth.

After ReadTrace has completed, the output folder contains a log file displaying the output in the command window. It contains a number of RML files, which have the naming convention SQL*nnnnn*.RML, where *nnnnn* is the session identifier (SPID), with one file created for each SPID in the source trace.

Limitations of ReadTrace

Until this point, everything sounds great: ReadTrace can be used in various scenarios and paired with OStress to generate production-like load for meaningful database performance testing. However, rarely is there a silver-bullet solution that works in every scenario, so this section outlines limitations and workarounds when SQL Server replication is employed and when Multiple Active Result Sets (MARS) are used.

There are some specific considerations when capturing a trace on servers using SQL Server Replication — since actions performed by replication agents will be included in the trace. When the trace is replayed replication statements may fail; therefore exluding these from the trace or stopping replication is often the best approach. Excluding the replication statements from the trace avoids replaying statements that may fail since this would not generate a representative workload. If the trace for replay contains only statements from genuine user activity, replication can be configured in the test environment to provide a meaningful test environment. When capturing the trace it is possible to use a filter to exclude replication traffic from the trace, consider using the application name as the filter criteria, as this is populated with the job name for all SQL Agent replication jobs.

When defining a filter for the first time, it can be helpful to define the filter using SQL trace and then script the trace definition; this will be provided complete with the column ID to be filtered. Further information on tracing with SQL Profiler is available in Chapter 10.

Using trace filters creates additional performance overhead because the filter is evaluated for every transaction, so test the impact by running the trace for a short period.

The Multiple Active Result Sets (MARS) feature was introduced with SQL Server 2005, and this presents some challenges because the current release of ReadTrace does not support MARS.

You can find additional details on the CSS SQL blog at `http://blogs.msdn.com/psssql/archive/2009/01/21/prb-rml-utilities-readtrace-and-how-to-workaround-mars.aspx`.

Reporter

Reporter is the utility that displays Reporting Services–based reports on the trace data after the ReadTrace data load is complete. The reports enable drill-through analysis to batch and statement level, providing excellent visibility of performance bottlenecks and scalability issues. The reports may be familiar because they're also provided to SQL Nexus when analyzing trace output, although Nexus also analyzes output from the PerfStats script.

Reporter is run automatically once the ReadTrace data load has completed it defaults to displaying the Performance Overview window shown in Figure 12-2. The chart provides an immediate visual representation of resource usage and potential bottlenecks.

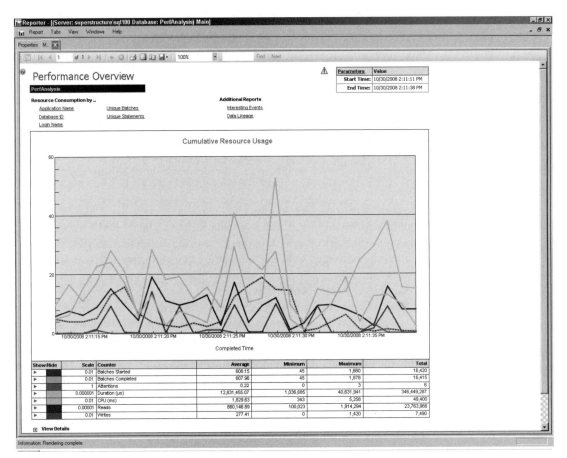

FIGURE 12-2

The hyperlinks above the chart provide drilldown access to additional charts with detailed aggregation using the query template functionality discussed earlier. This query template approach is used to identify unique batches and unique statements, and provide accurate performance comparison. Figure 12-3 shows the top unique statements from Reporter; from here it's immediately clear which single query has the highest cumulative duration, and any of the bars on the chart can be clicked for drill through to the statement template used.

Each click through opens a new tab within Reporter, and it's easy to navigate between these and close unwanted tabs using the menu bar. Two additional reports are included: Interesting Events and Data Lineage. The Interesting Events report shows details about frequency of events such as Attention events, exceptions, File autogrow and statement or procedure recompilation. A high number of occurrences of such events can negatively impact server performance and should be reviewed to determine if anything can be done to minimize occurrences.

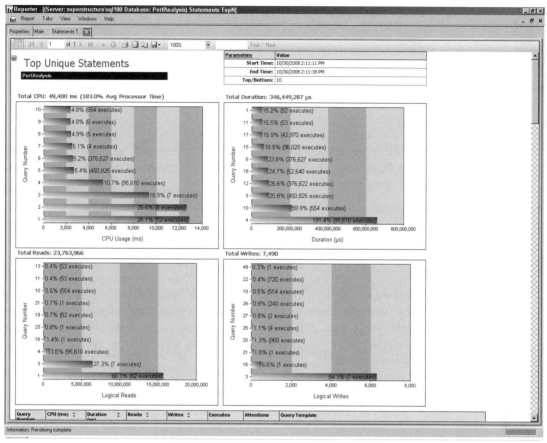

FIGURE 12-3

OStress

OStress is an ODBC utility that can be used to either replay a trace or stress-test a database server. OStress can replay SQL Server traces (once they've been converted to RML files using ReadTrace) or execute SQL scripts against a database server.

OStress can also generate a controlled workload for testing SQL Server. The utility is well suited to this use because OStress provides multi-threaded trace replay, which would be cumbersome with other native SQL Server tools such as SQLCMD or OSQL, as these provide no easy method to manage multiple sessions. In addition, as testing requirements scale up to hundreds of users with thousands of sessions, there are no out-of-the-box SQL Server tools suitable for this task, even Ostress.

Stress Mode

Using OStress in stress mode is designed to generate user activity in a controlled workload. Because the test can be readily repeated and workload is always controlled and identical, this can be a useful method for verifying the impact of changes. In stress mode, user activity is not replayed but commands are started in sequence, as quickly as possible.

Using OStress in stress mode means sessions and threads are completely independent, and there is no mechanism for sessions to be synchronized or started in any specific sequence (unlike replay mode, which does enforce sequencing).

Replay Mode

Using OStress in replay mode enables administrators to replay a workload, captured using SQL Trace and converted to RML using Read Trace, on a test server. This can be useful in many situations, such as upgrading SQL Server versions, deploying a service pack, or making significant hardware changes (e.g., evaluating the benefit of 64-bit).

While OStress is used to replay workload, it is necessary to run another data capture for comparison with the baseline from the original server. Depending on the purpose of the testing this may require PerfMon and trace data capture.

When replaying RML files, ORCA (described next) is used to ensure correct sequencing of activities. Every RML file contains details of the sequence number, including the next sequence number. The default sequencing mode used by OStress suppresses periods of inactivity while preserving sequencing to ensure that query execution occurs serially (as it did when the trace was taken), with any delays between statements suppressed. Alternately, the exact sequencing method can be used to provide like-for-like trace replay whereby waits are not suppressed, which may be useful if distributed transactions are used in the workload.

Getting Started with OStress

At its most simple, OStress can be used to execute an individual query and write the output to a folder. The syntax is self-descriptive:

```
Ostress.exe –Q"Select GETDATE()" -oc:\temp\output
```

All parameters are case sensitive, and -S is used to specify the server name if connecting to remote servers or named instances. Similarly, use -U, -P to specify credentials (i.e., username and password) if a SQL login is used for connection.

One of the characteristics that makes OStress attractive for database testing activity is its ease of use. Two parameters can be particularly useful when stress testing a database: -r, to increase the query repeat count; and -n, to increase the number of threads. Using this method, workload activity for testing can be consistently and conveniently repeated using an identical workload each time.

> *Most replay workloads contain a combination of data manipulation statements, such as inserts, delete, and update statements. In order to ensure fair and consistent testing, the dataset should be reverted to initial state between test iterations. The dataset can be reset by restoring a backup, restoring from a snapshot or utilizing a data reversion script.*

The following syntax illustrates how to execute the simple GETDATE function using 100 threads with repeat count 1000 (each thread executes the command 1,000 times):

```
Ostress.exe -Q"Select GETDATE()" -oc:\temp\output -n100 -r1000
```

When using OStress replay functionality, the -m parameter should be set to "replay," which will result in ORCA being used to control the replay. Also use the -i parameter to reference an RML or SQL file to be executed. Since ReadTrace creates one RML file for each SPID, when replaying a complete workload (often hundreds of files from a busy server), it is necessary to use a wildcard (*) to indicate that all RML files should be replayed, as shown in the following example:

```
Ostress.exe -ic:\tracedata\output\*.RML -oc:\temp\output -mreplay
```

Advanced OStress

In addition to the command-line options available with OStress, an .INI configuration file can be used to control aspects of the replaying behavior. A major benefit of using OStress is the ability to introduce random events such as timeouts or query cancellation when running a query test. The following sample .INI file provided with RML Utilities consists of three sections: Connection Options, Query Options, and Replay Options:

```
[Connection Options]
LoginTimeout=30
QuotedIdentifier=Off
AutocommitMode=On
DisconnectPct=0.0
MaxThreadErrors=0

[Query Options]
NoSQLBindCol=Off
NoResultDisplay=On
PrepareExecute=Off
ExecuteAsync=Off
RollbackOnCancel=Off
QueryTimeout=0
QueryDelay=0
MaxRetries=0
BatchDisconnectPct=0.0
CancelPct=0.00
CancelDelay=0
CancelDelayMin=0
CursorType=
CursorConcurrency=
RowFetchDelay=0

[Replay Options]
Sequencing Options=global sequence
::Sequencing Options=global sequence, dtc replay
DTC Timeout=
DTC Machine=(local)
Playback Coordinator=(local)
StartSeqNum=
StopSeqNum=
TimeoutFactor=1.0
```

A complete explanation of each option is provided in the RML Utilities user guide, but note that there are query options relating to query cancellation that can be useful for constructing tests as close to real user activity as possible. Table 12-2 summarizes these options.

TABLE 12-2: RML Utilities Options

INI FILE PROPERTY	EXPLANATION
CancelPct	Execute query cancellations x percent of the time. Must set ExecuteAsync=On.
CancelDelay	Queries are cancelled after the delay is reached. This setting controls the delay (in milliseconds) that OStress will wait for query completion. If set to a negative number queries can be cancelled at any time up to the absolute value specified. To ensure queries have at least some time to execute set the **CancelDelayMin.** This can be useful to simulate impatient users.
CancelDelayMin	Enforces a minimum time (in milliseconds) a query is allowed to execute before they are considered for cancellation. Only used when the **CancelDelay** is set to a random time.

ORCA

The OStress Replay Control Agent (ORCA) provides session tracking, sequencing, and distributed transaction control for OStress replay. When replaying trace data from a single host, no configuration is required for ORCA because OStress will start and configure ORCA automatically.

ORCA can also be used to coordinate multi-host trace replay. In this situation, multiple computers host instances of OStress and one instance of ORCA coordinates activities between hosts, as shown in Figure 12-4. If this replay method is required, the Playback coordinator element of the configuration .INI file on each OStress host should be configured to point to the ORCA host.

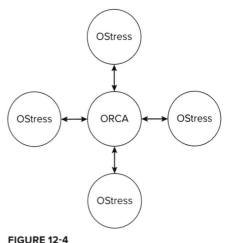

FIGURE 12-4

Bob Dorr and Keith Elmore have published step-by-step guidance for multi-machine replay using ORCA. You can find it on the Microsoft Customer Service and Support (CSS) blog for SQL Server: http://blogs.msdn.com/psssql/archive/2009/01/23/ inf-multi-machine-replay-using-orca-and-ostress.aspx.

PERFORMANCE TESTING

RML Utilities provides a method for replaying real user workload in a test environment. Replaying activity from genuine users on a repeatable basis means DBAs and engineers can verify the effect of changes, optimizations, and fixes without risk to service and the availability of the production platform. The high-level process looks as follows:

1. Back up production database.
2. Capture SQL trace.
3. Analyze TRC files with ReadTrace and create RML files.
4. Restore database to test server.
5. Set up Profiler trace on test server.
6. Replay RML files using OStress to generate base line.
7. Restore database.
8. Make optimizations/fixes etc.
9. Replay the RML files using OStress.
10. Analyze TRC files from the test server and compare using Reporter analysis.

Testing Scenarios

Start testing with a small number of short tests. Keeping each test cycle short and specific enables you to quickly capture results, and problems with the test environment can be identified and remedied quickly.

> *Consider setting the Max Degree of Parallelism value to 1 to prevent SQL Server from selecting parallel query plans. This can be a useful technique to restrict CPU performance on a test server, and it can bring performance problems such as missing indexes to the forefront earlier.*

Ensuring a Fair Test

Effective measurement of the impact of any change is necessary to determine whether the change led to the expected improvement, resulted in no change, or had a negative impact. Testing should be approached scientifically, whereby environmental factors are maintained between tests and a control test is carried out to determine a baseline, or reference point, for comparison.

There are two aspects to ensuring a fair test: *environment preparation* and *test execution*. Key to performance testing is ensuring that the test environment is representative of the production environment. Further, while testing, it's important to ensure that environmental factors are maintained (as much as reasonably possible), while changing only one controlled factor with each test.

When replaying a trace, always run a test in which no variables are changed. This provides a point of reference for comparison between the production and test environment before any changes are made. If differences are identified during this process, the results of all subsequent tests should take into account this difference.

There will likely be differences, so to simplify this process, it is good practice to take a baseline on the test system and compare against that, from which you can then work out the difference with the production system.

Environment Preparation

When performance testing, make sure that the test environment matches the production servers as closely as possible and that any differences are known. In addition, the impact of the delta (performance change) should be understood so this can be considered when interpreting test results.

A test environment designed for functional testing can be quite different from that designed for performance testing. When performance testing, you want the whole environment to match production because differences in server specification, such as number and speed of CPUs, memory, and storage performance, Operating System, Service Pack Level, and hotfixes may each have a significant impact.

Review the following list of considerations to ensure that the test environment matches production, or differences are understood and quantified:

➤ Network configuration (default gateway, DNS settings, local host files, VLAN membership and routing, etc.)

➤ Domain Config (OU, GPOs, security, location of Domain Controllers)

➤ Windows platform (x86, x64), Service Pack, and hotfix level

➤ Page file size and location

➤ Network connectivity and teaming configuration

➤ Storage Configuration (MPIO drivers and configuration, HBA queue depth, Storport drivers)

➤ Cluster configuration (dependencies, MSDTC)

➤ SQL Server edition, service pack, cumulative updates, and hotfix level

➤ Database data and log file placement

➤ Review `sp_configure` settings, especially the following:

    ➤ AWE

    ➤ Min and max server memory

    ➤ Max degree of parallelism

➤ Database settings, recovery model,

    ➤ Data file sizes, locations, number of, growth settings.

➤ Third party applications installed (anti-virus, backup agents, etc.)

Test Execution

When performing multiple tests in succession, there are a number of opportunities for results from one test to pollute results from a subsequent test. As such, take the following steps to reset the database environment between tests:

1. Restore the database.

2. Clear the buffer (data) cache.

3. Clear the procedure cache.

4. Warm the cache prior to testing.

CONSIDER USING DATABASE SNAPSHOTS

Restoring to a consistent point in time at the start of a test is crucial for repeatable testing. Doing a full restore for large databases can be time consuming and delay testing. As an alternative, consider creating a database snapshot prior to test execution. Once testing is complete, restore from the snapshot. This only replaces pages that have changed, and so reverting to your known starting point can be much faster.

There is performance overhead associated with maintaining a database snapshot, particularly with disk write activity, so consider the effect on the test results of maintaining the snapshot and only adopt this approach if the data proves the effect is small or consistent across all tests (i.e., self-canceling). Most databases are 80% read and 20% write; the higher the read percentage, the lower the impact the snapshot will have on performance. You may also consider the performance hit for write operations as valid additional disk IO in your testing if you are focusing on the read operations.

When executing SQL batches, either through workload or trace replay, it is usually necessary to restore a database backup. Without restoring the database state, batch executions could fail because of primary key violations caused by inserting duplicate records, or missing foreign keys causing statement failure. The performance effect of statements failing is usually significantly less than the impact of honoring those statements. In order to ensure a fair test, it is usually necessary to restore a database backup, unless a script can be generated to "reset" data.

> Performance of the test server will be closer to production server performance if the data cache is populated with useful data pages. Consider running a small batch to warm the cache prior to starting each test. Only warm the cache if this step will be carried out before every test, in order to prevent skewed results.

Clearing the buffer cache between test executions ensures that testing is fair between iterations. Use DBCC DROPCLEANBUFFERS to clear the buffer cache. Without clearing the buffer cache, the first test will forego some disk performance while data is retrieved from disk and loaded into the buffer cache in memory.

Following execution of the first test, the procedure cache is likely to be populated with compiled query plans that were generated by the Query Optimizer during execution of the first test. Use DBCC FREEPROCCACHE to empty the procedure cache.

Capturing a SQL Trace

Because Chapter 10 is dedicated to tracing in SQL Server and Profiler, there's no need to duplicate here the steps required to create a trace or the best practices for tracing. In brief summary: Always use server-side tracing to a dedicated (if possible) local disk. Avoid tracing to a UNC path; and be aware of USB disks, as performance can be a problem.

The samples folder within the RML Utilities folder contains three scripts pre-configured with the events necessary to capture the data required for replay and performance analysis with ReadTrace, eliminating a lot of the work required to build a trace. The trace definitions have filenames matching their purpose and create files that rollover to create a new file every 250MB; it will be necessary to specify the destination for trace files.

> Capture the trace during a period of normal activity or when problems are happening. Many decisions and recommendations may be drawn from the trace, and if the data within the trace is not representative, then the benefit of the entire exercise is negated.
>
> It is not good enough to capture a trace during periods of low activity (such as lunchtime or early morning). If, for example, the system has two primary user groups, such as call center staff during working hours and web traffic during the evening and weekends, then capture during both periods.

WORKING WITH DATABASE CLONES

Database clones are useful when investigating problems related to the SQL Server Query Optimizer. A database clone is a portable copy of a database schema and statistics only — there is no data. Clones can be used to generate estimated execution plans, and serve as a helpful troubleshooting tool.

You can create a database clone using the Script Wizard. Full instructions can be found in the Microsoft Knowledge Base article "How to generate a script of the necessary database metadata to create a statistics-only database in SQL Server 2005 and in SQL Server 2008" at http://support.microsoft.com/kb/914288.

Analyzing Large Datasets

When comparing the same workload performance between platforms it can be interesting to see statements that are executed differently. The statements executed differently can be reviewd to determine whether the difference provides a gain or loss in terms of performance. This approach can be useful to reduce risk on upgrades, changes, or migration projects; there's a technique presented in a document available on the SQL CAT team website (http://www.sqlcat.com) to assist with comparing query plans between two servers.

The document is called the Precision Performance technical note and contains a useful query that performs an outer join between the two databases containing the ReadTrace output. The query (code shown here) is used to compare execution plans and will help highlight statements which use a different plan between test iterations for further investigation.

Available for download on Wrox.com

```
select * from
(select p.PlanHashID as [PlanHashID_1],
b.HashID as [HashID_1],
count(*) as [Executes_1]
from SQL100TestA.ReadTrace.tblPlans p
inner join SQL100TestA.ReadTrace.tblBatches b on b.BatchSeq = p.BatchSeq
group by p.PlanHashID, b.HashID) as vwClone1
FULL OUTER join
(select p.PlanHashID as [PlanHashID_2],
b.HashID as [HashID_2],
count(*) as [Executes_2]
from SQL100TestB.ReadTrace.tblPlans p
inner join SQL100TestB.ReadTrace.tblBatches b on b.BatchSeq = p.BatchSeq
group by p.PlanHashID, b.HashID) as vwClone2
on vwClone1.HashID_1 = vwClone2.HashID_2
where vwClone1.PlanHashID_1 is NULL
or vwClone2.PlanHashID_2 is NULL
or vwClone1.PlanHashID_1 <> vwClone2.PlanHashID_2
```

This code available for download at wrox.com [compareplan.sql]

Once a statement has been identified as having the same hash ID, but differing (or missing) plan IDs between the two traces, Reporter can be used to investigate further. To use Reporter, copy the query hash ID from the compareplan.sql output, as shown in Figure 12-5.

	PlanHashID_1	HashID_1	Executes_1	PlanHashID_2	HashID_2	Executes_2
1	-5938266649235047858	9090740273285134311	1	-2273930034087599151	9090740273285134311	1
2	-5938266649235047858	9090740273285134311	1	-1637356510449767625	9090740273285134311	1
3	-5938266649235047858	9090740273285134311	1	-238731440282594729	9090740273285134311	1
4	-5938266649235047858	9090740273285134311	1	207378046287395295	9090740273285134311	1
5	-5938266649235047858	9090740273285134311	1	702850422845489797	9090740273285134311	1
6	-5938266649235047858	9090740273285134311	1	4962757797789336080	9090740273285134311	1
7	-2273930034087599151	9090740273285134311	1	-5938266649235047858	9090740273285134311	1
8	-2273930034087599151	9090740273285134311	1	-1637356510449767625	9090740273285134311	1
9	-2273930034087599151	9090740273285134311	1	-238731440282594729	9090740273285134311	1

FIGURE 12-5

Next, within Reporter locate a HashID tag, which is a hyperlink, and click this to display a dialog. Paste the query hash ID into the dialog as shown in Figure 12-6 to display the query text and plan.

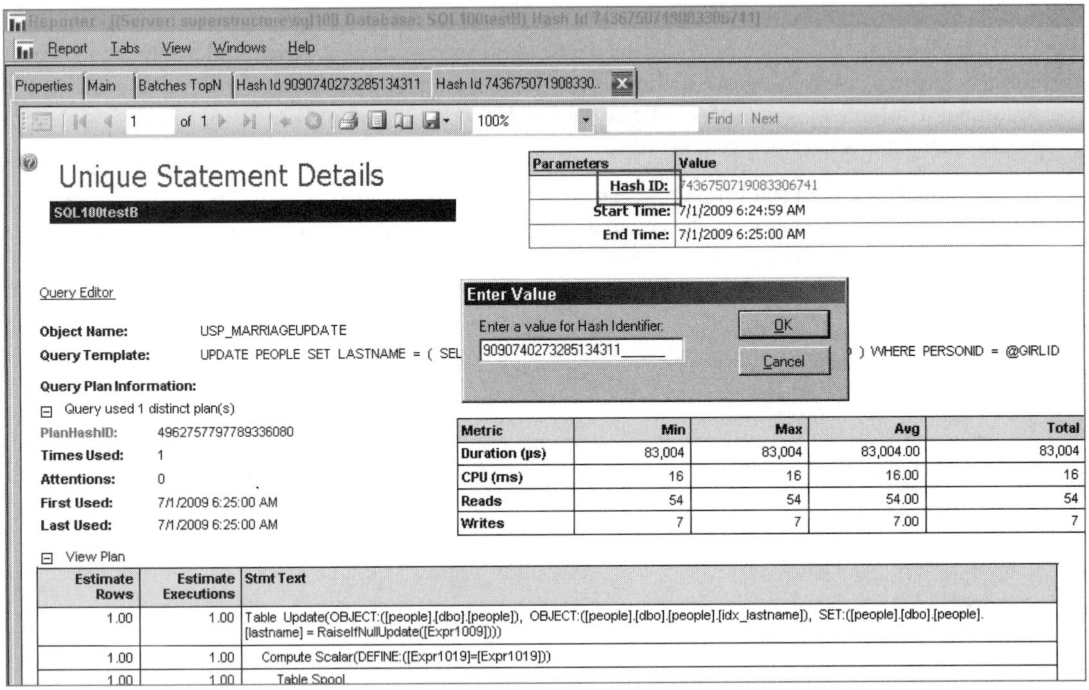

FIGURE 12-6

As you can see, effort is involved in retrieving low-level trace data for performance analysis, but the SQL Server tools are better than ever and still evolving. It's a skilled job that requires good knowledge of SQL Server components, tools, and utilities, as well as awareness of the application environment.

SUMMARY

RML Utilities provides valuable SQL Server support tools for fault-finding, verifying build, performance testing, and impact analysis when testing changes or new releases with workload captured in the production environment. Consider testing any significant environment changes such as software or hardware upgrades prior to implementation using RML Utilities for repeatable testing with measurable results.

ReadTrace will convert TRC files to RML files and generate a set of interactive reports including Top *n* worst-performing queries report. These reports allow you to drill down to look at information in more detail.

OStress can be used in two modes, either to replay a workload as it was captured from the server or to generate a workload based on a set of sql scripts allowing you to simulate many user sessions and activity.

The RML Utilities can be used to support repeatable testing useful when making any upgrade, environment change or when validating the effect of a change. Capturing a trace containing a representative workload and diligently resetting the test environment between iterations are key to ensuring reliable test results. Use RML Utilities to replay a workload and create a baseline for comparison between the production server and test server.

When replaying a trace to a test server, restore a backup first to ensure that the replay is valid. Run another trace while the replay is running and use the `compareplan.sql` query to identify changes to the query plan.

13

Bringing It All Together with SQL Nexus

WHAT'S IN THIS CHAPTER

➤ What SQL Nexus can do

➤ How to manage an effective data collection

➤ Loading data into the tool and using the reports to troubleshoot issues

➤ Adding custom reports

This chapter is about a troubleshooting tool called SQL Nexus that brings together all of the knowledge and skills covered in the book up to this point. To use the tool effectively you should be familiar with all the chapter topics covered so far.

SQL Nexus enables you to load and analyze SQL Server trace files, performance monitor logs, wait statistics, and locking and blocking information through a single tool.

It uses ReadTrace (part of RML Utilities and covered in Chapter 12) to process the SQL Trace files and provides the ReadTrace reports embedded in the tool for ease of use. It also analyzes blocking and wait statistics information collected by the PerfStats script (Chapter 11) and contains reports that enable you to drill down into that information too.

Figure 13-1 shows part of the Bottleneck Analysis report, which indicates CPU utilization on the server from which the data was collected, and SQL Server's contribution to it. You can also see an analysis of SQL Server wait types, which in this example indicates that 72% of SQL Server's wait time (Chapter 3) was spent waiting for locks.

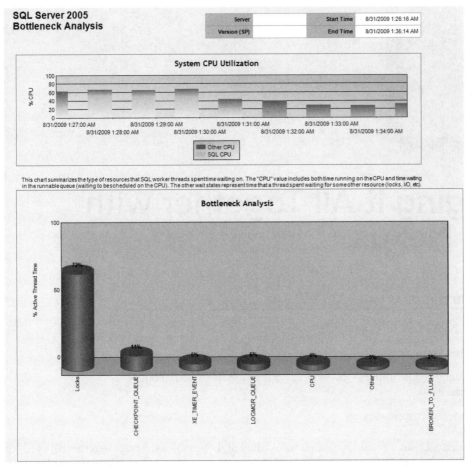

FIGURE 13-1

Figure 13-2 shows the Blocking Chains report from the same data collection, which provides a summary of the blocking chains detected and allows you to drill through to get full details of the sessions and statements involved. You'll see this example data collection toward the end of the chapter when SQL Nexus is used to examine the underlying problem.

The final screen to whet your appetite is shown in Figure 13-3, which depicts the Top Unique Batches embedded report produced by ReadTrace. While SQL Nexus doesn't enhance the ReadTrace reports themselves, producing them using SQL Nexus rather than using the ReadTrace command line interface will generally get you results much more quickly. Also, having them in context with the wait stats and blocking reports mentioned already adds a valuable dimension to your investigation.

This brief introduction to SQL Nexus shows you just a few of the benefits of using this tool. By the end of the chapter you will feel confident adding SQL Nexus to your troubleshooting toolset.

Blocking Chains

Start	End	Blocking Type	Duration (sec)	Blocked Sessions
8/31/2009 3:37:42 AM	8/31/2009 3:37:53 AM	LOCK BLOCKING	2	47
8/31/2009 3:37:53 AM	8/31/2009 3:38:04 AM	LOCK BLOCKING	6	49
8/31/2009 3:38:04 AM	8/31/2009 3:38:14 AM	LOCK BLOCKING	8	47
8/31/2009 3:38:14 AM	8/31/2009 3:38:26 AM	LOCK BLOCKING	7	49
8/31/2009 3:38:26 AM	8/31/2009 3:38:36 AM	LOCK BLOCKING	6	49
8/31/2009 3:38:36 AM	8/31/2009 3:38:47 AM	LOCK BLOCKING	7	48
8/31/2009 3:38:47 AM	8/31/2009 3:38:58 AM	LOCK BLOCKING	4	49
8/31/2009 3:38:58 AM	8/31/2009 3:39:09 AM	LOCK BLOCKING	6	200
8/31/2009 3:39:09 AM	8/31/2009 3:39:20 AM	LOCK BLOCKING	7	304
8/31/2009 3:39:20 AM	8/31/2009 3:39:41 AM	LOCK BLOCKING	21	47
8/31/2009 3:39:41 AM	8/31/2009 3:39:51 AM	LOCK BLOCKING	5	46
8/31/2009 3:39:51 AM	8/31/2009 3:40:02 AM	LOCK BLOCKING	7	46
8/31/2009 3:40:02 AM	8/31/2009 3:40:13 AM	LOCK BLOCKING	6	45
8/31/2009 3:40:13 AM	8/31/2009 3:40:24 AM	LOCK BLOCKING	5	45
8/31/2009 3:40:24 AM	8/31/2009 3:40:35 AM	LOCK BLOCKING	7	45
8/31/2009 3:40:35 AM	8/31/2009 3:40:46 AM	LOCK BLOCKING	5	43
8/31/2009 3:40:46 AM	8/31/2009 3:40:56 AM	LOCK BLOCKING	6	44
8/31/2009 3:40:56 AM	8/31/2009 3:41:06 AM	LOCK BLOCKING	6	44
8/31/2009 3:41:06 AM	8/31/2009 3:41:17 AM	LOCK BLOCKING	4	164
8/31/2009 3:41:17 AM	8/31/2009 3:41:28 AM	LOCK BLOCKING	3	40
8/31/2009 3:41:28 AM	8/31/2009 3:41:38 AM	LOCK BLOCKING	3	34
8/31/2009 3:41:38 AM	8/31/2009 3:41:48 AM	LOCK BLOCKING	3	34
8/31/2009 3:41:48 AM	8/31/2009 3:41:58 AM	LOCK BLOCKING	3	34
8/31/2009 3:41:58 AM	8/31/2009 3:42:09 AM	LOCK BLOCKING	3	30
8/31/2009 3:42:09 AM	8/31/2009 3:42:20 AM	LOCK BLOCKING	2	25
8/31/2009 3:42:20 AM	8/31/2009 3:42:30 AM	LOCK BLOCKING	1	106
8/31/2009 3:42:30 AM	8/31/2009 3:42:40 AM	LOCK BLOCKING	3	45
8/31/2009 3:42:40 AM	8/31/2009 3:42:51 AM	LOCK BLOCKING	1	14
8/31/2009 3:42:51 AM	8/31/2009 3:43:01 AM	LOCK BLOCKING	1	18
8/31/2009 3:43:01 AM	8/31/2009 3:43:11 AM	LOCK BLOCKING	2	70
8/31/2009 3:43:11 AM	8/31/2009 3:43:22 AM	LOCK BLOCKING	2	11
8/31/2009 3:43:22 AM	8/31/2009 3:43:32 AM	LOCK BLOCKING	0	12
8/31/2009 3:43:32 AM	8/31/2009 3:43:53 AM	LOCK BLOCKING	21	10

FIGURE 13-2

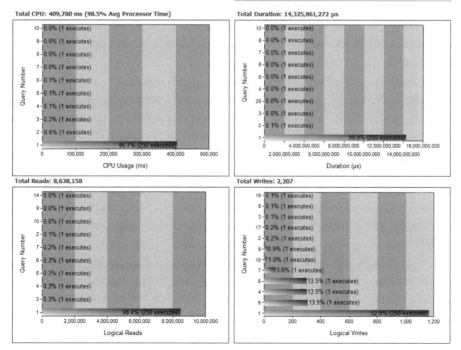

FIGURE 13-3

GETTING STARTED

The home of SQL Nexus is on the open-source community website CodePlex, at `http://codeplex` `.com/sqlnexus`. Here you'll find links to download the tool, prerequisites, as well as a discussion board and the full source code. This chapter is based on the latest version available at the time of writing, SQL Nexus 3.0.0.0.

Prerequisites

SQL Nexus requires either SQL Server 2005 or SQL Server 2008 with Service Pack 1 installed. If you're using SQL Server 2005, you also need to install the SQL Server 2008 SP1 Report Viewer, which can be found at `http://tinyurl.com/n5ux8f`. You'll also need to install the RML Utilities to get ReadTrace, which you can download here: `http://support.microsoft.com/kb/944837`.

Installation

Once you've installed the prerequisites you can start SQL Nexus by simply running `sqlnexus.exe` from the folder you've downloaded. There is no installation process.

Startup

Every time you run SQL Nexus you're presented with a dialog box to connect to SQL Server. The SQL Server instance to which you connect is used to store the results from processing a data collection. It is *not* the server you want to troubleshoot; SQL Nexus is an "offline" analysis tool, which means it analyzes data that has already been collected.

When you connect to a SQL Server instance, SQL Nexus will look for a database called "SQLNexus." If one is found, then the Recovery Model (see Chapter 1) will be set to Simple to ensure that the transaction log doesn't need to be managed. If the SQLNexus database doesn't exist, then one is created with a 50MB data file.

Now you're ready to import a data collection or start to plan one. Either way, you should read the next section to understand how to collect data that will give you the best results for SQL Nexus to analyze.

DATA COLLECTION

The key to data collection for SQL Nexus is the PerfStats script, covered in Chapter 11. While SQL Nexus doesn't require the use of PerfStats, using it does enable you to quickly configure a data collection that can be used by all the features in the tool, and it is usually the preferred method for ease of use and completeness.

The PerfStats script customizes a SQLDiag data collection (also covered in Chapter 11) to add a custom data collector for gathering information on locking and blocking issues and wait stats information. This information can be invaluable for troubleshooting performance issues, and the analysis and presentation of these details is a key strength of SQL Nexus.

Using PerfStats automates and consolidates a data collection that will give you the following results for importing into SQL Nexus:

➤ Performance Monitor logs (see Chapter 9)

➤ SQL Trace files (see Chapters 10 and 11)

➤ Locking, blocking, and wait stats information (see Chapter 11)

Is the Default Data Collection Good Enough?

By default, the PerfStats script collects a customized set of events and counters. This section explores whether or not you need to adjust what is captured in order to help with your troubleshooting or reduce the performance impact of the data collection.

Performance Monitor (PerfMon) Log

The Performance Monitor log captures all the SQL Server counters and the core Windows counters, so for most scenarios it isn't necessary to add to or modify the default settings. The size of the resulting log file is easily manageable, generally only hitting 100 or 200MB after a few hours, even on very busy servers; and the performance impact is negligible.

PerfStats Script

The PerfStats script itself doesn't have anything that you need to be worried about configuring for the purposes of SQL Nexus, and it will collect information on locks, latches, and wait types by default with very little performance impact.

SQL Trace

SQL Nexus uses ReadTrace (see Chapter 12) to analyze the trace files, but in order to use ReadTrace's full functionality you need to gather a few more events in your SQL Trace than the default PerfStats configuration allows. This code is available for download at www.wrox.com in the file PerfStatsScript2008.zip

If you download and uncompress PerfStats, you'll find a batch file called StartSQLDiagTrace2008.cmd, which uses an XML configuration file in the same folder called SQLDiagPerfStats_Trace2008.XML to determine what data to capture. Running this batch file will capture a Performance Monitor log; locking, blocking, and wait information, as well as a SQL Trace from all instances on the server.

However, the trace doesn't collect statement-level details or execution plans by default because they are frequent events and generate a lot of logging activity, which can then be difficult to process if you need to run a long trace. The problem in the majority of cases tends to be with the volume of data collected in a short period, rather than the data collection's impact on the server. However, you should approach it tentatively in your own environment to ensure that the data collection doesn't adversely affect the performance of any critical applications.

The default data collection will capture details at the stored procedure and batch level without execution plans. SQL Nexus/ReadTrace will work with this level of data, but you quickly find that not being able to drill down any further becomes frustrating when you're trying to troubleshoot a problem.

For that reason, I tend to favor short data collections that capture everything I need, so I run the collection with the extra events whenever possible. You do need to monitor the disk space used by the trace files, however, because they can easily store hundreds of megabytes a minute on a very busy system.

The default SQL Trace events collected by `StartSQLDiagTrace2008.cmd` are summarized below for easy reference:

- Database: Data File Autogrow
- Database: Data File Autoshrink
- Database: Log File Autogrow
- Database: Log File Autoshrink
- Errors and Warnings: Attention
- Errors and Warnings: Bitmap Warning
- Errors and Warnings: CPU Threshold Exceeded
- Errors and Warnings: EventLog
- Errors and Warnings: Exception
- Errors and Warnings: Execution Warnings
- Errors and Warnings: Hash Warning
- Errors and Warnings: Missing Join Predicate
- Errors and Warnings: OLE DB Errors
- Errors and Warnings: Sort Warnings
- Locks: Deadlock
- Locks: Escalation
- Locks: Timeout
- Objects: Auto Update Stats

- Performance: Plan Guide Successful
- Performance: Plan Guide Unsuccessful
- Security Audit: Login
- Security Audit: Login Failed
- Security Audit: Logout
- Security Audit: ServiceControl
- Server: Server Memory Change
- Server: PreConnect:Starting
- Server: PreConnect:Completed
- Sessions: ExistingConnection
- Sessions: PreConnect:Starting
- Sessions: PreConnect:Completed
- Stored Procedures: RPC:Completed
- Stored Procedures: RPC:Starting
- Stored Procedures: SP:CacheInsert
- Stored Procedures: SP:CacheRemove
- Stored Procedures: SP:Recompile
- Transactions: DTCTransaction
- Transactions: SQL Transaction
- T-SQL: SQL:BatchCompleted
- T-SQL: SQL:BatchStarting

These events provide a good baseline of SQL Server activity, but enabling the following additional events will enable you to drill down to the statement level and compare and review execution plans, albeit at the expense of increased overhead in the data collection:

➤ **Performance:** Show Plan Statistics

➤ **Stored Procedures:** SP:StmtCompleted

➤ **Stored Procedures:** SP:StmtStarting

➤ **T-SQL:** SQL:StmtCompleted

➤ **T-SQL:** SQL:StmtStarting

Modifying the Data Collection

Thankfully, adding and removing additional events and counters to your data collection is easy. All the events and counters are already listed in the sample XML configuration files, so all you need to do is set `enabled` to `true` or `false` against the items you want to modify.

For example, to add the missing events for SQL Nexus/ReadTrace to the data collection for `StartSQLDiagTrace2008.cmd`, you need to uncheck the read-only flag on `SQLDiagPerfStats_Trace2008.XML`, load it into Notepad or an XML editor, set the preceding counters to true, and then save the file. Figure 13-4 shows the section in the XML file for Performance Events, and the Show Plan Statistics event that has been enabled.

You can also choose which collectors are used, so you can disable collectors like PerfMon or SQL Trace if you're not interested in them for a specific data collection. The next section describes where the collectors are enabled and disabled.

```
<EventType name="Performance">
    <Event name="Degree of Parallelism (7.0 Delete)" enabled="fal
    <Event name="Degree of Parallelism (7.0 Insert)" enabled="fal
    <Event name="Degree of Parallelism (7.0 Select)" enabled="fal
    <Event name="Degree of Parallelism (7.0 Update)" enabled="fal
    <Event name="Execution Plan" enabled="false" id="68" />
    <Event name="Plan Guide Successful" enabled="true" id="217" /
    <Event name="Plan Guide unsuccessful" enabled="true" id="218"
    <Event name="Show Plan All" enabled="false" id="97" />
    <Event name="Show Plan Statistics" enabled="true" id="98" />
    <Event name="Show Plan Text" enabled="false" id="96" />
    <Event name="Showplan XML" enabled="false" id="122" />
    <Event name="Showplan XML For Query Compile" enabled="false"
    <Event name="Showplan XML Statistics Profile" enabled="false"
```

FIGURE 13-4

Collecting Data for a Specific Instance

By default, PerfStats will try to collect data from all the instances on the local machine on which it's run. This provides a quick out-of-the-box solution so that you can simply run the script without modification. However, you're more likely to be interested in one instance at a time, so it makes sense to explicitly specify the instance from which data should be collected.

To do this, you need to edit the XML configuration file as above, changing the "instance name" parameter from an asterisk(*) to the name of your instance. For example, if the SQL Server you connect to is MARS\PHOBOS, set the instance name parameter to PHOBOS. If you're collecting data from a default instance, then use MSSQLSERVER as the instance name.

It's also a good idea to explicitly specify the computer name (it's "." by default, which is a shortcut for local) for the data collection as well, to ensure that it doesn't work if you accidentally run it on the wrong server. In the preceding example, MARS is the computer name you would specify.

If you're collecting data from a failover cluster, you have to specify both parameters. The computer name is the first part of your virtual instance name, and the instance name is the second part. The physical node computer names are not used.

Figure 13-5 shows the parameter location with default values, and Figure 13-6 shows the parameters modified to collect data from a clustered instance called JUPITERv\ CALLISTO. Although JUPITERv is the computer name specified, it is the virtual server name for the instance, rather than the computer name of one of the physical nodes.

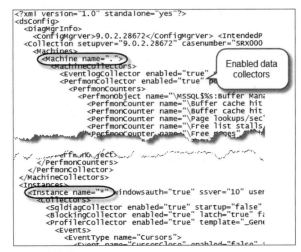

FIGURE 13-5

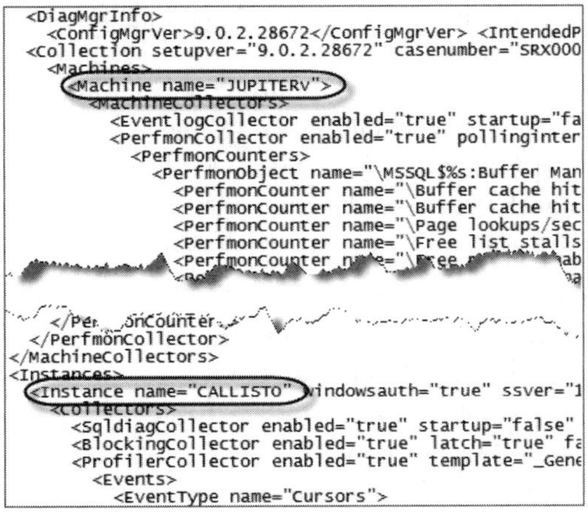

FIGURE 13-6

Knowing How Much Data to Collect

The simple answer to this question is to capture enough data to enable you to reproduce the issue you're trying to resolve. Unfortunately, that's not always possible when you're troubleshooting intermittent issues or on busy production servers that generate hundreds of megabytes of diagnostics data every minute.

There is no prescriptive answer that you can apply to every situation, but understanding how and where your data collection will grow and the limitations of SQL Nexus can help you determine for how long you should run a particular data collection.

The Performance Monitor logs take a snapshot of data every five seconds and roll over to a new file every 256MB. The total size of the PerfMon logs is only likely to be significant on very long data collections of tens of hours, and even then 1GB of data would be considered very large. The file size is normally insignificant compared to the SQL Trace data.

When you start the data collection, a subfolder called SQLDiagOutput is created. You can monitor that folder to keep an eye on how much data is being collected. You'll notice the PerfMon log (SQLDIAG.BLG) increase in size gradually but the SQL Trace files (*sp_trace.trc) are cached and written to the directory as they become full and another file is started. The SQL Trace trace files will roll over to a new file every 350MB.

On a busy SQL Server, it's very easy to generate tens or even hundreds of gigabytes of SQL Trace data; and while you may be able to import that much data, the resulting reports will be unusable.

As a test I imported 150GB of SQL Trace data collected over three hours on a busy SQL Server. Importing the data took eight hours on a quad-core machine with 16GB RAM and produced a 20GB SQLNexus database. It took a long time to import but was still manageable. However, I had to kill the first query that the ReadTrace report ran after it had been running for an hour because those timings make the reports useless for troubleshooting.

SQL Nexus can manage up to 10GB of SQL Trace data with relative ease, so you should aim to keep your data collection below that size to create a responsive set of reports on top of the data.

IMPORTING DATA

Once you've completed your data collection and installed SQL Nexus and its dependencies (see the "Getting Started" section) on a server or workstation where the processing won't affect the performance of anything essential, you can start importing the data you've collected.

Figure 13-7 shows the main SQL Nexus screen and highlights the location of the Import button and the resulting options. The first thing you'll need to do is specify the location of the data to import; this will normally be the SQLDiagOutput folder discussed in the last section.

The destination for the data load will be a database called SQLNexus, which was created when you connected to the SQL Server instance. The database can store data for only one instance at a time, so it is recreated each time you run an import. If you want to keep the results of previous imports, then you need to take a database backup before the next import. You'll be prompted each time to overwrite the database if there's existing data.

> *You can suppress the message to confirm you want to overwrite the existing database each time by selecting the option visible in Figure 13-7*

Clicking the Options link on the bottom left of the Data Import dialog will present you with a list of menu options; expanding the Importers menu gives you a list of the three types of data collection you can import — PerfMon logs, SQL Trace files, and PerfStats output — from which you can enable or disable the ones that you're interested in. This is also visible in Figure 13-7.

> *For security reasons the *.trc files are created with the same Windows security permissions as the database data files. In most environments this will mean that you don't have read permission to the files and the import will fail. Check the permissions on all the *.trc files in the SQLDiagOutput folder and assign yourself* Read & Execute *permissions where appropriate.*

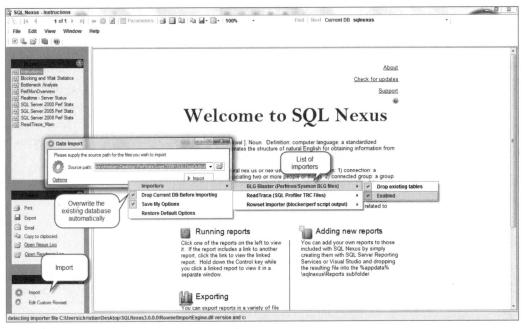

FIGURE 13-7

Once you've selected the importers to use, click the Import button on the Data Import window to start processing. If everything is imported correctly, you'll get a complete set of green bars and a status message for each file type as shown in Figure 13-8. Now that you've finished the data collection and import, you can start looking into what results have been produced.

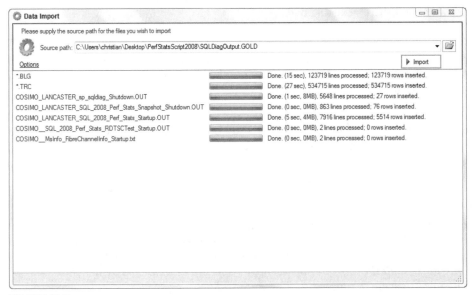

FIGURE 13-8

AVAILABLE REPORTS

The out-of-the-box reports include some overlap of functionality, and even deprecated reports, so it's worth reviewing each one to help you decide where to focus your attention.

The supplied reports are shown in Figure 13-9.

➤ **Instructions:** The "home page" for the tool provides quick links to the supplied help file.

➤ **Blocking and Wait Statistics:** Provides waits grouped into similar wait types and ranked by the total average wait time, as well as a list of all the blocking chains detected with drill-through capability. This is one of the most useful reports in the tool.

➤ **Bottleneck Analysis:** Contains a breakdown of CPU utilization across the time frame of the data collection, including the amount for which SQL Server was responsible. It also has a chart of the grouped wait types ranked by percent to highlight the most common bottleneck.

FIGURE 13-9

➤ **Real-time – Server Status:** This report, written for SQL Server 2005, provides a live dashboard showing the health of the SQL Server to which you connected on startup. This report doesn't work against SQL Server 2008 and has been deprecated, so it won't be updated.

➤ **SQL Server 2000 Perf Stats:** Reports on blocking chains collected from SQL Server 2000.

➤ **SQL Server 2005 Perf Stats:** A grouping of the Blocking and Wait Statistics and Bottleneck Analysis reports described above, along with a spinlock report for SQL Server 2005 (a *spinlock* is when a thread continually loops trying to acquire a lock rather than allowing itself to be rescheduled).

➤ **SQL Server 2008 Perf Stats:** A grouping of the Blocking and Wait Statistics and Bottleneck Analysis reports described above, along with a Spinlock report and a Query Hash report for SQL Server 2008 (*query hashing* is a new feature in 2008 that helps you to identify identical queries run with different variables or parameters for the purpose of aggregating performance statistics).

➤ **ReadTrace_Main:** The embedded ReadTrace report

EXAMPLE SCENARIO USING SQL NEXUS

In this section you're going to work through an entire example process — from data collection through to import and finally using the reports to help identify any problems.

The example database used is called "PeopleSQLNexus" and can be downloaded from www.wrox.com if you'd like to follow along. It contains four tables: people, girlsnames, boysnames, and lastnames.

The stored procedures in the database are as follows:

➤   `usp_peopleInsert`: Inserts a boy and a girl into the people table.

➤   `usp_generateDOB`: Generates random birth dates within the last 110 years. Used by `usp_peopleInsert`.

➤   `usp_loopPeopleInsert`: Runs `usp_peopleInsert` 10 times. Can be overridden by passing a value to the `@people` parameter.

➤   `usp_birthInsert`: Inserts a new boy and girl record with today's date as the date of birth.

➤   `usp_loopBirthInsert`: Runs `usp_birthInsert` 10 times. Can be overridden by passing a value to the `@people` parameter.

➤   `usp_marriageUpdate`: Matches a boy and girl together and updates the girl's surname to be the same as the boy's surname.

➤   `usp_loopMarriageUpdate`: Runs `usp_marriageUpdate` 10 times. Can be overridden by passing a value to the `@people` parameter.

➤   `usp_deathDelete`: Deletes a boy and a girl record from the people table.

➤   `usp_loopDeathDelete`: Runs `usp_deathDelete` 10 times. Can be overridden by passing a value to the `@people` parameter.

Configuring the Data Collection

For this example, you want to collect everything that SQL Nexus needs in order to provide you with a full set of reports. Thankfully, there isn't much to do to achieve this, as covered in depth earlier in the chapter.

I'm going to be using `StartSQLDiagTrace2008.cmd` for the data collection, which means I need to edit the `SQLDiagPerfStats_Trace2008.XML` configuration file to add COSIMO as the machine name and LANCASTER as the instance from which I want to collect data. I also need to enable the following events:

➤   **Performance:** Show Plan Statistics

➤   **Stored Procedures:** SP:StmtCompleted

➤   **Stored Procedures:** SP:StmtStarting

➤   **T-SQL:** SQL:StmtCompleted

➤   **T-SQL:** SQL:StmtStarting

If you need a reminder about how to do this, refer to the "Modifying the Data Collection" section earlier in the chapter.

Now that PerfStats has been configured, I can run `StartSQLDiagTrace.cmd` and wait for the "SQLDIAG data collection started" message before generating the workload.

Generating the Workload

To help generate the load, I'm going to use OStress (part of RML Utilities and covered in Chapter 12) to create multiple connections to simultaneously run a T-SQL script containing a workload against the peopleSQLNexus database. The workload script, shown in Listing 13-1, contains code to randomly run one of three stored procedures that generate either inserts, updates, or deletes.

LISTING 13-1: Workload script to use with OStress (Chapter13Workload.sql)

```
DECLARE @random INT = RAND(( DATEPART(mm, GETDATE()) * 100000 )
                     + ( DATEPART(ss, GETDATE()) * 1000 )
                     + DATEPART(ms, GETDATE()))
                     * 100

IF @random % 3 = 0
    EXEC dbo.usp_loopBirthInsert
ELSE
    IF @random % 3 = 1
        EXEC dbo.usp_loopMarriageUpdate
    ELSE
        IF @random % 3 = 2
            EXEC dbo.usp_loopDeathDelete
```

I've saved the preceding code in a T-SQL file so I can then pass it as a parameter to OStress as the workload file.

Here is the OStress command with the parameters that I'm going to use (the default location for OStress is C:\Program Files\Microsoft Corporation\RMLUtils):

```
ostress -Scosimo\lancaster -dpeopleSQLNexus -E -i"c:\temp\peopleworkload.sql" -n50
    -r5
```

My instance is COSIMO\LANCASTER, the database is peopleSQLNexus, and the workload file is saved in c:\temp. The workload script will be run 5 times from 50 different connections.

> *You can modify the size of the workload by changing the values for the -n parameter to reflect the number of connections to use and the -r parameter for the number of times to run the workload. You might want to do that if you find that the workload completes much faster or slower than you see described in this example.*

Before running OStress, first configure and start the PerfStats script so the data collection is started before the workload begins.

On my laptop, OStress took about four minutes to complete and I collected a 125MB SQL Trace file from PerfStats, along with the blocking and PerfMon logs, which were of negligible size.

Importing the Data

Before running the import, check the Windows file permissions on the *.trc files in the SQLDiagOutput folder. As mentioned earlier, security on the files is set to the same as the database data files to protect sensitive data. This means that you will have to manually assign yourself *Read & Execute* permissions in order to import successfully.

By default, the SQL Trace and PerfStats importers are selected so you shouldn't need to change anything for this example.

Looking at the Bottlenecks

Once the import is complete, you can begin looking at the reports to see if anything interesting was happening. First up is the Bottleneck Analysis report, shown in Figure 13-10. This report indicates significant CPU utilization from SQL Server and a severe locking problem. In this case, Locks is the only group of wait types that you need to worry about, showing 72% of the total wait time.

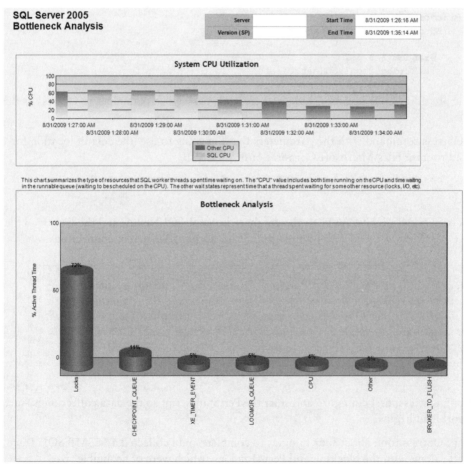

FIGURE 13-10

The next report to look at is Blocking and Resource Wait Statistics, to see if we can get more information on this locking problem. The report indicates that around 30 blocking chains were detected; in Figure 13-11, part of the detail is magnified to show the blocking duration and the number of blocked requests within the chain. The worst blocking duration was 21 seconds and the longest chain of blocked requests was 304.

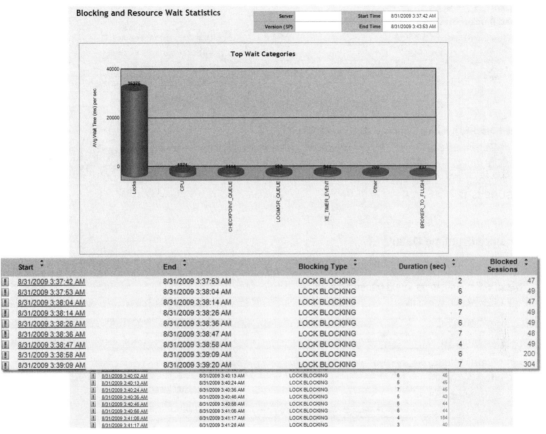

FIGURE 13-11

This report enables a drilldown for each chain, which is useful as you want to know the heads of all the blocking chains.

Figure 13-12 shows the first-level drilldown for the earliest detected blocking chain, which indicates that the head blocker was running a DELETE command. Drilling down again provides the detail shown in Figure 13-13, which indicates that the head blocker was running the usp_deathDelete stored procedure.

Within the stored procedure, the command causing the blocking problem is
"DELETE people WHERE personid = @boyid," which has an exclusive lock on the people table. This exclusive lock is then blocking other requests for update locks (LCK_M_U) and shared locks (LCK_M_S).

Blocking Chain Detail

Click here to copy text summary to clipboard:

Server	
Version (SP)	

Blocking Chain Statistics

Head Blocker Session ID	93	Blocking Duration (sec)	2
Blocking Start	8/31/2009 3:37:42 AM	Max Blocking Chain Size	47
Blocking End	8/31/2009 3:37:53 AM		

Head Blocker Statistics

Program Name	OSTRESS	Transaction Type	1-Read/write
Host Name	COSIMO	Transaction Isolation	2-Read Committed
NT User	cosimo\christian	Transaction Name	INSERT
Login Name	cosimo\christian	Trans Start (Duration)	8/31/2009 3:37:42 AM (0 sec)
		#Open Transactions	2

Head Blocker Runtime Summary (Session ID 93)

Runtime	Blocker Task State	Blocker Wait Category	Wait Time (ms)	Blocker Query Duration (ms)	Blocked Tasks	Blocker Command	Most Recent Head Blocker Query
2009-08-31 03:37:42.593	RUNNABLE		143	8095	47	DELETE	DELETE people ...

FIGURE 13-12

Session/Runtime Detail

Server	
Version (SP)	

Detail for Session ID 93 at 8/31/2009 3:37:42 AM

Program Name	OSTRESS	Transaction Type	1-Read/write
Host Name	COSIMO	Transaction Isolation	2-Read Committed
NT User	cosimo\christian	Transaction Name	INSERT
Login Name	cosimo\christian	Trans Start (Duration)	8/31/2009 3:37:42 AM (0 sec)
Last Query Start/End	8/31/2009 3:37:34 AM / 8/31/2009 3:37:34 AM	#Open Transactions	2
Wait Type			
Wait Time (ms)	143		

Exclusive Lock

Resource Description	ridlock fileid=1 pageid=203 dbid=7 id=lock5042dc0 mode=X associatedObjectId=72057594038517760
Procedure	CREATE PROCEDURE [dbo].[usp_deathDelete] AS
Query	⊞ DELETE people WHERE personid = @boyId -- Clean up before we are done

Runtime Snapshot

Snapshot Time: 2009-08-31T03:37:42.593

Session ID	Task State	Command	Blocking Session ID	Wait Type	Wait Duration (ms)	Wait Resource	Query	Request CPU (ms)
53	SUSPENDED	UPDATE	72	LCK_M_U	968	PAGE: 7:1:203	UPDATE people S...	2230
54	SUSPENDED	UPDATE	53	LCK_M_U	980	PAGE: 7:1:191	UPDATE people S...	437
55	SUSPENDED	UPDATE	54	LCK_M_U	903	PAGE: 7:1:191	UPDATE people S...	46
56	SUSPENDED	INSERT	72	LCK_M_S	2013	PAGE: 7:1:203	INSERT #girls (personId...	0
57	SUSPENDED	INSERT	72	LCK_M_S	2025	PAGE: 7:1:203	INSERT #girls (personId...	0
58	SUSPENDED	INSERT	72	LCK_M_S	2015	PAGE: 7:1:203	INSERT #girls (personId...	31
59	SUSPENDED	DELETE	93	LCK_M_U	152	RID: 7:1:334:6	DELETE people W...	187
60	SUSPENDED	INSERT	72	LCK_M_S	2012	PAGE: 7:1:203	INSERT #girls (personId...	31

FIGURE 13-13

Investigation into other blocking chains shows a similar story for `usp_marriageUpdate` as the head blocker.

After you know what code is involved, you can have a look at the ReadTrace_Main report to see what that can tell you.

ReadTrace provides the top-level reports shown in Figure 13-14.

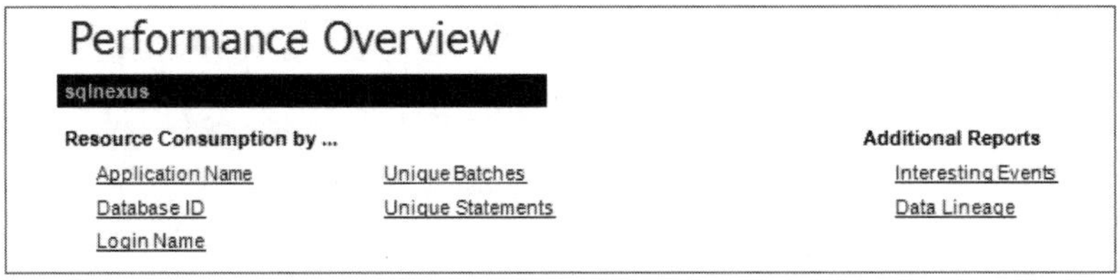

Performance Overview

sqlnexus

Resource Consumption by ...

Application Name   Unique Batches

Database ID   Unique Statements

Login Name

Additional Reports

Interesting Events

Data Lineage

FIGURE 13-14

The first report of interest is "Interesting Events," which you'll find on the right under "Additional Reports." Figure 13-15 shows some of the detail in this report, as described in the following list:

➤ **Auto Stats:** Indicates an event fired because statistics were automatically updated. Further investigation showed that many of the updates were for automatically generated statistics on the personid column in the people table, which might indicate a missing index.

Event Name	Trace Event ID	Number of Events
⊞ Auto Stats	58	124
⊞ Data File Auto Grow	92	3
⊞ Exception	33	41
⊞ Log File Auto Grow	93	6
⊞ Server Memory Change	81	1
⊞ Sort Warnings	69	1
⊞ SP:Recompile	37	43

FIGURE 13-15

➤ **Data File Autogrow:** Three autogrow events were detected; two for tempdb and one for peopleSQLNexus, indicating that the files were not properly sized for this workload. This is particularly important for tempdb (see Chapter 7).

➤ **Exception:** Exceptions indicate that something went wrong, but drilling down into the details indicates low-priority exceptions related to the data collection, so you can discount these events for this scenario.

➤ **Log File Autogrow:** Six autogrow events occurred for transaction logs: four for tempdb and two for peopleSQLNexus, indicating (as with the Data File Autogrow) that the logs were not sized correctly.

➤ **Server Memory Change:** Indicates a change in SQL Server memory usage. In this case it was an increase to 104MB so it's nothing to be concerned about.

➤ **Sort Warnings:** This occurs when a sort operation can't fit in memory and has to be spilled to disk. This might be worth investigating to try to remove the sort.

➤ **SP:Recompile:** This event triggers when statements are recompiled. Drilling into the detail shows a mix of recompiles for code involved in data collection and "deferred compiles" in the workload caused by the use of temporary tables in the code. There is nothing in here to be concerned about at this stage.

The following conclusions can be drawn from this report:

➤ Auto-created stats on `peopleid` in the people table may indicate a missing index. Numerous auto-update events indicate significant changes to the people table.

➤ Data and transaction log files were not sized appropriately, as indicated by autogrow events. This should be reviewed, but there are no indicators that this is the major cause of the blocking locks.

Next up is the Top Unique Batches report, shown in Figure 13-16.

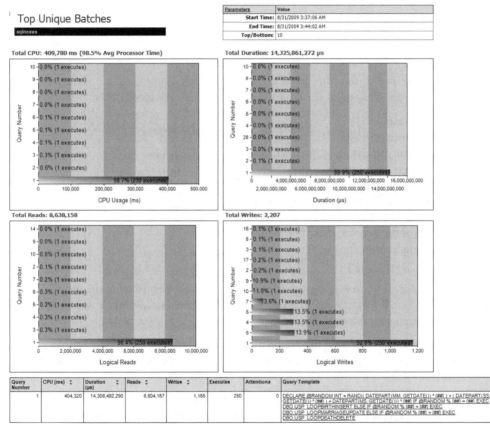

FIGURE 13-16

This report shows all the batches ranked by Total CPU, Total Duration, Total Reads, and Total Writes. However, the workload was run from a single batch, which then randomly ran different stored procedures, so the report at this level isn't of much use because there is only one batch.

Clicking the Query Template for Query Number 1 takes you to the statement-level report for the batch, which should be far more useful. Figure 13-17 shows an expanded fragment of this. The most expensive stored procedures and statements are highlighted.

Top Statements (Ordered By CPU)

Exe	Duration (μs)	CPU (ms)	Reads	Writes	Nest Level	Query Template
	9,467,128,093	287,233	3,266,572	455	1	⊟ EXEC USP_DEATHDELETE
	4,618,703,780	127,314	1,336,560	87	2	DELETE PEOPLE WHERE PERSONID = @BOYID
	4,281,924,522	124,021	1,336,415	104	2	DELETE PEOPLE WHERE PERSONID = @GIRLID
866	391,810,007	17,274	247,751	105	2	⊞ INSERT #BOYS (PERSONID) SELECT TOP (##) PERSONID FROM PEOPLE WHERE DOB >= @BEGINDATE AND DOB < @ENDDATE AND SEX = (STR) AND DOD IS NULL
852	154,538,452	16,424	251,566	112	2	INSERT #GIRLS (PERSONID) SELECT TOP (##) PERSONID FROM PEOPLE WHERE DOB >= @BEGINDATE AND DOB < @ENDDATE AND SEX = (STR) AND DOD IS NULL
850	1,105,014	454	27,700	0	2	DROP TABLE #BOYS
	4,829,512,849	114,529	5,209,444	682	1	⊟ EXEC USP_MARRIAGEUPDATE
	4,279,351,390	62,500	2,689,265	449	2	UPDATE PEOPLE SET LASTNAME = (SELECT LASTNAME PEOPLE WHERE PERSONID = @BOYID) WHERE PERSONID = @GIRLID
	176,602,717	23,754	1,207,238	110	2	INSERT #GIRLS (PERSONID) SELECT TOP (##) PERSOM PEOPLE WHERE DOB >= @BEGINDATE AND DOB < @ENDDATE AND SEX = (STR OD IS NULL
852	335,421,810	22,980	1,202,737	99	2	⊞ INSERT #BOYS (PERSONID) SELECT TOP (##) PERSONID FROM PEOPLE WHERE DOB >= @BEGINDATE AND DOB < @ENDDATE AND SEX = (STR) AND DOD IS NULL
850	800,005	676	33,814	0	2	DROP TABLE #GIRLS
850	1,064,013	541	34,465	0	2	DROP TABLE #BOYS
1	1,384,079	406	1,543	1	3	SELECT STATMAN(SC0, SB0000) FROM (SELECT TOP (##) PERCENT SC0, STEP DIRECTION (SC0) OVER (ORDER BY NULL) AS SB0000 FROM (SELECT PERSONID AS SC0 FROM DBO.PEOPLE TABLESAMPLE SYSTEM (##.(##) PERCENT) WITH (READUNCOMMITTED)) AS _MS_UPDSTATS_TBL_HELPER ORDER BY SC0, SB0000) AS _MS_UPDSTATS_TBL OPTION (MAXDOP (##))
800	11,055,302	2,134	27,570	28	1	⊟ EXEC USP_BIRTHINSERT
1,600	733,007	389	1,932	28	2	INSERT PEOPLE (FIRSTNAME, LASTNAME, DOB, SEX) VALUES(LIST)
800	358,001	326	4,000	0	2	SELECT @MAXGIRLS = COUNT(*) FROM GIRLSNAMES
800	352,001	297	4,000	0	2	SELECT @MAXLAST = COUNT(*) FROM LASTNAMES
800	276,000	295	4,000	0	2	SELECT @BOYSNAME = NAME FROM BOYSNAMES WHERE ID = @ID1
800	298,001	234	4,000	0	2	SELECT @GIRLSNAME = NAME FROM GIRLSNAMES WHERE ID = @ID2
2,750	142,006	46	0	0	1	WHILE @COUNTER < @PEOPLE
1,650	37,000	32	0	0	1	SET @COUNTER += (##)

FIGURE 13-17

This report indicates that two DELETE statements in usp_deathdelete and an UPDATE statement in usp_marriageupdate are the biggest consumers of CPU, a high number of reads relative to the batch, and, most interesting, all have a very selective WHERE clause against the personid column that was already identified as possibly missing an index (because it has auto-created statistics).

At this stage you can be pretty confident where the investigation is heading, but before committing to creating an index on personid, quickly check the execution plan by clicking on the statement to see how each one was accessing the people table to find the right personid.

Figure 13-18 shows a section of the Unique Statement Details report for one of the DELETE statements, and Figure 13-19 shows the same report for the UPDATE statement.

All the statements have to use table scans when accessing the people table to find a row by personid because there is no appropriate index to use.

The table is a *heap*, which means there is no clustered index, so the decision now is whether to create a clustered or nonclustered index on personid.

The two examples I have of searches using the WHERE clause have been very selective, which is good for nonclustered indexes. Personid has a unique identifier column type, which is quite large for a clustered index key (it will be used in every nonclustered index), so with nothing further to influence the decision you can create a nonclustered index instead of a clustered index.

The script to create the index is as follows:

```
CREATE NONCLUSTERED INDEX idx_peopleid
ON dbo.people (personId)
```

Unique Statement Details

sqlnexus

Parameters	Value
Hash ID:	5975663209613614764
Start Time:	8/31/2009 3:37:06 AM
End Time:	8/31/2009 3:44:02 AM

Query Editor

Object Name: USP_DEATHDELETE

Query Template: DELETE PEOPLE WHERE PERSONID = @BOYID

Query Plan Information:

Query used 1 distinct plan(s)

PlanHashID:	-6824718091740343892		
Times Used:	850		
Attentions:	0		
First Used:	8/31/2009 3:37:35 AM		
Last Used:	8/31/2009 3:43:39 AM		

Metric	Min	Max	Avg	Total
Duration (μs)	97,005	14,625,836	5,433,769.00	4,618,703,780
CPU (ms)	15	344	149.00	127,314
Reads	1,564	1,585	1,572.00	1,336,560
Writes	0	1	0.00	87

View Plan

Estimate Rows	Estimate Executions	Stmt Text
1.00	1.00	Table Delete(OBJECT:([peopleSQLNexus].[dbo].[people]))
1.00	1.00	Top(ROWCOUNT est 0)
1.00	1.00	Table Scan(OBJECT:([peopleSQLNexus].[dbo].[people]), WHERE:([peopleSQLNexus].[dbo].[people].[personid]=[@boyID]) ORDERED)

FIGURE 13-18

Unique Statement Details

sqlnexus

Parameters	Value
Hash ID:	7436750719083306741
Start Time:	8/31/2009 3:37:06 AM
End Time:	8/31/2009 3:44:02 AM

Query Editor

Object Name: USP_MARRIAGEUPDATE

Query Template: UPDATE PEOPLE SET LASTNAME = (SELECT LASTNAME FROM PEOPLE WHERE PERSONID = @BOYID) WHERE PERSONID = @GIRLID

Query Plan Information:

Query used 1 distinct plan(s)

PlanHashID:	4440756387780329122		
Times Used:	850		
Attentions:	0		
First Used:	8/31/2009 3:37:42 AM		
Last Used:	8/31/2009 3:43:37 AM		

Metric	Min	Max	Avg	Total
Duration (μs)	229,013	11,130,636	5,034,531.00	4,279,351,390
CPU (ms)	0	219	73.00	62,500
Reads	3,138	8,194	3,163.00	2,689,265
Writes	0	2	0.00	449

View Plan

Estimate Rows	Estimate Executions	Stmt Text
1.00	1.00	Table Update(OBJECT:([peopleSQLNexus].[dbo].[people]), SET:([peopleSQLNexus].[dbo].[people].[lastname] = RaiseIfNullUpdate([Expr1009])))
1.00	1.00	Table Spool
1.00	1.00	Compute Scalar(DEFINE:([Expr1009]=[Expr1016]))
1.00	1.00	Nested Loops(Left Outer Join)
1.00	1.00	Top(ROWCOUNT est 0)
1.00	1.00	Table Scan(OBJECT:([peopleSQLNexus].[dbo].[people]), WHERE:([peopleSQLNexus].[dbo].[people].[personid]=[@girlID]) ORDERED)
1.00	1.00	Assert(WHERE:(CASE WHEN [Expr1015]>(1) THEN (0) ELSE NULL END))
1.00	1.00	Stream Aggregate(DEFINE:([Expr1015]=Count(*), [Expr1016]=ANY([peopleSQLNexus].[dbo].[people].[lastname])))
1.00	1.00	Table Scan(OBJECT:([peopleSQLNexus].[dbo].[people]), WHERE:([peopleSQLNexus].[dbo].[people].[personid]= [@boyID]))

FIGURE 13-19

Testing the Resolution

Now that you've identified a new index to add, you'll want to see what difference it makes to your workload, so restore the peopleSQLNexus database to put it into the same state as before, add the new index, and then run PerfStats and the workload again with OStress.

In this case, the workload took about one minute to complete, which is a good sign, as it took four minutes to complete without the index. Still, is there anything that can be done to speed it up?

> *If your timings are considerably different to this you might want to go back and modify the workload to suit your machine as discussed previously in the section on Generating the Workload.*

Figure 13-20 shows the Blocking and Resource Wait Statistics report for the new data collection. It indicates a slightly more even distribution of waits, but clearly the PAGELATCH and CPU waits dominate; in addition, a blocking chain waited 23 seconds on the pagelatch wait type.

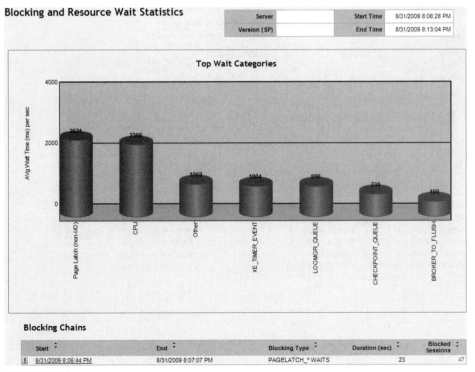

Server		Start Time	8/31/2009 8:06:28 PM
Version (SP)		End Time	8/31/2009 8:13:04 PM

Blocking Chains

Start	End	Blocking Type	Duration (sec)	Blocked Sessions
8/31/2009 8:06:44 PM	8/31/2009 8:07:07 PM	PAGELATCH_* WAITS	23	47

FIGURE 13-20

Drilling down through the blocking chain detail as before shows the cause of the latch wait: allocation contention in tempdb. Figure 13-21 shows part of the detail.

The wait resource is "2:1:1," which refers to `database_id:file_id:pagenumber`. Tempdb has a `database_id` of 2, so all the queries were waiting for the first page in the first file in tempdb. This page is known as the Page Free Space (PFS) page, and it is accessed during the allocation and de-allocation of space in a database.

These results indicate a condition known as *allocation contention*, which tempdb is particularly susceptible to. This problem and how to approach resolving it is covered in detail in Chapter 7.

If you've been following along with the example, have a look at Chapter 7 and try to resolve this issue before running the workload and measuring the results again. What's the next bottleneck? Can any of the other chapters in the first part of the book help you remove or reduce any more bottlenecks? How fast can *you* get the workload to run?

Session/Runtime Detail

	Server	
	Version (SP)	

Detail for Session ID 54 at 8/31/2009 8:06:44 PM

Program Name	OSTRESS	Transaction Type	1-Read/write
Host Name	COSIMO	Transaction Isolation	2-Read Committed
NT User	cosimo\christian	Transaction Name	DROPOBJ
Login Name	cosimo\christian	Trans Start (Duration)	8/31/2009 8:06:50 PM (-5 sec)
Last Query Start/End	8/31/2009 8:06:44 PM / 8/31/2009 8:06:44 PM	# Open Transactions	2
Wait Type			
Wait Time (ms)	30		
Resource Description	2:1:1		
Procedure	CREATE PROCEDURE [dbo].[usp_deathDelete] AS		
Query	⊞ INSERT #girls (personid) SELECT TOP 100 personid FROM p...		

Runtime Snapshot

Snapshot Time: 2009-08-31T20:06:44.610

Session ID	Task State	Command	Blocking Session ID	Wait Type	Wait Duration (ms)	Wait Resource	Query	Request CPU (ms)
53	RUNNABLE	INSERT	54	PAGELATCH_UP	24	2:1:1	INSERT #boys (personid ...	312
54	RUNNABLE	INSERT	0		30	2:1:1	INSERT #girls (personid ...	16
55	SUSPENDED	INSERT	54	PAGELATCH_UP	56	2:1:1	INSERT #girls (personid ...	312
56	SUSPENDED	INSERT	54	PAGELATCH_UP	5	2:1:1	INSERT #girls (personid ...	343
57	RUNNABLE	INSERT	54	PAGELATCH_UP	3	2:1:1	INSERT #boys (personid ...	219
58	SUSPENDED	INSERT	54	PAGELATCH_UP	24	2:1:1	INSERT #boys (personid ...	94
59	SUSPENDED	INSERT	54	PAGELATCH_UP	25	2:1:1	INSERT #boys (personid ...	124

FIGURE 13-21

ADDING YOUR OWN REPORTS

SQL Nexus also allows you to incorporate your own Reporting Services reports into the tool by simply copying the RDL files into the reports directory. However, at the time of writing, the latest version of the SQL Server 2008 SP1 Report Viewer doesn't support Reporting Services reports created using Business Intelligence Development Studio (BIDS)/Visual Studio 2008.

This means that until a new release of Report Viewer is available, you'll have to write your reports using the 2005 version of BIDS/Visual Studio if you want them to work in SQL Nexus.

Where Are the PerfMon Reports?

SQL Nexus 3.0.0.0 provides the facility to import your PerfMon logs into SQL Server but it doesn't provide any pre-built reports on the data, so to analyze PerfMon data you have four options:

➤ Don't import, and use the Performance Monitor tool to analyze the data (Chapter 9).

➤ Don't import, and just use the PAL tool (Chapter 9).

➤ Query the SQLNexus database directly.

➤ Write a custom SQL Nexus report to display the data.

Which option(s) you choose will depend on many factors. I tend to use the PAL tool and Performance Monitor most frequently because the logs I capture tend not to be very large, but I also import the PerfMon log into SQL Nexus to archive the data collection in a database backup with all the other data.

The website for this book on www.wrox.com includes a custom report written by James Boother from Live Software Solutions in the U.K. that works against the PerfMon data in the SQLNexus database. You can just drop it into the SQLNexus/Reports folder and it will be available from within the tool.

Figure 13-22 and 13-23 show a couple of the reports generated from PerfMon data in the SQLNexus database. In Figure 13-22 you can see Page Life Expectancy dropping as low as nine seconds on a server, which is an indicator of memory pressure (Chapter 2). Figure 13-23 is from a different data collection, showing the Average Disk Queue Length on a data file drive. There are a few spikes between 4 and 6, which might not be desirable but it would depend on the underlying disk configuration (Chapter 4).

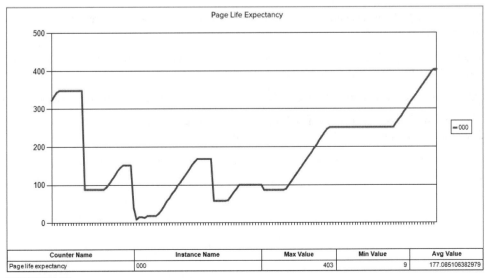

Counter Name	Instance Name	Max Value	Min Value	Avg Value
Page life expectancy	000	403	9	177.085106382979

FIGURE 13-22

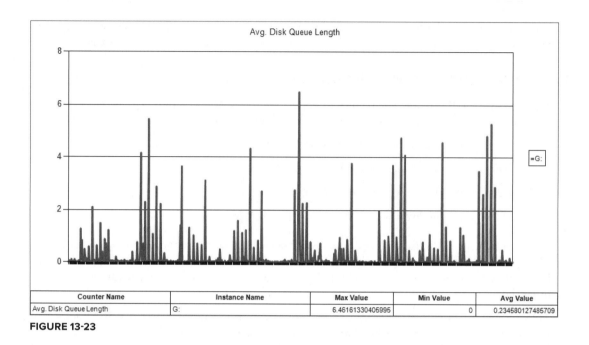

Counter Name	Instance Name	Max Value	Min Value	Avg Value
Avg. Disk Queue Length	G:	6.46161330405995	0	0.234580127485709

FIGURE 13-23

SUMMARY

This chapter has introduced you to the SQL Nexus troubleshooting tool, which makes it easy to process and review SQL Traces, PerfMon log files, and locking, blocking, and wait statistics.

The key points from this chapter are as follows:

➤ The key to SQL Nexus is getting the right data collection from the PerfStats script featured in Chapter 11.

➤ The Blocking and Wait Statistics report uses waits information to identify bottlenecks, and produces drilldowns for detected blocking chains.

➤ SQL Nexus uses ReadTrace to process SQL Trace files and embeds the reports within the tool.

➤ There are no built-in reports for PerfMon data but you can add you own custom report or download a sample report from the book's website.

➤ Continue to check `http://codeplex.com/sqlnexus` for new versions and news on updated dependencies.

14

Using Management Studio Reports and the Performance Dashboard

WHAT'S IN THIS CHAPTER

➤ How to get basic troubleshooting information by pointing and clicking in SQL Server Management Studio

➤ Where to get more reports from Microsoft for even deeper information

➤ The basics of building your own reports

SQL Server 2005 brought with it a number of built-in SQL Server Reporting Services reports for use inside SQL Server Management Studio. This allows users to get insight into all aspects of the database including schema information, engine health and performance. Database administrators could right-click on objects such as servers or databases, click Reports, and access a variety of graphical dashboards. These reports provide valuable troubleshooting data that SQL Server normally hides in difficult to access places like system tables and dynamic management views (DMVs).

> *Because most of the reports rely on the DMVs and the default trace, both of which were new in SQL Server 2005, they do not work on SQL Server 2000 instances.*

Service Pack 2 for SQL Server 2005 added the ability to include your own custom reports, and the Microsoft Customer Support Services (CSS) team for SQL Server took advantage of this feature to create a custom set of reports called the Performance Dashboard.

In SQL Server 2008, Microsoft shifted focus away from SSMS reports in favor of the new Management Data Warehouse (MDW). The MDW addresses some weaknesses of the Standard Reports and the Performance Dashboard, such as adding the capability to persist data beyond server restarts and combining data from multiple servers into a single repository (see Chapter 15). However, the MDW comes at the expense of added performance overhead and additional storage requirements. DBAs should investigate the option of using the Management Data Warehouse, but managing SQL Server isn't an all-or-nothing proposition: DBAs can get started with the Standard Reports and Performance Dashboard first to do quick and simple troubleshooting.

This chapter explains how to use some of the more powerful Standard Reports, how to use the Performance Dashboard reports in SQL Server 2008, where the data comes from, and how these reports can be used to troubleshoot database problems. Next, this chapter takes those reports to the next level by showing how DBAs can build their own: by utilizing some of the troubleshooting queries from other chapters of this book and making them available with a right-click from SQL Server Management Studio. Mastering this technique will make even the most junior database administrator a more efficient troubleshooter.

USING THE STANDARD REPORTS

Compared to querying the dynamic management views (DMVs), accessing the Standard Reports is deceptively simple. In the object explorer pane of SQL Server Management Studio right-click on any SQL Server 2008 or 2005 instance and then click Reports ➪ Standard Reports. A list of built-in reports is displayed, as shown in Figure 14-1.

This right-click Reports option is available on all nodes in the object explorer in SQL Server Management Studio; out-of-the-box reports are only available on certain nodes such as SQL Server Agent, Logins and individual databases. The reports list is context sensitive: It displays only the reports relevant to the object explorer node that was right-clicked. Some of these reports are completely self-explanatory, and serve more as educational material than troubleshooting tools. Rather than explain every report in every area of SSMS, this chapter explores the most powerful troubleshooting tools that a DBA will use most frequently.

> *Some of the reports discussed in this chapter rely on high levels of permissions and the existence of the default trace (discussed in Chapter 10). In environments where permissions have been locked down or the default trace has been disabled, some reports will not function.*

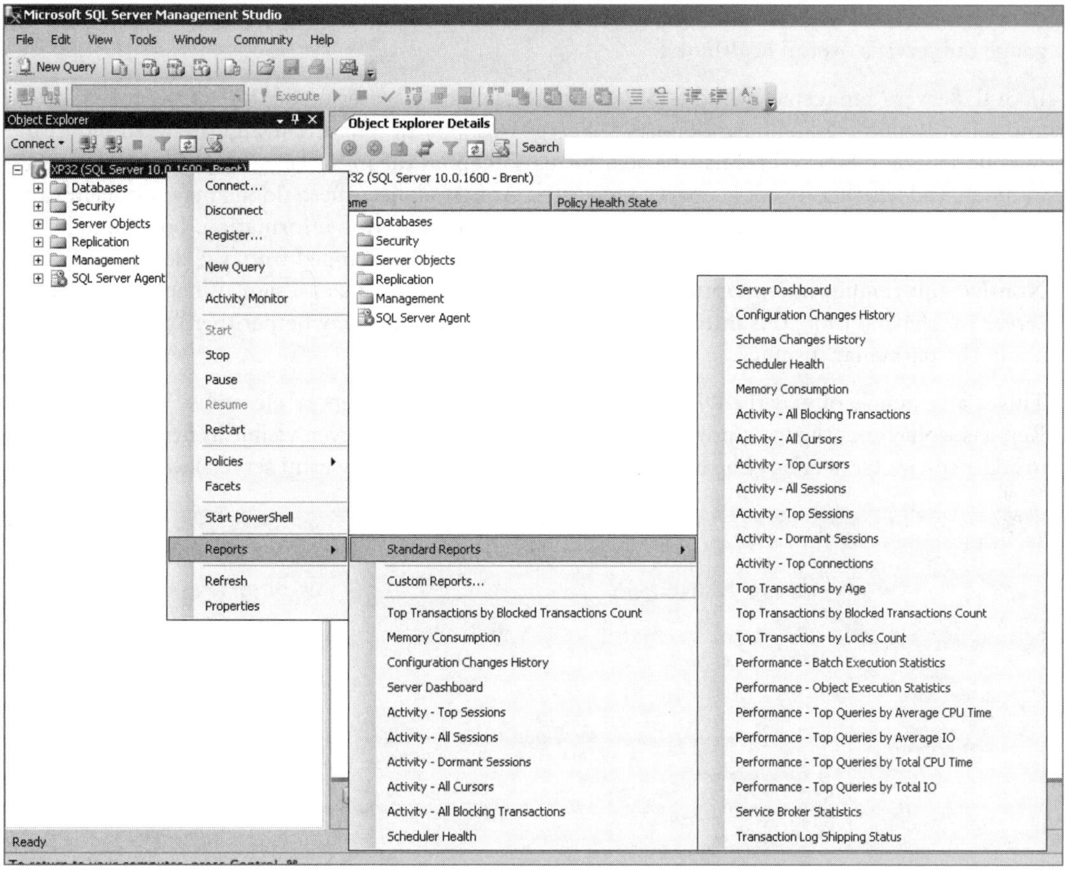

FIGURE 14-1

The reports are a good starting point for obtaining information, but they're built with a minimum of troubleshooting assistance. For example, exceptions and problems aren't necessarily highlighted: The report might note that a particular server has "clr enabled = 1" but the user doesn't know whether that's a good thing or a bad thing, or whether it's a variance from the company policy. There's no link to click in order to get more information about a particular setting. It's up to the DBA to determine what these settings mean and what action to take, and that's where this book comes in.

The following sections examine each of the reports to find out what parts of the reports need to be examined more closely and how these reports affect the troubleshooting discussed in other chapters.

Interpreting the Standard Server Reports

During troubleshooting, the database administrator focuses first on the database server as a whole. If something is wrong with the SQL Server configuration or performance, it affects every query on the system. Therefore, it helps to start by taking a look at the troubleshooting options available to gauge the server's overall health first.

In SQL Server Management Studio (SSMS), right-click on a server name in the Object Explorer, and select Reports ⇨ Standard Reports ⇨ Server Dashboard. A short, straightforward report like the one shown in Figure 14-2 lists basic information about the instance, such as its name, version number, and whether or not it's part of a cluster. At first glance, these tidbits may not seem valuable, but drilling deeper into the report provides useful troubleshooting information. For example, to see if the server has any configuration parameters that have been changed from the defaults expand the Non-Default Configuration Options section by clicking on the plus (+) sign. When approaching a server for the first time, this information helps the DBA determine whether there's anything unusual about the particular instance.

This is an example of why the DBA needs to learn about all of a report's features. With the Standard Reports, sometimes the most powerful features of a report aren't even visible at first — they're hidden inside a collapsible section. The next sections explore the most powerful server-level reports in detail.

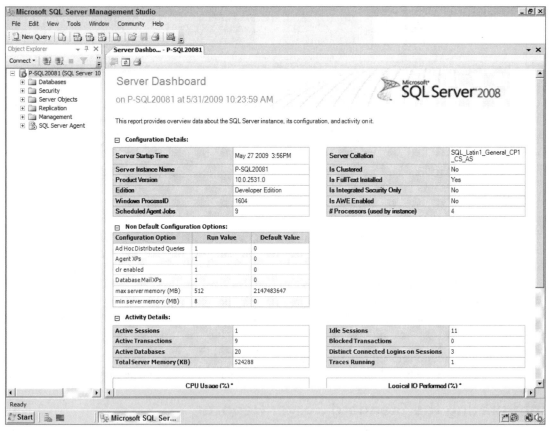

FIGURE 14-2

Reading the Server Dashboard Report

The name "Dashboard" implies that this report is a good place to get a fast overview of what the server's doing: Unfortunately, that's not the case. Don't run this report expecting to see a snapshot of the server's load or health. It doesn't trend history, doesn't show problems, and doesn't give the DBA a good sense of what's going on. It's simply a summary of the most basic configuration options on the server and some very rudimentary connection statistics.

The one valuable part of this report is the Non-Default Configuration Options, shown earlier, which indicates any server-level configuration settings that have been changed from SQL Server's default settings. This is a great place to start when troubleshooting a server for the very first time, or for the first time in several weeks or months. Glancing at this section can provide a concise picture of any configuration settings that may have a system-wide impact on performance.

In a simplified nutshell (not including some of the trace flag data, since that's more difficult to fetch and display), this section of the report is built by doing the following:

1. Building a table variable with SQL Server's default `sys.configurations` values (often viewed by DBAs with the `sp_configure` command)

2. Building a table variable with the current `sys.configurations` data

3. Joining those two table variables together to find any configurations that don't match the hard-coded default values

An abbreviated snippet of the first step is shown here:

```
declare @configurations_option_table table (
        name nvarchar(128)
,       run_value bigint
,       default_value bigint
);
insert into @configurations_option_table values(''Ad Hoc Distributed Queries'',0,0)
insert into @configurations_option_table values(''affinity I/O mask'',0,0)
insert into @configurations_option_table values(''affinity mask'',0,0)
insert into @configurations_option_table values(''Agent XPs'',0,0)
insert into @configurations_option_table values(''allow updates'',0,0)
insert into @configurations_option_table values(''awe enabled'',0,0)
insert into @configurations_option_table values(''blocked process threshold'',0,0)
insert into @configurations_option_table values(''c2 audit mode'',0,0)
insert into @configurations_option_table values(''clr enabled'',0,0)
```

Consider how this query could be adapted by database administrators. Rather than audit for non-default configuration settings, DBAs can write their own version of this report to audit a server, looking for configurations that deviate from the company's chosen standards. For example, the company may require that all user databases are encrypted with Transparent Data Encryption, and the DBA can write a report looking for any databases that have not been encrypted. The technique of writing custom reports is discussed later in the chapter.

Configuration Changes and Schema Changes Reports

If the Server Dashboard report shows a configuration change, the Configuration Changes History report can help the database administrator find out when it was made, and by whom. Figure 14-3 shows this report for an instance in which the Max Degree of Parallelism (maxdop) option has been changed to 1. It also indicates the user responsible for making the change.

For troubleshooting purposes, this is a good report to run when users complain that a server's performance degrades suddenly.

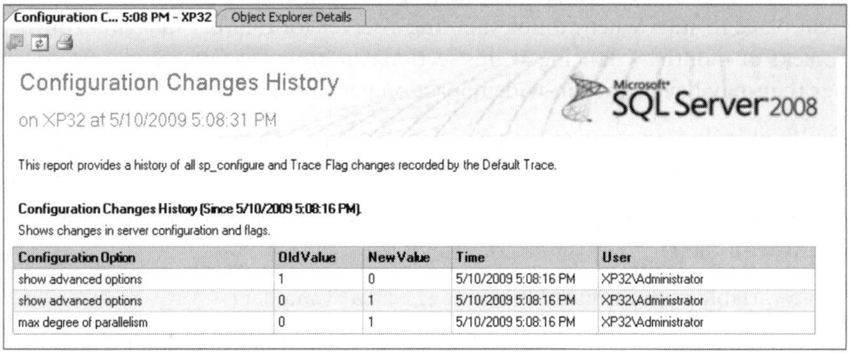

Configuration C... 5:08 PM - XP32 | Object Explorer Details

Configuration Changes History

on XP32 at 5/10/2009 5:08:31 PM

Microsoft SQL Server 2008

This report provides a history of all sp_configure and Trace Flag changes recorded by the Default Trace.

Configuration Changes History (Since 5/10/2009 5:08:16 PM).

Shows changes in server configuration and flags.

Configuration Option	Old Value	New Value	Time	User
show advanced options	1	0	5/10/2009 5:08:16 PM	XP32\Administrator
show advanced options	0	1	5/10/2009 5:08:16 PM	XP32\Administrator
max degree of parallelism	0	1	5/10/2009 5:08:16 PM	XP32\Administrator

FIGURE 14-3

Likewise, the Schema Changes History report, shown in Figure 14-4, shows all DDL changes made in all databases on the instance. This is especially helpful when users complain of sudden performance problems, because someone may have dropped an index or changed a stored procedure. This report is also useful when an application suddenly stops working for no apparent reason, because someone may have changed a table schema, thereby breaking queries.

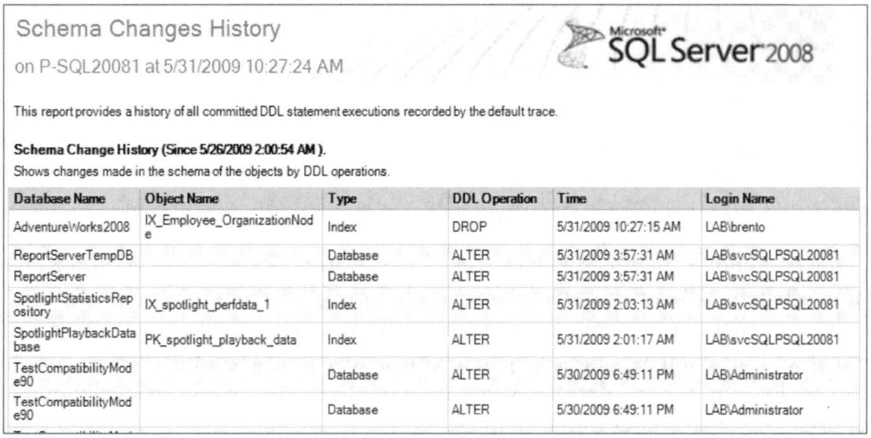

Schema Changes History

on P-SQL20081 at 5/31/2009 10:27:24 AM

Microsoft SQL Server 2008

This report provides a history of all committed DDL statement executions recorded by the default trace.

Schema Change History (Since 5/26/2009 2:00:54 AM).

Shows changes made in the schema of the objects by DDL operations.

Database Name	Object Name	Type	DDL Operation	Time	Login Name
AdventureWorks2008	IX_Employee_OrganizationNode	Index	DROP	5/31/2009 10:27:15 AM	LAB\brento
ReportServerTempDB		Database	ALTER	5/31/2009 3:57:31 AM	LAB\svcSQLPSQL20081
ReportServer		Database	ALTER	5/31/2009 3:57:31 AM	LAB\svcSQLPSQL20081
SpotlightStatisticsRepository	IX_spotlight_perfdata_1	Index	ALTER	5/31/2009 2:03:13 AM	LAB\svcSQLPSQL20081
SpotlightPlaybackDatabase	PK_spotlight_playback_data	Index	ALTER	5/31/2009 2:01:17 AM	LAB\svcSQLPSQL20081
TestCompatibilityMode90		Database	ALTER	5/30/2009 6:49:11 PM	LAB\Administrator
TestCompatibilityMode90		Database	ALTER	5/30/2009 6:49:11 PM	LAB\Administrator

FIGURE 14-4

Both of these reports pull their data from the default trace (see Chapter 10 for more information), so this report only goes back as far as the default trace data. The change will not appear in this report if:

➤ the SQL Server service has been restarted five times since the change was made; or

➤ the default trace has accumulated more than 100MB of data since the change.

Fetching data from the default trace files is not for the faint of heart, but Microsoft's code for these reports can serve as a starting point for building a custom auditing solution. The following query from the Configuration Changes report shows how the report fetches the current trace file name from sys.traces, opens it, and inserts the data into a table variable:

```
declare @d1 datetime;
declare @diff int;
declare @curr_tracefilename varchar(500);
declare @base_tracefilename varchar(500);
declare @indx int ;
declare @temp_trace table (
        textdata nvarchar(MAX) collate database_default
,       login_name sysname collate database_default
,       start_time datetime
,       event_class int
);

select @curr_tracefilename = path from sys.traces where is_default = 1 ;

set @curr_tracefilename = reverse(@curr_tracefilename)
select @indx  = PATINDEX(''%\%'', @curr_tracefilename)
set @curr_tracefilename = reverse(@curr_tracefilename)
set @base_tracefilename = LEFT
( @curr_tracefilename,len(@curr_tracefilename) - @indx) + ''\log.trc'';

insert into @temp_trace
select TextData
,       LoginName
,       StartTime
,       EventClass
from ::fn_trace_gettable( @base_tracefilename, default )
where ((EventClass = 22 and Error = 15457) or (EventClass = 116 and
TextData like ''%TRACEO%(%''))
```

Due to the limitations of data kept by the default trace, this code can be enhanced and run on a regular interval, which will enable all DDL changes to be captured. Persisting the data in a user database for later review will ensure the history of changes available permanently. This approach eliminates the need for DDL triggers at the database level, but it does have some weaknesses:

➤ **Security:** The DBA must ensure that malicious users cannot delete rows from the reporting table.

➤ **Service restarts:** A malicious user could rapidly restart the SQL Server service five times after making a DDL change, thereby purging the default trace history. (Obviously, that type of attack leaves other signatures.) To reduce the impact of such an attack, the DBA could create a startup stored procedure to automatically persist the data from the default trace.

➤ **Job monitoring:** If the data capture is performed via a SQL Agent job, then a malicious user could simply turn off the job or disable the schedule.

For higher security, or to investigate server configuration changes or schema definition changes that occurred in the past, the database administrator has another option: examining the transaction log backups. If the databases involved are in full recovery mode, and the log backups are available for the time when the change was made, then the log backups will help clarify the change.

SQL Server doesn't include a log-reading tool to audit the transaction logs and see what changes were made and by whom. However, some third-party utilities read the log backups to retrieve this information. Unfortunately, because the user data is not captured as part of the transaction logs, these utilities can only determine who made the change if the end user is still connected to the database.

AUDITING SCHEMA CHANGES

To capture schema changes for auditing or troubleshooting purposes, consider using a DDL trigger. DDL triggers can act when a schema change is made, initiating custom code to audit the event. They can log the schema change to a table for reporting purposes. Be aware that if the database application frequently builds and destroys user tables (not temp tables) as a regular operation, DDL triggers will incur a performance overhead.

Scheduler Health Report

In previous versions of SQL Server, some system administrators enabled Fiber Mode or Lightweight Pooling in order to improve performance. Microsoft KB article #319942 recommends this only in cases where the processors are doing more than 20,000 context switches per second. The Scheduler Health Report helps a database administrator determine whether a particular server is a good candidate for Fiber Mode by displaying the number of context switches per scheduler, as shown in Figure 14-5. Keep in mind that this report does not show a per-second number, but it can be refreshed periodically to get a quick idea of how many context switches are happening.

Memory Consumption Report

The Memory Consumption Report, shown in Figure 14-6, provides a current snapshot of how SQL Server is utilizing memory. Memory statistics are discussed in detail in Chapter 2.

This report is only a one-time peek into SQL Server's internals, and so DBAs should not make configuration decisions based on this report. When DBAs find themselves needing the kind of information in this report, it's time to consider using the Management Data Warehouse instead. The MDW captures and reports on this information over time, which is important for frequently changing data such as memory usage. For example, a SQL Server Agent job might be running every night and using a great deal of memory, and that information is crucial to making good configuration decisions.

Scheduler Health
on SWSSQLPRVS1 at 5/30/2009 10:00:33 AM

This report provides detailed activity data on each of the Instance's Schedulers.

Scheduler Status

Idle

Scheduler Details
Details of the workers, tasks & processes running under particular scheduler.

Scheduler ID	Status	CPU ID	# Preemptive Switches	# Context Switches	# Idle Switches	# Tasks	# Workers	Queue Length	# Pending IO Requests	Load Factor
⊞ 0	Idle	255	14,210,624	407,552,045	841,176,777	5	72	0	0	6
⊞ 1	Idle	255	19,127,955	211,047,283	513,372,172	7	73	0	0	7
⊞ 2	Idle	255	24,897,753	263,578,435	554,830,245	4	72	0	0	5
⊞ 3	Idle	255	24,151,840	236,258,802	540,286,625	6	72	0	0	8
⊞ 4	Idle	255	1,871,141	108,539,306	228,832,186	6	72	0	0	7

FIGURE 14-5

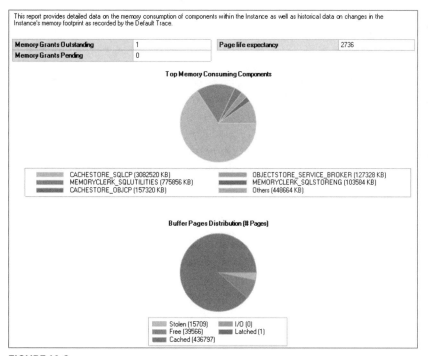

This report provides detailed data on the memory consumption of components within the Instance as well as historical data on changes in the Instance's memory footprint as recorded by the Default Trace.

Memory Grants Outstanding	1	Page life expectancy	2736
Memory Grants Pending	0		

Top Memory Consuming Components

CACHESTORE_SQLCP (3082520 KB)
MEMORYCLERK_SQLUTILITIES (775856 KB)
CACHESTORE_OBJCP (157320 KB)
OBJECTSTORE_SERVICE_BROKER (127328 KB)
MEMORYCLERK_SQLSTORENG (103584 KB)
Others (448664 KB)

Buffer Pages Distribution (# Pages)

Stolen (15709)
Free (39566)
Cached (436797)
I/O (0)
Latched (1)

FIGURE 14-6

Activity Reports

SQL Server Management Studio 2008's Activity Monitor has continued to improve over previous versions, giving the DBA better insight into CPU and memory issues on the server. However, viewing all current queries through Activity Monitor or by running sp_who can seem like drinking water from a fire hose. These Activity Reports help filter the current activity to just the queries the DBA needs to see.

If a user calls the IT department to complain that a server is busy, the DBA can check the following reports:

➤ **Activity – All Blocking Transactions:** This report is similar to running an sp_who2 and looking at the BlkBy column to see if any transaction is blocking another transaction.

➤ **Activity – All Cursors:** If a slow cursor-based query or, heaven forbid, a nested cursor, is chewing up a great deal of resources on a server, it's visible in this report. This is also useful for cursors that have not been closed, like if a user leaves SSMS open without finishing their running code.

➤ **Activity – Top Sessions:** This report, shown in Figure 14-7, breaks out the oldest, most CPU-intensive, memory-intensive, read-intensive, and write-intensive sessions. Unfortunately, while the report includes the workstation name and application, it doesn't include the login name, making it more difficult to contact the problem users. Nor does it display the SQL being executed by the user.

Activity - Top Sessions

on SWSSQLPRVS1 at 5/30/2009 10:09:56 AM

Microsoft® SQL Server 2008

This report identifies the top user Sessions on the Instance based on age, CPU utilization, memory utilization, and IOs.

⊞ **Top Oldest Sessions**

⊟ **Top CPU Consuming Sessions**

Session ID	Login Time	Last Request End Time	Host Name	Program Name	# Connections	CPU Time (ms.)	Memory Usage (KB)	Total Scheduled Time (ms.)	Total Elapsed Time (ms.)	# Reads	# Writes
84	5/24/2009 6:42:36 PM	5/30/2009 10:09:55 AM	FLMIRCRPR1	Windows Installer - Unicode	1	1,163,798.0 0	16	1,170,341.00	2,009,772.00	33,433	35,035
212	5/24/2009 6:42:40 PM	5/30/2009 10:09:21 AM	FLMIRCRPR1	Windows Installer - Unicode	1	1,161,916.0 0	16	1,171,602.00	1,788,788.00	35,382	33,920
188	5/22/2009 6:03:05 PM	5/30/2009 9:35:18 AM			1	668,233.00	16	680,289.00	2,288,846.00	17,929	194,542
324	4/29/2009 10:37:58 AM	5/30/2009 10:05:22 AM			1	160,347.00	16	164,702.00	902,056.00	63,372	163,216
205	5/22/2009 6:03:05 PM	5/30/2009 10:09:54 AM			1	113,325.00	16	117,153.00	1,544,954.00	5,746	37,781
735	5/30/2009 9:35:08 AM	5/30/2009 10:09:55 AM	SolarWinds	SolarWinds Network Management Tools	1	30,149.00	16	30,740.00	90,896.00	22	8,281
71	5/30/2009 9:35:16 AM	5/30/2009 10:09:53 AM	SolarWinds	SolarWinds Network Management Tools	1	23,445.00	16	24,111.00	113,806.00	305	30,124
127	4/29/2009 1:33:06 AM	5/30/2009 10:09:39 AM	SWSSQLPRVS1	SQLAgent - Alert Engine	1	17,015.00	16	251,427.00	585,864.00	204	30,965
75	4/29/2009 10:37:57 AM	5/30/2009 10:08:59 AM			1	13,823.00	16	13,880.00	15,271.00	122	0
195	5/30/2009 9:10:12 AM	5/30/2009 10:09:55 AM	FLMIRHPSIM1	iTDS	1	10,397.00	88	10,341.00	15,073.00	235	71

⊞ **Top Memory Consuming Sessions**

⊞ **Top Sessions By # Reads**

FIGURE 14-7

There are more Activity Reports, but they offer less troubleshooting value and are self-explanatory.

These reports get their data from DMVs such as `sys.dm_exec_sessions`, `sys.dm_exec_connections`, and `sys.dm_exec_requests`. One of the queries from the Top 10 Sessions report is shown here:

```
select top 10 s.session_id
    ,       s.login_time
    ,       s.host_name
    ,       s.program_name
    ,       s.cpu_time as cpu_time
    ,       s.memory_usage * 8 as memory_usage
    ,       s.total_scheduled_time as total_scheduled_time
    ,       s.total_elapsed_time as total_elapsed_time
    ,       s.last_request_end_time
    ,       s.reads
    ,       s.writes
    ,       count(c.connection_id) as conn_count
from sys.dm_exec_sessions s
left outer join sys.dm_exec_connections c  on ( s.session_id = c.session_id )
left outer join sys.dm_exec_requests r  on ( r.session_id = c.session_id )
where (s.is_user_process= 1)
group by s.session_id, s.login_time, s.host_name, s.cpu_time, s.memory_usage,
  s.total_scheduled_time, s.total_elapsed_time, s.last_request_end_time, s.reads,
s.writes, s.program_name
order by s.memory_usage desc
```

The problem with this query, and all of the activity queries, is that the `sys.dm_exec_sessions` DMV only shows data as long as the user remains connected. As soon as users disconnect, they no longer show up as top users on the system, no matter how many resources they consumed for any length of time. Therefore, these reports help to filter the Activity Monitor results, but they do not help paint a picture of the most active users on the system for a length of time.

When discussing some of the other reports in this chapter, you read about the possibility of storing the data in a user table for long-term reporting. That approach is less useful with the activity reports you've just looked at because the sessions, connections, and Requests-column data are cumulative: Every time the data is queried, SQL Server reports back the total amount of resource a particular session has used since the session was started. If you persist the data in a table every 60 seconds, you would not be able to sum up the records over time because the records themselves contain their sums.

Performance Executions Reports

The Performance – Object Execution Statistics report is a great example of how the Standard Reports come very close to providing value, yet fall just a bit short. Thankfully, it makes a good example of how to build better replacement reports. This report, shown in Figure 14-8, shows which database objects are undergoing the most reads, writes, and CPU time. Unfortunately, the report shows objects by their object number — not the most intuitive way to find objects in the database.

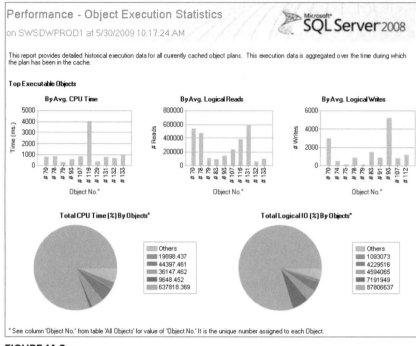

FIGURE 14-8

By using Profiler while this report runs, the database administrator can reverse-engineer the T-SQL it executes. The report starts by building a few table variables to store results, and then the first significant query hits the DMV sys.dm_exec_query_stats. It joins to sys.dm_exec_sql_text to get the exact SQL executed:

```
Select   sql_handle
     ,       sql_handle as chart_display_option
     ,       sql_handle as chart_display_optionIO
     ,       master.dbo.fn_varbintohexstr(sql_handle)
     ,       dense_rank() over (order by s2.dbid,s2.objectid) as SPRank
     ,       s2.dbid
     ,       s2.objectid
     ,       (select top 1 substring(text,(s1.statement_start_offset+2)/2, (case when
s1.statement_end_offset = -1  then len(convert(nvarchar(max),text))*2 else
s1.statement_end_offset end - s1.statement_start_offset) /2  ) from
sys.dm_exec_sql_text(s1.sql_handle)) as [SQL Statement]
     ,       execution_count
     ,       plan_generation_num
     ,       last_execution_time
     ,       ((total_worker_time+0.0)/execution_count)/1000 as [avg_worker_time]
     ,       total_worker_time/1000.0
     ,       last_worker_time/1000.0
     ,       min_worker_time/1000.0
     ,       max_worker_time/1000.0
     ,       ((total_logical_reads+0.0)/execution_count) as [avg_logical_reads]
     ,       total_logical_reads
```

```
    ,       last_logical_reads
    ,       min_logical_reads
    ,       max_logical_reads
    ,       ((total_logical_writes+0.0)/execution_count) as [avg_logical_writes]
    ,       total_logical_writes
    ,       last_logical_writes
    ,       min_logical_writes
    ,       max_logical_writes
    ,       ((total_logical_writes+0.0)/execution_count + (total_logical_reads+0.0)/
    execution_count) as [avg_logical_IO]
    ,       total_logical_writes + total_logical_reads
    ,       last_logical_writes +last_logical_reads
    ,       min_logical_writes +min_logical_reads
    ,       max_logical_writes + max_logical_reads
    from    sys.dm_exec_query_stats s1
    cross apply sys.dm_exec_sql_text(sql_handle) as  s2
    where   s2.objectid is not null and db_name(s2.dbid) is not null
    order by  s1.sql_handle;
```

It continues with additional SQL statements to get more information about the objects, total load for the SQL Server, and to rank the individual queries. The troubleshooting DBA may not be interested in these, however. Instead, it may make more sense to build a report based on just the preceding query, and join more DMVs to get more information (such as the object name) about the objects themselves. You'll explore this in more detail in the section "Building Custom Reports."

Performance Top Queries Reports

The phrase "Top Queries" implies best, but instead these reports should be renamed "Worst User Queries." These reports help the database administrator track down the worst problem queries for performance tuning without running a resource-intensive, round-the-clock Profiler trace. The report only reflects queries that are still in the execution plan cache, so the report results may not help a DBA troubleshoot a server under severe memory pressure or with high amounts of ad-hoc queries; but generally speaking, these are some of the best Standard Reports for performance tuning and pointing fingers. The report variants include Top Queries by Average CPU Time (shown in Figure 14-9), by Average I/O, by Total CPU Time, and by Total I/O.

When users complain of slow performance in an application, these reports help the DBA determine which exact queries are running behind the scenes. This is especially helpful when users can't reproduce the problem or it happens only sporadically: If the plan is still in the cache and it suddenly needs a large amount of CPU or I/O, it will be reflected in these reports. By drilling down, using the plus sign next to each query, the DBA can get more information. As shown in Figure 14-10, this includes compilation time, last execution time, CPU, I/O statistics, and the number of times the query was executed.

These reports don't include the execution plan for the query, and the query is not shown in a copy/paste-friendly format. Even if the DBA copies the query manually and generates an estimated execution plan, keep in mind that the execution plan may have changed since the query was executed. The inability to copy/paste report results means the DBA should get used to exporting this data to Excel or running the underlying report queries in SSMS in order to get the raw data.

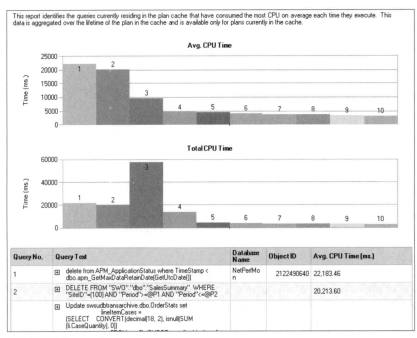

This report identifies the queries currently residing in the plan cache that have consumed the most CPU on average each time they execute. This data is aggregated over the lifetime of the plan in the cache and is available only for plans currently in the cache.

Query No.	Query Text	Database Name	Object ID	Avg. CPU Time (ms.)
1	⊞ delete from APM_ApplicationStatus where TimeStamp < dbo.apm_GetMaxDataRetainDate(GetUtcDate())	NetPerfMon	2122490640	22,183.46
2	⊞ DELETE FROM ''SWO''.''dbo''.''SalesSummary'' WHERE ''SiteID''=(100) AND ''Period''>=@P1 AND ''Period''<=@P2			20,213.60
	⊞ Update swsudbtransarchive.dbo.OrderStats set lineItemCases = (SELECT CONVERT(decimal(18, 2), isnull(SUM (li.CaseQuantity), 0))			

FIGURE 14-9

Query No.	Query Text		Database Name	Object ID	Avg. CPU Time (ms.)
1	⊟ delete from APM_ApplicationStatus where TimeStamp < dbo.apm_GetMaxDataRetainDate(GetUtcDate())		NetPerfMon	2122490640	22,183.46

Compilation Time	Last Execution Time	Total CPU Time (ms.)	# Total Logical IO	# Avg. Logical IO	# Logical Reads	# Logical Writes	# Executions
5/30/2009 2:15:11 AM	5/30/2009 2:15:12 AM	22,183.46	1,825,473	1,825,473.0 0	1,825,464	9	1

Query Text
delete from APM_ApplicationStatus where TimeStamp < dbo.apm_GetMaxDataRetainDate(GetUtcDate())

FIGURE 14-10

Top Transactions Reports

The Top Transactions Reports list transactions by Age (shown in Figure 14-11), by Blocked Transactions Count, and by Locks Count. Unfortunately, like the Activity reports, the Top Transactions Reports do not show historical data: They report only on the transactions that are open at the exact moment the report is run. As such, they are not particularly useful when trouble-shooting an event that has already taken place.

The Top Transactions reports are available at a database level as well. When troubleshooting performance in a specific database, the DBA can right-click on a database name to access the Standard Reports. Now it's time to examine the other reports that are available for individual databases.

Top Transactions by Age

on SWSSQLDV1 at 5/30/2009 10:15:02 AM

This report identifies the oldest transactions on the Instance.

Top Oldest Transactions

Determined by the time when the transactions were submitted to the server.

Tran. ID	Tran. Name	State	Tran. Type	Start Time	Isolation Level	Session ID	Login Name
⊟ 1357185 951	UpdateUsage	Active	Full Transaction	5/30/2009 10:14:51 AM	Read Committed	58	SWSGS\SQLSvcAgtF LMIRSQLDV1
	Database Name	**Tran. State**	**# Locks**	**First Update Time**			
	Control_State	Initialized	2				
	Currently Executing SQL Statement						
	dbcc updateusage ([Control_State]) WITH NO_INFOMSGS						

* The transactions span multiple databases on the same instance.
+ The transactions are distributed transactions.

FIGURE 14-11

Interpreting the Database Reports

In Management Studio, right-click on a database name in the Object Explorer and select Reports ➪ Standard Reports. SSMS 2008 displays a list of available reports, as shown in Figure 14-12.

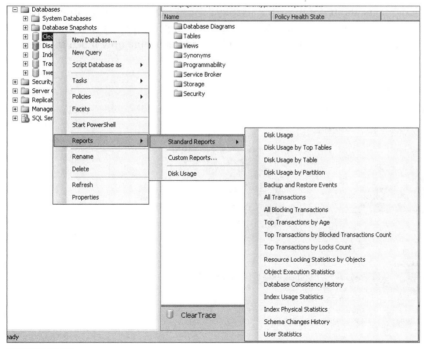

FIGURE 14-12

Some of these reports are identical to the server-level reports explored earlier in the chapter, except that they filter the troubleshooting data down to one database. The Top Transactions reports by database, for example, are the same as their server-level equivalents. However, a few additional reports need some explanation.

Disk Usage Reports

DBAs always need to monitor the use of storage and make sure their servers don't run out of storage. At the same time, DBAs are under cost pressures from the organization. Economic pressure, confined datacenter space, and the increasing power of CPUs introduced the concept of SQL Server *consolidation* - using less hardware to host more databases. More databases are sharing fewer storage arrays, which can lead to problems when one of the databases starts growing out of control. The frequent growth of one database can deplete a SQL Server out of drive space, and the DBA needs to determine which database is growing.

Another reason to monitor disk usage is for performance. SQL Server's default database file growth settings are not good for performance. The default data file growth setting is 1MB at a time, and the default log file growth setting is 10% at a time. Growing at just 1MB at a time is too small: The database's files can end up fragmented all over the physical drives in very tiny increments. Growing log files 10% at a time may be too large: In a data warehouse environment with large log files, the time spent growing the log file can bring the server to its knees for minutes at a time.

To help make better judgments about database file settings, consult the Disk Usage Report to see how much space is unused, and how much the files have grown lately. Expand the Data/Log Files Autogrow/Autoshrink Events section, shown in Figure 14-13, to determine how much the files have grown, and how long it took SQL Server to expand the files.

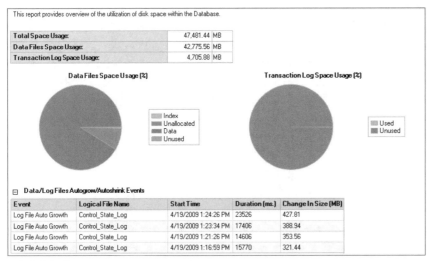

FIGURE 14-13

If the server is configured with Instant File Initialization as discussed in Chapter 7, then data file growth events should take a matter of a few milliseconds regardless of how large the file grows.

Log files, conversely, do not benefit from the Instant File Initialization performance improvements. Log files must always be cleared out as they grow, so the DBA needs to set the autogrowth amount carefully. Rather than let the log file grow when the server is under heavy load, consider pre-growing the log file to the largest practical size that should accommodate the server's load.

> *On the surface, AutoShrink might seem like an attractive option: SQL Server will automatically shrink a database that has empty space and thus free up space. However, this is a dangerous setting that causes performance problems. Shrink operations result in table fragmentation due to the way pages are moved to free up space at the end of the data file. If combined with growth operations you also get storage fragmentation. Depending on the database's file growth settings, a database might grow by 100MB to accommodate 10MB of data, then shrink by 90MB, and then grow by 100MB again, resulting in 10MB fragments of data scattered around the drives. When both AutoShrink and AutoGrow events show up in the Disk Usage report, they're evidence that you will have table and file level fragmentation. Consider disabling AutoShrink and pre-growing the database files to a size large enough to handle planned data growth.*

Backup and Restore Reports

Database administrators often troubleshoot backup job times by looking at the runtime durations of the SQL Server Agent jobs. For more granular detail, right-click on an individual database and choose the Backup and Restore Events report, shown in Figure 14-14. It lists the average duration for full, differential, and log backups.

This report provides historical data about Backup and Restore actions performed on the Database.

Average Time Taken For Backup Operations
The average duration is calculated using the history of various types of backup operations performed on this database.

Backup Type	Average Duration (min.)
Database	20.90
Database Differential	0.03
Log	0.00

Successful Backup Operations
Shows details of the successful backup operations performed on this database in the past.

Start Time	Duration (minutes)	Backup Type	Backup Size		Backup Name	Device Type	User Name	Recovery Model	Differential Base LSN	Last LSN
5/30/2009 1:02:01 PM	0.00	Log	1.69	MB		⊟ 7	SWSGS\SQLSvc ServerFLMIRSNS	FULL	Not applicable	15376600000230360 0001
	Physical Device Name									
	\\SWSNBMEDIA2\SQLBackup1\FLMIRSNSQLPR1\EDW_CatMan\EDW_CatMan_tlog_200905301302.BAK									
5/30/2009 12:47:00 PM	0.00	Log	1.69	MB		⊞ 7	SWSGS\SQLSvc ServerFLMIRSNS	FULL	Not applicable	15376600000230360 0001
5/30/2009 12:32:00 PM	0.00	Log	1.69	MB		⊞ 7	SWSGS\SQLSvc ServerFLMIRSNS	FULL	Not applicable	15376600000230360 0001
5/30/2009 12:17:00 PM	0.00	Log	1.69	MB		⊞ 7	SWSGS\SQLSvc ServerFLMIRSNS	FULL	Not applicable	15376600000230360 0001
5/30/2009 12:02:01 PM	0.00	Log	1.69	MB		⊞ 7	SWSGS\SQLSvc ServerFLMIRSNS	FULL	Not applicable	15376600000230360 0001

FIGURE 14-14

This report is not available at the server level, but by tracing the queries it runs, the database administrator can adapt the report's query to return results for all databases in alphabetical order:

```
select t1.database_name
,        t1.type as [type]
,        (avg(datediff(ss,backup_start_date, backup_finish_date)))/60.0 as
AverageBackupDuration
,        count(*) as BackupCount
from msdb.dbo.backupset t1
inner join msdb.sys.databases t3 on ( t1.database_name = t3.name )
group by t1.database_name, t1.type
order by t1.database_name, t1.type
```

In the result set, the Type column indicates the type of backup: D for full backups, I for differential backups, or L for transaction log backups.

Similarly, database-level reports can be run for all databases by calling that T-SQL code with the system stored procedure sp_msforeachdb. That stored procedure will run against each database and return the results separately. These reports could also be run for multiple servers with SSMS 2008's Group Query Execute feature.

On the SSMS report, clicking the plus (+) sign in the Device Type column yields more information about each individual backup file. This comes in handy when troubleshooting a broken LSN chain or problems with log shipping. Sometimes end users or developers do their own full backups out of sequence from the DBA's backup and recovery scheme, and the DBA will need to track down the location of the out-of-control backup file. This report shows the physical device name (tape or drive location) of the backup and the user who performed the backup. To simplify this troubleshooting, DBAs might consider building their own report to show all backups performed by an account other than the normal backup job account.

Index Usage Statistics Report

Adding indexes can be the fastest way to solve a performance problem. Repeated applications of that solution can be a pretty quick way to cause a performance problem. The more indexes a table has, the longer SQL Server takes to update the related indexes when the table data changes. To balance faster reads against slower inserts/updates/deletes, the database administrator needs to know how each index is used and how much it is being updated. The Index Usage Report, shown in Figure 14-15, shows how many times each index has been used in a query (user seeks/scans) versus how many times it has slowed down changes to data(user updates).

This data is accumulated from the time the SQL Server instance is started (or when the database has been restored, whichever is more recent). This can produce misleading data; if an index is heavily used for weeks and then suddenly is no longer needed due to a query change or the presence of a better index, the number of User Seeks and User Scans will still seem high. To mitigate this issue, the DBA needs to check the Last User Seek, Last User Scan, and Last User Lookup Time columns. If they are old, then the index has not been used recently even though the Seeks and Scans numbers will be high. However, be aware of database use histories, because if a database is only used once per month or once per quarter, the Last User Seek, Scan, and Lookup times won't be updated.

This report provides details on usage of individual Indexes within the Database as well as data on the cost of maintaining them.

⊟ **Index Usage Statistics**
Shows how the users and system use the indexes.

Table Name

⊟ dbo.Accounts

Index Name	Index Type	# User Seeks	# User Scans	# User Updates	Last User Seek Time	Last User Scan Time	Last User Lookup Time	Last User Update Time	# System Seeks	# System Scans	# System Updates
PK_Accounts	CLUSTERED	75133	142986	494	5/30/2009 9:24:02 AM	5/30/2009 9:29:02 AM	1/1/1900 12:00:00 AM	5/29/2009 10:31:25 PM	0	11	0

⊟ dbo.ActionDefinitions

Index Name	Index Type	# User Seeks	# User Scans	# User Updates	Last User Seek Time	Last User Scan Time	Last User Lookup Time	Last User Update Time	# System Seeks	# System Scans	# System Updates
IX_ActionDefinitions	NONCLUSTERED	0	0	7	1/1/1900 12:00:00 AM	1/1/1900 12:00:00 AM	1/1/1900 12:00:00 AM	5/18/2009 11:04:27 AM	0	0	0
PK_ActionDefinitions	CLUSTERED	23	3796306	23	5/19/2009 9:26:20 AM	5/30/2009 1:40:48 PM	1/1/1900 12:00:00 AM	5/19/2009 9:26:20 AM	0	0	0

⊟ dbo.ActiveAlerts

Index Name	Index Type	# User Seeks	# User Scans	# User Updates	Last User Seek Time	Last User Scan Time	Last User Lookup Time	Last User Update Time	# System Seeks	# System Scans	# System Updates
IX_ActiveAlerts	CLUSTERED	0	3882	46	1/1/1900 12:00:00 AM	5/29/2009 4:56:26 PM	1/1/1900 12:00:00 AM	5/28/2009 2:18:57 PM	0	0	0
PK_ActiveAlerts	NONCLUSTERED	0	46	46	1/1/1900 12:00:00 AM	5/28/2009 2:18:57 PM	1/1/1900 12:00:00 AM	5/28/2009 2:18:57 PM	0	0	0

⊟ dbo.AlertDefinitions

Index Name	Index Type	# User Seeks	# User Scans	# User Updates	Last User Seek Time	Last User Scan Time	Last User Lookup Time	Last User Update Time	# System Seeks	# System Scans	# System Updates
PK_AlertDefinitions	CLUSTERED	2562205	2348881	1804439	5/30/2009 1:40:48 PM	5/30/2009 1:40:48 PM	1/1/1900 12:00:00 AM	5/30/2009 1:40:48 PM	0	7412	0

FIGURE 14-15

Index Physical Statistics Report

As data is inserted, updated, and deleted in a table, the table and its indexes become fragmented. Index fragmentation slows down sequential operations such as range scans and read-ahead because the storage needs to hunt around for all the relevant pages. The Index Physical Statistics report, shown in Figure 14-16, helps clarify the extent of index fragmentation.

Index Physical Statistics
[SurveyReports]
on SWSSQLDV1 at 5/30/2009 2:06:11 PM

Microsoft®
SQL Server 2008

This report provides overview of the utilization of disk space within the Database.

Table Name

⊟ dbo.AdhocSurveyAssignments

Index Name	Index Type	# Partitions	Depth	Operation Recommended
pk_sa_fta_guid	CLUSTERED INDEX	⊟ 1	3	Reorganize

Partition No.	Avg. Fragmentation (%)	# Fragments	Avg. Pages Per Fragment	# Pages
1	12	102	8	848

⊟ dbo.AdhocSurveyCustomers

Index Name	Index Type	# Partitions	Depth	Operation Recommended
pk_sa_fta_guid_cust_sit eid	CLUSTERED INDEX	⊞ 1	3	.

⊟ dbo.AdhocSurveyDetailResponses

Index Name	Index Type	# Partitions	Depth	Operation Recommended
pk_sdr_frlID	CLUSTERED INDEX	⊞ 1	4	.

⊟ dbo.AdhocSurveyHeaderResponses

Index Name	Index Type	# Partitions	Depth	Operation Recommended
pk_shr_frhID	CLUSTERED INDEX	⊞ 1	3	.

⊟ dbo.AdhocSurveyHeaders

Index Name	Index Type	# Partitions	Depth	Operation Recommended
pk_sh_fth_guid	CLUSTERED INDEX	⊟ 1	2	Rebuild

Partition No.	Avg. Fragmentation (%)	# Fragments	Avg. Pages Per Fragment	# Pages
1	39	12	2	28

FIGURE 14-16

This report shows all clustered and nonclustered indexes in the database and their depth — the number of levels in the b-tree of the index. Clicking the plus (+) sign next to each partition yields more information about the object's average fragmentation, number of fragments, and number of pages overall.

If SQL Server determines that the DBA needs to take action on the table's fragmentation, it will display a recommendation of Rebuild or Reorganize for each partition. It's up to the DBA to script the recommended actions, unfortunately. When deciding which objects to tackle first, consider checking the number of pages in the object. Microsoft's whitepaper on index fragmentation in SQL Server 2000 indicates that DBAs should not be concerned with objects under 1,000 pages in size:

`http://technet.microsoft.com/en-us/library/cc966523.aspx`

> *The easiest way to stay on top of fragmented objects is to use maintenance plans to periodically rebuild or reorganize all indexes in a database. Unfortunately, this causes a lot of logged and locked operations, which affects performance while the maintenance plan runs. For databases over 100GB, consider writing scripts to reorganize and/or rebuild only the fragmented objects. Rebuilding only the most fragmented objects will reduce the performance impact on database mirroring and log shipping, which both slow down dramatically during index rebuilds.*

USING THE PERFORMANCE DASHBOARD

Microsoft's Product Support Services (PSS) team for SQL Server created a set of custom reports for SQL Server 2005 SP2 called the Performance Dashboard. These reports gave database administrators more powerful troubleshooting information about the health of their server. Sadly, the reports were not updated for SQL Server 2008, but with a few easy tweaks, the reports will work fine. Keep in mind, however, that they won't account for new SQL Server 2008 features like filestream data or spatial data. Here's how to install and configure the Performance Dashboard reports:

1. Download the SQL Server 2005 Performance Dashboard .msi file from the following URL:

   `www.microsoft.com/downloads/details.aspx?FamilyId=1d3a4a0d-7e0c-4730-8204-e419218c1efc`

2. Run this program on the workstation where the reports will be used with SQL Server Management Studio, not on the SQL Servers being monitored.

3. If multiple database administrators will be running the reports, they each need to run this .msi file. (MSI files are Windows setup programs or packages.) Take note of the exact installation path because the report files will be stored there. By default, this is `c:\Program Files\Microsoft SQL Server\90\Tools\PerformanceDashboard`.

4. After installation completes, open the target folder in Windows Explorer.

5. Copy the RDL files into `My Documents\SQL Server Management Studio\Custom Reports`. (This isn't a required step, but it will make it easier to use these reports faster.) If the folder doesn't exist, create it. It's created for the first time when a user opens SSMS and tries to open a custom report.

These reports rely on some additional functions included in the `setup.sql` script in the installation folder.

6. On all SQL Servers where the Performance Dashboard reports will be used, run that `setup.sql` script.

7. Launch SQL Server Management Studio.

8. Connect to a SQL Server 2005 or 2008 instance, and right-click the server name in Object Explorer.

9. Click Reports ➪ Custom Reports, and an Open File dialog will appear, as shown in Figure 14-17. If the RDL files were copied into My Documents, they'll appear immediately; otherwise, the user must navigate to the folder where the Performance Dashboard files were installed.

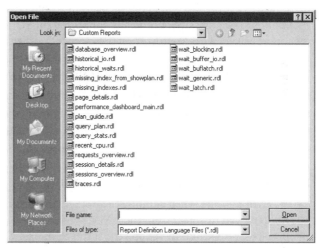

FIGURE 14-17

10. Open `Performance_dashboard_main.rdl`. This is the starting point for the dashboard, and all other reports are accessed as drilldowns from this report.

SQL Server will display a warning about running a custom report. Read this warning carefully before proceeding.

> *Custom reports contain queries that will be executed with the current user's logon credentials. If the user is a sysadmin, then the report queries will execute as a sysadmin. Only run custom reports from trustworthy sources, and review the queries first. Consider running the reports with the least-privileged login possible. Also consider keeping the reports in a secure location that can't be modified by other personnel. Since they include T-SQL code, someone else could change the RDLC files, causing them to run dangerous code under the DBA's login credentials.*

If the report executes successfully, it displays a bar chart and several tables. However, don't be alarmed if the report produces an error instead: There are several known issues with the report scripts, and they're very easy to fix. One fix is required for use on SQL Server 2008 servers, so the next section reviews a few key troubleshooting tips before moving on to interpreting the report results.

Troubleshooting Common Errors

After installing the Performance Dashboard Reports, they may not work out-of-the-box — especially with newer versions of SQL Server. This section covers several commonly experienced issues with the reports.

Be aware that this list can't contain every possible error on every SQL Server. Since the Performance Dashboard Reports aren't officially supported on SQL Server 2008 and beyond, the DBA can't open support tickets with Microsoft on these reports either.

"The stored procedures and functions required by the performance dashboard have not yet been installed."

The reports rely on code that isn't included with SQL Server 2005 or 2008. To install the add-on code, open the `setup.sql` file in the Performance Dashboard installation directory. Run that script on each SQL Server instance to be monitored.

"Invalid column name 'cpu_ticks_in_ms'."

This error appears when running the `setup.sql` script on a SQL Server 2008 instance. SQL Server 2008 removed this field from the DMV `sys.dm_os_sys_info` in the interest of higher accuracy in CPU clock resolution. In `setup.sql`, scroll to line 218 as shown:

```
select @ts_now = cpu_ticks / convert(float, cpu_ticks_in_ms) from
sys.dm_os_sys_info
```

Change that to read as follows:

```
select @ts_now = ms_ticks from sys.dm_os_sys_info
```

Execute the script again; it will run without errors.

"Difference of two datetime columns caused overflow at runtime."

Depending on how long a connection has been open, some reports can display this message. The solution is to open the `setup.sql` file distributed with the reports, go to line 272, and examine the following select statement:

```
select count(*) as num_sessions,
  sum(convert(bigint, s.total_elapsed_time)) as total_elapsed_time,
  sum(convert(bigint, s.cpu_time)) as cpu_time,
```

```
 sum(convert(bigint, s.total_elapsed_time)) - sum(convert(bigint, s.cpu_time)) as
wait_time,
 sum(convert(bigint, datediff(ms, login_time, getdate())))) - sum(convert(bigint,
s.total_elapsed_time)) as idle_connection_time,
 case when sum(s.logical_reads) > 0 then (sum(s.logical_reads) - isnull(sum(s.
reads), 0)) / convert(float, sum(s.logical_reads))
   else NULL
   end as cache_hit_ratio
from sys.dm_exec_sessions s
where s.is_user_process = 0x1
```

Line 276 causes a bug because it compares two dates using milliseconds. Change it to the following:

```
sum(convert(bigint, CAST ( DATEDIFF ( minute, login_time, getdate()) AS BIGINT)
*60000 + DATEDIFF ( millisecond, DATEADD ( minute, DATEDIFF ( minute, login_time,
 getdate() ), login_time ),getdate() ))) - sum(convert(bigint,
 s.total_elapsed_time)) as idle_connection_time,
```

Then rerun this `setup.sql` script on the SQL Server instance being monitored.

"Index (zero based) must be greater than or equal to zero and less than the size of the argument list."

This error appears when attempting to run a Performance Dashboard report on a database with the compatibility level of 80 (SQL Server 2000) instead of 90 (SQL 2005) or 100 (SQL 2008). The Performance Dashboard works only for databases with a compatibility level of 90 or higher.

"The 'version_string' parameter is missing a value."

This error appears when trying to run one of the Performance Dashboard drilldown reports directly. Instead, run `performance_dashboard_main.rdl` and then drill down to the relevant report.

Interpreting the Performance Dashboard Reports

After `setup.sql` has been successfully executed on the server and `performance_dashboard_main.rdl` runs, the results are shown (see Figure 14-18). The first difference between this report and the Standard Reports should be immediately obvious: drilldowns. By clicking on graph elements and hyperlinked words, the user can jump to other reports that have more information about an underlying problem. This screenshot shows two waiting requests, which the user can click on to find the performance bottlenecks.

The System CPU Utilization, Current Waiting Requests, and Current Activity sections of the report give the DBA a heads-up view of the SQL Server's current health. Clicking on each of their hyperlinks leads to more detailed information about that section. For example, clicking on User Requests yields a list of current queries, what they're waiting on, how long they've been waiting, and even the execution plan of the query. This information is useful for looking at what's currently happening, but the Performance Dashboard provides even more value in the Historical Information section.

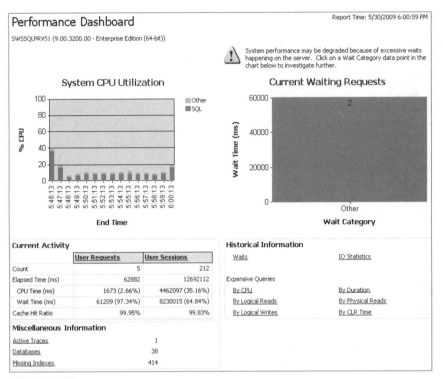

FIGURE 14-18

Historical Waits Report

The Waits link in the Historical Information section leads to the report shown in Figure 14-19. It can also be run independently by right-clicking on a SQL Server instance name, clicking Reports ➪ Custom Reports, and choosing `historical_waits.rdl` from the Performance Dashboard installation folder.

This report shows how long SQL Server has spent waiting on different resources, but it's not a complete picture. This report was originally designed for SQL Server 2005, and SQL Server 2008 introduced new waits. As a result, this report lumps a large number of events into the Other category. To understand why, review the code in the scalar function `msdb.MS_PerfDashboard.fn_WaitTypeCategory`, shown here:

```
create function [MS_PerfDashboard].[fn_WaitTypeCategory](@wait_type nvarchar(60))
returns varchar(60)
as
begin
        declare @category nvarchar(60)
        select @category =
                case
                        when @wait_type like N'LCK_M_%' then N'Lock'
                        when @wait_type like N'LATCH_%' then N'Latch'
                        when @wait_type like N'PAGELATCH_%' then N'Buffer Latch'
                        when @wait_type like N'PAGEIOLATCH_%' then N'Buffer IO'
                        when @wait_type like N'RESOURCE_SEMAPHORE_%' then
N'Compilation'
```

```
                         when @wait_type = N'SOS_SCHEDULER_YIELD' then N'Scheduler
Yield'
                         when @wait_type in (N'LOGMGR', N'LOGBUFFER',
N'LOGMGR_RESERVE_APPEND', N'LOGMGR_FLUSH', N'WRITELOG') then N'Logging'
                         when @wait_type in (N'ASYNC_NETWORK_IO',
N'NET_WAITFOR_PACKET') then N'Network IO'
                         when @wait_type in (N'CXPACKET', N'EXCHANGE') then
N'Parallelism'
                         when @wait_type in (N'RESOURCE_SEMAPHORE', N'CMEMTHREAD',
 N'SOS_RESERVEDMEMBLOCKLIST') then N'Memory'
                         when @wait_type like N'CLR_%' or @wait_type like N'SQLCLR%'
then N'CLR'
                         when @wait_type like N'DBMIRROR%' or @wait_type =
N'MIRROR_SEND_MESSAGE' then N'Mirroring'
                         when @wait_type like N'XACT%' or @wait_type like N'DTC_%' or
@wait_type like N'TRAN_MARKLATCH_%' or @wait_type like N'MSQL_XACT_%' or
@wait_type = N'TRANSACTION_MUTEX' then N'Transaction'
                         when @wait_type like N'SLEEP_%' or @wait_type
in(N'LAZYWRITER_SLEEP',
N'SQLTRACE_BUFFER_FLUSH', N'WAITFOR', N'WAIT_FOR_RESULTS') then N'Sleep'
                         else N'Other'
            end

        return @category
end
```

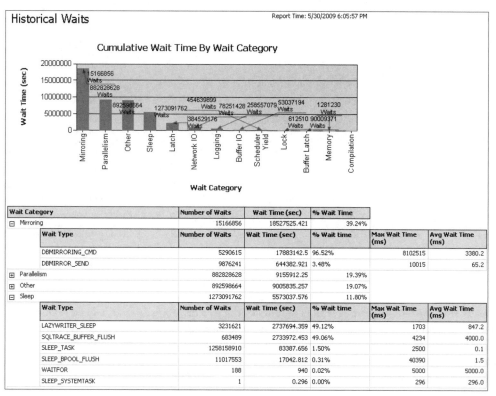

FIGURE 14-19

Any `wait_types` that weren't explicitly included in this function show up in the Other category. The good news is that the database administrator can modify this function to include new wait types, and any wait types that appear in subsequent versions of SQL Server.

Keep in mind that just because a wait statistic shows up, that doesn't mean it's a performance bottleneck. In this screenshot, database mirroring waits are the top statistic, but this server is running database mirroring in asynchronous mode. No queries were actually waiting for database mirroring to complete, so focusing on improving database mirroring performance wouldn't be the best use of the database administrator's time. Understanding the results of this report are the key to successful actions, so spend time in Chapter 3 before taking action on this report.

Missing Index Report

For a decade or more, database administrators have been eagerly awaiting the arrival of the mythical "self-tuning database server:" a database platform that automatically adds indexes where appropriate, removes indexes where they're no longer needed, and answers phone calls from irate users. While SQL Server 2008 is still not that version, the Missing Index Report, shown in Figure 14-20, gets one step closer.

Missing Index Report

Report Time: 5/30/2009 6:39:30 PM

This report shows potential indexes that the SQL Server optimizer identified during query compilation. These recommendations are specific recommendations targeting a specific query. Consider submitting your workload and the proposed index to the Database Tuning Advisor for a more comprehensive evaluation that could include partitioning, choice of clustered versus nonclustered index, and so forth.

Overall Impact	Database ID	Object ID	Unique Compiles	User Seeks	User Scans	Avg Total User Cost	Avg User Impact	Proposed Index
99.93	4	1954106002	281453	281452	0	50.30	99.93	CREATE INDEX missing_index_122 ON [msdb].[dbo
99.93	17	1817109564	2	2	0	72.05	99.93	CREATE INDEX missing_index_8751 ON [SWSUDB] [Status], [CreatedDate], [LastAttemptedDate], [Se [BuildDBVersion])
99.93	17	1817109564	1	1	0	72.05	99.93	CREATE INDEX missing_index_8850 ON [SWSUDB] [Status], [CreatedDate], [LastAttemptedDate], [Se [CurrentDBVersion], [BuildDBVersion])
99.93	30	1648724926	1	2	0	5.35	99.93	CREATE INDEX missing_index_262077 ON [SWO].[
99.89	17	1817109564	1	1	0	73.90	99.89	CREATE INDEX missing_index_258598 ON [SWSUD [FirstName], [LastName], [DomainId], [Password], [LastAttemptedDate], [Success], [Reason], [TestU [CurrentDBVersion], [BuildDBVersion], [email], [Fax [SendOrderEnable])
99.85	17	1008058677	73612	76029	0	23.49	99.85	CREATE INDEX missing_index_27 ON [SWSUDB].[d
99.7	8	546100986	6	19830	0	5.89	99.70	CREATE INDEX missing_index_676 ON [DWSurveys
99.61	16	149575571	6688	6688	0	3.56	99.61	CREATE INDEX missing_index_432 ON [Facsys51c]
99.58	30	560721050	1	1	0	7.70	99.58	CREATE INDEX missing_index_291796 ON [SWO].[
99.58	30	560721050	2	2	0	7.74	99.58	CREATE INDEX missing_index_292608 ON [SWO].[
99.57	30	560721050	27	699	0	7.53	99.57	CREATE INDEX missing_index_6575 ON [SWO].[db
99.41	18	1765581328	14	16	0	0.66	99.41	CREATE INDEX missing_index_49772 ON [SWSUDB
99.34	35	2073058421	11	381	0	0.69	99.34	CREATE INDEX missing_index_263552 ON [BOCMS [SI_PLUGIN_OBJECT]) INCLUDE ([ObjectID])
99.15	21	2119678599	2	81375	0	0.84	99.15	CREATE INDEX missing_index_10488 ON [TopazMa [Expiration_Date])
99.09	8	66099276	82	8254	0	7.75	99.09	CREATE INDEX missing_index_672 ON [DWSurveys
98.96	21	2119678599	3	111290	0	0.81	98.96	CREATE INDEX missing_index_10554 ON [TopazMa
98.9	19	738101670	2	2	0	35.09	98.90	CREATE INDEX missing_index_980419 ON [SWSUD ([FormResponseHeaderID], [FTI_GUID], [Entry_Da [TrackingNumber], [Created_Date], [Confirmation] [NTLogin])

FIGURE 14-20

This broadly inclusive report exposes the contents of the `sys.dm_db_missing_index_*` DMVs. The Overall Impact column shows how much faster the missing index would make related queries by taking into account the number of queries and how much faster they would be. A minor improvement in speed for a very frequently executed query would be more important than a major improvement in speed for a rarely executed query. On the other hand, in environments like data warehouses that run time-intensive overnight queries, improving the performance of a single query might be exactly what the DBA needs.

Don't blindly add every single recommended query, however; the database administrator needs to carefully examine these recommendations in relationship to each other and to the database's indexing strategy. Adding every index can sometimes result in a speed penalty instead of a speed gain. For example, note the output of the Missing Index Detail report shown in Figure 14-21. The bottom three recommended indexes are very similar; and in fact the index on CustomerID alone is completely redundant. Implementing the indexes on CustomerID and Status will fulfill the need for the index on CustomerID alone.

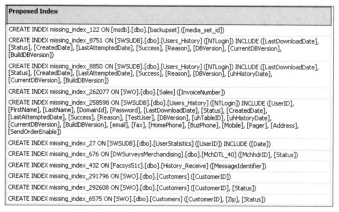

FIGURE 14-21

These are also accumulative stats, but can be cleared for a db by setting the DB in single user mode.

Like the Wait Stats report, this report demonstrates that it's not enough to simply run these Performance Dashboard reports and take action on them without understanding their contents. The database administrator must understand the concepts of performance tuning and troubleshooting, and apply them to the report results. After accumulating a wealth of knowledge about how SQL Server works, DBAs may want to extend the Performance Dashboard reports with their own personal expertise, or build new custom reports from scratch.

BUILDING CUSTOM REPORTS

Throughout their careers, effective database administrators accumulate knowledge about how to do a better job of monitoring and troubleshooting their servers. They collect scripts, tips, and software to automate tasks, and they reuse these tools as they move from company to company. Just as many DBAs build a folder of their favorite T-SQL scripts, they can also amass a group of Management Studio custom reports. These reports are simple text files, not much more complicated than T-SQL script files, that can be used anywhere and passed from DBA to DBA.

SSMS delivers these reports using SQL Server Reporting Services technology, but don't be scared off: Building custom reports doesn't require in-depth reporting expertise or business intelligence experience. In this section, you'll learn how to get started with Microsoft's report development tool, BIDS, build a sample report, and examine some good candidates for custom reporting.

Building a Custom Report with BIDS

Microsoft's Business Intelligence Development Studio (BIDS), shown in Figure 14-22, is a version of Visual Studio with a set of project types for the building of an entire BI solution. This tool is included on the SQL Server installation DVD, and can be selected during the installation process. If you already have visual studio installed, setup will add the BI project types to your existing install, if not it will install a version of Visual Studio. If it's not already on a workstation, simply rerun the SQL Server installation process and add the Business Intelligence Development Studio feature.

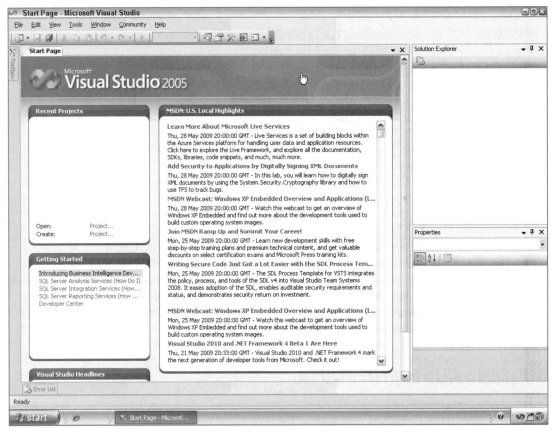

FIGURE 14-22

Sharp-eyed readers will notice that the window shows Visual Studio 2005, not 2008; this is not a publishing error. SQL Server Management Studio 2008's embedded reporting technology is not actually compatible with reports produced in BIDS 2008. So ironically, DBAs can't use SQL Server 2008 tools in order to build reports for SQL Server Management Studio 2008. Opening a BIDS 2008 custom report in SSMS 2008 results in the error message "The report definition is not valid."

The following section demonstrates the process for developing a custom report that will display database information. Start by building a simple report that queries sys.databases, by executing the following steps:

1. After installing and launching BIDS 2005, click File ➪ New Project, and select the Report Server Project.

2. Enter a solution name, report name and location, and click OK. For this example, use **DatabaseList** as the solution and report name. Take note of where the solution's files are stored because you'll need to open the files later in SQL Server Management Studio.

3. In the Solution Explorer window, right-click on Reports and choose Add New Report as shown in Figure 14-23. This will start the Report Wizard. If you wish to start with a blank report click on Add and then on Report.

4. Use the Report Wizard to build the first report. Connections to databases used by the report are called Data Sources, because this solution has no shared data sources yet, the first data source will be a new one.

5. For the data source name, enter the name of the instance to be queried, and use the Edit button to build a connection string. For now, don't check the button to make it a shared data source, because this won't be reused — you do not want the real reports to automatically pull their connection string information from the SQL Server Management Studio context.

6. After testing the connection string, click Next.

7. In the Report Query step, enter the following for the query:

   ```
   select * from master.sys.databases
   ```

8. Click Next. The Report Wizard will ask what type of report to generate; choose Tabular.

9. The Design the Table step, shown in Figure 14-24, enables the DBA to configure which fields from the recordset will be shown on the report. Enter the following fields in the Details area:

   ➤ name

   ➤ compatibility_level

   ➤ state

   ➤ recovery_model

   ➤ log_reuse_wait

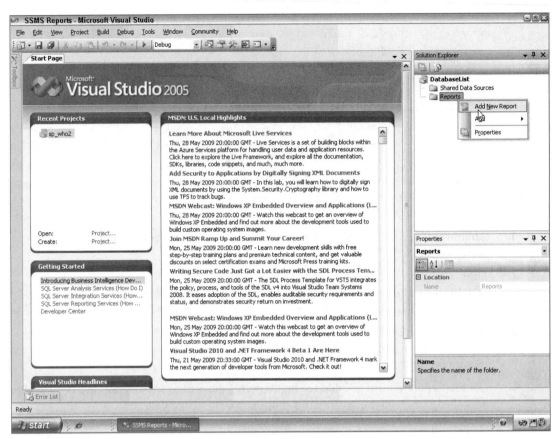

FIGURE 14-23

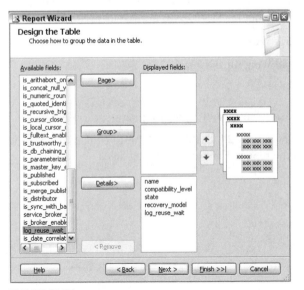

FIGURE 14-24

10. Click Finish, enter DatabaseList as the name of the report, and check the Preview Report box before clicking Finish again. If all goes well, the result will be a list of databases, as shown in Figure 14-25.

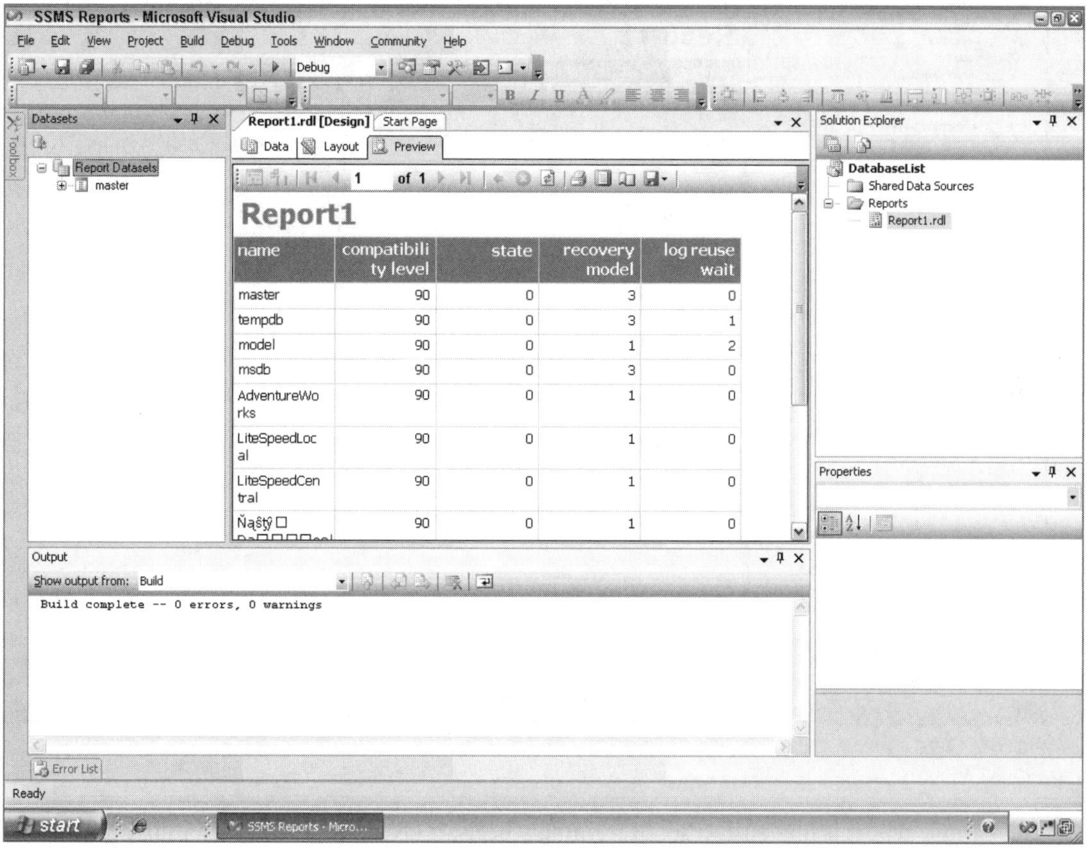

FIGURE 14-25

This report's configuration data was stored by BIDS in an RDL file, the name of which is shown in the Solution Explorer at the top right. In this screenshot, it was `Report1.rdl`. Congratulations — you have created a SQL Server Management Studio Custom Report. Open SSMS, connect to a SQL Server instance, right-click on the instance, and click Reports ➪ Custom Reports. Navigate to the RDL file that was just created by BIDS and open it. The results are shown in SQL Server Management Studio (see Figure 14-26).

Next, connect to a different SQL Server instance with different databases and use this custom report. Right-click on the instance name and click Reports ➪ Custom Reports, and then navigate to the RDL file. The report shows the database list for the currently connected server — not the database connection that was specified when the report was originally designed!

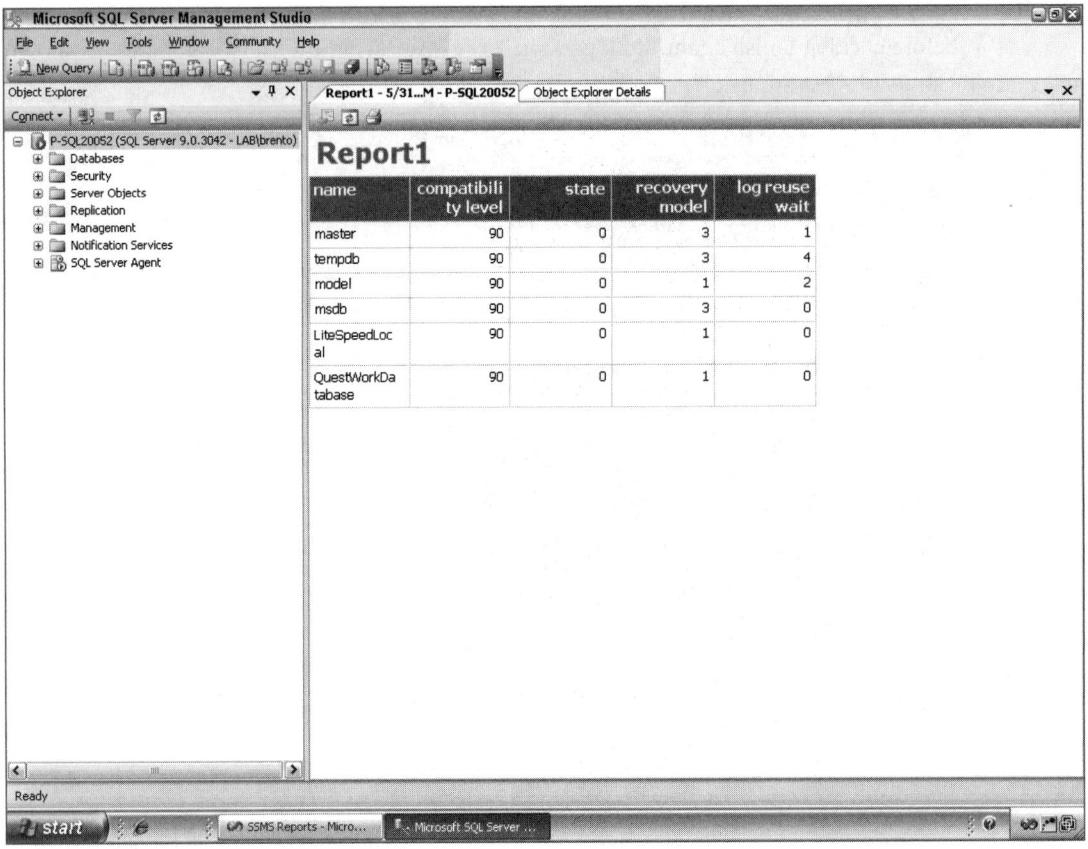

FIGURE 14-26

This sample report is obviously a set of training wheels; it gives the database administrator just a taste of how easy it is to create an SSMS Custom Report. From here, the next steps are designing better-looking reports and building more powerful datasets. The matter of report design is best left to SQL Server Reporting Services books, so instead the next section dives into building queries to drive reports.

Picking Custom Reports Candidates

Throughout this book, T-SQL query examples have been used to illustrate troubleshooting techniques, and many of these queries can be built into Custom Reports. The best candidates for custom reports are queries that involve numeric information that would be easier to understand in a graph. The worst candidates are queries whose results are frequently copied and pasted into other windows for subsequent querying.

SSMS custom reports can include more than just DMVs and default trace data. Systems management software such as Dell OpenManage, HP System Insight Manager, IBM Director, Microsoft SystemCenter, and VMware VirtualCenter can all use Microsoft SQL Server as a back end. Companies using these inventory systems can query that data in SSMS custom reports. Imagine running an SSMS report that included hardware information, virtual server host information, or patch levels. Keep in mind, however, that these repositories may live on other database servers, and the report would need to use linked server queries.

When writing custom reports, especially those that use business logic in stored procedures and functions, be cognizant of the differences between SQL Server versions. If there's a way to avoid using a T-SQL feature found only in newer versions of SQL Server, such as MERGE, then avoid it to improve compatibility. The more servers the report runs on, the more it will be used by peers, and the more it can be used on both SQL Server 2005 and 2008 servers.

Consider using a case-sensitive SQL Server for report development. Even though the other servers in the company may not be using a case-sensitive collation, this helps build a better result. Sooner or later, every DBA will be faced with a case-sensitive server, and it's better to plan for this eventuality in advance. By ensuring that all of the scripts and reports work on as many servers as possible, the DBA will be able to take quicker troubleshooting action regardless of how a broken server is configured.

SUMMARY

In SQL Server 2008 and 2005, Microsoft's new dynamic management views gave DBAs insight into what's happening inside the Storage Engine, and the SSMS reports helped surface that information. When troubleshooting SQL Server, DBAs can make their jobs easier by:

➤ Using the bundled Standard Reports to get a quick view of basic health metrics

➤ Installing the Performance Dashboard Reports to deliver more insightful information on problems

➤ Building their own reports modeled on the Performance Dashboard Reports for truly powerful analysis

However, when managing dozens or hundreds of servers in an enterprise, it might be easier to use more Microsoft technology rather than reinvent the wheel.

If building these custom reports sounds like too much work and testing, don't despair. In SQL Server 2008, Microsoft added another solution for monitoring performance of servers, databases, queries, and users: the Management Data Warehouse. The next chapter explores this new tool.

15

Using SQL Server Management Data Warehouse

WHAT'S IN THIS CHAPTER

➤ Purpose of the Management Data Warehouse (MDW)

➤ Configuring the MDW

➤ Creating custom collectors

➤ Reporting on the MDW

The Management Data Warehouse provides a solution to medium and long-term database performance data collection and reporting. When SQL Server 2005 was released, the user community became very excited about the visibility of systems internals provided by dynamic management views (DMVs) and dynamic management functions (DMFs). However, the DMVs have a limitation because data is not persisted between service restarts. This is a limitation because data that is useful for performance analysis, trending, and capacity analysis is lost each time the SQL Server service is restarted.

Performance Data Collection is the method of collecting SQL Server performance data organized as sets, from targets for consolidation and reporting in the MDW. Three System Data Collection Sets are created during the MDW setup and these provide server performance overview. Additionally MDW provides a framework for custom data collection that is useful for independent software vendors or applications that were developed in-house. The Management Data Warehouse is a relational data warehouse configured and managed within SQL Server Management Studio.

INTRODUCING MANAGEMENT DATA WAREHOUSE

The Management Data Warehouse is intended as a centralized repository for performance data from servers across an enterprise, providing an out-of-the-box solution to performance management for SQL Server administrators who are responsible for performance and capacity management.

The MDW is populated using *data collectors*. Three data collectors are set up as default by MDW setup wizard and further collectors can be configured as required. The MDW offers a scalable, customizable reporting solution that requires a minimal investment of configuration effort before providing value. The data collection solution utilizes SQL Server components such as SQL Server Agent jobs, SQL Server Integration Services to load performance data, and a relational data warehouse; and data is presented using SQL Server Reporting Services.

The MDW is not a monitoring solution, as it has no capability to configure acceptable performance or operational thresholds and alerts; and it doesn't provide real-time performance information (Activity Monitor provides this information). Nor does the MDW provide a centralized overview of all servers within an organization. In most medium-size and enterprise environments, it is still necessary for capacity and performance planning across the server estate, rather than on a per-server basis. However, used for the right purpose, MDW provides better insight than what was available before, as much of the valuable data available within DMVs can be harvested and stored for mid and long-term performance trending and analysis.

Background to MDW

In 2007, Tom Davidson and Sanjay Mishra of the SQL Server Customer Advisory Team (CAT) within Microsoft released a data warehouse and set of SQL Server Agent jobs for SQL Server 2005 called *DMVStats*. The purpose of DMVStats was to collect performance data from dynamic management views (DMVs) and store it within a data warehouse for reporting.

While DMVStats was an early incarnation of the MDW, the primary limitation of DMVStats was that it collected data only from a local instance. Writing data to a local data warehouse was a better solution than losing the data entirely, but the overhead of setup and ongoing management of many localized performance data warehouses made the solution cumbersome and unattractive to many organizations that require the data.

The Performance Dashboard for SQL Server 2005, released around the same time as Service Pack 2, used an updated version of the default trace to present a server performance report with drill-through capability, including detailed wait statistics and worst performing queries by reads, writes, duration, and CPU time. While the Performance Dashboard was extremely successful at making useful data more readily available to the DBA, it was still built on the default trace, which has a nonvolatile repository; therefore, performance data was lost with each service restart.

The MDW has been included in the core SQL Server product to provide customers with a built-in solution for central performance data capture and reporting — something that was previously available only in third-party products or with significant self-development effort.

MDW Architecture

The MDW consists of the following three key components:

➤ Data collection sets

➤ Data warehouse

➤ Reports

The Data Collection Sets are defined as SQL Server Agent jobs used to collect and upload data from target servers to the data warehouse. The data warehouse is a centralized repository for performance data storage. Reports are executed against the data warehouse to present data stored in the data warehouse.

Data Collection Sets

Data collection is necessary to retrieve performance data from the targets and store this in the data warehouse. Performance data collection is carried out by a user-mode process called DCEXEC.EXE that runs on each target server. This application is called by a SQL Server Agent job and is responsible for collecting performance data based on collection items defined in the collection set. Data collection is mainly performed using a SQL Server Integration Services (SSIS) package that controls data collection and upload.

Data collection sets can be configured in either cached mode or non-cached mode. Table 15-1 summarizes the differences between caching modes.

TABLE 15-1: Data Collection Caching Modes

MODE	DESCRIPTION
Cached	Data collection and upload jobs are two separate jobs configured on individual schedules. Supports continuous data collection and scheduled data uploads, e.g., collection could run every 60 seconds and upload every 20 minutes.
Non-cached	Collection and upload are a single job running on one schedule. The collector runs and uploads data at a configured frequency. Non-cached mode enables the collection and uploading of data on demand, as well as at intervals specified in the job.

There are two categories of data collections: System Data Collections and Custom Data Collections. System Data Collections are those configured out-of-the-box by the MDW (of which there are three), and Custom Data Collections are any user-defined Data Collection Sets.

The terminology for creating and managing data collections can be confusing because of the minor subtleties between component names. Figure 15-1 illustrates the hierarchy between collection sets, items, types, and providers.

The three System Data Collections are Disk Usage, Query Statistics, and Server Activity, and these are set up when the MDW is configured. Each Data Collection Set consists of one or more collection items. The Disk Usage collection has two collection items, one item for data files and a second for log files. These collection items use the T-SQL collector type to gather details about the data and log file sizes from system tables such as sys.database_files and sys.partitions for data file use and DBCC SQLPERF(LOGSPACE) to determine free space in the transaction log.

When defining custom collections, four collector types are available to gather data, as summarized in Table 15-2.

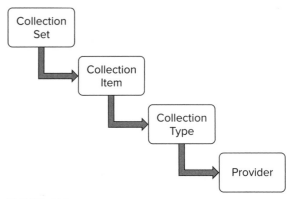

FIGURE 15-1

TABLE 15-2: Custom Collector Types

COLLECTOR TYPE	DESCRIPTION
T-SQL query	Executes a T-SQL query, storing the output in the data warehouse
SQL Trace	Loads output from SQL Trace into the data warehouse
Performance Counters	Collects Windows Performance Monitor (PerfMon) counters
Query Activity	Gathers query text and query plan for queries matching defined criteria

The MDW implementation is designed to reuse as much SQL Server infrastructure as possible, and as such leverages the functionality of SQL Server Agent to control data collection and perform uploads to the data warehouse. Each target will have two SQL Server Agent jobs for each collection set, with a suffix indicating the job function — for example, `collection_set_2_collection` and `collection_set_2_upload`.

One limitation of the MDW is that target instances for monitoring must be SQL Server 2008. Currently, there is no option to monitor earlier versions of SQL Server.

Data Warehouse

The data warehouse is the database used for storing data gathered by the data collectors. This is a regular SQL Server database that can be created and modified like any other database. The MDW is populated using SQL Server Agent to gather data, and SSIS to perform data upload to the MDW based on a schedule controlled through a SQL Server Agent job.

When the MDW is configured, a job is created named `mdw_purge_data[MDW]`, which is responsible for removing expired data from the MDW database based on the retention policy set in each collection set.

> *If the MDW becomes bloated, running this job manually may not help, as only expired data is purged. In order to reduce the size of a bloated MDW, first edit each collection set to reduce the retention period, then rerun the purge data job. By default, the purge data job runs daily at 02:00, although this can be altered if any conflicts occur.*

When the MDW is installed, two schemas are created: core schema and snapshot schema. The core schema is used to store metadata about data snapshots, such as source and time details. The snapshot schema is used to store data from the system collection sets and custom trace and Performance Monitor collection sets. A third collection set, custom_snapshots, is used when custom collection sets are created using the Generic T-SQL collector type. Books Online contains a detailed description of the schema and tables within MDW.

Reports

Reports are the interface to the data warehouse — these are SQL Server Reporting Services (SSRS) reports that present the data collected and stored in the MDW. Three reports are provided with the MDW:

- ➤ Server Activity History
- ➤ Disk Usage Summary
- ➤ Query Statistics History

These reports provide details on poorly performing queries, missing indexes, resource contention, and disk consumption. The reports provide drilldown functionality within each chart and offer a rounded overview of SQL Server performance.

While the data repository provides centralized data storage, the reports must still be launched by registering each server and expanding the Management and Data Collection folders before the right-click Reports option is available.

IMPLEMENTING MDW

The MDW is set up and configured from a wizard launched from SQL Server Management Studio. The wizard steps you through the process of setting up the MDW and starting data collection. There are two phases to implementing the MDW:

1. Configure the Management Data Warehouse.
2. Set up data collection.

The first step, configuring the MDW, is
required once only and creates the database
that will be used to store the performance
data for an organization. The second step,
setting up data collection, is required for
every server participating in the MDW, potentially every production SQL Server within an
organization.

Ensure SQL Server Agent is running and set to
auto-start, then expand the Management folder
within SQL Server Management Studio;
right-click Data Collection to launch the
Configure MDW Wizard. Figure 15-2 shows
the first dialog following the flash screen,
enabling you to choose a task to perform.

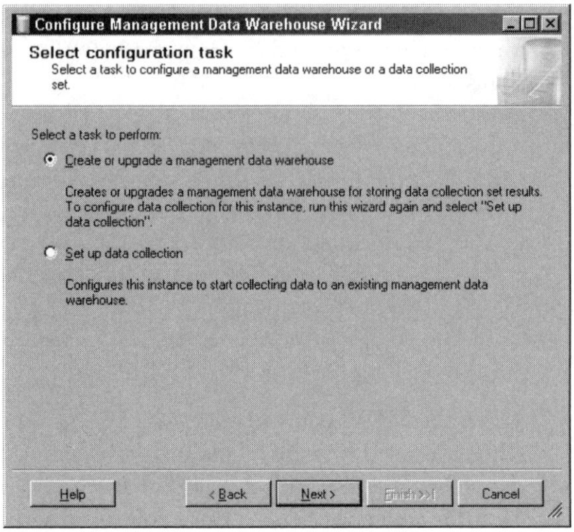

Table 15-3 summarizes the terms relating to
collection sets, types, and collection items.

FIGURE 15-2

TABLE 15-3: Collector Terms

COLLECTOR TERMS	DESCRIPTION
Collection Set	Group of related collection items, such as the system collection sets: disk usage, server activity, and query statistics
Collector Type	Logical wrapper for an SSIS package to collect then upload data to the MDW. Collector types include: T-SQL Query, SQL Trace, Performance Counter, and query activity.
Collection Item	Data gathered from a single data provider, e.g., value of a specific PerfMon monitor counter

Creating a Management Data Warehouse

The first step in implementing the MDW is to identify and configure the server that will be used to
host the data warehouse. In large organizations it may be possible to dedicate a SQL Server instance
or server to the MDW, but in all but the largest deployments a utility database server will suffice.
The process required to create the MDW consists of two steps:

1. Configure MDW storage.
2. Map logins and users.

The MDW should use a dedicated database, which you can create before the wizard is started (and
then select the required database from the drop-down) or create a new database. Ensure that the

data warehouse is sized appropriately; allow 250-500 MB data per instance per day. Additionally, apply best practices such as separating data and log files and configuring a fixed autogrow size for the MDW database. The MDW operates using a series of SQL Server Agent jobs that contain the database name. Therefore, changing the database name also requires changing these SQL Server Agent jobs to reference the new name.

The final step to complete setup of the MDW is to map users and logins. The MDW uses three database roles, mdw_admin, mdw_reader, and mdw_writer, and these should each be mapped to appropriate logins.

Set Up Data Collection

The Configure MDW Wizard should be run on each target (SQL Server instance) to configure the MDW destination. During this wizard, you'll be asked to provide security credentials and configure the cache location.

Because the MDW utilizes SQL Server Agent to control data collection and perform uploads, this should be running, preferably using a domain service account. The service account for SQL Server

Agent requires access to the MDW database, as the SSIS upload task will run to this destination. When troubleshooting, the SQL Server Agent logs can be useful, and you can launch a data collection log viewer by right-clicking on Data Collection and choosing View Logs. Figure 15-3 shows the dialog used to capture MDW connection details and control cache settings.

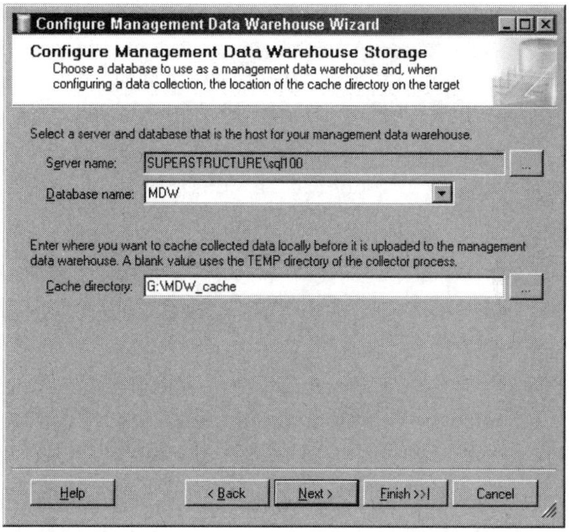

If the cache directory is not specified during the configuration wizard, the temp directory for the SQL Server Agent service account will be used. Because the cache folder can grow quite large, potentially affecting the read/write performance of the disk hosting the cache folder, it's a good practice to specify a location with sufficient capacity and where cache read/write activity will not impact I/O throughput of SQL Server.

FIGURE 15-3

System Collection Sets

The MDW is provided with three system collection sets out-of-the-box, and these provide server performance overview and baseline information. The *Disk Usage* collection set uses two collectors of the Generic T-SQL collector type (two different T-SQL scripts are used; the data file disk usage collector is shown in the following code example) to retrieve data and log file size for each database. Using the default settings, this data is collected every 60 seconds, uploaded to the MDW every six hours, and retained for 730 days:

```
DECLARE @dbsize bigint
DECLARE @logsize bigint
DECLARE @ftsize bigint
DECLARE @reservedpages bigint
DECLARE @pages bigint
DECLARE @usedpages bigint

SELECT @dbsize = SUM(convert(bigint,case when type = 0 then size else 0 end))
      ,@logsize = SUM(convert(bigint,case when type = 1 then size else 0 end))
      ,@ftsize = SUM(convert(bigint,case when type = 4 then size else 0 end))
FROM sys.database_files

SELECT @reservedpages = SUM(a.total_pages)
      ,@usedpages = SUM(a.used_pages)
      ,@pages = SUM(CASE
                        WHEN it.internal_type IN (202,204) THEN 0
                        WHEN a.type != 1 THEN a.used_pages
                        WHEN p.index_id < 2 THEN a.data_pages
                        ELSE 0
                    END)
FROM sys.partitions p
JOIN sys.allocation_units a ON p.partition_id = a.container_id
LEFT JOIN sys.internal_tables it ON p.object_id = it.object_id

SELECT
        @dbsize as 'dbsize',
        @logsize as 'logsize',
        @ftsize as 'ftsize',
        @reservedpages as 'reservedpages',
        @usedpages as 'usedpages',
        @pages as 'pages'
```

The *Query Statistics* system collection set consists of a single collection item for query statistics. Under the default configuration, this collection runs every 10 seconds, is uploaded to the MDW every 15 minutes, and data is retained for 14 days.

The *Server Activity* collection set consists of one Generic T-SQL collector type used to snapshot the following dynamic management views (DMVs):

➤ dm_os_waiting_tasks

➤ dm_os_latch_stats

➤ dm_os_process_memory

➤ dm_os_memory_nodes

➤ dm_os_schedulers

➤ dm_io_virtual_file_stats

The Server Activity Collection set uses a second collection item to gather Performance Monitor data. The two collection set properties are shown in Figure 15-4.

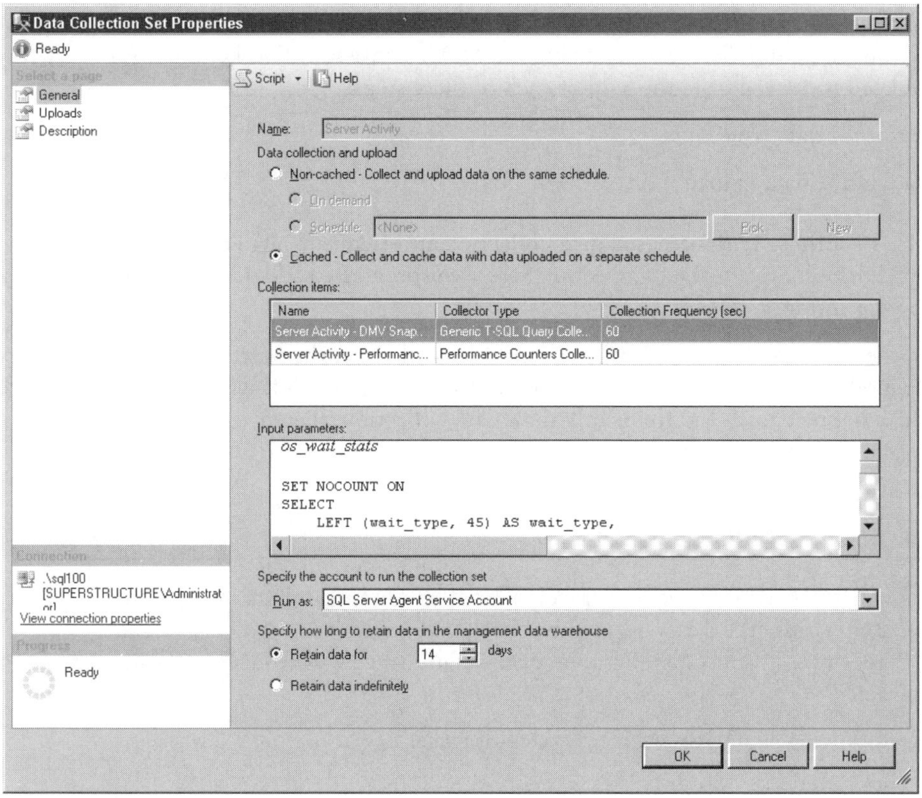

FIGURE 15-4

The Performance Counter collection item includes a subset of serverwide performance counters such as Memory, Logical Disk, and Processor, as well as SQL Server–specific counters such as Buffer Manager\Page Life Expectancy and SQL Statistics\Batch Requests/sec. Each collector runs every 60 seconds, uploading data every 15 minutes, and retaining data for 14 days by default.

Uses for MDW

In addition to the server performance information that is available from the MDW, the data collection infrastructure provides a framework for software vendors to construct their own data collection mechanisms. The MDW provides reusable components that can be leveraged to provide insight into custom applications, potentially providing application vendors with detailed application performance and usage information to improve their product and enable them to better support their customers.

Performance Overhead

Assuming the MDW is deployed as intended, a central data warehouse server is designated for the purpose of data storage and reporting functions. The aspect most DBAs are concerned with is overhead on the production SQL Servers. Deploying the MDW consists of two key steps for every target server,he overhead is derived from the load of each of these steps:

➤   Effect of the data collection

➤   Impact of the data upload

It is reasonable to surmise that increased data collection and frequency will result in increased overhead. The three default System Data Collection Sets are estimated to add 4% CPU overhead to each target SQL Server instance.

Additionally, the cache mode of each data collection set will affect the overhead on the target server. In non-cache mode there is a single step for data collection and upload, whereas the cache mode data upload can happen much less frequently than data collection, thereby reducing overhead. Using a local cache and decreasing the frequency of data upload will reduce the overhead of the MDW.

DISABLING THE DEFAULT TRACE

When using the MDW, the default trace will still be running, which may no longer be required because the data collected by the default trace (and more) is captured by the System Data Collectors. Disabling the default trace will reduce overhead on each target.

Use the following T-SQL to disable the default trace:

```
sp_configure 'default trace enabled', 0
reconfigure with override
go
```

The performance overhead of any custom collection set can be quantified by the impact of running the collection type outside the MDW framework. For example, configuring a SQL Trace to capture lock acquired and lock released events will generate many events on busy servers, as this is a very common occurrence in SQL Server. The effect of using SQL Trace to capture such events will be the same whether the start/stop of data capture is controlled by a server-side trace or through a Data Collection Set.

There's no free lunch when monitoring performance. Every attempt to observe server activity and resource performance has an affect on performance, and it's important to be sensitive to the server environment and resource usage when creating custom data collections. Test data collections carefully with a known workload (see Chapter 12 for details on replaying a SQL Trace), and validate that the impact is minimal. If there's any question whether data collection is the cause of a performance problem, stop collection for a short period and try to identify whether the problem disappears.

REPORTING FROM MDW

Reporting is the purpose of data collection and the whole purpose of the MDW. Previous incarnations of MDW, such as DMVStats and the Performance Dashboard (both for SQL Server 2005), were adopted widely because of the feature-rich drill-through reports. These reports enable DBAs to gain a systemwide view and drill down to specific problem query plans and wait statistics within a few mouse clicks.

The MDW provides three reports that present data captured in each of the three System Data Collection sets. Reports are launched from the right-click menu available on the Data Collection object within the Management folder. Each report contains a time control component that enables selection of the date range for the report. Use a wide date range for a long-term view of server activity and performance, or a narrow range when investigating a specific problem.

The Server Activity History, shown in Figure 15-5, provides a server performance overview, including resources such as CPU, memory, disk, and network, where total resource usage and SQL Server resource use alone are represented (such as % CPU Utilization and SQL Server % Processor time). Also included are SQL Server waits and general SQL Server activity, including Batches/sec, Logins/sec, and Compilations/sec. Clicking any of the chart lines enables drilling down for more detailed information — for example, clicking through the Memory Usage chart displays an additional report plotting Total Working Set and Page Reads/second.

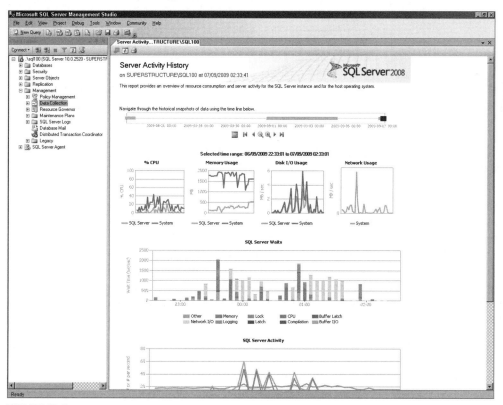

FIGURE 15-5

The second report provided is the Disk Usage report. As shown in Figure 15-6 this report displays the data and log file size and growth statistics for each database on the instance. This report's most useful aspect is displaying the average growth per day, and a trend line indicates rapid-growth databases.

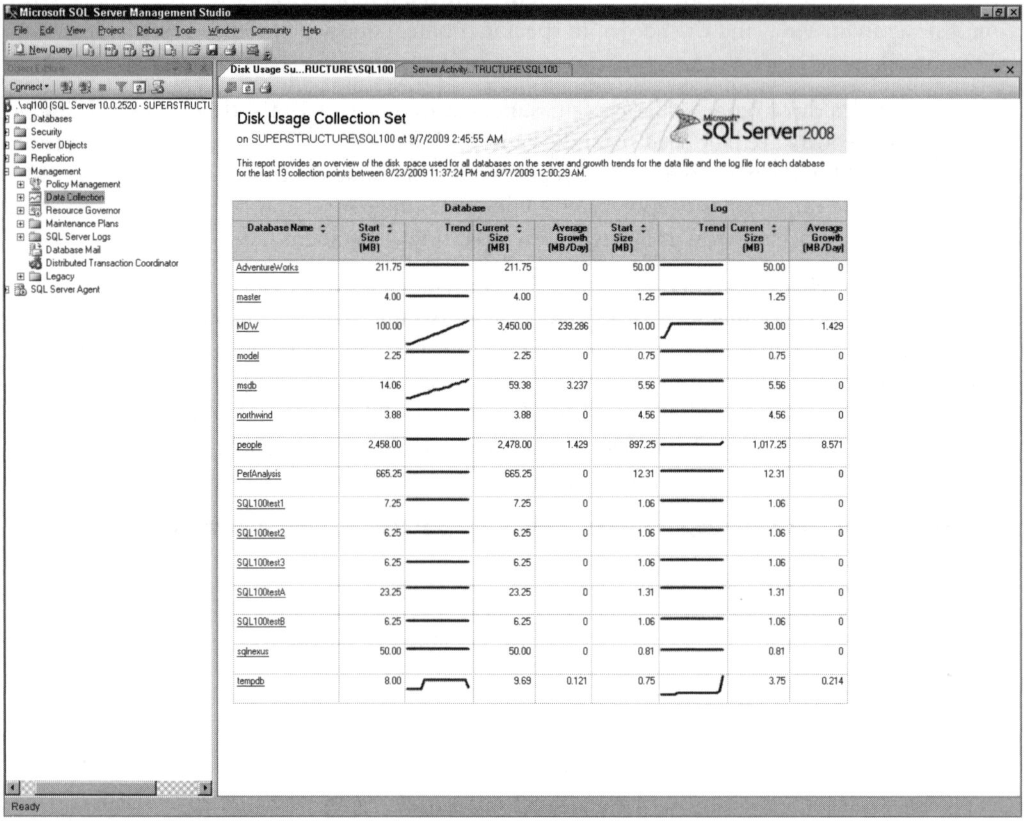

FIGURE 15-6

The third out-of-the-box report provided with the MDW is the Query Statistics report. This report presents the top 10 worst-performing queries, grouped by CPU time, duration, total I/O, physical reads, or logical reads. Figure 15-7 shows an example of the top 10 worst-performing queries by duration, including a clearly identifiable overall worst-performing query. The power of the MDW can be demonstrated by clicking either the vertical bar or the first query in the table (both behave the same), which provides a summary of the query execution statistics. The really interesting feature here is that the query plan is captured and stored, which means the graphic showplan can be subsequently retrieved.

In addition to the three reports provided with the MDW, additional custom reports can be designed and run fairly readily. By customizing the Report Definition Language (RDL) files that construct the reports provided with MDW, a pre-built report can be adapted as required.

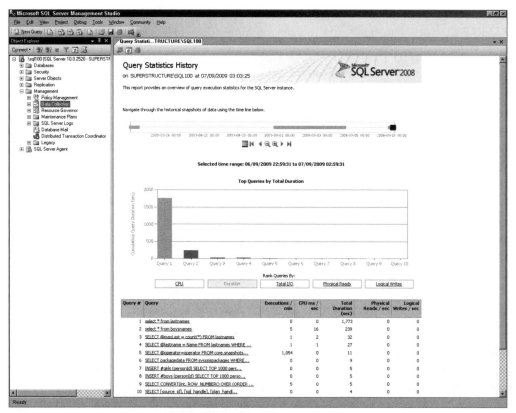

FIGURE 15-7

CUSTOM DATA COLLECTION AND REPORTING

The MDW provides a broad and powerful out-of-the-box performance data capture and reporting solution. It also offers more than a one-size-fits-all approach, as the MDW provides a framework for defining and managing custom data collections. Unlike the setup of the MDW, there's no wizard or interface within SQL Server Management Studio to support creation of custom data collection sets — this must be done through T-SQL scripts.

The scripts required to define a data collection can be written from scratch, or you could use SQL Server Management Studio to adapt an existing collection set to the purpose.

MDW provides four collector types to gather data: T-SQL query, PerfMon, SQL-Trace, and Query Activity (the query activity collector is only useful within the System Collection).

Defining Custom Collections

Custom collections provide extensibility, enabling DBAs to leverage the MDW infrastructure and adapt to specific organizational or technical requirements. To illustrate the flexibility of the MDW, the following example uses the People database (introduced in Chapter 13), where index fragmentation is captured nightly. Capturing index fragmentation each night enables volatile tables to be identified, which in turn potentially enables optimizations to be made, such as lowering the index fill factor to reduce page splits.

The following query can be used to identify fragmentation levels for every index within the People database:

```
SELECT object_name(IdxPhysStats.object_id) AS [Table],
    SysInd.name AS [Index],
    IdxPhysStats.Index_type_desc,
    IdxPhysStats.avg_fragmentation_in_percent,
    IdxPhysStats.avg_fragment_size_in_pages,
    IdxPhysStats.avg_page_space_used_in_percent,
    IdxPhysStats.record_count,
    IdxPhysStats.ghost_record_count,
    IdxPhysStats.fragment_count,
    IdxPhysStats.avg_fragment_size_in_pages
FROM sys.dm_db_index_physical_stats
(db_id(N'People'), NULL, NULL, NULL , 'DETAILED') IdxPhysStats
    JOIN sys.tables SysTab
WITH (NOLOCK) ON IdxPhysStats.object_id = SysTab.object_id
    JOIN sys.indexes SysInd
WITH (NOLOCK) ON IdxPhysStats.object_id = SysInd.object_id AND
IdxPhysStats.index_id = SysInd.index_id
```

The preceding T-SQL query can be built and tested within SQL Server Management Studio; and once the query is complete and robust enough for inclusion within a data collection set, the next step is to wrap the query in the T-SQL necessary to create a collection set.

The Disk Usage collection set (one of the System Collections) uses the Generic T-SQL collector type, and therefore provides a good base for adaptation for this purpose. The next code snippet was initially scripted from the Disk Usage collection set, and uses the index fragmentation query provided above.

To briefly narrate the code sample, the first part creates the collection set, including the name, expiration date, and schedule (which must be predefined). The second part defines the collector types that will be used — in this case, the Generic T-SQL query. In logical progression, the third part creates the collection item where the T-SQL query body is wrapped in XML; be careful to escape any single quotes with an additional quotation mark. The final part contains error handling and provides meaningful error messages.

```
Begin Transaction
Begin Try

-- Part 1
Declare @collection_set_id_1 int
Declare @collection_set_uid_2 uniqueidentifier
EXEC [msdb].[dbo].[sp_syscollector_create_collection_set]
    @name=N'Index Fragementation',
    @collection_mode=1,
    @description=N'Record daily index fragmentation',
    @logging_level=0,
    @days_until_expiration=90,
```

```
        @schedule_name=N'Every Night at 3AM',
        @collection_set_id=@collection_set_id_1 OUTPUT,
        @collection_set_uid=@collection_set_uid_2 OUTPUT

-- Part 2
Declare @collector_type_uid_3 uniqueidentifier
Select @collector_type_uid_3 = collector_type_uid
  From [msdb].[dbo].[syscollector_collector_types]
Where name = N'Generic T-SQL Query Collector Type';

-- Part 3
Declare @collection_item_id_4 int
EXEC [msdb].[dbo].[sp_syscollector_create_collection_item]
    @name=N'Collect index fragmentation',
    @parameters=N'<ns:TSQLQueryCollector xmlns:ns="DataCollectorType">
<Query><Value>
SELECT object_name(IdxPhysStats.object_id) AS [Table],
   SysInd.name AS [Index],
   IdxPhysStats.Index_type_desc,
   IdxPhysStats.avg_fragmentation_in_percent,
   IdxPhysStats.avg_fragment_size_in_pages,
   IdxPhysStats.avg_page_space_used_in_percent,
   IdxPhysStats.record_count,
   IdxPhysStats.ghost_record_count,
   IdxPhysStats.fragment_count,
FROM sys.dm_db_index_physical_stats
(db_id(''People''), NULL, NULL, NULL , ''DETAILED'') IdxPhysStats
   JOIN sys.tables SysTab
WITH (NOLOCK) ON IdxPhysStats.object_id = SysTab.object_id
   JOIN sys.indexes SysInd
WITH (NOLOCK) ON IdxPhysStats.object_id = SysInd.object_id
AND IdxPhysStats.index_id = SysInd.index_id
ORDER BY 1,5
</Value><OutputTable>Index Fragmentation</OutputTable></Query><Databases
 UseSystemDatabases="true" UseUserDatabases="true" />
</ns:TSQLQueryCollector>',
    @collection_item_id=@collection_item_id_4 OUTPUT,
    @collection_set_id=@collection_set_id_1,
    @collector_type_uid=@collector_type_uid_3

-- Error handling
Commit Transaction;
End Try
Begin Catch
Rollback Transaction;
DECLARE @ErrorMessage NVARCHAR(4000);
DECLARE @ErrorSeverity INT;
DECLARE @ErrorState INT;
DECLARE @ErrorNumber INT;
DECLARE @ErrorLine INT;
DECLARE @ErrorProcedure NVARCHAR(200);
SELECT @ErrorLine = ERROR_LINE(),
       @ErrorSeverity = ERROR_SEVERITY(),
       @ErrorState = ERROR_STATE(),
```

```
        @ErrorNumber = ERROR_NUMBER(),
        @ErrorMessage = ERROR_MESSAGE(),
        @ErrorProcedure = ISNULL(ERROR_PROCEDURE(), '-');
RAISERROR (14684, @ErrorSeverity, 1 , @ErrorNumber,
@ErrorSeverity, @ErrorState, @ErrorProcedure, @ErrorLine, @ErrorMessage);
End Catch;
GO
```

Once the data collection set has been created, it will be visible within SQL Server Management Studio but not yet started. Collection sets can be started by right-clicking Start Collection Set or using the `sp_syscollector_start_collection_set` stored procedure in MSDB.

The following query can be used to view the data collected by the T-SQL collector and display historic index fragmentation details:

```
SELECT
    [Table],
    [Index],
    Index_type_desc,
    avg_fragmentation_in_percent,
    avg_page_space_used_in_percent,
    record_count,
    fragment_count,
    avg_fragment_size_in_pages
FROM [MDW].[custom_snapshots].[Index Fragmentation]
```

This could be further enhanced by using a Reporting Services report to present the data retrieved from the MDW. A report designed in SQL Server Reporting Services can provide drill-through presentation for each table, showing the indexes and fragmentation levels plotted on a chart over time.

SSAS Monitoring Scripts for the MDW

The SQL Server Customer Advisory Team (SQLCAT) at Microsoft has produced a monitoring solution based on the MDW for SQL Server Analysis Services (SSAS). The solution is freely available via CodePlex (`http://www.codeplex.com/SQLSrvAnalysisSrvcs`) and extends the MDW functionality to SSAS. The Codeplex download includes a paper with configuration and deployment guidelines for the SSAS monitoring solution.

SUMMARY

The MDW provides a rapid-deployment solution for long-term SQL Server performance data collection and reporting. It offers a framework for custom data capture and reporting that can be leveraged by end users and software vendors to provide custom performance trending and diagnostic data.

Because the MDW does carry a small CPU overhead, testing should be carried out prior to production deployment to measure the impact of data collection sets and determine the optimal configuration of caching and upload scheduling. The MDW does not provide support for SQL Server 2000 or SQL Server 2005 targets, so its adoption is likely to be lower until all servers are upgraded.

INDEX

Q